BMW

KÖNEMANN

Rainer W. Schlegelmilch

Hartmut Lehbrink

Jochen von Osterroth

I would like to express my thanks to everyone who made it possible for this book to happen by allowing their cars to be used:
Ich danke allen, die mir die Verwirklichung dieses Buches durch die Bereitstellung ihrer Fahrzeuge ermöglicht haben:
Je remercie tous ceux qui m'ont permis de réaliser ce livre en mettant à ma disposition leurs voitures :
Hans-Friedrich Andexer, Udo Beckmann, Jochen Burgdorf, Helmut und Thomas Feierabend, Baldur Glaas, Günter Herz,
Dr. August Kau, Dr. Jürgen und Brigitte Klöckner, Michael Knittel, Prof. Dr. Gerhard Knöchlein, Dr. Bernhard Knöchlein,
Sepp Mayer, Jürgen Pollack, Karl Heinz Wedel.

I would also like to thank the members of the press department of BMW AG, BMW Mobile Tradition, BMW Motorsport Ltd. and the BMW office in Frankfurt/Main:
Ich bedanke mich ebenso bei den Mitarbeitern der Presseabteilung der BMW AG, der BMW Mobile Tradition, der BMW Motorsport Ltd. und der BMW Niederlassung Frankfurt am Main:
Je remercie tout autant les collaborateurs de BMW AG, de BMW Mobile Tradition, de BMW Motorsport Ltd. et de la succursale de BMW de Francfort/Main :
Franz Joseph Bötsch, Christian W. Eich, Richard Gerstner, Thomas Giuliani, "Bepi" Grassl, Helmut Grünwald, Franz Inzko, Fred Jakobs, Raimund Kupferschmid,
Klaus Kutscher, Uwe Mahla, Joachim Pietzsch, Bruno Santic, Christian Stockmann, Ali Strasser, Dirk-Henning Strassl, Walter Zeichner, Axel Zimmermann.

My gratitude to all those in positions of responsibility at Egelsbach, Michelstadt, Lauf-Lillinghof and Siegerland airports for their kind support when I was photographing there.
Für die freundliche Unterstützung bei meinen Aufnahmen danke ich den Verantwortlichen der Flugplätze Egelsbach, Michelstadt, Lauf-Lillinghof und des Flughafens Siegerland.
Je tiens à remercier les responsables des aéroports d'Egelsbach, Michelstadt, Lauf-Lillinghof et de l'aéroport du Siegerland pour leur aide amicale.

And finally, thanks are due to Hartmut Lehbrink and Jochen von Osterroth for their texts, as well as
Christian Maiwurm, Monika Dauer, Sabine Gerber and the Könemann team for the inspired way in which they handled the project.
Und zu guter Letzt gilt mein Dank Hartmut Lehbrink und Jochen von Osterroth für ihre Texte sowie
Christian Maiwurm, Monika Dauer, Sabine Gerber und dem Könemann-Team für die geniale Realisation.
Et, enfin, je dois aussi remercier Hartmut Lehbrink et Jochen von Osterroth pour leurs textes ainsi que
Christian Maiwurm, Monika Dauer, Sabine Gerber et l'équipe de Könemann pour la réalisation géniale.

Rainer W. Schlegelmilch

Photography: Rainer W. Schlegelmilch
Text: Hartmut Lehbrink, Jochen von Osterroth

Art direction: Peter Feierabend
Project manager: Sally Bald
Layout and typography: Christian Maiwurm
Typesetting: Georg Windheuser
Drawings: Jochen von Osterroth
Translation into English: Christian von Arnim, Stephen Hunter, Paul Motley
Translation into French: Jean-Luc Lesouëf
Contributing editor: Stefanie Becker
Production manager: Detlev Schaper
Production assistant: Nicola Leurs
Production: Mark Voges
Reproductions: Typografik, Cologne
Printing and binding: Partenaires Livres
Printed in France

ISBN 3-8290-0657-8
10 9 8 7 6 5 4 3 2 1

Contents · Inhalt · Sommaire

BMW V12 LMR	1999	35
Wartburg Motorwagen	1898	36
Dixi 3/15 PS	1927	44
BMW Wartburg DA3	1930	50
BMW 3/20 PS	1932	56
BMW 303	1933	64
BMW 315/1 Sport-Zweisitzer	1934	72
BMW 326 Cabriolet	1936	80
BMW 327	1937	88
BMW 328 Roadster	1936	106
BMW 328 Mille Miglia und Touring	1940	118
BMW 335	1939	130
BMW 325 Leichter Einheits-Pkw	1939	138
Veritas RS	1949	144
BMW 502 Cabriolet	1954	152
BMW Isetta 300	1956	162
BMW 502 3,2 Liter Super	1957	170
BMW 3200S Staatslimousine	1963	178
BMW 507	1956	184
BMW 503	1956	194
BMW 700LS	1962	206
BMW 3200CS	1962	214
BMW 1500	1962	220
BMW 2000CS	1965	226
BMW 1802 und 2002tii	1971	232
BMW 2002 turbo	1973	238
BMW 2500	1968	246
BMW 3.0CSi	1971	252
BMW 3.0CSL / 3.0CSL (IMSA)	1975	258
BMW 520	1972	264
BMW M1	1978	270
BMW 323i	1978	278
BMW 728i	1979	284
Brabham BMW BT52	1983	290
BMW 635CSi	1982	296
BMW 325iX touring	1988	306
BMW M3 Sport Evolution	1990	312
BMW 318i Cabrio (Kat)	1990	320
BMW 750iL	1987	326
BMW Z1	1988	332
BMW 850i	1989	340
BMW M5	1992	346
BMW M3	1992	356
BMW 318i Cabrio	1994	366
McLaren F1	1994	372
BMW 318ti compact	1994	382
BMW 320i touring	1995	388
BMW 740i	1996	392
BMW 540i	1996	398
BMW M roadster	1997	404
BMW 328i	1998	416
BMW V12 Le Mans	1998	422
BMW Z3 coupé 2.8	1998	430
BMW M5	1998	438
BMW X5	1999	446

6		Foreword by Albrecht Graf Goertz
8		Achievements in White and Blue – BMW in Retrospect
8	1916–1945	War, Peace and War Again Krieg, Frieden und wieder Krieg Guerre et paix, puis de nouveau la guerre
8	1916–1928	Engines from Munich Motoren aus München Moteurs de Munich
13	1928–1945	Success During Crisis and Catastrophe Karriere zwischen Krise und Katastrophe Carrière entre crise et catastrophe
19	1945–1962	Finding Their Feet Orientierungsstufe Changement de cap
19	1945–1952	Of Kitchen Accessories and Prodigal Sons Von Küchenzubehör und reuigen Satelliten Articles ménagers et transfuges repentants
21	1952–1962	Of Chubby-Cheeked Cherubs and Eggs on Wheels Von rundlichen Engeln und rollenden Eiern L'histoire de la Bavaroise plantureuse et l'œuf à roulettes
22	1962–1999	New Horizons Zu neuen Ufern Vers de nouveaux horizons
22	1962–1972	The "New Class" „Neue Klasse" La «Nouvelle Classe»
23	1972–1980	Crisis Management and Breaking New Ground Krisenmanagement und Abschied von der Nische Cellule de crise et abandon des créneaux
27	1980–1990	Firing on all Cylinders, from Two to Twelve Feuer aus allen Rohren: von zwei bis zwölf Zylindern Faire feu de tout bois : de deux à douze cylindres
31	1990–1999	BMW Worldwide Weißblau weltweit Bleu et blanc dans le monde entier
12	Inset:	Veni, Vidi, Dixi
14	Exkurs:	Veni, Vidi, Dixi
15	Encadré :	Veni, Vidi, Dixi
25	Inset:	The Discreet Charm of the Niche
26	Exkurs:	Vom scheuen Charme der Nische
28	Encadré :	Du charme indéfinissable du créneau
450		Specifications/Technische Daten/Spécifications
459		Glossary/Glossaire
460		Bibliography/Bibliographie

Foreword by Albrecht Graf Goertz

To be allowed to write a foreword at an age when I may be suspected of soon needing an obituary is sufficiently stimulating for me to put my ancestors on hold for a while before following in their footsteps. Allow me to take the opportunity presented by this book, with its impressive photos by Rainer Schlegelmilch and the texts by Hartmut Lehbrink and Jochen von Osterroth, to cast an eye back over my career as a designer, which was significantly influenced by BMW.

On a cold January day in 1914, a certain Count Albrecht Rudolf Moritz Eustach Friedrich-Wilhelm Alex Eduard von Schlitz, known as von Görtz, was born on the Brunkensen estate south of Hanover which had been in the family's possession since 1272. What a burden of a name I had been saddled with! In contrast to my elder brother, Eberhard, I was not so interested in country life. I had fallen in love with cars, and at ten years old I duly drew my first automobile, an Adler.

Since my effort at schooling had exhausted itself with secondary school, my mother – my father had died at a young age – apprenticed me to a bank as a clerk, first in Germany, then in England. From there I emigrated to the USA in 1936 in the search for creative freedom far from the pressures of national socialism.

The American GI Albrecht Goertz saw action in the islands of the Pacific, only to get stuck in Honolulu as the only one of 40,000 soldiers returning to the front. Chance?

And chance stepped in for a second time. Back in New York, I parked my home-built car, designed as early as 1938, in front of the Waldorf-Astoria hotel. The car caught the eye of a man standing in front of me. This was none other than the "Frenchman" Raymond Loewy, a genius at PR and all-round designer who could package more or less anything into a streamlined shape.

I became Loewy's pupil, yet neither the master's textbook, "Ugliness does not sell well", nor the theory taught in a Brooklyn design institute brought me much further forwards. Making use of Loewy's Studebaker connections, I started a period of helpful practical training with this automobile company which was so rich in tradition. Loewy tolerated this for two-and-a-half years before throwing me out with the "kind" words: "Goertz, you will never become a designer. You would do better to find yourself a rich wife."

In 1953 I opened my own studio in New York. One day, Maxie Hoffman, importer of European sports cars, told me that he would like to have a BMW sports car for the US market. The problem was, he said, winking at me, that it still had to be designed. I should make two sketches for BMW and send them to Hanns Grewenig, the sales director of the works. A prototype already presented by Loof did not accord with his ideas.

I sent the sketch off and after only 12 days received a telegram asking when I would come to Munich. With the next plane of course! A hectic time ensued, particularly as the first 1:5 model had to be reworked completely. As well as the roadster, to be called 507, BMW also wanted a spacious four-seater coupé/convertible, the 503.

Things were achieved which are only possible with a well-motivated team which is also prepared to work at weekends. And even for the head of development, Fritz Fiedler, it was – as so often – "no problem" when I just wanted to lower the engine a little in the 1:1 layout of the new 507 six months before the launch.

In the autumn of 1955 – we worked up to the last moment – BMW presented the 503 and the 507 in Frankfurt; I personally find the coupé the more beautiful car of the two. The 507 celebrated its New York launch in the spring of 1956. I was much

praised in the press, which considered the 507 to be a "miracle of design". Just between you, me and the gatepost: beautiful lines do not have to be invented, they simply have to be put in the correct relationship to one another. For me it is an expression of emotion.

In terms of aerodynamics, too, I am reluctant to lump everything together. With the 507 I did not have to bow to the influence of the wind tunnel, which exercises a decisive effect on automobile design today, although I did of course take aerodynamic considerations into account. Consider it rather as "streamlining" with the premise that the car should be able to do 136 mph (220 kph) with the appropriate transmission. This test was undertaken on a closed motorway – with the required result.

It is no coincidence that the BMW 700 was created in cooperation with Michelotti. I recommended my colleague over coffee in Geneva, and today I can reveal why: my fee was a little too high for the company, which was somewhat battered at the time.

While BMW blossomed in the 1960s, creative unrest drew me to the land of the lotus blossom. Just imagine, a "German-American" applying to design cars in Japan. The result is no secret: my design, the Datsun 240Z, is considered to be the best-selling sports car in the world. Like Loewy, I designed many things; even – for the government – the inside of Mexican classrooms. But before becoming sidetracked to Fissler cooking pots and Constructa washing machines, and Rowenta lighters and irons, let me turn my attention again to the subject of BMW and thus this magnificent book.

Apologies for this small diversion away from BMW! After all, I always took a great interest in the development of the white and blue marque and never allowed the connection to break off. I have often exchanged experiences with Dr. Wolfgang Reitzle, for many years Head of Development and Design. I will never forget my many meetings with proud 507 owners. 40 of these cars united on the old market place in Siena – an uplifting feeling.

A private letter from former BMW Chairman, Bernd Pischetsrieder, gave me particular pleasure. He had finally succeeded in buying a 507, a memorial to me, as it were. Long live nostalgia! And this you can indulge to the full with the present book. After all, Goertz drove an Isetta – in New York. Thanks to BMW of course!

When I venture on to the highway today in my M3 (living in Brunkensen again since 1990), I see much automotive monotony. On the other hand I am always surprised by the trends that are being set with nuances of design. I do not know whether my taste always corresponded to contemporary taste, but the multitude of cars which I cannot identify until I see their name on the trunk is disturbing. With BMW, everything forms an integrated whole, "corporate design", some of it of classic beauty.

In conclusion, allow me to add an afterword to the foreword in this impressive book. There is no point in hoarding the money I have earned with my designs. On the contrary, I want to pass on the experience I have gained over the years – and they are many – to young talent. The Goertz Foundation supports up-and-coming designers in worldwide competitions.

I hope that this BMW book – a splendid volume with its many illustrations – gives you much pleasure.

Presse sieht im 507 gar ein "formgestalterisches Wunderwerk". Ganz im Vertrauen – schöne Linien müssen nicht erfunden werden, man muß sie nur in das richtige Verhältnis setzen. Bei mir ein Ausdruck der Emotion.

Auch aerodynamisch will ich nicht gleich alles über einen Kamm scheren. Dem Einfluß des Windkanals, der heutzutage das Autodesign entscheidend prägt, muß ich mich beim 507 nicht beugen, wenngleich ich natürlich aerodynamische Gegebenheiten berücksichtigt habe. Betrachten Sie es eher als ein "Streamlining" aus der Hand mit der Prämisse, daß der Wagen mit entsprechender Übersetzung auch 220 "Sachen" fahren kann. Dieser Test erfolgt dann auf einer gesperrten Autobahn – mit dem geforderten Resultat.

Daß der BMW 700 in Zusammenarbeit mit Michelotti entsteht, ist kein Zufall. Ich habe den Kollegen bei einem Kaffee in Genf empfohlen und darf heute verraten, warum: Meine Honorarforderung ist für das damals etwas gebeutelte Unternehmen zu hoch.

Während BMW in den sechziger Jahren aufblüht, treibt mich die schöpferische Unruhe in das Land der Lotosblüten. Stellen Sie sich vor, da bewirbt sich ein "Deutsch-Ami" in Japan und will Autos entwerfen! Das Ergebnis ist bekannt: Mein Design, der Datsun 240Z, gilt als meistverkaufter Sportwagen der Welt. Wie Loewy entwerfe ich Verschiedenes, sogar das Interieur mexikanischer Schulklassen - als Staatsauftrag. Doch ehe ich von Fissler-Kochtöpfen und Constructa-Waschmaschinen auf Rowenta-Feuerzeuge und -Bügeleisen komme, möchte ich mich wieder dem Thema BMW und diesem prächtigen Buch widmen.

Sehen Sie mir bitte diesen kleinen Exkurs nach. Schließlich habe ich die Entwicklung der weißblauen Marke stets verfolgt und die Kontakte nie abreißen lassen. Mit Dr. Wolfgang Reitzle, lange Jahre Chef für Entwicklung und Konstruktion, habe ich oft Erfahrungen ausgetauscht. Unvergessen bleiben mir die vielen Treffen stolzer 507-Besitzer. 40 dieser Wagen auf dem alten Marktplatz von Siena vereint – für mich ein erhebendes Gefühl.

Besonders habe ich mich über ein privates Schreiben des ehemaligen BMW-Vorstandsvorsitzenden Bernd Pischetsrieder gefreut. Es sei ihm endlich gelungen, einen 507 zu kaufen, sozusagen mein Denkmal. Es lebe die Nostalgie! Und diese dürfen Sie im vorliegenden Buch in vollen Zügen genießen. Schließlich bin ich Fahrer einer Isetta gewesen – und das in New York. Dank BMW natürlich!

Wenn ich mich heute (seit 1990 wieder in Brunkensen) mit meinem M3 auf die Autobahn begebe, sehe ich viel automobiles Einerlei, bin aber andererseits überrascht, daß auch mit designerischen Nuancen Akzente gesetzt werden. Ich weiß nicht, ob ich mit meinem Geschmack immer richtig liege, doch die große Anzahl von Autos, die ich erst am Namen auf der Heckklappe erkenne, ist bedenklich. Bei BMW wirkt alles wie aus einem Guß, "corporate design", teilweise klassisch schön.

Zum Schluß möchte ich in diesem großartigen Buch ein Nachwort im Vorwort anbringen. Es ist müßig, daß ich das Geld zähle, das ich mit meinen Designs verdient habe. Vielmehr möchte ich meine im Laufe der Jahre - es sind nicht wenige - gesammelten Erfahrungen an junge Talente weitergeben. Die Goertz-Stiftung engagiert sich für den Designer-Nachwuchs in weltweiten Wettbewerben.

Viel Freude an diesem BMW-Buch – einem prächtigen Bildband zum Genießen – wünscht Ihnen

même dans la 507 un «chef-d'œuvre du design». Soit dit entre nous : il n'est pas nécessaire d'inventer de belles lignes, il faut seulement leur donner les proportions qui conviennent. Pour moi, c'est une expression de mon émotion.

Sur le plan aérodynamique, non plus, je ne veux pas tout jeter dans le même panier. Pour la 507, je n'ai pas besoin de me plier au diktat de la soufflerie qui, aujourd'hui, marque de son sceau l'ensemble du design automobile. Cela m'a pas empêché de prendre en considération certaines lois de l'aérodynamique. Considérez plutôt ceci comme un «streamlining» dessiné par intuition avec un cahier des charges qui veut que la voiture soit capable de rouler aussi à 220 km/h avec la démultiplication correspondante. Ce test est alors réalisé sur une autoroute fermée à la circulation - et le résultat souhaité est obtenu.

Si la BMW 700 est réalisée avec le concours de Michelotti, cela n'est pas le fruit du hasard. Buvant un café avec quelques collègues à Genève, je le leur ai recommandé et me permets de vous confier aujourd'hui pourquoi : mes prétentions étaient trop élevées pour l'entreprise alors moins florissante qu'aujourd'hui.

Alors que BMW connaît un vif essor dans les années 60, mon impétuosité créatrice me fait partir pour le pays des fleurs de lotus. Imaginez un «Germano-Américain» qui veut dessiner des voitures au Japon ! Le résultat est connu : mon enfant, la Datsun 240Z, est considéré comme la voiture de sport la plus vendue dans le monde. Comme Raymond Loewy, je dessine beaucoup, et même - sur commande de l'Etat - l'aménagement intérieur de salles de classe au Mexique. Mais avant de passer du thème des cocottes-minute Fissler et machines à laver Constructa aux briquets et fers à repasser Rowenta, je préfère me consacrer de nouveau au thème de BMW et, donc, à ce magnifique ouvrage.

Pardonnez-moi cette petite digression. J'ai en effet toujours suivi l'évolution de la marque à l'emblème bleu et blanc et n'ai jamais laissé les contacts se rompre. J'ai souvent échangé mes vues avec Dr Wolfgang Reitzle, longtemps chef du développement et de la construction. Je n'oublierai jamais les rencontres de fiers propriétaires de 507. Voir réunies 40 de ces voitures sur la vieille Place du marché de Sienne - quelle sensation émouvante !

Je me suis particulièrement réjoui d'une lettre que m'a envoyée à titre privé Bernd Pischetsrieder, ancien président du directoire de BMW. Il a enfin réussi, écrit-il, à acheter une 507, pour ainsi dire mon monument. Vive la nostalgie ! Et c'est cette nostalgie que vous pouvez boire à pleins traits dans le présent livre. Savez-vous que j'ai possédé et construit une Isetta - et ce à New York. Grâce à BMW, naturellement !

Quand je circule aujourd'hui (depuis 1990, je suis de nouveau à Brunkensen) avec ma M3 sur l'autoroute, je croise une multitude de voitures se ressemblant toutes. Je suis surpris que quelques touches de design permettent néanmoins de leur donner un accent particulier. Je ne sais pas si je réponds toujours aux attentes avec mon goût, mais le grand nombre de voitures que je ne reconnais que lorsque je lis leur nom sur la malle arrière me donne matière à réflexion. Avec BMW, tout semble couler de source, «corporate design», parfois d'une beauté classique.

Enfin, j'aimerais ajouter à la préface de cet ouvrage un épitaphe. Il serait fastidieux de vouloir compter l'argent gagné avec mes réalisations. Je préfère léguer mes expériences accumulées au cours des années - et il n'y en a pas peu - aux jeunes talents. La Fondation Goertz s'engage pour la jeune génération de designers en organisant des concours à l'échelle mondiale.

Prenez plaisir à lire ce livre sur BMW - un magnifique ouvrage photographique - c'est ce que vous souhaite.

Albrecht Graf Goertz

Achievements in White and Blue
BMW in Retrospect

War, Peace and War Again (1916–1945)

Engines from Munich (1916–1928)

They say that the achievements of many individuals lie behind any success story, but that the names of most fade into obscurity. The story of the origins of the Bayerische Motoren Werke (BMW) tends to lend support to this view, though it is hard to be sure in the absence of messages from the hereafter. And these are, as we all know, somewhat thin on the ground. On the other hand, the here and now offers messages of great reliability in the form of official records and notarized documents. In fact, as regards the birth of BMW, there is an embarrassment of riches in this respect, with no less than three relevant official documents in existence. Unfortunately, in our search for the truth, this situation turns out to be as much a hindrance as a help.

The first document is dated 7 March 1916 and is to be found in the Munich Register of Companies. It states that the Bayerische Flugzeugwerke AG (Bavarian Airplane Works, or BFW) had just been founded. Its purpose was to be "the manufacture and commercial distribution of airplanes and any related machinery, equipment and other objects, and further, in the pursuit of this purpose, the founding of other enterprises in any legally permissible form, or participation therein, and also the running of companies of any sort". The clerk noted that the capital stock amounted to one million marks.

The new company was very much following the trend of the times. The First World War had reached the halfway mark without any sign of a let-up, and anything related to aviation was booming. One of the founders was a certain Gustav Otto, son of the inventor Nikolaus August Otto. As the clerk's punctilious handwriting notes, he brought "the Otto plants, previously his property, along with all assets and liabilities" to the new company, receiving 432,782.44 marks in exchange. BFW's base of operations was the premises at Lerchenauer Straße 76, not far from Oberwiesenfeld – now a historic BMW site.

A second find, also in the Munich Register of Companies, dates from 21 July 1917. Here we read that Rapp Motorenwerke GmbH, of Schleißheimer Straße 288, had been renamed the Bayerische Motoren Werke GmbH, but only after the previous managing director, Karl Rapp, had left the company. The new managing director, Franz-Joseph Popp, made an entry on 5 October of the same year at the Imperial Patent Office to the effect that the company purpose was to produce "land, air and water vehicles, automobiles and bicycles, automobile and bicycle accessories, vehicle parts, stationary engines for solid,

Krieg, Frieden und wieder Krieg (1916–1945)

Motoren aus München (1916–1928)

Der Erfolg, so heißt es, hat viele Väter, nur daß sich mancher Anspruch und so manche Zuweisung im dunkeln verliert. Das Bild läßt sich mit den üblichen Retuschen auf die Ursprünge der Bayerischen Motoren Werke übertragen, zumal Rückmeldungen aus dem Jenseits bekanntlich ausgesprochen rar sind. Dafür hat das Diesseits ungemein verläßliche Dokumente zu bieten in Gestalt des amtlich Niedergelegten und des notariell Beglaubigten. In bezug auf die Geburtsstunde von BMW schafft allerdings der Plural Verwirrung, denn gleich drei Urkunden erweisen sich bei der Wahrheitssuche als ebenso hilfreich wie hinderlich.

Die erste, datiert mit 7. März 1916, findet sich im Münchener Handelsregister. Sie hält fest, man habe gerade die Bayerische Flugzeugwerke AG (BFW) ins Leben gerufen. Ihr Zweck und Ziel sei „die Herstellung und der gewerbsmäßige Vertrieb von Flugzeugen und allen damit im Zusammenhang stehenden Maschinen, Geräten und sonstigen Gegenständen, ferner im Rahmen dieses Zwecks auch die Errichtung anderer Unternehmungen in jeder rechtlich zulässigen Form oder die Beteiligung hieran und überhaupt der Betrieb von Gesellschaften jeder Art". Das Stammkapital, notiert der Schreiber, betrage eine Million Mark.

Die neue Marke liegt voll im Trend. Der Erste Weltkrieg verzeichnet Halbzeit ohne Pfiff und Pause, und alles boomt, was mit der Fliegerei zu tun hat. Unter den Gründern wird Gustav Otto genannt, Sohn des Erfinders Nikolaus August Otto. Er habe, so ist in pingeliger Handschrift vermerkt, in die neue Gesellschaft "die ihm bisher gehörenden Otto-Werke samt allen Aktiva und Passiva" eingebracht und dafür 432.782,44 Mark erhalten. Standort der BFW ist die Liegenschaft Lerchenauer Straße 76, unweit des Oberwiesenfelds – historischer BMW-Boden.

Zum zweiten Mal wird man am 21. Juli 1917 fündig, wieder im Handelsregister der Stadt München. Die bisherige Rapp Motorenwerke GmbH in der Schleißheimer Straße 288, steht da zu lesen, habe man umgewidmet zur Bayerische Motoren Werke GmbH, allerdings erst nachdem der alte Geschäftsführer Karl Rapp ausgeschieden sei. Der neue, Franz-Joseph Popp, läßt am 5. Oktober des gleichen Jahres beim Kaiserlichen Patentamt eintragen, die Firma habe es sich zum Anliegen gemacht „Land-, Luft- und Wasserfahrzeuge, Automobile und Fahrräder, Automobil- und Fahrradzubehör, Fahrzeugteile, stationäre Motoren für feste, flüssige und gasförmige Betriebsstoffe und

Guerre et paix, puis de nouveau la guerre (1916–1945)

Moteurs de Munich (1916–1928)

Le succès - dit-on - a de nombreux pères, mais il est parfois difficile de le revendiquer ou, inversement, d'en attribuer le mérite à quelqu'un. Avec les corrections d'usage, ce cliché vaut d'autant plus pour les origines des Bayerische Motoren Werke (BMW) qu'il est extrêmement rare que des voix se fassent entendre d'outre-tombe. En revanche, le temps présent permet de se prévaloir de documents d'une fiabilité à toute épreuve sous la forme de ce qui a été rédigé officiellement et authentifié par notaire. Quant à la date de naissance de BMW, la prolifération sème toutefois la confusion à ce propos. En effet, pas moins de trois actes officiels simultanés s'avèrent tout aussi utiles que déroutants dans la recherche de la vérité.

Le premier, daté 7 mars 1916, se trouve au registre du commerce de la ville de Munich. Il établit la création, ce jour-là, des Bayerische Flugzeugwerke AG (BFW). But de la société : «fabriquer et distribuer commercialement des avions et toutes les machines, appareils et autres objets s'inscrivant dans ce contexte ; en outre, dans le cadre de ce but, également créer d'autres entreprises sous une forme juridique légale ou participer à celles-ci et, d'ailleurs, exploiter des sociétés en tout genre.» Le capital social, a même précisé le greffier, était d'un million de marks.

La nouvelle marque a le vent en poupe. La Première Guerre mondiale vient de terminer sa première mi-temps, sans coup de sifflet ni interruption, et tout ce qui touche à l'aviation connaît un essor sans précédent. Parmi les fondateurs figure Gustav Otto, le fils de l'inventeur du moteur à quatre temps, Nikolaus August Otto. Il a, est-il précisé d'une écriture d'expert-comptable, apporté dans la nouvelle société «les usines Otto, dont il est jusque-là propriétaire, avec tous les actifs et passifs» et a reçu pour cela 432 782,44 marks. La BFW réside dans la propriété du 76 de la Lerchenauer Straße, non loin de l'Oberwiesenfeld – un sol historique pour BMW.

On fait une seconde découverte, le 21 juillet 1917, et de nouveau dans le registre du commerce de Munich. Ce qui s'appelait jusque-là Rapp Motorenwerke GmbH, au 288 de la Schleißheimer Straße, peut-on y lire, a été rebaptisé en Bayerische Motoren Werke GmbH, mais seulement après que Karl Rapp, l'ancien administrateur-gérant, ait démissionné. Le nouveau, Franz-Joseph Popp, fait enregistrer le 5 octobre de la même année, auprès de l'Office impérial des Brevets, que la firme s'est donné pour objectif de fabriquer «des véhicules terrestres, aéronautiques et amphibies, automobiles et

liquid and gaseous fuels, and their replacement and accessory parts" – a truly ambitious and diversified range of products. At the same time Popp registered the company's trademark, which still remains today – the stylized whirl of a rotating propeller surmounted by the letters BMW, plus two white and two blue quadrants, in homage to his Bavarian homeland.

Thus the production facilities, name and emblem were all in place, albeit as yet in the hands of different owners. Nevertheless things were afoot behind the scenes, though the marriage of the two companies would not come till later. There was to be no wedding night or honeymoon for the not-so-young couple, however, for in 1922 the Bayerische Motoren Werke moved lock, stock and barrel into the premises of the ailing Bayerische Flugzeugwerke, and the latter was promptly dissolved.

Up to that point, the BMW ship had always had to chart stormy waters. Karl Rapp, erstwhile employee of the Daimler-Motoren-Gesellschaft and survivor from the pioneering days of the automobile industry, was a resilient character and a fighter, but luck always seemed to be against him and by the end, he was simply too tired and too ill to continue. When in 1912 the first "Kaiserpreis für aeronautische Apparate" (Imperial Prize for Aeronautical Devices) was announced, he entered the competition with his biplane, powered by a 90 bhp four-cylinder overhead camshaft engine. However, the plane only succeeded in attracting derision and ridicule as it failed to become airborne, managing no more than a few clumsy kangaroo hops down the airfield. For the second "Kaiserpreis" in autumn 1914, he planned to enter a 125 bhp six-cylinder machine, but unfortunately this time the First World War intervened. However, the war did also create a demand for airplanes, but Rapp's aviation engines were plagued by vibration problems and fell into disrepute with the Prussian and Bavarian authorities, as complaints about it were practically a daily occurrence.

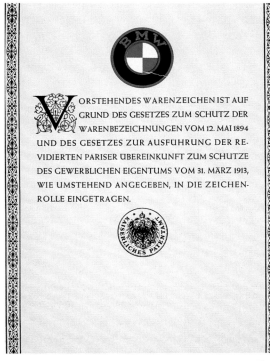

Registration of the BMW trademark at the Imperial Patent Office in Munich. The year is 1917.

Eintrag des BMW-Firmenzeichens beim Kaiserlichen Patentamt München. Man schreibt das Jahr 1917.

Inscription de l'emblème de la marque BMW à l'Office impérial des Brevets de Munich. Nous sommes en 1917.

On 29 November 1916, Franz-Joseph Popp made his approach to the Rapp Motorenwerke.

Am 29. November 1916 wird Franz-Joseph Popp bei den Rapp Motorenwerken vorstellig.

Le 29 novembre 1916, Franz-Joseph Popp se présente aux usines de moteurs Rapp.

deren Ersatz- und Zubehörteile" herzustellen, eine wahrlich ambitionierte und breit gefächerte Produktpalette. Zugleich meldet Popp das bis heute bestehende Markenzeichen an, das stilisierte Wirbelfeld eines Propellers mit den Lettern BMW im Kopfende sowie zwei weißen und zwei blauen Viertelkreisen als Verneigung vor der bayerischen Heimat.

Produktionsstätte, Name und Firmenzeichen sind damit vorhanden, wenn auch im Besitz verschiedener Personen. Schon spinnen sich Fäden hinüber und herüber, aber zur Ehe kommt es erst später. Allerdings bleiben dem nicht mehr ganz jungen Paar Hochzeitsnacht und Flitterwochen verwehrt, denn 1922 ziehen die Bayerischen Motoren Werke mit Sack und Pack in das Anwesen der maroden Bayerischen Flugzeugwerke um, die somit aufhören zu existieren.

Bis dahin muß sich das Schifflein BMW jedoch noch in aufgewühltem Fahrwasser behaupten. Das war schon immer so. Karl Rapp, als einstiger Kostgänger der Daimler-Motoren-Gesellschaft ein Stück Treibgut aus der Phase des automobilen Urknalls, ist zwar ein Stehaufmännchen, aber auch ein glückloser Kämpfer und daher am Ende krank und müde. Als 1912 der erste „Kaiserpreis für aeronautische Apparate" ausgelobt wird, bewirbt er sich mit einem Vierzylinder mit 90 Pferdestärken, bei deren Erzeugung eine obenliegende Nockenwelle im Spiel ist. Der Doppeldecker, der sich mit diesem Triebwerk in die Lüfte erheben soll, zieht mit ein paar neckischen Hüpfern lediglich Hohn und Spott auf sich. Beim zweiten Kaiserpreis im Herbst 1914 gedenkt man mit einem Sechszylinder mit 125 PS anzutreten. Aber diesmal kommt der Erste Weltkrieg dazwischen. Er erzeugt zugleich jedoch Nachfrage und Aufträge kommen herein. Aber Rapps Flugmotoren geraten bei den zuständigen preußischen und bayerischen Behörden ins Gerede und in Verruf, denn sie werden von Vibrationen gebeutelt. Reklamationen sind an der Tagesordnung.

bicyclettes, accessoires d'automobile et de bicyclette, pièces de véhicules, moteurs stationnaires pour combustibles solides, liquides et gazeux et leurs pièces de rechange et accessoires», une gamme de produits véritablement ambitieuse et très diversifiée. Simultanément, Popp fait breveter l'emblème, le tourbillon stylisé d'une hélice avec les lettres BMW sur la circonférence ainsi que deux quarts de cercle respectifs blancs et bleus en guise de révérence à sa patrie bavaroise.

Unité de production, nom et emblème existent donc déjà, mais ils se trouvent en possession de différents propriétaires. Ceux-ci commencent toutefois à tresser les liens qui vont les rapprocher. Le mariage ne sera malgré tout célébré que bien plus tard. Le couple plus très jeune n'aura malheureusement jamais le plaisir de fêter ni nuit de noces, ni lune de miel. En effet, en 1922, les Bayerische Motoren Werke prennent avec tambours et trompettes possession des terrains des moribondes Bayerische Flugzeugwerke qui disparaissent.

En attendant, le petit bateau de BMW aura encore dû surmonter de nombreuses tempêtes. Mais ce n'était pas la première fois. Karl Rapp, autrefois inscrit sur les listes salariales de la Daimler-Motoren-Gesellschaft et, en tant que tel, survivant de la phase du Big Bang automobile, est un homme qui retombe toujours sur ses pieds, mais aussi un battant qui n'a pas la bonne fortune à ses côtés et, à la fin, est tout simplement malade et fatigué. Lorsque, en 1912, on annonce que sera décerné le premier «Kaiserpreis für aeronautische Apparate» (prix impérial pour des appareils aéronautiques), il fait acte de candidature avec un quatre-cylindres de 90 ch muni d'un arbre à cames en tête. Le biplan que l'on espérait voir prendre les airs propulsé par ce moteur se contente de quelques bonds de cabri qui en font la risée générale. Lors de la collation du deuxième prix impérial, à l'automne 1914, il espère faire mieux avec un six-cylindres de 125 ch. Mais, cette fois-ci, c'est la Première Guerre mondiale qui fait capoter ses plans. En revanche, elle engendre aussi une demande et cela lui vaut des commandes. Les moteurs d'avion de Rapp font toutefois l'objet de critiques au sein des autorités prussiennes et bavaroises et ont mauvaise réputation. Ils sont handicapés par leurs vibrations. Les réclamations sont à l'ordre du jour.

Le banquier et conseiller commercial viennois Camillo Castiglioni, un personnage agile et maître d'un empire aussi ramifié que mystérieux, ne se laisse pas impressionner par la réputation douteuse du Rapp Motorenwerke. Il est habitué à jongler sans complexe avec les millions et c'est la raison pour laquelle il a été surnommé Castimillioni. Il acquiert une grande partie des actions de Rapp et veille à ce que le capital social soit majoré à 1,2 million de marks à l'automne 1916. Castiglioni est membre du conseil de surveillance d'Austro-Daimler, à Wiener Neustadt, dont il est également actionnaire. L'ancienne filiale autrichienne de Daimler tourne au maximum de ses capacités. Une commande sous licence pour 224 moteurs d'avions, ce qui représente un volume de dix millions de marks, devra donc être retransmise à une firme ayant une structure similaire – contre une commission juteuse, cela va de soi. Homme d'action, Castiglioni réunit lui-même sans hésiter les préalables nécessaires.

Pendant que l'infatigable banquier a surtout pour objectif de faire grossir sa fortune, un autre Autrichien s'intéresse surtout à la compétence. Franz-Joseph Popp est lieutenant-colonel de réserve de la marine austro-hongroise, ingénieur diplômé et expert du Ministère de la Guerre de la double

However, in the meantime the Viennese banker and entrepreneur Camillo Castiglioni had appeared on the scene. He seemed entirely unconcerned by Rapp Motorenwerke's dubious reputation. Castiglioni was an enigmatic figure. He was the head of a wide-ranging business empire of almost Byzantine complexity, and his casual juggling with multi-figure sums had earned him the popular nickname "Castimillioni". He had acquired a major slice of Rapp stock, thus ensuring that the company's capital stock had grown to 1.2 million marks by autumn 1916. Castiglioni was both a stockholder and member of the supervisory board of Austro-Daimler in Wiener Neustadt. The erstwhile Austrian Daimler subsidiary was working at full capacity, and as a result, a license contract for the manufacture of 224 airplane engines, worth ten million marks, was up for grabs for a firm of similar structure – in return for a hefty commission, naturally. Ever the man of action, Castiglioni set the whole deal up himself at short notice.

While the go-getting banker was chiefly interested in increasing his holdings, another Austrian was more concerned about competence. This was Franz-Joseph Popp, a Lieutenant in the reserves of the Austro-Hungarian marines, and a graduate engineer. As an aviation expert attached to the Royal Imperial War Ministry, his business was to keep himself up-to-date with the latest developments on the ground, whether at Benz, for example, or at NAG (Neue Automobil Gesellschaft: New Automobile Company). Accordingly, the authorities in Vienna made the award of this large contract conditional on Popp and a man of their choice keeping a close eye on the production of the 224 V12 power units, each developing 350 bhp, in Munich.

The thirty-year old Popp arrived in the Bavarian capital on 29 October 1916 with absolutely no idea that the job in hand was to become his life's work. He personally had not had any negative experiences with the Rapp engines. However, he was shocked at the company's cramped premises and the desolate state of its machinery and equipment. Despite this he put his faith in the company, and this was rewarded when he supported the appointment of the highly competent ex-Daimler engineer Max Friz. He had just applied for a position with Rapp, still smarting that his old boss Paul Daimler in Stuttgart had rejected out of hand his request for a raise of 50 marks a month.

On 1 January 1917, the Daimler renegade started work in Munich, against Karl Rapp's wishes, who saw his erstwhile colleague Friz as a potential rival. He was even more discontented that he now found himself working for a foreign power, and so he retired, a disappointed and disgruntled man. Franz-Joseph Popp became technical director. However, the company was still hindered by its poor reputation, and the only remedy was to create a new identity. And thus that fateful entry in the Munich Register of Companies, dated 21 July 1917.

Before long BMW had a successful Friz design to show, a six-cylinder airplane engine dubbed the IIIa. Friz's altitude-compensated carburetor meant that its 220 bhp at sea level was only reduced by half at 19,800 feet (6000 meters). Not without reservations, the War Ministry ordered 600 of them at a total cost of 13.2 million marks, and further orders followed. Schleißheimer Straße became a place of hectic activity, and in the end BMW itself was forced, due to insufficient capacity, to farm out some of the production on license, to Opel, Adler, the NAG, and MAN. The Prussian and Bavarian Ministry's misgivings that existing financial cover was too thin were quieted when the company went public on 13 August 1918, with capital stock of

Gänzlich unbeirrt vom schlechten Leumund der Rapp Motoren Werke bleibt der Wiener Bankier und Kommerzialrat Camillo Castiglioni, ein schillernder Zeitgenosse und Herrscher über ein gleichermaßen heimliches wie unheimliches Imperium. Wegen seines unbekümmerten Jonglierens mit vielstelligen Zahlen wird er im Volksmund auch Castimillioni genannt. Er erwirbt eine massive Portion der Rapp-Anteile und sorgt dafür, daß das Stammkapital im Herbst 1916 auf 1,2 Millionen Mark angewachsen ist. Natürlich geschieht dies nicht um Gottes Lohn. Castiglioni sitzt im Aufsichtsrat von Austro-Daimler in Wiener Neustadt und ist auch dort Teilhaber. Die einstige österreichische Daimler-Dependance ist voll ausgelastet. Ein

Advertisement by the Rapp Motorenwerke Munich of 1916, with an indication of the client.

Inserat der Rapp Motorenwerke München von 1916 mit dem Hinweis auf den Auftraggeber.

Annonce des usines de moteurs Rapp de Munich, en 1916, avec mention du client.

Lizenzauftrag über 224 Flugmotoren mit einem Volumen von zehn Millionen Mark winkt daher einer Firma mit ähnlicher Struktur – gegen deftige Provision, versteht sich. Als Mann der Tat schafft Castiglioni die Voraussetzungen kurzerhand selbst.

Während der umtriebige Bankier eher die Mehrung seines Besitzstandes im Sinn hat, geht es einem anderen Österreicher vor allem um Kompetenz. Franz-Joseph Popp ist Oberleutnant der Reserve bei der österreichisch-ungarischen Marine und Diplomingenieur und hält sich als Sachverständiger des kaiserlich-königlichen Kriegsministeriums für Flugmaschinen überall auf dem laufenden, bei Benz etwa oder der NAG (Neue Automobil Gesellschaft). Den Großauftrag knüpft die Wiener Behörde an eine Bedingung: Mit Popp müsse ein Mann ihrer Wahl und ihres Vertrauens die Fertigung der 224 V12-Triebwerke, jedes 350 PS stark, in München überwachen.

Am 29. Oktober 1916 trifft der Dreißigjährige in der bayerischen Metropole ein und ahnt nicht, daß sich der Job zur Berufung auswachsen wird. Persönlich hat er mit Rapp-Motoren

monarchie austro-hongroise, ce qui lui permet de se tenir au courant partout pour tout ce qui touche à l'aviation, chez Benz ou chez NAG (Neue Automobil Gesellschaft). Une clause conditionne la commande géante de l'administration viennoise: avec Popp, un homme de son choix et de sa confiance devrait surveiller la fabrication des 224 moteurs V12, chacun d'une puissance de 350 ch, à Munich.

Le 29 octobre 1916, le trentenaire arrive dans la métropole bavaroise et n'a absolument aucune idée que son métier va se métamorphoser en vocation. Personnellement, il n'a pas fait de mauvaises expériences avec les moteurs Rapp. Il est par contre frappé de stupeur en découvrant la modestie des locaux de l'entreprise et l'âge avancé de son parc de machines. Sans se laisser démonter, il investit sa confiance et cela portera ses fruits, d'autant plus qu'il soutient le recrutement de Max Friz, un ancien ingénieur de Daimler très capable. Il vient de se proposer à Rapp, écumant de fureur parce que son ancien chef Paul Daimler, à Stuttgart, a refusé d'un ton cassant sa demande d'augmentation de salaire de 50 marks par mois.

Le 1er janvier 1917, l'ancien mercenaire de Daimler prend ses fonctions à Munich, contre la volonté de Karl Rapp, qui voit dans son ancien collaborateur Friz un rival. Il est encore plus furieux de devoir se mettre au service d'une cause étrangère, si bien que, blessé et vexé, il décide de prendre sa retraite. Franz-Joseph Popp est ainsi nommé directeur technique. Et pourtant, la firme souffre encore de sa mauvaise réputation. La seule issue consiste donc à lui donner une nouvelle identité. Or cela implique une inscription au registre des sociétés de Munich, ce qui est fait le 21 juillet 1917.

En peu de temps, BMW peut présenter une création réussie de Friz, le moteur d'avion IIIa, un six-cylindres. Grâce au carburateur à haute altitude de Friz, à 6000 mètres d'altitude, il ne perd que la moitié des 220 ch qu'il avait au sol. Non sans scepticisme, le Ministère de la Guerre en commande 600 exemplaires pour un prix de 13,2 millions de marks. D'autres commandes vont suivre. La fébrilité s'installe dans l'usine de la Schleißheimer Straße et, finalement, les Bayerische Motoren Werke doivent elles-mêmes, par manque de capacités, attribuer des licences, à Opel, Adler, NAG et MAN. Les ministères prussien et bavarois ayant critiqué que l'envergure financière était trop réduite, BMW réplique en transformant la firme en société anonyme, le 13 août 1918. Le capital social s'élève à 12 millions de marks. Franz-Joseph Popp est nommé directeur général. A partir du moteur BMW IIIa, Friz développe le BMW IV, qui a encore une puissance de 250 ch à 3000 mètres d'altitude. A l'automne de cette année-là, BMW donne travail et salaire à 3500 collaborateurs.

La guerre, proclame Héraclite, est la mère de toutes choses. Si l'on prend au pied de la lettre le philosophe grec, BMW devient orpheline de sa mère à la fin de 1918: le Traité de Versailles la prive de toute base d'existence avec la stricte injonction des puissances victorieuses de cesser de fabriquer des moteurs d'avions. Il faut donc faire preuve de souplesse, ce qui est une autre qualité de Popp. Une commande passée par Knorr-Bremse AG, de Berlin, pour 10 000 circuits de freinage pour l'administration des chemins de fer bavaroise permet de voir venir, mais c'est une commande qui ne déclenche pas la passion.

Tenu de faire tourner l'affaire, Popp n'en oublie pas pour autant son vieux penchant: malgré l'interdiction de fabriquer des moteurs d'avions, le 9 juin 1919, le pilote Zeno Diemer, aux

12 million marks. Franz-Joseph Popp was appointed President. The BMW IV, which could generate 250 bhp even at 10,000 feet (3000 meters), was developed from the BMW IIIa. By autumn of that year BMW was providing gainful employment for a workforce of 3500.

War, according to Heraclitus, is the father of all things. Taking the ancient Greek sage's wise words literally, at the end of 1918 BMW suddenly found itself orphaned. The Treaty of Versailles robbed it of its livelihood at a stroke, as the victorious powers imposed a prohibition on the construction of aviation engines in Germany. Flexibility was called for, and once again Popp came up trumps. An order from the Berlin company Knorr-Bremse AG for 10,000 brake systems for the Bayerische Eisenbahnverwaltung (Bavarian Railway Authority) tided BMW over, though the job was carried out with no great enthusiasm.

However, the obligation to keep the show on the road did not lead Popp to forget the company's true direction. On 9 June 1919, despite the ban, the pilot Zeno Diemer soared in his DFW CIV over Oberwiesenfeld, after 87 minutes reaching the dizzy height of 32,208 feet (9760 meters) – a world record. The IV in the airplane's designation indicates that it belonged in the 200–300 bhp class. It was powered by a BMW IV engine – good publicity for the company. Unfortunately though, Diemer's feat was never recognized by the governing body FAI (Fédération Aéronautique Internationale), since Germany, as a defeated power, was not a member of the organization.

In the spring of 1922, Castiglioni purchased the Bayerische Flugzeugwerke's plant for BMW on Lerchenauer Straße and the Süddeutsche Bremsen AG (Southern German Brakes) moved into their previous premises.

Production now rested essentially on two products. First there was the 45/60 bhp engine, a rugged four-cylinder power unit with a cubic capacity of 8 liters, an overhead camshaft and weighing 11 hundredweight. It was known as the "Bayern-Motor" (Bavarian engine). It had truly universal applications: "The Bayern-Motor, a great success for the German automotive industry, ideal for motor boats, trucks, tractors, motorized plows and motorized bogies," as an advertisement in an automobile magazine proclaimed as early as 1921.

Secondly there was the M 2 B 15 "Bayern-Kleinmotor" (Bavarian mini-engine), designed by the BMW works superintendent Martin Stolle. This was an air-cooled two-cylinder 494 cc boxer engine generating 6.5 bhp at 2800 rpm. It was most suited for use in motorcycles and the smallest automobiles, such as the droll two-wheeled car made by Mauser-Werke, though only 25 of these were ever made, aiming at low-income buyers. On the other hand, the BMW R 32 motorcycle was the sensation of the 1923 Berlin and Paris Motor Shows. This was a milestone in motorcycle design with its tough and robust boxer power train, universal drive and double-tube frame.

At the same time, German aviation was getting back on to its feet after the restrictions of the Versailles Treaty were loosened a little in 1922. BMW made news with a number of spectacular publicity events. For example, on 18 December 1924 the Swiss Lieutenant Colonel Walter Mittelholzer embarked in his Junkers A-20 on the arduous flight from Zurich to Teheran, a flight that would take him over the 18,715 foot (5671 meters) peak Damavand in the Persian Elburz mountains. The heart of the machine was a BMW IV, once again bringing it to the attention of the decision-makers. After the specter of inflation

keine schlechten Erfahrungen gemacht. Verblüfft zeigt er sich indessen über die bescheidenen Räumlichkeiten des Unternehmens und die desolate Verfassung seines Maschinenparks. Gleichwohl investiert er Vertrauen, und das zahlt sich aus, zumal er die Anstellung des fähigen ehemaligen Daimler-Ingenieurs Max Friz unterstützt. Der hat sich gerade bei Rapp beworben, schäumend vor Wut, weil sein alter Chef Paul Daimler in Stuttgart seine Bitte um eine Gehaltserhöhung von 50 Mark im Monat schnöde zurückgewiesen hat.

Am 1. Januar 1917 tritt der Daimler-Renegat seinen Dienst in München an – gegen den Willen von Karl Rapp, der in seinem früheren Mitarbeiter Friz einen Rivalen wittert. Noch mehr

ärgert es ihn, daß er sich in den Dienst einer fremden Sache zu stellen hat, und so zieht er sich verletzt aufs Altenteil zurück. Technischer Direktor wird Franz-Joseph Popp. Doch noch immer krankt die Firma an ihrem schlechten Image. Da bleibt dem Unternehmen nur noch der Ausweg, in eine neue Identität zu schlüpfen. Diese bezeugt der Eintrag im Münchener Gesellschaftsregister vom 21. Juli 1917.

Binnen kurzem kann BMW eine gelungene Friz-Konstruktion vorweisen, den Flugmotor IIIa, einen Sechszylinder. Dank Friz' Höhenvergaser sind von seinen 220 PS am Boden in 6000 Metern Höhe nur die Hälfte abgeschmolzen. Nicht ohne Skepsis ordert das Kriegsministerium 600 Exemplare im Gegenwert von 13,2 Millionen Mark. Weitere Aufträge folgen. Hektische Betriebsamkeit kehrt in der Schleißheimer Straße ein, und schließlich vergeben die Bayerischen Motoren Werke mangels Kapazitäten selber Lizenzen an Opel, Adler, die NAG und an MAN. Auf die Einwände der preußischen und bayerischen Ministerien, die Kapitaldecke sei zu dünn, reagiert man am 13. August 1918 mit der Umwandlung in eine Aktiengesellschaft. Das Grundkapital beläuft sich auf 12 Millionen Mark. Zum Generaldirektor wird Franz-Joseph Popp ernannt. Friz entwickelt aus dem BMW IIIa den BMW IV, der noch in 3000 Metern Höhe mit 250 PS aufwartet. Im Herbst jenes Jahres stehen bei BMW 3500 Mitarbeiter in Lohn und Brot.

commandes de son DFW CIV, décolle de l'aérodrome d'Ober-wiesenfeld et atteint en 87 minutes l'altitude de 9760 m. Record du monde! Le «IV» de la fiche signalétique du moteur symbolise qu'il s'inscrit dans la classe des 200 à 300 ch. L'avion est propulsé par un moteur BMW IV – une bonne publicité. Le record d'altitude de Diemer ne sera toutefois jamais homologué par l'autorité de tutelle, la Fédération Aéronautique Internationale (FAI), car l'Allemagne vaincue ne figure pas parmi ses membres.

Au printemps 1922, Castiglioni achète au nom de BMW les terrains du Bayerische Flugzeugwerke dans la Lerchenauer Straße. La Süddeutsche Bremsen AG s'installe dans ses anciens locaux.

Agriculture, too, was rendered early services, as this advertisement from the magazine Jugend (Youth) of 1918 shows.

Auch um die Landwirtschaft macht man sich frühzeitig verdient, wie diese Anzeige in der Zeitschrift Jugend von 1918 zeigt.

On acquiert aussi, très tôt, du mérite dans l'agriculture, comme le prouve cette annonce dans la revue Jugend (Jeunesse) de 1918.

La firme a désormais pratiquement deux fers au feu. L'un d'eux est le moteur 45/60 PS, un quatre-cylindres rugueux de 8 litres de cylindrée à un arbre à cames en tête et d'un poids de 11 demi-quintaux surnommé «le moteur de Bavière». Il est véritablement d'une extrême polyvalence: «le moteur de Bavière, un grand succès de l'industrie automobile allemande, est en particulier idéal pour les bateaux à moteur, les camions, les tracteurs, les charrues motorisées, les autorails», proclame, dès 1921, une publicité faite dans une revue automobile allemande.

Le «petit moteur de Bavière», le M 2 B 15, un bicylindre à plat refroidi par air de 494 cm³ et 6,5 ch à 2800 tr/mn est une réalisation de Martin Stolle, directeur d'usine chez BMW. Il se prête surtout pour une utilisation dans les motos et voiturettes comme la bizarre voiture monovoie des usines Mauser, qui ne fera le bonheur que de 25 acheteurs. Mais la sensation des Salons de l'Automobile de Paris et de Berlin, en 1923, est la première motocyclette BMW R 32, qui est entrée dans les

Veni, Vidi, Dixi

The Fahrzeugfabrik Eisenach (Eisenach Vehicle Factory) came into being in 1896. Its founding father Heinrich Ehrhardt, a Thuringian country boy, is said to have been multi-talented. One of his achievements was commemorated in his feudal-sounding nickname "Der kleine Kanonenkönig" (The little cannon king), reflecting the fact that he was accredited with the invention of the barrel recoil damper for artillery. He was also ambitious: he aimed to set up the third automobile company in Germany after Daimler and Benz via construction under license of the French make Décauville, with de Dion-Bouton engines under the seat. Though 307 of Ehrhardt's Wartburg cars were produced at his tiny plant, expenses were greater than earnings, and in 1903 he unapologetically called it a day. His parting speech, an attempt to exonerate himself from all guilt, was a testament to his erudite classical education. It is said to have ended with the word "dixi", the standard closing formula of ancient Roman orators, meaning "I have spoken".

No sooner had he left than things began to look up. Without further ado, the product was named after Ehrhardt's parting shot, and the mysterious name had the desired effect. Between 1904 and 1929, 15,822 Dixis were sold. However, right from the start the name was applied to a bewildering variety of different models, from a 1.2-liter for the less well off, to a 5-liter, and culminating with "a huge 'Salonlimousine', a 7.3-liter luxury model (author's note), also available as a sports car or landaulet", as the glib promotional Dixi literature of the time put it. Among a number of features which were ahead of their time was the ingenious modular assembly system.

Business was so good that the loss-making parent company in Gotha was kept going by the Eisenach business. By 1926, though, ruin was staring them in the face. But then the speculator Jakob Schapiro incorporated both companies into his hydra-like organization. New problems were soon to rear their ugly heads. The car factory at Eisenach was required to take over production of a 2.3-liter six-cylinder 40 bhp car from Zyklon, another Schapiro acquisition which in the view of his experienced team of engineers, was an automotive catastrophe. They responded with an alternative design, a 3.5-liter 65 bhp machine which blithely ignored market realities and duly flopped as surely as the cuckoo's egg from the Zyklon camp in Mylau, Saxony.

The fate of the Dixi appeared to be sealed. But then Schapiro had a cunning plan. The most popular small car in Great Britain was the Austin Seven, from the Austin Motor Company in Birmingham. This was a Spartan driving machine, but despite that, as popular as darts. An agreement for its construction under license was quickly reached, and in June 1927, 100 Austin Sevens arrived in Eisenach, still with their original right-hand drive. In no time at all 7000 of the Dixi 3/15 PS had been sold – a point in their favor which did not escape Franz-Joseph Popp's attention any more than the discrete charm of this compact British machine did. However some things, he immediately saw, would have to be changed.

Der Krieg, lehrt Heraklit, sei der Vater aller Dinge. Nimmt man den alten Griechen beim Wort, werden die Bayerischen Motoren Werke Ende 1918 zur vaterlosen Gesellschaft. Der Versailler Vertrag entzieht ihnen durch die strikte Weisung der Siegermächte, den Bau von Flugmotoren einzustellen, die Existenzgrundlage. Flexibilität ist gefragt, Popp verfügt auch darüber. Ein Auftrag der Berliner Knorr-Bremse AG über 10.000 Bremsanlagen für die Bayerische Eisenbahnverwaltung hilft zunächst aus der Patsche, wird aber ohne Leidenschaft umgesetzt.

Über der Pflicht, die Geschäfte am Laufen zu halten, vergißt Popp nicht die Neigung: Am 9. Juni 1919 erhebt sich trotz des Verbots, Flugmotoren zu bauen Pilot Zeno Diemer mit seiner DFW CIV vom Oberwiesenfeld aus in die Lüfte und erreicht in

Dixi-land: 3/15 Dixis, lined up in front of the administration building of the BMW works in Eisenach.

Dixi-Land: Dixi-Wagen vom Typ 3/15, aufgereiht vor dem Direktionsgebäude der BMW-Werke Eisenach.

Pays de Dixi : Dixi 3/15 alignées devant le bâtiment des usines BMW d'Eisernach.

87 Minuten die lichte Höhe von 9760 Metern. Das ist Weltrekord. Die „IV" im Typensigel der Maschine besagt, daß sie in der Klasse 200–300 PS angesiedelt ist. Sie wird von einem BMW-IV-Motor angetrieben – das ist gute Werbung. Der Höhenflug Diemers erhält jedoch nie den Segen der Kontrollbehörde FAI (Fédération Aéronautique Internationale), da ihr das besiegte Deutschland nicht angehört.

Im Frühjahr 1922 ersteht Castiglioni für BMW das Anwesen der Bayerischen Flugzeugwerke in der Lerchenauer Straße. In die bisherigen Räumlichkeiten zieht die Süddeutsche Bremsen AG ein.

Die Produktion ruht nun im wesentlichen auf zwei Säulen. Da ist das Triebwerk 45/60 PS, ein knorriger Vierzylinder mit 8 Litern Hubraum, obenliegender Nockenwelle und 11 Zentnern Gewicht, genannt der „Bayern-Motor". Er ist universell verwendbar: „Der Bayern-Motor, ein großer Erfolg der deutschen Wärmewirtschaft, besonders geeignet für Motorboote, Lastwagen, Traktoren, Motorpflüge, Eisenbahnselbstfahrer", lockt schon 1921 ein Inserat in einer Autozeitschrift.

Um eine Konstruktion von BMW-Werksmeister Martin Stolle handelt es sich bei dem „Bayern-Kleinmotor" M 2 B 15, einem

annales de la moto mondiale avec son indestructible moteur boxer, sa transmission à cardan et sa partie cycle à doubles tubes.

L'aéronautique allemande reprend du poil de la bête dès lors que les conditions draconiennes du Traité de Versailles ont été légèrement allégées en 1922 déjà. BMW fait de la publicité pro domo avec des actions spectaculaires. Le 18 décembre 1924, par exemple, le lieutenant-colonel suisse Walter Mittelholzer, au manche à balai de son Junkers A-20, s'attaque à l'épuisant vol de Zurich à Téhéran à l'occasion duquel il doit franchir des sommets comme le Demãvend, qui culmine à 5671 mètres d'altitude dans le massif de l'Elbourz, en Perse. Le cœur qui bat dans l'appareil est le BMW IV qui, ainsi, se rappelle une fois de plus au bon souvenir des décideurs. Une fois que le spectre de l'inflation s'est dissipé, on majore le capital social de BMW à trois millions de reichsmarks à la fin de fin 1924. Une augmentation de capital est décidée en 1925, à cinq millions de reichsmarks, puis en 1927, à dix millions et, en 1928, à seize millions. A partir de 1926, Dr Emil Georg von Stauss siège au conseil de surveillance de la Bayerische Motoren Werke AG en qualité de représentant de la Deutsche Bank et, à partir de 1927, en tant que son président. Le numéro deux est Camillo Castiglioni. Simultanément, en un patient et intelligent jeu d'échecs, von Stauss commence, partout où cela lui est possible, à couper l'herbe sous le pied à l'influent, mais intrigant Autrichien.

Parfois, les deux hommes font cause commune, même si leurs motifs sont parfois profondément différents. L'avenir de BMW – là-dessus, les deux hommes sont unanimes – réside dans la construction d'automobiles. Ils n'envisagent toutefois pas de partir d'une feuille blanche et se mettent donc en quête d'un partenaire déjà bien établi, si possible quelqu'un qui jouisse d'une bonne réputation et se trouve pourtant en difficultés. Castiglioni, qui se pare entre-temps du titre honorifique et pompeux, mais sans signification réelle, de «Président des Bayerische Motoren Werke», joue les intermédiaires auprès de la direction de la Eisenacher Fahrzeugfabrik, une filiale de la Gothaer Waggonfabrik. Il lui rachète sa filiale qui se trouve à l'ombre de la Wartburg, le 14 novembre 1928, contre 200 000 reichsmarks versés en espèces et des actions de BMW pour une valeur nominale de 800 000 reichsmarks. Simultanément, les Bavarois reprennent les dettes de leur filiale adoptive de Thuringe, qui s'élèvent à onze millions de reichsmarks.

Carrière entre crise et catastrophe (1928–1945)

Les débuts de BMW en tant que constructeur d'automobiles sont modestes, mais le cap est le bon. La monoculture est de règle puisque le seul modèle construit est, pour l'instant, la 3/15 PS. Jusqu'à la mi-1929 encore, l'Anglaise naturalisée allemande continue d'être produite dans sa version de Thuringe, sauf qu'elle a le volant à gauche, en tant que Dixi 3/15 PS DA 1 (DA pour Dixi-Austin ou, aussi, pour Deutsche Ausführung – exécution allemande). A la fin du mois de juillet de cette année, la presse attentive et un public très intéressé découvrent dans les nouveaux salons d'exposition de BMW, au 5 de la

A legend in its own lifetime: the R 32, the first motorcycle of the Bayerische Motoren Werke.

Schon zu Lebzeiten eine Legende: die R 32, das erste Motorrad der Bayerischen Motoren Werke.

Du temps de sa production, déjà une légende: la R 32, la première moto des Bayerische Motoren Werke.

had subsided, BMW capital stock was set at three million reichsmarks at the end of 1924. This figure was raised to five million reichsmarks in 1925, to ten million in 1927, and to sixteen million in 1928. From 1926 onwards Dr Emil Georg von Stauss joined the supervisory board of Bayerische Motoren Werke AG as a representative of Deutsche Bank, becoming its president in 1927. The number two was Camillo Castiglioni, but von Stauss had begun a cunning and dogged tactical battle aimed at reducing the influence of the slippery Austrian wherever possible.

However, over some matters they could work in unison, albeit acting from very different motives. The general consensus, for example, was that the future of BMW lay in the construction of automobiles. They did not intend to start from scratch though, aiming rather to enter into partnership with a pre-existing manufacturer with a good reputation but running into difficulties. Castiglioni, now with the impressive-sounding but fairly meaningless honorary title "President of the Bayerische Motoren Werke" acted as an intermediary to the management of Eisenacher Fahrzeugfabrik (Eisenacher Automobile Factory), a subsidiary of Gothaer Waggonfabrik (Gothaer Railway Wagon Factory). On 14 November 1928, the subsidiary, located in Thuringia, eastern Germany, was duly sold to BMW in return for 200,000 reichsmarks in cash plus BMW shares to a nominal value of 800,000 reichsmarks. The Bavarian company also took on the Thuringian subsidiary's liabilities, amounting to eleven million reichsmarks.

Success During Crisis and Catastrophe (1928–1945)

BMW's first efforts as an automobile manufacturer were modest, but in the right direction. Initially they limited themselves to manufacturing the 3/15 PS. This native English machine continued to be built until mid-1929 in the Thuringian version, but now with the steering wheel on the left and designated the Dixi 3/15 PS DA 1 (DA standing for Dixi Austin or Deutsche Ausführung meaning German construction). By the end of July of that year, the BMW 3/15 PS DA 2 was introduced to an attentive press and to great public interest in BMW's new showrooms in Berlin's Gutenbergstraße 5. The car had been

luftgekühlten Zweizylinder-Boxer mit 494 ccm und 6,5 PS bei 2800 Umdrehungen pro Minute. Geeignet ist er vor allem für die Verwendung in Motorrädern und Kleinstautos wie dem skurrilen Einspur-Wagen der Mauser-Werke, der allerdings lediglich in einer Stückzahl von 25 Exemplaren unter die armen Leute gebracht wird. Zur Sensation der Pariser und Berliner Autosalons von 1923 wird die erste BMW-Maschine Typ R 32, ein Meilenstein im weltweiten Motorradbau mit ihrem robusten Boxer-Triebwerk, Kardanantrieb und Doppelrohrrahmen.

Doch auch die deutsche Fliegerei faßt wieder Tritt, nachdem die Beschränkungen des Versailler Vertrags schon 1922 ein wenig gelockert worden sind. BMW macht mit spektakulären Aktionen von sich reden. Am 18. Dezember 1924 etwa begibt sich der eidgenössische Oberleutnant Walter Mittelholzer mit seiner Junkers A-20 auf den beschwerlichen Flug von Zürich nach Teheran und muß dabei Gipfel wie den 5671 Meter hohen Demawend im persischen Elbursgebirge überwinden. Das Herz der Maschine ist der BMW IV, der sich damit erneut der geneigten Aufmerksamkeit der Entscheidungsträger empfiehlt. Nachdem der Spuk der Inflation verflogen ist, setzt man das BMW-Aktienkapital Ende 1924 auf drei Millionen Reichsmark fest. Erhöhungen folgen 1925 auf fünf Millionen, 1927 auf zehn Millionen und 1928 auf sechzehn Millionen. Ab 1926 sitzt Dr. Emil Georg von Stauss als Repräsentant der Deutschen Bank im Aufsichtsrat der Bayerischen Motoren Werke AG, ab 1927 als Vorsitzender. Zweiter Mann ist Camillo Castiglioni. Zugleich beginnt von Stauss, in einem klugen und zähen Schachspiel den Einfluß des wendigen und windigen Österreichers zu unterbinden, wo immer das möglich ist.

Gleichwohl zieht man gelegentlich an einem Strang, wenn auch aus unterschiedlichen Motiven. Die Zukunft von BMW, darüber herrscht Konsens, liege im Bau von Automobilen. Allerdings denkt man nicht an einen Start aus dem Stand, sondern sucht nach einem real existierenden Partner, vorzugsweise mit einem guten Namen, der dennoch in Nöten ist. Castiglioni, inzwischen mit dem pompösen, aber ziemlich unverbindlichen Ehrentitel „Präsident der Bayerischen Motoren Werke" bedacht, fungiert als Mittelsmann gegenüber dem Management der Eisenacher Fahrzeugfabrik, einer Filiale der Gothaer Waggonfabrik. Dieser kauft man den Zweigbetrieb im Schatten der Wartburg am 14. November 1928 ab, gegen 200.000 Reichsmark bar auf die Hand und BMW-Aktien im Nennwert von 800.000 Reichsmark. Zugleich übernehmen die Bayern Verbindlichkeiten der thüringischen Adoptivtochter in Höhe von elf Millionen Reichsmark.

Karriere zwischen Krise und Katastrophe (1928–1945)

Die Anfänge der Bayerischen Motoren Werke als Hersteller von Automobilen sind bescheiden, aber die Richtung stimmt. Zunächst beschränkt man sich auf die Herstellung des 3/15 PS in Monokultur. Noch bis Mitte 1929 wird der naturalisierte Engländer in der thüringischen Version weitergebaut, nun mit dem Lenkrad auf der linken Seite als Dixi 3/15 PS DA 1 (für Dixi-Austin oder auch Deutsche Ausführung). Ende Juli jenes Jahres wird in den neuen Schauräumen der Bayerischen Motoren Werke in der Berliner Gutenbergstraße 5 der aufmerksamen Presse und einem höchst aufgeschlossenen Publikum der BMW

Gutenbergstraße à Berlin, la BMW 3/15 PS DA 2 que Popp a adaptée au goût allemand grâce à de discrètes et réussies retouches et a également rendue plus sûre. En un paradoxe subtil, la publicité proclame que la nouvelle voiture est «plus grande à l'intérieur qu'à l'extérieur». En publicité, la marque n'a, dès cette époque, jamais fait preuve de modestie: «BMW pense à l'époque de demain», peut-on lire ailleurs.

Alors que, sur la première Dixi, l'effet du frein à main sur les roues avant et du frein à pédale sur les roues arrière était des plus souples, un freinage à câble sur les quatre roues confère à la DA 2 une décélération digne de ce nom. La calandre a une forme différente et l'emblème bleu et blanc bien connu a supplanté le logo de la Dixi, un centaure au galop avec la crinière flottant dans le vent.

La petite BMW est tout d'abord proposée au prix de 2500 reichsmarks en une version berline avec une carrosserie tout acier sans marchepied fabriquée par Ambi-Budd à Berlin. Pour son esthétique, BMW s'est inspirée de Lucien Rosengart, à Neuilly-sur-Seine, qui commercialise lui aussi des répliques sous licence de l'Austin Seven - traitées à la française. Elle possède des vitres à manivelle et non pas coulissant dans les portières, une lunette arrière plus grande et des sièges avant réglables. A cela s'ajoutent deux variantes décapotables, une tourer à quatre places et une biplace de construction allégée avec un châssis en bois recouvert de similicuir, le tout vendu au prix défiant toute concurrence de 2200 reichsmarks. BMW ne manque pas d'arguments face à ses concurrents dans le segment des voiturettes: l'Opel «Grenouille» toujours livrée en vert comme il se doit, sa concurrente directe, qui représente un tiers de la production automobile allemande en 1928 avec 42 741 exemplaires produits, coûte sensiblement le même prix. Une autre rivale, moins menaçante celle-là, la Hanomag 3/16 PS, coûte déjà 2800 reichsmarks.

Pour le reste, l'automobile a le vent en poupe. Naturellement, l'onde de choc du crash du 25 octobre 1929 à Wall Street avec ses remous consécutifs ébranle aussi le territoire de BMW à Munich et à Eisenach. En 1928, le personnel comprenant 2600 collaborateurs réalise un chiffre d'affaires de 27 millions de reichsmarks et de 34 millions en 1929 avec 3800 ouvriers (Eisenach compris). Le chiffre d'affaires passe à 36 millions de reichsmarks pour 3100 ouvriers en 1930 avant de retomber à 27 millions seulement pour 2900 collaborateurs en 1931. Le creux de la vague est atteint en 1932 lorsque BMW emploie 2800 ouvriers et que son chiffre d'affaires fond à 20 millions de reichsmarks.

Comparée à d'autres enterprises, la marque surmonte sans trop de dommages le cataclysme du Vendredi noir, ce qui est dû à plusieurs facteurs. D'une part, la 3/15 PS est la voiture prédestinée pour une période de crise. Le numéro de juin 1930 de la revue de l'entreprise munichoise *BMW Blätter* ne manque pas l'occasion, par galanterie teintée de sens des affaires, de vanter les qualités de la dame au volant. Mais elle loue aussi les atouts de la «voiture de 15 ch» comme tirelire mobile: elle n'est «pas seulement un allégement intellectuel, mais représente aussi une économie financière considérable». Pour une moyenne annuelle de 30 000 km, calcule l'auteur avec précision, son propriétaire peut se contenter de 5,11 pfennigs de coûts d'exploitation au kilomètre, ce qui est vraiment minime.

Naturellement, le succès de cette naine s'explique tout d'abord aussi par la voiturette elle-même, dont on ne peut que tomber amoureux, ainsi que Franz-Joseph Popp le constate déjà

cleverly restyled by Popp to suit German taste, and its safety had also been improved. The new model was, according to the somewhat paradoxical advertising, "bigger inside than out". Even in those days they were never short of a snappy slogan or two: "BMW has a vision for the world of tomorrow," was another.

While the Dixi's brakes were comparatively feeble, with just a handbrake for the front wheels and a foot brake for the rear ones, the model DA 2's cable-actuated four-wheel braking system provided a respectable amount of stopping power. The radiator grill had been redesigned, and the famous blue-and-white trade mark had replaced the Dixi emblem, a galloping centaur with a flowing head of hair.

This diminutive BMW was initially on sale from Ambi-Budd in Berlin at a price of 2500 reichsmarks, firstly as a sedan with all-steel bodywork and no running boards. For the styling, BMW had availed itself of the services of Lucien Rosengart of Neuilly-sur-Seine, who specialized in the construction under license of Austin Seven reproductions à la française. It was fitted with winding windows in place of the previous sliding ones, and with a larger rear windscreen and adjustable front seats. There were also two open-top versions, a four-seater tourer and also a lightweight construction two-seater with artificial leather coverings over a wooden frame, available at the give-away price of 2200 reichsmarks. This put BMW in a good position in the competitive small car market. Its direct competitor, the Opel "Laubfrosch", which left the factory a grass-green color, was responsible for over a third of all German automobile production in 1928, manufacturing a total of more than 42,741 cars, and costing roughly the same as the BMW. The much less threatening rival, the Hanomag 3/16 PS, would set you back 2800 reichsmarks.

All in all fate smiled on BMW. Of course the Wall Street Crash of 25 October 1929 and its long-term aftershocks did not spare BMW's home territory in Munich and Eisenach. In 1928 a workforce of 2600 achieved a turnover of 27 million reichsmarks, while in 1929, 3800 produced 34 million (including the Eisenach plant). In 1930 a workforce of 3100 were responsible for sales of 36 million reichsmarks, figures which fell in 1931 to 2900 and 27 million respectively. The low point was reached in 1932, when BMW's workforce fell to 2800, and their turnover to 20 million reichsmarks.

The fact that BMW survived Black Friday relatively unscathed, compared with other businesses, is due to several factors. Firstly, the 3/15 PS could have been tailor-made for the slump. The June 1930 edition of the Munich in-house publication *BMW Blätter* did not refrain from extolling the virtues of the lady at the wheel of the 15 bhp automobile, but was also quick to praise the money-saving virtues of the car itself, proclaiming that it represented "not just spiritual balm, but at the same time an outstanding financial saving". The meticulous author has calculated that, with an annual mileage of 18,645 miles (30,000 km), the owner's running costs come to a modest 5.11 pfennigs per kilometer.

Naturally the character of the car itself was responsible for a good deal of its success. It was a car that you just had to fall in love with, as Franz-Joseph Popp himself had observed when first viewing the original in Eisenach. As early as 1929 the BMW 3/15 PS and its creators made names for themselves via the motor sport successes of Max Buchner, Albert Kandt and Willi Wagner, who drove a brandnew 3/15 to victory in the

Veni, Vidi, Dixi

Die Fahrzeugfabrik Eisenach wird im Jahre 1896 ins Leben gerufen. Gründungsvater Heinrich Ehrhardt, Sohn eines thüringischen Waldbauern, gilt als Multitalent. Eine seiner Facetten spiegelt sich in seinem feudal-militanten Spitznamen „der kleine Kanonenkönig" wider: Man schreibt ihm die Erfindung der Rohrrücklaufbremse an Geschützen zu. Ehrgeizig ist er auch: Mittels Lizenzbauten des französischen Fabrikats Décauville mit de Dion-Bouton-Triebwerken unter dem Sitz möchte er sich nach Daimler und Benz als dritte Marke auf dem deutschen Markt einrichten. Obwohl 307 von Ehrhardts Wartburg-Wagen das winzige Werk verlassen, übersteigen die Ausgaben entschieden die Einnahmen. 1903 nimmt er seinen Hut. Seine Abschiedsrede – ein Versuch, sich von Schuld reinzuwaschen – zeugt von humanistischem Feinschliff. Sie soll mit „dixi" geendet haben, der stereotypen Schlußformel römischer Redner: „Ich habe gesprochen."

Kaum ist er weg, geht es bergauf. Kurzerhand benennt man das Produkt nach Ehrhardts Schlußwort. Der dynamisch-mysteriöse Begriff verfehlt seine Wirkung nicht. Zwischen 1904 und 1929 werden 15.822 Dixis unter das fahrende Volk gebracht. Dabei deckt der einheitliche Name von Anfang an eine strotzende Vielfalt von Varianten ab, vom 1,2-Liter für die weniger Betuchten unter den Freunden der Marke über einen 5-Liter bis hin zur „Salonlimousine (mit 7,3 Litern, Anm. d. Verf.) in Luxusausführung, auch als Sportwagen und Landaulet zu haben", wie es in der Dixi-Werbung voller Eigenlob heißt. Seiner Zeit weit voraus ist unter anderem ein ausgeklügeltes Baukastensystem.

Das Geschäft läuft so gut, daß das verlustträchtige Mutterhaus in Gotha von den Eisenachern mitgeschleppt werden muß wie ein siecher Greis. 1926 droht der Ruin. Dennoch verleibt der Spekulant Jakob Schapiro beide Unternehmen seiner Vielfirmen-Hydra ein. Neue Probleme erheben drohend ihr Haupt. Der Fahrzeugfabrik Eisenach wird zur Auflage gemacht, einen 2,3-Liter-Sechszylinder mit 40 PS von Zyklon zu übernehmen, einer anderen Schapiro-Erwerbung, in den Augen ihres erfahrenen Ingenieursteams eine automobile Katastrophe. Man antwortet mit einem Gegenentwurf, einem 3,5 Liter mit 60 PS, souverän am Markt vorbeigeplant und deshalb ebenso ein Flop wie das Kuckucksei aus der Zyklon-Garnison Mylau in Sachsen.

Unabwendbar scheint das „Dixi" am Ende der Grabrede auf Dixi. Da hat Schapiro eine clevere Idee. Großbritanniens Kleinwagen mit der größten Verbreitung ist der Seven der Austin Motor Company in Birmingham – eine spartanisch karge Fahrmaschine und dennoch populär wie der Dart-Sport. Über einen Lizenzbau hat man sich schnell geeinigt, und im Juni 1927 treffen 100 Austin Seven in Eisenach ein, noch im Urzustand mit Rechtslenkung. Im Nu sind 7000 Exemplare als Dixi 3/15 PS verkauft – ein Argument, dem sich Franz-Joseph Popp ebenso wenig entziehen kann wie dem diskreten Charme des britischen Winzlings. Einiges jedoch, das weiß er sofort, wird man wohl ändern müssen.

lors de l'inspection de l'original, à Eisenach. Dès 1929, le sport permet à la BMW 3/15 PS et à ses géniteurs de devenir célèbres lorsque trois compères – Max Buchner, Albert Kandt et Willi Wagner – au volant d'un exemplaire flambant neuf, gagnent la Coupe internationale des Alpes à la moyenne remarquable de 42 km/h. Un autre argument percutant pour les vendeurs est la possibilité de paiement à tempérament, introduite en avril 1929. De nombreux adeptes de BMW y recourent sans hésiter et payent leur DA 2 à raison de 24 mensualités à 107 reichsmarks chacune.

Pour le reste, aussi, Popp et son équipe ont la chance de leur côté, par exemple lorsqu'ils arrondissent vers le bas, en 1931, le programme de motocyclettes avec la monocylindre R 2 de 200 cm³. D'autres piliers sur lesquels la maison BMW repose en toute sécurité sont ses moteurs d'avions, par exemple le neuf-cylindres en étoile Hornet de 525 ch, copyright Pratt & Whitney. Un cinq-cylindres d'initialement 50 ch, puis 54 ch, qui est né sur la planche à dessin de l'ingénieur en chef Max Friz, est destiné aux avions de sport.

Back against the wall: the postal service does not want to do without the Dixi either. The spare wheel is fixed to the roof.

Mit dem Rücken zur Wand: Auch die Reichspost mag auf den Dixi nicht verzichten. Der Reservereifen ist auf dem Dach befestigt.

Le dos au mur: la Poste impériale, elle non plus, ne veut pas se passer de la Dixi. Le pneu de secours est fixé sur le toit.

Popp travaille d'arrache-pied pour agrandir et réorganiser le réseau de concessionnaires et de service après-vente, notamment les points de vente, chargés jusque-là des motocyclettes de la marque. Quelques concessionnaires de Mercedes sont également de la partie. Leurs programmes se complètent parce que, durant cette phase de dépression, les voitures de chez Daimler-Benz, toutes beaucoup plus coûteuses, sont plus difficiles à vendre et que l'on entretient en outre des relations amicales. De 1926, année de la fondation, à 1945, Franz-Joseph Popp est membre du conseil de surveillance de Daimler-Benz tandis que, de 1932 à la fin de la guerre, Dr Wilhelm Kissel – jusqu'en 1942 président du directoire de la firme à l'étoile de Stuttgart – siège au conseil de surveillance de BMW.

BMW relève le défi des années 30 avec la troïka motocyclettes, automobiles et moteurs d'avion. Cette dernière branche prend toutefois une telle ampleur que l'on doit vite créer une firme spécifique, la BMW Flugmotorenbau Gesellschaft mbH, à Munich, avec un capital social de 7,5 millions de reichsmarks, le 31 décembre 1934. La filiale d'Eisenach, aussi, qui reçoit de nombreuses commandes de développement des Forces aériennes, accède bientôt à l'autonomie.

Le catalogue des appareils propulsés par des moteurs BMW ressemble à un «Who's who» de l'aéronautique. On y trouve le légendaire Junkers 52, qui semble éternel, au même titre que le

Piggyback: Dixis being loaded in the works yard in Eisenach.

Huckepacksystem: Dixi-Verladung auf dem Werkhof in Eisenach.

En route: chargement de Dixi dans la cours de l'usine d'Eisenach.

International Alpenfahrt (Alpine Race) with an outstanding average speed of 26 mph (42 kph). Furthermore, the introduction of an installment plan in April 1929 proved to be a potent selling point, the offer being taken up by many BMW fans, who paid for their DA 2 in 24 monthly installments of 107 reichsmarks.

In other respects, too, Popp and his team held a strong hand, for example their range of motorcycles, which they rounded off in 1931 with the single-cylinder 200 cc R 2. A third mainstay of the BMW marque was its airplane engines, including the nine-cylinder radial engine Hornet, developing 525 bhp, manufactured under license from Pratt & Whitney. There was also a five-cylinder 50 bhp (later 54 bhp) engine, aimed at the sports airplane market, from the drawing-board of chief designer Max Friz.

Popp worked energetically on expanding and overhauling his distribution and service networks, in particular the centers which had hitherto dealt with the marque's motorcycles. This even included a few Mercedes dealers. During the Great Depression the much more expensive Daimler-Benz products were far harder to shift, and in any case relations between the two companies were cordial in those days. From the year of its formation in 1926 until 1945, Franz-Joseph Popp was a member of Daimler-Benz's supervisory board, and from 1932 until the end of the War, Dr Wilhelm Kissel, until 1942 President of Daimler-Benz's executive board, also sat on BMW's supervisory board.

BMW confronted the challenges of the 1930s on three fronts: motorcycles, automobiles and aviation engines. This latter division had in the meantime grown to such an extent that, with effect from 31 December 1934, it was hived off to Munich as BMW Flugmotorenbau Gesellschaft mbH (BMW Aviation Engine Construction Ltd), with capital stock of 7.5 million reichsmarks. And the branch in Eisenach, where intensive development work for the "Luftwaffe" was being undertaken, was soon trading as an independent entity.

The catalog of airplanes fitted with BMW power units reads like a "Who's Who" of aviation history. The legendary Junkers 52, along with the Dornier Wal and the Heinkel He 70 plane, are among its entries. Among the products to stem from the expert hands of chief designer Max Friz was the BMW 132, developed from the Pratt & Whitney engine the Hornet, which BMW had been constructing under license. This engine's 28 liter cubic capacity gave it a continuous output at 12,540 feet (3800 meters) of 625 bhp. In 1934, the year of the split, BMW's range of motorcycles included 200, 400 and 750 cc models, while the

3/15 PS DA 2 präsentiert, den Popp durch geschickte Retuschen dem deutschen Geschmack angepaßt und sicherer gemacht hat. Der Neue, so verheißt die Werbung in subtiler Paradoxie, sei „innen größer als außen". Um flotte Sprüche ist man schon damals nicht verlegen: „BMW denkt an die Zeit von morgen", heißt es an anderer Stelle.

Während im Dixi die Handbremse vergleichsweise milde auf die Vorderräder und die Fußbremse auf die Hinterräder einwirkt, sorgt am Modell DA 2 eine Seilzug-Vierradanlage für eine passable Verzögerung. Anders geformt ist die Kühlermaske, und das bekannte weißblaue Markenzeichen hat das Dixi-Emblem verdrängt, einen Zentauren in vollem Galopp mit flatterndem Haupthaar.

Für 2500 Reichsmark ist der kleine BMW zunächst als Limousine mit einer Ganzstahlkarosserie ohne Trittbretter von Ambi-Budd in Berlin erhältlich. Was das Styling anbelangt, hat man bei Lucien Rosengart in Neuilly-sur-Seine Anleihen gemacht, der seinerseits Lizenz-Nachbauten des Austin Seven in die Welt setzt – à la française. Sie wartet mit Kurbelfenstern anstatt der bisherigen Schiebefenster in den Türen, einer größeren Heckscheibe und verstellbaren Vordersitzen auf. Dazu kommen zwei offene Varianten, ein Tourer mit vier Plätzen sowie ein Zweisitzer in Leichtbauweise mit einem Kunstlederbezug über dem Holzrahmen zum Spottpreis von 2200 Reichsmark. Damit liegt BMW gut im Rennen und im Wettbewerb der Winzlinge: Der grasgrüne Opel Laubfrosch als direkter Konkurrent, 1928 durch eine Verbreitung von 42.741 Einheiten mit über einem Drittel an der deutschen Automobilproduktion beteiligt, kostet ungefähr genausoviel. Die Anschaffung des weit weniger bedrohlichen Rivalen Hanomag 3/16 PS schlägt mit 2800 Reichsmark zu Buche.

Trotz allem lacht BMW die Gunst der Stunde. Natürlich erschüttern die Schockwelle und die lang anhaltenden Nachbeben des Wall Street Crashs vom 25. Oktober 1929 auch das BMW-Territorium in München und Eisenach. 1928 erwirtschaftet eine Belegschaft von 2600 Mitarbeitern einen Umsatz von 27 Millionen Reichsmark. 1929 sind es 3800 bei 34 Millionen Umsatz (einschließlich Eisenach). 1930 erwirtschaften 3100 Kostgänger 36 Millionen Reichsmark und 1931 sind es nur noch 2900 bei 27 Millionen Umsatz. Die Talsohle ist 1932 erreicht, als BMW 2800 Werktätige beschäftigt und der Umsatz auf 20 Millionen Reichsmark zusammengeschmolzen ist.

Daß man aus dem Schatten des Schwarzen Freitags im Vergleich zu anderen Unternehmen relativ ungeschoren heraustritt, läßt sich auf mehrere Faktoren zurückführen. Zum einen wirkt der 3/15 PS wie maßgeschneidert für die Krise. Die Juni-Ausgabe der Münchener Hauspostille BMW Blätter von 1930 versäumt nicht, in gewinnorientierter Galanterie eine Lanze für die Qualitäten der Dame am Lenkrad zu brechen. Sie preist aber auch die Qualitäten des 15-PS-Wagens als mobiles Sparschwein: Er stelle „nicht nur eine geistige Entlastung dar, sondern zugleich eine außerordentliche finanzielle Erleichterung". Bei einem Jahresschnitt von 30.000 Kilometern, errechnet der Autor penibel, komme der Eigner mit moderaten 5,11 Pfennigen Betriebskosten pro Kilometer hin.

Verantwortlich für den Erfolg des Zwergs ist natürlich zunächst einmal das Wägelchen selbst, in das man sich einfach verlieben müsse, wie Franz-Joseph Popp bereits bei der Besichtigung des Originals in Eisenach feststellt. Schon 1929 gereicht dem BMW 3/15 PS und seinen Erzeugern der Sport zum Ruhme, als Max Buchner, Albert Kandt und Willi Wagner in einem

Veni, Vidi, Dixi

La Fahrzeugfabrik Eisenach (usine de voitures) est fondée en 1896. Son fondateur, Heinrich Ehrhardt, un fils de sylviculteur de Thuringe, est réputé pour ses multiples talents. Son martial surnom «le petit roi du canon» est, déjà, révélateur: c'est à lui que l'on attribue l'invention du frein de recul des canons d'artillerie. Qui plus est, il est ambitieux: à l'aide de Décauville françaises à moteur de type de Dion Bouton sous le siège, produites sous licence, il veut s'établir comme troisième marque sur le marché allemand après Daimler et Benz. Bien que 307 Wartburg d'Ehrhardt quittent la minuscule usine, les dépenses excèdent largement les recettes. En 1903, il jette l'éponge sans prévenir. Son discours d'adieu, une tentative de se laver de toute faute, témoigne de son éducation humaniste. Selon la légende, ce discours se serait terminé par «dixi», la formule stéréotype utilisée par les tribuns romains: «Dixi, j'ai parlé.»

À peine est-il parti que sa firme reprend du poil de la bête. Spontanément, on baptise le produit du dernier mot prononcé par Ehrhardt. Ce terme aussi dynamique que mystérieux ne manque pas son effet. Entre 1904 et 1929, 15 822 Dixi trouvent preneur. Dès le début, ce nom unique est apposé sur une grande diversité de modèles, le programme allant d'une 1,2 litre pour les moins riches parmi les amis de la marque à une 5 litres et même une «limousine de salon» (de 7,3 litres, note de l'auteur) en exécution de luxe, disponible aussi bien en tant que voiture de sport que landaulet», peut-on lire dans la fière publicité pro domo pour la Dixi. Son système de construction modulaire bien pensé, notamment, est très en avance sur son temps.

Les affaires marchent si bien que le groupe de Gotha, auquel appartient Dixi et qui n'engrange que des pertes, doit être traîné comme un boulet par la firme d'Eisenach. En 1926, la ruine menace. Ceci n'empêche pas le spéculateur Jakob Schapiro d'intégrer les deux entreprises à la nébuleuse de ses firmes. De nouveaux problèmes se font de plus en plus menaçants. L'usine de voitures d'Eisenach se voit contrainte de reprendre de Zyklon – une autre acquisition de Schapiro – une six-cylindres de 2,3 litres de 40 ch, une voiture qui est, aux yeux de son équipe d'ingénieurs expérimentés, un modèle sans avenir. Ils répliquent avec leur propre projet, une 3,5 litres de 60 ch qui ne répond absolument pas aux besoins du marché et est donc un échec retentissant, comme l'œuf de coucou de Mylau, la ville garnison de Zyklon, en Saxe.

«Dixi» semble devoir de nouveau s'imprimer, bien que l'on s'en défende bien, à la fin du discours d'enterrement de la Dixi. C'est alors que Schapiro a une idée intelligente. La voiturette la plus vendue de Grande-Bretagne est la Seven, fabriquée à Birmingham par l'Austin Motor Company, un engin spartiate et, pourtant, aussi populaire que le jeu de fléchettes. Il se met rapidement d'accord pour obtenir la licence et, en juin 1927, 100 Austin Seven arrivent à Eisenach, dans leur état original avec le volant à droite. En un rien de temps, il en vend 7000 exemplaires sous le nom de 3/15 PS – un argument auquel Franz-Joseph Popp peut tout aussi peu résister qu'au charme discret de cette minuscule voiture britannique. Il y a toutefois une chose qui lui vient immédiatement à l'esprit, il va absolument falloir y apporter quelques modifications.

three-wheeler delivery vans F 76 and F 79, their moderate fuel consumption ideal for the Depression years, were powered by motorcycle components and could be purchased tax-free and driven without a driver's license.

However, the company's most recent division, automobile construction, was becoming ever more important. A turning point here was the ending of the license agreement with Austin on 1 March 1932, which coincided with the introduction by BMW of the 3/20 PS, officially known as the 0,8 Liter/20 PS, bearing witness for all to see that their automobiles had now flown the nest. The only thing it had in common with its predecessor was the archaic front transverse leaf spring, but without the old rigid axle. The car's angular lines were in tune with contemporary style trends. The reviewers praised the appealing bodywork with which the 3/20 PS was fitted at the Mercedes-Benz body plant at Sindelfingen. Its successor, the 309, appeared two years later. The origin of the "3" as a model designation remains unclear. However, in what was to become standard future BMW usage, the two final digits indicate the capacity of each of its four cylinders: 845 cc, generously rounded up to 0.9 liters.

In contrast, the numbers 303 as the designation for the first BMW six-cylinder are difficult to interpret today. This model was launched in February 1933 at the Berlin Motor Show. Beneath its notched hood lay an 1173 cc engine, making it the smallest six-cylinder on the market. On top of this, the 303 was the first BMW with the unmistakable BMW front end, which would be familiar to future generations: the kidney shape, topped by the famous blue and white propeller. If you find the right street, a contemporary test driver enthused, the six-cylinder engine would enable you to "revel in the breathtaking feel of 100 kph (62.5 mph) speed". The men behind this machine were Fritz Fiedler, who had done outstanding work for Horch in the design of their eight and twelve-cylinder engines, and Rudolf Schleicher, who, after a period with Horch at the beginning of

Streamlined: Ernst Henne in 1931 during a world record drive on the Neunkirchner Allee between Vienna and Wiener Neustadt.

Stromlinie: Ernst Henne 1931 bei seiner Weltrekordfahrt auf der Neunkirchner Allee zwischen Wien und Wiener Neustadt.

Aérodynamique: Ernst Henne, en 1931, de son record du monde sur la Neunkirchner Allee entre Vienne et Wiener Neustadt.

the 1930s, had returned to BMW. The engine's essential character was superb. From the start it was subject to a continual development process involving several increases in cubic capacity, by the end of which it had grown in size to around two liters. The culmination of the earlier 3 series was the 326 of 1936. With sales of 15,936 cars between 1936 and 1941 it became the best-selling BMW of its era. As early as 1935, a construction license had been granted to Frazer-Nash of

13 cylinders: a Junkers 52 with nine combustion chambers flies nimbly over a BMW four-cylinder in 1983.

13 Zylinder: Eine Junkers 52 mit neun Verbrennungseinheiten überfliegt 1983 behäbig den BMW-Vierzylinder.

13 cylindres: un Junkers 52 à moteur à neuf cylindres survolant le bâtiment de BMW «à quatre cylindres» en 1983.

brandneuen Exemplar die internationale Alpenfahrt mit dem bemerkenswerten Schnitt von 42 Stundenkilometern gewinnen. Als Verkaufsargument erweist sich darüber hinaus die Möglichkeit der Teilzahlung, eingeführt im April 1929. Viele BMW-Anhänger machen bereitwillig davon Gebrauch und stottern ihren DA 2 in 24 Raten à 107 Reichsmark ab.

Auch sonst haben Popp und seine Männer eine glückliche Hand, zum Beispiel als sie 1931 das Motorradprogramm mit dem Einzylinder-Modell R 2 mit 200 ccm nach unten abrunden. Weitere Säulen, auf denen das Haus BMW sicher ruht, sind seine Flugmaschinen, etwa ein Neunzylinder-Sternmotor Typ Hornet mit 525 PS, Copyright Pratt & Whitney. Für Sportflugzeuge gedacht ist ein Fünfzylinder mit zunächst 50 PS und später 54 PS, der am Reißbrett des Chefkonstrukteurs Max Friz entsteht.

Energisch kümmert sich Popp um Ausweitung und Umgestaltung des Betriebs- und Servicenetzes, vor allem der Stützpunkte, die sich bislang um die Motorräder der Marke gekümmert haben. Auch ein paar Mercedes-Händler sind dabei. Die Programme ergänzen sich – während der Weltwirtschaftskrise lassen sich die durchweg weit teureren Produkte von Daimler-Benz viel schwerer absetzen – und überdies ist man einander freundschaftlich verbunden. Vom Gründungsjahr 1926 bis 1945 sitzt Franz-Joseph Popp im Aufsichtsrat von Daimler-Benz und Dr. Wilhelm Kissel, bis 1942 Vorstandsvorsitzender der Stuttgarter Firma mit dem Stern, sitzt von 1932 bis Kriegsende im Aufsichtsrat von BMW.

Den Herausforderungen der dreißiger Jahre begegnen die Bayerischen Motoren Werke dreispurig mit den Produktlinien Motorrad, Auto und Flugmotor. Letzterer Zweig erlangt indessen solche Bedeutung, daß man ihn mit Wirkung vom 31. Dezember 1934 kurzerhand als BMW Flugmotorenbau Gesellschaft mbH zu München mit einem Stammkapital von 7,5 Millionen Reichsmark ausgliedert. Auch die Filiale in Eisenach, wo man intensive Entwicklungsarbeit für die Luftwaffe leistet, firmiert bald mit einer selbständigen Identität.

Der Katalog der Maschinen, die durch BMW-Triebwerke beflügelt werden, liest sich wie ein „Who's who" der Lüfte. Die unsterbliche Legende Junkers 52 findet sich ebenso darunter wie die Dornier Wal und das Heinkel-„Schnellflugzeug" He 70. Unter den kundigen Händen von Chefkonstrukteur Max Friz entsteht aus dem Pratt & Whitney-Lizenzprodukt Hornet der BMW Typ 132, dessen 28 Liter Hubraum ihn auf 3800 Metern Höhe zu einer Dauerleistung von 625 PS befähigen. 1934, im Jahr der

Dornier Wal et l'«avion rapide» He 70 de Heinkel. Sous les mains habiles de l'ingénieur en chef Max Friz, le moteur Hornet de Pratt & Whitney produit sous licence donne bientôt naissance au BMW 132, auquel les 28 litres de cylindrée confèrent une puissance permanente de 625 ch à 3800 mètres d'altitude. En 1934, l'année de la scission, les motos BMW sont disponibles en 200, 400 et 750 cm³. Dans le même registre, BMW offre aussi les triporteurs F 76 et F 79, à la présentation spartiate comme il se doit en période de crise, qui sont exonérés d'impôts et peuvent être conduits sans permis.

Avec la construction d'automobiles, la branche la plus jeune de la maison prend de plus en plus d'importance. Une césure est, à ce point de vue, l'arrivée à expiration du contrat de licence signé avec Austin, le 1er mars 1932. A cette occasion, avec leur nouveau modèle 3/20 PS, appelé officiellement 0,8 Liter/20 PS, les Bavarois prouvent au monde entier que leurs voitures sont maintenant sevrées. Leur seul et unique point commun avec leur devancière est l'archaïque ressort à lames transversal à l'avant – mais désormais sans l'essieu rigide. Comme il est de règle à l'époque, le design cultive la religion de l'angle droit. Les commentateurs apprécient à l'unanimité les lignes séduisantes avec lesquelles la première série de la 3/20 PS est habillée à l'usine de carrosseries de Mercedes-Benz, à Sindelfingen. Elle est suivie, deux ans plus tard, par la 309. On ignore aujourd'hui encore le pourquoi et le comment du «3» dans sa dénomination. Mais les deux derniers chiffres indiquent déjà, comme cela allait devenir une coutume de BMW, la cylindrée de ses quatre chambres de combustion: 845 cm³, libéralement arrondis à 0,9 litres.

Inversement, on a aujourd'hui le plus grand mal à interpréter le chiffre 303 comme nom de la première six-cylindres de la marque, présentée au Salon de l'Automobile de Berlin en février 1933. Sous son capot aux multiples fentes latérales se dissimule, avec 1173 cm³, le plus petit moteur du marché qui présente une telle architecture. Et voilà encore une première: la 303 fend déjà la brise avec le visage inconfondable qu'afficheront les BMW des générations futures, les naseaux couronnés du célèbre tourbillon des hélices bleu et blanc. A condition de trouver la bonne route, se réjouit un essayeur contemporain, on peut, avec la nouvelle six-cylindres, «succomber à la sensation enivrante du 100 km/h». Quels sont les hommes derrière cette voiture? Fritz Fiedler, qui a acquis de grands mérites chez Horch avec les huit et douze-cylindres, et Rudolf Schleicher, qui, après un intermède chez Horch est également revenu chez BMW au début des années 30. Dans sa substance, le moteur est remarquable. Tout de suite débute en effet un processus de mûrissement continue au cours duquel se succéderont de nombreuses majorations de cylindrée qui atteindront leur paroxysme avec près de deux litres. Les premières «série 3» culminent avec la 326 de 1936. Avec 15 936 exemplaires fabriqués entre 1936 et 1941, ce sera la BMW la plus produite de son époque. Dès 1935, une licence est accordée à Frazer-Nash, à Isleworth, dans le comté anglais de Middlesex, licence qui est suivie d'innombrables 319 à conduite à droite ainsi que de châssis roulants pour les propres carrosseries du partenaire britannique.

Avec la 328, la voiture de sport de deux litres qui a remporté le plus de succès durant les années 30 défraye la chronique lors de sa première en obtenant une victoire de classe signée par Ernst Henne lors de la course de l'Eifel, sur le Nürburgring, le 14 juin 1936. Avec une moyenne de 101,5 km/h, la petite BMW blanche marche effrontément sur les brisées des grosses voitures à compresseur.

Isleworth, in the English county of Middlesex, supplying them with some 319 right-hand drives plus running gear, to which the British partner added its own coachwork.

The 328, the most successful 2-liter sports car of the 1930s, made a suitably dramatic debut when Ernst Henne achieved victory in his class at the Eifel race at the Nürburgring on 14 June 1936. His average speed of 63 mph (101.5 kph) brought the small white BMW into the midst of the big compressor cars.

Like John Surtees, Mike Hailwood or Johnny Cecotto in the postwar era, Henne was equally at home on two wheels or on four. On an icy November day in 1937, he flashed down the highway outside Frankfurt on a 500 cc motorcycle with stream-lined fairing, reaching a record speed of 279.503 kph (174 mph). Henne's reaction to this showed unrivaled cool: "Pretty good, huh?" After the 1933 German Motorcycle Grand Prix, the papers had a triple BMW triumph to report: in the 500 cc class, the old warhorse Peppi Stelzer took the honors, in the 1000 cc class Eduard Kratz won, while Theodor Schoth took the sidecar title. In the 1938 Mille Miglia, the two British drivers Alfred Fane and William James took the 2-liter title in their 328, also achieving eighth place in the overall classification. And in 1940 the racing Baron Huschke von Hanstein, accompanied by co-driver Walter Bäumer, was not to be fobbed off with a mere class victory: he won the overall victory in a 328 with a light alloy body from

Team prize for the BMW 315/1 in the 1934 International Alpine Race from Nice to Munich.

Mannschaftspreis für den BMW 315/1 bei der Internationalen Alpenfahrt 1934 von Nizza nach München.

Prix d'équipe pour la BMW 315/1 lors de la Coupe internationale des Alpes 1934 de Nice à Munich.

Touring at the same event, though this time on the triangular route Brescia-Cremona-Mantova, which that year replaced the usual giant circuit of whole of Italy. These are just a few examples of BMW's racing success.

"Racing improves the breed," as the English say. And that is not all; BMW's public image received just the boost it needed to make it stand out from its rivals. It sent out a message to the clientele and BMW devotees: BMWs are fresh, sporty and forever young, for people who keep a relaxed but firm hold on their lives.

Immediately after the start of the Second World War on 1 September 1939, the sale and delivery of motor vehicles to private individuals was prohibited. However, BMW's production of private cars somehow lingered on for a while, by a combination of underhand means and the blind eye turned by the authorities. By the end of that year, 480 cars of both the 321 and 326 models had been produced. By autumn 1940 just 201 cars had found owners. A few privileged people managed to have a wood carburetor fitted on the roof – an oven-like device

Spaltung, sind BMW-Zweiräder mit 200, 400 und 750 ccm erhältlich. Auf Kraftradkomponenten stützen sich die Dreirad-Lieferwagen F 76 und F 79, mit krisengerecht spartanischem Erscheinungsbild, steuerfrei und ohne Führerschein zu fahren.

Immer mehr an Bedeutung aber gewinnt der jüngste Sproß des Hauses – der Automobilbau. Ein wichtiges Datum ist in dieser Hinsicht die Beendigung des Lizenzvertrages mit Austin am 1. März 1932. Zugleich zeigen die Bayern mit der Neuent-wicklung 3/20 PS – offiziell 0,8 Liter/20 PS genannt – der Welt, daß ihre Autos flügge geworden sind. Nur noch die archaische vordere Querblattfeder teilt die Neuentwicklung mit dem Vorgänger – nun aber ohne die bisherige Starrachse. Das Design schwelgt im Stil der Zeit in rechten Winkeln. Die Rezensenten preisen die ansprechende Form, in welche die erste Serie des 3/20 PS im Mercedes-Benz-Karosseriewerk Sindelfingen gekleidet wird. Der Nachfolger 309 erscheint zwei Jahre später. Die Ursprünge der „3" in der Typenbezeichnung bleiben im Zwielicht. Aber die beiden letzten Ziffern erteilen analog zu künftigen BMW-Usancen Auskunft über den Hubraum seiner vier Verbrennungseinheiten: 845 ccm, aufgerundet zu 0,9 Litern.

Kaum entwirren läßt sich hingegen das Zahlenknäuel 303 als Bezeichnung für den ersten Sechszylinder der Marke, der auf der Berliner Autoausstellung im Februar 1933 debütiert. Hinter seiner seitlich vielfach aufgebrochenen vorderen Haube verbirgt sich mit 1173 ccm der in dieser Konfiguration kleinste Motor des Markts. Und noch eine Premiere: Der 303 streckt bereits das unverwechselbare BMW-Gesicht späterer Generationen in den Fahrtwind, die Niere, gekrönt vom bekannten weißblauen Propellerkreis. Wer die richtige Straße finde, frohlockt ein zeitgenössischer Tester, könne mit dem neuen Sechszylinder „das Gefühl des berauschenden Tempo 100 auskosten". Die Männer hinter dieser Maschine sind Fritz Fiedler, der sich bei Horch um die Acht- und Zwölfzylinder verdient gemacht hat, und Rudolf Schleicher, der ebenfalls nach einem Intermezzo bei Horch zu Beginn der dreißiger Jahre zu BMW zurückgekehrt ist. Die Substanz des Motors ist glänzend. Zugleich setzt ein kon-tinuierlicher Reifeprozeß ein, in den sich etliche Hubraum-vergrößerungen einlagern, bis bei rund zwei Litern ein Ende des Wachstums angezeigt scheint. Die frühen 3er kulminieren im 326 von 1936, denn mit 15.936 verkauften Exemplaren zwischen 1936 und 1941 wird er seiner Zeit zum BMW mit der größten Verbreitung. Schon 1935 vergibt man eine Lizenz an Frazer-Nash in Isleworth in der englischen Grafschaft Middlesex und läßt etliche 319 mit Rechtslenkung sowie rollende Chassis für eigene Aufbauten des britischen Partners folgen.

Einen standesgemäß dramatischen Einstand gibt der 328 – erfolgreichster 2-Liter-Sportwagen der dreißiger Jahre – durch einen Klassensieg von Ernst Henne beim Eifelrennen auf dem Nürburgring am 14. Juni 1936. Mit seinem Schnitt von 101,5 Stundenkilometern bricht der kleine weiße BMW in die Domäne der großen Kompressorautos ein.

Wie später ein John Surtees, Mike Hailwood oder Johnny Cecotto ist Henne auf zwei wie auf vier Rädern zu Hause. An einem eisigen Novembertag des Jahres 1937 huscht er auf einer stromlinienförmig verkleideten 500er mit dem Rekordtempo von 279,503 Stundenkilometern über die Autobahn bei Frank-furt. Hennes erster Kommentar zeugt von unnachahmlicher Gelassenheit: „Das ist doch sehr gut, oder?" Nach dem Großen Preis von Deutschland für Motorräder 1933 melden die Gazetten einen BMW-Dreifach-Triumph: Bei den 500ern

A l'instar de John Surtees, Mike Hailwood et Johnny Cecotto, Henne est aussi à l'aise sur deux roues que sur quatre. Par une glaciale journée de novembre 1937, au volant d'une moto de 500 cm³ à carénage aérodynamique, il signe un record de vitesse avec 279,503 km/h sur l'autoroute près de Francfort. Le premier commentaire de Henne témoigne de sa gouaille légen-daire: «C'est pas mal, non?» A l'issue du Grand Prix d'Allemagne pour motocyclettes de 1933, les manchettes des journaux annoncent un triomphal triplé BMW: en 500 cm³ avec le vieux renard de la course, Peppi Stelzer, avec Eduard Kratz en 1000 cm³ et avec Theodor Schoth en side-cars. Aux Mille Miglia de 1938, les deux Britanniques Alfred Fane et William James remportent la victoire avec leur 328 inscrite dans la catégorie deux-litres et terminent même 8e au classement général. En 1940, le rapide Baron Huschke von Hanstein, accompagné de son copilote Walter Bäumer, ne se contente pas de telles miettes pour son prochain succès: victoire au classement général au volant d'une 328 à carrosserie aluminium de Touring lors de la même manifestation, mais sur le circuit triangulaire Brescia-Crémone-Mantoue, qui, cette année-là, remplace la gigantesque boucle à travers l'Italie. Et ce ne sont là que quelques exemples.

«Racing improves the breed», disent les Anglais: la course anoblit la race. Mais il n'y a pas que cela: à cette époque, l'emblème de BMW acquiert aux yeux du public la notoriété qui la démarque positivement de l'anonymat des marques. Elle se fait ainsi connaître des clients, dont certains deviendront des disciples – frais, sportifs et d'une jeunesse durable, qui ont en main les choses de la vie, avec décontraction, mais d'une main de fer dans un gant de velours.

Ponctuellement pour le début de la Seconde Guerre mondiale, le 1 septembre 1939, le gouvernement interdit la vente et la livraison de toute automobile à des particuliers. Sous le manteau, mais non sans l'autorisation tacite des autorités compétentes, la production de voitures de tourisme chez BMW continue pendant un certain temps au compte-gouttes. Jusqu'à

Ernst Henne on 14 June 1936 on the way to victory at the Nürburgring.

Ernst Henne am 14. Juni 1936 auf dem Weg zum Sieg auf dem Nürburgring.

Ernst Henne, le 14 juin 1936, volant vers la victoire au Nürburgring.

la fin de 1939, BMW produira respectivement 480 exemplaires des 321 et 326. A l'automne 1940, elle n'aura plus vendu que 201 voitures. Quelques rares privilégiés ont fait équiper leur voi-ture d'un gazogène et sont même parvenus à se procurer pour leur roue de secours l'un de ces pneumatiques de plus en plus rares. Mais les choses ont depuis longtemps pris un cours inéluctable. En mai 1941, les chaînes s'arrêtent.

which burned wood to produce fuel – and even succeeded in getting hold of an increasingly scarce tire for the spare wheel. However, the writing had been on the wall for a long time, and by May 1941 the production lines finally fell silent.

Motorcycles, though, were still in demand and continued to be manufactured in some quantity. The heavy R 75, ideal for off-road use, became a legend for its all-round ruggedness. And of course the organized machinery of death and destruction demanded airplanes: in 1939 BMW acquired the Branden-burgische Motorenwerke in Berlin-Spandau, previously part of the Siemens group, and with a long tradition of aviation engine construction. Here and at BMW's other manufacturing plants in Munich and Eisenach, tens of thousands of aviation engines were produced between then and 1945. The 003 jet engine was essentially a technological nicety, of no real relevance to the outcome of the conflict of that time and at best of some value as a defiant gesture. The He 162 "Volksjäger" (people's fighter) – production start on 24 September 1944, maiden flight on 6 December 1944 – fitted with the 003, reached a speed of 522 mph (840 kph) at a height of 19,800 feet (6000 meters).

BMW motorcycles were used not just for peaceful purposes: parade on Adolf Hitler's birthday on 20 April 1936.

Nicht nur friedlichen Zwecken wurden BMW-Motorräder zuge-führt: Parade zum Geburtstag von Adolf Hitler am 20. April 1936.

Les motos de chez BMW ont aussi connu des applications martiales : parade pour l'anniversaire d'Adolf Hitler, le 20 avril 1936.

Meanwhile BMW itself had become a target for British and American bombers. As a shrewd precaution, certain branches of production had already been relocated to innocent-seeming rural locations such as Immenstadt, Kempten or Kaufbeuren, before the bombs began to fall thick and fast. Nevertheless, between 9 March 1943 and 22 September 1944, Plant I in Oberwiesenfeld was hit ten times and on 12 July 1944, 1117 bombers dropped more than 10,000 bombs, containing a total of 2727 tons of explosives. The chroniclers of the 8th and 15th American air fleets kept meticulous records, also noting that BMW Plant II in Allach was bombed nine times in 1944 alone.

By the time the unconditional surrender was signed in Reims on 7 May 1945, BMW had, like so much else, suffered severely as a result of the war. A third of the plant lay deserted in a wasteland of rubble and twisted steel. Hordes of plunderers fell like locusts on the mortally injured imperium and made off with yet more of its assets. On 1 October 1945 the American deputy garrison commander Lieutenant Colonel Eugene Keller issued an order for the entire Munich plant to be "packed in crates in preparation for shipment and subsequent destruction of the buildings".

gewinnt der alte Haudegen Peppi Stelzer, bei den 1000ern Eduard Kratz, bei den Gespannen Theodor Schoth. Bei der Mille Miglia 1938 landen die beiden Briten Alfred Fane und William James mit ihrem 328 einen Sieg bei den 2-Litern und arbeiten sich bis auf Rang acht im Gesamtklassement vor. 1940 begnügt sich der rasende Baron Huschke von Hanstein in Begleitung von Copilot Walter Bäumer nicht mehr mit solchen Almosen des Erfolgs: Gesamtsieg in einem von Touring in Leichtmetall gewandeten 328-„Innenlenker" bei der gleichen Veranstaltung, allerdings auf dem Dreieckskurs mit den Eckpunkten Brescia-Cremona-Mantua, der in jenem Jahr die Riesenrunde durch Italien ersetzt. Dies sind nur einige Beispiele für den Erfolg der Marke im Motorsport.

„Racing improves the breed", sagen die Engländer: Rennen veredeln die Rasse. Nicht nur das: Das BMW-Bild in der Öffent-lichkeit erhält damals jenen Kick, der es aus dem Markeneinerlei positiv heraushebt. Dies teilt sich zugleich den Kunden mit, unter denen auch BMW-Jünger sind: frisch, sportiv und dauer-haft jung; Menschen, die die Dinge des Lebens locker, aber unerbittlich im Griff haben.

Pünktlich zum Beginn des Zweiten Weltkriegs am 1. Sep-tember 1939 werden der Verkauf und die Auslieferung von Kraftfahrzeugen an Privatleute untersagt. Unter der Hand und mit der heimlichen Billigung der zuständigen Behörden plät-schert die PKW-Produktion bei BMW noch eine Zeitlang weiter. Bis zum Ende jenes Jahres entstehen jeweils 480 Exemplare der Typen 321 und 326. Im Herbst 1940 bringt man nur noch 201 Wagen an den Mann. Einige wenige Privilegierte haben ihrem Auto einen Holzvergaser auf den Buckel gepackt und einen der immer rarer werdenden Reifen für ihr Reserverad ergattert. Doch im Mai 1941 kommen die Bänder endgültig zum Stillstand.

Motorräder haben noch Konjunktur und werden weiter hergestellt. Die schwere geländegängige R 75 wird in ihrer knorrigen Solidität an allen Fronten zur Legende. Auch nach Flugzeugen verlangt die Maschinerie des organisierten Todes: 1939 hat BMW die damals zum Siemens-Konzern zählenden Brandenburgischen Motorenwerke in Berlin-Spandau erworben, die auf eine lange Tradition im Flugmotorenbau zurückblicken. Hier und in den anderen BMW-Fertigungsstätten in München und Eisenach werden bis 1945 Zehntausende von Flugmotoren gebaut. Eine technische Delikatesse, wenn auch nicht mehr von Bedeutung für die stattfindenden Kampfhandlungen und allen-falls noch als Drohgebärde tauglich, ist das Turbinenstrahltrieb-werk 003. Der „Volksjäger" Heinkel He 162 (Konstruktionsbeginn 24. September 1944, erster Flug 6. Dezember 1944) erreicht damit in 6000 Metern Höhe 840 Stundenkilometer.

Unterdessen sind die Bayerischen Motoren Werke selbst in das Visier der angloamerikanischen Bombergeschwader geraten. In weiser Voraussicht hat man bestimmte Produktionszweige bereits an unverfängliche ländliche Standorte wie Immenstadt, Kempten oder Kaufbeuren ausgelagert. Dann aber kommt es dennoch knüppeldick. Zwischen dem 9. März 1943 und dem 22. September 1944 wird Werk I im Oberwiesenfeld zehnmal heimgesucht. Allein am 12. Juli des vorletzten Kriegsjahres laden 1117 Maschinen über 10.000 Bomben mit 2727 Tonnen Spreng-stoff ab. Die Chronisten der 8. und 15. amerikanischen Luftflotte führen darüber pedantisch Buch und vermerken auch, dem BMW-Werk II in Allach habe man allein im Jahre 1944 neun Besuche der feindseligen Art abgestattet.

Als am 7. Mai 1945 in Reims die bedingungslose Kapitula-tion unterzeichnet wird, hat der Krieg auch BMW schlimme

The BMW Allach works, which escaped destruction, became a US Army supply and transport depot under German management.

Das unzerstört gebliebene BMW-Werk Allach wird unter deutscher Leitung ein Nachschub- und Fahrzeugdepot der US Army.

L'usine BMW d'Allach, épargnée par les bombardements, sera transformée, mais sous direction allemande, en un dépôt du train de l'armée américaine.

Seules les motocyclettes ont encore la cote et sont encore fabriquées. Sa solidité à toute épreuve sur tous les fronts élève la lourde R 75 tout-terrain au rang de légende. La machine d'extermination organisée a également besoin d'avions : en 1939, BMW a acquis les Brandenburgische Motorenwerke, à Berlin-Spandau, qui appartenaient alors au groupe Siemens et qui pouvaient se prévaloir d'une longue tradition pour la construction de moteurs d'avions. Ici et dans les autres unités de fabrication de BMW à Munich et Eisenach, on fabriquera des dizaines de milliers de moteurs d'avions jusqu'en 1945. Le réacteur 003 représente un summum de la technique, mais il ne jouera plus aucun rôle dans les hostilités qui s'achèvent et il n'est donc rien de plus qu'un tigre de papier. Le «chasseur du peuple», le Heinkel He 162 (dont la construction débute le 24 septembre 1944 et qui fait son premier vol le 6 décembre 1944), atteint ainsi la vitesse de 840 km/h à 6000 mètres d'altitude.

Pendant ce temps, BMW est elle-même devenue la cible des escadrilles de bombardiers alliés. Par prudence, on a transféré certains secteurs de la production dans des sites idylliques d'une tranquillité trompeuse comme Immenstadt, Kempten ou Kaufbeuren. Mais la revanche n'en sera que plus sévère. Entre le 9 mars 1943 et le 22 septembre 1944, l'Usine I d'Oberwiesenfeld est bombardée à dix reprises. Rien que le 12 juillet 1944, 1117 appareils déversent plus de 10 000 bombes avec 2727 tonnes d'explosifs. Les chroniqueurs de la 8e et 15e escadrille américaine tiennent leurs comptes avec une précision de bénédictins et font remarquer aussi que l'Usine II de BMW, à Allach, a été neuf fois la cible d'attaques ennemies rien qu'en 1944.

Lorsque les Allemands signent leur capitulation sans condition, le 7 mai 1945 à Reims, la guerre a laissé de profondes cicatrices dans le microcosme de BMW également. Un tiers des installations est à l'abandon dans un désert de pierre et d'acier. Des hordes de pilleurs s'abattent comme un nuage de criquets sur l'empire à l'agonie et lui ôtent tout ce qui lui reste de substance. Le 1er octobre 1945, l'adjoint au commandant de la garnison américaine, le lieutenant-colonel Eugene Keller, donne l'ordre «d'emballer dans des caisses de bois et d'expédier par bateau» tous les équipements des usines de Munich, puis de raser celles-ci.

Par bonheur, selon un dicton allemand, «on ne mange pas la soupe aussi chaude qu'on la cuit» et l'usine d'Allach est

Fortunately not everything was as black as it was painted, especially since the Allach plant was converted into a repair center for US military airplanes, the largest US spare parts storage facility on German territory. The Eisenach plant survived relatively unscathed, initially being confiscated "in the interests of the people of Thuringia", and then taking on a legally dubious identity under the aegis of the Soviet state-owned joint-stock company Awtowelo. The rise and fall of the Bayerische Motoren Werke had encompassed less than 30 years.

Wunden geschlagen. Ein Drittel der Anlagen liegt verödet in einer Wüste aus Stein und Stahl. Horden von Plünderern fallen wie Heuschrecken über das waidwunde Imperium her und entziehen ihm weitere Substanz. Am 1. Oktober 1945 ergeht die Anweisung des stellvertretenden amerikanischen Standortkommandanten Oberstleutnant Eugene Keller, die verbliebenen Münchener Maschinen „in Lattenverschläge zur Verschiffung zu verpacken" und die Werksanlagen zu schleifen.

Zum Glück wird nicht alles so heiß gegessen, wie es gekocht wird, zumal das Werk Allach zum Reparaturzentrum für amerikanische Militärfahrzeuge und zum größten US-Ersatzteillager auf deutschem Territorium umgewidmet wird. Die Filiale Eisenach ist relativ glimpflich davongekommen und wird, zunächst „zugunsten des thüringischen Volkes" enteignet, unter der sowjetischen staatlichen Aktiengesellschaft Awtowelo weitergeführt. Zwischen Aufstieg und Fall der Bayerischen Motoren Werke lagen knapp 30 Jahre.

transformée en centre de réparation pour les camions militaires américains et en plus grand entrepôt de pièces détachées des Etats-Unis sur le territoire allemand. La filiale d'Eisenach s'en est tirée relativement bien et, après avoir été confisquée «en faveur du peuple de Thuringe», est placée sous la tutelle de la société anonyme étatique soviétique Awtowelo. A peine 30 ans se seront écoulés entre l'essor et la chute des Bayerische Motoren Werke.

Finding Their Feet (1945–1962)

Of Kitchen Accessories and Prodigal Sons (1945–1952)

The plan of the American Finance Minister Henry Morgenthau Junior was to return the Germans to stone age status as farmers and ranchers living in a fertile landscape unsullied by any dark satanic mills. The simple range of BMW products during the immediate postwar years would have warmed the cockles of his heart: cooking pots, baking sheets and whisks, for example, as well as bicycles and agricultural machinery for sowing and harrowing.

The head of the works police in Allach was Georg Meier, known to all as "Cast-iron Schorsch". His name was one of some renown, the robust Bavarian having won the Isle of Man Tourist Trophy for BMW in 1939. Meier urged that they should find their feet amidst all the chaos and confusion by returning to the manufacture of motorcycles, bearing in mind their previous success in this sector. The beginnings were modest but nevertheless impressive: the R 24, with a single 250 cc cylinder and a four-speed foot gearshift, was launched at the Geneva Motor Show in March 1948, albeit in the form of a hastily cobbled-together dummy machine. However, by the end of 1949 alone 9459 were sold, providing their proud owners with a basic set of motorized wheels, and at the Milbertshofen plant a workforce of 2600 was once again on the payroll.

When the quarter-liter cubic capacity limit imposed by the occupying powers was lifted in 1950, production quickly switched to the long-planned 500 cc R 51, a gem of a machine with telescopic rear forks and a two-cylinder boxer power unit producing a highly pleasing engine note. Soon after this came the 600 cc R 67, and then the R 68 sports version, which with a top speed of 99 mph (160 kph) was the fastest production machine on the German market, as BMW themselves stressed with understandable pride. In 1954, motorcycle production reached its peak for the time being, with a production of 29,699 machines. Then came an abrupt turnaround, as the motorcycle boom subsided, a victim of the growing confidence of the

Orientierungsstufe (1945–1962)

Von Küchenzubehör und reuigen Satelliten (1945–1952)

Nach den Plänen des amerikanischen Finanzministers Henry Morgenthau junior sollen die Deutschen in den Steinzeit-Status von Ackerbauern und Viehzüchtern zurückgeführt werden, wohnhaft in blühenden und von keinerlei qualmenden Schloten verschandelten Landschaften. Das BMW-Sortiment der unmittelbaren Nachkriegsjahre hätte ihm gewiß zur hellen Freude gereicht: Kochtöpfe, Backbleche und Schneebesen, Fahrräder, Landmaschinen zum Säen und Eggen.

Chef der Werkspolizei in Allach ist Georg Meier, den alle Welt „Gußeiserner Schorsch" nennt. Sein Name hat einen guten Klang: Der kernige Bayer hat 1939 für BMW die Tourist Trophy auf der Isle of Man gewonnen. Meier mahnt, man solle inmitten des Chaos Tritt fassen und den Bau von Motorrädern wieder aufnehmen, angesichts früherer Erfolge auf diesem Sektor. Die Anfänge sind bescheiden und dennoch eindrucksvoll: die R 24 mit einem Zylinder von 250 ccm und Viergang-Fußschaltung wird auf dem Genfer Salon im März 1948 vorgestellt, wenn auch noch als zügig zusammengeschusterte Attrappe. Allein bis Ende 1949 verhelfen 9459 Exemplare ihren stolzen Besitzern zu elementarer Motorisierung, während im Werk Milbertshofen schon wieder 2600 Mitarbeiter auf den Gehaltslisten stehen.

Als die von den Besatzungsmächten verhängte Hubraumbeschränkung auf einen Viertelliter aufgehoben wird, rüstet man 1950 umgehend mit der längst geplanten R 51 mit 500 ccm auf, einem Schmuckstück mit Teleskop-Hinterradfederung und einem Zweizylinder-Boxertriebwerk von einschmeichelndem Klang. Bald darauf wird die R 67 mit 600 ccm angeboten, schließlich die Sportversion R 68, mit 160 Stundenkilometer Spitze die schnellste deutsche Serienmaschine, wie man in wohlverstandenem Eigenlob herausstellt. 1954 erreicht die Motorradfertigung mit 29.699 Exemplaren einen vorläufigen Höhepunkt, der gleichzeitig den Umschwung bringt. Angekratzt von der Tischleindeckdich-Mentalität des Wirtschaftswunders, flaut der Boom ab, denn am Zweirad klebt

Changement de cap (1945–1962)

Articles ménagers et transfuges repentants (1945–1952)

Si les plans du Ministre américain des Finances Henry Morgenthau junior étaient devenus réalité, les Allemands seraient retombés à l'âge de pierre et seraient devenus un peuple de paysans et d'éleveurs vivant dans un paysage rural où n'aurait plus fumé la moindre cheminée d'usine. Le jeune assortiment de BMW durant les années de l'immédiat après-guerre aurait assurément suscité la plus grande joie chez celui-ci : casseroles, plaques de four et fouets, par exemple, bicyclettes, machines agricoles pour semer et herser.

Le chef des vigiles de l'usine d'Allach est Georg Meier, que tout le monde connaît sous son surnom de «Schorsch». Son nom sonne bien : le pétulant Bavarois a remporté pour BMW, en 1939, le Tourist Trophy organisé sur l'Ile de Man. Meier insiste pour que l'on reprenne conscience de ses origines, en plein milieu du chaos, et que l'on se remette à construire des motocyclettes en s'inspirant des succès remportés jadis dans ce domaine. Les débuts sont modestes et, pourtant, impressionnants : il s'agit de la R 24 monocylindre de 250 cm³ à commande à quatre vitesses au pied, présentée au Salon de Genève de mars 1948, qui n'était, en réalité, qu'une maquette d'exposition. Fin 1949, déjà, 9459 exemplaires permettent à leurs fiers propriétaires de se déplacer de façon élémentaire alors qu'à l'usine de Milbertshofen, les effectifs s'élèvent de nouveau à 2600 collaborateurs.

Lorsque les puissances d'occupation suppriment le plafonnement de cylindrée à 250 cm³, BMW peut lancer immédiatement, en 1950, la R 51 de 500 cm³ depuis longtemps dans les cartons, un véritable bijou de la mécanique avec suspension arrière télescopique et bicylindre à plat au ronronnement mélodieux. Elle est bientôt suivie de la R 67, de 600 cm³, puis de la version sport R 68, qui est la plus rapide moto allemande de série avec une vitesse de pointe de 160 km/h, comme le proclame la publicité de BMW, qui n'a jamais mis sa lumière sous le boisseau. En 1954, la production de motos atteint déjà 29 699

"Wirtschaftswunder" years. Two-wheel vehicles were still stigmatized as a poor man's means of transport, and everyone was now looking to the sunlit uplands of the private sedan car.

From 1945 to 1947 the executive board consisted of Kurth Donath, Hanns Grewenig and Heinrich Krafft von Dellmensingen. Representations were regularly made to this triumvirate to produce a new BMW car, but they always rejected them out of hand. The marque's four-wheel tradition did live on to some extent, in exile and incognito, in mutant form. As part of the war reparations, H.J. Aldington, the managing director of the Bristol airplane works in Filton, England, received the plans for the BMW 327/28. Until 1948, its designer Fritz Fiedler was involved in the deal, not least due to the old friendship that existed between the two. In the spring of 1947, the Bristol 400, a blatant copy of the 327 coupé, was launched. Its successors, however, rapidly departed from the original design.

The fates of two prodigals who left the BMW fold for a period before receiving a generous welcome back were strikingly similar. The first of these was Ernst Loof of Bad Godesberg, once the head of styling at BMW, who left to manufacture racing and sports cars based on the 328 under the name Veritas from 1948 onwards. He gained a modest reputation in motor sport, and at the German Grand Prix of 1950 Tony Ulmen even achieved fourth place driving a Veritas. However, there was never enough money and things soon began to go downhill, and at the end of his freedom flight in 1953, Loof ended up back in the BMW styling department in Munich. Then there was Alex von Falkenhausen, at the end of the war head of the design office, who also went off to seek his fortune via the construction of sporty cars with a strong element of 1930s BMW incorporated into the design. However, the market niche identified by his firm AFM (short for Alexander von Falkenhausen, Munich) proved not to be sufficiently lucrative, and in 1954 the wiry nobleman returned to the Munich fold and once again did sterling service for the company as head of its racing division, where, over the years, he slowly took on the mantle of a gray eminence.

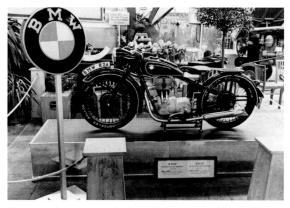

Prototype of the R 24 at the Hanover Export Fair in May 1948. The machine turned into a big seller.

Prototyp der R 24 bei der Exportmesse in Hannover im Mai 1948. Die Maschine wird ein Renner.

Le prototype de la R 24 à la Foire des Exportations de Hanovre en mai 1948. Cette moto sera un best-seller.

noch immer das Odium des Vehikels für arme Leute, und jedermann trachtet nach den höheren Weihen überdachter Fortbewegung.

Der Vorstand besteht in den Jahren 1945 bis 1947 aus den Herren Kurth Donath, Hanns Grewenig und Heinrich Krafft von Dellmensingen. Immer wieder wird an dieses Triumvirat der Wunsch nach einem neuen Auto von BMW herangetragen und dennoch stets verworfen. Die Vierradtradition des Hauses blüht gewissermaßen im Exil weiter, inkognito und in der Form von Mutanten. Als Reparationsleistung erhält H. J. Aldington, Generaldirektor der Bristol-Flugzeugwerke im englischen Filton, die Pläne des BMW 327/28. Konstrukteur Fritz Fiedler ist bis 1948 in dem Deal inbegriffen, nicht zuletzt aus alter Freundschaft zwischen den beiden Männern. Im Frühjahr 1947 stellt man den Bristol 400 vor, eine unverhohlene Raubkopie des Coupés 327, dessen Nachfolger sich indessen rasch vom Original entfernen.

Verblüffend ähnlich verlaufen die Schicksale zweier Satelliten, die sich eine Zeitlang aus der BMW-Atmosphäre lösen und schließlich in diese zurückkehren, ohne zu verglühen. Da ist der Bad Godesberger Ernst Loof, einst Styling-Chef, der unter dem Namen Veritas ab 1948 Renn- und Sportwagen auf der Basis des 328 herstellt. Er bringt es in der Tat zu mäßigem sportlichem

A Bristol 400 with Count G. Lurani and Frazer-Nash boss H. J. Aldington at the 1949 Mille Miglia.

Ein Bristol 400 mit dem Grafen G. Lurani und Frazer-Nash-Boß H. J. Aldington bei der Mille Miglia 1949.

Une Bristol 400 avec le comte G. Lurani et le chef de Frazer-Nash, H. J. Aldington, lors des Mille Miglia de 1949.

Ruhm, und beim Großen Preis von Deutschland 1950 belegt Veritas-Pilot Toni Ulmen sogar den vierten Platz. Überall fehlt es jedoch an Geld und bald geht es bergab. Nach dem Ende seines emanzipatorischen Ausflugs landet Loof 1953 wieder in der Styling-Abteilung in München. Da ist außerdem Alex von Falkenhausen, bei Kriegsende Leiter des Konstruktionsbüros, der ebenfalls mit dem Bau von sportiven Autos mit BMW-Ingredienzien der dreißiger Jahre sein Glück versucht. Die von seinem Unternehmen AFM (für Alexander von Falkenhausen, München) angepeilte Marktlücke erweist sich indes als wenig ergiebig. 1954 kehrt auch der drahtige Edelmann in den Schoß der Münchener Mutter zurück. Er macht sich als Leiter der Rennabteilung erneut um die Firma verdient und erlangt im Laufe der Zeit den Rang einer grauen Eminenz.

Rounded: this 600 experimental car from 1950 with its air-cooled two-cylinder engine never received its passing-out certificate.

Rundling: Dieser Versuchswagen Typ 600 von 1950 mit seinem luftgekühlten Zweizylinder erhält nie das Reifezeugnis.

Tout en rondeurs: cette voiture expérimentale, une 600 de 1950 à bicylindre refroidi par air, ne sera jamais fabriquée en série.

exemplaires, ce qui est un record provisoire. Mais cela ne va pas sans aléas: sous l'influence négative de la mentalité de nantis rassasiés du miracle économique, le soufflé commence à se dégonfler. En effet, les deux-roues traînent toujours l'hypothèque de véhicules de pauvres et chacun aspire légitimement à avoir un toit sur la tête dans ses déplacements.

De 1945 à 1947, le directoire se compose de Kurth Donath, Hanns Grewenig et Heinrich Krafft von Dellmensingen. Ce triumvirat entend toujours la même doléance - que BMW fabrique une nouvelle voiture - et la rejette toujours. C'est en quelque sorte en exil, incognito et sous la forme de mutants que renaît la tradition des quatre roues de la maison. Au titre des réparations, H. J. Aldington, directeur général des usines d'avions Bristol à Filton, en Angleterre, a reçu les plans de la BMW 327/28. Jusqu'en 1948, l'ingénieur Fritz Fiedler fait partie intégrante de la transaction, ce qui est aussi dû en partie à la vieille amitié qui lie les deux hommes. Au printemps 1947, on assiste à la présentation de la Bristol 400, un plagiat éhonté du coupé 327, dont le successeur va toutefois vite se démarquer de l'original.

Les destins des deux satellites qui se dissocient pendant un certain temps de la nébuleuse de BMW avant de finir par la rejoindre présentent une similitude frappante. Il s'agit d'abord d'Ernst Loof, de Bad Godesberg, jadis chef styliste de BMW, qui, sous le nom de Veritas, produit à partir de 1948 des voitures de course et de sport sur la base de la 328. Il obtient même une certaine notoriété sportive puisque, lors du Grand Prix d'Allemagne de 1950, Toni Ulmen, pilote de Veritas, remporte la quatrième place. Mais tout le monde manque d'argent et, bientôt, la déchéance est irrésistible, si bien qu'à l'issue de sa tentative d'émancipation, Loof atterrit de nouveau au bureau de style de Munich, en 1953. L'autre est Alex von Falkenhausen, directeur du bureau d'études à la fin de la guerre, qui cherche son salut en construisant des voitures sportives à partir d'ingrédients BMW des années 30. Le créneau du marché que vise sa société AFM (pour Alexander von Falkenhausen, Munich) s'avère vite peu porteur. En 1954, le noble à la silhouette élancée revient dans le giron de la maison-mère, à Munich, et recommence à y gagner ses galons comme directeur du service Course où, au fil du temps, il endosse le rôle d'eminence grise.

Of Chubby-Cheeked Cherubs and Eggs on Wheels (1952–1962)

On the borderline between the past and the future, half conservative, half innovative, the BMW 501 was launched at the 1951 Frankfurt Motor Show. In itself, the car was a success, and met with enthusiastic acclaim from all sides, rapidly being given the affectionate nickname the "baroque angel". Even Pinin Farina, whose own body design for the 501 was rejected by BMW's executive board, was fulsome in his praise of the design team responsible, Alfred Böning and Peter Szimanowski. A mood of optimism reigned, but in fact the car proved to be a false dawn. The sumptuous curves of the four-door sedan, which was supplied exclusively in black, were a financial liability: just pressing the front wing, for example, involved three or four different production stages. The asking price of 15,150 marks was exorbitant when set against an average monthly income of 350 marks, and had to be steadily reduced in later versions. The original 65 bhp developed by the 2-liter six-cylinder engine at 4400 rpm had to lug around a dead weight of 2955 lbs (1340 kg). What is more, the 501 was up against the Mercedes 220, while the eight-cylinder 502, produced from 1954 onwards, was in competition with the Mercedes 300, and despite the clear quality of these automobiles, they were not much more than a Bavarian article of faith in the war of prestige with their Stuttgart rivals.

Count Goertz's two beautiful creations, the 503 and 507, failed to achieve anything like the expected response from the American market in 1955, where they had been hoping to spark a hectic stampede to the dealers. With sales of 412 of the 503 and just 252 of the 507, they ended up as pricy rarities and monuments to an ill-thought-out models policy, as did the 3200CS of 1961. Seductively styled by star couturier Nuccio Bertone, the big coupé, with sales of just 603 cars, did BMW's image no harm but emptied its coffers. A total of 23,120 six and eight-cylinder BMWs were sold in what was practically an act of charity by the company, as they were sold at a total loss of 76 million marks, or 3250 marks per car.

In a tightrope act between two extremes, to prevent the company bleeding to death at the top end of the automobile market, BMW's policy was to introduce mini cars at the other end of the market. From 1955 onwards, the Isetta "Motocoupé", a modish, whimsical and disarmingly practical car, provided meager profits. It was very much targeted at the less well off: "For just 5.80 marks two adults and a child can travel about 230 kilometers (143 miles)", as the advertisement proudly proclaimed. The "rolling egg" or "cuddle box" was not even spared the rigors of motor sport, being entered in the 1955 Mille Miglia. From 1957 onwards the "large" Isetta BMW 600 offered more car for your money, while the various members of the BMW 700 family, introduced from 1959, almost looked like real cars.

Meanwhile, the 1959 financial year had eaten up the last of the company's reserves. An injection of 15 million marks from the Bremen wood entrepreneur Hermann Krages in 1957 had disappeared like snow in the spring sunshine, and the company appeared incapable of surviving under its own steam. The management and major banks saw no other way out than affiliation to their arch-rival Mercedes-Benz. However, at a memorable annual meeting of shareholders on 9 December 1959, the 39th in the history of the company, the workforce,

Von rundlichen Engeln und rollenden Eiern (1952–1962)

Auf dem Grenzstreifen zwischen gestern und morgen, halb konservativ, halb innovativ, wird der BMW 501 auf der IAA 1951 präsentiert, eine runde Sache, allerdings nur im eigentlichen Sinne des Wortes. Gewiß, allenthalben wird ihm begeisterte Akklamation zuteil. Bald stellt sich der freundliche Spottname „Barockengel" ein. Sogar Pinin Farina, dessen eigener Karosserie-Entwurf für den 501 vom BMW-Vorstand verschmäht wurde, zollt dem zuständigen Team Alfred Böning und Peter Szimanowski hohes Lob. Aufbruchstimmung macht sich breit, aber der Start führt direkt in eine Sackgasse. Die üppigen Kurven des ausschließlich in vornehmem Schwarz gelieferten Viertürers schlagen teuer zu Buche: Die vorderen Kotflügel zum Beispiel müssen in drei bis vier Arbeitsgängen gepreßt werden. Der Preis von 15.150 Mark ist angesichts eines Durchschnittseinkommens von 350 Mark saftig und wird in späteren Versionen schrittweise reduziert. Die ursprünglich 65 PS bei 4400 Umdrehungen pro Minute des 2-Liter-Sechszylinders haben ein massives Stück Eisen mit 1340 Kilo Leergewicht zu bewegen. Wie sich zuvor der 501 am Mercedes 200 messen lassen mußte, so muß sich der Achtzylinder 502 ab 1954 den Vergleich mit dem Mercedes 300 gefallen lassen – trotz unzweifelhafter Qualitäten doch eher ein bayerischer Glaubensartikel im Prestigeduell gegen die Stuttgarter.

Die beiden schönen Geschöpfe des Grafen Goertz namens 503 und 507 lösen 1955 keineswegs den erhofften Widerhall und die erwartete ungestüme Kauflust auf dem amerikanischen Markt aus. Sie werden mit 412 gefertigten Exemplaren des 503 und lediglich 252 des 507 zu kostbaren Raritäten und prächtigen Monumenten einer unbedachten Modellpolitik, ebenso wie der 3200CS von 1961. Verführerisch eingekleidet von Star-Couturier Nuccio Bertone, pflegt das große Coupé in der schwachen Verbreitung von 603 Stück zwar das Image, leert aber die Kassen. Insgesamt werden 23.120 Sechs- und Achtzylinder unter das fahrende BMW-Volk gebracht, ein Akt von geradezu mildtätigem Charakter, denn er wird mit einem Verlust von 76 Millionen Mark – 3250 Mark pro Auto – verkauft.

Der mißlichen Situation begegnet das Werk mit einem Hochseilakt zwischen den Extremen: Damit die Bayerischen Motoren Werke in den oberen Segmenten der Wagenhierarchie nicht verbluten, sollen Automobilzwerge die Kassen füllen. Ab 1955 fährt das „Motocoupé" Isetta – poppig, drollig und entwaffnend praktisch – magere Gewinne ein. Es ist fürwahr ein Angebot für schmale Geldbeutel: „Für ganze 5,80 DM fahren zwei Erwachsene und ein Kind rund 230 Kilometer weit", frohlockt die Werbung. Sogar gegen Sporteinsätze wie bei der Mille Miglia 1955 ist das „rollende Ei" oder die „Knutschkugel" nicht gefeit. Ab 1957 bietet die „große Isetta", der BMW 600, mehr Auto für das gleiche Geld, und beinahe schon wie richtige Autos sehen schließlich die Mitglieder der BMW-700-Familie ab 1959 aus.

Das Geschäftsjahr 1959 hat indes die letzten Reserven des Unternehmens aufgezehrt. Eine Finanzspritze des Bremer Holzkaufmanns Hermann Krages 1957 in Höhe von 15 Millionen Mark ist verpufft wie Spucke auf einer glühenden Herdplatte. Eine Sanierung aus eigener Kraft scheint nicht möglich. Verwaltung und Großbanken sehen keinen anderen Ausweg als die Anlehnung an den alten Rivalen Mercedes-Benz. Aber in der denkwürdigen Hauptversammlung vom 9. Dezember 1959, der

L'histoire de la Bavaroise plantureuse et de l'œuf à roulettes (1952–1962)

A la ligne de césure entre hier et demain, la BMW 501, aussi conservatrice que novatrice, est présentée au Salon de l'Automobile de Francfort de 1951 avec ses rondeurs rassurantes. Elle récolte de tous bords des acclamations enthousiastes et elle reçoit vite son surnom bienveillant d'«ange baroque». Pinin Farina lui-même dont le propre prototype de carrosserie pour la 501 a été refusé par le directoire de BMW, ne tarit pas d'éloges envers ses pères, l'équipe réunie autour d'Alfred Böning et Peter Szimanowski. L'ambiance est à l'optimisme, mais le départ sur les chapeaux de roue mène vite dans un cul-de-sac. Les courbes plantureuses de la quatre-portes commercialisée exclusivement dans un noir très distingué coûtent trop cher: les ailes avant, par exemple, doivent être embouties en trois ou quatre étapes. Son prix de 15 150 marks est astronomique comparé au revenu moyen de 350 marks par mois, à tel point que, pour les versions ultérieures, il sera diminué étape par étape. Les 65 ch (à 4400 tr/mn) que développe à l'origine le six-cylindres de deux litres doivent traîner un poids mort imposant de 1340 kg. De même que la 501 est mesurée à l'aune de la Mercedes 220, la 502 huit-cylindres de 1954 le sera à celle de la Mercedes 300, qui restera, malgré des qualités manifestes, une profession de foi envers la Bavière dans le duel de prestige contre Mercedes.

Les deux magnifiques réalisations du comte Goertz baptisées 503 et 507 ne déclenchent pas, en 1955, l'enthousiasme escompté et l'on est déçu de constater que l'on ne se les arrache pas sur le marché américain. Commercialisées à raison de 412 exemplaires pour la 503 et de seulement 252 pour la 507, elles resteront des raretés précieuses et des monuments arrogants d'une politique commerciale insuffisamment réfléchie, au même titre que la 3200CS de 1961. Habillée d'une robe séductrice par le couturier vedette Nuccio Bertone, le gros coupé diffusé au nombre confidentiel de 603 exemplaires redore le blason de BMW, mais vide ses caisses. Au total 23 120 six et huit-cylindres feront le bonheur de quelques heureux propriétaires, acte d'abnégation bienfaisante, car elle est vendue avec une perte de 76 millions de marks, soit 3250 marks par voiture.

Acte d'équilibrisme entre deux extrêmes: pour que BMW ne devienne pas exsangue dans les segments supérieurs de la hiérarchie automobile, des naines à quatre roues vont devoir remédier à la situation. A partir de 1955, l'Isetta «Motocoupé» – irrésistible, drôle et désarmante par son caractère pratique – permet d'engranger de maigres bénéfices. C'est véritablement une offre pour les bourses à plat: «Pour en tout et pour tout 5,80 marks, deux adultes et un enfant peuvent couvrir 230 km/h», proclame la publicité. Il y en a même qui font courir les Mille Miglia de 1955 à «l'œuf à roulettes» ou «au pot de yaourt», ainsi qu'on l'a surnommée. A partir de 1957, la «grosse Isetta» la BMW 600, offre plus de voiture pour son argent et les rejetons de la famille BMW 700, apparue en 1959, ressemblent déjà presque à de véritables voitures.

L'exercice 1959 a, en revanche, englouti les ultimes ressources de l'entreprise. Une injection d'argent par le négociant en bois brêmois Hermann Krages, en 1957, de 15 millions de marks, a fondu comme neige au soleil. Toute guérison de ses propres forces semble exclue. La direction et les grandes banques ne voient pas d'autre issue qu'un rapprochement avec sa vieille rivale, Mercedes-Benz. Mais, lors de la mémorable

dealers and minor stockholders joined forces to battle for the company's independence amid tumultuous scenes. Their stand awakened the interest of major stockholder Dr Herbert Quandt, and he took over a large slice of BMW stock. A new executive board was appointed, and a team of experts and an active works council also made a positive contribution. This time the direction was right, as they returned to once-familiar terrain: the middle ground. Aviation engine business also began to pick up. Rock bottom had been reached, and recovery was finally under way.

New Horizons (1962–1999)

The "New Class" (1962–1972)

When production of the new mid-range BMW 1500 began in February 1962, BMW had finally found its way home after all the errors and confusion of the postwar reconstruction period, and was back on the territory it had successfully occupied during the 1930s. Acclaimed as the star of the 1961 Frankfurt Motor Show, the straightforward no-frills lines of the 1500 subscribed to the old Prussian ideal of unassuming solidity, a value system that places content before style. The reaction of the trade press was one of fulsome praise: "Deeply hidden, but all the more deeply felt for that, the heart of the German car buyer yearns for a quality, which cannot be entirely satisfied by economical mass production cars," and the BMW 1500 was tailor-made to satisfy just that yearning, as *auto motor und sport* observed, clearly in a reflective mood at the time. Initially, BMW was barely able to meet the demand it had stirred up; with a production of 50 cars a day, supply was far less than worldwide demand. However, the company responded rapidly and energetically. While stockpiles of unsold 700 series cars faced an uncertain future, production facilities for the "New Class" were being expanded, development capacity was being increased and a special sales organization was being set up. True to Goethe's dictum that all isolation is despicable, the range of models was extended to suit a variety of tastes. It extended from the original 1500 to the 1800 TISA in 1964, a special edition of 200 aimed at sporting drivers, right up to the 2000tii in 1969.

1966 saw the birth of the compact two-door 1600-2, a car where BMW strategists were partially responsible for inventing and developing a new dimension for the automobile. By 1975 the 1600-2, with its attractively sturdy appearance, had shattered all previous BMW production records with total sales of 252,786. At the end of the 1960s, BMW also returned to its six-cylinder tradition, this time with greater success: the three big 1968 models, the 2500 and 2800 sedans and the 2800CS coupé immediately met with a rave reception, being hailed in reviews as a crowning achievement of European automobile construction.

All in all, BMW now had a program in place which left it excellently equipped to face the future. Over the next few years production and sales records tumbled with monotonous regularity. Motorcycle sales were also recovering, as the two-wheeler came to be viewed not as an alternative but as a

39. in der Geschichte des Hauses, kämpfen Belegschaft, Händler und Kleinaktionäre in tumultartigen Szenen um die Eigenständigkeit ihrer Firma. Ihr Feuer weckt das Interesse des Großaktionärs Dr. Herbert Quandt, der eine große Anzahl der BMW-Anteile übernimmt. Ein neuer Vorstand wird eingesetzt, sachkundige Spezialisten und ein aktiver Betriebsrat helfen mit. Die Richtung stimmt und führt sogar auf altvertrautes Terrain: Der Mittelweg ist der richtige. Das Flugzeugtriebwerksgeschäft belebt sich ebenfalls. Die Talsohle ist durchmessen.

Zu neuen Ufern (1962–1999)

„Neue Klasse" (1962–1972)

Mit dem Produktionsbeginn des Mittelklassewagens Typ 1500 im Februar 1962 findet das Unternehmen nach den Irrungen und Wirrungen der Wiederaufbauphase zu seinen Domänen zurück, die seit den späten dreißiger Jahren brachliegen. Als Star der IAA 1961 gefeiert, huldigt der schlicht und schnörkellos geformte Bayer gleichsam dem preußischen Imperativ der gehaltvollen Bescheidenheit: „Mehr Sein als Schein". Fast hymnisch schallt auch das Echo der Fachpresse zurück: „Tief versteckt, aber um so sicherer geborgen, befindet sich im Herzen des deutschen Autokäufers eine Sehnsucht nach Gediegenheit, die von preiswerten Großserienwagen nur unvollkommen erfüllt werden kann." Und just dieser Sehnsucht komme der BMW 1500 entgegen, merkt etwa *auto motor und sport* nachdenklich an. Anfangs kann man die Nachfrage, die man geweckt hat, kaum befriedigen: Mit 50 Einheiten am Tag ist das Angebot weitaus geringer als die weltweite Nachfrage. Die Reaktion erfolgt rasch und energisch. Während noch ganze Halden von 700ern unverkauft einer ungewissen Zukunft entgegendämmern, werden bereits die Produktionsanlagen für die „Neue Klasse" erweitert, die Entwicklungskapazitäten aufgestockt, eine gezielte Verkaufsorganisation geschaffen. Getreu der Goetheschen Devise, alle Vereinzelung sei verwerflich, fächert man die Baureihe filigran auf, um vielen unterschiedlichen Geschmäckern gerecht zu werden. Sie spannt sich vom Ur-Typ

Collected works: the first BMW 1500s being delivered to the dealers in 1963. Light colors were preferred.

Gesammelte Werke: Die ersten BMW 1500 werden 1963 an die Händler ausgeliefert. Man bevorzugt helle Farben.

Œuvres réunies : les premières BMW 1500 sont remises aux concessionnaires en 1963. Les couleurs claires ont la cote.

assemblée générale du 9 décembre 1959, la 39e dans l'histoire de la maison, personnel, concessionnaires et petits actionnaires en viennent presque aux mains pour préserver l'autonomie de leur firme. Leur enthousiasme suscite l'intérêt du grand actionnaire Dr Herbert Quandt, qui rachète une grande partie des actions BMW. Un nouveau directoire est institué, des spécialistes compétents et un comité d'entreprise actif y mettent aussi leur grain de sel. Le cap choisi est le bon et ramène sur un terrain où l'on se meut en pleine confiance : la voie médiane est la bonne voie. Le segment des moteurs d'avions s'envole lui aussi de nouveau. Le creux de la vague est bientôt franchi.

Vers de nouveaux horizons (1962–1999)

La «Nouvelle Classe» (1962–1972)

En lançant la production de la 1500 du segment intermédiaire, en février 1962, l'entreprise revient, après les errements de la phase de reconstruction, à son domaine de prédilection qu'elle avait négligé depuis la fin des années 30. Célébrée comme la grande vedette du Salon de l'Automobil de Francfort de 1961, la Bavaroise aux lignes sobres et sans fioritures sacrifie simultanément à l'impératif prussien de la modestie trompeuse selon la devise «être plus que paraître». La presse spécialisée rivalise de commentaires élogieux : «Profondément dissimulée, mais d'autant plus sûre se trouve au cœur de l'acheteur de voiture allemand une soif de confort et de luxe que les voitures de grande série bon marché ne peuvent apaiser que de façon incomplète», et ce serait justement au-devant de ces acheteurs que va la BMW 1500, note *auto motor und sport* sur un ton pensif. Dès le début, BMW a le plus grand mal à satisfaire les besoins qu'elle a elle-même suscités : avec 50 unités par jour, l'offre est loin de suffire à la demande du monde entier. La réaction ne se fait pas attendre et elle est d'autant plus énergique. Alors que des parkings entiers sont encombrés de 700 invendues et dont l'avenir est plus qu'incertain, les chaînes de production sont d'ores et déjà agrandies pour la «Nouvelle Classe», les capacités de développement sont augmentées et un réseau de distribution efficace mis en place. Selon la devise de Goethe qu'il peut être fatal de se concentrer sur une seule action, la gamme s'enrichit rapidement pour satisfaire les goûts les plus divers. Elle va de la 1500 d'origine à la 2000tii produite en 1969 en passant par la 1800 TISA de 1964, construite en une édition confidentielle de 200 exemplaires pour combler les amateurs de conduite sportive.

1966 est l'année de naissance de la compacte 1600-2 à deux portes avec laquelle les commerciaux réunis sous le signe des «naseaux» ont, en quelque sorte, inventé une nouvelle dimension de l'automobile. Avec ses lignes râblées, mais attrayantes, elle va, jusqu'en 1975, avec 252 786 exemplaires, battre tous les records de production dans l'histoire de la marque. A la fin des années 60, BMW fait en outre revivre sa tradition du six-cylindres. Et, cette fois-ci, cela en vaut la peine : les trois grosses BMW de 1968, les berlines 2500 et 2800 ainsi que le coupé 2800CS, récoltent immédiatement les commentaires et les éloges enthousiastes des milieux spécialisés, qui y voient les meilleurs représentantes de la construction automobile européenne.

supplement to the motor car. In 1969 just 5000 motorcycles were sold, but after the launch of the R 50/5, R 60/6 and R75/5 in 1970, sales rose sharply to more than 12,000, and just two years later production had risen to more than 21,000.

By the beginning of the 1970s the lean years of tough lessons and reconstruction were history, and years of plenty beckoned. BMW's new pride was reinforced by a string of motor sport triumphs, and racetrack success was consciously used as a marketing tool. Slightly modified production sedans won the Spa 24-hour race in 1965, and in 1968 the Touring Cars Grand Prix at the Nürburgring, driven by Dieter Quester and Hubert Hahne, who also achieved considerable success in the 1970 Formula 2 season. A powerful visual symbol of the new BMW identity came in the form of the four-cylinder administrative building which soared heavenwards from 1972 on Munich's Petuelring, facing the similarly avant-garde Olympiapark,

Single cylinder and V8 – this combination proved unpalatable in the 1950s.

Einzylinder und V8 – dieser Spagat erweist sich in den fünfziger Jahren als wenig bekömmlich.

Monocylindre et V8 – dans les années 50, ce grand écart s'avérera peu favorable au constructeur.

constructed that same year, providing it with a counterpart, and at the same time offering a certain counterpoint. In 1972, annual sales exceeded two billion marks for the first time; a further major investment was the expansion of the Dingolfing works, purchased from Glas in 1967.

Crisis Management and Breaking New Ground (1972-1980)

With the launch of the 520 in 1972, the Milbertshofen car manufacturer began, after a four-year development period, to open up new territory to the industry, without departing from its existing credo: the car was sporty, but with a generous portion of comfort and discreet luxury, created to a certain extent for the heads of expanding families, an intention underlined by the new designation. The new car soon came to be known as the "fiver" (5 series). It later became part of an all-round numbering system, as the compact cars came to be known as the 3 series from 1975, the big coupés from 1976 as the 6 series and the top-of-the-range BMWs from 1977 as the 7 series, while from 1989 onwards the 8 series heralded the coming golden age of the touring sports sedan. As in the 1930s, additional digits after the initial 3, 5 or 7 give information about the cubic capacity of each model.

1500 über den 1800 TISA anno 1964, einem Angebot nach Maß für den Sportfahrer in einer Kleinauflage von 200, bis hin zum 2000tii von 1969.

In das Jahr 1966 fällt die Geburtsstunde des kompakten zweitürigen 1600-2, mit dem die Strategen im Zeichen der Niere gewissermaßen eine weitere Dimension des Automobils erfinden und erschließen. Von gedrungen-attraktiver Anmut, wird er bis 1975 mit einer Stückzahl von 252.786 alle bisherigen Produktionsrekorde der Marke in den Schatten stellen. Ende der sechziger Jahre nimmt BMW zudem seine Sechszylinder-tradition wieder auf, und diesmal lohnt es sich: Die drei großen Achtundsechziger, die Limousinen 2500 und 2800 sowie das Coupé 2800CS, werden als Spitzenerzeugnisse europäischen Autobaus begeistert aufgenommen und erhalten überaus wohlwollende Rezensionen.

Mit diesem Programm ist man trefflich gerüstet. In den nächsten Jahren erzielt man immer neue Fertigungs- und Absatzrekorde. Auch das Motorradgeschäft belebt sich, als das Zweirad nicht mehr als Alternative, sondern als Ergänzung zum Auto in die Garage gestellt wird. Nachdem 1969 nur knapp 5000 Maschinen verkauft werden konnten, bringt das Jahr 1970 mit den neuen Modellen R 50/5, R 60/6 und R 75/5 die Wende. Die Produktion steigt auf über 12.000 Exemplare, schon zwei Jahre später sind es mehr als 21.000.

Anfang der siebziger Jahre ist die Lehr- und Aufbauphase Vergangenheit und Herrenjahre sind angesagt. Der neue Stolz bei BMW gründet nicht zuletzt auf eine Unzahl von Trophäen im Sport, den man durchaus als Marketingmedium versteht. Seriennahe Limousinen erringen Siege beim 24-Stunden-Rennen von Spa 1965 oder 1968 beim „Großen Preis der Tourenwagen" auf dem Nürburgring unter Dieter Quester und Hubert Hahne, die 1970 auch für Erfolge in der Formel 2 sorgen. Als symbolträchtig-sichtbarer Ausdruck der neuen BMW-Identität reckt sich seit 1972 das vierzylindrige Verwaltungs-gebäude am Münchener Petuelring gen Himmel, in bevorzugter Panoramalage gegenüber dem gleichermaßen avantgar-distischen Olympiapark aus dem gleichen Jahr – Pendant und zugleich auch ein bißchen Kontrapunkt zu diesem. Der Jahres-umsatz überschreitet 1972 erstmals zwei Milliarden Mark. Schwerpunkt weiterer Investitionen ist der Ausbau des Werks Dingolfing, das 1967 von Glas erworben wurde.

Krisenmanagement und Abschied von der Nische (1972–1980)

Mit dem 520 von 1972 beginnen die Milbertshofener Auto-macher nach vier Jahren Entwicklungszeit, dem Markt Neuland abzugewinnen, ohne mit ihrem bisherigen Credo zu brechen: Sportlich gibt er sich, aber versetzt mit einem guten Schuß Komfort und dezentem Luxus, sozusagen wie geschaffen für die Vorstände expandierender Familien. Diese Intention besiegelt der neue Name. Volkes Stimme nennt den Novizen bald salopp den „Fünfer". Er wird künftig Teil eines sinnträchtigen Systems, denn die Kompakten, das sind ab 1975 die 3er, die großen Coupés ab 1976 die 6er und die Oberklassen-BMW ab 1977 die 7er, während man mit dem 8er von 1989 die Beletage des kommoden Reisesportwagens betritt. Als Zusatzinformation sind der Status-zahl, wie gelegentlich schon in den dreißiger Jahren, Hinweise auf das Volumen der jeweiligen Maschine beigegeben.

Avec un tel programme, BMW est parfaitement armée pour l'avenir. Au cours des années qui suivent, elle bat record sur record pour la fabrication et la vente. Le segment de la moto, lui aussi, fait bien plus que végéter, d'autant plus que les deux-roues ne sont plus considérées comme une alternative, mais bel et bien comme un complément à la voiture qu'elles côtoient parfois dans le garage. Alors que, en 1969, à peine 5000 motos seulement ont été vendues, l'année 1970 marque un change-ment de cap avec les nouveaux modèles R 50/5, R 60/6 et R 75/5. La production grimpe à plus de 12 000 et à plus de 21 000 deux ans plus tard déjà.

Au début des années 70, les années d'apprentissage et de démarrage appartiennent depuis longtemps à une époque révo-lue. Des années de vaches grasses sont annoncées pour l'avenir. La nouvelle fierté chez BMW s'appuie aussi et surtout sur la multitude de trophées remportés en compétition, que l'on conçoit comme un instrument de marketing. Des berlines proches de la série remportent par exemple des victoires aux 24 Heures de Spa en 1965 ou 1968 ainsi qu'au «Grand Prix des voitures de tourisme» du Nürburgring avec Dieter Quester et Hubert Hahne, qui sont aussi une garantie de succès en Formule 2 en 1970. Expression visible de loin, et au grand symbolisme, de la nouvelle identité de BMW, le siège social à quatre cylindres, qui longe le grand boulevard du Petuelring, s'élève depuis 1972 dans le ciel de Munich, à un emplacement prestigieux, vis-à-vis du Parc olympique de la même année, autre symbole d'avant-garde auquel il correspond comme un écho et fait en même temps aussi un peu contrepoids. En 1972, le chiffre d'affaires annuel dépasse pour la première fois le seuil des deux milliards de marks. Un temps fort d'autres investissements est l'agrandissement de l'usine de Dingolfing, rachetée à Glas en 1967.

Cellule de crise et abandon des créneaux (1972–1980)

Avec la 520 dévoilée en 1972, le constructeur automobile de Milbertshofen commence prudemment, après quatre années de développement, à défricher de nouvelles terres sans renier son credo traditionnel : sportive sans doute aussi, mais avec un doigt de confort et de luxe discret, elle est tout désignée pour les chefs de famille aisés parmi sa clientèle. Ce nouveau nom matérialise bien cette intention. En Allemagne, dans le langage populaire, la nouvelle voiture est rapidement surnommée «la Cinq». A l'avenir, elle fera partie intégrante d'une hiérarchie bien claire. En effet, les compactes, ce seront à partir de 1975 les série 3, les gros coupés seront à partir de 1976 les série 6 et les BMW du segment de luxe, à partir de 1977, les série 7 alors que la vocation de la série 8, à partir de 1989, sera de représenter BMW dans le segment des voitures de grand tourisme de luxe. A titre

The opening of the new administrative headquarters and of the low-slung BMW museum right next door were not the only causes for celebration in 1973; it also marked the 50th anniversary of BMW motorcycle production. Half a million machines had been manufactured to date, 21,122 of them the previous year alone. And that same year, Dingolfing began production under the sign of the whirling blue and white propeller, and the 100,000th BMW would roll off the production line there on 7 November 1975. By 1973 the new plant was already responsible for massive growth as the workforce increased by 12 percent and production by 8 percent.

The shockwaves from the energy crisis – one quarter real, three quarters skilfully engineered – did not have a major impact on BMW, and merely led to a minor setback during 1974, when a workforce of 25,805 produced 188,965 cars, achieving a turnover of 2492 million marks. The corresponding figures for 1973 were 27,737 employees producing 197,446 automobiles and a turnover of 2608 million marks, and for 1975 28,989 employees producing 221,298 vehicles and a turnover of 3,254,500 million marks.

The new-found awareness of energy-related issues that the crisis sparked did not sit easily with BMW's sporty image, and many viewed powerful cars such as the 2002 turbo with its bulging flared fenders as an affront to public taste. In the teeth of all this, however, BMW Motorsport GmbH, the subsidiary set up in 1972, was making an indelible mark under its quietly efficient boss Jochen Neerpasch. The CSL coupés with their mighty spoilers powered from victory to victory throughout 1973, as BMW drivers won 11 of the 16 Formula 2 races that season, with the inevitable 2-liter four-cylinder machines breathing down their necks, Alex von Falkenhausen having produced a small run of 50 of these. Jean-Pierre Jarier became European champion in his March 732, one of six to use a BMW power unit between then and 1982.

BMW had long since started thinking on a global scale: in France, Italy and Belgium distribution and customer service had been taken over by BMW subsidiaries. Suitably-sized networks of dealerships and garages were set up, while in South Africa the importer's existing assembly facility was converted into an autonomous production plant. The United States had long since become the most important export market, and no less than 80 BMW clubs bespoke the car's virtual cult status among its faithful following there. In 1974, for example, 35,877 BMWs were shipped to the States, and in November that year BMW of North America became a Bavarian bridgehead in the spiritual home of the motorcar.

The addition to the range in January 1975 of the BMW 1502 proved to be more than just a nostalgic last hurrah for the legendary 02 model range. Over the next two years more than 70,000 of this classic were shifted, despite the fact that sales head Hans-Erdmann Schönbeck had introduced a two-door 3 series model, a new compact automoblie with pleasingly contemporary lines and technology to match. The BMW range was becoming ever larger, offering a glittering array of different models. At the 1976 Geneva Spring Motor Show, the stars of the show were the two new coupés, the 630CS and 633CSi, allowing head of development Bernhard Osswald and designer Paul Bracq to leave BMW on an impressive high note.

Equally spectacular was the R 100 RS, which came with full fairing and an integrated cockpit as standard, and blasted to 62.5 mph (100 kph) in 4.6 seconds. Since January of that year

Gründe zum Feiern liefert 1973 nicht nur der Einzug in den „Vierzylinder" und in das einer Schüssel ähnelnde BMW-Museum gleich nebenan, sondern auch ein Jubiläum der besonderen Art: Seit einem halben Jahrhundert fertigt man Motorräder. Eine halbe Million waren es bisher insgesamt, im Jahr zuvor allein 21.122 Stück. Zugleich nimmt Dingolfing im Zeichen des weißblau wirbelnden Propellers die Produktion auf. Am 7. November 1975 wird dort der 100.000. BMW vom Band laufen. Schon 1973 sorgt der neue Standort für massive Zuwächse mit 12 Prozent mehr Mitarbeitern und einem Produktionsplus von 8 Prozent.

Admired and scolded: "Nischen-Paul" Hahnemann.

Viel bewundert und viel gescholten: „Nischen-Paul" Hahnemann.

Très admiré mais souvent en butte aux critiques: Paul Hahnemann surnommé «Paul la niche».

Die Ausläufer der zu einem Viertel realen, zu drei Vierteln geschickt eingefädelten Energiekrise erreichen die Bayerischen Motoren Werke nur in abgeschwächter Form, mit einem kleinen Einbruch 1974. Zu diesem Zeitpunkt beschäftigt man 25.805 Mitarbeiter, baut 188.965 Autos und erzielt einen Umsatz von 2492 Millionen Mark. 1973 waren es 27.737 Kostgänger, 197.446 Automobile, 2608 Millionen Mark Umsatz. 1975 wird sich eine Belegschaft von 28.989 um 221.298 Fahrzeuge und 3254,5 Millionen Mark Umsatz verdient machen.

Dabei verträgt sich das just entdeckte Energiegewissen kaum mit dem sportiven BMW-Image. Manch einer empfindet Kraft-Wagen wie den Typ 2002 turbo mit seinen schwellenden Kotflügelverbreiterungen geradezu als Affront. Gleichwohl macht die 1972 ins Leben gerufene BMW Motorsport GmbH unter ihrem stillen, aber effizienten Chef Jochen Neerpasch unüberhörbar auf sich aufmerksam: Die mächtig geflügelten CSL-Coupés driften 1973 von Sieg zu Sieg, und 11 von 16 Formel-2-Läufen gewinnen BMW-Piloten, im Rücken den unvermeidlichen 2-Liter-Vierzylinderrennmotor, von dem Alex von Falkenhausen eine kleine Serie von 50 Exemplaren aufgelegt hat. Europameister wird Jean-Pierre Jarier auf dem March 732 – einer von sechs Titeln mit BMW-Triebwerken bis 1982.

d'information supplémentaire, la combinaison de chiffres révèle, comme dans les années 30 déjà, quelle est la cylindrée du moteur respectif qui se trouve sous le capot.

En 1973, BMW a plusieurs raisons de se réjouir: non seulement l'inauguration du «quatre-cylindres» ainsi que du musée BMW en forme de coupelle à toit plat, juste à côté, mais aussi un anniversaire d'une saveur toute particulière: on fabrique des motos depuis un demi-siècle. Un demi-million, jusqu'à ce jour, et pas moins de 21 122 exemplaires rien que pour l'année précédente. Simultanément, Dingolfing entame sa production sous le symbole de l'hélice bleue et blanche. Le 7 novembre 1975, la 100 000e BMW y sortira de chaîne. Dès 1973, la nouvelle unité de fabrication se rentabilise avec des augmentations flatteuses: 12 % pour les effectifs et 8 % pour la production.

Les derniers remous d'une crise énergétique pour un quart bien réelle, mais pour les trois quarts mise en scène avec adresse, n'atteignent BMW qu'avec une violence relative et se traduisent par une légère baisse de la production en 1974. On emploie alors 25 805 collaborateurs, construit 188 965 voitures et réalise un chiffre d'affaires de 2492 millions de marks. En 1973, ces chiffres étaient de 27 737 pour les effectifs, 197 446 pour les voitures et 2608 millions de marks pour le chiffre d'affaires. En 1975, les effectifs sont de 28 989 personnes, qui produisent 221 298 voitures et réalisent un chiffre d'affaires de 3254,5 millions de marks.

Et pourtant, la conscience que toute énergie est éphémère est peu conciliable avec l'image sportive de BMW. Nombreux sont ceux qui ressentent alors comme un affront le lancement de la 2002 turbo avec ses élargisseurs d'ailes démesurés et son aileron avant agressif. Simultanément, la BMW Motorsport GmbH créée en 1972 se profile de plus en plus sur le devant de la scène sous la conduite de son chef aussi silencieux qu'efficace, Jochen Neerpasch. En 1973, les coupés CSL aux énormes ailerons aérodynamiques volent de victoire en victoire et les pilotes BMW gagnent 11 des 16 manches de Formule 2 avec, dans le dos, l'incontournable quatre-cylindres de deux litres dont Alex von Falkenhausen a produit une petite série de 50 exemplaires. Jean-Pierre Jarier, sur une March 732, est sacré champion d'Europe, l'un des six titres que remporteront les moteurs BMW jusqu'en 1982.

La stratégie est depuis longtemps planétaire: en France, Italie et Belgique, des filiales BMW assurent la distribution et le service après-vente. Le réseau de concessionnaires et d'ateliers est conçu spécifiquement en fonction de l'ordre de grandeur nécessaire. En Afrique du Sud, l'ancienne unité de montage de

Full of ideas: Jochen Neerpasch.

Unerschöpflicher Ideenreichtum: Jochen Neerpasch.

Jamais à court d'idées: Jochen Neerpasch.

The Discreet Charm of the Niche

Paul Georg Hahnemann, born in 1912 in Strasbourg, was the man of action and power before Eberhard von Kuenheim. Anyone looking for visible evidence of his influence need only take a look at the Munich skyline: Hahnemann's monument, just half a meter shorter than the Frauenkirche, is the BMW administrative building, called the "Vierzylinder" (four cylinder), or simply "Der Turm" (the tower). He successfully championed the design of Vienna professor Karl Schwanzer in 1970 in the teeth of general opposition, victorious here as he had been in so many battles since autumn 1961, with his sleeves rolled up and with the ready garrulousness of an itinerant preacher, always ready with a pithy saying or an earthy anecdote, the right man at the right time.

When he responded to the call from the BMW major shareholder Quandt to become head of the sales department, Hahnemann was head of marketing at Auto-Union in Düsseldorf. He found the Bayerische Motoren Werke in a terrible state. In 1962 a workforce of 9189 managed to knock up 52,934 automobiles for an annual turnover of 295 million marks. When Hahnemann resigned on 27 October 1971, BMW's workforce numbered 23,307, the turnover had risen to 1.9 billion marks and production to 164,701 units.

Hahnemann later identified four main factors behind this dramatic turnaround. Firstly, he totally rationalized the product range. At the bottom of the range, the Isetta 600 and 700 were scrapped, as were the prestigious flops, the 501 and 502, and also the Bertone coupé at the top end. In their place he introduced the "New Class", comprising the 1500 (production of which commenced on 25 August 1962), the 1800 (1963), the 2000 (1966), and their respective variants. Hahnemann incessantly preached the wisdom of the niche. This was a psychological variable, vaguely defined via notions such as youthful, sporty, maneuverable or classy, not least designed to differentiate BMW products from those of big brother Daimler-Benz. Bavarian politician Franz-Josef Strauß christened the go-getting manager "Nischen-Paul" ('Paul the niche') at a celebration to mark Strauß's 50th birthday in 1965, and "Nischen-Paul" he remained. The ranks of journalists, always looking for a good catchphrase, were particularly fond of using the BMW chieftain's *nom de guerre*. For all that, the 1968 six-cylinder 2500 and 2800 seemed tantamount to a head-on attack on the Stuttgarters. Hahnemann, though, performed verbal somersaults in his attempts to justify their introduction in terms of his philosophy of the niche.

The second factor cited by Hahnemann was the acquisition of Bavaria's other automobile manufacturer, the struggling firm Glas of Dingolfing. The company changed hands on 10 November 1966 for a purchase price of 9.1 million marks; BMW also took on the firm's debts of 50 million marks. The claustrophobic confines of the original Munich plant at Milbertshofen were by then working at full capacity, with a daily production of 450 units. The Glas deal meant more space and labor, and thus new capacity. The third factor stressed by Hahnemann was the network of BMW dealerships, which the competition initially dismissed contemptuously as "puncture repair men". "The other half of BMW is out there, in distribution, in repairs and in aftersales care," he would monotonously repeat like a religious mantra. And the final factor: the construction of the "Turm", a symbol for all that had been achieved, and a vehicle for the long-term promotion of the company.

Despite all his achievements, Paul G. Hahnemann left BMW full of anger. Too often, he had crossed swords with Herbert Quandt, and "Nischen-Paul's" habit of viewing the sales division as the measure of all things just did not fit in with the business climate at the beginning of the 1970s. Furthermore, his familiar and robust relations with the executive board went too much against the board leadership principle Quandt was seeking to introduce. Hahnemann and von Kuenheim's personalities were just too different; on 1 January 1970, von Kuenheim had become president of BMW's executive board, and intended to be one in more than just name.

What would Hahnemann do after the parting of the ways? As an ex-member of BMW's upper echelons, Hahnemann's pension was more than sufficient to keep body and soul together, but at the tender age of 60 he felt far too young to resign himself to long walks along the banks of the Isar in the company of his dog Sonja. The advice of friends that he should amuse himself and keep in shape with regular skiing was rejected out of hand. As a younger man he had always been a winner in sport and he was not about to give anyone the opportunity to say: "Look at the old fool trying to pretend he's a teenager."

The suggestion in 1972 of the Transport Minister of the time, Georg Leber, that company rescuer Paul G. Hahnemann could turn around the ailing Bundesbahn as its President, was also little to his liking. For one thing, Hahnemann knew that within such a complex set-up he would be able to achieve little. Instead he took on the office equipment firm Pohlschröder, and between 1972 and 1976 wiped out its bank debts of 50 million marks and brought it back into profit. He persuaded the Hamburg salvage ship owner Ulrich Harms to acquire the ailing enterprise, and then talked him into giving the firm up again once it had recovered, thus allowing two giants of the sector, Strafer of Strasbourg and Steelcase of the USA, to each buy 50 percent of Pohlschröder. When these two companies merged to form a group at the beginning of the 1980s, it was rumored that Hahnemann had played the role of go-between and marriage broker for the two. He denied this with a twinkle in his eye, insisting that he had just been the personal adviser of Strafer's boss, Henry Lachman.

Not all of the professional rescuer's lesser enterprises went according to plan. For example, his effort to get the body-conscious Germans interested in the Singaporean wonder ointment "Tiger Balm" was not the greatest of successes. Notwithstanding this, right up until 1990 Hahnemann, now in his late 70s, was still putting in a solid 35-hour week at his Pohlschröder desk in his offices in Munich-Bogenhausen. When not occupied in safeguarding or proliferating his holdings, he took a keen interest in the academic careers of his two daughters Carolin and Suzan, both gifted philology students at the University of Munich. At the end he too achieved a philosophical peace of mind, his search for harmony extending even to his views on the contemporary automobile industry. Here Hahnemann felt considerable empathy for Daimler-Benz boss Edzard Reuter. In terms of achievements, he greatly admired Eberhard von Kuenheim.

Paul G. Hahnemann passed away in January 1997. "Nischen-Paul" had long since given way to an older and wiser man.

BMW Motorrad GmbH (BMW Motorcycle) of Berlin had become an organizationally independent entity. In the benign and publicity-friendly presence of West German President Walter Scheel, the cornerstone was laid in 1977 for modern motorcycle manufacture in the former and future capital of Germany, though this was overshadowed by the sensation created by the launch of the 7 series in January. The range of six-cylinder power units was extended downwards with the addition of a small 2-liter engine, not without some rhetorical allusions to old traditions and the glorious past.

That past was in the foreground in any case, since BMW was now celebrating its 50th anniversary as a car manufacturer, marking the occasion with a string of records: almost five billion marks in turnover, and production figures of 31,515 motorcycles and 290,236 automobiles. Executive board president von Kuenheim's belief that a figure of 350,000 was feasible by 1982 proved in reality to be less than optimistic, as the actual figure was 378,769. In 1978 half of all BMW engines had six cylinders, a number which in Munich had practically achieved the status of a tenet, and which was greeted in the trade press with great acclamation; devotees of the straight six held that nothing was

Längst denkt man bei BMW global: In Frankreich, Italien und Belgien übernehmen eigene Tochtergesellschaften Vertrieb und Kundendienst. Das Händler- und Werkstättennetz wird paßgerecht auf die notwendige Größenordnung zugeschnitten. In Südafrika baut man den bisherigen Montagebetrieb des Importeurs zum autarken Fertigungsort aus. Zum wichtigsten Exportmarkt haben sich längst die Vereinigten Staaten entwickelt, wo nicht weniger als 80 Markenklubs zu Stätten kultischer Verehrung der bayerischen Technik geworden sind. 1974 beispielsweise werden 35.877 BMW nach Übersee verfrachtet, und im November konstituiert sich „BMW of North America" als bajuwarischer Brückenkopf im Autoland Nummer eins.

Daß ab Januar 1975 der Typ 1502 angeboten wird, erweist sich als mehr als nur ein nostalgisches Ausklingen der legendären Modellreihe 02. In den nächsten beiden Jahren lassen sich über 70.000 Exemplare dieses Klassikers absetzen, obwohl Verkaufsleiter Hans-Erdmann Schönbeck im Juli mit dem zweitürigen 3er den neuen Kompakten in zeitgemäß-gefälliger Linienführung und entsprechender Technik vorstellt. Doch das BMW-Spektrum vergrößert sich weiter und erglänzt in bunter

l'importateur se transforme en un site de production autarcique. Il y a des lustres que les Etats-Unis sont devenus le principal marché d'exportation et l'on n'y compte pas moins de 80 clubs de marques qui s'adonnent au culte de la marque bavaroise. En 1974, 35 877 BMW prennent la direction des Etats-Unis où, en novembre, se constitue «BMW of North America» en tant que tête de pont bavaroise dans l'eldorado de l'automobile.

Le lancement de la 1502, en janvier 1975, est plus qu'un simple rappel nostalgique de la légendaire gamme 02. Les deux années suivantes, BMW vend plus de 70 000 de cette classique bien que le directeur des ventes, Hans-Erdmann Schönbeck, avec la nouvelle série 3 à deux portes, lance une nouvelle compacte aux lignes séduisantes tout à fait dans l'air du temps et avec une technique qui représente l'état de l'art. Mais le programme de BMW ne cesse de s'enrichir et brille par sa diversité. Au premier Salon du Printemps, à Genève en 1976, déjà, les deux coupés 630CS et 633CSi suscitent de nouvelles envies, sublimes cadeaux d'adieu du chef du développement, Bernhard Osswald, et du designer Paul Bracq.

Une autre création aussi spectaculaire est la R 100 RS, équipée en série d'un carénage intégral et d'un cockpit digne

Vom scheuen Charme der Nische

Paul Georg Hahnemann, 1912 in Straßburg geboren, ist der Macher und Motor vor Eberhard von Kuenheim. Wer nach sichtbaren Spuren seines Wirkens sucht, wird im Stadtbild von München fündig. Hahnemanns Denkmal ist einen halben Meter niedriger als die Frauenkirche: das BMW-Bürogebäude, auch „Vierzylinder" oder schlicht „Der Turm" genannt. Er boxt den Entwurf des Wiener Professors Karl Schwanzer 1970 gegen den allgemeinen Widerstand durch, so wie er seit Herbst 1961 vieles durchgeboxt hat: hemdsärmelig, von der rüden Beredsamkeit eines Wanderpredigers und immer für starke Sprüche und pralle Anekdoten gut – der richtige Mann zur richtigen Zeit.

Als ihn der Ruf von BMW-Großaktionär Quandt ereilt, zukünftiger Leiter des Verkaufs zu werden, ist Hahnemann Marketingchef bei der Auto-Union in Düsseldorf. Die Bayerischen Motoren Werke sind in miserabler Verfassung. 1962 klempnern 9189 Mitarbeiter an 52.934 Automobilen und einem Jahresumsatz von 295 Millionen Mark. Als Hahnemann am 27. Oktober 1971 kündigt, stehen 23.307 Mitarbeiter auf der BMW-Gehaltsliste. Der Umsatz wird sich auf 1,9 Milliarden Mark belaufen, die Produktion bei 164.701 Einheiten liegen.

Die Ursachen für diese reife Leistung ordnet Hahnemann später vier Feldern zu. Zum einen entrümpelt er die Modellpalette. Die Einstiegsmodelle Isetta 600 und 700 am unteren Ende des Spektrums fliegen ebenso heraus wie die Prestige-Flops 501 und 502 und das Bertone-Coupé am oberen Ende. Dafür setzt er die „Neue Klasse" auf die richtige Schiene – den 1500 (die Bänder laufen am 25. August 1962 an), den 1800 (1963) und den 2000 (1966) mit ihren verschiedenen Varianten. Unablässig predigt Hahnemann die Lehre von der Nische. Das ist eine psychologische Größe, vage definiert durch Werte wie jugendlich, sportlich, handlich oder gediegen, nicht zuletzt, um die BMW-Produkte gegen die des großen Bruders Daimler-Benz abzugrenzen. „Nischen-Paul" nennt Franz-Josef Strauß den umtriebigen Manager 1965 anläßlich einer Feier zu Strauß' 50. Geburtstag, und „Nischen-Paul" bleibt ihm auf den Leib geschrieben wie eine Tätowierung. Vor allem die auf dergleichen begierige Zunft der Journalisten läßt sich den Kriegernamen des BMW-Häuptlings genüßlich auf der Zunge zergehen. Die

Sechszylinder 2500 und 2800 von 1968 kommen allerdings schon einer frontalen Attacke auf die Untertürkheimer gleich. Hahnemann scheut indes keine rhetorische Mühe, sie in seine Ideologie der Nische einzubeziehen.

Zum zweiten setzt Hahnemann den Erwerb des ins Schlingern geratenen bayerischen Autoherstellers Glas in Dingolfing durch. Die Übergabe findet am 10. November 1966 statt. Der Kaufpreis beträgt 9,1 Millionen Mark, außerdem übernimmt BMW die Schulden des Unternehmens in Höhe von 50 Millionen Mark. In der klaustrophobischen Enge des Stammwerks München-Milbertshofen hat man mit einer Tagesproduktion von 450 Einheiten das Ende der Fahnenstange erreicht. Der Glas-Deal bedeutet Areal und Arbeitskräfte und somit Kapazität. Zum dritten bringt Hahnemann das BMW-Händlernetz auf Vordermann, das die Konkurrenz anfänglich hämisch als die „Schlauchflicker" abqualifiziert hat. „Die andere Hälfte von BMW findet draußen statt, beim Vertrieb, in Wartung und Pflege", wiederholt er mit der einprägsamen Mechanik einer Gebetsmühle. Zum vierten errichtet er den „Turm", Sinnbild für Erreichtes, Vehikel wohl auch für eine Selbstdarstellung über den Tag hinaus.

Dennoch verläßt Paul G. Hahnemann die BMW im Zorn. Zu oft ist er mit Herbert Quandt aneinandergeraten. Zu wenig paßt Nischen-Pauls Gepflogenheit, das Verkaufsressort zum Maß aller Dinge zu machen, Anfang der siebziger Jahre in die Landschaft. Zu sehr reibt sich sein kumpelhafter Umgang mit dem Vorstand am Direktorialprinzip, das Quandt anstrebt. Zu verschieden sind die Persönlichkeiten Hahnemanns und von Kuenheims, der seit dem 1. Januar 1970 BMW-Aufsichtsratsvorsitzender ist und es nicht nur dem Namen nach sein möchte.

Was nach dem Bruch kommt? Als ehemaligem Mitglied der BMW-Spitze steht Hahnemann ein Ruhegehalt zu, mit dem sich Butter, Brot und Bier gewiß bestreiten lassen. Im zarten Alter von knapp 60 Jahren fühlt sich der Frührentner indes noch zu jung für ausgedehnte Spaziergänge am Isarufer in Begleitung seines Hundes Sonja. Den Rat von Feunden, sich mit reichlich Skifahren bei Laune und bei Kondition zu halten, tut er ab: Als junger Mann habe er im Sport stets zu den Besten gezählt, und

niemand solle jetzt lästern: „Schau mal, der alte Knacker, wie sich abrackert."

Auf mangelnde Gegenliebe stößt 1972 auch das Angebot des damaligen Verkehrsministers Georg Leber, der gelernte Profi-Sanierer Paul G. Hahnemann solle als Präsident die marode Bundesbahn aus den roten Zahlen fahren. Als Einzelner, weiß dieser, wird er in einem so komplizierten Apparat wenig ausrichten können. Dafür steuert Hahnemann den Büroausstatter Pohlschröder, der mit 50 Millionen Mark bei den Banken in der Kreide steht, zwischen 1972 und 1976 wieder in die schwarzen Zahlen. Er überredet den Hamburger Bergungsreeder Ulrich Harms zum Erwerb des maroden Unternehmens, luchst diesem jedoch den inzwischen wieder intakten Havaristen wieder ab. So können sich zwei Branchenriesen mit jeweils 50 Prozent bei Pohlschröder einkaufen, Strafer in Straßburg und Steelcase in den USA. Als sich diese beiden zu Beginn der achtziger Jahre zu einer Gruppe zusammenfinden, munkelt man, Hahnemann habe sich als Postillon d'amour und Heiratsvermittler um diesen Bund fürs Leben verdient gemacht. Er winkt da in augenzwinkernder Bescheidenheit ab, er sei lediglich der persönliche Berater von Strafer-Boß Henry Lachman.

Nicht immer von einem Happy-End gekrönt sind kleinere Aktivitäten des Berufssanierers, etwa der Versuch, den körperbewußten Deutschen für die Wundersalbe „Tiger Balm" aus Singapur zu erwärmen. Die ungebrochene Erwerbstätigkeit des Spätsiebzigers erfordert 1990 eine stramme 35-Stunden-Woche am Pohlschröder-Schreibtisch in seinem Büro in München-Bogenhausen. Wenn er nicht um Wahrung und Mehrung seines Besitzstandes bemüht ist, verfolgt er mit lebhaftem Interesse die akademische Laufbahn seiner Töchter Carolin und Suzan, begabten Philologiestudentinnen an der Münchener Universität. Auch er selbst betrachtet die Dinge am Ende abgeklärt, philosophisch, auf Harmonie bedacht, selbst was die zeitgenössische Autoszene betrifft. So fühlt sich Hahnemann menschlich Daimler-Benz-Boß Edzard Reuter verbunden. Was den Erfolg anbelangt, bewundert er Eberhard von Kuenheim.

Längst leise und weise geworden, stirbt Paul G. Hahnemann im Januar 1997.

---

quite as good or as smooth as this tried-and-tested power unit. 50 percent of all cars and 75 percent of all motorcycles went for export.

To sum up, just 20 years after the company's near-terminal illness, BMW found itself in the sunlit uplands where growth and increased sales had become the norm, even in times when others were struggling against a stagnant economic situation. In autumn 1979, BMW could look back on a postwar production of three million automobiles, 90,000 of the 7 series alone had been produced and sold since its introduction, taking BMW into the heart of Mercedes-Benz territory; BMW had long since lost all fear of its arch-rival.

Meanwhile, the Motorsport GmbH was launching its latest masterpiece – the 535i. Possessing all the charisma of its rivals from the Via Emilia, the mid-engine M1 coupé embarked on a glittering career on roads and racetracks, at the Procar races for example, a Grand Prix sideshow in which amateur drivers pit their skills against the exclusive ranks of the Grand Prix drivers, taking on those with the fastest times from the training sessions.

The Motorrad GmbH returned to motor sport with the R 80 GS, immediately taking second place in the European motocross championship and winning both the German and

Vielfalt. Schon auf dem Frühjahrssalon in Genf 1976 werden neue Begehrlichkeiten durch die beiden Coupés 630CS und 633CSi erweckt, mit denen sich Entwicklungschef Bernhard Osswald und Designer Paul Bracq eindrucksvoll von BMW verabschieden.

Ebenso spektakulär ist die R 100 RS mit ihrer serienmäßigen Vollverkleidung und Integral-Cockpit, die in 4,6 Sekunden auf Tempo 100 spurtet. Seit Januar 1976 hat sich die BMW Motorrad GmbH in Berlin organisatorisch emanzipiert. Im wohlwollenden und werbewirksamen Beisein von Bundespräsident Walter Scheel wird 1977 in der alten und künftigen Hauptstadt der Grundstein für eine moderne neue Zweiradmanufaktur gelegt, überstrahlt gleichwohl vom Aufsehen, das das Erscheinen des 7ers im Januar erregt. Die Bandbreite der Sechszylindertriebwerke wird nach unten durch einen kleinen 2-Liter erweitert, nicht ohne rhetorische Anspielungen auf alte Gepflogenheiten und die glorreiche Vergangenheit.

Diese Vergangenheit rückt ohnehin ins Blickfeld, denn auch der Autohersteller BMW wird 50 und würdigt dieses Ereignis mit Rekordzahlen: fast fünf Milliarden Mark Umsatz, 31.515 Motorräder, 290.236 Automobile. Die Vision des Vorstandsvorsitzenden von Kuenheim, 1982 seien 350.000 machbar, wird

d'une voiture, qui abat le 0 à 100 km/h en 4,6 secondes. Depuis janvier 1976, la BMW Motorrad GmbH, qui a son siège à Berlin, s'est émancipée sur le plan de l'organisation. En la présence bienveillante et médiatique du Président fédéral Walter Scheel est posée, en 1977, dans l'ancienne et future capitale, la première pierre d'une nouvelle et moderne usine de deux-roues, manifestation encore nimbée de la stupéfaction qu'a suscitée la parution de la série 7 en janvier. La gamme des six-cylindres est complétée vers le bas par un petit deux-litres qui n'est pas sans rappeler une vieille coutume d'une époque depuis longtemps révolue et un passé glorieux.

Celui-ci se rappelle d'ailleurs au bon souvenir de tous puisque BMW constructeur d'automobiles, elle aussi, fête son cinquantenaire, un événement célébré avec de nombreux records : près de cinq milliards de marks de chiffre d'affaires, 31 515 motos produites et 293 236 voitures construites. La vision du président du directoire, Eberhard von Kuenheim, qui prétend que 350 000 voitures sont un chiffre réaliste pour 1982, est rattrapée par la réalité, une correction s'impose – vers le haut : de facto, ce nombre sera de 378 769. En 1978, la moitié des moteurs de BMW ont six cylindres, un chiffre qui est presque élevé au rang de dogme à Munich et suscite les applaudis-

Eberhard von Kuenheim, Chairman of the board of BMW AG in 1989.

Eberhard von Kuenheim, Vorstandvorsitzender der BMW AG, anno 1989.

Eberhard von Kuenheim, président du directoire de BMW AG, en 1989.

World championships in the 750 cc class. In Steyr, Austria, the first sod was cut for the engine plant there, after the signing a year earlier of an agreement with Steyr-Daimler-Puch AG worth two billion Austrian Schillings, for the development and production of diesels.

von der Wirklichkeit korrigiert – nach oben: de facto sind es 378.769. Anno 1978 weist die Hälfte aller BMW-Motoren sechs Zylinder auf, eine Zahl, die in München fast in den Rang eines Dogmas erhoben wird und unermüdlichen Applaus durch die Fachpresse erhält: In weitem Umkreis gebe es nichts Besseres und Geschmeidigeres als dieses Reihentriebwerk. 50 Prozent aller Wagen und 75 Prozent aller Zweiräder werden dem Export zugeführt.

Überhaupt: 20 Jahre nach dem fast letalen Siechtum des Unternehmens sonnt man sich im Zauber der großen Zahlen, werden Wachstum und Steigerung zur Norm, sogar in Zeiten, in denen andere im Gestrüpp einer unerquicklichen Wirtschaftslage strauchELN. Im Herbst 1979 blicken die Bayerischen Motoren Werke auf die lange Reihe von drei Millionen gefertigten Autos seit Kriegsende zurück. Seit ihrer Einführung sind allein 90.000 7er produziert und abgesetzt worden – mitten hinein ins Mercedes-Benz-Land, vor dem man längst jegliche Schwellen- und Berührungsängste verloren hat.

Mit dem 535i legt die Motorsport GmbH ihr neuestes Meisterstück vor. Das mit dem vollen Charisma seiner Konkurrenten von der Via Emilia ausgestattete Mittelmotor-Coupé M1 beginnt seine glanzvolle Karriere auf Straße und Piste, etwa bei den Procar-Rennen im Rahmen der Grand Prix, wo die Trainingsschnellsten aus dem exklusiven Feld der Formel-1-Piloten sich mit Horden von ehrgeizigen Privatfahrern raufen.

Die Motorrad GmbH meldet sich mit der R 80 GS im Rennsport zurück, belegt gleich den zweiten Platz in der Gelände-Europameisterschaft und stellt sowohl den Weltmeister als auch den deutschen Meister in der Klasse über 750 ccm. Im österreichischen Steyr tut man den ersten Spatenstich für das dortige Motorenwerk: Schon ein Jahr früher wurde mit der Steyr-Daimler-Puch AG ein Abkommen getroffen über die Entwicklung und den Bau von Dieselmotoren, Volumen: zwei Milliarden Schillinge.

sements infatigables de la presse spécialisée : de tout ce qui a six cylindres sous la culasse, il n'y a rien de mieux ni de plus velouté que ce moteur en ligne. La moitié des voitures et les trois quarts des motos prennent la direction des marchés d'exportation.

D'ailleurs : 20 ans après l'agonie qui a failli être fatale à l'entreprise, les Bavarois rosissent de fierté à la lecture de chiffres qui sont aussi des records tandis que la croissance et l'augmentation deviennent une norme, même à une époque à laquelle d'autres piétinent dans les chausse-trappes d'une situation économique décourageante. A l'automne 1979, BMW peut se prévaloir d'avoir fabriqué trois millions de voitures depuis la fin de la guerre. Depuis la création de cette gamme, elle a produit et vendu pas moins de 90 000 série 7, marchant ainsi sans vergogne sur les plates-bandes de Mercedes-Benz à l'égard de laquelle l'on a, depuis longtemps, perdu tout sentiment d'appréhension et toute inhibition.

Avec la 535i, la Motorsport GmbH administre une nouvelle fois la preuve de son incomparable savoir-faire. Le coupé M1 à moteur central qui dégage autant de charisme que ses concurrentes de la Via Emilia commence sa carrière impressionnante sur les routes et sur les pistes, notamment lors des courses de Procar en lever de rideau des Grands Prix de Formule 1 : les pilotes choisis parmi les mieux classés aux essais sont alors confrontés à des hordes de concurrents privés qui ne sont pas disposés à s'en laisser remontrer.

Avec la R 80 GS, Motorrad GmbH fait sa réapparition en compétition motocycliste et remporte d'emblée la seconde place au championnat d'Europe d'enduro, fournissant aussi «accessoirement» le champion du monde et le champion d'Allemagne dans la catégorie des plus de 750 cm3. Dans la ville autrichienne de Steyr, le premier coup de pioche est donné pour une future usine de moteurs : un an plus tard, déjà, un accord avait été passé avec Steyr-Daimler-Puch AG relatif au développement et à la construction de moteurs diesel. Volume de la transaction : deux milliards de schillings.

Firing on all Cylinders, from Two to Twelve (1980–1990)

While the flying Swiss Marc Surer secured the fifth European Formula 2 championship for BMW in 1980, in Munich they were already reviewing the continued use of the production four-cylinder block in motor sport. The only mountain in motor sport yet to be climbed by BMW was the blue riband event, Formula 1. This job fell to Paul Rosche. Within the company he became known as "Camshaft Paul". Before very long the serried ranks of skeptics and know-it-alls had been silenced as Nelson Piquet secured a first victory for Brabham BMW at the Canadian Grand Prix in Montreal on 13 June 1982, and in 1983 the piercing-eyed Brazilian secured the world title. Like the Brabham BMW Formula 1 car, the aristocratic but nimble 745i sedan, BMW's flagship since 1980, was powered by an exhaust supercharger and supplied with fuel by the L-Jetronic electronically controlled injection system, as were its sister cars, the 728i, 732i and 735i.

In June 1981, a thoroughly revised 5 series consigned its predecessor to well-deserved retirement, and 16 months later the 1,000,000th car of the series rolled off the Dingolfing production line. In the meantime, BMW Iberica S.A. of Madrid

Feuer aus allen Rohren: von zwei bis zwölf Zylindern (1980–1990)

Als der rasende Eidgenosse Marc Surer 1980 die fünfte Europameisterschaft in der Formel 2 an die BMW-Fahnen heftet, macht man sich in München bereits Gedanken um die weitere Verwendung des serienmäßigen Vierzylinderblocks im Rennsport. Als Steigerung und Krönung bleibt nur noch die Formel 1. Mit dieser Aufgabe betraut ist Paul Rosche, in firmeninterner Analogie zur einstigen Verkaufsikone „Nischen-Paul" Hahnemann salopp „Nocken-Paul" genannt. Binnen kurzem bringt er den nörgelnden Chor der Skeptiker und Besserwisser zum Verstummen: Am 13. Juni 1982 siegt Nelson Piquet erstmals mit dem Brabham BMW beim Großen Preis von Kanada in Montreal, und 1983 gewinnt der feueräugige Brasilianer zudem auch noch die Weltmeisterschaft. Wie der Brabham zwangsbeatmet durch einen Abgasturbolader, wird die großbürgerlich-agile Limousine 745i, die seit Mitte 1980 die BMW-Hierarchie krönt, ebenso von dem elektronisch geregelten Einspritzsystem L-Jetronic gespeist wie ihre Schwestern 728i, 732i und 735i.

Im Juni 1981 schickt der umfassend retuschierte 5er seinen Vorgänger aufs verdiente Altenteil. 16 Monate später wird das Werk Dingolfing das 1.000.000. Exemplar der Baureihe insge-

Faire feu de tout bois: de deux à douze cylindres (1980–1990)

Lorsque le rapide Helvète Marc Surer remporte, en 1980, le cinquième titre de champion d'Europe de Formule 2 pour les couleurs de BMW, on réfléchit depuis longtemps déjà sur l'utilisation ultérieure du bloc quatre-cylindres de série en compétition automobile. Seule la catégorie reine, la Formule 1, entre encore en ligne de compte. C'est l'affaire de Paul Rosche, que l'on surnomme familièrement «Paul la came» par analogie à «Paul le créneau» Hahnemann, l'ancien pape de la vente. En peu de temps, Paul Rosche fait taire les critiques des sceptiques et de ceux qui croient toujours tout savoir mieux que les autres: le 13 juin 1982, Nelson Piquet, au Grand Prix du Canada organisé à Montréal, remporte la première victoire avec la Brabham BMW et, en 1983, le Brésilien aux yeux d'aigle enfonce le clou en coiffant la couronne de champion du monde. Alimentée comme la Brabham par un turbocompresseur, la grosse et luxueuse limousine 745i couronnant la hiérarchie BMW depuis la mi-1980, est animée d'un système d'injection à commande électronique L-Jetronic au même titre que ses sœurs, les 728i, 732i et 735i.

En juin 1981, la série 5 retravaillée en profondeur justifie un départ en retraite mérité de sa devancière. 16 mois plus tard,

Du charme indéfinissable du créneau

Paul Georg Hahnemann, né en 1912 à Strasbourg, c'est la cheville ouvrière et la locomotive qui a précédé Eberhard von Kuenheim. Quiconque se met en quête de témoignages visibles de son action sera récompensé par la silhouette de Munich. Le monument de Hahnemann est 50 cm moins élevé que la «Frauenkirche»: il s'agit des tours de bureaux de BMW, que l'on appelle aussi les «quatre-cylindres» ou, tout simplement, «la tour». En 1970, il impose le projet du professeur viennois Karl Schwanzer envers et contre tout, de même que, depuis l'automne 1961, il a imposé bien d'autres projets envers et contre tout, en parlant sans ambages, avec l'élocution entraînée d'un prédicateur itinérant, toujours connu pour ses bons mots et ses anecdotes inénarrables, le bon homme au bon moment.

Hahnemann est chef du marketing chez Auto-Union, à Düsseldorf, lorsqu'il apprend que le grand actionnaire de BMW, Herbert Quandt, l'a choisi comme futur directeur des ventes. BMW est dans une constitution misérable. En 1962, 9189 ouvriers «bricolent» 52934 voitures pour un chiffre d'affaires annuel de 295 millions de marks. Au moment de la démission de Hahnemann, le 27 octobre 1971, 23307 salariés sont à la solde de BMW. Le chiffre d'affaires est passé à 1,9 milliard de marks et la production s'élève à 164701 voitures.

Hahnemann donnera plus tard quatre explications à ce résultat flatteur. En un premier temps, il élague le programme. Les Isetta 600 et 700, voitures d'entrée de gamme, sont envoyées au placard au même titre que, à l'autre bout de l'échelle, les 501 et 502 de prestige à l'échec retentissant ou le coupé Bertone. En revanche, il lance la «Nouvelle Classe» sur les rails, la 1500 (dont la production débute le 25 août 1962), puis la 1800 (1963) et la 2000 (1966) dans leurs différentes versions. Infatigablement, Hahnemann prêche la doctrine du créneau. Il s'agit d'un paramètre psychologique, vaguement défini par des notions comme jeune, sportif, maniable ou luxueux, aussi et surtout pour délimiter les produits de BMW vis-à-vis de ceux de sa grande sœur, Daimler-Benz. En 1965, lors des cérémonies pour le cinquantenaire de Franz-Josef Strauß, celui-ci surnomme l'infatigable manager «Paul le créneau», un surnom qui lui collera à la peau de façon aussi inamovible qu'un tatouage. Pour la gent toujours avide de sensations que sont les journalistes, notamment, le nom de guerre du chef de BMW est un surnom bienvenu pour fleurir leurs reportages. Créneau ou pas créneau, les six-cylindres 2500 et 2800 de 1968 sont bel et bien une attaque de front dirigée contre Untertürkheim. Hahnemann ne néglige pour autant aucun effort de rhétorique pour les intégrer dans son idéologie du créneau.

En un deuxième temps, Hahnemann impose la reprise du constructeur automobile bavarois Glas, à Dingolfing, au bord de la faillite. Le passage du flambeau a lieu le 10 novembre 1966 et le prix d'achat est de 9,1 millions de marks. Pourtant, BMW accepte de régler les obligations de l'enterprise s'élévant à 50 millions de marks. Dans l'étroitesse claustrophobique de l'usine-mère de Munich-Milbertshofen, BMW était, en effet, finalement confrontée à une production quotidienne limitée de façon incompressible à 450 exemplaires. La transaction avec Glas est synonyme d'espace et de main-d'œuvre – autrement dit de capacités. Troisième coup de fanfare, Hahnemann donne un sérieux coup de balai dans le réseau de concessionnaires de BMW – concessionnaires que leurs concurrents surnommaient ironiquement «bidouilleurs de chambres à air». «L'autre moitié de BMW travaille à l'extérieur, dans la distribution, l'entretien et le service après-vente», se plaît-il à répéter avec la régularité d'un moulin à prières tibétain. Quatrième fait d'armes, il édifie la «tour», symbole du chemin qui a été couvert et a, sans aucun doute aussi, pour but de véhiculer la fierté de soi pendant les décennies qui viennent.

Et pourtant, Paul G. Hahnemann quittera BMW dans la zizanie. Ses conflits avec Herbert Quandt auront été trop fréquents. Au début des années 70, la volonté de Paul le créneau de faire des ventes l'aune à laquelle doit être mesuré tout le reste est trop inconciliable avec les conceptions de cette époque. Au directoire, son style de copain fort en gueule entraîne trop de frictions avec le principe directorial auquel aspire Herbert Quandt. Trop différentes sont aussi les personnalités de Hahnemann et von Kuenheim, qui, depuis le 1er janvier 1970, officie comme président du conseil de surveillance de BMW et entend ne pas l'être seulement sur le papier.

Que se passe-t-il après la rupture? En tant qu'ancien membre de la direction de BMW, Hahnemann a droit à une pension qui permet sans aucun doute de financer aisément la bière, le pain et, aussi, le beurre pour le tartiner. A l'âge relativement jeune de 60 ans, le préretraité s'estime en revanche encore trop vert pour de longues promenades sur les rives de l'Isar en compagnie de sa chienne Sonja. Il rejette sans hésiter le conseil que lui donnent des amis de conserver sa bonne humeur et sa bonne forme en pratiquant le ski à forte dose: jeune homme, il a toujours été parmi les meilleurs de son sport et il ne veut maintenant entendre personne se moquer de lui: «Regarde le vieux croulant comme il se donne du mal.»

En 1972, l'offre soumise par le Ministre des Transports de cette époque, Georg Leber, qui veut recruter Paul G. Hahnemann, reconnu comme sauveur professionnel d'entreprises, et le nommer président de la Bundesbahn en plein déficit, suscite tout aussi peu d'enthousiasme. Il sait que lui seul ne pourrait guère obtenir de résultats dans une structure aussi compliquée. En revanche, de 1972 à 1976, Hahnemann reprend en main le fabricant de meubles de bureau Pohlschröder, qui est endetté de 50 millions de marks auprès des banques, et lui fait écrire de nouveau des bilans positifs. Il convainc l'armateur hambourgeois Ulrich Harms, spécialisé dans le sauvetage de navires, d'acquérir l'entreprise agonisante avant de lui racheter cet «havariste» entre-temps de nouveau en plein essor. Ainsi deux géants de ce secteur peuvent-ils reprendre respectivement 50 % de Pohlschröder, Strafer à Strasbourg et Steelcase aux Etats-Unis. Lorsque ces deux firmes fusionnent en un seul groupe, au début des années 80, on murmure que Hahnemann aurait joué le rôle de postillon d'amour dans cette union pour la vie. Il dénie, dans un clin d'œil de modestie, et rétorque qu'il a seulement été le conseiller personnel de Henry Lachman, le P.D.G. de Strafer.

Les activités secondaires de ce sauveteur professionnel ne se terminent pas toujours par un «happy-end», ce qui est par exemple le cas de la tentative d'inculquer les bienfaits de la pommade miracle «Baume du tigre» de Singapour aux Allemands épris de leur condition physique. Quoi qu'il en soit, en 1990, cette débauche d'activités impose encore à ce septuagénaire avancé une semaine de largement 35 heures à son bureau Pohlschröder dans sa société de Munich-Bogenhausen. Lorsqu'il ne s'efforce pas d'accroître sa fortune, il suit attentivement la carrière universitaire de ses filles Carolin et Suzan, étudiantes douées en philologie à l'Université de Munich. A la fin, lui-même voit les choses avec plus de calme, philosophiquement, épris d'harmonie, même en ce qui concerne les milieux de l'automobile de son temps. Ainsi, sur le plan humain, Hahnemann se sent-il très proche d'Edzard Reuter, le P.D.G. de Daimler-Benz. Quant au succès, il admire Eberhard von Kuenheim.

Paul G. Hahnemann meurt en janvier 1997. Mais, alors, Paul le créneau est depuis longtemps devenu silencieux – et sage.

---

had become the 12th foreign distribution company, and a daring attempt had been made to gain a foothold in a precarious market with the setting up of BMW Japan. By 1982, 3800 new BMWs were traversing the dusty roads of Spain, while 5300 had made the long journey to the land of the rising sun. This was to be the prologue to a success story, as Japanese BMW registrations multiplied sixfold over the following eight years. The launch of the new 3 series was set against the exotic backdrop of Morocco, and production of the 2,000,000th of these now not-so-compact BMWs was already in sight. Milbertshofen had long since reached its full capacity of 500 cars a day, and so a new plant was set up at Regensburg. On 17 November 1986, the first 3 series cars left Regensburg's Plant 6, and as always they were in great demand despite the challenge from the Mercedes-Benz 190, signaling the Stuttgart company's intention of competing with the Bavarians head-on in this market niche.

As an economically-oriented enterprise, BMW never lost sight of those potential purchasers who themselves think along

samt melden. In der Zwischenzeit hat man mit der BMW Iberica S.A. in Madrid die 12. Auslandsvertriebsgesellschaft ins Leben gerufen und sich mit der Tochter BMW Japan keck auf einen prekären Markt vorgewagt. 1982 verkehren bereits 3800 neue BMW auf den Straßen Spaniens, während 5300 den langen Weg ins Land der aufgehenden Sonne gefunden haben. So liest sich der Prolog zu einer Erfolgsstory: Die Zulassungszahlen dort werden sich in den folgenden acht Jahren versechsfachen. Von exotischem Ambiente umfächelt ist die Vorstellung des neuen 3ers in Marokko, just als die Produktion von Numero 2.000.000 des nun nicht mehr ganz so kompakten BMW in Sicht ist. In Milbertshofen sind mit der Produktion von 500 Autos täglich längst die Grenzen jeglichen Wachstums erreicht, und so besiedelt man Neuland in Regensburg. Am 17. November 1986 werden die ersten 3er das dortige Werk 6 verlassen, gefragt wie eh und je trotz des Herausforderers Mercedes-Benz 190, mit dem die Untertürkheimer ihrerseits auf Kollisionskurs zu den Bajuwaren gegangen sind.

l'usine de Dingolfing annonce la fabrication du 1000000e exemplaire de cette gamme. Entre-temps, avec la BMW Iberica S.A., à Madrid, la 12e société de distribution à l'étranger a été créée et les Bavarois se lancent, non sans courage, sur un marché incertain avec leur filiale BMW Japon. En 1982, 3800 nouvelles BMW circulent déjà sur les routes d'Espagne alors que 5300 ont pris la (longue) direction du Pays du Soleil levant. On croirait y voir le prologue d'une «success story»: au cours des huit années suivantes, le nombre des immatriculations dans ce pays va sextupler. La présentation de la nouvelle série 3, au Maroc, a lieu dans une ambiance d'exotisme juste au moment où le 2000000e exemplaire d'une BMW, qui n'est maintenant plus aussi compacte qu'à l'origine, est en vue. A Milbertshofen, avec 500 voitures par jour, on a depuis longtemps déjà atteint les limites de la croissance possible et il faut une nouvelle usine. On la construira à Ratisbonne. Le 17 novembre 1986, les premières série 3 quittent cette Usine 6, toujours aussi demandées et appréciées malgré la 190 de son challenger Mercedes-Benz

economical lines, thus the appearance in 1983 of the 525e (eta concept) and the 524td. The turbo-diesel, which incidentally had almost five million test miles (eight million kilometers) under its belt, was produced by BMW Motoren Gesellschaft mbH in Steyr, which had now become a pure BMW enclave within Austrian territory. Right from the start, one of the top priorities was to get away from the traditional image of the diesel as a rickety, rough-sounding crawler; this six-cylinder engine went about its business with the discretion of an English butler. On top of that, with 115 bhp at 4800 rpm, it was not short of power, albeit hardly in the same class as the mighty M 635CSi which came out a few months later, developed from the power unit of the M1, which from 1985 onwards was also to give the M5 a helping hand.

1983 also saw the market launch of a whole new generation of motorcycles, the K 100 with its water-cooled electronically-controlled four-cylinder engine. And bowing to the contemporary demand for all-wheel drive vehicles, the 325iX with its permanent four-wheel drive was introduced in 1985, and the three-cylinder K 75 was added to the motorcycle range that same year. Falling export sales due to the unfavorable exchange rate with the dollar were compensated for by increased domestic demand, not least due to falls in the price of crude oil.

The 100th anniversary of the invention of the automobile in 1986 was an emotive date for arch-rival Daimler-Benz more than anyone else, but BMW turned the occasion to their advantage by launching the new 7 series in all its glory. The highly-respected trade journal *auto motor und sport,* regarded by many readers as having a pronounced leaning towards Mercedes-Benz, put the 735i ahead of the Mercedes S class in a comparative test. The development of the new top-of-the range model had cost a cool one-and-a-half billion marks, with 480 7 series sedans being put through the most arduous of paces during more than two million miles (three million kilometers) of testing. But the labor of love had not been in vain, and the first year's production sold out before you could say 'electronic fuel injection'.

The launch of the sleek new M3, a 195 bhp high-performance sedan fitted with spoilers and a four-cylinder four-valve engine set the course for future production-car based motor sport. Also quite an achievement was the production of 5000 vehicles within 12 consecutive months, as required by the governing body FISA's race regulations. The European Touring Car Championship was won by the Venetian Roberto Ravaglia in a 635CSi. BMW motorcycles also achieved a noteworthy success when the K 100 RS was chosen as motorcycle of the year for the fourth year in succession by trade journal *MOTORRAD.*

The reception of the twelve-cylinder 750iL was similarly pleasing. At its launch in 1987 at the Geneva Spring Motor Show, the acclaim of the assembled trade journalists was unanimous and enthusiastic: it passed the test with flying colors. As a counterpoint to the new flagship of the BMW marque, in autumn that year the Z1 was introduced at the Frankfurt Motor Show. This somewhat idiosyncratic variation on the roadster theme was the work of the subsidiary BMW Technik GmbH, which had been founded in 1986. In the motorcycle sector there were also a couple of novelties: the endurance machines R 80 GS and R 100 GS. Their most noteworthy characteristic was the new patented double joint swinging fork. The M3 was soon busy accumulating victories and championships. Also serving as the driver's off-circuit company car, the M3 had many

Als gewinnorientiertes Unternehmen verlieren die Bayerischen Motoren Werke auch die wirtschaftlich denkenden potentiellen Kunden nicht aus den Augen. 1983 erscheinen der 525e (eta-Konzept) und der 524td im Programm. Der Turbodiesel, mit fast acht Millionen Testkilometern auf dem Buckel, ist das Produkt der BMW Motoren Gesellschaft mbH in Steyr, inzwischen eine reine BMW-Enklave auf österreichischem Terrain. Zu den Aufgaben dieses Triebwerks zählte von Anfang an, das traditionelle Image vom rachitisch lahmenden und dennoch ruppigen Selbstzünder zu beheben: Der Sechszylinder versieht seinen

They called him "Camshaft Paul": racing car engineer Rosche.

Sie nannten ihn „Nocken-Paul": Rennmotoreningenieur Rosche.

On le surnommait «Paul la came»: l'ingénieur et motoriste Rosche.

Dienst mit der Diskretion eines englischen Butlers. Er steht überdies mit 115 PS bei 4800 Umdrehungen pro Minute gut im Saft, wenn auch weit entfernt von der ungestümen Potenz des M 635CSi ein paar Monate später, hervorgebracht vom Triebwerk des M1, das ab 1985 auch dem M5 auf die Sprünge helfen wird.

Ebenfalls 1983 bringt man eine völlig neue Generation von Motorrädern auf den Markt, die K 100 mit einer wassergekühlten, elektronisch gesteuerten Vierzylindermaschine. Ein artiger Knicks vor dem allradelnden Zeitgeist: der 325iX mit seinem permanenten Vierradantrieb anno 1985, als das Zweiradspektrum um die Dreizylindermaschine K 75 ergänzt wird. Einbußen beim Export wegen des ungünstigen Wechselkurses zum Dollar lassen sich durch eine erhöhte Nachfrage im Inland ausgleichen, nicht zuletzt weil die Rohölpreise zurückgegangen sind.

Den 100. Geburtstag des Automobils 1986, ein emotionsträchtiges Datum vor allem für den Dauerrivalen Daimler-Benz, nutzt BMW zu einem kraftvollen weißblauen Akzent. Der neue 7er kommt glänzend an. Das angesehene Fachblatt *auto motor und sport,* von vielen Lesern einer ausgeprägten Affinität zum Stuttgarter Stern bezichtigt, siedelt in einem Vergleichstest den 735i vor der Mercedes S-Klasse an. Lohnende Liebesmüh, denn 1,5 Milliarden Mark zehrte die Entwicklung des neuen Großen auf. 480 Exemplare einer Vorserie des 7ers durchlitten auf drei Millionen Testkilometern schwere Autoschicksale. Dafür ist die erste Jahresproduktion im Nu verkauft.

Mit der Vorstellung des pausbackigen geflügelten M3, einer 195 PS starken, flinken Hochleistungslimousine mit einem Vierzylinder-Vierventiler, stellt man die Weichen für die künftigen seriennahen Motorsport. Ein Kunststück auch dies: Zur Homologation bei der Legislative FISA muß eine Verbreitung von 5000 Stück in 12 aufeinanderfolgenden Monaten nachgewiesen werden. Die Europameisterschaft der Tourenwagen gewinnt der Venezianer Roberto Ravaglia auf dem 635CSi. Das BMW-Zweirad erringt ebenfalls einen höchst willkommenen Sieg, als die K 100 RS vom Fachjournal *MOTORRAD* zum vierten Mal hintereinander zur Maschine des Jahres erkoren wird.

avec laquelle le constructeur de Untertürkheim entend croiser le fer avec les Bavarois.

Dédiées à l'économie de marché, BMW ne perd pas des yeux les clients potentiels qui ont le sens de l'économie. En 1983, la 525e (concept eta) et la 524td font leur apparition au programme. La turbodiesel, qui a accompli près de huit millions de kilomètres en essai, est le produit de la BMW Motoren Gesellschaft mbH sise à Steyr, qui est entre-temps devenue une pure enclave de BMW en terre autrichienne. Le cahier des charges était exigeant: balayer l'image traditionnelle de moteurs lymphatiques et simultanément bruyants et sales, qui hypothéquait le moteur diesel. Le six-cylindres accomplit sa tâche avec la discrétion d'un serviteur britannique. Qui plus est, avec 115 ch à 4800 tr/mn, il ne manque pas de vigueur même si, naturellement, il est à des années-lumière de la puissance époustouflante de la M 635CSi, par exemple, qui sortira quelques mois plus tard et est propulsée par le moteur de la M1, moteur qui fera aussi de la M5, en 1985, l'une des stars parmi les voitures routières.

Toujours en 1983, BMW lance sur le marché une génération complètement nouvelle de motocyclettes, la K 100 avec un moteur à quatre cylindres à refroidissement liquide et gestion électronique. Révérence polie à la traction intégrale qui est dans tous les esprits à cette époque est la 325iX à quatre roues motrices de 1985 lorsque la gamme des deux-roues est complétée par la K 75 à moteur à trois cylindres. Une baisse des ventes aux exportations en raison du taux de change défavorable du dollar est compensée par l'augmentation de la demande en Allemagne, aussi et surtout parce que les prix du pétrole brut ont chuté.

BMW profite du centenaire de l'automobile, en 1986, qui est surtout une date riche en émotions pour son éternelle rivale Daimler-Benz, pour mettre un accent visible en bleu et blanc. La nouvelle série 7 est accueillie à bras ouverts par les acheteurs. La

Flawless: BMW K 100 – with a seat height of 29.94 inches (76 cm) it was suitable also for smaller people.

Tadellose Figur: BMW K 100, mit einer Sitzhöhe von 760 mm auch für kleine Leute geeignet.

Silhouette irréprochable: la BMW K 100, aussi à la portée des petits gabarits avec une hauteur de selle de 76 cm.

revue spécialisée réputée *auto motor und sport,* que nombre de ses lecteurs accusent d'avoir une affinité prononcée pour l'étoile de Stuttgart, place la 735i avant la Mercedes classe S lors d'un essai comparatif. BMW voit ses efforts récompensés: elle a investi 1,5 milliard de marks dans le développement de son nouveau navire amiral. 480 série 7 de pré-série ont enduré trois millions de kilomètres d'essais et de tortures, un destin que l'on ne souhaite à aucune voiture. La première année de production est vendue instantanément.

opportunities to demonstrate its robustness, and after several spectacular but minor accidents on public roads, those involved, including the Italian Ivan Capelli, declared themselves, tongue-in-cheek, founders of the "M3 Destruction League".

The existing 5 series was getting a little outmoded and long in the tooth, and in 1988 the changing of the guard duly came. The new model was such a success that it even cut a little into sales of BMW's own 3 series. Meanwhile, at the IFMA Motor Show the BMW Motorrad GmbH launched the K 1, a tremendously sporty machine incorporating the welcome innovation of two-wheel ABS.

While the 6 series coupé had complemented the first 7 series sedan, this time things were the other way round, with the larger number complementing the smaller: at the 1989 Frankfurt Motor Show the 850i was launched as an adjunct to the latest 7 series. With its feline coiled-spring looks, it bristled with character tempered by a velvety smoothness. The launch of the 850i overshadowed another important development: the introduction of the catalytic converter on all BMW turbo diesels.

The worldwide demand for the whole range of BMWs was so great that, for the first time in the company's history, the year's production and sales broke the half million barrier, with a total of 511,476, of which 332,658 were destined for export. The ever-increasing demand for BMWs, now exclusively fitted with injection engines, was met by introducing continued production during works holidays, first at Dingolfing and then later in Munich and Regensburg too. Driving for the Schnitzer team, Roberto Ravaglia won a coveted title for the fourth successive year when he took the German Touring Car Championship.

Although sales were very sluggish in the five new eastern German states after the Berlin Wall came down, BMW prepared logistically for brisker trade by expanding its network of dealerships. One of the first BMW support centers in the eastern states was the firm Heinz Melkus of Dresden established in 1990. At around the same time BMW was making headlines in the business press with the beginnings of a program of diversification. In the spring, they purchased the KHD Luftfahrttechnik (aviation technology) division from Klöckner-Humboldt-Deutz, and in the summer they founded BMW Rolls-Royce AeroEngines GmbH in Oberursel as a joint venture with Rolls-Royce, throwing in the new acquisition as part of the deal, never forgetting the symbolic message of the blue and white emblems. Naturally, Eberhard von Kuenheim let it be known, this moment reminded him of BMW's origins. On the other hand, when the *Sunday Times* reported in July 1992 that BMW was interested in the automobile division of the historic English company, this was flatly denied.

BMW's latest subsidiary, BMW Fahrzeugtechnik (vehicle technology) GmbH is situated on land steeped in history. This plant, located in the Eisenach industrial district Deubachshof, has been producing large tools since 1992. On the occasion of BMW's first Research Day, the FIZ Forschungs- and Ingenieurzentrum (Research and Engineering Center) was opened on Hanauer Straße in Munich, creating jobs for more than 6000 scientists and engineers, plus their support teams.

Towards the end of the year the third generation 3 series was launched at the Istres test site in the South of France, initially in a four-door version fitted with the latest four-cylinder engine and the current four-valve straight six. Since 1988, BMW had been the sole motorcycle manufacturer to offer an anti-block braking system, fitting it to both the K 100 and the K 75.

Ähnlich Vergnügliches widerfährt dem Zwölfzylinder 750iL, der auf dem Genfer Salon im Frühjahr 1987 seinen Einstand gibt. Als einhelliges Urteil über den Kandidaten braust es durch die abgebrühte Zunft der Motor-Schreiber wie Donnerhall: summa cum laude. Als Kontrapunkt wird dem neuen Flaggschiff der BMW-Flotte auf der IAA im Herbst der Z1 zur Seite gestellt, eine eigenwillige Interpretation der 1986 gegründeten BMW Technik GmbH zum Thema Roadster. Novitäten gibt es auch bei den Motorrädern mit den Enduros R 80 GS und R 100 GS. Deren hervorstechendstes Merkmal ist die neue, patentierte Doppelgelenkschwinge, BMW Paralever genannt. Der M3 sammelt bereits emsig Siege und Meisterschaften. Als Dienstwagen seiner Piloten hat er häufig auch abseits der Piste seine Robustheit unter Beweis zu stellen. Nach mehreren ebenso spektakulären wie glimpflichen Unfällen im Straßenverkehr schließen sich die Betroffenen, wie zum Beispiel der Italiener Ivan Capelli, schelmisch zu einer "M3 Destruction League" zusammen.

Da der real existierende 5er ein wenig in die Jahre und aus der Mode gekommen ist, findet 1988 die fällige Wachablösung statt. So gut ist der Neue gelungen, daß er sogar dem 3er aus dem gleichen Hause ein wenig das Wasser abgräbt. Mit der K 1 präsentiert die BMW Motorrad GmbH anläßlich der IFMA ein ungemein sportliches Instrument und wartet mit der willkommenen Innovation Zweirad-ABS auf.

Während einst das 6er Coupé auf die erste 7er Limousine einstimmte, handhabt man es diesmal umgekehrt: Auf der IAA 1989 erscheint das 850i als Pendant zum jüngsten 7er, katzenhaft geduckt und voll strotzenden Temperaments, das gleichwohl wie auf Samtpfötchen daherkommt. In seinem Schlagschatten – und dennoch wichtig – vollzieht sich die Einführung des Katalysators für alle BMW Turbodiesel.

Die Nachfrage nach dem Modellprogramm ist weltweit so stark, daß erstmals in der Geschichte des Unternehmens innerhalb eines Jahres mit 511.476 Automobilen mehr als eine halbe Million Fahrzeuge produziert und abgesetzt werden. 332.658 davon gehen ins Ausland. Der ständig steigenden

Top motorcycle K 1, launched at the IFMA Motor Show in Cologne in September 1988.

Top-Zweirad K 1, vorgestellt auf der IFMA in Köln im September 1988.

Un deux-roues de très haute gamme: la K 1 présentée à l'IFMA de Cologne en septembre 1988.

Nachfrage nach den nur noch mit Einspritzmotoren ausgestatteten Bayern-Mobilen begegnet man schließlich damit, daß erst in Dingolfing, später auch in München und Regensburg während der Betriebsferien weitergearbeitet wird. Als Pilot des Schnitzer-Teams gewinnt Roberto Ravaglia mit der Deutschen Tourenwagen Meisterschaft zum vierten Mal hintereinander ein angepeiltes Championat.

Avec la présentation de la M3, une rapide berline à hautes performances dont les arches de roues joufflues et les ailerons trahissent la sportivité et qui est propulsée par un quatre-cylindres à quatre soupapes de 195 ch, BMW pose les jalons pour la compétition automobile proche de la série d'un proche avenir. Autre performance: pour son homologation par la FISA, il est nécessaire d'en avoir produit 5000 exemplaires en 12 mois consécutifs. Le Vénitien Roberto Ravaglia, sur une 635CSi, remporte le championnat d'Europe des voitures de tourisme. Sur deux roues, les BMW remportent aussi une victoire chaleureusement accueillie lorsque la K 100 RS est sacrée «moto de l'année» pour la quatrième fois consécutive par la revue spécialisée *MOTORRAD*.

La douze-cylindres 750iL, qui fête sa première au Salon de Genève au printemps 1987, peut elle aussi être assurée d'un tel succès. Les journalistes spécialisés, qui en ont pourtant vu de toutes les couleurs, rendent un verdict unanime sur le nouveau navire amiral: summa cum laude. Aux antipodes de ce magnifique bâtiment de la flotte BMW est présentée au Salon de l'Automobile de Francfort de l'automne 1987, la Z1, une interprétation très personnelle de la société BMW Technik GmbH, fondée en 1986, sur le thème du roadster. Mais il y a aussi des nouveautés dans le segment des motos avec les enduros R 80 GS et R 100 GS. Leur principale caractéristique technique est la nouvelle fourche oscillante à double articulation que BMW a fait breveter sous le nom de «Paralever». La M3, quant à elle, engrange déjà sans répit victoires et titres de championnat. En tant que voiture de fonction de ses pilotes en dehors des pistes aussi, elle doit souvent administrer la preuve de sa solidité: après plusieurs accidents aussi spectaculaires que sans conséquences dans la circulation de tous les jours, ces mauvais larrons, tel l'Italien Ivan Capelli, se regroupent ironiquement en une «M3 Destruction League».

La série 5, de son côté, commence à avoir des rides et n'est plus au top de la mode. La relève est assurée en 1988. La nouvelle est si réussie qu'elle coupe même un peu l'herbe sous le pied de la série 3 de la même écurie. Avec la K 1, la BMW Motorrad GmbH présente, à l'occasion de l'IFMA, un modèle ultrasportif qui se distingue par une innovation bienvenue, un ABS de moto.

Alors que, jadis, le coupé de la série 6 avait annoncé la première limousine de la série 7, cette fois-ci, les choses se passent inversement: au Salon de l'Automobile de Francfort de 1989, la 850i est présentée comme alternative à la toute dernière série 7, trapue comme un tigre prêt à bondir et regorgeant de tempérament, mais sans sortir ses griffes de ses pattes de velours. Elle en ferait presque oublier une innovation pourtant importante: l'introduction du pot catalytique pour toutes les BMW turbodiesel.

Le monde entier s'arrache les BMW, tous modèles confondus, si bien que, pour la première fois dans l'histoire de l'entreprise, BMW produit et vend bel et bien plus d'un demi-million de voitures en l'espace d'une année: 511 476, dont 332 658 destinées à l'étranger. La demande croissante de Bavaroises, qui ne sont plus équipées que de moteurs à injection, oblige finalement à continuer de travailler pendant les vacances annuelles, tout d'abord à Dingolfing puis, plus tard, aussi à Munich et Ratisbonne. Roberto Ravaglia, pilote de l'équipe Schnitzer, avec le championnat d'Allemagne des voitures de tourisme, remporte pour la quatrième fois consécutive un championnat dont BMW avait fait son objectif avoué.

Seat in the glasshouse: BMW Research and Engineering Center (FIZ) in the North of Munich.

Sitz im Glashaus: BMW-Forschungs- und Ingenieurzentrum FIZ im Münchener Norden.

Dans la maison de verre : le centre de recherche et d'ingénierie (FIZ) de BMW, dans la banlieue nord de Munich.

Now came a further first: a three-way catalytic converter for the models K 1 and K 100 RS. And there had also been the usual good news on the sporting front, for example victories in the 24-hour races at both the Nürburgring and in Spa.

Obwohl die Verkäufe unmittelbar nach dem Fall der Mauer in den fünf neuen Bundesländern nur schleppend anlaufen, bereitet man sich logistisch mit der Erweiterung des Händlernetzes auf mehr vor. Einer der ersten ostdeutschen BMW-Stützpunkte ist die Firma Heinz Melkus im Jahr 1990 in Dresden. Zu diesem Zeitpunkt versorgen die Bayerischen Motoren Werke die Wirtschaftspresse bereits durch beginnende Diversifikation mit Schlagzeilen. Im Frühjahr kauft man Klöckner-Humboldt-Deutz den Zweig KHD Luftfahrttechnik ab. Im Sommer gründet BMW in einem Joint Venture mit Rolls-Royce die BMW Rolls-Royce Aero Engines GmbH in Oberursel und bringt gleichsam als Morgengabe die Neuerwerbung mit in den Deal ein, immer vor dem Hintergrund der symbolischen Botschaft des weißblauen Emblems. Natürlich, sagt Eberhard von Kuenheim, erinnere er sich in diesem Augenblick der Ursprünge von BMW. Als hingegen die *Sunday Times* im Juli 1992 meldet, die Bayern seien am Autozweig der britischen Edelmarke interessiert, winken diese kühl ab.

Auf geschichtsgetränktem Boden begibt man sich auch mit der jüngsten Tochter BMW Fahrzeugtechnik GmbH. Im Eisenacher Gewerbeviertel Deubachshof fertigt dieses Werk ab 1992 Großwerkzeuge. Im Rahmen des ersten BMW Forschungstages wird das Forschungs- und Ingenieurzentrum FIZ an der Hanauer Straße in München eröffnet. Es schafft Arbeitsplätze für über 6000 Wissenschaftler und Ingenieure sowie ihre Teams.

Gegen Ende des Jahres wird auf dem Testgelände von Istres in Südfrankreich die dritte 3er Generation vorgestellt, zunächst ein Viertürer mit den neuesten Vierzylindern und den aktuellen Vierventil-Reihensechszylindern. Schon seit 1988 bietet BMW als einziger Zweiradhersteller ein Antiblockiersystem an, nun nicht mehr nur für die K 100, sondern auch für die K 75. Eine weitere Premiere: der geregelte Katalysator für die Modelle K 1 und K 100 RS. Auch im Sport hat man wie üblich Erfreuliches vorzuweisen, zum Beispiel Doppelsiege bei den beiden 24-Stunden-Rennen auf dem Nürburgring und in Spa.

Bien que les ventes ne démarrent tout d'abord que lentement dans les cinq nouveaux Länder immédiatement après la chute du Mur, BMW met en place la logistique nécessaire en étendant rapidement son réseau de concessionnaires. L'une des premières antennes de BMW dans l'ex-Allemagne de l'Est est la société Heinz Melkus, à Dresde, qui est fondée en 1990. BMW fournit déjà des informations à la presse économique avec l'annonce d'une diversification prochaine. Au printemps, BMW achète à Klöckner-Humboldt-Deutz sa filiale KHD Luftfahrttechnik (technique aéronautique). En été, en un «joint venture» avec Rolls-Royce, BMW fonde la BMW Rolls-Royce Aero Engines GmbH, à Oberursel, et amène simultanément, en guise de dot, sa nouvelle acquisition, toujours bien consciente du message symbolique de l'emblème bleu et blanc. Naturellement, dira plus tard Eberhard von Kuenheim, il se rappela à ce moment-là les origines de BMW. Lorsque le *Sunday Times* annonce, en juillet 1992, que les Bavarois sont également intéressés à la branche automobile de cette marque britannique de prestige, Munich fait la sourde oreille.

Avec la dernière filiale, la BMW Fahrzeugtechnik GmbH, elle revient sur un terrain historique. Dans la zone industrielle de Deubachshof, à Eisenach, cette usine fabrique à partir de 1992 de grosses machines-outils. A l'occasion des premières Journées BMW de la Recherche, le centre de recherche et d'ingénierie FIZ est inauguré à la Hanauer Strasse, à Munich. Il crée des emplois pour plus de 6000 scientifiques et ingénieurs ainsi que leurs équipes.

Vers la fin de l'année, la troisième génération de la série 3 est présentée à Istres, dans le midi de la France, tout d'abord sous la forme d'une quatre-portes avec le tout nouveau quatre-cylindres et les modernes six-cylindres en ligne à quatre soupapes. Depuis 1988 BMW est l'unique constructeur de motos à proposer un système d'antiblocage, non seulement pour la K 100, mais aussi pour la K 75. Autre première : le pot catalytique réglé pour les modèles K 1 et K 100 RS. En compétition aussi, on peut se prévaloir de nombreux succès : ainsi des doublés aux deux courses de 24 Heures, au Nürburgring et à Spa.

BMW Worldwide (1990–1999)

On its 75th birthday in 1991, BMW was anything but a frail old-timer of a company, dreaming of days gone by. A judicious glance in the rear view mirror was accompanied by the more important act of reading the road ahead, with special reference to the technology of the future. At the Frankfurt Motor Show, a thoroughbred electric car bearing the famous blue and white emblem, called simply the E1, was waiting in the wings to make its noiseless entrance. A preview of the future is also to be found among the exhibits in the BMW Museum under the heading "Zeithorizonte" (time horizons), which in equal parts delves into the history of the car and looks ahead at the automobile world of tomorrow.

Once again, BMW emerged relatively unscathed from the global recession of the early 1990s. Falling export sales were more than made up for by increasing demand for BMW's products in the new eastern German states. As from September 1991, ABS was fitted as standard in all production BMWs. In autumn, along with a number of other social benefits, a new

Weißblau weltweit (1990–1999)

An ihrem 75. Geburtstag 1991 sind die Bayerischen Motoren Werke weit davon entfernt, als gebrechlicher Firmen-Senior längst Vergangenem nachzuträumen. Zum wohldosierten Blick in den Rückspiegel gesellt sich vor allem der nach vorn, hin zu den Technologien der Zukunft. Auf der IAA wartet ein reinrassiges Elektroauto mit dem weißblauen Sigel, schlicht E1 genannt, auf seinen lautlosen Einsatz. Eine Vorschau auf Künftiges decken auch die Exponate des BMW-Museums unter dem Motto „Zeithorizonte" ab, ein Ausflug in die Geschichte ebenso wie in die Zukunft zum Auto von morgen und seinem Umfeld.

Die globale Unruhe Anfang der neunziger Jahre läßt BMW wieder relativ ungeschoren. Einbußen auf den Exportmärkten lassen sich durchaus wettmachen, weil sich in den neuen Bundesländern die Nachfrage nach automobiler Markenware aus Bayern belebt. Ab September 1991 gehört ABS zur Grundausstattung aller serienmäßigen BMW. Im Herbst wird – neben anderen sozialen Segnungen im BMW-Land – ein neues Arbeits-

Bleu et blanc dans le monde entier (1990–1999)

En 1991, année de sa 75e anniversaire, BMW est loin de rêver du bon vieux temps à un âge où l'homme, normalement, est depuis longtemps à la retraite. Si l'on jette bien évidemment un coup d'œil dans le rétroviseur, on regarde surtout vers l'avenir, en l'occurrence les technologies de l'avenir. Au Salon de l'Automobile de Francfort, une voiture à propulsion purement électrique sous le logo bleu et blanc, sobrement baptisée E1, attend de prendre la route en silence. Les modèles exposés au Musée BMW sous la devise «Zeithorizonte» (Déroulement temporel) lèvent aussi un coin du voile sur l'avenir, rappel de l'histoire aussi bien que projection de la voiture de demain avec son environnement.

Une fois de plus, les troubles planétaires du début des années 90 épargnent presque BMW. Le manque-à-gagner sur les marchés d'exportation est largement compensé par les nouveaux Länder, où la demande d'automobiles en provenance de Bavière ne fait qu'augmenter. A partir de septembre 1991, l'ABS fait partie de la dotation de série de toutes les BMW.

system of working hours was introduced at the Munich site, whereby personnel working hours were decoupled from production facility running times.

In 1992 a two-door model was added to the 3 series, which was immediately declared to be a coupé on the strength of its pleasingly sporting lines. In the dramatic and picturesque surroundings of the Monaco Grand Prix in May, the thorougbred McLaren F1 was presented, a co-production with the English Formula 1 constructor, and a spectacular collection of sheer superlatives. These include the price tag of 1.5 million marks, rather tending to rule out the average salary earner as a potential customer. Similarly, opportunities to test this projectile's top speed of 231 mph (371 kph) tend to be limited, especially at rush hour in big cities. Even highly experienced car drivers can find this monster a little hot to handle, as McLaren boss Ron Dennis and future BMW boss Pischetsrieder demonstrated when they each managed the costly feat of writing off an F1.

The widest product range in the company's history was responsible for a new production record. When the factory gates were closed for the Christmas break on 23 December 1992, 598,000 automobiles had left the plants, including 100,000 3 series coupés. More than 35,000 motorcycles were sold during the same period, also a new record, suitably marking the 70th

Restrained optimism: Chairman of the board until January 1999, Bernd Pischetsrieder.

Verhaltener Optimismus: Vorstandsvorsitzer bis Januar 1999 Bernd Pischetsrieder.

Optimisme contenu : le président du directoire jusqu'en janvier 1999, Bernd Pischetsrieder.

anniversary of two-wheeler production. After a meticulous search for an ideal location in the United States, BMW selected Greenville, near Spartanburg in South Carolina, and in September 1994 the first 318i rolled off the production line.

On 13 May 1993 Bernd Pischetsrieder became the new president of the executive board. Pischetsrieder, who hails from Munich, faced a double challenge. Firstly, he replaced the masterful Prussian Eberhard von Kuenheim, who turned BMW from a medium-sized car and motorcycle manufacturer into

zeitmodell für den Standort München eingeführt, durch das die persönliche Dienstzeit der Werktätigen von der Laufzeit der Produktionsanlagen abgekoppelt werden kann.

1992 erweitert man das 3er Spektrum um einen Zweitürer, wegen seiner gefällig-sportiven Linie kurzerhand als Coupé deklariert. In das dramatisch-pittoreske Ambiente des Grand Prix de Monaco im Mai eingebettet wird die Präsentation des Vollbluts McLaren F1, entstanden in Koproduktion mit der britischen Monoposto-Manufaktur und spektakuläres Puzzle aus lauter Superlativen. Einer davon ist sein Preis von 1,5 Millionen Mark, der eine große Zahl von Erwerbstätigen aus dem Kreis der möglichen Kunden ausgrenzt. Auch läßt sich die Spitze des flachen Projektils – 371 Stundenkilometer – zumindest zu den Hauptstoßzeiten des Straßenverkehrs in Ballungsräumen selten ausfahren. Daß selbst kundige Autofahrer mit soviel Feuer ihre liebe Not haben, beweisen in Bälde sowohl McLaren-Boß Ron Dennis als auch der künftige BMW-Chef Pischetsrieder, indem sie je einen F1 zerstören.

Die bislang breiteste Produktpalette in der Geschichte des Unternehmens ist die Basis für einen neuen Produktionsrekord. Als am 23. Dezember 1992 die Fabriktore geschlossen werden, haben 598.000 Automobile die Werke verlassen, davon 100.000 3er Coupés. Mehr als 35.000 Motorräder waren es im gleichen Zeitraum, ebenfalls ein Bestwert pünktlich zum 70. Jubiläum der Zweiradfertigung. Am Ende einer sorgfältigen Standortsuche in den Vereinigten Staaten entscheidet man sich für Greenville bei Spartanburg in South Carolina, wo im September 1994 der erste 318i vom Band rollen wird.

Am 13. Mai 1993 bekommt das Unternehmen mit Bernd Pischetsrieder einen neuen Vorstandsvorsitzenden. Der Münchener blickt gelassen einer doppelten Herausforderung entgegen: Zum einen beerbt er den souveränen Ostpreußen Eberhard von Kuenheim, der die BMW AG von einem Auto- und Motorradhersteller im Mittelfeld zu einem der 15 größten Wirtschaftsunternehmen in Deutschland und zur Weltmarke von hohem Ansehen geführt hat. Zum anderen rütteln die Ausläufer der weltweiten Wirtschaftskrise nun auch an den Pforten von BMW. Gleichwohl bleibt man im schwarzen Bereich und wärmt sich an der Genugtuung, am Ende mit 534.000 Einheiten mehr hergestellt zu haben als Daimler-Benz mit 508.000. Für Gesprächsstoff sorgt der Auftritt auf der IAA in Frankfurt, wo sich BMW unter dem Slogan „Mobilität ist Leben" als Anbieter ebendieser Mobilität empfiehlt. Diese Mobilmachung neuen Stils bedeutet unter anderem, daß man nun auch Trekking- und Mountainbikes aus eigener Fertigung feilbietet.

Schon zu Beginn des Jahres 1994 gibt man sich offensiv auf etlichen Kriegsschauplätzen. Am 31. Januar wird bekannt, BMW habe Rover und damit englische Schmankerl wie den Mini, den Land Rover und den Range Rover sowie die brachliegende Legende MG erworben. Die frohe Botschaft kommt aus heiterem Himmel, da die Bindungen der Briten an den japanischen Giganten Honda stärker zu sein schienen. Die Gründe für den Überraschungskauf erläutert Bernd Pischetsrieder in der strengen Sprache der offiziellen Statements: „Die Produktprogramme der beiden Hersteller ergänzen sich fast ideal. Unsere regional unterschiedlichen Stärken werden sich potenzieren. Unser Ziel ist es jetzt, zwei unabhängige starke Automobilunternehmen in Zukunft gemeinsam in den Wettbewerb zu führen." Im übrigen speist man in wohlüberlegter Dramaturgie drei Novitäten in den Markt ein: die Kurzversion des 3ers, einen neuen 7er, der nur noch von Acht- und Zwölf-

A l'automne – outre d'autres bienfaits sociaux dans la mère-patrie du BMW – un nouveau schéma de temps de travail est instauré pour le site de Munich : il permet de découper les horaires de travail personnels des actifs du temps de fonctionnement des équipements de production.

En 1992, la gamme de la série 3 s'enrichit d'une deux-portes que l'on baptise sans hésiter coupé en raison de ses lignes sportives et séduisantes. Dans l'ambiance aussi dramatique que pittoresque du Grand Prix de Monaco, en mai, a lieu la présentation d'un pur-sang baptisé McLaren F1, une coproduction réalisée avec le constructeur de monoplaces britannique qui est un spectaculaire puzzle de superlatifs. Son prix de 1,5 million de marks en est un bon exemple. Un grand nombre d'actifs risquent donc de ne pas faire partie de la clientèle potentielle. Par ailleurs, la vitesse de pointe de ce projectile tapi sur la route, 371 km/h, pourra rarement être exploitée, tout au moins aux heures de pointe de la circulation dans les grandes agglomérations. Même des conducteurs aussi confirmés que Ron Dennis, le P.D.G. de McLaren, ou le futur chef de BMW, Bernd Pischetsrieder, prouvent qu'il n'est pas aisé de juguler tant de tempérament : chacun d'eux détruira une F1.

La gamme jusqu'ici la plus diversifiée dans l'histoire de l'entreprise est une plate-forme idéale pour un nouveau record de production. Lorsque l'usine ferme ses portes, le 23 décembre 1992, 598 000 voitures sont sorties de chaîne, dont 100 000 coupés de la série 3. Plus de 35 000 motos ont été produites durant la même période, ce qui est également un record, juste à temps pour le 70e anniversaire de la fabrication de deux-roues. A l'issue d'une longue quête pour trouver le site idéal aux Etats-Unis, on s'est mis d'accord sur Greenville, près de Spartanburg, en Caroline du Sud, où, en septembre 1994, la première 318i sortira de chaînes.

Le 13 mai 1993, l'entreprise voit un nouveau PDG prendre la barre avec Bernd Pischetsrieder comme président du directoire. Le Munichois ne se laisse pas impressionner par le double défi à relever : d'une part, il reprend le drapeau d'Eberhard von Kuenheim, authentique noble de Prusse orientale, qui a transformé BMW AG de constructeur de voitures et de motos de taille moyenne en l'une des 15 plus grandes entreprises économiques d'Allemagne et marque mondiale de grand prestige. D'autre part, les ondes de choc de la crise économique mondiale ébranlent maintenant aussi les fondations de BMW. Ceci n'empêche pas que les bilans soient toujours positifs et, à la fin de l'exercice, on peut tout au moins se féliciter, avec 534 000 voitures, d'en avoir fabriqué plus que Daimler-Benz avec 508 000. Au Salon de l'Automobile de Francfort, où BMW proclame le slogan « La mobilité, c'est la vie », les Munichois font sensation en présentant ce qu'ils entendent par mobilité. Cette mobilisation d'un nouveau genre sous-entend notamment la vente de vélos de trekking et de VTT de fabrication maison.

Dès le début de l'année 1994, BMW passe à l'offensive dans tous les registres : le 31 janvier, la marque annonce que BMW a acquis Rover et, par la même occasion, quelques modèles britanniques de grande réputation comme la Mini, la Land Rover et la Range Rover ainsi que la légendaire MG à l'agonie. Ce message frappe d'autant plus de stupéfaction que tout le monde croyait que les liens unissant le constructeur britannique au géant japonais Honda étaient plus forts que jamais. Bernd Pischetsrieder explique dans la langue de bois de la déclaration officielle les motifs de cet achat surprise : «Les programmes des deux constructeurs se complètent de manière presque idéale.

one of the 15 biggest business enterprises in Germany, also enjoying an excellent reputation on world markets. Secondly, the shockwaves of the global depression were now buffeting BMW. Despite this, the company remained in the black and had the satisfaction at the end of the year of having sold more units than Daimler-Benz, with figures of 534,000 as against 508,000. On top of this, BMW's showing at the Frankfurt Motor Show was a major talking point, as they put themselves forward as suppliers of mobility, under the slogan "Mobilität ist Leben" (Mobility is Life). Among other things, this new emphasis on mobility involved adding trekking and mountain bikes, manufactured by BMW themselves, to the company's range of products.

Right from the beginning of 1994 BMW went on the offensive on several fronts. On 31 January, it was announced that BMW had acquired Rover, and with it such desirable English brand names as Mini, Land Rover and Range Rover, as well as the dormant legend MG. This welcome news came as a bolt from the blue, since the British company's links with the Japanese giant Honda had seemed stronger than ever. The reasons for this surprise acquisition were given by Bernd Pischetsrieder in the sober language of the official statement: "The product ranges of the two manufacturers complement each other almost perfectly. Our differing regional strengths will be reinforced. Our goal now is to lead two strong, independent automobile enterprises into the future, presenting a united front to our competitors". The year also saw the carefully orchestrated introduction of three new products: a short version of the 3 series, a new 7 series, now powered exclusively by eight and 12-cylinder engines, and a new 5 series of discrete and restrained appearance. BMW de Mexico S.A. in Toluca became the 16th BMW subsidiary, and in Peking a BMW agency rolled up its sleeves and got down to work.

The headlong rush towards internationalization once again made the headlines during 1995. BMW signed an agreement for the CKD (completely knocked down, i.e. delivered in parts) assembly of motorcycles in Indonesia, set up a subsidiary in Brazil, acquired Designworks (USA) as a BMW subsidiary, set up an automobile assembly facility in Vietnam and their first dealership on the Philippines, and yet more BMW subsidiaries were founded in Norway, Finland and South Korea. And with the Z3, a product of the Spartanburg plant, a BMW was launched that for the first time had not been produced in Germany. Hollywood provided invaluable free publicity when, in the latest James Bond film, the spy with the license to kill dispensed justice to the bad guys driving a Z3, in place of the speedy machines from Aston Martin and Lotus that had accompanied him in the past. Critics pointed out that the Z3 looked good but was underpowered. This was put right in 1996 by the introduction of a six-cylinder version and in 1997 by the appearance of the M roadster with its flared fenders. In the meantime, the BMW motorcycle division set a new record with sales of around 50,000.

Both production and turnover records tumbled once again in 1996 as car sales reached 1,150,000 (made up of 644,100 BMWs and 507,254 Rovers), augmented by motorcycle sales of 50,500, and the turnover rose to 52.3 billion marks, double the figure at the end of the 1980s. BMW and its satellites employed a workforce of 116,112. The 5 and 7 series were voted by the readers of *auto motor und sport* the best cars in the world. The BMW Rolls-Royce aviation engines received their international

zylindern befeuert wird, und einen neuen 5er von dezentzurückhaltendem Erscheinungsbild. Mit der BMW de Mexico S.A. in Toluca wird die 16. Tochtergesellschaft gegründet und in Peking krempelt eine BMW-Vertretung die Ärmel hoch.

Ein ungestümer Drang zur Internationalisierung spiegelt sich in den Schlagzeilen des Jahres 1995 wider: BMW schließt einen Vertrag ab über die CKD-Montage (für „completely knocked down", d. h. in Teilen angeliefert) von Motorrädern in Indonesien, BMW ruft eine Tochtergesellschaft in Brasilien ins Leben, Designworks (USA) wird BMW-Tochter, BMW eröffnet einen Automobilmontagebetrieb in Vietnam und einen ersten Händlerbetrieb auf den Philippinen, BMW-Tochtergesellschaften werden in Norwegen, Finnland und Südkorea gegründet. Mit dem Z3, einem Produkt der Filiale Spartanburg, geht erstmals ein BMW-Auto an den Verkaufsstart, das nicht in Deutschland produziert wird. Hollywood leistet Schützenhilfe: Bei seiner jüngsten Schurken-Hatz rückt James Bond der organisierten Niedertracht mit einem Z3 zu Leibe wie früher schon mit flinken Erzeugnissen von Aston Martin und Lotus. Schön, aber zu schwach motorisiert sei der Neue, mäkeln manche. Also schafft man mit der Sechszylindervariante von 1996 und mit dem ab 1997 bärenstark und mit üppigen Kotflügelverbreiterungen daherkommenden M roadster Abhilfe. Die BMW-Sparte Motorrad verbucht mit rund 50.000 Verkäufen einen neuen Bestwert.

Rekorde erzielen 1996 auch Produktion und Umsatz des Konzerns: 1,15 Millionen Automobile (644.100 BMW und 507.254 Rover im weiteren Sinne) sowie 50.500 Motorräder erreichen ihre glücklichen Kunden. Der Umsatz steigt auf 52,3 Milliarden Mark, doppelt soviel wie Ende der achtziger Jahre. 116.112 Mitarbeiter werken für BMW und seine Trabanten. Der 5er und der 7er werden von den Lesern von *auto motor und sport* zu den besten Autos der Welt gewählt. Die BMW-Rolls-Royce-Flugtriebwerke erhalten ihre internationale Zulassung. Die Entscheidung für neue Produktionskapazitäten fällt zugunsten eines Motorenwerks im englischen Hams Hall und eines gemeinsamen Unternehmens mit der Chrysler Corporation, das in Südamerika kleinere Vierzylindermotoren herstellen wird.

Die beiden ungleichen Exponate M coupé und Zweiradstudie C1 auf der Frankfurter IAA 1997 verbindet, daß ihre Fahrer ein festes Dach über dem Kopf vor den Unbilden der Witterung

Side entrance: the C1 concept car, a potential city vehicle for the next millennium.

Für Seiteneinsteiger: die Studie C1, ein potentielles Stadtgefährt für das nächste Jahrtausend.

Voiture ou scooter? Le prototype C1, un engin urbain pour le prochain millénaire.

Nos points forts, qui sont différents sur le plan régional, vont se conjuguer. Notre objectif consiste maintenant à relever en commun la concurrence de l'avenir avec deux entreprises automobiles indépendantes et fortes.» Pour le reste, selon une dramaturgie bien réfléchie, BMW lance sur le marché trois nouveautés: une version raccourcie de la série 3, une nouvelle série 7 désormais propulsée exclusivement – dans tous les sens du terme – par des huit et douze-cylindres et une nouvelle série 5 au style discret qui est une grande réussite. Avec BMW de Mexico S.A., à Toluca, la 16e filiale prend forme et, à Pékin, une représentation de BMW relève ses manches.

Les manchettes des journaux de 1995 reflètent une volonté irrésistible d'internationalisation: BMW passe un contrat pour un montage CKD (pour «completely knocked down», c'est à dire livrées en pièces détachées) de motos en Indonésie et crée une filiale au Brésil tandis que Designworks (aux Etats-Unis) devient une filiale de BMW, qui inaugure aussi une chaîne de montage au Vietnam et ouvre sa première succursale aux Philippines; des filiales BMW sont aussi fondées en Norvège, en Finlande et en Corée du Sud. Avec la Z3, qui est fabriquée dans la filiale de Spartanburg, la première BMW de l'histoire qui n'ait pas été produite en Allemagne apparaît sur le marché. Avec un coup de pouce bienveillant de Hollywood: dans son dernier thriller, James Bond s'attaque à la criminalité organisée avec une Z3, à l'instar de son prédécesseur au volant d'immortelles Aston Martin et Lotus. Certains critiquent que cette Z3 est, certes, fort belle, mais pas assez musclée. On y remédie donc avec la version six-cylindres en 1996 et fait taire toutes les mauvaises langues, en 1997, avec le M roadster aux passages de roues élargis. La catégorie motocyclettes de BMW signe un nouveau record avec environ 50 000 motos vendues.

Autres records, en 1996, pour la production et le chiffre d'affaires réalisés par le groupe avec 1,15 million de voitures (644 100 BMW et 507 254 Rover) et 50 500 motos qui vont combler leurs propriétaires. En hausse, le chiffre d'affaires passe à 52,3 milliards de marks, soit deux fois plus qu'à la fin des années 80. 116 112 salariés œuvrent pour BMW et ses firmes satellites. Les lecteurs d'*auto motor und sport* consacrent la série 5 et la série 7 comme meilleures voitures du monde. Les usines de moteurs d'avions BMW/Rolls-Royce obtiennent leur agrément international. La décision pour de nouvelles capacités de production est prise en faveur d'une usine de moteurs sise à Hams Hall, en Angleterre, et d'un «joint venture» avec la Chrysler Corporation, qui va fabriquer de petits moteurs à quatre-cylindres en Amérique du Sud.

Un point commun à deux modèles aux antipodes l'un de l'autre, le M coupé et le prototype de scooter-moto C1, au Salon de l'Automobile de Francfort de 1997, est qu'un toit en dur protège leur pilote des intempéries. Simultanément, Munich jette le gant à Daimler-Benz dans la catégorie reine de la compétition automobile aussi en annonçant que BMW fera son retour en Formule 1 en l'an 2000 – en tant que partenaire de l'écurie Williams. La vedette sur le stand de BMW au 32e Motor Show de Tokyo, en octobre, est le gros cabriolet Z07, reprenant la tradition longtemps négligée de la 507, bien qu'il ne s'agisse que d'un spécimen unique. Chacun espère évidemment que BMW n'en restera pas là.

En 1998, il s'avère que le *Sunday Times* avait finalement raison en 1992, mais avec un retard certain: BMW AG s'intéresse au département Automobile de la marque de prestige Rolls-Royce. A la fin d'une guerre acharnée et aux nombreux

Well-known face: the Z7 roadster, available as the Z8 from spring 2000, is delightfully reminiscent of the legendary 507 from the 1950s.

Bekanntes Gesicht: Der Z7 Roadster, als Z8 lieferbar ab Frühjahr 2000, zitiert liebevoll die Legende 507 der fünfziger Jahre.

Visage connu : le roadster Z7, livrable à partir du printemps de l'an 2000, sous le nom de Z8 rappelle délicieusement la légende 507 des années 50.

license. The decision over new production capacity fell in favor of an engine plant in Hams Hall, England and a joint enterprise with the Chrysler Corporation, which would produce small four-cylinder engines in South America.

Two very different exhibits at the Frankfurt Motor Show in 1997, the M coupé and the motorcycle one-off, the C1, had one thing in common: both protected their drivers from the elements with a roof. At the same time, BMW threw down the gauntlet to Daimler-Benz in motor sport's blue riband event as well, announcing their return to Formula 1 in the year 2000, as partners to the Williams team. The eye-catcher at the 32nd Tokyo Motor Show in October was the large Z07 convertible, in the long-neglected tradition of the 507. Though only a one-off, hopefully it will not remain that way.

In 1998 it turned out that the *Sunday Times* had been right all along in 1992. BMW AG really was interested in acquiring the automobile division of the blue-blooded Rolls-Royce marque. After a long and confusing wrangle with the Volkswagen group, BMW announced in a press release on 28 July that they had acquired the rights to the Rolls-Royce name for 40 million pounds sterling. Rolls-Royce Motor Cars was granted a license to manufacture and distribute Rolls-Royce cars until 31 December 2002. Thereafter, BMW will take over the distribution, while the Silver Seraph will continue to be produced in collaboration with the plant in Crewe, but new Rolls-Royce cars will be produced by BMW itself at an as yet unconstructed new plant in Great Britain. This will be run by a new company to be formed in due course, with Rolls-Royce represented by a seat on the supervisory board.

Speaking about the fundamental change to the situation after the sale of Rolls-Royce Motor Cars by Vickers on 4 July, Bernd Pischetsrieder had the following to say: "We have always stressed how well Rolls-Royce would complement our group's brand portfolio. Thus we are looking forward all the more to running this marque in the future in line with its time-honored traditions and bringing out products of the highest technological level. We are convinced that we have taken the necessary steps to this end for all those involved both here and in Great Britain."

Rolls-Royce of course is a jewel in the crown of English heritage. For BMW, the road from the first crude airplane engine to this dual citizenship has been long and hard.

schützt. Zugleich wirft man Daimler-Benz den Fehdehandschuh auch im Spitzensport mit der Ankündigung hin, die Bayerischen Motoren Werke würden im Jahre 2000 in die Formel 1 zurückkehren – als Partner des Williams-Rennstalls. Blickfang auf der 32. Motor Show in Tokio im Oktober ist das große Cabriolet Z07 in der lange vernachlässigten Tradition des 507, wenn auch nur ein Unikat. Es wird, wie jedermann hofft, nicht dabei bleiben.

1998 erweist sich, allerdings mit Verzögerung, daß die *Sunday Times* 1992 doch recht hatte: Die BMW AG interessiert sich in der Tat für die Abteilung Automobile der Nobelmarke Rolls-Royce. Am Ende eines verwirrenden Gerangels mit dem VW-Konzern erwirbt BMW, wie in einer Pressemitteilung vom 28. Juli ausgeführt wird, die Rolls-Royce-Namensrechte für 40 Millionen Pfund Sterling. Man erteilt Rolls-Royce Motor Cars eine bis zum 31. Dezember 2002 befristete Lizenz für die Fertigung und den Vertrieb von Rolls-Royce-Fahrzeugen. Im Anschluß daran wird BMW den Vertrieb selbst übernehmen, den Silver Seraph in Kooperation mit dem Werk in Crewe weiter produzieren und weitere Rolls-Royce-Fahrzeuge in einer neu zu errichtenden Fertigungsstätte in Großbritannien in eigener Regie herstellen. Diese wird von einer neu zu gründenden Gesellschaft betrieben werden, in der Rolls-Royce mit einem Platz im Aufsichtsrat vertreten sein wird.

Zur grundlegenden Änderung der Situation nach dem Verkauf von Rolls-Royce Motor Cars durch Vickers am 4. Juli äußert sich Bernd Pischetsrieder wie folgt: „Wir haben immer betont, wie gut Rolls-Royce zum Marken-Portfolio unseres Konzerns paßt. Umso mehr freuen wir uns nun darauf, diese Marke im Sinne ihrer Tradition und mit technisch höchstwertigen Produkten in die Zukunft zu führen. Wir sind der Überzeugung, damit die richtigen Schritte für alle Beteiligten eingeleitet zu haben – bei uns und in Großbritannien."

Rolls-Royce, wohlgemerkt, das ist englisches Urgestein vom feinsten. Vom ersten rauhen Flugmotor bis hin zur zweiten Staatsbürgerschaft der spärlich bekleideten Emily in Deutschland führte ein langer Weg.

rebondissements avec le groupe Volkswagen, BMW acquiert les droits pour le nom de Rolls-Royce pour la somme de 40 millions de livres sterling, comme on peut le lire dans un communiqué de presse daté du 28 juillet. On accorde une licence limitée jusqu'au 31 décembre 2002 à Rolls-Royce Motor Cars pour fabriquer et distribuer les somptueuses Rolls-Royce. Ensuite, BMW reprendra la barre, continuera de produire la Silver Seraph en coopération avec l'usine de Crewe et fabriquera sous sa propre régie d'autres Rolls-Royce dans une nouvelle unité de fabrication qu'elle a l'intention d'ériger en Grande-Bretagne. Cette usine sera gérée par une société qui sera fondée en temps utile et où Rolls-Royce sera représentée avec un siège au conseil de surveillance.

Après un changement dramatique de situation suite à la vente de Rolls-Royce Motor Cars par Vickers, le 4 juillet, Bernd Pischetsrieder prend position en ces termes: «Nous avons toujours souligné combien Rolls-Royce allait à la perfection avec le portefeuille de marques de notre groupe. Nous nous réjouissons d'autant plus de pouvoir diriger cette marque à l'avenir dans l'esprit de sa tradition et avec des produits d'une très grande sophistication technique. Nous sommes convaincus d'avoir pris ainsi les bonnes mesures pour tous les partenaires impliqués – chez nous et en Grande-Bretagne.»

Rolls-Royce, entendons-nous bien, c'est une entreprise anglaise qui remonte aux fondations de l'empire britannique. Longue a été la route qui a mené du moteur d'avion bruyant à la seconde nationalité de l'Emily symboliquement vêtue, la nationalité allemande.

New face: on 29 January 1999, Joachim Milberg, previously head of Engineering and Production, is elected Chairman of the board.

Neues Gesicht: Am 29. Januar 1999 wird Joachim Milberg, bis dato zuständig für Engineering und Produktion, zum neuen Vorstandsvorsitzenden erkoren.

Nouveau visage : Joachim Milberg, responsable jusqu'à présent de l'ingénierie et de la production, est nommé président du directoire le 29 janvier 1999.

BMW V12 LMR 1999

Alongside the preparations for making a Formula 1 comeback with Williams Grand Prix Engineering, the new BMW V12 LMR sports car is being built at BMW Motorsport Ltd in Grove, England. The "R" stands for roadster. The renaissance of open sporty road cars is accompanied at BMW by the comeback of open two-seaters on the racetrack.

At the launch of the V12 LMR in January 1999 in the skiing paradise of Kitzbühel, the director of BMW Motorsport, Gerhard Berger, emphasized that the open BMW had still been something of an exotic contender in between all those fixed-roof prototypes when it was used at Le Mans in 1998, but that it has proved to be a genuine trendsetter. As everyone knows, Audi immediately followed with the R8.

If the BMW ancestry of the 1998 V12 LM was difficult to see, the new car has once again been given very typical BMW looks, including the headlight surrounds, shaped underneath in a similar fashion to the 3 series BMW. The aerodynamically and stylistically refined outer skin hides a single-piece carbon-fiber monocoque body.

Chief engineer John Russell had started as early as the summer of 1998 with testing many of the new components of the LMR in the LM. To accord with the regulations, this high-tech piece of equipment weighs 1984 lbs (900 kg). A 24-gallon (90 liter) tank feeds the proven V12 engine, which has become still a little lighter and more efficient.

Parallel zu den Vorbereitungen für das Formel-1-Comeback mit Williams Grand Prix Engineering entsteht bei BMW Motorsport Ltd in Grove, England, der neue Sportwagen BMW V12 LMR. Das "R" steht für Roadster. Mit der Renaissance offener sportlicher Straßenautos geht bei BMW das Comeback der offenen Zweisitzer auf der Rennstrecke einher.

Bei der Präsentation des V12 LMR im Januar 1999 im Skiparadies Kitzbühel betont BMW-Motorsport-Direktor Gerhard Berger, daß der offene BMW beim Einsatz in Le Mans 1998 zwischen den geschlossenen Prototypen noch wie ein Exot gewirkt habe, nun aber voll im Trend liege. Bekanntlich zog Audi mit dem R8 sofort nach.

Konnte man beim V12 LM von 1998 die BMW-Herkunft äußerlich nur erahnen, so hat der Neue wieder ein äußerst BMW-typisches Gesicht bekommen, in das sogar die Scheinwerfer-Abdeckungen, die nach Art des 3er BMW unten ausgespart wurden, mit einbezogen sind. Unter der aerodynamisch und stilistisch ausgefeilten Außenhaut befindet sich ein neu entworfenes einteiliges Kohlefaser-Monocoque.

Chef-Ingenieur John Russell hatte schon im Sommer 1998 damit begonnen, viele neue Komponenten des LMR im LM zu testen. Dem Reglement entsprechend wiegt das High-Tech-Gerät 900 Kilo. Ein 90-Liter-Tank speist den bewährten V12, der noch etwas leichter und effizienter geworden ist.

En marge des préparatifs du come-back en Formule 1 avec Williams Grand Prix Engineering naît, chez BMW Motorsport Ltd, à Grove, Angleterre, la nouvelle voiture de sport BMW V12 LMR. Le «R» signifie roadster. La renaissance des décapotables sportives de route va de pair, chez BMW, avec le retour des biplaces découvertes sur les circuits.

Lors de la présentation de la V12 LMR, en janvier 1999, dans le paradis du ski de Kitzbühel, en Autriche, Gerhard Berger, le directeur de la compétition chez BMW, rappelle que la BMW découverte, lors de son engagement au Mans en 1998, avait encore fait l'effet d'un oiseau exotique parmi les prototypes fermés. Or elle a fait école puisque, de notoriété publique, Audi, lui a immédiatement emboîté le pas avec la R8.

Alors qu'avec la V12 LM de 1998, on ne pouvait, extérieurement, que deviner ses origines BMW, la nouvelle barquette a, elle, le visage typique des BMW où l'on retrouve même les carénages de phares avec le double arrondi inférieur comme pour la série 3. Sous la carrosserie aérodynamiquement et esthétiquement raffinée se dissimule une nouvelle monocoque en fibre de carbone d'un seul tenant.

Dès l'été 1998, l'ingénieur en chef, John Russell, avait commencé à faire tester de nombreux éléments de la LMR dans la LM. Conformément au règlement, cet engin high-tech pèse 900 kg. Un réservoir de 90 litres alimente le V12 éprouvé qui est toutefois encore un peu plus léger et plus efficace.

Wartburg Motorwagen 1898

On 3 December 1896, a bank consortium led by Privy Councilor and Group Chairman Dr Heinrich Ehrhardt founded the Fahrzeugfabrik Eisenach AG vehicle factory with the intention of building military vehicles and bicycles. Dr Ehrhardt with his Rheinmetall Group was a growing competitor of Krupp and was to pump 1.25 million goldmarks into the new company at Eisenach. The resourceful businessman had realized the potential of the Imperial Army as a profitable source of major orders. Ambulances and ammunition trucks, in addition to mobile kitchens, were all items appearing in large quantities on the commander's list of provisions.

There was another product intended for use outside the battlefield being sold in large quantities. This product was a bicycle with ratios designed for uphill cycling via a shaft drive, tailor-made for cycling up to the Wartburg castle. So the first mountain bike was named after the Landgrave of Thuringia's former seat and Martin Luther's refuge during the Reformation.

A new reformation was occuring, but this time Luther did not need to spill any ink to make Ehrhardt understand its consequences: he clearly saw the success that Daimler and Benz enjoyed with their volume-produced motorcars. To save both the time and money involved in an original development, Erhardt obtained the manufacturing license for the French Decauville-Voiturettes.

Like the bicycle, this car was also christened "Wartburg." Presented in Düsseldorf at the first German motor show in September 1898, it appeared alongside names such as Benz, Daimler, Opel and Dürkopp. Despite such stiff competition, it acquitted itself well.

This vehicle was also known as the "Wartburg motorized carriage" because of its carriage shape. Depending on how many people were sitting on the coach box and the opposite bench, it could reach road speeds of up to 28 mph (45 kph). There were alternative two-cylinder engines available: an aircooled design (479 cc, 3.5 bhp) and a water-cooled motor delivering 5 bhp. Initially, the transmission only had two speeds, a third being introduced later.

The front suspension technology offered leaf-sprung comfort, recognizable today, but a lack of rear axle suspension meant that passengers' backs suffered. A single steering bar was employed, a conventional steering wheel was only introduced for the new generation of motorcars in 1902/03. This did not seem to affect the car's sporty characteristics. "Wartburg" cars gained excellent double victories in the major Dresden-Berlin and Aachen-Bonn car races of 1899. The carriage car won a total of 22 gold medals, including an award for elegance.

Of the six original cars remaining today, one is still capable of performing at competition level. This Wartburg, chassis number 88, had slumbered like Sleeping Beauty from 1903 to 1959 in Landsberg/Lech before being woken up by the Munich vintage car enthusiast Georg Schlautkötter.

Wiesloch 1964: Schlautkötter's Wartburg caused a sensation at the Bertha Benz memorial rally, demanding that the fire brigade leap into action. At the turn of the century, the local constabulary in Wiesloch stipulated that the fire brigade spray the streets with water whenever a motorcar was filled with petrol from a pharmacy. This is exactly what happened at the veteran event in which this car took part.

Den Bau von Militärfahrzeugen und Fahrrädern im Visier, gründet am 3. Dezember 1896 ein Bankenkonsortium unter Leitung des Geheimen Baurats Generaldirektor Dr.-Ing. e.h. Heinrich Ehrhardt die Fahrzeugfabrik Eisenach AG. 1,25 Millionen Goldmark pumpt der findige Unternehmer, der mit seinem Rheinmetall-Konzern bereits Krupp Konkurrenz macht, in das Eisenacher Werk, denn dicke Rüstungsaufträge winken. Sanitäts- und Munitionswagen sowie Feldküchen – allesamt in größerer Stückzahl – stehen auf der Beschaffungsliste des Berliner Kriegsministeriums.

Aber auch ein ziviles Nebenprodukt findet reißenden Absatz. Ein Fahrrad mit Bergübersetzung und Kardanantrieb – ideal für Fahrten hinauf zur Wartburg. Und so wird dieses erste „Mountain-Bike" nach dem ehemaligen Sitz der Landgrafen von Thüringen und Zufluchtsort Martin Luthers benannt.

Um Ehrhardt auf die bevorstehenden Umwälzungen des 20. Jahrhunderts vorzubereiten, bedarf es keines Reformators. Schwarz auf weiß gedruckt sieht Erhardt die Erfolge der Firmen Daimler und Benz im Bau serienmäßiger Motorwagen. Um die Kosten einer eigenen Entwicklung zu sparen und Zeit zu gewinnen, erwirbt er die Lizenz zum Nachbau der französischen Decauville-Voiturettes.

Wie das Fahrrad auf den Namen „Wartburg" getauft, stellt sich das Lizenz-Produkt im September 1898 auf der ersten deutschen Automobil-Ausstellung in Düsseldorf dem Vergleich mit Benz, Daimler, Opel und Dürkopp, und der fällt gut aus!

Wegen seiner Kutschenform auch „Wartburg-Kutschierwagen" genannt, läuft dieses Gefährt je nach Anzahl der Passagiere auf dem Kutschbock und dem gegenüberliegenden

Kinderbänkchen bis zu 45 Stundenkilometer. Zwei Zweizylindermotoren stehen zur Auswahl: Ein luftgekühltes Triebwerk (479 ccm, 3,5 PS) und ein wassergekühlter Motor, der 5 PS leistet. Das Getriebe beschränkt sich erst auf zwei, dann drei Gänge.

Während die Vorderradaufhängung geradezu modern anmutet, malträtiert die ungefederte Hinterachse die Bandscheiben der Passagiere. Gelenkt wird mit einer Kurbel. Erst die junge Motorwagen-Generation 1902/03 bekommt ein Lenkrad. Der Sportlichkeit tut es keinen Abbruch, denn in den großen Rennen Dresden–Berlin und Aachen–Bonn anno 1899 erringen die Wartburg Doppelsiege. Insgesamt 22 Goldmedaillen – darunter auch Edelmetall für seine Eleganz – heimst der Kutschwagen ein.

Von den sechs erhaltenen Exemplaren des Ur-Wartburg ist eines noch wettbewerbsfähig. Dieser Wagen mit der Chassis-Nummer 88 hatte von 1903 bis 1959 in Landsberg/Lech einen Dornröschen-Schlaf gehalten, ehe ihn der Münchner Oldtimer-Enthusiast Georg Schlautkötter weckte.

Wiesloch 1964: Der Wartburg Schlautkötters erregt bei der Bertha-Benz-Gedächtnis-Rallye Aufsehen und sorgt für einen Einsatz der Feuerwehr. Beim Betanken eines Motorwagens mit Benzin – aus der Apotheke (so eine Anordnung der Wieslocher Gendarmerie der Jahrhundertwende) – muß die Feuerwehr die Straße spritzen. So geschieht es auch bei dieser Veteranenveranstaltung.

Le 3 décembre 1896, un consortium bancaire dirigé par Heinrich Ehrhardt, ingénieur diplômé honoris causa, fonde la Fahrzeugfabrik Eisenach AG dans l'intention de construire des véhicules militaires et des bicyclettes. L'offensif industriel qui se pose déjà en concurrent de Krupp avec son groupe Rheinmetall injecte 1,25 millions de marks or dans l'usine d'Eisenach, car il a en vue d'importantes commandes d'armes. Des ambulances et transporteurs de munitions ainsi que des cuisines de campagne – le tout en nombre très important – figurent dans les carnets de commandes des stratèges à Berlin.

On s'arrache aussi un produit secondaire civil. Il s'agit d'une bicyclette avec dérailleur pour la montagne et transmission à cardan – idéale pour monter sur la Wartburg. Et c'est ainsi que ce premier «vélo tout-terrain» est baptisé du nom de l'ancien siège des Landgraves de Thuringe où Luther trouva refuge lors de la Réforme.

Mais Ehrhardt n'a pas besoin de copier Luther jetant son encrier. Il observe les succès de Daimler et de Benz qui construisent en série des automobiles. Pour s'épargner les coûts de sa propre réalisation et gagner du temps, il acquiert la licence de la voiturette française Decauville.

Baptisée, comme la bicyclette, du nom de «Wartburg», la voiture construite sous licence est exposée en septembre 1898 au premier Salon de l'Automobile d'Allemagne, à Düsseldorf, où on la compare aux Benz, Daimler, Opel et Dürkopp. Et la comparaison est flatteuse!

Surnommé «coche Wartburg» en raison de sa forme rappelant celle d'une calèche, ce véhicule peut atteindre 45 km/h selon le nombre de personnes qu'il transporte sur le banc et la banquette opposée pour enfants. Pour les moteurs, on a le choix entre deux deux-cylindres: l'un refroidi par air (479 cm³, 3,5 ch) et l'autre refroidi par eau, qui développe 5 ch. La boîte a tout d'abord deux, puis trois vitesses.

Alors que la suspension avant est un parangon de modernisme, l'essieu arrière non suspendu maltraite la colonne vertébrale des passagers. La direction est à manivelle. Il faudra attendre la jeune génération de voitures à moteur de 1902/03 pour voir apparaître un volant. Cela ne porte aucunement préjudice à la sportivité puisque, lors des grandes courses Dresde-Berlin et Aix-la-Chapelle-Bonn organisée en 1899, les Wartburg signent un magnifique doublé. La voiturette rafle au total 22 médailles d'or, dont un prix d'élégance.

Des six exemplaires qui existent encore, un seul est encore en mesure de courir. Cette Wartburg, numéro de châssis 88, avait sommeillé dans une grange de 1903 à 1959 à Landsberg/Lech avant d'être réveillée par Georg Schlautkötter, un Munichois fanatique de voitures de collection.

Wiesloch 1964 : lors du rallye commémoratif Bertha-Benz, la Wartburg de Schlautkötter fait sensation, mais doit faire appel aux pompiers. Lors du ravitaillement d'une voiture à moteur en benzène de pharmacie - selon les instructions de la gendarmerie de Wiesloch de la fin du XIXᵉ et du début du XXᵉ siècle - les pompiers doivent inonder la route. Et c'est donc ce que l'on fait lors de cette concentration de voitures anciennes.

A technically interesting vehicle: this delicate-looking motor vehicle, just over 4 feet (1.25 meters) wide, is steered by a hand crank via a rack-and-pinion and started with a hand wheel located alongside the driver's seat. During travel, the magneto ignition can be adjusted using two levers.

Ein technisch interessantes Fahrzeug: Der filigran wirkende, nur 1,25 Meter breite Motorwagen wird per Handkurbel über Zahnstangen gelenkt und mit einem Handrad, das sich neben dem Fahrersitz befindet, angeworfen. Während der Fahrt läßt sich die Magnetzündung an zwei Hebeln verstellen.

Une voiture intéressante sur le plan technique : cette automobile à l'aspect fragile, de seulement 1,25 m de large, possède une direction à manivelle et crémaillère. Son moteur est lancé à l'aide d'un volant placé à côté du siège du conducteur. Deux manettes permettent de régler l'allumage magnétique durant la conduite.

Wartburg Motorwagen 1898   39

Wartburg Motorwagen 1898

The engine sits unprotected beneath the "coach-box", generating 3.5 bhp in the air-cooled version and 5 bhp in the water-cooled version. A feature that stands out is the linkage of the cam-adjusted rear wheel brakes. The front wheel suspension, with its encased helical springs and overhead transverse springs, is also ahead of its time.

Ungeschützt unter dem „Kutscherbock" arbeitet der Motor, der luftgekühlt 3,5 PS und wassergekühlt 5 PS leistet. Auffällig ist das Gestänge der mit Nocken verstellbaren Hinterradbremse. Die Vorderradaufhängung mit gekapselten Schraubenfedern und hochliegender Querfeder ist ebenfalls ihrer Zeit voraus.

Le moteur, d'une puissance de 3,5 ch dans la version à refroidissement par air et de 5 ch dans l'exécution à refroidissement liquide est exposé aux intempéries sous la banquette de cocher. Bien visible, la timonerie du frein arrière réglable par cames. La suspension du train avant, avec ressorts hélicoïdaux protégés de la poussière et ressort transversal surélevé, est également en avance sur son temps.

Dixi 3/15 PS 1927

Strange but true: BMW cars are of British ancestry. Financially troubled, the Eisenach Dixi factory could not make use of the bank loan available for mass production of a small car as there was no own automotive design. The stock exchange speculator Jakob Schapiro, who had interests in several wagon and car companies, also controlled the Dixi factory. Without hesitation, Schapiro decided to buy the license to build the Austin Seven. This uncomplicated car with its 750 cc four-cylinder engine had sold strongly in Britain since 1922.

As well as the manufacturing license, Schapiro immediately obtained 100 Austin Sevens for the first Dixi 3/15 PS customers. These preliminary cars were sold with few alterations: even UK right-hand drive and braking only for the two rear wheels were retained.

In December 1927, the factory began producing its own Dixi 3/15 PS, type DA1. DA stood for Dixi Austin or "Deutsche Ausführung" meaning "German construction". A touring version of this diminutive car, just 970 lbs (440 kg), was created using the original plans and production documents from England. The 15 bhp were achieved at 3000 rpm, giving the vehicle a top speed of 47 mph (75 kph). Fuel consumption was correspondingly modest: 39.5 miles to the gallon (6 liters per 100 km). Just 42 tourers were built in December 1927, sales scheduled to begin in January 1928.

When BMW took over the busy but broke Dixi factory on 16 November 1928 for ten million reichsmark, production of the 3/15 initially continued unchanged. In 1928/29, 9308 Dixi DA1s left the factory in the shadow of Wartburg castle. The majority (4831 units) were tourers. The BMW-badged DA2, a considerable development of the basic Austin design, was mass-produced from summer 1929 onward. Thew DA2 saw Eisenach cars begin to carry the BMW name.

In the final months of production, the Dixi was available through special finance deals (discounts and 24 monthly installments). The DA1 was provided with a battery since the original magneto ignition was unreliable. No longer did customers gamble with the brakes ("they work more ... or less"), but BMW would improve this aspect.

As well as the tourer and limousine (for three large or four smaller passengers), the open-top two-seater was very popular. Dixi prices were between 2750 and 3200 reichsmark, a real market niche!

"It accords with the wishes of the sporting lady and the gentleman driver, who wish to drive a light two-seater vehicle with modern lines and elegant exterior", claimed BMW as it took over the Dixi legacy. What would "Grandfather" Austin say in the 1990s, now that BMW has again adopted British "grandchildren" at Rover and Rolls-Royce?

Eigentlich ist der Urahn aller BMW ein Brite. Die Eisenacher Dixi-Werke sind in finanziellen Schwierigkeiten, und dem Bankkredit für eine Serienfabrikation eines Kleinwagens steht keine brauchbare Entwicklung gegenüber. Börsenspekulant Jakob Schapiro, der an mehreren Waggon- und Fahrzeugfirmen beteiligt ist und auch die Dixi-Werke kontrolliert, besorgt kurzerhand eine Nachbau-Lizenz des Austin Seven. Dieser unkomplizierte Wagen mit einem 750-ccm-Vierzylindermotor verkauft sich auf der Insel seit 1922 prächtig.

Schapiro erwirbt nicht nur die Lizenz, sondern läßt auch gleich 100 Austin Seven kommen, um sie als erste Dixi 3/15 PS zu verkaufen. Diese „Vorabserie" geht fast unverändert – sogar noch mit Rechtslenkung – an die Kunden.

Im Dezember 1927 beginnt die Eigenproduktion des Dixi 3/15 PS, Typ DA1. Dabei steht „DA" als Kürzel für „Dixi Austin" oder für „Deutsche Ausführung". Nach Originalplänen und Fertigungsunterlagen aus England entsteht das 440 Kilo leichte Wägelchen in der Tourer-Version. Die 15 PS werden bei 3000 Umdrehungen pro Minute erreicht und beschleunigen das Gefährt auf bis zu 75 Stundenkilometer. Ähnlich bescheiden ist der Verbrauch: sechs Liter auf 100 Kilometer. 42 Tourer werden im Dezember 1927 gebaut, der Verkaufsbeginn wird auf Januar 1928 festgelegt.

Als BMW am 16. November 1928 für 10 Millionen Reichsmark die hochverschuldeten, aber emsig produzierenden Dixi-Werke übernimmt, wird der 3/15 erst einmal unverändert weitergebaut. 1928/29 verlassen 9308 Dixi DA1 das Werk in Sichtweite der Wartburg. Den Hauptanteil trägt die Produktion des

Tourers mit 4831 Einheiten. Der DA2, eine erheblich weiter-
entwickelte Konstruktion, geht im Sommer 1929 parallel vom
Band und trägt erstmals den Namen BMW.

Zurück zum Dixi, der in den letzten Monaten seiner
Fertigung zu Sonderpreisen erhältlich ist – Rabatte und Raten-
zahlung in 24 Monaten. Dem DA1 wird eine Batterie eingebaut,
da die Magnetzündung des Austin-Originals unzuverlässig
arbeitet. Auch der Unsicherheitsfaktor Bremsen („they work
more … or less") wird behoben.

Neben Tourer und Limousine (für drei große oder vier
kleinere Passagiere) erfreut sich der offene Zweisitzer großer
Beliebtheit. Die Dixi-Preise liegen zwischen 2750 und 3200
Reichsmark – eine echte Marktnische!

„Er entspricht dem Wunsche der sporttreibenden Dame und
des Herrenfahrers, die ein leichtes zweisitziges Fahrzeug mit
moderner Linienführung und elegantem Äußeren zu steuern
wünschen." Mit dieser Werksaussage übernimmt der BMW das
Erbe des Dixi. Was hätte „Großvater" Austin wohl gesagt, hätte
er gewußt, daß BMW mit Rover und Rolls-Royce Jahrzehnte
später wieder englische „Enkel" adoptieren würde?

L'ancêtre des BMW est en réalité une Anglaise. Retour en
arrière : les usines Dixi d'Eisenach rencontrent des
difficultés financières et le crédit accordé par les
banques pour la fabrication en série d'une petite voiture ne
correspond à aucune automobile digne de ce nom. Un
spéculateur, Jakob Schapiro, qui tire les ficelles de plusieurs
firmes de wagons et d'automobiles et contrôle aussi les usines
Dixi, procure sans hésiter une licence pour une réplique de
l'Austin Seven. Pas compliquée pour un brin, cette voiture avec
un petit moteur à quatre cylindres de 750 cm³ se vend comme
des petits pains en Angleterre depuis 1922.

Outre la licence, Schapiro fait venir dans la foulée 100
Austin Seven pour pouvoir vendre les premières Dixi 3/15 PS.
Cette série préliminaire est vendue aux clients pratiquement
sans modification – elles ont même encore le volant à droite.

En décembre 1927 commence la production à Eisenach de
la Dixi 3/15 PS, type DA1 (pour Dixi Austin et, à partir de 1928,
pour «Deutsche Ausführung», exécution allemande). Selon les
plans originaux et les dossiers de fabrication d'Angleterre, cette
voiturette de 440 kg est fabriquée en version tourer. Les 15 ch
sont délivrés à 3000 tr/mn et confèrent à l'engin une vitesse de
75 km/h. La consommation est modeste: 6 litres aux 100 km.
42 tourer sont construites en décembre 1927 et le début de la
commercialisation est fixé à janvier 1928.

Quand BMW reprend pour 10 millions de reichsmarks les
usines Dixi grevées de dettes, mais qui tournent au régime de
production maximum, le 16 novembre 1928, la 3/15 est, en un
premier temps, construite sans modification. En 1928/29,
9308 Dixi DA1 quittent l'usine à un jet de pierre de la Wartburg.

Avec 4831 exemplaires, la tourer représente la part du lion de
la production. La DA2, un modèle beaucoup plus perfectionné,
est produite parallèlement à partir de l'été 1929. Et seule la DA2
porte le nom BMW.

Mais revenons à la Dixi qui, durant ses derniers mois de
production, est vendue à un prix spécial (avec ristourne et
même payable en 24 mensualités). La DA1 est pourvue d'une
batterie, car l'allumage magnétique de l'Austin d'origine n'est
pas fiable. Le comportement des freins («they work more … or
less») est, lui aussi, revu et corrigé. Avec la tourer et la berline
(pour trois grands ou quatre petits passagers), la biplace
découverte jouit aussi d'une grande popularité. Les Dixi coûtent
entre 2750 et 3200 reichsmarks. Un véritable créneau!

«Elle répond aux besoins de la dame sportive et du
gentleman-driver qui souhaitent conduire une légère voiture
biplace aux lignes modernes et à l'allure élégante», proclame le
slogan publicitaire de BMW lors de la reprise de l'héritage de la
Dixi. Qu'aurait dit le «grand-père» Austin, s'il avait su que BMW,
après Rover, tente encore, avec Rolls-Royce, d'adopter une
autre «petite-fille» anglaise?

The galloping centaur – the symbol of the Dixi works at Eisenach – captured the hearts of motorists. It stands at the prow of the DA1, of which 9308 were produced during 1928 and 1929, under license to Austin. The tourer model depicted here accounted for the bulk of production.

Der galoppierende Zentaur – Symbol der Dixi-Werke Eisenach – stürmt mit dem DA1 in die Herzen der Automobilisten. 1928/29 werden 9308 Exemplare davon nach Austin-Lizenz gebaut. Der Hauptanteil der Produktion entfällt auf das hier abgebildete Tourer-Modell.

Le centaure au galop – emblème des usines Dixi d'Eisenach – prend d'assaut le cœur des automobilistes avec la DA1. En 1928/29, 9308 voitures de ce type sont construites sur licence Austin. Le modèle tourer illustré ici a représenté la part du lion de la production.

In the cockpit of the Dixi, instruments, switches and levers are reduced to a bare minimum. The fuel supply when idling is regulated by a lever fitted on the rim of the steering wheel. For the sake of simplicity, this also serves to bring the car to a standstill. The footbrake operates on the rear wheels and the handbrake on the front wheels.

Im Cockpit des Dixi sind Armaturen, Schalter und Hebel auf das Notwendigste reduziert. Das Standgas wird über einen Hebel auf dem Lenkradkranz reguliert. Er dient der Einfachheit halber auch gern zum Abstellen des Motors. Die Fußbremse wirkt auf die Hinterräder, während die Handbremse vorne greift.

Dans le cockpit de la Dixi, les cadrans, leviers et manettes se limitent au strict minimum. Un levier sur la couronne du volant permet de régler le ralenti. Astuce géniale, on s'en sert aussi pour couper le moteur. La pédale de frein agit sur les roues arrière alors que le frein à main agit sur le train avant.

Taking a look under the hood, the Dixi's engineering comes across as simple but functional: the Klaxon fitted above the 15 bhp engine with its laterally-mounted sidedraft carburetor may be a few decibels less loud than modern horns, but it is certainly more original.

Einfach, doch funktionell präsentiert sich die Dixi-Technik auch bei einem Blick unter die Haube: Die „Tröte" über dem 15-PS-Motor mit seitlich stehendem Flachstromvergaser ist heutigen Hupen zwar um einige Dezibel unterlegen, dafür aber umso origineller.

Simple et pourtant fonctionnelle, telle est la mécanique de la Dixi également lorsque l'on soulève le capot: la corne qui trône sur le moteur de 15 ch à carburateur horizontal placé sur le côté est, certes, beaucoup moins puissante que les fanfares d'aujourd'hui, mais nettement plus originale.

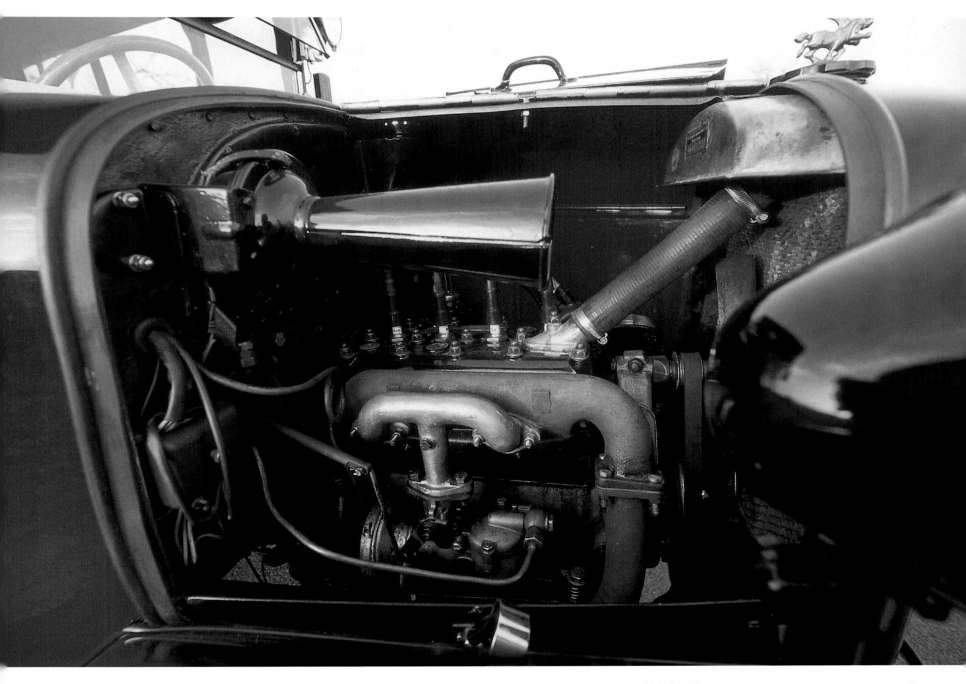

BMW Wartburg DA3 1930

Mr W. from Munich is entitled to call himself the Croesus of veteran cars, for his stock of BMWs of the 3/15 PS category has been likened to a Dixi band with 20 soloists. The tone is set by a particularly beautiful Wartburg DA3. Machines such as the DA3 appear just six times in the archive lists of Jürgen Pollack, membership officer of the BMW Veteran Club.

On the subject of the DA3, Pollack defers to another expert: "I'm sure that Kasimirowicz in Düsseldorf will know more about that." Helmut Kasimirowicz, who has already assisted several BMWs to return to their old glory, including a rare express pick-up truck, knows more: "I know another three DA3 owners, I'm one of them."

The DA3 of Jürgen and Brigitte Klöckner possesses an original chassis with number and associated documentation which was only produced 150 times. Conversation about the refinements of the engine with copper suction pipe and double exhaust immediately turns to a special carburetor. Tested by the motor magazine *Motor und Sport* in 1930, the "Atmos carburetor" produced a performance increase of 1.4 bhp.

In the DA3, weighing no more than 904 lbs (410 kg) with its aluminium chassis, 18 to 19 bhp were sufficient to produce a car with "a full personality and spirit and all the signs of a thoroughbred sports car," wrote *Motor und Sport*.

On 17 April 1931, *ADAC-Motorwelt* added: "The low air resistance of the light and racy sports chassis contributes to the achievement of a good speed." When the windscreen – made of shatter-proof glass back then – was folded, the agile little DA3 neared 62.5 mph (100 kph).

Steering and handling of the small car surprised its contemporaries. A lowered front axle with transverse leaf-sprung suspension enabled a ride height reduction of almost 4 inches (10 cm) compared to the DA2, benefitting roadholding.

The sporting attributes also included the spare wheel fixed to the side of the bonnet, an absence of doors and the instruments. The latter were restricted to a roller speedo and an oil pressure gauge flanking the ignition switch.

In his *Motor und Sport* report of 1930, the author noted: "The Wartburg is a car for good drivers. Bad drivers do not deserve to own this automobile." Probably the best Wartburg driver was Robert "Bobby" Kohlrausch, born in Eisenach in 1904. Professionally, Bobby advanced from apprentice fitter in the Dixi works to engineer. The motorcycle which his father gave him as a reward for his hard work – modified as a racing machine by Bobby – earned him many cups, but also almost cost him his life. On the promise of never racing motorcycles again, his Dad gave him a BMW. So began an incredible career with 62 wins and four world records. Nobody had said anything about four-wheeler motor sports. Each year in May, when the "DA pilgrims" are engaged in their pilgrimage to Eisenach, one of the most beautiful Kohlrausch cups is reverently passed around.

Herr W. aus München darf sich Oldtimer-Krösus nennen, denn sein Bestand an BMW der 3/15-PS-Kategorie gleicht einer „Dixi-Band" mit 20 „Solisten". Den Ton gibt freilich ein besonders schönes Exemplar des Typs DA3 Wartburg an. Solche DA3-Raritäten finden sich lediglich sechsmal in den Archiv-Listen von Jürgen Pollack, dem Mitglieder-Betreuer des BMW-Veteranen-Clubs.

Beim Thema DA3 verweist Pollack gern an einen Kenner: „Sicherlich weiß da der Kasimirowicz aus Düsseldorf noch mehr." Helmut Kasimirowicz, der schon einigen BMW, so auch einem seltenen Eil-Lieferwagen, zu altem Glanz verholfen hat, weiß tatsächlich mehr: „Ich kenne drei weitere DA3-Eigner, einer davon bin ich."

Der DA3 von Dr. Jürgen und Brigitte Klöckner verfügt über ein Originalfahrgestell mit Nummer und dazugehörigem Brief, wie er nur 150 Mal ausgestellt wurde. Angesichts des Motors – mit kupfernem Ansaugrohr und doppeltem Auspuff – kommt die Sprache sofort auf eine spezielle Vergaserbestückung. Solchermaßen exerziert von den Testern der Fachzeitschrift *Motor und Sport* im Jahre 1930, bringt ein sogenannter „Atmos-Vergaser" einen Leistungszuwachs von 1,4 PS.

Bei dem nur 410 Kilo leichten DA3 mit Aluminium-Karosserie sorgen 18 bis 19 PS für „eine vollwertige Autopersönlichkeit mit Temperament und allen Anzeichen eines gutrassigen Sportwagens" (so *Motor und Sport*).

Und die *ADAC-Motorwelt* vom 17. April 1931 fügt hinzu: „Der geringe Luftwiderstand der leichten und schnittigen Sportkarosserie trägt zu einer guten Fahrgeschwindigkeit bei." Bei heruntergeklappter Windschutzscheibe, die bereits aus

splitterfreiem Glas besteht, kommt das behende Wägelchen an die 100-km/h-Marke heran.

Lenkung und Handling des schmalen Wagens erstaunen die Zeitgenossen. Eine durchgekröpfte Vorderachse mit Querfeder macht es nicht nur möglich, das Auto gegenüber dem DA2 um fast 10 Zentimeter tieferzulegen, sondern verbessert auch die Straßenlage.

Sportliche Attribute sind auch das seitlich neben der Motorhaube montierte Reserverad, der türlose Einstieg und die Instrumentierung, die sich auf einen Walzentacho, das Öldruckmanometer und das dazwischenliegende Schalt-Zündschloß beschränkt.

In einem *Motor und Sport*-Bericht von 1930 vermerkt der Autor: „Der Wartburg ist ein Wagen für gute Fahrer. Schlechte Fahrer verdienen nicht den Besitz dieses Automobils." Der wohl beste Wartburg-Lenker ist Robert „Bobby" Kohlrausch, 1904 in Eisenach geboren. Beruflich bringt es Bobby vom Schlosserlehrling in den Dixi-Werken bis zum Ingenieur. Das vom Vater als Lohn des Fleißes geschenkte Motorrad – von Bobby zur Rennmaschine umgebaut – fährt viele Pokale ein, kostet ihn aber auch fast das Leben. Gegen das Versprechen, nie mehr Motorradrennen zu fahren, spendiert der Papa einen BMW. Es ist der Beginn einer unglaublichen Karriere mit 62 Siegen und vier Weltrekorden. Von vier Rädern war ja nicht die Rede! Jedes Jahr im Mai, wenn die „DA-Pilger" gen Eisenach ziehen, wird einer der schönsten Kohlrausch-Pokale andächtig herumgereicht.

Monsieur W., de Munich, peut légitimement se considérer comme un Crésus parmi les amateurs de voitures anciennes, car sa collection de BMW de la catégorie 3/15 PS évoque un «orchestre de Dixi» avec 20 «solistes». C'est toutefois un superbe exemplaire du type Wartburg DA3 qui donne le ton. De telles raretés comme les DA3 ne se trouvent qu'à six exemplaires dans les archives de Jürgen Pollack, qui gère le club des propriétaires de vieilles BMW.

Sur le thème de la DA3, Pollack vous renverra cependant volontiers à un connaisseur: «Je pense que Kasimirowicz, de Düsseldorf, en sait encore plus». Helmut Kasimirowicz, qui a déjà restauré plus d'une BMW, dont une rare fourgonnette de livraison expresse, en sait en effet plus: «Je connais trois autres propriétaires de DA3, et je suis l'un d'eux.»

La DA3 de Dr Jürgen Klöckner et de son épouse Brigitte possède un châssis original avec le numéro et la carte grise d'origine, qui n'a été délivrée qu'à 150 exemplaires. Quand on évoque les raffinements du moteur avec tubulure d'aspiration en cuivre et double pot d'échappement, on ne peut pas manquer de parler immédiatement de sa dotation particulière en carburateur. Lors d'un essai réalisé par la revue spécialisée *Motor und Sport* en 1930, un carburateur «Atmos» donne un gain de puissance de 1,4 ch.

Avec un poids de seulement 410 kg pour la DA3 à carrosserie aluminium, 18 ou 19 ch garantissent «une personnalité d'automobile à part entière avec du tempérament et tous les signes d'une voiture de sport de bonne race» (citation de *Motor und Sport*).

L'*ADAC-Motorwelt* du 17 avril 1931 ajoute: «La faible résistance aérodynamique de la légère et racée carrosserie sport contribue à une bonne vitesse». Avec son pare-brise rabattu, déjà en verre de sécurité, cette rapide petite voiture peut franchir les 100 km/h.

Le volant et le maniement de cette étroite voiture étonnent ses contemporains. Un essieu avant galbé avec ressort transversal permet de la surbaisser de près de 10 cm par rapport à la DA2 et est aussi tout bénéfice pour la tenue de route.

D'autres signes de sportivité sont la roue de secours montée sur le côté du capot moteur, l'absence de portières et le tableau de bord constitué d'un tachymètre à tambour, d'un manomètre d'huile et d'une clef de contact entre les deux.

Dans un reportage de *Motor und Sport* de 1930, l'auteur souligne: «La Wartburg est une voiture pour bons conducteurs. Un mauvais conducteur ne mérite pas de posséder une telle automobile.» Le meilleur conducteur de Wartburg est sans aucun doute Robert «Bobby» Kohlrausch, né en 1904 à Eisenach. Il fait carrière d'apprenti-ajusteur aux usines Dixi jusqu'à devenir ingénieur. Une fois transformée par Bobby en machine de course, la motocyclette que lui a offerte son père pour le récompenser de son travail rapporte de nombreuses coupes, mais lui coûte presque la vie. Contre la promesse de ne plus jamais courir en moto, son père lui offre une BMW: ce sera le début d'une incroyable carrière avec 62 victoires et quatre records du monde. Il n'avait, en effet, jamais promis de ne pas courir sur quatre roues! Chaque année en mai, lorsque le «pèlerinage des DA» prend la direction d'Eisenach, on se transmet respectueusement de main en main l'une des plus belles coupes de Kohlrausch.

A motor magazine observed in 1930 that "the Wartburg is a car for good drivers." And apparently they were happy to crank up the 18 bhp engine in all weathers in order to get behind the wooden steering wheel and go for a spin. The folding windscreen was already made of shatter-proof glass and stays up "as an exception".

1930 heißt es in einer Fachzeitschrift: „Der Wartburg ist ein Wagen für gute Fahrer." Und die werfen den 18-PS-Motor offenbar bei jedem Wetter an, um sich hinter das dicke Holzlenkrad zu klemmen. Die umlegbare Windschutzscheibe besteht bereits aus splitterfreiem Glas und bleibt „ausnahmsweise" oben.

En 1930, une revue spécialisée proclame: «La Wartburg est une voiture pour les bons conducteurs qui apparemment n'hésitent pas à mettre en marche le moteur de 18 ch par tous les temps pour se glisser derrière l'épais volant en bois. Le pare-brise rabattable est déjà en verre de sécurité et reste rarement à la verticale.

BMW Wartburg DA3 1930

The tapering tail of the bodywork is a striking feature. Its lightweight aluminium construction was the major factor in keeping the car's weight down to a mere 904 lbs (410 kg). The high power-to-weight ratio gave the car a top speed of 56 mph (90 kph).

Auffällig ist das spitz zulaufende Heck der leichten Aluminiumkarosserie, die zu dem niedrigen Wagengewicht von nur 410 Kilo entscheidend beiträgt. Das Leistungsgewicht ermöglicht stattliche 90 Stundenkilometer.

Une caractéristique de la carrosserie – en aluminium, ce qui explique en grande partie le faible poids de la voiture, seulement 410 kg – est son arrière boatstail. Son rapport poids/performance avantageux lui permettait d'atteindre jadis la vitesse respectable de 90 km/h.

Max Friz, an engine designer who had left Daimler-Motoren-Gesellschaft due to unfulfilled salary expectations and a lack of interest in his project for high altitude flight-engines, was one of BMW's first pioneers. He was a genius in his field, capable of finding the engine to suit any purpose, especially to power planes, but also trucks, boats and motorbikes.

The BMW license agreement with Austin came to an end on 1 March 1932. As it had, in any case, been a thorn in his flesh, Friz, who had since become a company director, began to work on his own design for a two-stroke car engine with front-wheel drive transmission. Immersing himself in engine practice and suspension theory, Friz was forced to concede that the proposal of Eisenach staffers to adapt designs which were already in existence was a quicker means of achieving his objectives.

Transforming these designs to create the first proper BMW began with an engine whose stroke was lengthened by 80 mm while the original bore was retained. This extended stroke could deliver 20 bhp as opposed to the previous rating of 15 bhp, a fact mirrored by the new creation's name: 3/20 PS (PS is a German alternative measure of realistically rating horsepower). The modifications made to the crankshaft drive, cylinder head and side-mounted camshaft (now driven by a duplex chain instead of cast iron spur gears) meant that the design was effectively brand new.

One of the biggest departures from the British original could be seen in the chassis. The main features constituted a central frame (instead of U-section rails) and a propshaft extended right back to the swing axle. The front axle, one of the

components most in need of updating, remained unaltered. Therefore, the driving characteristics continued to be somewhat less than driver-friendly, particularly since the new car's sturdy, but heavy body (from Daimler-Benz at Sindelfingen) meant that it weighed 396 lbs (180 kg) more than the earlier 3/15 DA2.

Daimler-Benz built all four designs: limousine, tourer, convertible and roadster. What was even more confusing was the type designation AM 1 for "1. Auto München" (1st Munich car). One of the special car bodies did, however, come from Munich: a cute roadster by Ludwig Weinberger. Some 7215 chassis (AM 1-4) were manufactured from April 1932 to the end of 1934, all destined to cater for a wide variety of designs. 53 were destined for pick-up trucks.

Four of the 59 BMW 3/20s listed in the BMW Veteran Club Germany have the same owner: the lucky man is a Dutchman from Gouda. A Warsaw owner is even more fortunate: in addition to an AM 4, he owns a truly rare model, the 1932 AM 1 Roadster.

Die Daimler-Motoren-Gesellschaft hat er wegen unerfüllter Gehaltswünsche und allgemeinem Desinteresse an seinem Höhenflugmotoren-Projekt verlassen. Bei BMW ist der Motorenkonstrukteur Max Friz einer der Männer der ersten Stunde, ein genialer Kopf, der allem, „was kreucht und fleucht" – besonders Flugzeugen, aber auch Lastwagen, Booten und Motorrädern – die richtigen Triebwerke verpaßt.

Der Lizenzvertrag mit Austin, der Friz ohnehin ein Dorn im Auge ist, wird zum 1. März 1932 gekündigt, und sofort macht sich Friz – inzwischen zum Direktor avanciert – an eine eigene Konstruktion. Das Ziel ist ein Zweitakter mit Frontantrieb. In Motorenpraxis und Fahrwerkstheorie tiefschürfend, muß Friz bald erkennen, daß der Vorschlag der Eisenacher, Vorhandenes umzukonstruieren, schneller zum Ziel führt.

Die Mutation zum richtigen BMW beginnt beim Motor, dessen Hub unter Beibehaltung der Bohrung auf 80 Millimeter verlängert wird. 20 statt 15 PS bringt die so erzielte Hubraumvergrößerung, und damit steht auch der Name des Debütanten fest: 3/20 PS. Änderungen an Kurbeltrieb und Zylinderkopf sowie der Antrieb der seitlichen Nockenwelle über eine Duplexkette anstelle der gußeisernen Stirnräder sprechen für eine „Fast-Neukonstruktion".

Noch mehr vom Insel-Original entfernt man sich beim Chassis. Wichtigste Merkmale sind der Zentralrahmen anstelle des U-Profils und eine bis nach hinten zur Pendelachse durchlaufende Kardanwelle. Ausgerechnet die Vorderachse, die eigentlich nach einer besseren Lösung verlangt, bleibt unverändert. Und so bleiben auch die Fahreigenschaften äußerst gewöhnungsbedürftig, zumal der Wagen mit seiner

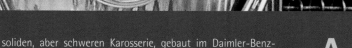

BMW 3/20 PS 1932

soliden, aber schweren Karosserie, gebaut im Daimler-Benz-Werk Sindelfingen, 180 Kilo mehr wiegt als der 3/15 DA2.

Daimler-Benz baut alle vier Aufbauten: Limousine, Tourer, Cabriolet und Roadster. Umso mehr verwirrt die Typenbezeichnung AM 1 für „1. Auto München". Immerhin stammt eine der Sonderkarosserien aus der Isar-Metropole: ein schnuckeliger Roadster von Ludwig Weinberger. Von April 1932 bis Ende 1934 werden 7215 Fahrgestelle (AM 1-4) für die verschiedensten Aufbauten gefertigt. Davon erhalten 53 einen Lieferwagenaufbau.

Von den 59 im BMW-Veteranen-Club Deutschland e.V. registrierten 3/20 befinden sich vier in einer Hand: Ein Holländer aus Gouda ist der Glückliche. Es gibt aber auch einen Überglücklichen, und der kommt aus Warschau: Ihm gehört neben einem AM 4 eine echte Rarität, der AM 1 Roadster von 1932.

Après avoir quitté la Daimler-Motoren-Gesellschaft qui n'avait pas accepté sa demande d'augmentation de salaire et ne portait aucun intérêt à son projet de moteur d'avion, le motoriste Max Friz est, chez BMW, l'un des hommes de la première heure. C'est un génie qui dessine des moteurs idéaux pour «tout ce qui rampe et tout ce qui vole» – en particulier des avions, mais aussi des camions, bateaux et motos.

Le contrat de licence signé avec Austin, qui a de toute façon toujours été la bête noire de Friz, est résilié le 1er mars 1932 et, immédiatement, Friz – entre-temps promu directeur – s'attaque à sa propre construction: un moteur à deux temps pour une voiture à traction avant. Parfait connaisseur de la pratique des moteurs et de la théorie des châssis, Friz doit admettre que la proposition des ingénieurs d'Eisenach consistant à adapter quelque chose de préexistant mènera plus vite à destination.

La mutation en une véritable BMW commence avec le moteur, dont la course est allongée à 80 mm pour un alésage inchangé. L'augmentation de cylindrée permet ainsi d'obtenir 20 ch au lieu de 15 et, par la même opération, donne son nom à la voiture: 3/20 PS. Des modifications de l'embrayage et de la culasse ainsi que de la prise de force pour l'arbre à cames latéral à l'aide d'une chaîne duplex – et non plus d'engrenages en fonte – justifient le qualificatif de construction presque complètement nouvelle.

Pour le châssis, on est encore plus éloigné de l'original. Les caractéristiques les plus importantes sont le cadre central (à la place de profilés en U) ainsi que la transmission par cardan allant jusqu'à l'essieu arrière oscillant. Quant à l'essieu avant, qui mériterait pourtant d'être amélioré, il reste tel quel. Le comportement demande donc, pour le moins, une certaine accoutumance, d'autant plus que la voiture à la solide, mais lourde carrosserie (fabriquée par l'usine Daimler-Benz de Sindelfingen) pèse 180 kg de plus que la 3/15 DA2.

Daimler-Benz assemble chacune des quatre carrosseries: berline, tourer, cabriolet et roadster. La dénomination AM 1 pour «1ère Auto Munich» est d'autant plus troublante. Toujours est-il que l'une des carrosseries spéciales est née dans la métropole des bords de l'Isar: il s'agit d'un joli petit roadster signé Ludwig Weinberger. D'avril 1932 à la fin de 1934 sont construits 7215 châssis (AM 1-4) pour les carrosseries les plus diverses (dont 53 en exécution camionnette).

Sur les 59 BMW 3/20 enregistrées auprès du BMW-Veteranen-Club Deutschland e.V. (club des collectionneurs de vieilles BMW), quatre se trouvent aux mains d'un seul homme: l'heureux collectionneur est un Hollandais de Gouda. Mais il y en a un autre qui a encore plus de chance, et celui-ci réside à Varsovie: il est le propriétaire non seulement d'une AM 4, mais aussi d'une authentique rareté, le roadster AM 1 de 1932.

A "real" BMW, whose engine generated 20 bhp thanks to the increased cubic capacity.
59 of these BMW 3/20s are still on the BMW Veteran Club's lists.

Ein „richtiger" BMW, dessen Motor dank einer Hubraumvergrößerung 20 PS leistet. Noch 59 dieser
BMW 3/20 sind im BMW-Veteranen-Club registriert.

Une «vraie» BMW dont le moteur développe 20 ch grâce à l'augmentation de cylindrée.
Le registre du club des collectionneurs de vieilles BMW fait encore état de 59 exemplaires de ces
BMW 3/20.

BMW 3/20 PS 1932

The body was mounted on the central box frame in Sindelfingen – by Daimler-Benz.

Auf dem Zentralkastenrahmen werden in Sindelfingen die Aufbauten gesetzt – von Daimler-Benz!

Les carrosseries sont montées sur le cadre à caisson central à Sindelfingen – par Daimler-Benz!

The BMW 3/20 PS is a rock-solid vehicle, but at 1430 lbs (650 kg) a relatively heavy one. Despite this, 7215 chassis were produced for a variety of different bodies, even including 53 pick-up trucks.

Der BMW 3/20 PS ist zwar ein grundsolides, aber mit 650 Kilo Gewicht doch ein relativ schweres Vehikel. Immerhin werden 7215 Fahrgestelle für verschiedene Aufbauten – darunter auch 53 Lieferwagen – gefertigt.

La BMW 3/20 PS est, certes, une voiture inusable, mais, avec ses 650 kg, tout de même relativement lourde. 7215 châssis seront néanmoins construits pour différentes carrosseries – dont 53 camionnettes.

The dashboard is compact and well-designed. Underneath the hood, plenty of spare room is left by the small straight-cylinder engine with its laterally-mounted camshaft driven by a duplex chain.

Gebündelte Ordnung herrscht auf dem Amaturenbrett. Viel Platz unter der Haube läßt der kleine Reihenmotor, dessen seitliche Nockenwelle über eine Duplexkette angetrieben wird.

Tout est bien ordonné sur le tableau de bord. Le petit moteur en ligne dont l'arbre à cames latéral est actionné par une chaîne duplex est loin d'occuper tout le compartiment moteur.

BMW 303 1933

The 3/20 formula delivered 5 bhp per cylinder. How do you get 30 bhp? Correct, install six cylinders. So a miniscule BMW engine was born; 1173 cc, meaning it was the smallest automotive six cylinder of all time. Like the whole BMW 303 car, it was an interim solution, but provided a basis for follow-up designs of the 1930s.

The six cylinders featured long stroke dimensions, measuring 56 x 80 mm, utilizing overhead valves. The pressurized lubrication now took a liter and a half more oil than a 3/20 and the carburation system had also been uprated with two Solex sidedraft carburetors.

The engineers from Eisenach developed a modern frame design with tubular steel longitudinal beams and four box-section cross beams. The 309, 315, 315/1, 319 and 329 models also followed this construction. New conscientious solutions had also been researched and developed for the suspension, which had previously been the car's Achilles' heel: control arms and transverse springs at the front, semi-elliptic springs at the live axle rear. This was an enormous technological advance on BMW's DA and AM predecessors.

Thanks to fine-tuning of shock absorbers and springs alongside direct rack and pinion steering, the 303 provided a completely new driving sensation. Pleasure in driving was disseminated and marketed by an advertising campaign involving a 1250 mile (2000 km) publicity trip through the German Reich.

Every fourth car of the 2300 BMW 303s built was a four-window convertible. The models on offer – only in production for a year – were completed by special designs, such as the Gläser sports convertible. Only two examples were manufactured of the tourer and the convertible limousine bodies.

The Wartburg area was still covered by the snow which fell in the winter of 1933/34: by then it was already clear that the 303 was old hat. In February, the exterior of the subsequent BMW 315 model was trimmed to give a final body style, one made unmistakable by six parallel cooling slots on each side of the hood. A 1.5 liter engine (to which the "fifteen" numeral after the "three" prefix refers in 315) was completed and installed from April onwards.

Theoretically, the increase in cubic capacity should, in percentage terms, produce 8 bhp more. That prediction was inaccurate, for an increase of only 4 bhp was achieved. This was, however, enough to enable the European 100 kph (62.5 mph) barrier to be breached.

5 PS pro Zylinder lautet die Gleichung beim 3/20. Wie kommt man also auf 30 PS? Richtig, indem man mit sechs Zylindern rechnet! So entsteht bei BMW mit 1173 ccm der hubraumschwächste automobile Sechszylinder aller Zeiten - eine Interimslösung wie das ganze Auto, aber eine Grundlage für die Folgekonstruktionen der dreißiger Jahre.

Über den sechs langhubigen Zylinderröhrchen mit je 56 x 80 mm liegen im Zylinderkopf hängende Ventile. Gegenüber dem 3/20 passen anderthalb Liter Öl mehr in den Druckumlauf, und auch das Vergasersystem wird der neuen Situation gerecht.

Die Ingenieure aus Eisenach entwickeln eine moderne Rahmenkonstruktion mit Stahlrohrlängsträgern und vier Kastenquerträgern. Auf dieser Basis entstehen auch die Modelle 309, 315, 315/1, 319 und 329. Für die Radaufhängungen, den bisherigen Schwachpunkt, gibt es ebenfalls durchdachte Lösungen: vorn mit Querlenkern und -feder, hinten mit halbelliptischen Blattfedern - ein enormer technischer Fortschritt gegenüber den DA- und AM-Vorgängern.

Dank der gefühlvollen Abstimmung von Stoßdämpfern und Federn und einer direkten Zahnstangenlenkung vermittelt der 303 ein völlig neues Fahrgefühl. Fahrfreude kommt auf, und die wird bei einer 2000 Kilometer langen Tour durch das Deutsche Reich werbewirksam vermittelt und vermarktet.

Jeder vierte der 2300 gebauten 303 ist ein Cabriolet mit vier Fenstern. Seltene Sonderaufbauten wie das Sport-Cabriolet von Gläser runden das Angebot dieser Baureihe, die nur ein Jahr lang in Produktion bleibt, ab. Vom Tourer und der Cabrio-Limousine werden jeweils nur zwei Fahrzeuge gefertigt.

Die Wartburg hüllt noch der Schnee des Winters 1933/34 ein, da ist schon klar, daß der 303 bereits Schnee von gestern ist. Im Februar wird das Outfit auf das Nachfolgemodell BMW 315 getrimmt, leicht erkennbar an den sechs unterteilten Kühlschlitzfeldern auf jeder Seite der Motorhaube. Auch der 1,5-Liter-Motor, für den die 15 hinter der 3 steht, ist fertig und wird ab April eingebaut.

Die Rechnung, daß das neue Modell nun proportional zur Hubraumvergrößerung 8 PS mehr an die Räder bringen könnte, geht freilich nicht auf: Es sind lediglich vier Pferdestärken mehr, aber genug, um die „Schallgrenze" von 100 Stundenkilometern zu erreichen.

Comme pour la 3/20, l'équation fait état de 5 ch par cylindre. Comment obtient-on donc 30 ch? Vous avez raison, avec six cylindres! C'est ainsi que naît chez BMW un minuscule moteur qui est, avec ses 1173 cm³, l'automobile six-cylindres de plus petite cylindrée de tous les temps. C'est une solution intérimaire pour toute la voiture, mais elle jettera les bases des réalisations suivantes des années 30.

Les six minuscules cylindres à longue course aux cotes respectives de 56 x 80 mm ont des soupapes suspendues. Le circuit d'huile renferme un litre et demi de plus que celui de la 3/20 et le système de carburateur est, aussi, adapté à son nouvel environnement.

Les ingénieurs d'Eisenach mettent au point un châssis-cadre moderne avec longerons longitudinaux en tube d'acier et quatre poutres transversales en caisson – un châssis en échelle que reprennent également les modèles 309, 315, 315/1, 319 et 329. Pour les suspensions, le talon d'Achille de ces voitures jusqu'à cette époque, on trouve également des solutions: des bras et ressorts transversaux à l'avant et des ressorts semi-elliptiques à l'arrière. C'est un énorme progrès sur le plan mécanique par rapport aux DA et AM de la génération précédente.

Grâce à d'excellents tarages des amortisseurs et des ressorts ainsi qu'à une direction à crémaillère directe, la 303 donne des sensations de conduite absolument inédites. On ressent un réel plaisir de conduite – une tournée publicitaire de 2000 km à travers le Reich allemand assure la propagation et la commercialisation de cette philosophie.

Près d'un quart des 2300 BMW 303 construites sont des cabriolets à quatre fenêtres. De rares carrosseries spéciales comme le Sport-Cabriolet de Gläser complètent le programme de cette voiture qui ne sera produite que pendant un an. Deux seuls exemplaires sont construits de la tourer et de la berline cabriolet.

La Wartburg frissonne encore sous le manteau de neige de l'hiver 1933/34, mais il est déjà clair que la 303 n'en est déjà plus à son printemps. En février, son esthétique est alignée sur celle de sa benjamine, la BMW 315, aisément reconnaissable aux six fentes de refroidissement de chaque côté du capot moteur. Le moteur de 1,5 litre symbolisé par le «quinze» derrière le «trois» est mûr techniquement et fait son apparition en avril.

L'équation selon laquelle l'augmentation de cylindrée pourrait se traduire proportionnellement par 8 ch supplémentaires n'est pas correcte puisqu'ils ne sont qu'au nombre de quatre – mais cela suffit pour atteindre le «mur du son» des 100 km/h.

The BMW 303 saw the birth of the characteristic BMW kidney-shaped radiator grill and marked the launch of a completely new range of models. The first bodies were still produced in Sindelfingen, but mass production was at Ambi-Budd in Berlin.

Der BMW 303 markiert die Geburtsstunde der BMW-Nieren und den Beginn einer völlig neuen Baureihe. Die ersten Karosserien entstehen noch in Sindelfingen, der Serienbau erfolgt dann bei Ambi-Budd in Berlin.

La BMW 303 marque la naissance des naseaux chez BMW et le début d'une gamme inédite. Les premières carrosseries sont encore réalisées à Sindelfingen, mais la construction en série a lieu chez Ambi-Budd à Berlin.

The new engine, with twin vertical carburetors and developing 30 bhp, was the smallest six-cylinder automobile of all time with its cubic capacity of 1.2 liters.

Der neue Motor, der mit seinen zwei Vertikalvergasern 30 PS leistet, ist mit 1,2 Litern Hubraum der kleinste automobile Sechszylinder aller Zeiten.

Le nouveau moteur, qui développe 30 ch avec ses deux carburateurs verticaux, est avec 1,2 l le plus petit six-cylindres de toute l'histoire de l'automobile.

BMW 303 1933

For the 303 the engineers from Eisenach developed a modern frame incorporating tubular steel longitudinal beams and box-section cross members. The bodywork styling found great favor with motorists, as a promotional tour through the German Reich revealed, but the car's performance left something to be desired.

Für den 303 haben die Ingenieure aus Eisenach eine moderne Rahmenkonstruktion mit Stahlrohrlängsträgern und Kastenquerträgern entwickelt. Die Form der Karosserie findet bei den Automobilisten – wie sich bei einer Werbetour durch das Deutsche Reich herausstellt – großen Anklang. Die Leistung läßt indes noch Wünsche offen.

Pour la 303, les ingénieurs d'Eisenach ont conçu un châssis moderne à caissons avec des longerons longitudinaux creux en acier et des poutres transversales. Comme le révèle une campagne publicitaire qui a traversé tout le Reich allemand, sa carrosserie est tout à fait du goût des automobilistes, mais sa puissance laisse encore à désirer.

BMW 303 1933

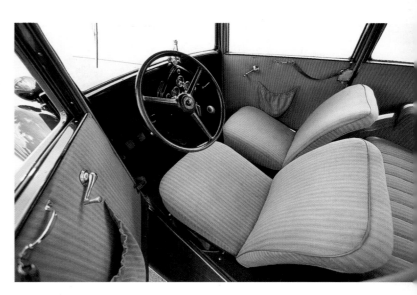

The hinged windscreen ensures fresh air at the wheel and plenty of ventilation for the roomy interior. Just nine examples of the 56 mph (90 kph) BMW 303 are registered with the Veteran Club.

Für Frischluft am Steuer und Ventilation im geräumigen Innenraum sorgt die ausstellbare Windschutzscheibe. Von den 90 Stundenkilometer schnellen BMW 303 sind im Veteranen-Club lediglich noch neun Exemplare registriert.

Le pare-brise relevable permet de profiter de l'air frais au volant et d'aérer l'habitacle spacieux. Selon le club des collectionneurs de BMW, il existe encore neuf exemplaires de cette BMW 303 capable d'atteindre 90 km/h.

BMW 315/1 Sport-Zweisitzer 1934

In 1933 a dramatic change took place. BMW abandoned its small-volume, four-cylinder baby engine and redesigned it as a six-cylinder. The result was an 1173 cc engine, which was the smallest in the world. It only took a few weeks before engineers at Eisenach recognized the engine's potential and increased the volume to 1490 cc. This motor move provided the basis for the BMW 315, which sold a total 9765 units to be highly successful. The bigger engine also laid the foundations for an attractive small sports car providing 40 bhp. It proved to be so successful in motor sport that the English company Frazer-Nash acquired the license to build it.

BMW engine size was increased again to achieve sporting success in the two-liter class. That 1911 cc development produced 55 bhp at 4000 rpm and an 81 mph (130 kph) top speed, 10 kph more than the smaller six-cylinder engine delivered.

Both sport two-seaters, the 315/1 and the 319/1, look almost identical. The "bigger brother" boasts three decorative strips on the grills on the side of the hood and features a small ventilator window, slightly reducing drafts around the necks of passengers. This sport two-seater should only be driven open-topped, for the raised fabric folding top gives a rather ugly appearance. A coupé top, designed by the Vereinigte Werkstätten München (workshop for car bodies and coach building) remained a short-lived oddity and was not a styling triumph.

In contrast to the 315 sport convertible and the 319/1 edition from the Munich BMW dealer and specialist bodywork producer, Ludwig Weinberger, the 315/1 Sport-Zweisitzer was notable for the delicate and refined style of its covered rear wheels.

All in all, the 315/1 was an uncomplicated vehicle with a simple chassis (at the front: lower control arm suspension, transverse spring on top, plus rigid rear axle suspension via semi-elliptic spring). Interestingly, it already used an electric fuel pump for the 11-gallon (42 liter) tank. Maneuverability and a good power-weight ratio destined the 315/1 for motor sport, its only occasional drawback being the erratic drum brakes.

Both sport two-seaters correspond to the classic idea of a roadster, starting with the spartan cockpit. Two large round instruments dominate: the tachometer on the left and the speedometer with odometer on the right. Two smaller round instruments for water temperature and oil pressure, as well as many little levers and push-buttons (located above the glove compartment) are the only dashboard decorations. The small front windscreen with its parallel wipers is adjustable.

Even the doors, with their recessed armrests, are pure roadster: there are no handles to open them; a small lever inside works the mechanism. Of course there are no bumpers or external mirrors. One thing which is important, however, is the spare wheel, situated where you would expect the trunk to be.

1933 vollzieht sich ein Umsturz: BMW wendet sich von seinem hubraumschwachen Vierzylindermotörchen ab und steigt auf sechs Zylinder um. Heraus kommt der mit 1173 ccm kleinste Sechszylinder der Welt. Welche Möglichkeiten in diesem Triebwerk stecken, erkennt man in Eisenach schon nach wenigen Wochen und vergrößert das Volumen auf 1490 ccm. Das ist die Basis des mit insgesamt 9765 Einheiten recht erfolgreich verkauften BMW 315, eine Baureihe, zu auch ein attraktiv aussehender kleiner Sportwagen mit 40 PS gehört. Dieser ist im Motorsport so erfolgreich, daß die englische Firma Frazer-Nash das Recht zum Lizenzbau erwirbt.

Um auch in der 2-Liter-Klasse sportlich reüssieren zu können, wird der Motor nochmals vergrößert. Aus 1911 ccm werden bei 4000 Touren 55 PS geholt. Das bedeutet 130 Stundenkilometer Spitze - zehn mehr als mit dem kleineren Sechszylinder möglich sind.

Beide Sport-Zweisitzer, der 315/1 und der 319/1, unterscheiden sich optisch kaum. Der „große Bruder" protzt mit drei Zierleisten auf den seitlichen Motorhauben-Gittern und verfügt über ein kleines Ausstellfenster, das die Luftverwirbelung im Nackenbereich der Passagiere etwas reduziert. Diese Sport-Zweisitzer sollte man nur offen fahren, denn das geschlossene Stoffverdeck wirkt ziemlich ungehobelt. Ein Coupé-Aufsatz, entworfen von den Vereinigten Werkstätten in München, das stilistisch wenig gelungen ist, bleibt kurzlebiges Kuriosum.

Im Gegensatz zum 315 Sport-Cabriolet und der 319/1-Ausgabe des Münchner BMW-Vertreters und Sonderkarosserie-Herstellers Ludwig Weinberger wirkt der 315/1 Sport-Zweisitzer zierlich und mit seinen abgedeckten Hinterrädern elegant.

Insgesamt gesehen ist der 315/1 ein unkompliziertes, sportliches Fahrzeug mit simplem Fahrwerk - vorn verfügt er über einen Querlenker unten, eine Querfeder oben und hinten über eine starre Aufhängung mit Halbfedern. Interessant ist, daß er bereits eine elektrische Benzinpumpe für den 42-Liter-Tank aufweist. Wendigkeit und gutes Leistungsgewicht prädestinieren diesen Wagen zum motorsportlichen Einsatz, wo Freude und Erfolg nur ab und zu durch Schwächen der Trommelbremsen getrübt werden.

Beide Sport-Zweisitzer entsprechen den klassischen Roadster-Idealen, beginnend mit dem spartanischen Cockpit. Ins Blickfeld fallen zwei große Rundinstrumente: links die Uhr und rechts der Tachometer mit Kilometerzähler. Zwei kleinere Rundinstrumente für Wassertemperatur und Öldruck sowie einige Hebelchen und Zugknöpfe (selbst über dem Handschuhfach) sind die einzige Zierde des Armaturenbretts. Die knapp bemessene Frontscheibe mit den Parallelwischern ist verstellbar.

Aber auch die mit Armausschnitten versehenen Türen erinnern an einen Roadster: Griffe zum Öffnen fehlen, die Schlösser betätigt ein Hebelchen von innen. Natürlich sind auch keine Stoßstangen und Außenspiegel vorhanden. Wichtig ist allerdings das Reserverad, das sich dort befindet, wo man den Kofferraum vermutet.

1933 est une année révolutionnaire. BMW met au placard ses asthmatiques quatre-cylindres de petite cylindrée pour se tourner vers les six-cylindres. Avec 1173 cm³, c'est le plus petit six-cylindres du monde. On en fait le constat à Eisenach en quelques semaines et majore sa cylindrée à 1490 cm³. Il est l'âme de la BMW 315 qui connaîtra un succès enviable puisqu'elle sera vendue au total à 9765 exemplaires, une BMW 315 qui sera aussi épaulée par une séduisante petite voiture de sport de 40 ch. Celle-ci remporte tant de succès en compétition que la firme britannique Frazer-Nash acquiert le droit de la construire sous licence.

Pour lui assurer le succès sportif dans la catégorie deux litres également, la cylindrée de son moteur est encore majorée. Les 1911 cm³ délivrent 55 ch à 4000 tr/mn : la vitesse de pointe est de 130 km/h, dix de plus qu'avec le petit six-cylindres.

Sur le plan esthétique, il est bien difficile de distinguer les deux biplaces de sport, la 315/1 et la 319/1. La «grande sœur» frime avec trois joncs décoratifs sur les grilles d'aération latérales du capot moteur et possède un petit déflecteur qui réduit légèrement les courants d'air à hauteur de la nuque des passagers. On ne peut, en effet, conduire cette biplace de sport pratiquement qu'en décapotable, car la capote en toile fermée dégrade la beauté des lignes. Un hard-top dessiné par les Vereinigte Werkstätten München (atelier de carrosserie et d'automobiles de Munich), qui n'est pas non plus une grande réussite esthétique, ne connaîtra qu'un destin éphémère.

Contrairement à la 315 cabriolet sport et à la 319/1 carrossée par Ludwig Weinberger, un concessionnaire munichois de BMW qui fabrique aussi des carrosseries spéciales,

la 315/1 sport biplace semble frêle et est avec ses roues arrière carénées bien élégante.

Globalement, la 315/1 est une voiture sportive et peu compliquée avec un châssis simple (bras transversaux inférieurs et ressort transversal supérieur à l'avant et, à l'arrière, suspension rigide à ressorts semi-elliptiques). Un détail intéressant est qu'elle possède déjà une pompe à essence électrique pour son réservoir de 42 litres. Maniabilité et un bon rapport poids-puissance prédestinent pour la compétition cette voiture dont le seul talon d'Achille est une faiblesse presque chronique des freins à tambour.

Les deux biplaces de sport correspondent au schéma classique du roadster, à commencer par leur cockpit spartiate. Deux gros cadrans circulaires sautent aux yeux : à gauche, l'horloge et, à droite, le tachymètre avec compteur journalier. Deux cadrans ronds de plus petit diamètre pour la température d'eau et la pression d'huile ainsi que quelques petites manettes et boutons (même au-dessus de la boîte à gants) sont la seule décoration du tableau de bord. De petite dimension, le pare-brise à essuie-glaces parallèles est réglable.

Quant aux portières servant d'accoudoirs, elles sont dans le plus pur style des roadsters : il n'y a pas de poignées pour les ouvrir, un petit levier actionne de l'intérieur le mécanisme. Naturellement, il n'y a pas non plus de pare-chocs ni de rétroviseurs extérieurs. La roue de secours, par contre, est indispensable et se trouve là où l'on pense trouver le coffre.

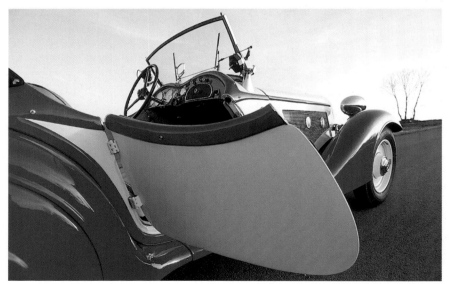

Sporty elegance and performance to match are the main features of the 315/1, which also had considerable success on the racetrack. The clock and speedometer, reading up to 93 mph (150 kph), are the dominant features of this roadster dashboard.

Sportliche Eleganz und ein ansprechendes Leistungspotential kennzeichnen den 315/1, der sich auch mit vielen rennsportlichen Meriten schmücken darf. Die Uhr und ein Tacho, der bis zu 150 Stunden-kilometer anzeigt, sind die beherrschenden Rundinstrumente auf dem Roadster-Armaturenbrett.

Elégance sportive ainsi qu'un potentiel intéressant caractérisent la 315/1 qui remportera de nombreux lauriers en compétition. Deux cadrans circulaires, la montre et le tachymètre gradué jusqu'à 150 km/h, trônent sur le tableau de bord du roadster.

BMW 315/1 Sport-Zweisitzer 1934

BMW 315/1 Sport-Zweisitzer 1934

Harmony of form and function from all angles. The front windscreen of the stylish automobile is adjustable, the soft top is easy to operate, and the tapered "trunk" at the rear only has room for the spare wheel.

Harmonie von Form und Funktion aus jeder Perspektive. Die Frontscheibe des schnittigen Fahrzeugs ist verstellbar, das Verdeck leicht zu bedienen, und in dem auch nach hinten abgerundeten „Kofferraum" findet lediglich das Reserverad Platz.

Harmonie des formes et de la fonction quelle que soit la perspective : le pare-brise de cette élégante voiture s'ouvre et la capote s'escamote aisément, mais le «coffre» arrondi n'héberge que la roue de secours.

BMW 315/1 Sport-Zweisitzer 1934

The elegant lines of the twin-seater 315/1, whose cladded rear wheels and long, sweeping wings accentuate the chic design.

Einfach chic ist die Linienführung des 315/1 Zweisitzers, dessen abgedeckte Hinterräder die elegante Note ebenso betonen wie die langgestreckten vorderen Kotflügel.

Elles sont d'un grand chic, les lignes de la 315/1 biplace dont les roues arrière carénées soulignent la note élégante au même titre que les interminables ailes avant.

BMW 326 Cabriolet 1936

The 326 proved to be the most successful prewar BMW, despite the fact that it was thought to be somewhat conservative when it was presented in February 1936. This model had a 50 bhp six-cylinder engine, which fired the imagination of bodywork designers. Some 5500 convertibles were built in addition to more than 10,000 sedans, whose bodies were manufactured in Berlin-Johannisthal.

Coach builders Autenrieth in Darmstadt were a major player in the automotive sector and offered two-door as well four-door body designs. A 1938 prototype caused a sensation with its safety-conscious sliding doors. This was a beautiful car, one which is still in the best of health lovingly preserved to this day.

The convertible offered by the Vereinigte Werkstätten München for car bodies and coach building listed two doors, four seats, four windows. The two-seater convertibles by Drauz, Weinberger and Gläser were far sportier. Erdmann & Rossi's roadster appealed to the purists and could provide drivers with a wonderful slipstream sensation, one broken only by the windscreen.

The bumpers turned out to be a means by which the passage of each succeeding year could be determined: they appeared in pairs until 1938 and in a single blade from 1939. In the year of the car's "birth", the 326 had disc wheels, followed by perforated rims from 1937.

As already indicated, the "crowning glory" was the new six-cylinder engine, which had 1971 cc instead of 1911 cc and therefore took the two-liter class to the limit. This extremely long-stroke engine (66 x 96 mm equals a bore-to-stroke ratio of 1.45) made a compact cylinder block possible due to the small gaps between cylinders.

The crankshaft and the four-bearing camshaft with a duplex chain drive were correspondingly small. A pair of down-draft Solex 26 BFLV carburetors were part of the basic 326 equipment range. For reasons of cost, BMW decided to install just one carburetor in the 320 and 321 models, although this was at the expense of 5 bhp.

Depending on the version and equipment range, a 326 convertible cost between 5800 and 8000 reichsmarks. The chassis and engine alone cost 4450 reichsmarks. All in all, this mid-range convertible was relatively expensive, which made the strong sales figures even more surprising.

Als erfolgreichster BMW der Vorkriegsgeschichte entpuppt sich der 326, der bei seiner Vorstellung im Februar 1936 einen eher biederen Eindruck macht. Doch der 50-PS-Sechszylindermotor dieses Typs beflügelt offenbar die Phantasie der Karosserieschneider. Denn neben mehr als 10.000 Limousinen, deren Karosserien in Berlin-Johannisthal entstehen, werden auch 5500 Cabriolets gebaut.

Autenrieth in Darmstadt ist groß im Geschäft und bietet vier- und zweitürige Ausführungen an. 1938 wird ein vielbestaunter Prototyp mit Sicherheits-Schiebetüren vorgestellt, ein bildhübscher Wagen, der sich noch heute „bester Gesundheit" erfreut.

Zwei Türen, vier Sitze, vier Fenster, so lautet die Cabriolet-Offerte der Vereinigten Werkstätten für Karosserie- und Wagenbau in München. Weitaus sportlicher wirken die zweisitzigen Cabriolets von Drauz, Weinberger und Gläser. Erdmann & Rossis Roadster wendet sich an die Puristen und bietet ein nur von der Windschutzscheibe getrübtes Fahrtwind-Erlebnis.

Die Jahrgänge lassen sich an den Stoßstangen ablesen: Bis 1938 sind sie doppelt, ab 1939 nur noch einfach ausgeführt. Im „Geburtsjahrgang" sind die 326 mit Scheibenrädern ausgestattet, die ab 1937 durch Lochfelgen ersetzt werden.

Des „Pudels Kern" ist aber der neue Sechszylinder, der mit 1971 ccm (zuvor 1911 ccm) die 2-Liter-Klasse voll ausschöpft. Dieser extreme Langhuber (66 x 96 mm entsprechen einem Bohrung-Hub-Verhältnis von 1,45) ermöglicht wegen seiner kurzen Zylinderabstände einen kompakten Block.

Entsprechend kurz sind die Kurbelwelle und die vierfach gelagerte Nockenwelle mit Duplex-Kettenantrieb. Zwei

Vertikalvergaser Solex 26 BFLV gehören zur Grundbestückung, während sich BMW aus Kostengründen bei den Modellen 320 und 321 auf einen Vergaser beschränkt und somit fünf PS „verschenkt".

Je nach Ausführung und Ausstattung müssen zwischen 5800 und 8000 Reichsmark für ein 326 Cabriolet bezahlt werden. Allein 4450 Reichsmark kostet das Fahrgestell mit Motor. Damit ist dieses Mittelklassecabriolet vergleichsweise teuer. Umso mehr überraschen die Verkaufszahlen.

La 326 sera la BMW produite en plus grand nombre durant l'avant-guerre bien que, durant sa présentation en février 1936, elle ait laissé une impression plutôt brave, mais le six-cylindres de 50 ch de cette version donne apparemment des ailes à l'imagination des constructeurs, car, en plus des plus de 10 000 mille berlines dont les carrosseries sont montées à Berlin-Johannisthal, BMW fabrique également 5500 cabriolets.

Autenrieth, à Darmstadt, fait lui aussi de bonnes affaires avec ses exécutions à deux et quatre portes. En 1938, il présente un prototype à portières de sécurité coulissantes qui fait sensation, une magnifique voiture qui est aujourd'hui encore merveilleusement en forme.

Deux portes, quatre places, quatre fenêtres, telle est la formule pour les cabriolets proposés par les Vereinigte Werkstätten München. Mais les cabriolets biplaces de Drauz, Weinberger et Gläser sont autrement plus sportifs. Le roadster d'Erdmann & Rossi se destine aux puristes et offre des sensations de décapotable que ne tempère qu'un petit pare-brise.

Les millésimes respectifs se distinguent par leurs pare-chocs: jusqu'en 1938, ils sont doubles, puis uniquement simples à partir de 1939. Durant l'année de leur naissance, les 326 possèdent des jantes à voile plein, puis des jantes perforées à partir de 1937.

Mais le morceau de bravoure mécanique est le nouveau six-cylindres en ligne qui, avec une cylindrée de 1971 cm^3 (contre 1911 cm^3), exploite à fond la classe deux litres. Ce moteur à course extrêmement longue (66 x 96 mm donnent un rapport alésage-course de 1,45) autorise un bloc compact grâce aux faibles intervalles entre les cylindres.

D'autant plus courts sont donc le vilebrequin et l'arbre à cames à quatre paliers avec entraînement par chaîne duplex. Deux carburateurs verticaux Solex 26 BFLV font partie de la dotation de série alors que, par souci d'économie, BMW se contente d'un seul carburateur, et renonce ainsi à 5 ch, pour les versions 320 et 321.

Selon l'exécution et la finition, une 326 Cabriolet coûte entre 5800 et 8000 reichsmarks. A lui seul, le châssis avec moteur coûte 4450 reichsmarks. Dans l'ensemble, ce cabriolet du segment intermédiaire est relativement cher et son succès est donc d'autant plus surprenant.

The four seats, four side windows and two large doors of this BMW 326 Cabriolet make for a well-heeled mid-range car with a generously equipped interior offering plenty of passenger comfort.

Vier Sitze, vier Seitenfenster und zwei große Türen offeriert dieses BMW 326 Cabriolet: die gehobene Mittelklasse mit einem reich ausgestatteten Interieur und viel Fahrkomfort.

Cette BMW 326 Cabriolet offre quatre places, quatre vitres latérales et deux grandes portières: un certain luxe, déjà, avec un habitacle richement équipé et un grand confort.

The driver's gaze is drawn over the large three-spoke steering wheel through the windscreen (no longer adjustable) to the free-standing headlamps. By the time the BMW 327 came along, these had been integrated into the wings.

Über das große Dreispeichenlenkrad fällt der Blick durch die nicht mehr ausstellbare Windschutzscheibe auf die freistehenden Lampen. Beim BMW 327 werden diese bereits in die Kotflügel integriert sein.

Derrière le grand volant à trois branches, le regard porte, à travers un pare-brise désormais fixe, sur les phares proéminents. Sur la BMW 327, ceux-ci seront déjà intégrés aux ailes.

The six-cylinder engine developed 50 bhp. The striking double fenders of the 326 disappeared from the BMW range in 1939.

Der Sechszylindermotor mobilisiert 50 PS. Die geteilten, besonders markanten Doppelstoßstangen des 326 verschwinden 1939 aus dem BMW-Programm.

Le six-cylindres délivre 50 ch. Les doubles pare-chocs divisés de la 326, particulièrement marquants, disparaîtront du programme BMW en 1939.

BMW 326 Cabriolet 1936

A successful model: more than 5500 of this attractive Cabriolet were sold, despite the price tag of almost 8000 reichsmarks. Apart from a few exceptions, Autenrieth of Darmstadt built the Cabriolet bodies.

Erfolgsmodell: Mehr als 5500 dieser attraktiven, nahezu 8000 Reichsmark teuren Cabriolets werden verkauft. Bis auf wenige Ausnahmen, führt Autenrieth in Darmstadt den Cabriolet-Aufbau durch.

Un grand succès commercial : plus de 5500 exemplaires de ce joli cabriolet qui coûtait près de 8000 reichsmarks seront vendus. A quelques rares exceptions près, les carrosseries seront l'œuvre d'Autenrieth, de Darmstadt.

BMW 326 Cabriolet 1936

BMW 327 1937

r Reif from Chemnitz was one of the few fortunate
people who were able to purchase the highly attractive BMW 327 convertible during the War. This
stylish black design from Eisenach cost 7500 reichsmark. When
Reif received the bill dated 12 May 1941, he could not know
that his car, chassis and engine number 87306, would be the
last of its kind to be made by BMW. Number 87307 was built in
1948 by the Soviet state company "Awtowelo" in a version
identical to the 327 built before the War.

The 2+2 seater sports convertible was publicly unveiled in
winter 1937. Initially it was difficult to target the right sales
groups for the 327. Beauty and elegant lines, the capacity for
storing a medium-sized case and a portable typewriter, and a
rating of 55 bhp were not high priorities for buyers in this
price category. Perhaps it was ideal for a traveling journalist
with entourage?

Sales were therefore sluggish. When an 80 bhp version
appeared in 1938 (327/28) to meet demands for performance
and sportiness, strangely enough sales for the basic 327 also
picked up. A total of 1124 convertibles and 179 coupés were
built. In May 1941, the last coupé was supplied to the Brazilian
consul-general de Louza-Ribeiro in Hamburg.

Like its predecessors, which were also equipped with a
2-liter engine (BMW 320, 321 and 326), the 327 had a low
slung box-section chassis, on which car bodies manufactured
by Ambi-Budd coachworks in Berlin-Johannisthal were used.
Ambi-Budd and Autenrieth in Darmstadt were BMW's largest
suppliers of car bodies in the 1930s.

Hurth and ZF supplied the four-speed transmission (with

freewheel facility in first and second gear). The drive ratio was
identical in both types, and the differences in the individual
gears were minor. What was different was how the doors were
hinged – at the front in the convertible and at the back in the
coupé.

After the dismantling of Ambi-Budd, the BMW chassis tools
of the 321, 326 and 327 types went to Awtowelo in East
Germany. The Russians and East German successor EMW
(Eisenacher Motoren Werk) manufactured 491 BMW 327
descendants between 1952 and 1954. The EMW 327-3, an
attractive coupé with a large rear window, was also
manufactured.

Just as it had many devotees amongst the leaders of the
Third Reich, the 327 sports convertible became, in its postwar
model, a status symbol for loyal and prominent Socialist Party
comrades. Fans of veteran BMWs consider the 327 to be one of
the most beautiful convertibles of its time.

err Reif aus Chemnitz gehört zu den wenigen Glücklichen, die in Kriegszeiten das äußerst attraktive Cabriolet BMW 327 erwerben dürfen. 7500 Reichsmark kostet
dieser vornehmlich in Schwarz ausgelieferte Wagen aus
Eisenach. Als Reif die am 12. Mai 1941 ausgestellte Rechnung
erhält, weiß er noch nicht, daß sein Wagen mit der Fahrgestell-
und Motornummer 87 306 der letzte aus der dortigen
BMW-Produktion ist. Nr. 87 307 wird 1948 von der staatlichen
sowjetischen Gesellschaft „Awtowelo" in unveränderter Vor-
kriegsausführung gebaut.

Ausgerechnet im Winter 1937 wird das 2+2sitzige Sport-
Cabriolet der Öffentlichkeit vorgestellt. Zunächst findet es nicht
die richtige Zielgruppe, denn Schönheit und elegante Linienführung, die Möglichkeit, neben den Passagieren auch noch
einen mittelgroßen Koffer und eine Reiseschreibmaschine
unterzubringen sowie 55 PS Leistung sind in dieser Preis-
kategorie weniger gefragt - ideal höchstens für einen Reise-
journalisten mit Anhang!

Der Verkauf läuft schleppend an. Als 1938 eine 80-PS-
Version (327/28) kommt, um dem Verlangen nach Leistung und
Sportlichkeit stattzugeben, beschleunigt sich seltsamerweise
auch der Absatz des 327. Insgesamt werden 1124 Cabriolets
und 179 Coupés gebaut. Das letzte Coupé wird im Mai 1941
dem brasilianischen Generalkonsul de Louza-Ribeiro in
Hamburg ausgehändigt.

Wie seine ebenfalls mit dem 2-Liter-Motor ausgerüsteten
Vorgänger (BMW 320, 321 und 326) hat der 327 einen Tiefbett-
Kastenrahmen, auf den Karosserien vom Preßwerk Ambi-Budd
in Berlin-Johannisthal gesetzt werden. Ambi-Budd und

Autenrieth in Darmstadt sind in den dreißiger Jahren die größten BMW-Karossiers.

Die Vierganggetriebe liefern Hurth (mit Freilauf im ersten und zweiten Gang) und ZF. Bei beiden ist die Antriebsübersetzung gleich und die Differenz in den einzelnen Gängen nur geringfügig. Unterschiedlich ist allerdings der Anschlag der Türen – beim Cabriolet vorn, beim Coupé hinten.

Awtowelo heißt die Firma, die bei der Demontage von Ambi-Budd den Zuschlag für den Erhalt der BMW-Karosserie-Werkzeuge für die Typen 321, 326 und 327 erhält. Die Russen und der DDR-Nachfolgebetrieb EMW (Eisenacher Motoren Werk) fertigen zwischen 1952 und 1954 noch 491 Abkömmlinge des BMW 327. Unter der Bezeichnung EMW 327-3 entsteht auch ein hübsches Coupé mit großem Heckfenster.

Schon bei den Größen des Dritten Reiches beliebt, wird das Nachkriegsmodell des 327 Sport-Cabriolets zum Statussymbol linientreuer SED-Parteifunktionäre. BMW-Veteranen-Freaks gilt der 327 als eines der schönsten Cabriolets seiner Zeit.

Monsieur Reif, de Chemnitz, est l'un des rares heureux élus qui, durant la guerre, a eu le droit d'acheter une BMW 327, un cabriolet très réussi. Cette voiture d'Eisenach – livrée presque toujours en noir – coûtait 7500 reichsmarks. Lorsque Reif reçoit la facture le 12 mai 1941, il ignore encore que sa voiture avec le numéro de châssis et de moteur 87306 est la dernière produite sous le label BMW. En 1948, la n° 87307 sera construite dans une version d'avant-guerre inchangée la compagnie soviétique nationale «Awtowelo».

Au cours de l'hiver 1937, le cabriolet sportif 2+2 est présenté au grand public. Mais il ne trouve pas d'emblée le groupe cible qui lui convient, car sa beauté et l'élégance de ses lignes alliées à la possibilité de transporter, outre les passagers, également une valise de taille moyenne et une machine à écrire avec 55 ch sous le capot, sont assez peu demandées dans ce segment de prix. Elle est idéale, au mieux, pour un journaliste de voyage avec sa cour!

C'est ainsi que les ventes sont hésitantes. Lorsqu'apparaît, en 1938, une version de 80 ch (327/28) qui répond aux désirs de plus grande puissance et de plus de sportivité, les ventes de la 327 décollent bizarrement elles aussi. Au total, 1124 cabriolets et 179 coupés seront construits. Le dernier coupé sera remis, en mai 1941, au consul général brésilien de Louza-Ribeiro à Hambourg.

Comme ses devancières (BMW 320, 321 et 326) également propulsées par un moteur de deux litres, la 327 possède un châssis à caisson surbaissé sur lequel est boulonnée la carrosserie montée par Ambi-Budd (emboutissage), à Berlin-

Johannisthal. Durant les années 30, Ambi-Budd et Autenrieth de Darmstadt seront les deux principaux carrossiers de BMW.

Les boîtes à quatre vitesses sont fournies par Hurth (avec moyeu de roue libre pour la première et la deuxième vitesse) et par ZF. Toutes les deux possèdent la même démultiplication et l'étagement est également assez proche. La différence se situe au niveau des portières – sur le cabriolet, elles sont articulées à l'avant, sur le coupé à l'arrière.

Lors du démontage d'Ambi-Budd, Awtowelo a été choisie pour reprendre les outillages de carrosserie de BMW des versions 321, 326 et 327. De 1952 à 1954, les Russes et l'entreprise est-allemande EMW (Eisenacher Motoren Werk), qui prendra sa succession, fabriqueront encore 491 dérivés de la BMW 327. Sous la dénomination EMW 327-3, ils fabriqueront également un joli coupé avec une grande lunette arrière.

Déjà apprécié des dignitaires du IIIe Reich, le modèle d'après-guerre qui succédera à la 327 Sport-Cabriolet deviendra un symbole de réussite pour les fonctionnaires du Parti socialiste fidèles à la ligne imposée. Les amoureux des BMW de collection considèrent la 327 comme l'un des plus jolis cabriolets de son époque.

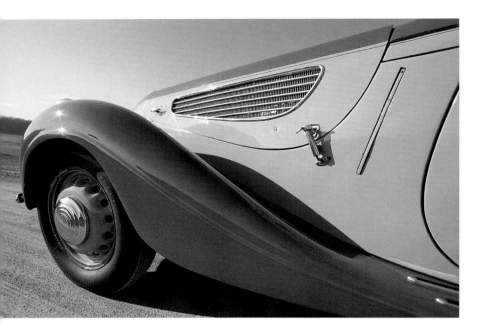

The elegant headlamps, mounted between the wings and the radiator hood, set the tone for the striking appearance of the BMW 327. Enthusiasts regard it as one of the most beautiful convertibles of the 1930s.

Die elegant in den Übergang von Kotflügel zu Kühlerhaube eingebetteten Scheinwerfer unterstreichen die ansprechende Optik des BMW 327. Kenner zählen ihn zu den schönsten Cabriolets der dreißiger Jahre.

Les phares élégamment positionnés à la ligne de césure entre les ailes et le capot soulignent l'esthétique réussie de la BMW 327. Les connaisseurs y voient l'un des plus jolis cabriolets des années 30.

The option of having the 80 bhp engine of the BMW 328 fitted in the 327/28 meant the otherwise somewhat underpowered 327 Cabriolet had plenty of "oomph", and with a top speed of 78 mph (125 kph) it gave motorists a lot of car for their money.

Mit der Option auf den Einbau des 80-PS-Motors des BMW 328 (als 327/28) kommen auch die nicht so stark motorisierten 327 Cabriolets „richtig in Fahrt" – 125 Stundenkilometer bereiten wohl Vergnügen.

Avec la possibilité de faire monter le moteur de 80 ch de la BMW 328 dans la 327/28, même les 327 cabriolets moins puissamment motorisés «décoiffent» – 125 km/h suffisent absolument pour se faire plaisir.

BMW 327 Sport-Cabriolet 1937

The 327 Cabriolet with its 55 bhp, elegant white spoked steering wheel and matching horn ring is stylish rather than sporting.

Eher vornehm als sportlich lassen sich die 55 PS des 327 Cabriolets mit dem eleganten weißen Speichenlenkrad und dem passendem Hupring lenken.

Le fringant volant blanc à trois branches avec la commande de klaxon circulaire incitera plutôt à conduire avec élégance que sur un rythme sportif la 327 Cabriolet de 55 ch.

BMW 327 Sport-Cabriolet 1937

From October 1938 onwards, coupé versions of the 327 and the 327/28 were available. In contrast to the Cabriolet, the door is hinged at the rear.

Ab Oktober 1938 sind der 327 und der 327/28 auch als Coupé erhältlich. Im Gegensatz zum Cabriolet ist der Türanschlag beim Coupé vorn.

A partir d'octobre 1938, la 327 et la 327/28 sont également disponibles en une version coupé. Contrairement aux cabriolets, les portes sont articulées à l'arrière.

BMW 327 Sport-Coupé 1938

Available as an option: the 80 bhp straight-six engine with V-valves and three Solex downdraft carburetors.

Wahlweise erhältlich: der Sechszylinder-Reihenmotor (80 PS) mit V-förmig hängenden Ventilen und drei Solex-Fallstromvergasern.

Alternative séduisante: le six-cylindres en ligne de 80 ch à soupapes suspendues en V et trois carburateurs Solex inversés.

BMW 327 Sport-Coupé 1938

Captivating lines and timeless beauty: the sweeping tail of the Coupé with a bulge where the spare wheel is housed.

Bestechende Linienführung und zeitlos schön: das gestreckte Heck des Coupés mit den spezifischen Rundungen, die sich der Reserveradausbuchtung im Kofferraumdeckel anpassen.

Lignes irrésistibles et beauté intemporelle : la poupe étirée du coupé aux galbes typés qui épousent l'emplacement ménagé pour la roue de secours dans le couvercle de malle.

A rare collector's item: only 179 coupés of the 327 and 86 of the 327/28 were produced by Autenrieth and Ambi-Budd.

Ausgesprochene Raritäten: Nur 179 Coupés des BMW 327 und 86 des BMW 327/28 wurden insgesamt von Autenrieth und Ambi-Budd gebaut.

Extrêmement rares : 179 coupés seulement de la 327 et 86 de la 327/28 ont été construits, au total, par Autenrieth et Ambi-Budd.

The 327/28 Cabriolet: stylish down to the last detail, from the indicator fitted flush with the door to the integrated headlamps, and the 327 chassis combined with the 80 bhp engine of the 328.

Das 327/28 Cabriolet ist chic bis ins kleinste Detail: der Einbauwinker vor der Tür, die integrierten Scheinwerfer und das Fahrwerk des 327, kombiniert mit dem 80-PS-Motor des 328.

Le cabriolet 327/28 est chic jusque dans les moindres détails: le signal de direction devant la portière, les phares intégrés et le châssis de la 327 combiné au moteur de 80 ch de la 328.

BMW 327/28 Cabriolet 1938

With the partial cladding of the rear wheel usually present on the 327/28s removed, the perforated rims can be seen to good effect. The color-contrasted contours of the wings are another pleasing feature.

Ohne die Teil-Hinterradabdeckung, die beim 327/28 eigentlich üblich ist, kommen die Lochfelgen besonders gut zur Geltung. Auch die farblich abgesetzten Kotflügelkonturen treten so besser hervor.

Sans le carénage partiel des roues arrière, normalement utilisé sur les 327/28, les jantes perforées se mettent particulièrement bien en évidence. Mais les contours d'ailes de couleur contrastée y gagnent également.

BMW 327/28 Cabriolet 1938

The three-spoke steering wheel with the white rim, the large round instruments, the clock on the glove compartment door and the lavish leather upholstery were all the rage at the time.

Damals voll im Trend: das Drei-speichenlenkrad mit weißem Kranz, große Rundinstrumente, ein Handschuhfach mit Uhr und üppige Ledersitze.

Très à la mode autrefois: le volant à trois branches à couronne blanche, de grands cadrans circulaires, une boîte à gants avec montre et d'accueil-lants fauteuils en cuir.

The two-liter power unit: a straight-six engine with V-valves, timed by the laterally-mounted camshaft according to a simple principle, three downdraft carburetors and 80 bhp at 5000 rpm.

Die 2-Liter-Kraftquelle: 6 Zylinder in Reihe, V-förmig hängende Ventile, deren Steuerung über die seitlich liegende Nockenwelle nach einem überaus einfachen Prinzip erfolgt, drei Fallstromver-gaser und 80 PS bei 5000 U/min.

Coup d'œil sous le capot: six-cylindres en ligne de deux litres, soupapes suspendues en V commandées par l'arbre à cames latéral selon un principe simple, trois carburateurs inversés et 80 ch à 5000 tr/mn.

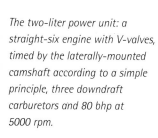

BMW 328 Roadster 1936

A feast for the eyes: slim fenders which extend full length, with elegantly integrated headlights. In sports tradition, no bumpers cover the small BMW kidneys at the front of the radiator of this roadster. The BMW 328 is not only a benchmark symbol of automotive esthetics but it also promises endless soft top fun.

Two leather belts secure the hood, which covers an engine capable of producing 80 bhp at 4500 rpm, a motor fed by three downdraft carburetors. To avoid developing a completely new engine, the existing six-cylinder unit was provided with a cylinder head whose brilliant design was worth a patent certificate in itself. Its tuning potential enabled power increases up to 120 bhp without difficulty, or 136 bhp for the final factory racing versions.

A consistently lightweight construction of only 1782 lbs (810 kg) and a balanced chassis ensured the best behavior even on the worst roads. This was a full-blooded sports car without any moodiness to spoil the fun. There is just one small fault: changing gear is like entering a labyrinth.

With the agility of a weasel, the 328 could outmaneuver many more powerful cars in the sports category, and on the racetrack it became a sporting legend in just three years with 405 wins and 154 second places. Indeed, races often featured internal BMW warfare, for there were starting grids made up exclusively of 328s.

The achievements of the racing version with the avant-garde aerodynamics of Carrozzeria Touring in Milan is worth a chapter in its own right. The series 328 also provided the basis for two streamlined versions built by the Wendler coachworks in Reutlingen, which reduced the drag coefficient and allowed very high maximum speeds.

Just 464 cars were built up to 1940. Frazer-Nash, British BMW importer since 1932, also built the 328 under license, converting it to right-hand drive.

The engine of the 328 experienced a comeback in postwar Britain and was used for several vehicles in the UK. Fritz Fiedler, one of the leading BMW designers, developed versions for Bristol and AFN. Last but not least, the Swiss automobile conversion company, Sbarro, contributed to the paeans of praise for the 328 with a replica in more recent times.

What was the 328? A classic or a vintage car? Perhaps a prestige badge for the company, a trendsetter of the 1930s for the sports cars of the postwar period? Maybe it was even a myth? Cult objects are a matter of taste. In the case of the 328, it is a fact that this timelessly elegant roadster has survived the era of automotive tin boxes and has remained forever youthful.

Eine Augenweide sind die schlanken, ganz nach hinten gezogenen Kotflügel mit den elegant integrierten Lampen. Keine Stoßstange verdeckt die sportlich schmalen BMW-Nieren vor dem Kühler dieses Roadsters. Der BMW 328 ist nicht nur ein Symbol automobiler Ästhetik, sondern verheißt auch schier endloses Cabriolet-Vergnügen.

Zwei Ledergurte sichern die Haube um das 80 PS bei 4500 U/min leistende Triebwerk, das von drei Fallstromvergasern beatmet wird. Um eine Neuentwicklung zu sparen, hat man den herkömmlichen Sechszylinder mit einem Zylinderkopf bestückt, dessen geniale Konstruktion eine Patenturkunde wert ist. Dieses Tuning erlaubt klaglos weitere Kraftschübe bis 120 PS und für die Rennversionen noch mehr.

Die konsequente Leichtbauweise (nur 810 Kilo) und ein ausgewogenes Fahrwerk sorgen für bestes Fahrverhalten selbst auf schlechtesten Straßen – ein Vollblutsportler ohne Launen. Kleines Manko: Die Schaltwege ähneln einem Labyrinth.

Mit der Wendigkeit eines Wiesels umkreist der 328 so manchen PS-Protz in der sportlichen Kategorie, und auf dem Rennparkett wird er mit 405 Siegen und 154 zweiten Plätzen in gerade mal drei Jahren zum Sportwagenmythos, wobei der Sieger oft als „primus inter pares" auftritt, denn letztlich gibt es Startfelder, die sich ausschließlich aus BMW 328 rekrutieren.

Das Ruhmesblatt der Rennversionen mit avantgardistischer Aerodynamik von Carrozzeria Touring in Mailand ist ein eigenes Kapitel wert. Aber auch auf Basis des serienmäßigen 328 werden von dem Karrosseriewerk Wendler in Reutlingen zwei Stromlinien-Exemplare gebaut, die den Luftwiderstandsbeiwert senken.

Bis 1940 werden 464 Exemplare gebaut. Frazer-Nash, seit 1932 britischer BMW-Importeur, führt die BMW 328 ein und baut sie auf Rechtslenkung um. Der Motor des 328 erlebt im Nachkriegs-England ein Comeback und beflügelt so manches Fahrzeug der Insel. Fritz Fiedler, einer der maßgeblichen BMW-Konstrukteure, entwickelt Derivate für Bristol und AFN. „Last but not least" stimmt der Schweizer Autoveredler Sbarro mit einer Replika in das Hohelied auf den 328 ein.

Was ist er nun eigentlich: ein Klassiker, ein Oldtimer, ein Firmenaushängeschild, ein Trendsetter der dreißiger Jahre für die Sportwagen der Nachkriegszeit oder gar ein Mythos? Kultobjekte sind Ansichtssache, aber beim 328 ist Tatsache: Dieser zeitlos elegante Roadster hat jede „Blechkultur" überlebt und wirkt noch immer jung.

Un délice pour les yeux sont les minces ailes qui s'enfuient vers l'arrière avec leurs phares élégamment intégrés. Aucun pare-chocs ne couvre les naseaux d'une minceur sportive de la BMW devant le radiateur de ce roadster. La BMW 328 n'est pas seulement un symbole d'esthétique automobile, elle incarne aussi le plaisir radieux et infini de la conduite en cabriolet.

Deux courroies de cuir fixent le capot sous lequel ronronne un moteur qui délivre 80 ch à 4500 tr/mn grâce à trois carburateurs inversés. Pour éviter de nouveaux développements, BMW a coiffé le six-cylindres conventionnel d'une culasse si géniale qu'elle mérite une déposition de brevet. Cette cure de vitamines permet sans difficulté de faire monter la puissance jusqu'à 120 ch et encore plus pour les versions course.

Une construction allégée systématique (seulement 810 kg) et un châssis équilibré lui inculquent un comportement sans défaut même sur les plus mauvaises routes. Un pur-sang sans allure. Elle n'a qu'un petit défaut: la grille est un véritable labyrinthe.

Avec sa maniabilité de belette, la 328 tourne autour de bien des voitures de sport beaucoup plus puissantes et, sur les pistes du monde entier, avec 405 victoires et 154 deuxièmes places en tout juste trois ans, elle devient un mythe parmi les voitures de sport, voire un «primus inter pares», car il y a parfois des plateaux qui se recrutent exclusivement de 328.

Il vaut la peine de consacrer un chapitre spécifique au tableau de chasse des versions course à l'aérodynamique d'avant-garde signée par Carrozzeria Touring à Milan. Mais, sur la base de la 328 de série aussi, la carrosserie Wendler, à Reutlingen, construit deux exemplaires aérodynamiques qui en diminuent le Cx.

Jusqu'en 1940, 464 exemplaires seront construits. Frazer-Nash, importateur de BMW en Grande-Bretagne depuis 1932, importe les 328 et les transforme pour la conduite à gauche. Dans l'Angleterre de l'après-guerre, le moteur de la 328 connaît une renaissance et donne des ailes à certaines voitures d'outre-Manche. Fritz Fiedler, l'un des grands ingénieurs de BMW, en développe les dérivés pour Bristol et AFN. «Last but not least», le préparateur suisse Sbarro chante une dernière élégie à la 328 avec une admirable réplique.

Mais comment la décrire? Est-ce une classique, un vétéran, une carte de visite, un faiseur de mode des années 30 pour les voitures de sport de l'après-guerre ou même un mythe? Sur les objets de culte, les avis sont partagés. Mais, pour la 328 une chose est acquise: ce roadster d'une élégance intemporelle a survécu à toutes les modes et reste jeune aujourd'hui encore.

A long slender kidney grill and sporting lines with no frills or flourishes and also no fender: the 328 is without doubt one of the most beautiful roadsters ever built. With its patented hood catch involving two leather straps to hold the engine hoods together, it has achieved cult status among BMW enthusiasts.

Eine schmale lange Niere und eine sportliche Linienführung ohne Schnörkel oder Stoßstangen: Der 328 ist zweifelsohne einer der schönsten Roadster, die je gebaut wurden. Mit den zwei Lederriemen, deren Patentverschlüsse die Motorhauben zusammenhalten, ist er ein automobilistisches Kultobjekt.

Des naseaux minces et étroits ainsi que des lignes sportives sans fioritures ni pare-chocs: la 328 est incontestablement l'un des plus jolis roadsters qui aient jamais été construits. Avec les deux courroies en cuir dont les fermetures brevetées maintiennent fermées les ailes du capot, c'est un objet de culte pour tout amateur d'automobiles.

DA-U 328

The slender running board, the scooped-out door rim leaving the driver free to steer unhindered, the unadorned instruments, switches and levers and the small hinged windows to deflect the airflow: that is what the cockpit of a genuine roadster should look like. Add to that an 80 bhp six-cylinder engine and all the ingredients for a successful motor sport career are in place.

Ein enger Einstieg, ein ausgesparter Türrand, damit die Lenkbarbeit nicht behindert wird, Armaturen, Schalter und Hebel ohne jegliche Verzierung und kleine Ausstellfenster zur Ableitung des Luftstroms: So sieht das Cockpit eines echten Roadsters aus. Dazu ein Sechszylinder mit 80 PS und alles ist wie geschaffen für den Motorsport.

Un accès étroit, une portière échancrée pour ne pas faire obstacle aux bras tournant le volant, des cadrans, manettes et leviers sans les moindres fioritures et de petits déflecteurs latéraux pour dévier les courants d'air: voilà à quoi ressemble le cockpit d'un authentique roadster avec, cerise sur le gâteau, un cylindre de 80 ch. Tous les atouts sont réunis pour connaître le succès en compétition.

BMW 328 Roadster 1936

The "legend on wheels" stood out for its excellent power-to-weight ratio and its superb handling.

Die „Legende auf Rädern" zeichnet sich durch ein günstiges Leistungsgewicht und exzellente Fahreigenschaften aus.

La «légende sur roues» se distingue par un rapport poids/puissance favorable et une excellente tenue de route.

BMW 328 Roadster 1936

Based on the BMW 328, the bodywork designer baron Reinhard of König-Fachsenfeld came up with this streamlined body whose drag coefficient is 0.38, a remarkable figure for those days.

Auf Basis des BMW 328 entwirft der Formgestalter Reinhard Freiherr von König-Fachsenfeld diese Stromlinienkarosserie, deren Luftwiderstandsbeiwert bei 0,38 liegt und für damalige Zeiten recht beachtlich ist.

Sur la plate-forme de la BMW 328, le styliste Reinhard baron de König-Fachsenfeld dessine cette carrosserie aérodynamique dont le Cx – 0,38 – est vraiment remarquable pour cette époque.

The Fachsenfeld design, on the basis of a patent by Paul Jaray, was produced at the Wendler bodywork plant in Reutlingen. Two prototypes were built, one of which can be seen in the Deutsches Museum in Munich, while the other one, illustrated here, is in the hands of a private BMW collector from Nuremberg.

Der Entwurf von Fachsenfeld nach einem Patent von Paul Jaray wird vom Karosseriewerk Wendler in Reutlingen realisiert. Zwei Prototypen werden gebaut, von denen einer im Deutschen Museum in München zu sehen ist. Dieser hier ist im Besitz eines privaten BMW-Sammlers aus Nürnberg.

Le croquis de Fachsenfeld selon un brevet de Paul Jaray est réalisé par le carrossier Wendler, de Reutlingen. Deux prototypes seront construits, dont l'un est exposé au Deutsches Museum de Munich, celui-ci étant la propriété d'un collectionneur privé de BMW de Nuremberg.

BMW 328 Fachsenfeld 1938

Fachsenfeld did a huge amount of detail work to get the drag coefficient down, such as the curved windows and the flush door handles. Without the radiator ribs the drag coefficient would have been as low as 0.29.

Zur Reduzierung des Luftwiderstandsbeiwerts leistet Fachsenfeld enorm viel Detailarbeit, zu der abgerundete Scheiben und versenkte Türgriffe gehören. Ohne die Kühlrippen auf der Motorhaube hätte der Cw-Wert sogar nur bei 0,29 gelegen.

Pour obtenir un Cx optimal, Fachsenfeld n'a négligé aucun détail, telles les vitres arrondies et les poignées intégrées aux portières. Sans les ailettes de refroidissement sur le moteur, le Cx aurait même été de seulement 0,29.

BMW 328 Mille Miglia und Touring 194

The success of the BMW 328 series from that Eifel race of June 1936, in which Ernst Henne came, saw and conquered, was overwhelming. But BMW wanted more than to win against itself, as had happened in the special race for 2-liter sports cars in the German Grand Prix of 1938.

Prepared for higher honors, an aluminium body was slipped over a tubular steel frame with box-section cross beams. This beautiful, lightweight roadster with its flowing side lines and rear wheel arches (covered if desired), was supplemented with a coupé by the Italian bodyshop Carrozzeria Touring.

This was more than fashion from Milan: the racing coupé corresponded to the aerodynamically favorable droplet form, but with a slightly raised rear end. The influence of Professor Wunibald Kamm, who was hired by BMW in his capacity as the founder of the motor vehicle and engine research institute at Stuttgart technical university, is unmistakable. The so-called "Kamm tail" became famous in many subsequent performance cars.

Peace prevailed just for the 1939 edition of the "24 Heures du Mans". A trio of works BMWs fought the long-distance battle on the Sarthe circuit, including a Touring coupé with the number 26 and registration number IIA 58 116. For safety reasons the two leather belts over the hood are mandatory as was the extraordinary extra light. The small coupé was fast and tough, romping about among the larger-engined cars and racing to the finish. Its crew – Prince Max of Schaumburg-Lippe/Hans Wencher – was unexpectedly fifth in the overall rankings, including, of course, victory in its class with an average 83 mph (132.8 kph).

Then came the War. No reason for Italians to miss a race. Late in April in 1940, the "Gran Premio Brescia delle Mille Miglia" was held. Again the familiar registration number IIA 58 116 made its way in the fastest time from the Piazza Vittoria in Brescia, via Crimona and Mantua, back to Brescia. A crazy average speed of 104 mph (166.7 kph) is set. That meant the Touring coupé – then driven by baron Fritz Huschke von Hanstein/Walter Bäumer – left their rivals comfortably behind. BMW also used three new roadsters, which came in third, fifth and sixth. A racing saloon with Kamm streamlining driven by count Lurani, retired.

Subsequently, the world was set on fire. As if nothing was happening, Carrozzeria Touring developed a new Spider on the basis of the 328. A delicious aerodynamic morsel, but one never to be enjoyed.

Die Erfolgsserie des BMW 328 seit jenem Eifelrennen 1936, als Ernst Henne kam, sah und siegte, ist überwältigend. Doch BMW will mehr als sich selbst besiegen, wie beim Sonderlauf der 2-Liter-Sportwagenklasse im Rahmen des Großen Preises von Deutschland 1938.

Um für höhere Weihen gewappnet zu sein, wird über einen Stahlrohrrahmen mit Kasten-Querträgern eine Aluminium-karosserie gestülpt. Diesem hübschen Leichtgewicht-Roadster mit seitlich fließenden Übergängen und wahlweise abdeckbaren Hinterradausschnitten stellt die italienische Karosserie-schmiede Carrozzeria Touring ein Coupé zur Seite.

Es ist mehr als Mailänder Mode: Das Renncoupé entspricht der aerodynamisch günstigen Tropfenform, jedoch mit leicht hochgezogenem Heck. Der Einfluß von Professor Wunibald Kamm, der als Gründer des Forschungsinstituts für Kraftfahr-wesen und Fahrzeugmotoren an der TH Stuttgart von BMW engagiert wird, ist unverkennbar. Das sogenannte „Kamm-Heck" prägt auch heutige Autogenerationen.

Noch ist Frieden! Unter den drei Werks-BMW, die 1939 die Langstreckenschlacht „24 Heures du Mans" an der Sarthe bestreiten sollen, ist auch ein Touring-Coupé mit der Startnummer 26 und dem Kennzeichen IIA 58 116. Aus Sicherheitsgründen dürfen die beiden Ledergurte über der Motorhaube ebensowenig fehlen wie ein voluminöser Zusatzscheinwerfer. Das kleine Coupé erweist sich als schnell und hart im Nehmen, tummelt sich unter den Hubraum-Größen und hält brav durch. Die Besatzung Max Prinz zu Schaumburg-Lippe/Hans Wencher belegt einen unerwarteten 5. Platz im Gesamtklassement, der natürlich den Klassensieg (Schnitt 132,8 km/h) beinhaltet.

Dann bricht der Krieg aus – für Italiener kein Grund, ein Rennen ausfallen zu lassen! In den letzten Apriltagen des Jahres 1940 steht der „Gran Premio Brescia delle Mille Miglia" auf dem Plan. Und wieder bahnt sich der Wagen mit dem Kennzeichen IIA 58 116 am schnellsten den Weg von der Piazza Vittoria in Brescia über Cremona und Mantova zurück nach Brescia. Ein Wahnsinns-Schnitt von 166,7 km/h, mit dem das Touring-Coupé – diesmal von Baron Fritz Huschke von Hanstein (Beifahrer Walter Bäumer) pilotiert – die Konkurrenz hoffnungslos abhängt. BMW setzt außerdem drei neue Roadster ein, die die Plätze 3, 5 und 6 belegen. Eine Rennsportlimousine mit Kamm-Stromlinienform, vom Conte Lurani pilotiert, fällt aus.

Die Welt brennt, doch als sei nichts geschehen, entwickelt Carrozzeria Touring einen neuen Spider auf Basis des 328: ein aerodynamischer Leckerbissen, dessen Genuß den Automobilenthusiasten versagt bleibt.

La série de succès remportés par la BMW 328 depuis la fameuse course de l'Eifel de 1936 – Ernst Henne vint, vit et vainquit – est sans précédent. Mais BMW veut plus que se vaincre elle-même, comme lors de la manche spéciale de la catégorie pour voitures de sport jusqu'à deux litres en marge du Grand Prix d'Allemagne de 1938.

Pour la préparer à une plus grande consécration, un châssis en tube d'acier avec poutres transversales est coiffé d'une carrosserie en aluminium. Ce joli roadster allégé aux flancs fluides et avec carénages de roues arrière démontables est épaulé par un coupé signé par Carrozzeria Touring, en Italie.

C'est plus que la mode de Milan : le coupé de course possède la forme en goutte d'eau aérodynamiquement idéale, mais avec un arrière légèrement surélevé. L'influence du professeur Wunibald Kamm, le fondateur de l'institut de recherche en automobiles et moteurs de véhicules à l'université technique de Stuttgart que BMW a recruté, est incontestable. L'arrière «Kamm» marque encore de son sceau les générations de voitures d'aujourd'hui.

Derniers jours de paix, 1939, «24 Heures du Mans» : parmi les trois BMW d'usine qui s'alignent pour la course d'endurance sur le circuit de la Sarthe figure aussi un coupé Touring avec le numéro 26 et la plaque minéralogique IIA 58 116. Pour des motifs de sécurité, les deux courroies de cuir sur le capot moteur doivent être présentes au même titre qu'un volumineux phare supplémentaire. Le petit coupé s'avère rapide et endurant et il se mêle même vaillamment aux plus grosses cylindrées. L'équipage prince Max zu Schaumburg-Lippe/Hans Wencher obtient une cinquième place inattendue au classement général,

qui va évidemment de pair avec une victoire de classe (à la moyenne de 132,8 km/h).

La guerre éclate. Pour les Italiens, ce n'est pas une raison d'annuler les courses. Fin avril 1940, le «Gran Premio Brescia delle Mille Miglia» figure au programme. Et c'est de nouveau la voiture immatriculée IIA 58 116 qui rejoint le plus vite la Piazza Vittoria à Brescia, après avoir bouclé la boucle par Crémone et Mantoue. A une moyenne fantastique de 166,7 km/h avec laquelle le coupé Touring – piloté cette fois-ci par le baron Fritz Huschke von Hanstein (avec Walter Bäumer comme coéquipier) – surclasse totalement la concurrence. BMW engage en outre trois nouveaux roadsters qui terminent 3e, 5e et 6e. Une berline sport-compétition à carrosserie aérodynamique Kamm, pilotée par le comte Lurani, doit par contre abandonner.

Le monde brûle. Comme si rien ne se passait, Carrozzeria Touring met au point un nouveau Spider sur la base de la 328, un chef-d'œuvre d'aérodynamique dont les fanas d'automobile ne pourront jamais profiter.

These three streamlined racing roadsters contested the 1940 Mille Miglia, ending up in third, fifth and sixth places. Overall victory went to a lightweight BMW Touring coupé. The Mille Miglia's aluminum bodywork considerably reduced its weight and also gave it a certain aerodynamic advantage.

Der Einsatz von drei dieser stromlinienförmigen Renn-Roadster bei der Mille Miglia 1940 endet mit den Plätzen drei, fünf und sechs. Der Gesamtsieg geht an ein BMW-Leichtbau-Coupé von Touring. Die Aluminium-Außenhaut des Mille Miglia bringt neben der erheblichen Gewichtseinsparung auch einige aerodynamische Vorteile.

L'inscription de ces trois roadsters de course aérodynamiques aux Mille Miglia de 1940 est récompensée par les troisième, cinquième et sixième places. Une BMW Coupé à carrosserie Touring allégée remporte la victoire au classement générale. Outre une économie de poids non négligeable, la carrosserie en aluminium de la version Mille Miglia a aussi des avantages aérodynamiques.

The superb styling of the bodywork plus a number of engineering innovations from the racetrack would no doubt have been incorporated into the production cars before long. The War meant that all such plans had to be shelved.

Die herrliche Karosserieform sowie einige im Rennfahrzeug erprobte technische Innovationen wären sicherlich kurze Zeit später in Serie gegangen. Aufgrund des Krieges werden derartige Pläne „ad acta" gelegt.

La magnifique carrosserie ainsi que quelques innovations techniques testées sur les voitures de course auraient assurément fait leur apparition en série un peu plus tard, mais la guerre empêcha la réalisation de tels projets.

The timeless beauty and aerodynamic qualities of the 328 Mille Miglia continued to influence the
design of many sports cars after the Second World War.

*Das zeitlos schöne und aerodynamisch vorteilhafte Design des 328 Mille Miglia bestimmt nach
dem Zweiten Weltkrieg die Formgebung einiger Sportwagen.*

*Après la Seconde Guerre mondiale, la beauté intemporelle et le style aérodynamique de la
328 Mille Miglia serviront de modèle pour de nombreuses voitures de sport.*

After the 328's success in the Mille Miglia, the Italian bodywork designer Carrozzeria Touring
came up with this optimized racing Spider convertible with its uninterrupted belt line.

*Auf Basis des 328 entsteht nach dem Erfolg bei der Mille Miglia bei der italienischen Karosserie-
schmiede Carrozzeria Touring dieser optimierte Renn-Spider mit durchgehender Gürtellinie.*

*Après le succès de la 328 aux Mille Miglia, BMW fait réaliser chez le carrossier italien Carrozzeria
Touring ce Spider de compétition optimisé à la ligne de ceinture d'un seul jet.*

BMW 328 Touring 1941

BMW 328 Touring 1941 125

BMW kidney grills and lamps are integrated into the rounded nose of this prototype of the Touring, causing virtually no turbulence.

BMW-Nieren und Lampen sind nahezu verwirbelungsfrei in den abgerundeten Bug des Prototypen von Touring integriert.

Les naseaux BMW et les phares sont intégrés pratiquement sans générer de tourbillons dans la proue tout en galbes du prototype de Touring.

Some styling details from the "Super-leggera", the shell of the Touring Spiders, which can be seen today in the BMW Museum in Munich.

Hier einige Styling-Details der „Super-leggera"-Außenhaut des Touring Spiders, der heute im BMW-Museum in München steht.

Quelques détails du style de la carrosserie «Superleggera» du Spider Touring, qui est aujourd'hui exposé au Musée BMW de Munich.

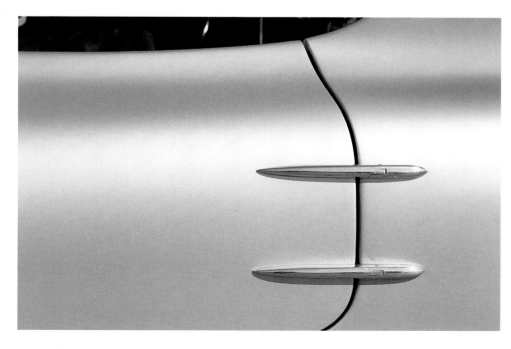

The racing version of the BMW six-cylinder was never short of power. The Mille Miglia Roadster
of 1940 developed 130 bhp at 5750 rpm, and an altered compression and larger outlet valves
allowed 136 bhp to be reached at 6000 rpm.

An Kraft mangelt es der kontinuierlich weiterentwickelten Rennversion des BMW-Sechszylinders
nicht. Mit 130 PS bei 5750 U/min entspicht sie der Leistung des Mille-Miglia-Roadsters von 1940.
Durch geänderte Kompression und größere Auslaßventile werden dann sogar 136 PS bei
6000 U/min erzielt.

Le six-cylindres de la BMW dans sa version course, perfectionné en permanence, ne manque pas
de puissance. Avec 130 ch à 5750 tr/mn, il est aussi puissant que le roadster Mille Miglia de 1940.
Un taux de compression supérieur et des soupapes d'échappement de plus grand diamètre
permettent même d'obtenir 136 ch à 6000 tr/mn.

By racing car standards the cockpit of the Touring looks positively comfortable. The large fuel tank was mounted directly behind the two-man crew.

Für ein Rennfahrzeug beinahe komfortabel mutet das Cockpit des Touring an. Der große Tank befindet sich direkt im Nacken der Besatzung.

Le cockpit de la Touring mérite presque le qualificatif de confortable pour une voiture de course. Le grand réservoir se trouve directement derrière la nuque de l'équipage.

BMW 328 Touring 1941   129

BMW 335 1939

The "cake" consisting of the large cars with three to four liters cubic capacity was apparently already shared out by autumn 1938. A good half of that sales cake went to the Ford V8, whilst Opel received a large portion thanks to its Admiral. Add Daimler Benz, Auto-Union, Borgward and Stoewer to the picture, and the cake was virtually consumed. A small piece of cream was left over for the 140 bhp, extravagantly expensive Maybach SW 38.

BMW aimed for their slice of the luxury cake with a 3.5-liter engine. Shortly after the test department moved from Eisenach to Munich, the six-cylinder motors, long-stroke engines displacing 3485 cc, were demonstrating the potential to deliver flagship performance of 90 bhp at 3500 rpm.

A mobile experimental lab, which was basically an extended BMW 326, aroused the interest of the Aldington brothers, owners of BMW's British partner and importer, Frazer-Nash. They presented this 335 prototype, equipped with right-hand drive, a lavish leather interior, and the Frazer-Nash BMW emblem, at the London Motor Show in October 1938.

This classy example of automotive technology stole the show from all its competitors, including the roomy US V8 limousines. Overjoyed, the Aldington brothers were able to keep this car, since BMW had already progressed with the development of the 335 to such an extent that it was ready for launch in volume production. Some adjustments were made to its physical appearance, since larger wheels made it necessary to widen the fenders.

Everything was ready on 17 February 1939. On that date, BMW presented the 335 as a limousine in Berlin, flanked by a convertible and a coupé. The 335 was praised both by experts and the public alike. With a power-to-weight ratio of 42.77 lbs/1 bhp (19.44 kg/1 bhp) – best value in this category – the newcomer was just as accelerative as it was physically appealing.

Before the War forced BMW to change its priorities, just 415 examples of 335 were built. Their variety was astonishing, particularly amongst the convertibles, for 24 chassis were built with individual designs, mainly by Autenrieth. The Darmstadt company still managed to supply three coupés in 1945. At that time, Ernst Henne had the only works coupé built using Autenrieth components.

What was probably the most beautiful BMW of all was created by the Swiss chassis artist Herrmann Graber: a jewel of a car with a rear elegantly extended. As was Graber practice, this 335 was painted in stylish black and equipped with green leather seats, so this convertible was a BMW enthusiast's dream. The man for whom this dream came true was Dr Bernhard Knöchlein from Franconia, owner of this unique carriage.

Der „Kuchen" der großen Wagen mit drei bis vier Litern Hubraum scheint im Herbst 1938 verteilt zu sein. Die V8 von Ford machen gut die Hälfte aus, Opel sichert sich mit dem Admiral ein großes Stück, und mit Daimler-Benz, Auto-Union, Borgward und Stoewer bleibt vom Kuchen so gut wie nichts übrig – nur ein kleines Sahnestück: der 140 PS starke, sündhaft teure Maybach SW 38.

In diese PS-Klasse steigt BMW mit seinem 3,5-Liter-Motor ein. Und man beeilt sich. Schon kurz nach dem Umzug der Versuchsabteilung von Eisenach nach München lassen die Sechszylindertriebwerke, Langhuber mit 3485 ccm, ihr Leistungspotential (90 PS bei 3500 U/min) erahnen.

Ein rollendes Versuchslabor, im Prinzip ein verlängerter BMW 326, erregt das Interesse der Gebrüder Aldington, Herren über den britischen Partner und Importeur Frazer-Nash. Sie präsentieren diesen 335-Prototypen, versehen mit Rechtslenkung, üppigem Lederinterieur und Frazer-Nash-BMW-Emblem, im Oktober 1938 auf der London Motor Show.

Das edle Einzelstück stiehlt allen Konkurrenten, einschließlich den dicken V8-Limousinen aus den USA, die Show. Zu ihrem größten Glück dürfen die Aldington-Brothers diesen Wagen behalten, da BMW mit anderen Versuchsträgern in der Entwicklung des 335 schon zur Serienreife gelangt ist. Die Optik erfährt noch Korrekturen, da die größeren Räder Kotflügelverbreiterungen erforderlich machen.

Am 17. Februar 1939 ist es soweit. In Berlin stellt BMW den 335 als Limousine vor, flankiert von einem Cabriolet und einem Coupé. Fachwelt und Publikum sind begeistert. Mit seinem Leistungsgewicht von 19,44 Kilo pro PS – Bestwert in dieser

Kategorie – glänzt der Neue mit seiner Technik ebenso wie mit dem schwungvollen Äußeren.

Obwohl nur 415 Wagen gebaut werden, ehe der Krieg auch bei BMW andere Prioritäten setzt, ist die Vielfalt – gerade bei den Cabriolets – erstaunlich. Allein 24 Fahrgestelle werden mit Einzelaufbauten, vornehmlich von Autenrieth, versehen. So liefert das Darmstädter Werk noch 1945 drei Coupés aus. Ernst Henne besitzt zu dieser Zeit das einzige Werks-Coupé, aufgebaut mit Teilen von Autenrieth.

Den wohl schönsten BMW überhaupt kreiert der Schweizer Karosseriekünstler Herrmann Graber: eine automobile Pretiose mit elegant nach hinten gestrecktem Heck. Vornehm schwarz lackiert und – wie bei Graber üblich – mit grünen Ledersitzen ausgestattet, ist dieses Cabriolet der Traum eines jeden BMW-Enthusiasten. Für einen BMW-Liebhaber ist er Realität: Dr. Bernhard Knöchlein aus Franken ist der Besitzer des einmaligen Gefährts.

A l'automne 1938, le «gâteau» des grosses voitures de trois à quatre litres de cylindrée semble être partagé entre les convives. Les Ford V8 en accaparent largement la moitié; avec l'Admiral, Opel s'assure elle aussi un bon morceau du gâteau tandis que Daimler-Benz, Auto-Union, Borgward et Stoewer se partagent les miettes. Mais il y a encore la cerise sur le gâteau: la Maybach SW 38 de 140 ch au prix astronomique.

Sans perdre de temps, BMW se lance dans ce segment de puissance avec son moteur de 3,5 l. En effet, peu après que le service des essais ait déménagé d'Eisenach à Munich, les six-cylindres, des moteurs à course longue de 3485 cm³, font une première démonstration de leur potentiel (90 ch à 3500 tr/min).

Une voiture-laboratoire, en principe une BMW 326 allongée, suscite l'intérêt des frères Aldington, gérants du partenaire et importateur britannique de Frazer-Nash. Ils présentent ce prototype 335 doté d'une direction à droite avec une fastueuse sellerie cuir et un emblème Frazer-Nash-BMW au Motor Show de Londres d'octobre 1938.

Cette somptueuse voiture vole la vedette à toutes ses concurrentes, y compris les grosses limousines V8 américaines. Comblés de bonheur, les frères Aldington peuvent même conserver cette voiture, car BMW a pratiquement mené à maturité le développement de la 335 avec d'autres voitures expérimentales. L'esthétique subira encore quelques corrections, car les roues de plus grand diamètre exigent des ailes plus larges.

Le 17 février 1939, le grand jour est arrivé. BMW présente la 335 en version berline, escortée d'un cabriolet et d'un coupé, à Berlin.

Milieux spécialisés et grand public sont enthousiasmés. Outre son rapport poids/puissance de 19,44 kilos par cheval (le record dans cette catégorie), la nouvelle voiture se distingue également par sa technique et ses lignes d'une grande vivacité.

Bien que 415 voitures seulement aient été construites avant que la guerre ne fasse valoir ses droits chez BMW, la diversité est étonnante, notamment pour les cabriolets. Pas moins de 24 châssis ont été habillés d'une carrosserie spéciale, le plus souvent signée Autenrieth. Ainsi l'usine de Darmstadt fournira-t-elle encore trois coupés en 1945. Ernst Henne possède à cette époque le seul coupé d'usine qui ait été monté à partir de pièces réalisées chez Autenrieth.

C'est incontestablement l'artiste carrossier suisse, Herrmann Graber, qui aura signé la plus belle BMW de tous les temps: un bijou d'automobile avec une poupe élégante aux lignes étirées vers l'arrière. D'une grande distinction avec sa peinture noire et – comme toujours chez Graber – ses sièges en cuir vert, ce cabriolet est le rêve de tous les amoureux de BMW. Il n'y a qu'une seule personne pour qui il soit une réalité: Dr Bernhard Knöchlein, de Franconie, est le propriétaire de cette voiture unique dans tous les sens du terme.

BMW 335 1939

In 1939 BMW entered the top end of the market with the launch of the 335. This one-off, built by Herrmann Graber in Switzerland, is in a class of its own. It is now in the possession of a German BMW enthusiast.

Mit dem 335 steigt BMW 1939 in die Oberklasse auf. Eine Klasse für sich ist dieses von Herrmann Graber in der Schweiz gefertige Einzelstück, das sich derzeit im Besitz eines deutschen BMW-Enthusiasten befindet.

Avec la luxueuse 335, BMW monte en gamme en 1939. Ce spécimen unique, carrossé en Suisse par Herrmann Graber, est un modèle exceptionnel qui se trouve actuellement en possession d'un Allemand, fanatique de BMW.

The 335 dashboard has an extravagant appearance, with its round instruments set in rounded-off rectangular housing. The steering wheel with four spokes instead of three is a new feature.

Extravagant gibt sich das Armaturenbrett des 335. Als ginge es um die Quadratur des Kreises, wurden die Rundinstrumente in abgerundete Rechteckfassungen gesetzt. Neu ist auch das Lenkrad mit vier anstelle von drei Speichen.

Le tableau de bord de la 335 est extravagant. Comme si l'on avait voulu résoudre la quadrature du cercle, les cadrans circulaires sont insérés dans un encadrement carré. Autre nouveauté : le volant possède maintenant quatre et non plus trois branches.

Tilted slightly towards the back for reasons of space is the long 3.5-liter straight-cylinder power unit, with its two vertical staged dual-register carburetors, developed 90 bhp at 3500 rpm.

Aus Platzgründen leicht nach hinten geneigt ist das lange 3,5-Liter-Reihentriebwerk, das mit zwei Vertikal-Doppelregistervergasern 90 PS bei 3500 U/min leistet.

Par manque de place, le long 3,5 litres en ligne est légèrement incliné vers l'arrière. Avec ses deux doubles carburateurs verticaux à registre, il développe 90 ch à 3500 tr/mn.

One people, one Reich, one Führer ... one chassis!" The propaganda slogans of the Third Reich might be extended thus in respect of the passenger vehicle for the German armed forces. The German army procurement office demanded a standard passenger vehicle in three weight classes. With exact instructions regarding the chassis, the order for the light version was awarded to Stoewer, Hanomag and BMW. No external changes were permitted. Emblems giving any indication of the manufacturer were forbidden.

As well as an engine of the manufacturer's choice – the only requirement was that it should fit under the bonnet and to the transmission – the profile of technical requirements specified permanent all-wheel drive, four limited slip differentials, and selectable, spindle-linked, four-wheel steering. Stoewer started production as early as 1936 and manufactured 7500 examples altogether, although not all of them had four-wheel steering. Hanomag produced 2000 units. BMW production started in April 1937 and carried on until summer 1940 and resulted in somewhere between 3225 and 3259 vehicles being produced, all called BMW 325.

A short wheelbase gave over-sensitive handling. Also, extremely complicated technology, and an unfavorable power-weight ratio, restricted the military usefulness of these vehicles. Transporting the 2.2 tons maximum permissible weight was hard work even for the strongest engine – BMW used its proven six-cylinders, achieving 50 bhp with two Solex updraft carburetors. The 325 was not suitable for the fabled German Blitzkrieg attacks, hobbled by a fuel tank range of just 150 miles (240 km). These standard specification military vehicles met

their "Stalingrad" defeats well before the Russian campaign began. All were withdrawn from the arms supply programs before the winter of 1942.

Today the 325 is a real rarity. Only one roadworthy vehicle is known to exist, one which Udo Beckmann, a motor mechanic from Siegen, has saved from "death in action" by loving restoration. This 325, built in 1939 and supplied to the German army in May 1940, was provided with a large equipment box for communications purposes, in place of one seat and a door. This storage proved useful postwar, thus this 325 served years in Austria with the mountain rescue and fire brigade.

Driving skill is required to handle the all-wheel drive and steering systems, particularly in rough terrain and on winding roads. Beckmann's 325 rolls to the "front" today, without its radio equipment but with spade and searchlight. Then it does not head for the desert, as it did with Rommel, but to a BMW veterans' meeting. Once there, a photo of the Field Marshal in a 325 will be proudly passed around.

Ein Volk, ein Reich, ein Führer ... ein Fahrgestell!" So ließe sich die Propagandaparole des Dritten Reiches hinsichtlich der Personenkraftwagen für die Wehrmacht erweitern, denn das Heereswaffenamt setzt auf Einheits-Pkw, gestaffelt nach drei Gewichtsklassen. Mit genauen Chassis- und Fahrwerksvorgaben geht der Auftrag für die leichte Version an Stoewer, Hanomag und BMW. Äußerliche Abweichungen sind nicht erlaubt. Embleme, die auf den Hersteller schließen lassen, sind verboten.

Das technische Anforderungsprofil sieht neben Motoren eigener Wahl – sie müssen nur unter die Haube und an das Getriebe passen – permanenten Allradantrieb, vier Sperrdifferentiale und eine hinten abstellbare Vierrad-Spindellenkung vor. Stoewer beginnt bereits 1936 mit der Produktion und fertigt insgesamt rund 7500 Wagen, freilich nicht alle mit Vierrad-Lenkung. Hanomag produziert 2000 Einheiten. Bei BMW, wo der Produktionsstart im April 1937 erfolgt und bis zum Sommer 1940 gefertigt wird, entstehen zwischen 3225 und 3259 Wagen, genannt BMW 325.

Zu kurzer Radstand, empfindliche, da sehr aufwendige Technik und ein ungünstiges Leistungsgewicht schränken die Truppentauglichkeit dieses Fahrzeugs ein. Selbst für den stärksten Motor, den BMW-Sechszylinder, der mit zwei Solex-Steigstromvergasern 50 PS leistet, bedeutet das Bewegen von 2,2 Tonnen zulässigen Gesamtgewichts Schwerstarbeit – nichts für Blitzkriege, zumal der Tank im Gelände nach 240 Kilometern leer ist. So erleben die Einheits-Pkw ihr Stalingrad bereits in der Anfangsphase des Rußlandfeldzugs. Noch vor dem Winter 1942 werden sie aus dem Rüstungsprogramm genommen.

BMW 325 Leichter Einheits–Pkw 1939

Heute ist der 325 eine absolute Rarität. Bekannt ist nur ein fahrtaugliches Exemplar, das Udo Beckmann, ein Kfz-Meister aus Siegen, durch liebevolle Restaurierung vor dem „Heldentod" bewahrt hat. Dieser 325, der 1939 gebaut und im Mai 1940 an die Wehrmacht ausgeliefert wurde, ist für Fernmeldezwecke mit einem großen Gerätekasten bestückt. Dafür fallen ein Sitz und eine Tür weg. Diese Konfiguration ist auch in Friedenszeiten brauchbar, und so dient dieser Wagen noch geraume Zeit in Österreich bei Bergwacht und Feuerwehr.

Fahrerisches Können ist beim Umgang mit dem Allradantriebs- und Lenkungssystem gefordert, besonders im Gelände und auf kurvenreichen Straßen. Wenn Beckmanns 325, ohne Funkgerät zwar, aber versehen mit Feldspaten und Suchscheinwerfer, heute wieder an die „Front" rollt, dann geht's nicht wie bei Rommel in die Wüste, sondern zum BMW-Veteranentreffen, wo dann stolz das Foto des Generalfeldmarschalls in einem 325 herumgereicht wird.

Un peuple, un Reich, un Führer ... et un châssis!» Ainsi pourrait-on transposer la devise de propagande du IIIᵉ Reich dans le domaine des voitures particulières pour la Wehrmacht, car les services des achats de l'Armée exigent un seul type de voitures particulières en fonction de trois catégories de poids différentes. Avec un cahier des charges précis pour le châssis et les trains roulants, la commande pour la version légère est attribuée à Stoewer, Hanomag et BMW. Aucune divergence extérieure n'est autorisée. Tout emblème indiquant le constructeur est interdit.

Outre des moteurs de son propre choix – ils doivent seulement entrer sous le capot et aller avec la boîte de vitesses – le cahier des charges prévoit une traction intégrale permanente, quatre différentiels autobloquants et une direction à broche sur les quatre roues, les deux roues arrière étant débrayables. Stoewer inaugure la production dès 1936 et fabrique au total environ 7500 voitures, dont toutes ne possèdent toutefois pas quatre roues directrices. Hanomag en produit 2000 exemplaires. Chez BMW (début de la production en avril 1937, fabrication jusque durant l'été 1940), entre 3225 et 3259 voitures sont construites, baptisées BMW 325.

Un empattement trop court, une technique peu fiable parce que trop sophistiquée et un rapport poids/puissance défavorable restreignent les possibilités d'utilisation par la troupe. Même pour le moteur le plus puissant – le six-cylindres BMW à deux carburateurs Solex verticaux développant 50 ch –, déplacer un poids total en charge autorisé de 2,2 tonnes représente un travail de forçat. On est donc loin des guerres éclairs, d'autant plus que, en tout-terrain, le réservoir est sec au bout

de 240 km. Ainsi ces voitures vivent-elles leur «Stalingrad» avant même que ne commence la campagne de Russie et l'hiver 1942 n'a même pas commencé qu'elles disparaissent du programme des achats militaires.

Aujourd'hui, la 325 est une rareté absolue. On ne connaît qu'un seul exemplaire apte à rouler, celui d'Udo Beckmann, un mécanicien automobile de Siegen, qui l'a préservé de la «mort des héros» en la restaurant avec amour. Cette 325, construite en 1939 et livrée à la Wehrmacht en mai 1940, comporte un grand caisson à appareils pour les télécommunications (ce qui a imposé le sacrifice d'un siège et d'une portière). Utilisable également en période de paix, cette voiture a encore servi longtemps en Autriche pour les secours de montagne et les pompiers.

Un certain savoir-faire est nécessaire pour rouler avec la traction intégrale et les quatre roues directrices, en particulier en tout-terrain et sur routes sinueuses. Lorsque la 325 de Beckmann, sans appareil de transmission, mais avec sa pelle-bêche et son projecteur orientable, roule de nouveau «vers le front» aujourd'hui, elle ne part pas à la rencontre du désert comme au temps de Rommel, mais aux concentrations de vieilles BMW où l'on se passe alors fièrement de main en main la photo du général feld-maréchal dans une 325.

Required by the German army procurement office: all-wheel drive and steering. The wheel suspension's double wishbone axles are each fitted with two helical springs.

Vom Heereswaffenamt gefordert: Allradantrieb und -lenkung. Die Doppel-Querlenker der Radaufhängungen sind mit je zwei dieser Schraubenfedern versehen.

Le cahier des charges de l'armée est exigeant: traction et direction intégrales. Les doubles bras transversaux des suspensions ont chacun deux de ces ressorts hélicoïdaux.

BMW 325 Leichter Einheits-Pkw 1939　　　141

The BMW six-cylinder engine generates 50 bhp, which had to struggle to shift a two-tonner such as the version with a telecommunications equipment box shown here. The 325 is a great rarity, and this example is the only roadworthy one still in existence. After the War, it did service in the Austrian mountain rescue and fire departments.

50 PS leistet der BMW-Sechszylinder. Das bedeutet Schwerstarbeit beim Bewegen eines Zweitonners, der hier in der Ausführung mit einem Gerätekasten für Fernmelder gezeigt wird. Der 325 gilt als absolute Rarität, und fahrbereit ist offenbar nur noch dieses Exemplar, das nach dem Krieg der Bergwacht und Feuerwehr in Österreich gedient hat.

Le six-cylindres BMW développe 50 ch. Il est donc à la peine avec cette voiture de deux tonnes vue ici dans l'exécution avec caisse à équipement de télécommunication. La 325 est un modèle considéré comme rarissime entre tous et, apparemment, seul cet exemplaire, utilisé pour les secours en montagne et les pompiers en Autriche après la guerre, est encore capable de rouler.

BMW 325 Leichter Einheits-Pkw 1939　　143

Veritas RS 1949

When an automotive development engineer, a businessman and a former world cycling champion decide to set up a company in the devastation that was postwar Germany, manufacture of a utilitarian vehicle immediately would seem likely. Perhaps a moped with a trailer? Or mini-vans, rubble-clearing vehicles or bicycles with passenger cars?

Completely wrong! The BMW engineer, Ernst Loof, the businessman, Lorenz Dietrich, and the ex-cycling star, Werner Miethe, wanted to build racing cars and sedan racers. This was supposed to happen in Munich-Allach, but the Americans did not give their consent, although Miethe also had US citizenship. The three moved instead to Meßkirch in Baden, because the French seemed to be more amenable to the project.

The hour of truth started with the name: Veritas. That was the name of the 1.5 and 2-liter cars built in factory ruins from remaining BMW components. However, winning cars were built as early as 1948 in the strangest of conditions, which demonstrated unbelievable powers of improvisation. The BMW motorbike legend and Auto-Union Grand Prix driver Georg Meier brought BMW its first win in this period in a non-formula racing cars class.

Karl Kling, who was actually working for Daimler Benz, also joined the unofficial BMW team. In 1949 – the small company's best year – Veritas headed the German racing scene. Helmut Glöckner and Karl Kling won both sports car classes at 1.5 and 2 liters. Toni Ulmen also performed well with Veritas racing cars.

Most of the 32 saloon racers were built in 1949. These Veritas RS had a lightweight, lattice-type chassis design with an aluminum "skin". Because they were hand-made like all Veritas vehicles, each looked very different. The BMW from Carrozzeria Touring served as a model for the design.

Thanks to the modified crankshaft and a new cylinder head, ratings of 120 to 125 bhp were delivered from the basic engine (six-cylinder BMW 328). Depending on the ratio, the 2-liter RS could reach road speeds of up to 125 mph (200 kph). Coping with unexpected transverse accelerations required outstanding driver skills, since the RS was prone to slight instability.

The 1949 Veritas RS also attracted buyers from outside Germany. The alterations performed included body work, upgrading the electrical system and adding a fuel pump, but were generally minor. By the end of 1950, over 60 competition and motor sports Veritas were built.

Defeat in sporting events and lack of success in tests on road vehicles meant the graceful end for this vehicle marque. The upper echelons of motor sport witnessed the finale at the Nürburgring. Loof, after the split with his partners, launched a short production run in the buildings previously owned by Auto-Union. Spohn from Ravensburg supplied him with the last of the line bodies. The Veritas type "Nürburgring" was to be Loof's last design, for he died shortly after the Veritas.

Wenn ein Automobil-Entwicklungsingenieur, ein Kaufmann und ein ehemaliger Radrenn-Weltmeister im zerbombten Nachkriegsdeutschland beschließen, eine Firma zu gründen, denkt man unwillkürlich an die Fertigung eines nützlichen Fahrzeugs: Mofa mit Anhänger, Kleinstlastwagen, Trümmer-Räumfahrzeug oder Fahrrad mit Beiwagen.

Völlig falsch! Der BMW-Ingenieur Ernst Loof, Kaufmann Lorenz Dietrich und Ex-Radstar Werner Miethe wollen Renn- und Rennsportwagen bauen. Das soll in München-Allach geschehen, doch die Amerikaner sind dagegen, obwohl Miethe sich auch als US-Bürger ausweisen kann. Die drei Herren weichen also nach Meßkirch im Badischen aus, da sich die Franzosen dem Projekt aufgeschlossen zeigen.

Die Stunde der Wahrheit beginnt mit der Namensgebung. Veritas – so heißen die zunächst in einer Fabrikruine zusammengebauten Wagen mit 1,5- und 2-Liter-Motoren aus BMW-Restbeständen. Unter abenteuerlichen Umständen und mit unglaublicher Improvisationskunst entstehen bereits 1948 Siegerwagen. Georg Meier, BMW-Motorrad-Legende und Grand-Prix-Fahrer der Auto-Union, holt den ersten Erfolg in einer formelfreien Rennwagenklasse.

Der eigentlich in Daimler-Benz-Diensten stehende Karl Kling steigt ebenfalls in das Team ein. 1949 steht die kleine Firma auf dem Zenit ihrer Entwicklung: Veritas beherrscht die deutsche Rennszene. Mit Helmut Glöckner und Karl Kling gewinnt man in beiden Sportwagenklassen (1,5 und 2 Liter). Toni Ulmen hält sich bei den Rennwagen schadlos.

Die meisten der insgesamt 32 Rennsportwagen werden

1949 gebaut. Diese Veritas RS weisen eine leichte Gitterrohr-Rahmenkonstruktion mit einer „Haut" aus Aluminium auf, die – handgefertigt wie alles bei Veritas – recht unterschiedlich ausfällt. Optisches Vorbild ist der BMW von Carrozzeria Touring.

Dank einer geänderten Kurbelwelle und einem neuen Zylinderkopf werden aus dem Basis-Motor (Sechszylinder BMW 328) zwischen 120 und 125 PS herausgeholt. Je nach Übersetzung erreicht der 2-Liter-RS bis zu 200 Stundenkilometer. Höhere Querbeschleunigungen verlangen viel fahrerisches Können, da der RS nicht ganz verwindungssteif ist.

Der Veritas RS des Baujahres 1949 findet aufgrund seiner Erfolge auch Käufer im Ausland. Die Änderungen – Karosseriearbeiten, Umrüstung der Elektrik, zusätzliche Benzinpumpe etc. – sind meistens geringfügig. Bis Ende 1950 werden mehr als 60 Wettbewerbsautos und Sportwagen gebaut.

Sportliche Niederlagen und erfolglose Versuche mit Straßensportwagen führen letztlich zum Exitus der Marke. Dieser vollzieht sich an prominenter Stelle: am Nürburgring, wo Loof – nach der Trennung von seinen Partnern – in den ehemaligen Auto-Union-Hallen eine Kleinserie begonnen hat. Die Karosserie liefert ihm die Ravensburger Firma Spohn. Dieser Wagen, Typ „Nürburgring", ist Loofs letzte Konstruktion. Kurz nach dem Aus von Veritas stirbt er.

Quand un ingénieur de développement en automobile, un commercial et un ancien champion du monde cycliste décident, dans l'Allemagne bombardée de l'après-guerre, de fonder une firme, on pense automatiquement qu'ils veulent fabriquer un quelconque véhicule à caractère utilitaire : un vélomoteur avec remorque, une mini-camionnette, un camion servant à déblayer les ruines ou un vélo avec side-car.

Eh bien, pas du tout! L'ingénieur BMW Ernst Loof, le commercial Lorenz Dietrich et l'ex-vedette de la petite reine Werner Miethe veulent construire des voitures de course et de sport. Ils choisissent pour cela Munich-Allach, mais les Américains s'y opposent bien que Miethe puisse se prévaloir d'être citoyen américain. Faisant contre mauvaise fortune bon cœur, les trois hommes optent pour Meßkirch, dans le pays de Bade, car les Français se révèlent accueillants au projet.

L'heure de vérité sonne au moment de baptiser la voiture : Veritas. Tel est le nom qu'arborent d'abord les voitures à moteur de 1,5 et 2 litres assemblées dans une usine en ruines à partir de stocks de pièces BMW. Dans des circonstances très aventureuses et avec un art consommé de l'improvisation, ils produisent déjà des voitures victorieuses en 1948. Georg Meier, légende de la compétition motocycliste chez BMW et pilote de Grand Prix pour Auto-Union, remporte la première victoire en catégorie voitures de course de formule libre.

Bientôt, Karl Kling, pourtant au service de Daimler-Benz, rejoint lui aussi l'écurie. En 1949 – la petite firme atteint alors son zénith – Veritas domine les milieux de la compétition en Allemagne : avec Helmut Glöckner et Karl Kling, la marque remporte les deux classes de voitures de sport (1,5 et 2 litres). Dans la catégorie voitures de course, Toni Ulmen défend avec les honneurs les couleurs de la marque.

La majorité des voitures de course, 32 au total, seront construites en 1949. Ces Veritas RS possèdent un léger châssis tubulaire habillé d'une «peau» en aluminium, toutes les carrosseries étant légèrement différentes parce que fabriquées à la main, comme tout chez Veritas. La source d'inspiration esthétique est la BMW de Carrozzeria Touring.

Grâce à un vilebrequin modifié et à une nouvelle culasse, le moteur de base (le six-cylindres de la BMW 328) développe entre 120 et 125 ch. Selon la démultiplication, la RS de deux litres peut flirter avec le 200 km/h. Les accélérations transversales exigent beaucoup de doigté de la part du pilote, car la rigidité torsionnelle n'est pas le fort de la RS.

En raison de ses succès, la Veritas RS de 1949 trouve aussi preneur à l'étranger. Le plus souvent, les aménagements – travaux de carrosserie, modification du système électrique, pompe à essence supplémentaire etc. – se réduisent à leur plus simple expression. Jusqu'à la fin de 1950, plus de 60 voitures de course et de sport sortent de chaînes.

Des défaites sportives et l'échec subi avec les voitures de sport de route sonnent finalement le glas de la marque. Le point final est mis en un haut lieu de la compétition automobile : au Nürburgring où Loof – qui s'est séparé de ses associés – a commencé une petite série dans les anciens ateliers d'Auto-Union. La société Spohn, de Ravensburg, lui fournit les carrosseries. Cette voiture, le type «Nürburgring», est la dernière construction de Loof. Il décédera peu après la disparition de la Veritas.

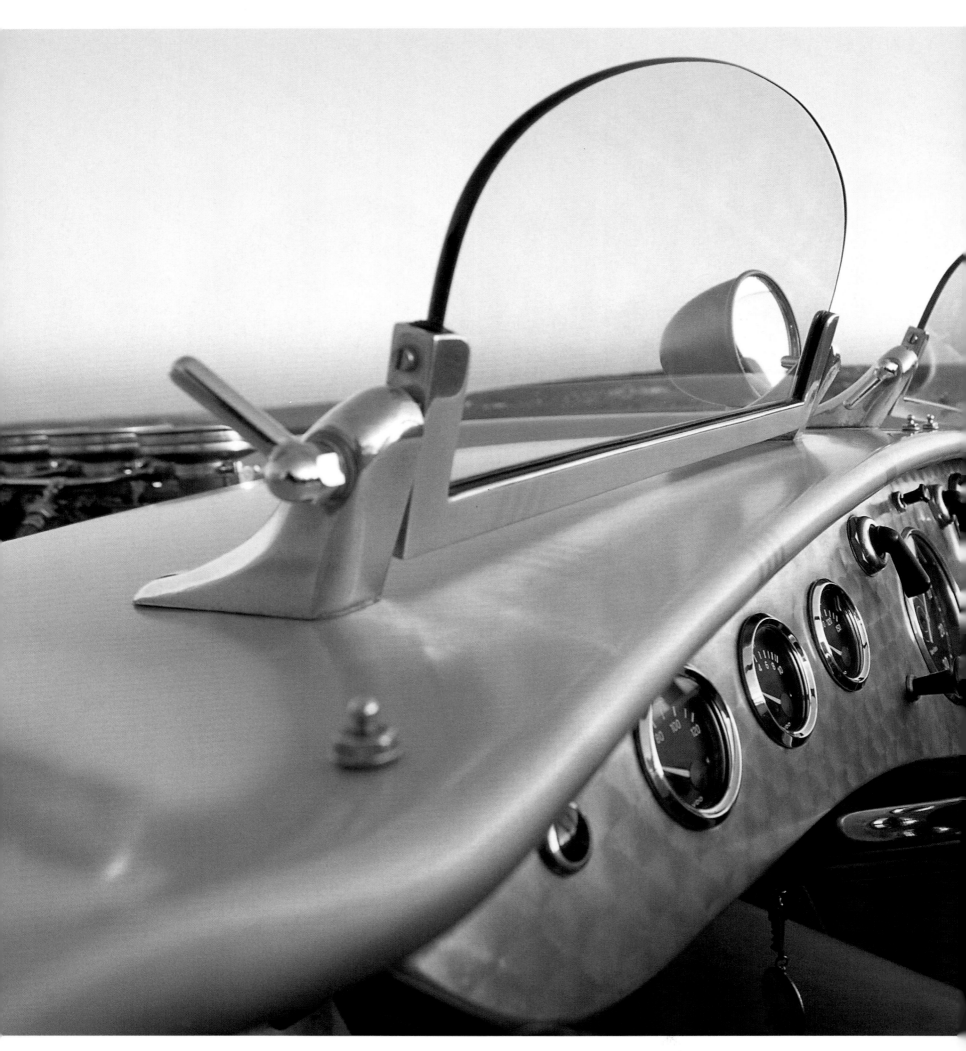

Veritas RS 1949

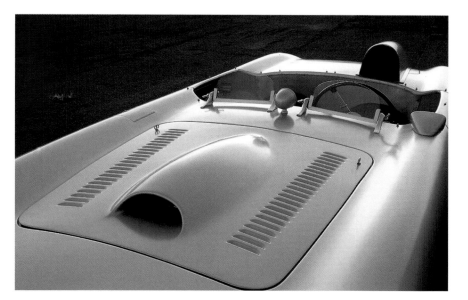

Beneath the adjustable windscreen the Veritas driver has an uninterrupted view of the rev counter, speedometer and oil pressure gauge, plus four other round instruments. With its three Solex carburetors, the two-liter six-cylinder engine developed 125 bhp.

Unter den verstellbaren Scheiben hat der Veritas-Pilot ständig Drehzahlmesser, Tacho, Öldruck-messer und vier weitere Rundinstrumente im Visier. Mit drei Solex-Vergasern entfaltet der 2-Liter-Sechszylinder 125 PS.

Sous le coupe-vent réglable, le pilote de la Veritas a constamment sous les yeux le compte-tours, le tachymètre, le manomètre d'huile et quatre autres instruments circulaires. Avec trois carbura-teurs Solex, le six-cylindres de 2 litres développe 125 ch.

Veritas RS 1949

The well-conceived and successful design of the RS made it a piece of high fashion on the racetrack. The headrests serve a purely aerodynamic purpose.

Durchdacht und gelungen: Form und Funktion des RS-„Gewandes" zählen 1949 zur Haute Couture im Rennwagenbau. Die Nackenstütze hat lediglich eine aerodynamische Funktion.

Bien congue et réussie: forme et fonction de la «robe» de la RS appartiennent à la haute couture parmi les voitures de course de 1949. Le carénage d'appuie-tête n'a qu'une fonction aérodynamique.

Bonjour Madame, please take your seat behind the ivory-colored wheel of the 22,000 mark BMW 502 Cabriolet. The advertising brochure for this noble car with the first German V8 engine of the postwar period totally ignored the man's world; only women, catching the admiring glances of men, were shown in this convertible. Indeed, the steering wheel with column shift gear lever, indicator and horn appeared to be made for delicate hands. The proper signal effect was produced by two Bosch musical horns behind the front bumper.

The wooden dashboard had a semi-circular speedo, which went up to 112 mph (180 kph), and the arrangement of the instruments gave a relaxed and light impression. The bias was defintely feminine: little levers and buttons below the Becker "Grand-Prix" radio, ready to play "In the Mood" – Glenn Miller inviting the ladies out into the fresh country air. After all, the top was easy for ladies to operate, as the BMW advertising emphasized.

The purring of the 2.6-liter engine was drowned in the sound of the wind. The engine, with light alloy block, wet cylinder liners and five-bearing crankshaft, was thoroughly modern, a 100 bhp power source. The overhead valves were mounted in pairs to be activated by tappets, push rods and rocker arms. The camshaft was driven by a duplex roller chain.

Ladies, cruising down the boulevard with their 502 Cabriolet, were probably not particularly interested in recitations of technical engine data. Only fuel consumption, and thus opening a purse, was of interest: 16.3 miles to the gallon of Super and 0.26 pints of oil every 62.5 miles (14.5 liters Super and 0.15 liters oil per 100 km). The switch to the auxiliary tank

had to be made after a good 250 miles (400 km). The coolant level for the radiator, too, needed to be inspected regularly.

Technical matters take over again with the ZF 4-speed manual transmission with full synchromesh on all forward gears, the gearbox itself being located under the front seats. A propshaft with two rubber joints linked the clutch to transmission. The connection to the final drive with hypoid bevel gears was by a secondary universal-joint propeller shaft, its joints on needle-roller bearings.

The excellent heating, once the radiator coolant had heated up to the proper temperature, and solid workmanship – the only draught came from the vents intended for that purpose – made this convertible truly winter-proof. However, it was less advisable to use this 3087 lbs (1400 kg) car – up to 4365 lbs (1980 kg) when fully laden – on snow and ice. Altogether, Baur in Stuttgart built a little over 130 convertibles and coupés with the 2.6-liter engine. Autenrieth produced some 50 special tops for the 502, some of them varying significantly and even diverging from the BMW specifications, which earned them no favours with BMW when it came to placing new orders.

Bonjour Madame, nehmen Sie Platz hinter dem elfenbeinfarbenen Steuer des 22.000 Mark teuren BMW 502 Cabriolets. Die Werbebroschüre des edlen Wagens mit dem ersten deutschen V8-Motor der Nachkriegszeit negiert die Männerwelt völlig. Nur weibliche Personen, die bewundernden Blicke der Männer erhaschend, führen dieses Cabriolet vor. In der Tat sind das Lenkrad mit Gangschaltung, Blinker und Hupring wie geschaffen für zarte Hände. Für die richtige Signalwirkung sorgen zwei Bosch-Fanfaren hinter der vorderen Stoßstange.

Auch das „holzgetäfelte" Armaturenbrett mit dem halbkreisförmigen Tacho, dessen Anzeige bis zu 180 km/h reicht, und die Verteilung der Instrumente wirken locker und leicht – feminin eben wie auch die Hebelchen und Knöpfchen unterhalb des „Grand-Prix"-Radios von Becker, das gerade „In the mood" spielt. Glenn Miller lädt die Damen zu einem Open-Air-Ausflug ein. Schließlich ist das Verdeck für Damen leicht zu betätigen, wie es explizit in der BMW-Werbung steht.

Das Surren des 2,6-Liter-Motors geht im Fahrtwind unter. Eine moderne, 100 PS starke Kraftquelle ist dieses Triebwerk mit Leichtmetallblock, nassen Zylinderlaufbüchsen und fünffach gelagerter Kurbelwelle. Die Ventile hängen parallel und werden durch Stößel, Stoßstangen und Kipphebel betätigt. Über eine Duplex-Rollenkette erfolgt der Nockenwellenantrieb.

Damen, die mit ihrem 502 Cabriolet über den Boulevard flanieren, interessiert dieses Defilee technischer Motordaten wohl kaum. Nur der Verbrauch und der damit einhergehende Schwund im Portemonnaie spielen eine Rolle: 14,5 Liter Super und 0,15 Liter Öl auf 100 Kilometer dürfen es schon sein. Nach

BMW 502 Cabriolet 1954

gut 400 Kilometern ist der Griff zum Reservehahn unumgänglich, und auch der Kühlwasserstand sollte ab und zu beobachtet werden.

Technisch wird es wieder bei dem unter den Vordersitzen angeordneten ZF-Viergang-Zahnradgetriebe mit Sperrsynchronisation der Vorwärtsgänge. Von der Kupplung zum Getriebe läuft eine Kardanwelle mit zwei Gummigelenken. Eine Gelenkwelle mit nadelgelagerten Gelenken stellt die Antriebsverbindung zum Hinterachsgetriebe mit Hypoid-Kegelrädern her.

Die Heizung, die gut funktioniert, sobald das Kühlwasser die entsprechende Temperatur erreicht hat, und die solide Verarbeitung - es zieht nur über die dafür vorgesehenen Düsen herein - machen das Cabriolet wirklich winterfest. Sich mit dem 1400 Kilo schweren Wagen (beladen bis 1980 Kilo) auf Schnee und Eis zu bewegen, ist weniger ratsam. Insgesamt baut Baur in Stuttgart etwas mehr als 130 Cabriolets und Coupés mit dem 2,6-Liter-Motor. Autenrieth stellt etwa 50 Sonderaufbauten für den 502 her, teilweise recht verschieden und sogar abweichend von den BMW-Vorgaben - nicht gut für ein „Au revoir" bei der Vergabe von Werksaufträgen.

Bonjour Madame, prenez donc place derrière le volant ivoirin du BMW 502 Cabriolet qui coûte 22 000 marks. Le prospectus de la prestigieuse voiture avec le premier moteur V8 allemand de l'après-guerre fait totalement abstraction du monde masculin : seules de jolies femmes qui attirent les regards admirateurs des hommes conduisent ce cabriolet. De fait, le volant avec levier de changement de vitesses, clignotants et anneau de klaxon est comme prédestiné pour de douces mains de femmes. Deux klaxons Bosch ronflants derrière le pare-chocs avant signalent son arrivée à qui veut l'entendre.

Le tableau de bord en bois avec le tachymètre en demi-cercle gradué jusqu'à 180 km/h et la répartition des instruments évoquent eux aussi la décontraction et la légèreté. Tout aussi féminins sont les petits leviers et boutons sous l'autoradio Becker «Grand Prix» qui joue «In the mood». Glenn Miller invite les dames à un concert en plein air. Enfin, la capote est facile à manier par la gent féminine, comme le laisse entendre explicitement la publicité BMW.

Le ronflement du moteur de 2,6 litres est couvert par les bruits aérodynamiques. Ce moteur à bloc en alliage léger, chemises humides et vilebrequin à cinq paliers est un propulseur moderne et puissant de 100 ch. Les soupapes suspendues sont parallèles et actionnées par des coupelles, des poussoirs et des culbuteurs. L'arbre à cames est entraîné par une chaîne à rouleaux duplex.

Les dames qui se plaisent à flâner sur les boulevards avec leur 502 Cabriolet ne prêteront qu'une oreille distraite à cette énumération de caractéristiques techniques. Elles s'intéresseront tout au plus à la consommation et, par conséquent, à l'ouverture du porte-monnaie : la consommation est de 14,5 litres de super et de 0,15 litre d'huile aux 100 km. Tous les 400 km, la procédure consistant à passer sur le réservoir de secours se rappelle à votre bon souvenir. Mais il ne faut pas oublier non plus de contrôler de temps à autre le niveau d'eau de refroidissement.

Pour la transmission, on retrouve la boîte ZF à engrenages à quatre rapports avec synchronisation des rapports avant qui se trouve sous les sièges avant. L'embrayage est relié à la boîte par un cardan avec deux articulations à palier en caoutchouc. Des articulations à roulements à aiguilles assurent la liaison entre la boîte du pont arrière à engrenages coniques hypoïdes.

Le chauffage performant, dès que l'eau de refroidissement a atteint la température correspondante, et la grande qualité de finition - l'air ne pénètre qu'à travers les ouïes prévues à cette fin - rendent le cabriolet réellement à l'épreuve de l'hiver. Il est toutefois peu conseillé de s'aventurer sur la neige et le verglas avec cette voiture qui pèse 1400 kg (et même jusqu'à 1980 kg à pleine charge). Au total, Baur de Stuttgart, construit un peu plus de 130 cabriolets et coupés avec le moteur de 2,6 litres. Autenrieth assemble une cinquantaine de carrosseries spéciales de la 502, certaines divergeant fortement ou parfois même totalement des instructions de BMW, ce qui n'est pas l'idéal pour un «au revoir» au moment de la passation des commandes par l'usine.

Portrait of a BMW 502. A total of more than 130 cabriolets and coupés, based on the 2.6-liter eight-cylinder 502, were built at the Baur bodywork plant in Stuttgart.

Konterfei eines BMW 502. Insgesamt werden von der Stuttgarter Karosseriefabrik Baur mehr als 130 Cabriolets und Coupés, basierend auf dem 502 mit 2,6-Liter-Achtzylinder, gebaut.

Profil d'une BMW 502. Au total, le carrossier Baur de Stuttgart, construira plus de 130 cabriolets et coupés, tous sur la plate-forme de la 502 à moteur huit cylindres de 2,6 litres.

The 15' 6" (4.7 meter) long convertible is based on a box-section frame with strong tubular cross members. The chassis and body are welded together. It was available in two and four-door models.

Das 4,7 Meter lange Cabriolet ruht auf einem Kastenrahmen mit starken Rohrquerträgern. Chassis und Aufbau sind miteinander verschweißt. Es ist zwei- oder viertürig lieferbar.

Le cabriolet de 4,7 mètres de long possède un châssis à caissons avec de solides poutres transversales. Le châssis et la carrosserie sont soudés l'un à l'autre. Deux versions sont disponibles : à deux ou quatre portes.

The V proudly displayed on the trunk of this BMW indicates that this is the first German V8 engine of the postwar era. It developed 100 bhp at 4800 rpm.

Stolz trägt dieser BMW das V-Zeichen auf dem Koffer-raumdeckel. Es steht für den ersten deutschen V8-Motor der Nachkriegszeit: Leistung 100 PS bei 4800 U/min.

Cette BMW arbore fièrement un V sur son couvercle de malle. Il trahit la présence du premier moteur V8 allemand de l'après-guerre. Puissance: 100 ch à 4800 tr/mn.

BMW 502 Coupé 1955

Ready to pounce: a rarity and an eyecatcher, this 106 mph (170 kph) coupé was manufactured in small numbers by Baur between 1955 and 1958.

Rarität und deshalb Blickfang: Das wie zum Sprung geduckt wirkende, 170 km/h schnelle Coupé wird von Baur zwischen 1955 und 1958 in kleiner Stückzahl gefertigt.

Une rareté qui attire immanquablement le regard : ce coupé qui évoque un félin prêt à bondir est capable de croiser à 170 km/h et a été construit en nombre limité par Baur de 1955 à 1958.

BMW 502 Coupé 1955   159

The Coupé roof with the drop-center rim stops short of the steel disc wheels, giving the tail of the car an elongated appearance.

Das noch vor den Stahlscheibenrädern mit Tiefbettfelge auslaufende Coupé-Dach streckt optisch die Heckpartie mit dem umgreifenden Stoßfänger.

Le toit du Coupé qui se termine avant même les roues à voile d'acier avec jante à base creuse allonge visuellement la partie arrière avec les pare-chocs mordant sur les ailes.

Stylish and contemporary: the white steering wheel and controls, plus a wood-paneled dashboard and leather seats. The engine is fitted with a dual-throat downdraft carburetor and a large air filter. The firing sequence 1-5-4-8-6-3-7-2 is conspicuous on the cylinder head cover.

Vornehm und zeitgemäß: Lenkrad und Bedienelemente in weiß, holzgetäfeltes Armaturenbrett und Ledersitze. Der Motor ist mit einem Doppel-Fallstromvergaser und großem Luftfilter bestückt, auffallend ist die Zündreihenfolge 1-5-4-8-6-3-7-2 auf dem Zylinderkopfdeckel.

Elégants et tout à fait dans le style de leur temps : volant et manettes de commande de couleur blanche, tableau de bord en bois et sièges en cuir. Le moteur est alimenté par un double carburateur inversé et respire à travers un grand filtre à air. L'ordre d'allumage – 1-5-4-8-6-3-7-2 – est affiché bien lisiblement sur le couvre-culasse.

BMW Isetta 300 1956

The "cuddle box", as it was nicknamed, was a miniature car to fall in love with, a bench with a cabin on wheels: ideal for lovers! Desired by vintage car fans not just as an easy-to-park funmobile, this mini car with motorbike engine is officially called "Motocoupé Isetta".

Apart from the engine and numerous changes to details, the Isetta 250 outwardly reflected the prototype of the Italian company Iso, from which BMW bought the license plus body-work tools. The engine already existed and came from the BMW R 25 motorcycle, a four-stroke single-cylinder engine offering 12 bhp.

The original version, with wrap-round window at the rear, hinged windows and opening roof, looked like an aircraft cockpit. In 1956 the Isetta 250 was given a big sister with carlike characteristics, the Isetta 300. The figures show the progression in engine size from 245 to 298 cc. This produced a "powerful" jump in performance: just 1 bhp!

The tiny engine chugged and burbled along behind the passenger seat. The capacity of the petrol tank (3.5 gallons or 13 liters) was as modest as the fuel consumption (43 miles per gallon/5.5 liters per 100 km). The rear wheels, only 20 inches (52 cm) apart, were driven by a short transverse propshaft and a duplex chain bathed in oil. A little lever on the left-side panel was available for the driver to poke about mightily in the four-speed transmission: best operated by double declutching, for there was no synchronization.

Road holding – the Isetta was not a car which easily tipped over – was acceptable, and at 53 mph (85 kph) maximum speed, the Isetta could keep up with the traffic flow. A length of just

over six feet (2.35 meters), a front-opening door, room for the beer crate in front of the passenger seat, and the shopping bags in the luggage space, are the attributes of this compact car. The Isetta has for more than 40 years been what the current Swatch Smart is still trying to attain.

Expectations were still modest in the 1950s. So an Isetta generally served as a car for all seasons: the drive to work as well as the holiday trip over the Alps to the Italian beaches.

As a classic car, the Isetta is still extremely serviceable in everyday use. That is particularly evident in city traffic and its lack of parking spaces. Have you ever tried parking a Corsa, Twingo or Polo at right angles to the traffic flow? Being able to get out forwards directly onto the pavement is also something appreciated by Prince Leopold of Bavaria on ice cream runs with the children. His Royal Highness, whose Isetta is painted in the Bavarian national colors, would not want to be without this midget of a car in his private family car fleet.

More than half of the 136,367 BMW Isettas built in Munich utilized the smaller engine, a question of the category of driver's license in Germany. The British imported the Isetta with just a single rear wheel owing to local laws which allowed three wheelers to be driven on a motorcycle license, with no requirement to take a separate car test.

Die „Knutschkugel", so der Volksmund, ist ein Kleinst-wagen zum Lieben und Verlieben, eine Bank mit Kabine auf Rädern – ideal für Liebespaare! Das Mini-Auto mit Motorrad-Motor, von Oldtimer-Fans heute nicht nur als park-raumsparendes Spaßmobil gefragt, trägt die offizielle Bezeich-nung „Motocoupé Isetta".

Vom Motor und zahlreichen Detailänderungen abgesehen entspricht die Isetta 250 dem Prototyp der italienischen Firma Iso, von der BMW die Nachbaulizenz samt Preßwerkzeugen kauft. Der Motor ist ein alter Bekannter und stammt vom BMW-Motorrad R 25, ein Viertakt-Einzylinder mit 12 PS.

Die Ur-Version der Isetta mit hinterer Panoramascheibe, Klappfenstern und Faltdach wirkt wie ein Flugzeug-Cockpit. 1956 bekommt die Isetta 250 eine große Schwester mit auto-mobilen Zügen, die Isetta 300. Die Zahlen drücken den Hub-raumzuwachs von 245 auf 298 ccm aus. Damit verbunden ist ein „gewaltiger" Leistungsschub: 1 PS!

Hinter dem Beifahrersitz tuckert und blubbert das kleine Motörchen. Bescheiden wie der Verbrauch (5,5 Liter) ist auch das Tankvolumen (13 Liter). Der Antrieb auf die nur 52 Zenti-meter auseinanderstehenden Hinterräder erfolgt über eine quer liegende kurze Gelenkwelle und eine Duplex-Kette, die sich in einem Ölbad suhlt. Mit einem Hebelchen, links an der Seiten-wand, darf in dem 4-Gang-Getriebe kräftig herumgerührt werden – am besten mit Zwischengas, denn eine Synchro-nisation existiert nicht.

Die Straßenlage – kein Umfaller-Wägelchen – ist passabel, und eine Höchstgeschwindigkeit von 85 Stundenkilometern reicht zu jenen Zeiten aus, um im Verkehrsfluß mitzuschwim-

men. 2,35 Meter Länge, eine sich nach vorn öffnende Tür, Platz für den Bierkasten vor dem Beifahrersitz und die Einkaufsbeutel auf der Ablage sind Attribute eines gelungenen Kompaktfahrzeugs. Was der Smart noch werden will, ist die Isetta schon seit mehr als 40 Jahren.

In den fünfziger Jahren sind die Ansprüche noch bescheiden, und die Isetta dient in den meisten Fällen als Auto für alle Fälle: für die Fahrt zur Arbeit ebenso wie für die Urlaubstour über die Alpen an Italiens Strände.

Als Oldtimer ist die Isetta noch äußerst alltagstauglich. Das zeigt sich besonders im von Parkplatznöten gebeutelten Großstadtverkehr. Versuchen Sie einmal, mit einem Corsa, Twingo oder Polo quer zur Fahrtrichtung einzuparken! Direkt nach vorn auf den Bürgersteig aussteigen zu können, schätzt auch Leopold Prinz von Bayern, wenn er mit seinen Kindern zur Eisdiele fährt. Königliche Hoheit, dessen Isetta in den bayerischen Landesfarben lackiert ist, möchten den automobilen Winzling in seinem privaten Wittelsbacher Fuhrpark nicht missen.

Mehr als die Hälfte der 136.367 in München gebauten BMW Isetta begnügt sich mit dem Motor mit kleinerem Hubraum – in Deutschland eine Frage der Führerscheinklasse. Die Briten hingegen importieren die Isetta mit nur einem Hinterrad – ebenfalls eine Frage der Führerscheinklasse, denn in Großbritannien darf man die Dreiräder mit dem Motorradführerschein fahren.

Le «pot de yaourt», comme on l'a vite surnommée, est une micro voiture dont on ne peut que tomber amoureux – un banc avec cabine sur roues, idéal pour les couples d'amoureux! La mini-voiture à moteur de moto, qui n'a pas seulement la cote auprès des fanas de voitures anciennes parce qu'elle est aussi compacte que ludique, porte officiellement le titre de «Motocoupé Isetta».

A part le moteur et plusieurs changements de détails, l'Isetta 250 est, extérieurement, identique au prototype de la firme italienne Iso, à laquelle BMW rachète la licence de construction et les presses d'emboutissage. Le moteur existe déjà. Il s'agit de celui du moto BMW R 25, un monocylindre à quatre temps de 12 ch.

La version originale à lunette panoramique, vitres entrebâillantes et toit pliant ressemble à un cockpit d'avion. En 1956, l'Isetta 250 est rejointe par une grande sœur qui ressemble plus à une voiture, l'Isetta 300. Les chiffres traduisent la hausse de cylindrée de 245 à 298 cm^3, laquelle va de pair avec un bond «gigantesque» pour la puissance: 1 ch!

Le petit moteur ronronne derrière le siège des passagers. La consommation (5,5 litres) est aussi réduite que le volume du réservoir (13 litres). La transmission aux roues arrière séparées l'une de l'autre par seulement 52 cm, est assurée par un court cardan transversal et une chaîne duplex qui barbote dans un bain d'huile. Un petit levier accolé à la paroi latérale de gauche permet de sélectionner les quatre rapports: de préférence avec double débrayage, car il n'y a pas de synchronisation.

La tenue de route est correcte – contrairement aux apparences, la voiturette ne se renverse pas – et, avec 85 km/h,

l'Isetta nage dans la circulation comme un poisson dans l'eau. 2,35 m de long, une porte ouvrant vers l'avant, de la place pour une caisse de bière devant le siège du passager et les sacs des courses sur la plage arrière sont des caractéristiques de cette compacte voiture. Ce que la Smart veut encore devenir, l'Isetta l'est déjà depuis plus de 40 ans.

Dans les années 50, on est encore modeste et l'Isetta sert, dans la majorité des cas, de voiture pour tous les cas: pour aller au travail aussi bien que pour partir en vacances au-delà des Alpes, sur les plages d'Italie.

Toute ancienne qu'elle soit, l'Isetta a encore parfaitement sa place dans la circulation de tous les jours. On le constate particulièrement dans les grandes agglomérations où l'on cherche souvent en vain une place de stationnement. Essayez donc de vous garer de travers avec une Corsa, une Twingo ou une Polo! Le Prince Leopold de Bavière apprécie de pouvoir descendre de l'avant sur le trottoir lorsqu'il emmène ses enfants au glacier du coin. Son Altesse Royale, dont l'Isetta est peinte aux couleurs nationales de la Bavière, ne se séparerait pour rien de cette minuscule automobile dans son parc privé des Wittelsbacher.

Plus de la moitié des 136 367 BMW Isetta qui ont été construites à Munich se contentent du moteur de plus petite cylindrée, ce qui était une question de catégorie de permis de conduire en Allemagne. Si les Britanniques n'importent l'Isetta qu'avec une seule roue arrière, ceci est dû à la catégorie de permis de conduire, puisqu'en Grande-Bretagne, il est possible de conduire un véhicule à trois roues avec un permis pour motos.

BMW Isetta 300 1956

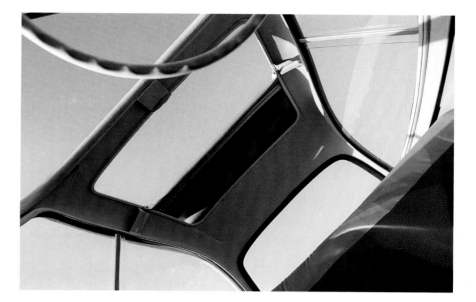

You get into the Isetta with its folding roof from the front. The "dashboard", which consists solely of a speedometer and the ignition lock, swings outwards with the door when it is opened. The gear lever for the four-speed transmission is fitted to the left-hand side wall. Top speed in fourth gear was 53 mph (85 kph), and 0 to 50 mph (0 to 80 kph) took around 40 seconds.

Von vorn erfolgt der Einstieg in die Isetta-Kabine mit Faltdach. Das „Armaturenbrett", lediglich aus Tacho und Zündschloß bestehend, schwenkt mit der Tür mit. Links an der Seitenwand befindet sich der Hebel für die Viergang-Schaltung des Klauengetriebes. Höchstgeschwindigkeit im vierten Gang: 85 Stundenkilometer, Beschleunigung auf 80 „Sachen" in rund 40 Sekunden!

L'accès à la cabine de l'Isetta à toit pliant s'effectue par l'avant. Le «tableau de bord» qui se compose uniquement d'un tachymètre et d'une serrure de clef de contact est solidaire de la porte. A gauche contre la paroi latérale se trouve le levier de la boîte à quatre vitesses à crabots. Vitesse maximum en quatrième: 85 km/h, accélération de 0 à 80 en environ 40 secondes.

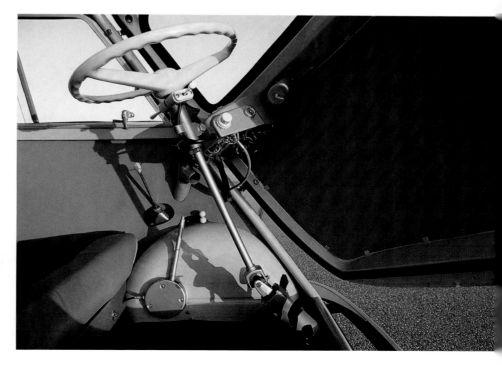

BMW Isetta 300 1956

BMW Isetta 300 1956

Originally the Isetta had a glass dome, but in 1956 this was replaced by the roof design illustrated, with its sliding windows. The car was also fitted at that time with free-standing headlamps and a modified tail. The "trunk" was externally mounted.

Anfänglich besaß die Isetta noch eine Glaskuppel, die 1956 diesem Dachaufbau mit Schiebefenstern wich. Außerdem erhielt der Wagen freistehende Scheinwerfer und ein modifiziertes Heck. Der „Kofferraum" liegt extern.

A l'origine, l'Isetta possédait encore une coupole en verre qui a fait place, en 1956, à ce type de toit à vitres coulissantes. En outre, la voiture a reçu des phares proéminents et son arrière a été modifié. Le «coffre» se trouve à l'extérieur.

The tiny four-stroke, single-cylinder, forced-air-cooled engine developed 12 bhp in the Isetta 250, and one bhp more in the Isetta 300. Fuel economy was, not surprisingly, good, at around 43 miles per gallon (5.5 liters per 100 km).

Das von Gebläseluft gekühlte Viertakt-Einzylindermotörchen liefert 12 PS bei der Isetta 250 und ein PS mehr bei der Isetta 300 – sparsame Triebwerke, die 5,5 Liter auf 100 Kilometer verbrauchen.

Le petit monocylindre à quatre temps refroidi par turbine délivre 12 ch sous le capot de l'Isetta 250 et un cheval de plus sous celui de l'Isetta 300 – des moteurs économiques qui consomment 5,5 litres/100 km.

BMW Isetta 300 1956

BMW 502 3,2 Liter Super 1957

The 501 and the 502, the first large postwar BMW sedans, had the unfortunate distinction of being nicknamed the "Bavarian baroque angels", although the rounded lines of these magnificent powerful limousines were extremely well-proportioned and, in aerodynamic terms, created relatively little turbulence.

The BMW 502 entered the annals of automotive history with its status of being the first German eight-cylinder car of the postwar era. It was based on the strong box-section frame with the tubular cross beams of the 501, welded to the solid steel body. The main visual difference from the 501 was the large panoramic rear window.

As the most powerful model in the range, the 502 3.2 Liter Super developed 140 bhp thanks to two dual-throat downdraft carburetors. This enabled the heavyweight carriage to attain road speeds of at least 109.3 mph (175 kph) and accelerate from 0 to 62.5 mph (0 to 100 kph) in a reported 14.5 seconds.

Undeniably the V8 with its light alloy engine block and wet cylinder lines marked the beginning of a new era of engine technology. Interestingly, the transmission was not directly flanged on to the engine. This resulted in a shorter secondary propshaft to the rear axle. The steering column was also abbreviated and was activated via a bevel gear, which enabled a steering wheel ratio of 3.5 turns lock-to-lock; the turning circle equalled that of today's 7 series.

The low numbers of the 3.2 Liter Super sold, which cost 20,000 marks when it was introduced, might have been acceptable on the grounds of prestige, but they were uneconomical. When all of the 502 3.2-liter cars produced between 1955 and

1964 are added together, the total comes to 3840. Not exactly a profitable business.

On the other hand, BMW could at last show the world that its products were worthy of competing with Mercedes-Benz. As a direct result of the 502, a variety of convertible and coupé versions were all individually produced by the car body manufacturers Baur of Stuttgart and Autenrieth of Darmstadt.

Thanks to its workmanlike and professional standards of finish, the prestigious external appearance and the high levels of driving comfort, the "baroque angels" truly earned the rating of "heavenly".

Bayerische Barockengel", mit dieser volkstümlichen Bezeichnung müssen die ersten großen Nachkriegs-limousinen von BMW – die Typen 501 und 502 – leben, obwohl die Rundungen der stattlichen Karossen durchaus gut proportioniert sind und aerodynamisch gesehen relativ wenig Verwirbelungen bilden.

Als erster deutscher Achtzylinderwagen der Nachkriegszeit geht der BMW 502 in die Annalen der Automobilgeschichte ein. Er basiert auf dem äußerst stabilen Kastenrahmen mit Rohrquerträgern des 501, mit dem die Ganzstahlkarosserie verschweißt ist. Vom 501 unterscheidet ihn optisch die große Panoramaheckscheibe.

Als stärkstes Modell der Serie entwickelt der 502 3,2 Liter Super dank zweier Doppel-Fallstromvergaser 140 PS. Damit kommt das schwere Gefährt auf rund 175 Stundenkilometer.

Dem bayerischen V8 mit seinem Leichtmetallblock und nassen Zylinderlaufbüchsen muß attestiert werden, eine neue Ära der Motorentechnik eingeleitet zu haben. Interessanterweise ist das Getriebe nicht direkt an den Motor angeflanscht. Daraus resultiert eine kürzere Kardanwelle zur Hinterachse. Auch die Lenksäule fällt kurz aus und läuft über ein Kegelrad, das dreieinhalb Lenkraddrehungen ermöglicht. Der Wendekreis entspricht dem der heutigen 7er Serie.

Die Stückzahlen des 3,2 Liter Super, der bei seiner Einführung knapp 20.000 Mark kostet, liegen in einer Größenordnung, die aus Prestigegründen akzeptabel sein mag, sich aber wirtschaftlich nicht rechnet. Die Summe aller von 1955 bis 1964 gebauten 502 3,2-Liter-Wagen beläuft sich auf gerade mal 3840 Fahrzeuge – ein Zuschußgeschäft!

Andererseits hat BMW dokumentiert, daß man Mercedes-Benz etwas entgegenzusetzen hat. Diverse Cabriolet- und Coupé-Ausführungen der Karosseriehersteller Baur in Stuttgart und Autenrieth in Darmstadt rankten sich, individuell gefertigt, um den 502.

Für solide und saubere Verarbeitung, das repräsentative Äußere und den hohen Fahrkomfort verdienen die „Barockengel" jedenfalls das Prädikat „himmlisch gut"!

L'«ange baroque de Bavière» est le surnom populaire qu'arborent les premières grandes berlines d'après-guerre de BMW, les 501 et 502, bien que leurs imposantes carrosseries tout en longueur affichent de belles proportions et soient d'une assez grande finesse aérodynamique.

La BMW 502 entrera dans les annales de l'histoire de l'automobile en tant que première huit-cylindres allemande de l'après-guerre. Elle reprend le châssis à caissons, extrêmement solide, à tubes transversaux de la 501 sur lequel la carrosserie tout en acier est soudée. Elle se distingue de la 501 par la grande lunette arrière panoramique.

Modèle le plus puissant de la série, la 502 3,2 Liter Super développe 140 ch grâce à ses deux carburateurs double-corps inversés. Cela permet à la lourde voiture d'atteindre allègrement 175 km/h.

On doit reconnaître que le V8 bavarois à bloc en alliage léger et chemises humides inaugure une ère nouvelle dans la technique des moteurs. Détail intéressant, la boîte de vitesses n'est pas accolée directement au moteur. Cela se traduit par un arbre de transmission plus court jusqu'à l'essieu arrière. La colonne de direction, elle aussi, est courte et est reliée à une roue conique qui autorise trois tours et demi de butée à butée. Le diamètre de braquage est sensiblement identique à celui de la série 7 d'aujourd'hui.

Acceptable sur le plan du prestige, le nombre d'exemplaires produits de la 3,2 Liter Super, qui coûte près de 20 000 marks lors de sa commercialisation, est d'un ordre de grandeur qui en fait une voiture non rentable. Si l'on additionne toutes les 502

de 3,2 litres construites de 1955 à 1964, on obtient le nombre de 3840 voitures. Une production déficitaire, donc!

En revanche, BMW a administré la preuve qu'elle pouvait répliquer à Mercedes-Benz. Diverses versions cabriolet et coupé signées par les carrossiers Baur, à Stuttgart, et Autenrieth, à Darmstadt – fabriquées sur commande spéciale – ont complété la gamme 502.

Pour la qualité et la solidité de sa finition, son allure représentative et son grand confort de conduite, l'«ange baroque» mérite incontestablement le qualificatif de «conduite comme sur un nuage».

Every porter's dream, the doors of the BMW 502 open at a flick of the wrist. The interior, with its sofa-like rear seat and sumptuously upholstered front seats, conveys the comfortable atmosphere of a cosy living-room.

Davon träumt jeder Portier: Der Einstieg zu diesem BMW läßt sich mit einem Handgriff öffnen. Das Interieur mit der couchähnlichen Rückbank und den gut gepolsterten Vordersitzen vermittelt eine behagliche Wohnzimmeratmosphäre.

Le rêve de tout voiturier : une poignée suffit pour découvrir l'entrée de cette BMW. L'habitacle avec le véritable divan à l'arrière et les fauteuils avant aux épais coussins distille une atmosphère de salon douillet.

The top model of the large type 501 and 502 BMW sedans, popularly known as the "Bavarian baroque angels", was the 3.2 Liter Super. The production version of this heavyweight cruiser had a maximum speed of 109 mph (175 kph), while the tuned engine of the sedan illustrated here was capable of 125 mph (200 kph).

Unter den großen BMW-Limousinen der Typen 501 und 502, volkstümlich „bayerische Barockengel" genannt, ist der 3,2 Liter Super das Spitzenmodell. Die Serienversion des schweren Gefährts kommt auf 175 km/h. Die hier gezeigte Limousine mit „frisiertem" Triebwerk erreicht die 200-km/h-Marke.

Parmi les grandes limousines BMW des séries 501 et 502 que la gouaille populaire surnommait les «anges baroques de Bavière», la 3,2 Liter Super est la plus aboutie. La version de série de cette lourde voiture atteint 175 km/h. La limousine présentée ici, dont le moteur a été préparé, culmine à 200 km/h.

BMW 502 3,2 Liter Super 1957

The V8 engine, with its twin Zenith 32NDIX dual-throat downdraft carburetors, developed 140 bhp at 4800 rpm, while this version is capable of 160 bhp at 5600 rpm. Another non-standard feature of the 3.2 Liter Super is the Nardi sports steering wheel with its wooden rim.

Der V8-Motor leistet mit zwei Doppel-Fallstromvergasern der Marke Zenith 32NDIX 140 PS bei 4800 U/min, ist aber in dieser Version auf 160 PS bei 5600 U/min steigerungsfähig. Ebenfalls nicht Standard beim 3,2 Liter Super: das Nardi-Sportlenkrad mit Holzkranz.

Le moteur V8 à deux double carburateurs inversés, de marque Zenith 32NDIX, développe 140 ch à 4800 tr/mn, mais tolère, dans cette version, jusqu'à 160 ch à 5600 tr/mn. Le volant sport Nardi à couronne de bois n'est également pas le volant normal de la 3,2 Liter Super.

BMW 3200S Staatslimousine 1963

After the memorable financial crisis AGM in winter 1959, BMW was well and truly on the road to recovery. The small 700 was selling very well, admittedly with a narrow profit margin, and success seemed to be just round the corner with the new middle-class BMW 1500.

Accompanying that boost in confidence, the company's thoughts turned to the large V8 limousines, whose production had fallen to 661 in 1960. They were due for an update, particularly since the official specifications now prohibited rear doors which opened towards the front.

The BMW chief designer, Wilhelm Hofmeister, implemented his proposed modifications on the solid technical basis of the 160 bhp aluminium V8 3200S: an extended roof to provide more headroom in the rear compartment, modified rear door hinges, an enlarged boot, and an additional headlamp on the fenders. Rear seat passengers were provided with fresh air by a large steel sunroof, which would become more and more important. However, matters did not progress beyond this prototype, simply because BMW stopped manufacturing large cars.

This car was initially used as a status symbol in the company car fleet. But BMW was soon to enjoy the kudos associated with having built a car for a state official. Alfons Goppel, premier of Bavaria since 1962, occasionally borrowed this flagship. The aforementioned steel sunroof proved to be particularly valuable for state visitors, who only had to stand in front of the rear seats to enjoy the spectator applause.

The attempt to intruduce this BMW to the politicians in Bonn proved a failure. Dr Konrad Adenauer's chauffeur was faithful to Mercedes. This also proved to be the case with the second launch in September 1965 in which the 505 was supposed to be BMW's answer to the Adenauer Mercedes 300. No more than two prototypes of this BMW Pullman limousine were manufactured. One of them ended its days in the BMW museum with the 3200Si prototype, and the other had to endure the indignities of commerce, advertising French fries, before the honor she deserved was restored to her by a BMW vintage car collector.

BMW ist seit der denkwürdigen Hauptversammlung im Winter 1959 auf dem Wege der Sanierung. Der kleine 700er verkauft sich – wenngleich mit geringer Gewinnmarge – recht gut, und mit dem neuen Mittelklassemodell BMW 1500 winkt der Erfolg.

Solchermaßen den Rücken gestärkt, macht sich das Unternehmen Gedanken über die Fortführung der großen V8-Limousinen, deren Stückzahl 1960 auf 661 gesunken ist. Die Modernisierung ist fällig, zumal Änderungen der Zulassungsvorschriften hinten angeschlagene Fondtüren verbieten.

Auf der soliden technischen Basis des 3200S mit seinem V8-Leichtmetallmotor mit 160 PS verwirklicht BMW-Designchef Wilhelm Hofmeister seine Modifikationsvorschläge: Strecken des Daches, um mehr Kopfraum im Fond zu erzielen, geänderter Türanschlag hinten, Vergrößerung des Kofferraums und Zusatzscheinwerfer in den Kotflügeln. Für die Frischluft auf der Rücksitzbank sorgt ein überdimensionales Stahlschiebedach, das noch Bedeutung erlangt. Es bleibt bei diesem Prototyp, denn BMW stellt die Produktion der großen Wagen ein.

Zunächst dient dieser Wagen zu repräsentativen Zwecken im Werksfuhrpark. Doch dann kann sich BMW den Orden, eine Staatskarosse gebaut zu haben, ans Revers heften. Bayerns Ministerpräsident Alfons Goppel, seit 1962 Landesvater, leiht sich des öfteren dieses einmalige Flaggschiff aus. Besonders bei Staatsbesuchen kommt das bereits erwähnte Stahlschiebedach zur Geltung. Wer auch immer bejubelt werden möchte, kann vor den Rücksitzen stehend die Ovationen entgegennehmen.

Ein Versuch, diesen BMW auch in Bonn zum Einsatz zu bringen, scheitert. Dr. Konrad Adenauers Chauffeur bleibt

Mercedes treu. Das bestätigt sich auch beim zweiten Anlauf im September 1965, bei dem BMW mit dem 505 eine weitere Antwort auf den Mercedes 300 von Adenauer geben will. Es bleibt bei zwei Prototypen dieser Pullman-Limousine. Der eine wandert – wie auch der 3200Si Prototyp – ins BMW-Museum, der andere dient dem schnöden Mammon und wirbt für Pommes frites, ehe er von einem BMW-Oldtimer-Sammler den ihm gebührenden Ehrenplatz zugewiesen bekommt.

Depuis la mémorable assemblée générale en hiver 1959, BMW est de nouveau dans la voie de la guérison. La petite 700 se vend bien – même si elle ne génère pas des bénéfices extraordinaires – et le succès est garanti au nouveau modèle du segment intermédiaire, la BMW 1500.

Les reins de nouveau solides, l'entreprise réfléchit à la descendance des grosses limousines V8, qui n'ont plus été produites qu'à 661 exemplaires en 1960. Une modernisation s'impose, d'autant plus que des modifications des normes d'homologation bannissent désormais les portières arrière s'ouvrant dans le sens contraire de la marche.

Sur la base mécanique solide de la 3200S au V8 en alliage léger de 160 ch, le chef styliste de BMW, Wilhelm Hofmeister, concrétise ses propositions de modifications: allongement du toit pour augmenter l'espace disponible pour la tête à l'arrière, modification des charnières de portières arrière, agrandissement du coffre et phares supplémentaires dans les ailes. Un toit coulissant en acier de grande dimension, qui allait plus tard prendre de l'importance, ouvre de grands horizons aux passagers des fauteuils arrière. Ce prototype restera un modèle unique, car BMW suspend la production des grosses limousines.

Cette voiture sert d'abord de véhicule de représentation dans la flotte de l'usine. Mais BMW finit malgré tout par pouvoir accrocher à son revers une distinction, celle d'avoir construit une limousine officielle représentative. Le ministre-président bavarois Alfons Goppel, qui préside depuis 1962 aux destinées du Land, emprunte fréquemment ce navire amiral unique. En particulier lors des visites officielles, le toit coulissant susmentionné fait étalage de tous ses avantages. Quel que soit celui qui veut se faire acclamer, il lui suffit de se mettre debout devant les sièges arrière pour recevoir les ovations.

BMW tente aussi de prendre pied à Bonn dans le fief de la marque à l'étoile – en vain. Le chauffeur de Dr Konrad Adenauer est un fidèle de Mercedes. La seconde tentative de BMW, en septembre 1965, de répliquer à la 300 d'Adenauer avec la 505 se solde également par un échec. Il n'y aura que deux prototypes de cette limousine pullman. Comme la 3200Si prototype aussi, l'une passera sa retraite au Musée BMW et l'autre sera sacrifiée sur l'autel du mercantilisme puisqu'elle fera de la publicité pour une marque de frites avant de reprendre la place d'honneur qui lui revient chez un collectionneur de BMW.

The Staatslimousine, based on the model 3200 Super, featured a slightly raised roof providing plenty of headroom for back seat passengers, an elongated tail and a modified rear door catch. It never got beyond a prototype version which saw sporadic service as an official car of the Bavarian State Government.

Leicht erhöhtes Dach mit viel Platz für die Passagiere im Fond, verlängertes Heck und geänderter Türanschlag hinten – so die Realisation der Staatslimousine, basierend auf dem Modell 3200 Super. Es bleibt bei einem Prototypen, der sporadisch der bayerischen Landesregierung dient.

Un toit légèrement surélevé avec beaucoup d'espace pour les passagers de la banquette arrière, une poupe allongée et une modification des charnières de portières arrière – voici comment obtenir une limousine d'apparat sur plate-forme de 3200 Super. Il n'en existera que ce prototype qui sera utilisé de façon sporadique par le gouvernement régional de Bavière.

The large supplementary headlamps and the pontoon-shaped trunk are striking features. The 160 bhp version of the 3.2-liter V8 engine powers the BMW, taking it up to a top speed of 118 mph (190 kph). Beneath the wood-paneled dashboard we see a large loudspeaker tastefully tucked away – perhaps for playing the national anthems.

Auffällig sind die größeren Zusatzscheinwerfer und die Pontonform des Kofferraums. Die 160-PS-Version des 3,2-Liter-V8-Motors bringt das „Flaggschiff" in Schwung und auf 190 km/h. Gediegen ist das holzverkleidete Armaturenbrett unter dem ein großer Lautsprecher – wohl zum Abspielen der Nationalhymnen – montiert ist.

Différences frappantes: des phares d'appoint de plus grand diamètre et la forme en ponton du coffre. La version de 160 ch du V8 de 3,2 litres donne des ailes à ce navire amiral et lui permet d'atteindre 190 km/h. Luxueux: le tableau de bord en bois sous lequel se trouve un grand haut-parleur – sans aucun doute pour jouer les hymnes nationaux.

BMW 3200S Staatslimousine 1963 183

BMW 507 1956

Otto von Schlitz was hereditary marshal of the arch-diocese of Fulda in the year 1100. He was also the ancestor of the counts von Schlitz, known as von Goertz, a family who collected assorted honors for more than 800 years. Albrecht Count Goertz added a colorful image to the family history, for he had been resident in the US since 1936 and became a leading international design guru. For BMW's 507, first postwar pure sports car from BMW, creator Goertz built himself a monument.

Externally, the 507 would do honor to any Ferrari: an excitingly beautiful, harmoniously curved body line with an aggressive interpretation of the BMW kidney trademark styling cues, transformed into an appearance like the mouth of a shark. The aluminium skin of the car barely covers its technical elements, so there is nothing surplus to requirements. A small but unmistakable styling element is the grid with cooling slits and BMW symbol on the front wings. This only partly fulfils its task, since it barely covers the wheel.

A strong box frame, which offered excellent protection against side impacts, was the foundation of the Goertz-designed BMWs 507 and 503. The refined V8 engine with two Zenith dual-throat downdraft carburetors produces 150 bhp. Depending on the rear axle transmission ratio, this brought 122.5 to 137.5 mph (196 to 220 kph).

Space at the rear of the vehicle was constricted, containing a 29-gallon (110 liter) tank behind the seats. Probably for safety reasons, this large amount of fuel directly behind the backs of the passengers in the car was reduced to a 17-gallon (65 liter) tank surrounding the spare wheel.

"A car to set the pulse racing" was the contemporary comment in the influential magazine *ADAC-Motorwelt* (published by the German automobile club, ADAC). This referred primarily to the looks of the 507, but also covered the small difference between the unladen and the permitted maximum weight – a mere 375 lbs (170 kg). A well-built member of the affluent society with a little luggage was thus forced to find a "light" lady to take along for driving pleasure à deux in the 507.

Acceleration from 0 to 62.5 mph (0 to 100 kph), with a driver of normal weight at the wheel, of between 11 and 11.5 seconds is appropriate for a sports car of this caliber. Disc brakes, however, were only enjoyed by the last of the total 254 cars built.

The dream car of the 1950s – Elvis had a 507, too – and on the most wanted lists of classic car freaks today, the 507 could be supplied with a properly fitted hardtop. It could compare with the Mercedes 300 SL, for the latter was just a few marks cheaper in 1956.

A few details can be a nuisance in the 507. The distance of the steering column to the driver can be adjusted telescopically, but it can only be reduced: a blessing for people with short arms, but a nuisance for anyone of elongated build. The arrangement of various push buttons and levers on the dashboard is also far from ergonomic. A small windshield-wiped field and little possibility of adjusting the seats, are items one would put up with – if only one could count oneself among those happy people who can proudly call themselves BMW 507 owners.

Otto von Schlitz, um 1100 Erbmarschall des Hochstiftes Fulda, ist Urahn der Herren von Schlitz, genannt von Goertz, die 800 Jahre lang Meriten aller Art eingeheimst haben. Albrecht Graf Goertz fügt der Familiengeschichte eine farbige Metapher hinzu. Er lebt seit 1936 in den USA und ist Designer. Mit dem ersten Nachkriegssportwagen von BMW, dem 507, setzt sich Goertz ein Denkmal.

Das Äußere des 507 würde jedem Ferrari zu Ehre gereichen: eine aufregend schöne, harmonisch geschwungene Karosserie-linie mit einer aggressiv wirkenden Interpretation der BMW-Niere, die eher einem Haifischmaul gleicht. Die Aluminium-schale des Wagens bedeckt so gerade den technischen Kern. Es gibt also keinerlei unnötige Überhänge. Kleines, aber unver-wechselbares Stylingelement sind die Gitter mit Kühlschlitzen und BMW-Emblem in den vorderen Kotflügeln. Diese werden ihrer Bestimmung nur teilweise gerecht, da sie das Rad kaum abdecken.

Ein stabiler Kastenrahmen, der viel Schutz gegen seitlichen Aufprall bietet, ist das tragende Element der Goertz-Wagen 507 und 503. 150 PS leistet der kultivierte V8-Motor mit zwei Doppel-Fallstromvergasern von Zenith. Je nach Hinterachs-übersetzung resultieren daraus 196 bis 220 Stundenkilometer.

Recht eng geht es im Fahrzeugheck zu, das zunächst ein 110-Liter-Tank hinter den Sitzen füllt. Wohl aus Sicherheits-gründen wird die große Benzinmenge direkt im Rücken der Fahrzeuginsassen zugunsten eines 65-Liter-Tanks, der das Reserverad umschließt, reduziert.

„Ein Herzklopfen erzeugendes Fahrzeug" – dieses eher auf die Optik des 507 bezogene zeitgenössische Statement der

ADAC-Motorwelt gilt auch für die geringe Differenz zwischen Leer- und zulässigem Gesamtgewicht. Es sind lediglich 170 Kilo. Ein schwergewichtiger Wohlstandsbürger mit etwas Gepäck ist für das Fahrvergnügen zu zweit im 507 quasi gezwungen, eine zarte Frau mitzunehmen.

Die Beschleunigung von 0 auf 100 Stundenkilometer – mit einem normalgewichtigen Menschen am Steuer – zwischen 11 und 11,5 Sekunden, ist angemessen für einen Sportwagen dieses Kalibers. In den Genuß von Scheibenbremsen kommen allerdings nur die letzten der insgesamt 254 gebauten Wagen.

Das Traumauto der fünfziger Jahre (auch Elvis hatte einen 507) und der Oldtimer-Freaks von heute, lieferbar mit einem gelungenen und gut angepaßten Hardtop, muß den Vergleich mit dem Mercedes 300 SL nicht scheuen, denn dieser ist 1956 sogar ein paar Mark billiger.

Beim 507 stören lediglich einige Details. So läßt sich der Abstand des Lenkrads zum Fahrer teleskopisch verstellen, aber nur in einem Bereich, der Menschen mit kurzen Armen entgegenkommt, während Fahrer mit „großer Reichweite" keine optimale Sitzposition finden. Auch die Anordnung diverser Zugknöpfe und Hebel des Armaturenbretts ist nicht glücklich gelöst. Kleines Wischerfeld und wenig Sitzverstellmöglichkeiten sind freilich Dinge, an die man sich gewöhnen könnte, würde man zu den Glücklichen gehören, die sich stolz Besitzer eines BMW 507 nennen dürfen.

Otto von Schlitz, maréchal de l'abbatiale de Fulda vers 1100, est l'ancêtre des seigneurs von Schlitz, nommés von Goertz, qui ont accumulé des mérites en tout genre au cours de plus de huit siècles. Le comte Albrecht von Goertz ajoute à la saga de la famille une touche supplémentaire de couleur: depuis 1936, il vit aux Etats-Unis et est designer. Avec la première BMW de sport de l'après-guerre, la 507, son créateur von Goertz s'édifie son propre monument.

Les lignes de la 507 feraient honneur à toute Ferrari: une carrosserie d'une beauté excitante, aux galbes harmonieux et avec une interprétation agressive des naseaux de BMW, une proue qui ressemble plutôt à une gueule de requin. La coque en aluminium de la voiture couvre tout juste sa mécanique. Il n'y a donc pas de porte-à-faux superflus. Un élément de style, minuscule mais particulier, est la grille avec fentes de refroidissement et emblème BMW dans l'aile avant. Celle-ci ne mérite d'ailleurs guère son nom puisqu'elle couvre à peine la roue.

Un solide cadre à caissons qui offre une bonne protection contre les collisions latérales est l'épine dorsale des 507 et 503 de Goertz. Le velouté V8 à double carburateur inversé Zénith développe 150 ch. Selon le rapport de pont, la vitesse de pointe oscille entre 196 et 220 km/h.

L'espace est plutôt compté à l'arrière, où un réservoir de 110 litres occupe beaucoup de place derrière les sièges. Par sécurité, l'importante quantité d'essence logée directement dans le dos des passagers est réduite en faveur d'un réservoir de 65 litres qui encercle la roue de secours.

«Une voiture qui donne des battements de cœur»: ce constat de la revue *ADAC-Motorwelt* de cette époque, qui fait surtout allusion à l'esthétique de la 507, vaut aussi pour la faible différence entre le poids à vide et le poids total autorisé – seulement 170 kilos! Pour le plaisir de rouler à deux en 507, tout bon bourgeois aisé avec un tant soit peu d'embonpoint et quelques bagages est déjà contraint à emmener avec lui une femme «légère».

Les accélérations de 0 à 100 km/h (avec un conducteur de poids normal au volant) sont dignes d'une voiture de sport de ce calibre avec entre 11 et 11,5 secondes. Seules les dernières des 254 voitures construites au total bénéficieront toutefois de freins à disques.

La voiture de rêve des années 50 (Elvis Presley avait lui aussi une 507) et des fanas de voitures anciennes d'aujourd'hui, qui était livrable avec un hardtop esthétique et bien étanche, s'est toujours vue comparée à la Mercedes 300 SL qui, en 1956, coûte même quelques marks de moins.

Seul quelques détails sont gênants avec la 507. Si la colonne de direction télescopique est réglable, on ne peut que diminuer son éloignement par rapport au conducteur: ce qui est une bénédiction pour ceux qui ont de petits bras est un véritable problème pour ceux qui sont affublés d'«ailes d'albatros». De même, l'agencement des divers boutons et leviers sur le tableau de bord n'est pas parfaitement ergonomique. Un champ d'essuyage réduit du pare-brise et de faibles possibilités de réglage des sièges sont des choses auxquelles on peut s'habituer et s'habituerait – à condition de figurer parmi les heureux élus qui peuvent se prévaloir d'être les fiers propriétaires d'une BMW 507.

The BMW 507, with its harmoniously flowing lines and aggressive version of the BMW kidney grill, is one of Count Goertz's most beautiful designs.

Sicherlich ist der BMW 507 mit seiner harmonisch geschwungenen Karosserielinie einerseits und der aggressiv wirkenden Interpretation der BMW-Niere andererseits eines der schönsten Designs des Grafen Goertz.

La BMW 507 avec sa carrosserie aux galbes élégants d'une part, et l'interprétation quelque peu agressive des naseaux de BMW d'autre part, est sans aucun doute l'un des plus beaux dessins du comte von Goertz.

Hans Stuck Senior performed the role of works representative for the dream sports car of the 1950s – though Goertz himself preferred the hardtop version. Among the many stars who drove this exciting machine was King of Rock 'n Roll, Elvis Presley.

Für den Traum-Sportwagen der fünfziger Jahre – Goertz selbst favorisiert die Hardtop-Version – fungiert Hans Stuck senior als Werksrepräsentant. Zu den Stars, die das aufregende Auto fahren, gehört auch Elvis Presley.

Hans Stuck senior joue le rôle d'ambassadeur de l'usine pour la voiture de sport de rêve des années 50 – dont von Goertz lui-même préfère la version hard-top. Elvis Presley sera l'une des vedettes qui s'offriront cette voiture excitante.

The sports steering wheel later added to the 507 cockpit by the German Nardi importer did nothing to detract from the roadster feeling, while the 4.50 E x 16 steel rims also contributed to the motor sport appearance.

Das nachträglich dem 507-Cockpit zugestandene Sportlenkrad des deutschen Nardi-Importeurs stört das Roadster-Feeling keineswegs. Motorsport-Optik auch bei den 4,50 E x 16 Stahlfelgen.

Le volant sport de l'importateur allemand Nardi concédé ultérieurement au cockpit de la 507 ne porte en aucun cas préjudice à son style roadster. Les jantes en acier de 4,50 E x 16 font aussi flotter un parfum de compétition.

This classic V8 engine with its light alloy block and twin dual-throat downdraft carburetors developed 150 bhp, rising to 165 bhp in the US version. This allowed top speeds of up to 137.5 mph (220 kph), depending on the rear axle ratio.

150 PS, in der US-Ausführung sogar 165 PS, leistet der klassische V8-Motor mit einem Leichtmetallblock und zwei Doppel-Fallstromvergasern. Damit sind je nach Hinterachsübersetzung Geschwindigkeiten von bis zu 220 Stundenkilometern möglich.

Le V8 classique à bloc en alliage léger et deux carburateurs double-corps inversés développe 150 ch et même 165 ch dans la version américaine. Il permet de rouler, selon le rapport de pont, jusqu'à 220 km/h.

The side air vents of the 507, reintroduced forty years later on the Z3, are unmistakable. The box-section frame, barely concealed by the bodywork, is painted black to make the belt line appear lower-slung.

Unverkennbar – beim Z3 40 Jahre später wieder aufgegriffen – sind die seitlichen Luftschlitze des 507. Der von der Außenhaut nur knapp bedeckte Kastenrahmen ist schwarz lackiert, damit die Gürtellinie niedriger wirkt.

Inconfondables et reprises, 40 ans plus tard, pour la Z3 : les fentes d'aération latérales de la 507. Le châssis à caissons qu'habille à grand peine la carrosserie est peint de couleur noire pour que la ligne de ceinture semble plus basse.

BMW 503 1956

As well as the 507, Count Albrecht Goertz designed "an elegant luxury travel sports car from the stable of the large BMW eight-cylinder cars" (factory jargon). This design, outstanding owing to its long bonnet and the projecting BMW kidney grill at the front, made its debut as the 503 at the Frankfurt Motor Show during September 1955.

The engine, a light alloy V8 with wet cylinder liners and a separate transmission which was not directly bolted on to the engine, was taken from the 502. The same applied to the descriptive full protection frame. It was not until December 1957 that the transmission, which was situated under the front seats, was bolted to the engine. Then the gear change on the steering column was replaced with a lever on the transmission tunnel.

Convertible and coupé are designed for four passengers, always assuming that those in the rear seats are not too large. "The interior is designed for sporty but comfortable driving," as the 503 brochure put it. Today such coupés are described as having 2+2 seating, offering less accomodation in the rear than a 4-seater.

The 503 convertible folding mechanism was sophisticated. It was the first German automobile to have an electrically operated power-top; cranking the side windows up and down is also completed by electric motors.

The aluminium body, captivating with its neat, snugly-fitting manufacture, limited the weight of the car to 3303 lbs (1500 kg). At this kerb weight, 140 bhp manage to produce acceleration of 13 seconds from 0 to 62.5 mph (100 kph) and a top speed of 119 mph (190 kph). The petrol tank, situated behind the rear axle and with a space for the spare wheel, held 20 gallons (75 liters), sufficient for approximatey 280 miles (450 km).

Like the 507, the last of the 503s enjoyed disc brakes on the front wheels. Also like the 507, the price – 29,500 marks for the convertible in 1956 – was within range of the Mercedes 300 SL. Only just over 400 of these noble 503 beasts, which needed to be subsidized by BMW, found a buyer. The 503 filled a market niche which was too small to make it economically viable. Today's owners of these flamboyant rarities therefore have all the more reasons to rub their hands together in glee.

Neben dem 507 entwirft Albrecht Graf Goertz „einen eleganten Reisesportwagen aus der Reihe der großen BMW-Achtzylinder" (Werks-Jargon). Dieses Fahrzeug, das durch seine lange Motorhaube und die wulstig nach vorn stehenden BMW-Nieren auffällt, wird als 503 auf der Frankfurter Automobilausstellung im September 1955 vorgestellt.

Das Triebwerk, ein V8 aus Leichtmetall mit nassen Zylinderlaufbüchsen und ein separates, nicht an den Motor angeflanschtes Getriebe, werden aus dem 502 übernommen, ebenso der sogenannte Vollschutzrahmen. Erst im Dezember 1957 wird das unter den Vordersitzen liegende Getriebe mit dem Motor verblockt, die Lenkradschaltung von einem Hebel auf dem Kardantunnel abgelöst.

Cabriolet und Coupé sind für vier Passagiere ausgelegt, vorausgesetzt, daß die im Fond sitzenden von kleinerem Wuchs sind. „Der Innenraum ist auf sportliche wie bequeme Fahrweise ausgelegt", so der 503-Prospekt. Aus damaliger Sicht ist dieser Beschreibung nichts hinzuzufügen.

Bequem ist sicherlich der Faltmechanismus des Cabrioletverdecks, der erstmalig bei einem deutschen Auto elektrisch betätigt wird, und auch die Kurbelarbeit zum Heben und Senken der Seitenscheiben übernehmen Elektromotoren.

Dank der Aluminiumkarosserie, die durch ihre saubere und paßgenaue Fertigung besticht, kann das Wagengewicht auf 1500 Kilo beschränkt werden. Bei diesem Gewicht erreichen die 140 PS eine Beschleunigung von 0 auf 100 Stundenkilometer in 13 Sekunden und eine Höchstgeschwindigkeit von 190 Stundenkilometern. Der hinter der Hinterachse liegende und mit einer Ausbuchtung für das Reserverad versehene

Kraftstofftank faßt 75 Liter. Das genügt für eine Strecke von rund 450 Kilometern.

Wie beim 507 kommen die letzten 503 noch in den Genuß von Scheibenbremsen an den Vorderrädern. Und wie beim 507 rangiert der Preis – 29.500 Mark für das Cabriolet 1956 – im Bereich dessen, was man für einen Mercedes 300 SL ausgeben muß. Nur etwas mehr als 400 dieser Edelstücke, bei denen BMW sogar noch ein paar Mark zuschießen muß, finden ihre Käufer. Der 503 füllt eine Marktnische, die zu klein für eine wirtschaftlich rentable Fertigung ist. Umso mehr reiben sich heute die Besitzer dieser extravaganten Rarität die Hände.

Outre la 507, le comte Albrecht von Goertz dessine «une élégante voiture de sport de voyage pour la gamme des grosses BMW huit-cylindres» (dans le jargon de l'usine). Cette voiture qui surprend par son long capot moteur et les proéminents naseaux BMW est présentée sous le nom de 503 au Salon de l'Automobile de Francfort en septembre 1955.

Le moteur, un V8 en alliage léger à chemises humides et avec boîte de vitesses séparée non accolée au bloc, est repris de la 502, tout comme le cadre à protection intégrale. Il faudra attendre décembre 1957 pour que la boîte de vitesses placée sous le siège avant rejoigne le moteur et que le sélecteur au volant soit remplacé par un levier sur le tunnel de transmission.

Le cabriolet et le coupé sont prévus pour quatre passagers à condition que ceux de l'arrière soient de petite taille. «L'habitacle est conçu pour un style de conduite sportif et décontracté», peut-on lire dans le prospectus de la 503. Aucun commentaire ne doit être ajouté à ce constat de cette époque.

La commande de capote qui, pour la première fois sur une voiture allemande, est électrique est confortable et le déplacement des vitres latérales est aussi assuré par des moteurs électriques.

Grâce à la carrosserie en aluminium qui séduit par sa finition et l'exactitude de son montage, le poids de la voiture peut être limité à 1500 kg. Avec un tel poids, les 140 ch permettent des accélérations de 0 à 100 km/h en 13 secondes et une vitesse de pointe de 190 km/h. Le réservoir d'essence placé derrière l'essieu arrière avec une auge pour la roue de secours a une capacité de 75 litres – assez pour une autonomie d'environ 450 km.

Comme pour la 507, la dernière 503 bénéficie, elle aussi, de freins à disques sur les roues avant. Et, comme pour la 507, le prix – 29 500 marks pour le cabriolet de 1956 – concurrence celui de la Mercedes 300 SL. Un peu plus de 400 exemplaires de ces superbes voitures, qui coûtent même quelques marks à BMW, trouvent preneurs. La 503 comble un créneau qui est trop petit pour être rentable. Aujourd'hui, les propriétaires de cette extravagante rareté s'en frottent d'autant plus les mains.

BMW 503 1956

Designed as a "touring sports car" by the designer and long-time resident of New York, Albrecht Count Goertz, the BMW 503 was ready to go on sale in May 1956. Only 273 coupés and 139 convertibles were sold in four years.

Als „Reisesportwagen" von dem lange Zeit in New York lebenden Designer Albrecht Graf Goertz entworfen, wird der BMW 503 ab Mai 1956 ausgeliefert. Nur 273 Coupés und 139 Cabriolets werden in vier Jahren gebaut.

Conçue en tant que voiture de sport et de grand tourisme par le designer allemand le comte Albrecht von Goertz, qui a longtemps vécu à New York, la BMW 503 est commercialisée en mai 1956. 273 coupés et 139 cabriolets seulement seront conçus en quatre ans.

BMW 503 1956

With the powerfully forward-jutting BMW kidneys and a long hood, the 503's aluminum bodywork was an impressive piece of work. It was based on an extremely stable box frame with tubular cross members.

Wuchtig nach vorn stehende BMW-Nieren und eine lange Motorhaube: Die Aluminiumkarosserie des 503 ist imposant. Sie ruht auf einem äußerst stabilen Kastenrahmen mit Rohrquerträgern.

Avec les naseaux BMW qui semblent jaillir du capot moteur interminable, la carrosserie en aluminium de la 503 est imposante. Elle repose sur un châssis à caissons à poutres transversales creuses extrêmement solide.

The convertible had a top speed of 118 mph (190 kph). Its top was electrically operated -
a first among German cars. With a showroom price of just under 30,000 marks in 1956,
it was, however, the preserve of an elite class of purchaser.

Das Cabriolet, dessen Verdeck elektrisch betätigt werden kann - übrigens erstmals bei
einem deutschen Auto -, erreicht 190 Stundenkilometer. Es ist aber 1956 mit einem
Neupreis von knapp 30.000 Mark einer elitären Käuferschicht vorbehalten.

Le cabriolet, dont la capote peut recevoir une commande électrique- ce qui est une
première sur une voiture allemande -, atteint 190 km/h. Mais, avec un prix de près de
30000 marks en 1956, il ne sera à la portée que d'une clientèle élitaire.

There was room for larger pieces of luggage, too, in the rear of the 503. The spare wheel and petrol tank were "harmoniously" positioned under the floor of the trunk. The tank had been specially shaped to accommodate the wheel.

Auch größere Gepäckstücke finden im Heck des 503 Platz. Unter dem Kofferraumboden liegen das Reserverad und der Tank „einträchtig" nebeneinander. Der Tank hat eigens für den Reifen eine Aussparung.

Le coffre de la 503 ne craint pas les bagages encombrants. Sous son plancher se trouvent, en bonne compagnie, la roue de secours et le réservoir. Le réservoir lui-même comporte un évidement pour le pneu.

The distinctive panels in which the headlights are set harmonized stylistically with the
kidney shape: an image which shows that Goertz' design was fully in tune with
contemporary taste.

Die markanten Blenden der Scheinwerfereinfassungen harmonieren stilistisch mit der
Nieren-Form: ein Konterfei, mit dem Goertz voll und ganz den Zeitgeschmack trifft.

Les enjoliveurs marquants des phares sont, esthétiquement, en parfaite harmonie avec la
forme des naseaux : un profil avec lequel Goertz touche la fibre sensible de ses
contemporains.

BMW 503 1956

In order to ensure that the round instruments could be seen better, the four spokes of the steering wheel had to move out of the way. Electrically operated windows and adjustable backrests meant additional controls. The V8 engine with two dual-throat downdraft carburetors produced 140 bhp.

Zur besseren visuellen Erfassung der Rundinstrumente müssen die vier Lenkradspeichen zur Seite weichen. Ein elektrischer Fensterheber und die Sitzlehnenverstellung ergänzen die Vielfalt der Bedienelemente. Der V8 mit zwei Doppel-Fallstrom-vergasern produziert 140 PS.

Il a fallu déplacer sur le côté les quatre branches du volant pour mieux placer les cadrans circulaires dans le champ de vision du conducteur. Des lève-vitres électriques et des dossiers de siège réglables complètent les multiples manettes de commande. Le moteur V8 à deux carburateurs double-corps inversés développe 140 ch.

Wolfgang Denzel, a technically-gifted man who was also a competent racing driver, was hungry for success as BMW's general importer for Austria. He dreamt of a really small, rear-engined BMW car for the middle class. What was so beautiful about the BMW 600 anyway? It was nothing more than a four-seater Isetta.

Denzel submitted his ideas to BMW in November 1957. The ideas received approval from the factory and, since the draft was conscientiously crafted, Denzel was asked that he should create a prototype with the Turin designer Michelotti. A few months later, the beautiful BMW 700 materialized. At the 1959 Frankfurt Motor Show, the 700 made its debut either as the coupé or a two-door sedan.

It caused a sensation and volume production was implemented immediately. The sedan, a value-for-money car designed for use by anyone, achieved a sales total which surpassed 60,000 units in the period 1959–62. Out of almost 30,000 coupés (1959–64), there were 9436 sport and CS versions alone.

The 700 coupé participated in motor racing on an impressively widespread basis. In 1959/60 alone, it had the distinction of winning 67 victories and being second 41 times. Drivers such as Hans Stuck senior (German champion at the age of 60) managed to keep competitors with larger engines at bay with the coupé. A further tuned 700 RS offered 70 bhp and a 125 mph (200 kph) top speed which put an end to the Fiat Abarth's domination of the winning positions in the smallest capacity classes. No less than 19 of these BMW motor racing open-top designs took victories, mainly at the great hill-climbing events such as Trento-Bondone, Gaisberg, Schauinsland and Roßfeld.

Meanwhile the sedan received a larger interior, achieved by adding 6.3 inches (16 cm) to the wheelbase. BMW extended the rear to accommodate a four-cylinder engine, intended to vault the 700 (with an LS badge suffix) further into the middle class. The overall addition of 13 inches (32 cm) was of particular benefit to the rear passengers, because the planned change of engine was abandoned, resulting in a cavity between the boxer engine and rear bulkhead. A "workshop-friendly" layout improved access.

However, the proven two-cylinder's power was increased from 30 to 32 bhp in February 1963, although this had little impact on the car's driving performance. The trunk in the nose of the car was divided between the spare wheel – an additional crumple zone behind the bumper – and a 7.9-gallon (30 liter) tank, leaving just enough room for one large suitcase.

The combination of a pleasing interior – an effective dashboard layout with a 2-spoke steering wheel offering a good grip, a sporty gearshift and quality seats – and a tasteful exterior made this car a hit with customers. Great roadholding, 75 mph (120 kph) top speed and reasonable fuel consumption (31.5 miles per gallon of Super/7.5 liters per 100 km) were all contributing factors to its sales success. In three years some 92,416 LS sedans, in addition to 1730 LS coupés, were built.

Wolfgang Denzel – technisch begabt, als Rennfahrer ganz passabel und als BMW-Generalimporteur für Österreich erfolgshungrig – träumt von einem richtigen kleinen BMW-Mittelklassewagen mit Heckmotor. Was ist denn schon der BMW 600? Doch nicht mehr als eine viersitzige Isetta!

Denzel bringt seine eigenen Vorstellungen zu Papier und präsentiert diese im November 1957 im Werk. Den Münchnern ist es recht, und da die Entwürfe „Hand und Fuß" haben, schlagen sie Denzel vor, zusammen mit dem Turiner Designer Michelotti einen Prototypen auf die Räder zu stellen. Ein bildhübscher Wagen, der BMW 700, entsteht innerhalb weniger Monate. Auf der Frankfurter Automobilausstellung 1959 feiert der 700 als Coupé und zweitürige Limousine Premiere.

Die Resonanz ist gewaltig, und die Serienproduktion läuft sofort an. Die Limousine, ein preiswertes Gefährt für jedermann, wird von 1959 bis 1962 in mehr als 60.000 Einheiten verkauft. Auf knapp 30.000 Coupés (1959–64) kommen allein 9436 Sport- und CS-Ausführungen. Motorsport auf breiter Ebene wird eindrucksvoll praktiziert. Allein 1959/60 feiert das Coupé 67 Siege und 41 zweite Plätze. Fahrer wie Hans Stuck – mit 60 Jahren noch deutscher Meister – hängen mit dem Coupé sogar hubraumstärkere Konkurrenten ab, und mit dem Erscheinen des 700 RS, der mit 70 PS eine Spitzengeschwindigkeit von 200 Stundenkilometern erreicht, bricht BMW in die Domäne der siegesgewohnten Fiat Abarth ein. Gleich 19 dieser BMW-Rennsport-Spider werden auf die Siegerstraßen, vornehmlich bei großen Bergpreisen wie Trento-Bondone, Gaisberg, Schauinsland und Roßfeld, geschickt.

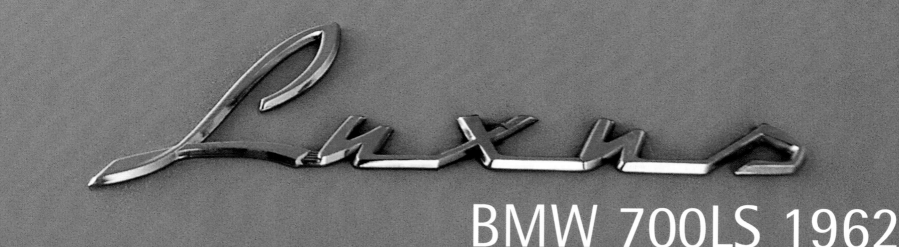

BMW 700LS 1962

Mehr Innenraum durch 16 Zentimeter längeren Radstand sowie ein verlängertes Heck zur Aufnahme eines Vierzylindertriebwerks sollen den 700 mit dem Zusatz „LS" in die Mittelklasse heben. Die Gesamtverlängerung von 32 Zentimetern kommt vornehmlich den Fondpassagieren zugute, denn die vorgesehene Ummotorisierung erweist sich als Flop, so daß zwischen Boxermotor und Heckschürze ein Hohlraum entsteht. „Werkstattfreundlich" nennt man das.

Immerhin wird im Februar 1963 die Potenz des Zweizylinders von 30 auf 32 PS angehoben, was sich in den Fahrleistungen allerdings kaum bemerkbar macht. Den Kofferraum im Wagenbug teilen sich das Reserverad – als zusätzliche Knautschzone hinter dem Stoßfänger –, ein 30-Liter-Tank und obendrauf das restliche Volumen für einen großen Koffer.

Ein gefälliges Interieur – ein übersichtliches Armaturenbrett mit griffigem Zweispeichenlenkrad, sportlichem Schaltknüppel und guten Sitzen – sowie das ansprechende Äußere treffen den Geschmack der Kunden. Die ordentliche Straßenlage, eine Spitzengeschwindigkeit von 120 Stundenkilometern und ein vernünftiger Verbrauch (7,5 Liter Super) tragen zum Verkaufserfolg bei. In drei Jahren werden 92.416 LS-Limousinen gebaut, zu denen sich noch 1730 LS-Coupés gesellen.

Wolfgang Denzel, génie de la mécanique, bon pilote de course et, en tant qu'importateur exclusif de BMW pour l'Autriche, affamé de succès, rêve d'une vraie petite BMW du segment intermédiaire à moteur arrière. Qu'est, en effet, la BMW 600 – si ce n'est une espèce d'Isetta à quatre places.

Denzel réalise quelques croquis de son concept qu'il présente en novembre 1957 à l'usine. Celui-ci est du goût des Munichois et, comme ses plans semblent prometteurs, ils proposent à Denzel de réaliser un prototype conjointement avec le styliste turinois Michelotti. Une très jolie petite voiture, la BMW 700, naît quelques mois plus tard. Elle fêtera sa première en tant que coupé et berline à deux portes au Salon de l'Automobile de Francfort de 1959.

Le succès est immense et la production en série débute immédiatement. La berline, un engin à la portée de chacun, est produite à plus de 60 000 exemplaires de 1959 à 1962. Sur les près de 30 000 coupés (1959-1964), pas moins de 9436 sont des versions sport et CS. Elles démocratisent en quelque sorte la compétition automobile. Rien qu'en 1959/1960, le coupé engrange 67 victoires et 41 deuxièmes places. Des pilotes comme Hans Stuck (encore champion d'Allemagne à 60 ans) surclassent même des concurrentes de plus forte cylindrée avec le coupé qui bat en brèche les Fiat Abarth pourtant abonnées à la victoire lorsqu'apparaît la 700 RS (70 ch, 200 km/h de vitesse de pointe). Pas moins de 19 de ces Spider de compétition de BMW coiffent des couronnes de laurier, notamment lors des Grands Prix de la montagne comme Trento-Bondone, Gaisberg, Schauinsland et Roßfeld.

Un empattement allongé de 16 cm ainsi qu'une poupe de plus grande longueur pour recevoir un moteur à quatre cylindres ont un objectif : faire rejoindre le segment intermédiaire à la 700 désormais qualifiée de «LS». Cet allongement total de 32 cm bénéficie en première ligne aux passagers de la banquette arrière, car le changement de motorisation est un échec. Le boxer original est si petit qu'il n'emplit même pas le compartiment moteur et évite ainsi des contorsions aux mécaniciens lors des révisions.

En février 1963, le deux-cylindres voit sa puissance passer de 30 à 32 ch, ce qui ne change toutefois pratiquement rien aux performances. La roue de secours – en tant que zone de déformation programmée supplémentaire derrière le pare-chocs –, un réservoir de 30 litres et assez d'espace pour une grosse valise se partagent le volume du coffre à l'avant.

Un habitacle séduisant (avec un tableau de bord bien agencé et un volant à deux branches, un levier de changement de vitesses sportif au centre et de bons sièges) ainsi que des lignes très réussies sont tout à fait du goût de la clientèle. Une tenue de route correcte, une vitesse de pointe de 120 km/h et une consommation raisonnable (7,5 litres de super aux 100 km) contribuent à son succès commercial. En trois ans, 92 416 berlines LS sont construites, auxquelles s'ajoutent encore 1730 coupés LS.

Encouraged by the success of the BMW 700, the Munich factory built the LS, an extra 13 inches (32 cm) in length, from 1962 onwards. This luxury was of particular benefit to the rear passengers and the trunk size.

Ermutigt durch den Erfolg des BMW 700 baut das Münchener Werk ab 1962 den 32 Zentimeter längeren LS. Dieser „Luxus" kommt besonders den Fondpassagieren und dem Kofferraumvolumen zugute.

Encouragée par le succès remporté par la BMW 700, l'usine de Munich construit, à partir de 1962, la LS à l'empattement allongé de 32 cm. Ce luxe bénéficie en particulier aux passagers de la banquette arrière et au volume du coffre.

The LS – a competitor of the DKW Junior de luxe – filled BMW's coffers: 92,416 of
these small sedans were sold.

Mit dem LS – einem Konkurrenten des DKW Junior de luxe – füllt der Münchener
Konzern durch den Verkauf von 92.416 dieser kleinen Limousinen seine Kassen.

Avec la LS – qui fait concurrence à la DKW Junior de luxe – le groupe munichois
remplit son tiroir-caisse en vendant 92 416 exemplaires de ces petites berlines.

BMW 700LS 1962   209

Sober and functional: the cockpit of the 700LS with its two large round instruments – speedo and clock. The two-cylinder boxer engine with one downdraft carburetor left a lot of space in the rear. The 30 bhp unit was given an additional 2 bhp of performance in 1963.

Nüchtern und funktionell ist das Cockpit des 700LS mit zwei großen Rundinstrumenten – Tacho und Uhr. Der Zweizylinder-Boxermotor mit einem Fallstromvergaser läßt im Heck viel Platz. 1963 erhält der 30-PS-Triebling einen Leistungszuwachs von 2PS.

Sobre et fonctionnel: le cockpit de la 700LS avec ses deux grands instruments circulaires – le tachymètre et la montre. Le bicylindre à plat à carburateur inversé laisse beaucoup d'espace à l'arrière. En 1963, le petit moteur de 30 ch voit sa puissance augmenter de 2 ch.

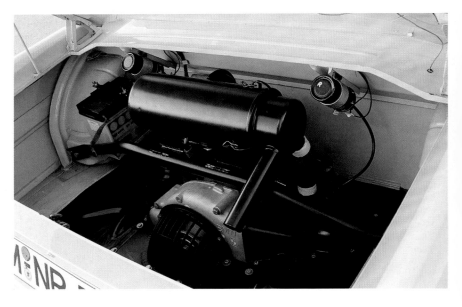

When the attractive BMW 700 coupé and sedan were shown at the Frankfurt Motor Show in the autumn of 1959, the response was tremendous. BMW received sufficient advance orders for two whole production years.

Bei der Präsentation des attraktiven BMW 700 Coupé samt Limousine auf der Frankfurter Automobilausstellung im Herbst 1959 ist die Resonanz gewaltig. BMW erhält Vorbestellungen für zwei komplette Produktionsjahre.

Lors de la présentation de l'attrayante BMW 700 Coupé aux côtés de la berline, au Salon de l'Automobile de Francfort de l'automne 1959, le succès est sensationnel. BMW reçoit des commandes anticipées pour deux années complètes de production.

BMW 700 Coupé 1959

The spare wheel positioned behind the rounded nose - like a sort of bumper - and the fuel tank left little luggage space in the trunk of this rear-engined car. The small coupé scored undreamed-of success as the basic vehicle for motor sport, a success to which Hans Stuck, at the age of 60, contributed a German championship title.

Das hinter dem runden Bug – quasi als Puffer – stehende Reserverad und der Tank lassen dem Hecktriebler nur wenig Gepäckraum. Als Basisfahrzeug für den Motorsport erntet das kleine Coupé ungeahnte Erfolge, zu denen Hans Stuck im Alter von 60 Jahren einen deutschen Meistertitel beisteuert.

La roue de secours placée à la verticale derrière la proue arrondie – en espèce de butoir – et le réservoir ne laissent que peu de place pour les bagages dans le coffre de cette voiture à moteur arrière. Le petit coupé remportera des succès inouïs en compétition automobile, notamment avec Hans Stuck qui y contribuera avec un titre de champion d'Allemagne... à l'âge de 60 ans.

BMW 3200CS 1962

All of the designs coming from the pen of motorcar designer Nuccio Bertone were distinguished by time-less and therefore understated elegance. What was so attractive about the Maestro's work was his ability to unite clear lines and technical practicalities. The people in Munich believed that Bertone's reputation enhanced BMW's profile, as would a four-seater coupé, due to replace the slow-selling 503.

When the Italian creation made its debut at the Frankfurt Motor Show in September 1961, it was met with universal acclaim. The sturdiness of the car body was unmistakable and provided yet another example of Bertone's quality workmanship. The cars from Turin started arriving via Munich for sale at the start of 1962.

The fresh wind blowing through the nearby Alps seemed to lend the BMW V8 even more power. With a compression of 9:1, the light alloy engine equipped with two dual-throat downdraft carburetors delivered 160 bhp at 5600 rpm. Despite a corresponding increase in the torque figures, the specific fuel consumption values were more favorable than those of the 140 bhp 3200L. That meant 15 miles per gallon (16 liters per 100 km) of Super grade gas fuel consumption in normal use.

The combination of good taste and practicality proved to be just as successful in Bertone's cabin as it had been in the exterior. Large doors and the absence of a B-pillar facilitated access to the rear compartment. In addition to the steering column gear shift – with the scarcely audible meshing of gear teeth underneath the front seats – there was a stick shift for the propshaft center tunnel.

Like the 507, the frame consisted of a box section with tubular cross beams. This provided a strong foundation for Bertone's attractive solid steel body design. The chassis was also identical to the one used in the 507, following the American adage, "If it ain't broke, don't fix it."

Public roads were not graced with many production examples of the 3200CS. Only 602 coupés were made during the four years of its production run. Only one convertible variant was manufactured. It was intended for the man who wished to make BMW profitable once more – Dr Herbert Quandt, BMW's major shareholder.

Zeitlose und daher eher unauffällige Eleganz schwingt bei allen Entwürfen des Autodesigners Nuccio Bertone mit. Der Maestro besticht durch die klare Linienführung seiner Entwürfe, die sich stets an der Technik orientieren. Bertones Renommee, so findet man in München, steht BMW gut zu Gesicht, und ein viersitziges Coupé, das den schwer verkäuflichen 503 ablösen soll, ebenfalls.

Als die italienische Kreation im September 1961 auf der Frankfurter Automobilausstellung debütiert, erntet sie einhelliges Lob. Die Karosserie strahlt Solidität aus und unterstreicht Bertones Fertigungsqualität. Anfang 1962 treffen die ersten Wagen aus Turin in München ein.

Mit dem frischen Wind, der da über die Alpen weht, wird dem V8-Triebwerk noch mehr Kraft eingehaucht. Mit einer Verdichtung von 9:1 liefert der mit zwei Doppel-Fallstromvergasern bestückte Leichtmetallmotor 160 PS bei 5600 Umdrehungen ab. Trotz Anhebung der Drehmomentkurve fallen die spezifischen Verbrauchswerte günstiger aus als beim 140-PS-Motor des 3200L, was den Benzinverbrauch von 16 Litern Super auf 100 Kilometern Normalbetrieb jedoch nicht tangiert.

Gediegen und funktionell wie das Äußere präsentiert Bertone den Innenbereich. Große Türen und der Verzicht auf eine B-Säule erleichtern den Zutritt zum Fond. Neben der Lenkradschaltung – die Getriebezähne mahlen kaum hörbar unter den Vordersitzen – wird auch ein Schalthebel auf dem Kardantunnel angeboten.

Wie beim 507 besteht der Rahmen aus einem Kasten mit Rohrquerträgern – eine äußerst stabile Basis, über die Bertone

seine hübsche Ganzstahlkarosserie gestülpt hat. Auch das Fahrwerk ist vom 507. Bewährtes soll man nicht neu erfinden!

Was die Produktionszahlen anbelangt, gehört auch der 3200CS zu den seltenen Erscheinungen im Straßenbild. Nur 602 Coupés entstehen in vier Jahren Bauzeit. Die Produktion einer Cabrioletvariante beschränkt sich auf ein Unikat für den Mann, der BMW wieder schwarze Zahlen bescheren will: BMW-Großaktionär Dr. Herbert Quandt.

Une élégance intemporelle et, donc, plutôt discrète, marque de son sceau toutes les créations du couturier automobile Nuccio Bertone. Le maestro est célèbre pour son coup de crayon incisif qui s'oriente toujours sur la mécanique. La renommée de Bertone – estime-t-on à Munich – siérait fort bien à BMW, de même qu'un coupé à quatre places qui remplacerait la 503 difficile à vendre.

Lorsque la création italienne fait ses débuts en septembre 1961, au Salon de l'Automobile de Francfort, elle remporte des éloges sans partage. La carrosserie dégage une impression de grande solidité et témoigne de la qualité de finition qui a fait la réputation de Bertone. Début 1962, les premières voitures de Turin arrivent à Munich.

Dans le sillage de la brise de fraîcheur qui franchit les Alpes, le moteur V8 gagne lui aussi en puissance. Avec un taux de compression de 9:1, le moteur en alliage léger à deux carburateurs double-corps inversés développe 160 ch à 5600 tr/mn. Malgré l'amélioration de la courbe de couple, les taux de consommation spécifiques sont meilleurs que ceux de la 3200L avec 140 ch, ce qui n'affecte cependant en rien le tribut à payer à la pompe avec 16 litres de super aux 100 km en conduite normale.

Bertone a réalisé un habitacle aussi luxueux et fonctionnel que la carrosserie elle-même. De grandes portières et l'absence de pied central facilitent l'accès à l'arrière. Outre le changement de vitesses au volant – presque silencieuse, la boîte se trouve sous les sièges avant – on peut aussi opter pour un levier sur le tunnel de transmission.

Comme pour la 507, le châssis consiste en une échelle avec poutres transversales – une plate-forme d'une extrême solidité que Bertone a coiffée de sa jolie carrosserie tout acier. Les trains roulants, eux aussi, sont ceux de la 507. Pourquoi changer une équipe qui gagne?

Les chiffres de production font aussi de la 3200CS un modèle que l'on a rarement l'occasion de croiser sur sa route. 602 coupés seulement seront construits en quatre ans. La production de cabriolets se limite à un spécimen unique destiné à l'homme qui veut absolument de nouveau faire sortir BMW du rouge : Dr Herbert Quandt, l'actionnaire majoritaire de BMW.

Nuccio Bertone designed a four-seater coupé, which was given the designation BMW 3200CS in accordance with its engine size, as a successor to the 503. This elegant car did not achieve high sales figures either.

Als Nachfolgemodell des 503 entwirft Nuccio Bertone ein viersitziges Coupé, das entsprechend seinem Hubraum als BMW 3200CS bezeichnet wird. Auch diesem eleganten Wagen sind keine hohen Verkaufszahlen beschieden.

Pour succéder à la 503, Nuccio Bertone dessine un coupé à quatre places baptisé, en raison de sa cylindrée, BMW 3200CS. Cette élégante voiture ne remportera pas, elle non plus, un très grand succès commercial.

BMW 3200CS 1962

For the first time, the company emblem appeared on the C-pillar of a BMW. It represented the circular area of a propeller in the Bavarian state colors. The V8 engine had achieved 160 bhp by 1962. Bertone's all-steel BMW creation – with its lines typical of the maestro – was given large doors and retractable side windows but did not have the B-pillar which can be a nuisance when getting into a car. The attractive coupé had a top speed of 125 mph (200 kph).

Erstmals taucht das Firmenemblem auf – an der C-Säule eines BMW. Es stellt eine Propellerkreis-fläche in den bayerischen Landesfarben dar. Der V8 ist 1962 bei 160 PS angelangt. Bertones BMW-Kreation aus Ganzstahl – in der Linienführung typisch für den Maestro – verfügt über große Türen und versenkbare Seitenscheiben und verzichtet auf die beim Einsteigen störende B-Säule. 200 Stundenkilometer erreicht das schmucke Coupé.

L'emblème de la marque figure pour la première fois sur le montant de toit postérieur d'une BMW. Il représente une hélice en rotation avec les couleurs de la Bavière. En 1962, le V8 délivre 160 ch. La carrosserie tout acier dessinée par Bertone pour la BMW – dont les lignes trahissent la patte du maestro – comporte de grandes portières et des vitres latérales descendantes sans montant de toit central entravant l'accès à la voiture. Cet élégant coupé tutoie les 200 km/h.

BMW 1500 1962

Many motorsists awaited – the BMW drivers and owners amongst them with true longing – for BMW to build a middle-class car. Suddenly it appeared at the Frankfurt Motor Show in September 1961, as if born of the measures to return the company to profitability, measures which had been introduced so recently. The show BMW was still a prototype – one whose badge number, 1500, reflected the size of the four-cylinder engine in cubic centimeters. It was a plain type designation for a car which BMW described as a "new class".

The public and motoring press immediately placed the newcomer from Bavaria on a pedestal, and it rode back to the factory for fine-tuning on a wave of enthusiasm. It was above all the successful overall technical concept as well as its smart appearance which turned the car into a true alternative to the mid-range cars from American-owned multi-nationals Ford and Opel (GM), based at Cologne and Rüsselsheim.

The engine, initially rated at 75 bhp, had 80 bhp coaxed out of it at 5500 rpm by the time volume production started in October 1962. The small trick here was to raise the compression ratio from 8.2 to 8.8.

"Flexibility at lower engine speeds, phenomenal power at the higher ones," was the promise made by the BMW brochure. They had moved its performance – 94 mph (150 kph) and acceleration from 0 to 62.5 mph (0 to 100 kph) in 16.8 seconds – right into the sports car bracket.

While the Solex downdraft carburetors were changed for a more efficient version from the same manufacturer in 1964, the new transmission with Porsche locking synchronization was

a "revelation". One which made the floor gear shift a pleasure to operate.

The beautifully shaped four-door monocoque steel body was based on a chassis which predicted the 4-wheel future at BMW. It was equipped with McPherson struts and coil springs at the front as well as trailing arms at the back.

Unfortunately the 1500, which was otherwise very solidly built, was prone to occasional technical hiccups. These kind of mechanical gremlins were eliminated in its successor, the BMW 1600.

The bare look behind the wheel – three circular instruments and the space for the radio – was no obstacle to sales. At a purchase price of something less than 9500 marks, the demand was considerably higher than the daily production output of 50 cars. By increasing capacity in 1963, a total of 23,807 cars were produced before the model was discontinued in 1964. By that time, the 1600 was already starting production, and a 1.8-liter model was selling well.

Viele Autofahrer – die markentreuen unter ihnen sogar sehnsüchtig – haben den Bau eines Mittelklassewagens von BMW erwartet. Auf der Frankfurter Automobilausstellung im September 1961 steht er plötzlich da, als sei der jüngst erfolgten Sanierungsphase der BMW AG frisch entsprungen. Noch ist es ein Prototyp, dessen Zahlenkombination 1500 die Hubraumgröße des Vierzylindermotors widerspiegelt – eine schlichte Typenbezeichnung für ein Auto, das BMW als die „neue Klasse" bezeichnet.

Das Publikum und die Fachpresse heben den Neuling aus bajuwarischen Landen sofort auf einen Sockel, und eine Welle der Begeisterung trägt ihn zum Feinschliff zurück ins Werk. Vor allem das gelungene technische Gesamtkonzept sowie das adrette Erscheinungsbild lassen den 1500 als verlockende Alternative zu den Mittelklassewagen aus Köln und Rüsselsheim erscheinen.

Dem zunächst nur 75 PS starken Triebwerk werden bis zur Serienproduktion im Oktober 1962 80 PS bei 5500 Umdrehungen in der Minute entlockt. Der kleine Trick dabei ist die Anhebung der Verdichtung von 8,2 auf 8,8.

„Elastizität in den niederen, ungestüme Kraft in den oberen Drehzahlbereichen", verheißt der BMW-Prospekt und rückt die Fahrleistungen – 150 Stundenkilometer, Beschleunigung von 0 auf 100 in 16,8 Sekunden – in den Bereich von Sportwagenwerten.

Während die Solex-Fallstromvergaser 1964 gegen eine effizientere Version dieses Herstellers ausgetauscht werden, ist das neue Getriebe mit Porsche-Sperrsynchronisation eine „Offenbarung", in der man mit dem Mittelschalthebel gern

herumrührt. Die formschöne viertürige Pontonkarosserie aus Stahl steht auf einem Fahrwerk, das mit McPherson-Federbeinen und Schraubenfedern vorn sowie Schräglenkern hinten bei BMW die technische Zukunft der rollenden Basis einläutet.

Leider befallen das an sich sehr solide gebaute Fahrzeug ab und zu kleinere technische „Hustenanfälle". Beim Nachfolger, dem 1600, plagen solche inneren Gebrechen den BMW-Fahrer nicht mehr.

Es ist für den Verkauf nicht hinderlich, daß das Armaturenbrett etwas dürftig aussieht – drei Rundinstrumente und die Aussparung für das Radio. Bei etwas weniger als 9500 Mark Kaufpreis ist die Nachfrage ungleich höher als die Produktionszahl von 50 Autos, die pro Tag vom Band rollen. Durch eine Kapazitätserhöhung 1963 werden letztlich bis 1964 23.807 Wagen gebaut. Da läuft der 1600 bereits an und das 1,8-Liter-Modell auf Hochtouren.

De nombreux automobilistes attendent – et même avec nostalgie pour les fidèles de la marque – que BMW construise une voiture du segment intermédiaire. Au Salon de l'Automobile de Francfort de septembre 1961, elle est soudain là, comme s'il s'agissait du résultat tout récent de la guérison tout juste achevée de la BMW SA. Il s'agit encore d'un prototype dont la combinaison de chiffres, 1500, trahit la cylindrée du quatre-cylindres, une dénomination sobre pour une voiture que BMW qualifie de «nouvelle classe».

Le grand public et les milieux spécialisés élèvent immédiatement un monument à la nouvelle petite Bavaroise et une vague d'enthousiasme l'accompagne jusqu'à son retour à l'usine pour une ultime mise au point. Le concept technique global réussi, surtout, ainsi que l'élégance de ses lignes en font une authentique alternative à ses concurrentes de Cologne et de Rüsselsheim.

Lors de sa production en série en octobre 1962, le moteur qui ne développait initialement que 75 ch en délivre 80 à 5500 tr/mn. Clef de l'énigme: le taux de compression a été majoré de 8,2 à 8,8.

«Souplesse à bas régime, force irrésistible à haut régime», promet le prospectus de BMW qui met en exergue ses performances – 150 km/h, de 0 à 100 km/h en 16,8 secondes – lesquelles la situent dans le segment des voitures de sport.

Alors que les carburateurs inversés Solex disparaissent en 1964 en faveur d'une version plus efficace de la même marque, la nouvelle boîte de vitesses à synchronisation Porsche est un chef-d'œuvre que l'on taquine volontiers avec le levier central. La jolie carrosserie ponton à quatre portes en acier trône sur un châssis qui inaugure, chez BMW, l'avenir mécanique des nouvelles plates-formes avec jambes élastiques McPherson et ressorts hélicoïdaux à l'avant ainsi que bras obliques à l'arrière.

Malheureusement, de petites «quintes de toux» viennent entraver de temps à autre la bonne marche de cette voiture en soi très solide. Avec sa remplaçante, la 1600, ce genre de malaise épargne totalement le conducteur de BMW.

Le fait que l'aménagement intérieur soit un peu frustre – trois cadrans circulaires et le réceptacle de l'autoradio – ne fait absolument pas obstacle à son succès commercial. Pour un prix légèrement inférieur à 9500 marks, la demande est très nettement supérieure à la production quotidienne, qui est de 50 voitures. Une augmentation des capacités, en 1963, permet finalement de produire 23 807 voitures jusqu'en 1964. Mais, à ce moment là, la 1600 et la version à moteur de 1,8 litre tournent déjà à plein régime.

BMW 1500 1962

Its external appearance and four-cylinder engine, just under 1500 cc, as well as a modern chassis, made this car so popular that it exceeded the capacity of the BMW production lines.

Das äußere Erscheinungsbild und der Vierzylindermotor mit knapp 1500 ccm sowie ein fortschrittliches Fahrwerk machen diesen Wagen so beliebt, daß er die Fließbandkapazitäten von BMW übersteigt.

Le style réussi et le moteur à quatre cylindres de près de 1500 cm³ ainsi que les liaisons à la route modernes rendent cette voiture si populaire qu'elle excède les capacités de production de BMW.

BMW 1500 1962

Spaciousness, comfortable seating and details such as a padded horn button all reflected the "new class" in the interior of the BMW 1500. The only thing slightly out of character was the painted dashboard.

Geräumigkeit, Sitzkomfort und Details wie die Hupenknopfpolsterung spiegeln die „neue Klasse" auch im Interieur des BMW 1500 wider. Lediglich das lackierte Armaturenbrett stört hier ein wenig.

Habitabilité, confort et richesse des détails, comme le capitonnage du bouton de klaxon, reflètent la «nouvelle classe» également à l'intérieur de la BMW 1500. Seul le tableau de bord peint semble un peu déplacé ici.

The front section, with the headlights and BMW kidney aligned in the grill, made a welcome change from other mid-range sedans. This also applied to the consistent emphasis of the waistline, with a chrome strip around the car integrating door handles and front indicators.

Die Frontpartie mit den im Grill auf einer Ebene liegenden Lampen und BMW-Nieren hebt sich von anderen Mittelklasse-Limousinen wohltuend ab. Das gilt ebenso für die konsequente Betonung der Gürtellinie rundum durch eine Chromleiste mit integrierten Türgriffen und vorderen Blinkern.

La proue avec les phares et les naseaux BMW intégrés sans cassure dans la calandre se démarque avec bonheur de celle des autres berlines du segment intermédiaire. On peut en dire autant de la ligne de ceinture, soulignée par un jonc chromé qui intègre les poignées de portières et les clignotants avant.

BMW 1500 1962

It was in total euphoria that BMW presented its chic coupé in the summer of 1965. This was characterized by its large windows and the absence of a center pillar. It was billed as "the reincarnation of the BMW 327". The most prominent features of the new look BMW were the flat wrap-around headlamps with integrated indicators. The oval reflectors earned the nickname of "slanted eyes" and were referred to inside BMW as "Asian eyes".

Technically, the coupé seemed to have been a prelude to the 2-liter sedans, which were launched in 1966. The 2000CS was already equipped with the 1990 cc engine capable of delivering 100 bhp with a single downdraft carburetor and 120 bhp with two double-barrel sidedraft carburetors. The chassis and the two-section propellor shaft were also taken from the sedan.

The majority of the 13,691 coupés leaving the Karmann works in Osnabrück over six years were fitted with a manually operated transmission and delivered 120 bhp (2000CS). The 100 bhp version (2000C), most of which were equipped with a ZF automatic transmission, was less popular.

To allow the 2-liter to run more smoothly, the chain drive of the overhead camshaft was equipped with sliding rails and an oil damped tensioning fixture. The transmission was also overhauled via wider stronger teeth and an expanding ring synchronizer. Accordingly, the diameter of the clutch was enlarged.

The car's "legs" were equipped with elastic mountings and, as was usual for that time, a special duct was fitted to allow cool air to reach the front brake discs. The dashboard and center console were given a businesslike and functional look. The four electric switches on the center console for window actuation were a nice and unfamiliar luxury toy for contemporary drivers.

Although the 2000CS was not the sportiest vehicle on the market, since it took 12 seconds to go from 0 to 62.5 mph (100 kph), but this acceleration figure was in keeping with the performance/weight ratio. The top speed of 115 mph (185 kph) was only slightly lower than that of the 1800TI/SA with 130 bhp.

The 2000CS was not expected to become a sporty machine. It was a four-seater which also had enough room for suitcases and bags – an apple for the pragmatist's eye, a medium-sized machine helping its drivers to see and be seen. To put it more simply: quite a lot of car for DM 17,000.

From February 1966, BMW offered a sporting four-door limousine (the 2000TI) identical with the 2000CS in engine, transmission and chassis. The former was replaced as early as 1968 by the tilux, which with its square headlights was compromised for contemporary taste.

Euphorisch präsentiert BMW im Sommer 1965 als „Wiedergeburt des BMW 327" ein schickes Coupé ohne Mittelpfosten und mit viel Fensterfläche. Auffälligstes Merkmal des neuen BMW-Gesichts sind die flachen, seitlich herumgezogenen Scheinwerfer mit integrierten Blinkern. Vom Volksmund bald „Schlitzaugen" genannt, findet man für die Ovalreflektoren auch in der werksinternen Terminologie einen sinnentsprechenden Begriff: „Asiatenaugen".

Technisch gesehen stellt das Coupé einen Vorgriff auf die 2-Liter-Limousinen des Jahrgangs 1966 dar. Es hat bereits den 1990-ccm-Motor, der mit einem Fallstromvergaser 100 PS und mit zwei Doppel-Flachstromvergasern 120 PS leistet. Auch das Fahrwerk und die zweigeteilte Kardanwelle werden von der Limousine übernommen.

Von den insgesamt 13.691 Coupés, die das Werk von Karmann in Osnabrück innerhalb von sechs Jahren verlassen, haben die meisten ein handgeschaltetes Getriebe und 120 PS (2000CS). Die 100-PS-Version (2000C), vornehmlich mit einer ZF-Automatik ausgerüstet, wird weniger gern gekauft.

Um das 2-Liter-Triebwerk zu mehr Laufruhe zu erzielen, wird der Kettenantrieb der obenliegenden Nockenwelle mit Gleitschienen und einer ölgedämpften Spannvorrichtung versehen. Auch das Getriebe mit verbreiterten Zahnrädern wird überarbeitet und erhält eine Spreizring-Synchronisierung. Analog fällt der Kupplungsdurchmesser größer aus.

Die „Beine" des Autos bekommen eine elastische Lagerung, und den Scheibenbremsen - wie damals üblich, nur vorn - wird durch einen Kunstgriff Kühlluft zugefächelt. Armaturenbrett und Mittelkonsole wirken aufgeräumt und funktionell. Ein

BMW 2000CS 1965

schönes Spielzeug für die Zeitgenossen sind die vier Schalter der elektrischen Fensterheber auf der Mittelkonsole.

Eine Beschleinigung von 0 auf 100 Stundenkilometer in 12 Sekunden entspricht nicht Sprinterwerten, aber dem Leistungsgewicht. Die Endgeschwindigkeit (185 km/h) liegt dagegen nur knapp unter der des 1800TI/SA mit 130 PS.

Sportliche Ambitionen werden mit dem 2000CS noch nicht verknüpft. Er ist ein Viersitzer, in dem auch einige Koffer und Taschen Platz finden, ein Beau für Pragmatiker, ein schickes Automobil zum Sehen und Gesehenwerden oder einfacher ausgedrückt – ziemlich viel Auto für 17.000 Mark.

In Motor, Getriebe und Fahrwerk mit dem 2000CS identisch, offeriert BMW ab Februar 1966 mit dem 2000TI auch eine sportliche viertürige Limousine. Diese wird bereits 1968 vom tilux – mit seinen Rechteck-Scheinwerfern ein Zugeständnis an den Zeitgeschmack – abgelöst.

Dans l'euphorie, BMW présente durant l'été 1965 la «réincarnation de la BMW 327», un coupé d'un grand chic sans pied médian et avec de généreuses surfaces vitrées. La caractéristique de style la plus frappante du nouveau visage de la BMW est ses phares allongés qui mordent sur le côté avec leurs clignotants intégrés. La gouaille populaire les surnomment rapidement «yeux bridés» alors que, dans la terminologie interne de la marque, les réflecteurs ovales ont un nom bien à eux: «yeux d'Asiatique».

Sur le plan mécanique, le coupé annonce les berlines de 2 litres du millésime 1966. Il possède déjà le moteur de 1990 cm^3 qui développe 100 ch avec un carburateur inversé et 120 ch dans la version à deux carburateurs double-corps inversés. Les trains roulants et l'arbre de transmission en deux éléments, aussi, sont repris de la berline.

Sur un total de 13 691 coupés qui sortiront de l'usine Karmann à Osnabrück en six ans, la majorité possèdent une boîte manuelle et un moteur de 120 ch (2000CS). La version de 100 ch (2000C), la plus souvent équipée d'une boîte automatique ZF, ne recueille pas tous les suffrages.

Pour accroître la douceur de fonctionnement du moteur de 2 litres, l'entraînement des chaînes de l'arbre à cames supérieur est assuré par des rails glissants avec un dispositif de tension baignant dans l'huile. La boîte de vitesses à engrenages élargis, elle aussi, est retravaillée et reçoit une synchronisation à anneaux d'écartement. Logiquement, le diamètre de l'embrayage augmente lui aussi.

Les «jambes» de la voiture possèdent des paliers élastiques et les freins à disques – uniquement à l'avant comme cela était alors la tradition – sont mieux refroidis grâce à une prise d'air spéciale. Le tableau de bord et la console médiane sont bien agencés et fonctionnels. Les quatre commandes des vitres électriques sur la console médiane sont un petit gadget bien apprécié des conducteurs de cette époque.

Les 12 secondes pour le 0 à 100 km/h ne sont pas un chiffre spectaculaire, mais elles reflètent le rapport poids/puissance. La vitesse de pointe (185 km/h) est, par contre, très proche de celle de la 1800TI/SA de 130 ch.

La 2000CS n'a pas encore d'ambitions sportives. Il s'agit d'une quatre-places qui peut aisément emmener également quelques valises et sacs – une belle voiture pour conducteurs pragmatiques, une voiture de promenade de taille moyenne pour voir et être vu ou, tout simplement, vraiment beaucoup de voiture pour 17 000 marks.

Avec la 2000TI, identique à la 2000CS pour le moteur, la boîte de vitesses et le châssis, BMW propose, à partir de février 1966, une sportive berline à quatre portes. Dès 1968, celle-ci sera remplacée par la tilux qui, avec ses phares rectangulaires, fait une concession aux goûts esthétiques de cette époque.

This coupé, with its strong appeal to contemporary taste, lacking a central pillar and with a great deal of window area, stood out particularly because of its headlights – also called "slanted eyes" – which were wrapped round to the side to integrate the indicators.

Das dem Zeitgeschmack stark angepaßte Coupé ohne Mittelpfosten und mit viel Fensterfläche fällt besonders durch die seitlich herumgezogenen Scheinwerfer – auch „Schlitzaugen" genannt – auf.

Le coupé qui reflète fidèlement le goût de son époque avec l'absence de montant central de pavillon et ses géné-reuses surfaces vitrées se distingue particulière-ment par les phares mordant sur les côtés.

Dashboard and central console with their sensibly arranged instruments and controls – the four controls for the electrical windows in front of the gear lever could hardly be missed – were appropriate for the outfit of the coupé. The 1990 cc engine anticipated the 1966 two-liter sedan.

Armaturenbrett und Mittelkonsole mit sinnvoll angeordneten Instrumenten und Schaltern – die vier elektrischen Fensterheber vor dem Schaltknüppel sind nicht zu übersehen – passen zum Erscheinungsbild des Coupés. Der 1990-ccm-Motor ist bereits ein Vorgriff auf die 2-Liter-Limousine des Jahrgangs 1966.

Le tableau de bord et la console médiane avec les instruments et manettes agencés ergonomiquement – les quatre lève-vitres électriques devant le levier de vitesses sautent aux yeux – vont avec le style extérieur du coupé. Le moteur de 1990 cm³ annonce déjà la berline de deux litres du millésime 1966.

BMW 2000CS 1965

BMW 1802 und 2002tii 1971

It requires special skills to cater for almost all tastes with a single model series. To put this ideal into practice, so that the product is also widely accepted, is the art of marketing. This is what happened between 1966 and 1977. BMW stretched the range of their "02 series" to extremes, from a 75 bhp economy model to the powerful 170 bhp turbo 2002. Commercial success proved this policy right: 863,203 cars were sold.

In the middle range there were two models which supplied optimum value for their price: the 1802 (90 bhp, 104 mph/ 167 kph) for 10,435 marks and the 2002tii (130 bhp, 119 mph /190 kph) which cost at least 2000 marks more.

The four-cylinder short-stroke engine (with 1766 cc for the 1802 and 1990 cc for the 2002tii) turned out to be an extremely reliable, lively engine. That the injection engine of the 2002tii with its 40 extra bhp only consumed 0.22 of a gallon (1 liter) more than the carburetor version may have been due to the efficient metering of the Kugelfischer injection pump. Both 02s had good roadholding, although it was worth installing the rollover bar in the 1802 which was standard in the 2002tii.

The 02 series went into the winter of 1973 with pepped-up looks – black radiator grill, rectangular instead of circular rear lights – and with safety equipment such as headrests and seatbelts. The rear-wheel drive of the tii proved powerful in the snow as was attested by contemporary test reports.

The normal production specification could be uprated in both versions: a sporty five-speed transmission was available as an option. Of course the brakes – discs at the front, drums at the rear – were larger for the 2002tii, and enlarged HR tires did justice to the greater loads encountered by the tii version.

The tii still had a good advantage over the 1802, sprinting from 0 to 62.5 mph (100 kph) in just 10 seconds. But that did not particularly worry the typical BMW 1802 buyer who might be lagging behind by two seconds. This was not the sportsman on the road, this was a man who wanted reliability, space and comfort from his vehicle at a reasonable price, whilst being able to keep up with the highway traffic flow.

From September 1973, BMW built larger tanks into the rear of the 1802 and 2002tii to increase the range. The bonus distance? Approximately 19 miles (30 km). With price increases of 33 per cent in four years, the cars reflected contemporary trends. The economic recession which was beginning to make itself sharply felt did not affect sales. Thus the 1802 achieved 83,351 and the 2002tii 38,703 units in the sales statistics, benchmarks to stand until the 3 series set new standards in July 1975.

Mit einer Modellreihe fast jeden Geschmack zu treffen, bedarf eines besonderen Riechers. Diese Idee dann so umzusetzen, daß das Produkt auch akzeptiert wird, ist die hohe Kunst des Marketings – so geschehen in den elf Jahren zwischen 1966 und 1977, in denen BMW mit den „02ern" eine Modellreihe in extreme Richtungen ausweitet – vom 75-PS-Sparmobil bis zum 170-PS-Turbo-Kraftpaket. Der Erfolg gibt dieser Modellpolitik recht: 863.203 verkaufte Autos.

Mittendrin liegen zwei Modelle, die für ihren Preis einen optimalen Gegenwert liefern: der 1802 (90 PS, 167 km/h) für 10.435 Mark und der gut 2000 Mark teurere 2002tii (130 PS, 190 km/h).

Der Vierzylinder-Kurzhubmotor (mit 1766 ccm beim 1802 und 1990 ccm beim 2002tii) erweist sich als ein äußerst zuverlässiges, temperamentvolles Triebwerk. Daß der 40 PS stärkere Einspritzmotor des 2002tii nur einen Liter Benzin mehr schluckt als der Vergaser, mag an der guten Dosierung der Kugelfischer-Einspritzpumpe liegen. Gut auf der Straße liegen beide, wobei sich beim 1802 der Einbau von Drehstabstabilisatoren, die beim 2002tii serienmäßig sind, empfiehlt.

Optisch aufgepäppelt – mit schwarzem Kühlergrill, eckigen statt runden Heckleuchten – und mit Sicherheitskomponenten wie Kopfstützen und Sicherheitsgurten ausgestattet, gehen die 02er in den Winter 1973. Daß auch der Heckantrieb des tii die Kraft in den Schnee bringt, attestieren ihm entsprechende Fahrberichte.

Der normale Gang der Dinge läßt sich bei beiden Ausführungen beschleunigen. Gegen Aufpreis gibt es ein sportliches Fünfganggetriebe. Natürlich sind die Bremsen,

vorne Scheiben- und hinten Trommelbremsen, beim 2002tii größer dimensioniert, und HR-Reifen werden den größeren Belastungen gerecht.

Beim Sprint aus dem Stand auf 100 Stundenkilometer hat der tii mit 10 Sekunden die Nase vorn. Den typischen Käufer des BMW 1802 stört es aber nicht, daß er da zwei Sekunden hinterherhinkt. Er ist nicht der Sportler auf der Straße, sondern ein Mann, der von seinem Fahrzeug Zuverlässigkeit, Platz und Komfort zu einem günstigen Preis erwartet, und dennoch in der Lage sein will, im Autobahnverkehr gut im Fluß zu bleiben.

Zur Erhöhung der Reichweite stattet BMW ab September 1973 den 1802 und den 2002tii mit größeren Tanks aus. Der Distanzgewinn beträgt rund 30 Kilometer. Mit Preissteigerungen von 33 Prozent in vier Jahren liegen beide Wagen im Trend der Zeit, und die sich andeutende Wirtschaftsrezession tangiert den Absatz offenbar nicht. So bringt es der 1802 auf 83.351 und der 2002tii auf immerhin 38.703 Einheiten in der Verkaufsstatistik, ehe im Juli 1975 die 3er Reihe neue Maßstäbe setzt.

Répondre à presque tous les goûts avec une seule gamme n'est pas à la portée de tout le monde. Mais réussir cette gageure avec un produit qui est largement plébiscité relève de l'art du marketing. C'est ce qui s'est passé entre 1966 et 1977, lorsque BMW a, avec les «02», décliné une gamme dans deux directions extrêmes – du modèle d'appel de 75 ch à la version sportive à moteur turbo de 170 ch. Le succès légitime a posteriori cette politique puisque BMW en a vendu pas moins de 863 203 exemplaires.

Au cœur de cette gamme, il y a deux modèles qui donnent une contre-valeur optimale pour leur prix: la 1802 (90 ch), 167 km/h) pour 10 435 marks et la 2002tii (130 ch, 190 km/h), qui coûte largement 2000 marks de plus.

Le quatre-cylindres à course courte (de 1766 cm³ pour la 1802 et de 1990 cm³ pour la 2002tii) se révèle être un moteur d'une extrême fiabilité en dépit de son vif tempérament. Si le moteur à injection de la 2002tii, plus puissant de 40 ch, ne consomme qu'un litre de plus que la version à carburateur, cela est sans doute dû au bon réglage de la pompe d'injection Kugelfischer. Toutes les deux ont une bonne tenue de route, mais il est recommandé d'équiper la 1802 des barres de torsion stabilisatrices qui équipent en série la 2002tii.

Légèrement modifiées esthétiquement – calandre noire, feux arrière rectangulaires et non plus ronds – et dotée d'éléments de sécurité comme des appuie-tête et des ceintures de sécurité, les 02 sont bien armées pour l'hiver 1973. Les essais réalisés durant cette saison témoignent que la propulsion arrière de la tii ne connaît pas de problèmes de transmission même sur la neige.

Il est possible d'accélérer le «cours normal des choses» pour les deux versions: contre supplément, BMW propose une sportive boîte manuelle à cinq vitesses. Naturellement, les freins – à disques à l'avant et à tambours à l'arrière – sont de plus grandes dimensions pour la 2002tii et des pneus HR répondent mieux aux sollicitations supérieures.

La tii ne perd pas son temps en route puisqu'il lui suffit de dix secondes pour passer de 0 à 100 km/h. La BMW 1802 demande deux secondes de plus, mais cela ne dérange en rien ses acheteurs typiques. Il ne s'agit pas d'un conducteur sportif sur route, mais d'un homme qui attend de sa voiture fiabilité, habitabilité et confort à un prix intéressant et qui soit malgré tout en mesure de suivre aisément le rythme de la circulation sur autoroute.

Pour augmenter l'autonomie, BMW installe à partir de septembre 1973 des réservoirs de plus grande capacité dans les 1802 et 2002tii. Gain: une trentaine de kilomètres. Avec une augmentation de prix de 33 % en quatre ans, les deux voitures sont tout à fait dans l'air du temps et la récession économique qui s'esquisse n'affecte en rien les ventes. Ainsi la 1802 se vendelle à raison de 83 351 exemplaires et la 2002tii, même de 38 703, avant que la série 3 ne vienne ouvrir un nouveau chapitre en juillet 1975.

Outwardly, the two-door 02 series BMW gave a delicate and unassuming effect. But the 130 bhp performance of the 2-liter engine in the 2002tii, with Kugelfischer fuel injection, was enough to make an impression.

Äußerlich wirken die zweitürigen 02er BMW zierlich und unscheinbar. Aber mit den 130 PS, die der 2-Liter-Motor im 2002tii mit Kugelfischer-Einspritzpumpe leistet, läßt sich Staat machen.

Extérieurement, les BMW 02 à deux portes semblent fragiles et n'attirent pas le regard. Mais, avec les 130 ch que délivre le moteur de deux litres de la 2002tii à injection Kugelfischer, il ne faut pas se fier aux apparences, car leurs conducteurs peuvent épater la galerie.

A discreet hint of the 2-liter engine under the hood was provided by the radiator grill, black except for two ribs. The designation at the rear specified the model.

Ein dezenter Hinweis auf das 2-Liter-Triebwerk unter der Haube ist der bis auf zwei Rippen geschwärzte Kühlergrill. Die Bezeichnung auf dem Heck gibt den jeweiligen Typ an.

Une allusion discrète au deux-litres qui œuvre sous le capot: la calandre teinte en noir à l'exception de deux rainures chromées. Le logotype à l'arrière indique de quelle version il s'agit.

Of the 863,000 02 series cars which were built, the share in the sales statistics of the 119 mph (190 kph) 2002tii amounted to 38,703 units.

Von den 863.000 gebauten Wagen der 02er Reihe beträgt der Anteil des 190 Stundenkilometer schnellen 2002tii in der Verkaufsstatistik 38.703 Einheiten.

Sur les 863 000 exemplaires vendus de la série 02, 38 703 sont des 2002tii qui flirtent avec les 190 km/h.

At first it is just a slight whistling sound at 4000 rpm, which grows into the "sweet roll of thunder" when the performance potential arrives alongside 6400 rpm. In the 2002 turbo, BMW took account of the resolution of the international ruling body of motor sport (FISA = Fédération Internationale du Sport Automobile) in Paris that future rallies would only be open to production sedans.

Thus a very powerful machine was presented to the public at the Frankfurt Motor Show in 1973. A specific bhp per liter performance of 85 bhp outdid even the Porsche Carrera RS (80 bhp/liter). The magical letters "turbo" were an incentive to use the accelerator, but for some BMW shareholders, all this extrovert badging was like a red rag to a bull. They demanded that these "unreasonable" letters be removed from the cars, or at least from those supplied in Germany.

Assertive owners of the "turbo" were, of course, inclined to advertise to an even greater extent their four-wheeled power symbol, whose hot exhaust gases caused the vanes of the charger to whiz up to an almost unbelievable speed of 90,000 rpm. But it was not only the stripes of BMW Motorsport GmbH and the standard front spoiler which identified the 2002 turbo as the basis of a sporting car. Massive widening of the fenders and a rear spoiler gave the game away: here was the signal to attack in motor sport.

The interior transmitted a hint of sportiness: bucket seats, leather steering wheel and a speedometer which went to 150 mph (240 kph) with room for even higher speeds. This potential was restricted in the production version, and only really came into play beyond 4500 rpm. Power was shut off

after mere moments of glory by a mundane contact breaker that was regulated by centrifugal force.

The understeering performance was a trait that a keen BMW driver, hitherto used to correcting sliding rear wheels during fast cornering, had to practice. However, drivers who were not averse to occasional excursions on to the north loop of the Nürburgring, quickly acclimatized to the effective brakes, which showed little fade. Back in 1973, internally ventilated discs with four-piston calipers at the front and enlarged brake drums at the rear represented state of the art technology. The same praise did not apply to fuel consumption at 12.5 miles per gallon or 19 liters per 100 km. Its thirst for petrol was such that the petrol tank, enlarged to 18.5 gallons (70 liters), was empty after only 250 miles (400 km) of driving.

But anyone who likes to enjoy his driving pleasure to the full, wants to overtake on country roads without difficulty, and gets his kicks from the swing of the turbocharger boost gauge needle will not be too bothered by the dictates of the petrol pump. They sound their horn for the chase – with turbo power.

Erst ist es nur ein leichter Pfeifton bei 4000 Umdrehungen, der sich zu einem „süßen Donnergrollen" erhebt, wenn das Leistungspotential vehement bis auf 6400 Touren ansteigt. Mit dem 2002 turbo hat BMW einem Beschluß der obersten internationalen Automobilsportbehörde FISA (Féderation Internationale du Sport Automobile) in Paris Rechnung getragen, wonach der Rallyesport künftig nur noch mit Serien-Tourenwagen zu bestreiten ist.

Was für ein Kraftpaket, das sich auf der IAA 1973 dem Publikum präsentiert! Mit einer spezifischen Literleistung von knapp 85 PS wird sogar der Porsche Carrera RS (80 PS/Liter) überflügelt. Der magische Schriftzug „turbo" reizt zum Gas geben. Für einige Aktionäre der BMW AG ist der „turbo" eher ein Reizwort. Sie fordern – zumindest für die in Deutschland ausgelieferten Wagen – ein Verbot der „unzumutbaren" Lettern.

Ambitionierte Besitzer des BMW turbo neigen zu noch größerer Plakatierung ihres vierrädrigen Kraftsymbols, dessen heiße Abgase die Schaufeln des Laders in die unglaubliche Rotationsgeschwindigkeit von nahezu 90.000 Umdrehungen pro Minute versetzen. Doch nicht nur das Streifendesign der BMW Motorsport GmbH und der serienmäßige Frontspoiler identifizieren den 2002 turbo als Basissportler. Wuchtige Kotflügelverbreiterungen und ein Heckspoiler verraten, daß hiermit auch im Motorsport zum Angriff geblasen werden soll.

Das Interieur vermittelt einen Hauch von Sportlichkeit: Schalensitze, Lederlenkrad und ein Tacho, der bis 240 km/h reicht – Spielraum für noch mehr Potential. Dieses ist in der Serienversion beschränkt, setzt erst jenseits von 4500 Touren richtig ein und wird nach Momenten der Kraft und Herrlichkeit

BMW 2002 turbo 1973

durch einen banalen fliehkraftgeregelten Unterbrecherkontakt abgeriegelt.

Gewöhnungsbedürftig ist das untersteuernde Fahrverhalten für einen BMW-Fahrer, der bislang gewohnt war, schnellen Kurvenpassagen mit dem Einfangen des Wagenhecks zu begegnen. Schnell gewöhnt sich der Freund gelegentlicher Ausritte auf die Nordschleife des Nürburgrings dagegen an die effektvoll – kaum Fading – arbeitenden Bremsen. Innenbelüftete Scheiben mit Vierkolbensätteln vorn und vergrößerte Bremstrommeln hinten sind 1973 modernster Stand der Technik. Vom Verbrauch (19 Liter bei Vollgas) kann man das weniger behaupten. Der Benzindurst ist so ausgeprägt, daß der auf 70 Liter vergrößerte Treibstofftank bereits nach 400 Kilometern normalen Fahrbetriebs leer ist.

Doch wer den Fahrspaß in vollen Zügen genießen will, auf Landstraßen problemlos überholen kann und sich am Ausschlag der Nadel des Ladedruckanzeigers Adrenalinstöße holt, den interessiert das Diktat der Zapfsäule wenig. Er bläst mit Turbo-Power zum Halali!

On ne perçoit tout d'abord qu'un léger sifflement à 4000 tr/mn, qui se mue en un «délicieux coup de tonnerre» à 6400 tr/mn lorsque l'on exploite tout le potentiel. Avec la 2002 turbo, BMW a tenu compte d'une résolution prise par la Fédération Internationale du Sport Automobile (FISA), à Paris, qui exige que, désormais, seules les voitures de tourisme de série puissent participer aux rallyes.

Quelle boule de muscles se présente là au public au Salon de l'Automobile de Francfort de 1973. Avec une puissance au litre de près de 85 ch, elle bat même la Porsche Carrera RS (80 ch/litre). L'emblème magique «turbo» incite à enfoncer l'accélérateur. Pour quelques actionnaires de BMW SA, cela fait l'effet de la muleta sur le taureau. Ils exigent, tout au moins pour les voitures livrées en Allemagne, une suppression du graphisme provocant.

Les propriétaires ambitieux de la «turbo» sont, au contraire, plutôt enclins à afficher encore plus visiblement le potentiel de leur bête de la route dont les gaz d'échappement brûlants font tourner les ailettes du turbocompresseur au régime incroyable de près de 90000 tr/mn. Mais il n'y a pas que les bandes décoratives de la BMW Motorsport GmbH et l'aileron avant de série qui identifient la 2002 turbo comme excellente base pour la course. De massifs élargisseurs d'ailes et un aileron arrière trahissent qu'elle a aussi pour vocation la compétition automobile.

Le cockpit ne fait pas mystère de cette vocation de sportivité : baquets, volant cuir et un tachymètre gradué jusqu'à 240 km/h, avec de la marge pour encore plus de potentiel. Celui-ci est limité dans la version de série, qui ne commence vraiment à pousser qu'à partir de 4500 tours et où, après quelques instants de gloire et de splendeur, un banal rupteur actionné par la force centrifuge met un terme à cette débauche de puissance.

Le comportement demande une certaine accoutumance de la part des pilotes de BMW, jusqu'ici habitués à franchir rapidement les virages en contrôlant le décrochement de l'arrière. L'amateur de cavalcades échevelées occasionnelles sur la boucle Nord du Nürburgring s'est vite habitué aux freins efficaces et pratiquement insensibles au fading : en 1973, les disques ventilés à quatre pistons l'avant et tambours de plus grande dimension à l'arrière représentent l'état de l'art. On ne peut pas en dire autant de la consommation (19 litres à plein gaz). Sa soif est telle que le réservoir de carburant agrandi à 70 litres est déjà complètement sec au bout de 400 kilomètres de conduite normale.

Mais celui qui veut boire à plein trait le plaisir de conduite, doubler quand il le veut sur les petites routes de campagne et ressentir une poussée d'adrénaline chaque fois que l'aiguille du manomètre de pression atteint la butée ne s'intéresse guère à la facture à la pompe à essence. Il sonne l'hallali – turbo à fond.

The front spoiler with its BMW Motorsport stripes and widened wings clearly indicated that this
02 series BMW was intended to be used as a basis for motor sport.

Der Frontspoiler im BMW-Motorsport-Streifendesign und die Kotflügelverbreiterungen machen
deutlich, daß dieser 02er BMW als Basisauto für den Motorsport gedacht ist.

L'aileron avant avec les bandes de couleur typiques de BMW Motorsport et les élargisseurs d'ailes
joufflus indiquent sans équivoque que cette BMW 02 est conçue comme base pour la compétition
automobile.

From its roof to the tread of its 185/70HR tires, considered wide at the time, the 2002 turbo provided Bavarian power without compare. Sales were moderate due to the generally bad economic situation. No more than 1670 deliveries were made.

Vom Dach bis hin zur damals als breit geltenden 185/70HR-Sohle ist der 2002 turbo ein „Kraft-Bayer" sondergleichen. Aufgrund der allgemein schlechten wirtschaftlichen Lage läuft der Verkauf mäßig. Der Wagen wird insgesamt nur 1670 Mal ausgeliefert.

Du toit aux pneus de 185/70HR, ce qui n'était pas rien à cette époque, la 2002 turbo roule des mécaniques. Mais la conjoncture économique n'est pas favorable aux sportives de cet acabit et cette voiture ne sera, au total, produite qu'à 1670 exemplaires.

BMW 2002 turbo 1973   243

244   BMW 2002 turbo 1973

Bucket seats, leather steering wheel, speedo up to 150 mph (240 kph) and gauge for the turbo charger: appropriate equipment for this eight-second sprinter from 0 to 62.5 mph (100 kph). The 2-liter unit unleashed a snarling 170 bhp.

Schalensitze, Lederlenkrad, Tacho bis 240 km/h und Druckanzeige für den Abgas-turbolader: Dies sind die standesgemäßen Attribute des 8-Sekunden-Sprinters (von 0 auf 100 km/h). In dem 2-Liter-Aggregat werden 170 PS fauchend entfacht.

Baquets, volant cuir, tachymètre gradué jusqu'à 240 km/h et affichage de la pression du turbocompresseur, cette sprinteuse qui passe de 0 à 100 km/h en 8 secondes affiche fièrement ses attributs. Le moteur de deux litres délivre 170 ch qui piaffent d'impatience.

BMW 2002 turbo 1973

BMW wanted an upper mid-range car to invade Mercedes territory. The two new six-cylinder engines were designed accordingly: 2.5 liters at 150 bhp and 2.8 liters at 170 bhp. But equipment, dimensions and pricing were also aimed at their counterparts from Mercedes. "Heavy guns" in the form of a ride level device and a limited slip differential as standard equipment were used by the luxuriously equipped 2800 to go into battle against Mercedes. The battle of material goodies ended in withdrawal by BMW to a less costly position. Nevertheless, the limited slip differential continued to be available – albeit at extra cost.

The 2500 model got off to a better start: between September and Christmas 1968, 2560 of these four-door sedans came off the production line and at the end of the nine-year production period, it was almost 95,000, most of them with manual transmissions. Over 17,000 comfort-conscious BMW customers left the hard work to the ZF automatic transmission with hydraulic torque converter and three-speed planetary gears.

The new six-cylinder four-stroke in-line engine with a seven-bearing crankshaft and overhead camshaft had a compression ratio of 9:1 and turned out to be extremely refined. It was also an ideal foundation for engine derivatives up to 3.3 liters. It was not easy on the fuel, for the 20.5-gallon (78 liter) tank in the rear was insufficient for 312.5 miles (500 km), even when driven with fuel economy in mind.

The driving comfort which one expected from a BMW 2500 was taken care of by independent suspension with McPherson struts having lower control arms at the front and semi-trailing arms at the rear. As befits a luxury car, a servo-assisted hydraulic dual circuit brake system supported disc brakes all round. This spacious sedan was properly equipped: a functional dashboard with circular instruments and a broad central console. There was a manageable steering wheel, comfortable body-shaped seats (from 1973 also height-adjustable, provided with headrests), and sensibly organized compartments for odds and ends or maps.

Another practical detail awaited discovery on opening the trunk. On the inside was a large folding case with 30 tools to cover all eventualities. Whether the three spare spark plugs would have cured any breakdown was never put to the test. The engine was durable and deep-chested: it could accelerate a 2500 with two passengers – a total of around one-and-a-half tons – to 119 mph (190 kph). Not bad for a 1960s sedan.

Mit einem Wagen der gehobenen Mittelklasse will BMW auf Mercedes-Terrain vorstoßen. Entsprechend sind die beiden neuen Sechszylindertriebwerke ausgelegt: 2,5 Liter mit 150 PS und 2,8 Liter mit 170 PS. Aber auch Ausstattung, Abmessungen und das Preis-Leistungs-Verhältnis zielen auf die Pendants mit dem Stern. Mit „schweren Geschützen", nämlich serienmäßiger Niveauregulierung und einem Sperrdifferential, zieht der luxuriös „eingerichtete" 2800 ins Feld gen Untertürkheim. Die „Materialschlacht" endet mit dem Rückzug auf eine weniger aufwendige Basis. Immerhin kann das Sperrdifferential, nunmehr gegen Aufpreis, als Extra weiterhin bestellt werden.

Besser läuft die Produktion des 2500 an. Von September bis Weihnachten 1968 gehen 2560 dieser viertürigen Limousinen vom Band, und nach der neunjährigen Produktionszeit sind es nahezu 95.000, vornehmlich mit Schaltgetriebe ausgerüstet. Etwas mehr als 17.000 komfortbewußte BMW-Kunden überlassen die Hebelarbeit der ZF-Automatik mit hydraulischem Wandler und Dreigang-Planetengetriebe.

Der neue Sechszylinder-Viertakt-Reihenmotor mit siebenfach gelagerter Kurbelwelle und obenliegender Nockenwelle ist 9:1 verdichtet und erweist sich als äußerst kultiviert: ein ideales Basistriebwerk für Derivate bis zu 3,3 Litern. Sparsam ist er freilich nicht, denn der 78-Liter-Tank im Heck reicht selbst bei schonender Fahrweise nicht einmal für 500 Kilometer.

Für einen Fahrkomfort, wie man ihn vom BMW 2500 erwartet, sorgen die Einzelradaufhängungen mit Federbeinen – vorn an Quer-, hinten an Schräglenkern. Standesgemäß sorgt eine servounterstützte hydraulische Zweikreisbremse mit vier

BMW 2500 1968

Scheibenbremsen für angemessene Verzögerung. Die geräumige Limousine ist ordentlich „eingerichtet": funktionelles Armaturenbrett mit Rundinstrumenten und breiter Mittelkonsole, griffiges Lenkrad, bequeme, körpergerecht geformte Sitze (ab 1973 auch in der Höhe regulierbar und mit Kopfstützen versehen) und sinnvoll verteilte Ablagen für Kleinigkeiten und Atlanten.

Auch beim Aufklappen des Kofferraumdeckels entdeckt man ein praktisches Detail. An der Innenseite befindet sich ein großes Klappetui mit 30 Werkzeugen für alle Fälle. Ob die drei Reservezündkerzen einen Motorschaden „kurieren" können, ist nie ausprobiert worden. Das Triebwerk erweist sich als standhaft und bringt den Wagen mit zwei Passagieren – zusammen rund anderthalb Tonnen – auf 190 Stundenkilometer: recht passabel für eine Limousine der sechziger Jahre.

BMW veut marcher sur les plates-bandes de Mercedes avec une voiture du segment intermédiaire supérieur. Les deux nouveaux six-cylindres sont conçus en conséquence: 2,5 litres de 150 ch et 2,8 litres de 170 ch. Mais la finition, les dimensions et le rapport prix/prestations rivalisent exactement avec ceux de la marque à l'étoile. D'une grande «sophistication mécanique», à savoir avec un correcteur d'assiette en série et un différentiel autobloquant, la 2800 traitée plus luxueusement passe à l'attaque contre Untertürkheim. La «bataille» se termine par une «victoire à la Pyrrhus» qui impose une plus grande modestie mécanique. Au moins, le différentiel autobloquant – maintenant proposé en option – peut toujours être commandé contre supplément.

La stratégie connaît plus de succès avec la 2500: de septembre à Noël 1968, 2560 de ces limousines à quatre portes sortent des chaînes et, après neuf ans de production, on en compte 95 000, presque toutes avec boîte manuelle. Un peu plus de 17 000 acheteurs de BMW ayant le goût du confort laissent à la boîte automatique ZF planétaire à trois rapports et convertisseur hydraulique la charge de changer de vitesse.

Le nouveau six-cylindres en ligne à quatre temps avec vilebrequin à sept paliers et arbres à cames en tête a un taux de compression de 9:1 et s'avère extrêmement cultivé. Une excellente base, donc, pour monter en cylindrée jusqu'à 3,3 litres. Il n'est malheureusement pas économique puisque même le réservoir de 78 litres à l'arrière n'autorise pas une autonomie de 500 kilomètres en conduite «coulée».

Des suspensions à roues indépendantes avec jambes élastiques – avec bras transversaux à l'avant et bras obliques à l'arrière – garantissent le confort que l'on est en droit d'attendre d'une BMW 2500. Comme il se doit, le double circuit de freinage à assistance hydraulique est à disques sur les quatre roues. Spacieuse, la limousine est parfaitement «aménagée»: un tableau de bord fonctionnel avec des cadrans circulaires et une large console médiane, un volant qui tombe bien en mains, des sièges confortables et ergonomiques (également réglables en hauteur et avec appuie-tête à partir de 1973) et des vide-poches bien placés pour les petites bricoles et les cartes géographiques.

Lors de l'ouverture du couvercle de malle, aussi, on découvre un détail pratique: celui-ci comporte une mallette d'outillage intégrée avec une trentaine d'outils pour parer à toutes les éventualités. Quelqu'un aura-t-il jamais pu réparer une panne de moteur avec les trois bougies de réserve que l'on y trouve? Le moteur s'avère endurant et, avec deux personnes à bord – soit au total un poids d'environ une tonne et demie – il propulse cette voiture à 190 km/h, une performance vraiment flatteuse pour une limousine des années 60.

The imposing exterior of the 2500, with its double-headlamp front and slightly bulging tail. The car marked a deliberate attempt by BMW to encroach on Mercedes territory.

Wuchtige Doppelscheinwerferfront und ausladendes Heck: Der 2500, mit dem BMW 1968 gezielt auf Mercedes-Terrain vorstößt, hat auch repräsentativen Chrom zu bieten.

Une proue agressive à phares doubles et une poupe interminable : sur le plan extérieur, aussi, la 2500 avec laquelle BMW marche résolument sur les plates-bandes de Mercedes en 1968 ne manque pas d'atouts.

The dashboard, center console and storage shelf are functional and well-designed. The six-cylinder in-line engine, with its block angled 30° to the right, generated 150 bhp.

Klar gegliedert und funktionell angeordnet präsentieren sich Armaturenbrett und Mittelkonsole mit Ablagefach. 150 PS aktiviert der Sechszylinder-Reihenmotor mit einem um 30° zur rechten Seite geneigten Block.

Bien agencés et fonctionnels, telles sont les caractéristiques du tableau de bord et de la console médiane avec vide-poches. Le six-cylindres en ligne, dont le bloc est incliné de 30° sur la droite, développe 150 ch.

BMW 2500 1968

Almost 95,000 of this comfortable upper mid-range car were produced by BMW over a nine-year period.

Nahezu 95.000 dieser komfortablen Wagen der gehobenen Mittelklasse werden in neun Jahren bei BMW produziert.

Près de 95 000 de ces voitures confortables du segment supérieur seront produites chez BMW en neuf ans.

BMW 3.0CSi 1971

Much admired at the Paris Motor Show in the autumn of 1968, BMW presented the 2800CS as a commitment to large sporty coupés. The chassis of this slim car without a B-pillar was simply the consistent further development of the 2000CS and was built by Karmann. Final assembly and the installation of the six-cylinder engine were at Dingolfing, a new BMW site in 1967. Here Hans Glas had failed in the construction of his top-of-the-range coupés and was forced to hand over his factory to BMW. The CS swiftly developed and soon the small "i" behind the CS indicated the transition to an injection engine. Simultaneously, the engine size was increased to 2985 cc – hence the 3.0 badge.

A strong 200 bhp engine catapulted the 3087 lbs (1400 kg) CSi to 137.5 mph (220 kph). As early as 1972, it was slimmed down by 286 lbs (130 kg) and the engine size was increased to 3003 cc for a special CSL version, the L standing for lightweight. CSL customers were rewarded with a tangible increase in acceleration from 0 to 62.5 mph (100 kph). The coupé's heart, that highly revving engine, remained refinement personified. But such refinement is expensive: 13.5 miles to the gallon (17.5 liters per 100 km) driven hard made frequent gas station stops inevitable, despite a 18.5-gallon (70 liter) tank. This at a time when European petrol prices rocketed.

Which coupé driver is going to allow an oil crisis to spoil his fun behind the wheel? BMW, believing that it had to respond to a period of economic challenge with a 2.5-liter economy version, produced a flop. The strange calculation of dropping 50 bhp, losing rapid acceleration and the top speed of 137.5 mph (220 kph), all to save two-thirds of a gallon (3 liters)

was hardly worth noting, so there were only 844 buyers. Even savings of about 4000 marks were insufficient. Some options, which came as standard on the CSi, had to be added on.

The opposite trend was indicated. The CSL coupé with huge front spoiler, wind splitters and rear spoiler was aimed at sporting activities, its luxury accessories removed for weight reasons. The sports package was supplemented by gigantic wing structures at the rear of the car and a roof spoiler. This fixed the outline of the racing coupé – except for widening the fenders.

The success story of the coupés (2800CS from 1968 to 1971, 3.0CS/CSi from 1971 to 1975) was reflected in healthy production figures. If the 844 "economy" 2.5 coupés are included, more than 30,000 cars were built, 8142 of them the CSi.

Auf dem Pariser Autosalon im Herbst 1968 viel bestaunt, stellt BMW den 2800CS als Bekenntnis zu großen sportlichen Coupés vor. Freilich ist die Karosserie des schlanken Wagens ohne B-Säule nichts anderes als eine konsequente Weiterentwicklung des 2000CS und wird bei Karmann gebaut. Die Endmontage und der Einbau des Sechszylindermotors erfolgen in Dingolfing. Hier ist Hans Glas am Bau solcher Oberklassecoupés gescheitert und hat sein Werk an BMW abtreten müssen. Der CS entwickelt sich rasant, und bald symbolisiert das kleine „i" hinter dem CS den Übergang zum Einspritzmotor. Gleichzeitig wird der Hubraum auf 2985 ccm vergrößert – deshalb 3.0.

200 PS wuchten den immerhin 1400 Kilo schweren Wagen auf 220 Stundenkilometer. Bereits 1972 wird der CSi um 130 Kilo abgespeckt, und das Triebwerk bekommt 3003 ccm Hubraum. Diese Ausführung wird CSL genannt. Mit einer deutlich besseren Beschleunigung von 0 auf 100 Stundenkilometer werden die Käufer des Coupés belohnt. Das Herzstück, der drehfreudige Motor, überzeugt durch seine Laufkultur. Aber diese Kultur kostet etwas: 17,5 Liter Super bei allzu scharfer Gangart machen trotz des 70-Liter-Tanks häufige Tankstopps unumgänglich und das bei rapide steigenden Benzinpreisen.

Doch welcher Coupéfahrer läßt sich schon das Fahrvergnügen durch eine sogenannte Ölkrise verderben? Im Glauben, den wirtschaftlich schweren Zeiten mit einer 2,5-Liter-Sparversion begegnen zu müssen, erlebt BMW einen Reinfall. Die Rechnung, auf 50 PS, eindrucksvolle Beschleunigungserlebnisse und Geschwindigkeiten um 220 Stundenkilometer verzichten zu können, um pro Tankfüllung läppische drei Liter

zu sparen, begreifen nur 844 Käufer. Selbst die Ersparnis von rund 4000 Mark lockt nicht, da einige Extras, die beim CSi zum Serienumfang gehören, dagegen aufgerechnet werden müssen.

Der Trend geht genau in die andere Richtung. Das CSL-Coupé mit überdimensionalem Frontspoiler, Windsplits und Heckspoiler zielt auf sportliche Aktivitäten, zumal auf Luxus-accessoires aus Gewichtsgründen verzichtet wird. Ein gigantisches Flügelwerk für das Wagenheck und ein Dachspoiler ergänzen das Sportpaket. Damit steht das Outfit des Rennsport-Coupés bereits – bis auf Kotflügelverbreiterungen – fest.

Die Erfolgsstory der Coupés (2800CS von 1968 bis 1971, 3.0CS/CSi von 1971 bis 1975) schlägt sich in einer ansehnlichen Produktion nieder. Einschließlich der 844 „Sparbrötchen" werden mehr als 30.000 Wagen gebaut, 8142 davon sind CSi.

Au Salon de l'Automobile de Paris, à l'automne 1968, sous les yeux étonnés des nombreux visiteurs, BMW dévoile la 2800CS, profession de foi envers les gros coupés sportifs. La carrosserie de l'élégante voiture sans montant de pavillon central n'est toutefois rien d'autre qu'une extrapolation intelligente de la 2000CS et est construite chez Karmann. Le montage final et le mariage avec le six-cylindres ont lieu à Dingolfing. Dans cette ville, Hans Glas avait fait faillite en voulant construire de tels coupés du segment supérieur et avait dû céder son usine à BMW. La CS connaît un développement rapide et, bientôt, le petit «i» derrière le CS signale la présence d'un moteur à injection. Simultanément, la cylindrée passe à 2985 cm³ – d'où le 3.0.

200 ch catapultent à 220 km/h cette voiture qui pèse tout de même 1400 kg. Dès 1972, elle est allégée de 130 kg et le moteur a une cylindrée de 3003 cm³. Cette version est appelée CSL. L'acheteur du coupé CSL est récompensé par de bien meilleures accélérations pour le 0 à 100 km/h. Enthousiasmant par sa spontanéité à monter en régime, le moteur séduit par son velouté. Mais cette culture a son prix : malgré un réservoir de 70 litres, les 17,5 litres de super consommés quand on roule à bride abattue imposent des ravitaillements fréquents et ce, alors que le prix de l'essence augmente tout aussi rapidement.

Mais quel amateur de coupés accepterait de se laisser gâcher le plaisir par un soi-disant choc pétrolier? BMW, croyant répliquer avec une version économique de 2,5 litres en période de difficultés économiques, subit un échec cinglant: seuls 844 acheteurs saisissent la bizarre équation – renoncer à 50 ch, à la sensation des accélérations et à des vitesses d'environ 220 km/h

pour économiser trois malheureux litres par ravitaillement. Même l'économie d'environ 4000 marks n'est pas un argument, car il faut y ajouter quelques options qui font partie de l'équipement de série sur la CSi.

La tendance va exactement dans le sens contraire. Le coupé CSL avec imposant aileron avant, windsplits et becquet arrière affiche effrontément sa sportivité, d'autant plus que des accessoires de luxe ont été bannis pour économiser du poids. Le kit sport est complété par un impressionnant becquet arrière et un aileron de toit. Le gréement du coupé compétition est à la mesure de ses ambitions – à l'exception des élargisseurs d'ailes.

La «success story» des coupés (2800CS de 1968 à 1971, 3.0CS/CSi de 1971 à 1975) se traduit par un succès commercial sans précédent – y compris les 844 exemplaires de la «version économique», plus de 30000 voitures sont construites, dont 8142 CSi.

The 3.0CSi coupé was a huge success for BMW during the first half of the 1970s, selling a total of 8142. Total production of the CS range of coupés exceeded 30,000.

Als äußerst erfolgreiches Coupé in der ersten Hälfte der siebziger Jahre entpuppt sich der 3.0CSi, den BMW 8142 Mal verkauft. Insgesamt sind es sogar mehr als 30.000 CS-Coupés, die vom Band laufen.

La 3.0CSi, dont BMW vendra 8142 exemplaires, est l'un des coupés qui remportera le plus de succès durant la première moitié des années 70. Au total, ce sont même plus de 30.000 coupés de la famille CS qui sortiront des chaînes.

The type plate on the tailgate makes it abundantly clear that this is a CS with a 3-liter injection engine.

Unübersehbar verkündet das Typenschild auf der Heckklappe, daß es sich hier um einen CS mit dem 3-Liter-Einspritzmotor handelt.

Le logotype sur la malle arrière affiche fièrement qu'il s'agit ici d'une CS à moteur à injection de 3 litres.

Beneath the hood resides a six-cylinder engine with electronically-controlled Bosch fuel injection. It generates 200 bhp at 5300 rpm.

Unter der Haube macht sich ein Sechszylinder mit elektronisch gesteuerter Bosch-Benzineinspritzung breit. Bei 5300 Umdrehungen werden 200 PS frei.

Un six-cylindres à injection électronique Bosch occupe le compartiment moteur. Il délivre 200 ch à 5300 tr/mn.

The commentator was left speechless and the spectators around the bumpy airfield track in Sebring in Florida shouted their approval: cheerful Hans Stuck from Germany's Bavarian state provided an interview featuring three pithy answers and a protracted mountain-country yodel. Such vocal gymnastics from deepest Bavaria graced many of the famous US racetracks in 1975, from East Coast Daytona and Watkins Glen to the sunny Californian tracks of Monterey, Riverside and Laguna Seca.

BMW hoped to be rewarded with extra exports as a result of its participation in the American IMSA (International Motor Sports Association) Championship. BMW Motorsport GmbH entered the 3.0CSL winged coupé – a great racing success in Europe ever since its 1973 debut. The sunshade on the CSL's windshield bore the legend in large capital letters: "Bavarian Motor Works". That prevented any misunderstanding of the BMW abbreviation in the States. Incredibly, newspapers had written "British Motor Works" as the translation of BMW. That was before the Munich CSLs raced in the New World, and nobody made that mistake again.

The core team of two white racing coupés with the Motorsport GmbH stripes included the Bavarian Stuck, the fast Swede Ronnie Peterson, British long distance specialist (formerly of Porsche and Ferrari) Brian Redman, and a youngster from the US by the name of Sam Posey. A strong and – as it turned out – a successful team. They certainly had no intention of lagging behind their winning European counterparts, including Hagen-born Siggi Müller, who drove a CSL owned by Rüdiger Faltz (Essen) to win the European touring car title.

The appearance of the IMSA coupé differed from the European CSL in its large air intakes for the transmission, rear axle and engine oil coolers, these being integrated within vast fender extensions. The rear fenders had to be huge to cover the 16 inch-wide Dunlop rollers with appropriate BBS wheels. These racing wheels were naturally equipped with central wheel studs to facilitate rapid wheel changes.

Magnesium wheel uprights, aluminum wheel hubs and the aluminum casings of the Bilstein gas shock-absorbers tubes reduced kerb weight. The adjustable top spring plates meant that the distance from the ground could be immediately controlled to suit each race circuit. Similarly suspension springs of many different poundage rates were also sent across the Atlantic from Munich to cater for the different racetrack characteristics.

To achieve better weight distribution, the trunk was filled up with the fuel tank, dry sump oil tank, brake bias control, an automatic fire-extinguisher system, battery, pioneering hydraulic system for the experimental ABS anti-lock braking and an alternator. Two large gas filler necks distinguished the trunk deck, under a large rear CSL wing.

The twin side exhaust pipes replicated a lion's roar when the 430 bhp engine – increased to at least 450 by the end of the season – ran flat out. Bavarian lions have a loud roar. Otherwise Stuck, with a talent as divine as opera star Caruso, would not have had anything to yodel about.

Dem Streckensprecher verschlägt es die Sprache, und die Zuschauer rund um die holprige Flugplatzpiste von Sebring in Florida johlen vor Begeisterung: Frohnatur Hans Stuck aus „Bavaria, Germany" hat gerade ein Interview gegeben – drei kurze, aber kernige Antworten und einen langen Jodler! Diese urbayerische Stimmbandverrenkung erschallt 1975 noch auf vielen bekannten US-Racetracks zwischen Daytona, Watkins Glen und den sonnigen kalifornischen Pisten von Monterey, Riverside und Laguna Seca.

BMW erwartet sich von dem Engagement in der amerikanischen IMSA-Serie (International Motor Sports Association) deutliche Exportimpulse. Und so setzt die BMW-Motorsport GmbH werkseitig die schon seit 1973 in Europa äußerst erfolgreichen 3.0CSL-Flügel-Coupés ein. Um eine Fehlinterpretation des Kürzels "BMW" in den Staaten auszuschließen, steht in großen Lettern auf der Windschutzscheibenblende des CSL „Bavarian Motor Works". Man sollte es nicht glauben, aber vor dem Auftauchen der Münchener in der Neuen Welt hatte ein Blatt tatsächlich „British Motor Works" geschrieben.

Die Stammcrew der beiden weißen Coupés mit den Streifen der Motorsport GmbH bilden neben dem Bayern Hans-Joachim Stuck der schnelle Schwede Ronni Peterson, der britische Allround-Pilot und Langstreckenspezialist (auf Porsche und Ferrari) Brian Redman sowie der Amerikaner Sam Posey - eine starke Truppe und, wie sich herausstellt, erfolgreich obendrein. Was die Siege angeht, möchte man seinen Kollegen in Europa – der Hagener Siggi Müller holt auf einem CSL von Rüdiger Faltz (Essen) den Tourenwagen-Europameistertitel – in nichts nachstehen.

BMW 3.0CSL/3.0CSL (IMSA) 1975

Optisch unterscheiden sich die IMSA-Coupés von den in Europa eingesetzten CSL durch große Luftschächte für die Ölkühler von Getriebe, Hinterachse und Motor in den hinteren Kotflügelverbreiterungen. Diese fallen gewaltig aus, denn sie müssen 16 Zoll breite Dunlop-Walzen mit ebenso großen BBS-Felgen abdecken. Natürlich sind diese Räder für schnelle Radwechsel mit Zentralverschlüssen versehen.

Für Gewichtsersparnis sorgen Magnesium-Radträger, Aluminiumradnaben und Alurohre in den Bilstein-Gasdruck-stoßdämpfern. Über geschraubte Federteller läßt sich der Bodenabstand regulieren, und für die unterschiedlichen Rennstrecken-Charakteristika haben die Münchener Federn aller erdenklichen Härtegrade über den Teich geschippert.

Aus Gründen der besseren Gewichtsverteilung ist der untere Bereich des „Kofferraums" vollbepackt mit dem Tank sowie Ölsumpf, Bremskraftregler, Feuerlöschbombe, Batterie, Hydrauliksystem für das ABS und Lichtmaschine. Zwei große Einfüllstutzen zieren den „beflügelten" Kofferraumdeckel.

Der Sound der beiden seitlichen Auspuffrohre erinnert an das Gebrüll von Löwen, sobald sich die 430 PS – zu Saisonende sollen es gut 450 gewesen sein – voll entfalten. Es hat auch niemand bestritten, daß ein bayerischer Löwe gut brüllen kann. Sonst hätte der „Strietzel" Stuck ja nichts zum Jodeln.

Le speaker en perd la parole et les spectateurs massés aux abords de la cahoteuse piste tout autour de l'aéroport de Sebring, en Floride, hurlent de plaisir : le gai luron Hans Stuck, de «Bavaria, Germany», vient de donner une interview – trois réponses brèves, mais percutantes et un interminable jodler! Ce trémolo antédiluvien typiquement bavarois résonnera souvent, en 1975, sur beaucoup de prestigieux «racetracks» américains entre Daytona, Watkins Glen et les pistes ensoleillées de Monterey, Riverside et Laguna Seca, en Californie.

BMW espère que son engagement dans la série américaine IMSA (International Motor Sports Association) donnera un coup de fouet à ses exportations vers les Etats-Unis. Et c'est ainsi que la BMW Motorsport GmbH engage ses coupés à ailerons 3.0CSL qui remportent déjà un très grand succès en Europe depuis 1973. Pour parer à toute interprétation erronée de l'abréviation BMW aux Etats-Unis, «Bavarian Motor Works» figure en lettres capitales sur la banderole pare-soleil ornant le pare-brise des CSL. C'est incroyable mais avant l'apparition des Munichois sur le Nouveau continent, un journal avait déjà pris le nom de BMW comme l'abrevation de «British Motor Works».

Outre le Bavarois Hans-Joachim Stuck, l'équipage de base des deux coupés blancs avec les banderoles bleues et rouges de la Motorsport GmbH sont le rapide Suédois Ronnie Peterson, le pilote britannique touche-à-tout et spécialiste de l'endurance (sur Porsche et Ferrari) Brian Redman ainsi que l'Américain Sam Posey. Une équipe de choc et, comme on allait le constater, gagnante. Côté victoires, ils veulent être à la hauteur de leurs collègues qui se battent sur les circuits européens, comme par exemple Siggi Müller, de Hagen, qui coiffe la couronne de

champion d'Europe des voitures de tourisme sur une CSL de Rüdiger Faltz (Essen).

Sur le plan visuel, les coupés IMSA se distinguent des CSL engagées en Europe par de grandes prises d'air pour les radiateurs d'huile de la boîte de vitesses, du pont arrière et du moteur dans les ailes arrière élargies. Celles-ci sont gigantesques, car elles doivent héberger de larges pneus Dunlop de 16 pouces avec des jantes BBS de mêmes dimensions. Naturellement, ces roues comportent un moyeu de fixation central pour garantir un échange rapide de pneumatiques.

Par souci de poids, les paliers de roues sont en magnésium, les moyeux de roues et les tubes des amortisseurs à gaz Bilstein en aluminium. Des coupelles de ressort vissées permettent de modifier la garde au sol et, pour répondre aux différentes caractéristiques des circuits, les Munichois ont emmené outre-Atlantique des ressorts de toutes les duretés possibles et imaginables.

Pour obtenir une meilleure répartition du poids, le «coffre» est rempli avec le réservoir à essence, la lubrification à carter sec, les répartiteurs de la puissance de freinage, l'extincteur réglementaire, la batterie, le système hydraulique pour l'ABS et l'alternateur. Deux grosses goulottes de remplissage décorent le couvercle de malle orné d'un gigantesque aileron.

La sonorité des deux gros pots d'échappement latéraux rappelle les feulements d'un lion dès que vrombissent les 430 ch – qui sont même largement 450 à la fin de la saison. Personne n'a jamais contesté qu'un lion bavarois ne sache feuler puissamment. Sinon, «Strietzel» Stuck ne pourrait pas pousser la tyrolienne.

During the 4-hour touring car classic race on the north loop of the Nürburgring in 1975, the Faltz-Alpina 3.0CSLs – here the car of Müller/Peltier who came second – were clearly dominant.

Beim 4-Stunden-Touren-wagen-Klassiker auf der Nordschleife des Nürburgrings 1975 dominieren die Faltz-Alpina-3.0CSL klar – hier der Wagen der Zweit-plazierten Müller/Peltier.

Lors des 4 Heures du Nürburgring pour voitures de tourisme, sur le circuit nord du Nürburgring, en 1975, la domination des Faltz-Alpina-3.0CSL – ici la voiture de Müller/Peltier qui finiront deuxièmes – est évidente.

1000-km-Nürburgring (D), 1975

Hans-Joachim Stuck (left, at the Nuremberg 200 mile race) wrote motor sport history for BMW in Europe with the 3.0CSL, as he did with the IMSA version of the coupé with its prominent spoilers and his start number of 25.

Hans-Joachim Stuck (links beim 200-Meilen-Rennen von Nürnberg) schreibt mit dem 3.0CSL in Europa für BMW ebenso Motorsportge-schichte wie mit der IMSA-Ausführung des Flügel-Coupés mit „seiner" Startnummer 25.

Hans-Joachim Stuck (à gauche lors des 200 Miles de Nuremberg) écrit un chapitre d'histoire de la compétition automobile pour BMW avec la 3.0CSL en Europe et fait de même aux Etats-Unis avec la version IMSA du coupé bardé d'ailerons arborant le 25, numéro de Stuck.

Norisring (D), 1975

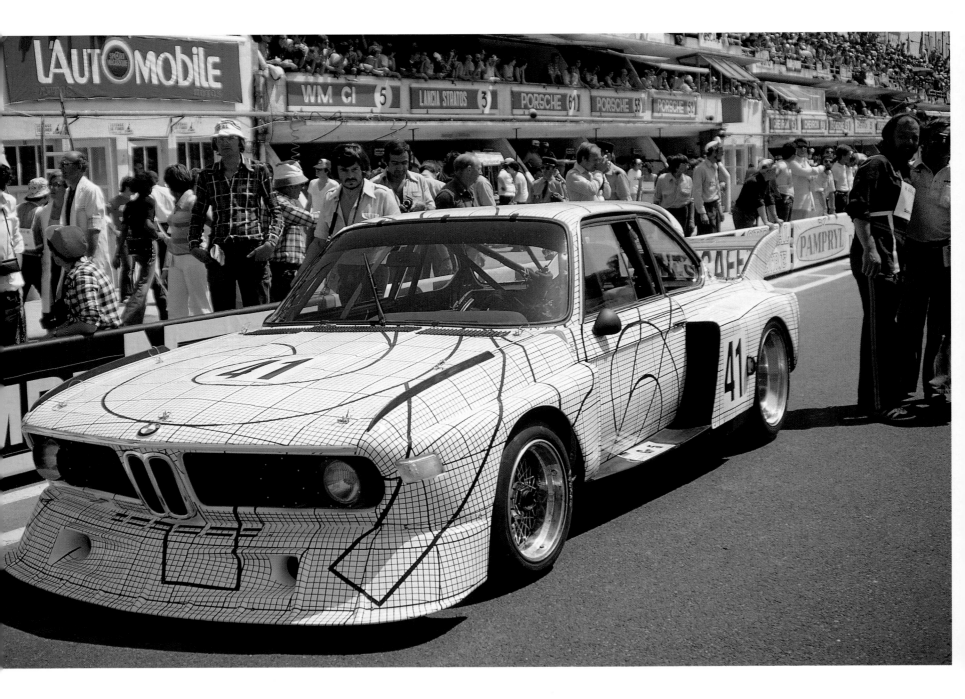

Art and motor sport: with his coordinate paper design, the American artist Frank Stella intended to depict high-tech precision on the works 3.0CSL. Unfortunately, the work of art on the "stage" of Le Mans 1976 only had a life of 2 hours 16 minutes.

Kunst und Motorsport: Mit den Linien auf dem Millimeterpapier will der amerikanische Künstler Frank Stella auf dem Werks-3.0CSL High-Tech und Präzision darstellen. Leider ist dem Kunstwerk auf der „Bühne" von Le Mans 1976 nur eine Lebensdauer von zwei Stunden und 16 Minuten beschieden.

Art et compétition automobile : avec son dessin au papier millimétrique sur la 3.0CSL d'usine, l'artiste américain Frank Stella veut représenter la haute technologie et la précision. Malheureusement, sur le «catwalk» du Mans en 1976, on ne pourra admirer l'œuvre d'art que pendant deux heures et 16 minutes.

US safety regulations as demonstrated by the 3.0CSL (IMSA): the driver's door was welded shut – Stuck inserted his long frame through the net (replacing the side windows) – and there were additional brackets for the rear windscreen. In the 1975 season the six-cylinder produced 450 bhp. Pictured here, the automobile "High Priest" Paul Rosche and his masterpiece.

US-Sicherheitsvorschriften am Beispiel des 3.0CSL (IMSA): eine zugeschweißte Fahrertür – der Einstieg für den langen Stuck erfolgt durch das Netz (statt Seitenscheibe) – und die zusätzlich mit Klammern gehaltene Heckscheibe. Bis zu 450 PS gibt der Sechszylinder in der Saison 1975 ab. Rechts im Bild der „Motor-Papst" Paul Rosche und sein Meisterwerk.

Normes de sécurité à l'américaine à l'exemple de la 3.0CSL (IMSA): une porte conducteur soudée – le longiligne Stuck doit se glisser à bord après avoir déplacé le filet (il n'y a plus de vitre latérale) – et une lunette arrière maintenue en place par des brides supplémentaires. Le six-cylindres produit jusqu'à 450 ch dans la saison 1975. On y voit Paul Rosche, le «pape» de la construction automobile, et son œuvre.

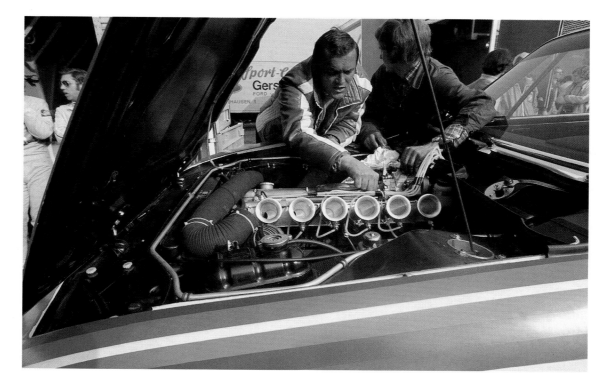

BMW 520 1972

The first of a new BMW generation saw the light of an automotive day in September 1972: the 520. It heralded the start of the middleweight 5 series. Although this BMW partially owed its physical appearance to the planned six-cylinder engine, its heart was a four-cylinder engine. And this heartbeat was simply not enough for a vehicle at the top end of the middle class. This fact was only taken into account five years later, when all BMW 520s had a new six-cylinder implant.

The four-cylinder required some automotive surgery. Changing the combustion chambers to what are known as "3-sphere turbulence combustion chambers" prompted a compression ratio increase, therefore optimizing the mixture combustion and increasing both performance and fuel efficiency. More functional changes came for environmental reasons: the new Stromberg downdraft carburetor with automatic start improved emission control, particularly in cold starts.

The only problems encountered were related to the vehicle's performance. A 115 bhp engine required almost 13 seconds to bring a car weighing 2805 lbs (1275 kg) from 0 to 62.5 mph (100 kph); to make matters worse, there were 44.1 lbs (20 kg) extra with the automatic. At the top end, speeds of up to 109.3 mph (175 kph) were attained and the fuel injection car which delivered 130 bhp could reach 114.3 mph (183 kph).

The addition of longer wheelbases, wider track and anti-roll bars to the tried and tested chassis with McPherson struts at the front, and a triangulated trailing arm at the rear, was so effective that only a mild "pedicure" was required: fine-tuning the suspension. Helpful cornering characteristics – there were

early signals of slight oversteer – and high levels of driving comfort were both 520 plus points.

The safe chassis with strengthened struts and special beam rigidity in the sub-frame were worthy of special note. Computer calculations predicted what could be crumpled in an accident, and what should remain intact.

High standards were, of course, expected of a car which cost 15,000 marks without any extras in 1972. The efficient interior did not let anyone down. The dashboard lit up in impressive muted orange shades whenever the lights were switched on, but what was most striking was the volume of fresh or heated air which could be displaced every 60 seconds.

The 520 came with either a five-speed or an automatic transmission and options even included the seatbelts. Yet it offered so much for its price that over 45,000 new 5 series were sold in 1973 alone.

Die „Erstgeburt" einer neuen BMW-Generation erblickt im September 1972 das Licht der Autowelt: der 520, mit dem die 5er Reihe anfängt. Auch wenn er sich optisch ein wenig an den großen Sechszylindern orientiert, ist sein Herz ein Vierzylinder. Und das schlägt eigentlich zu schwach für ein Fahrzeug der gehobenen Mittelklasse. Erst fünf Jahre später trägt man diesem Umstand Rechnung und implantiert neue Sechszylinder in den BMW 520.

Einen kleinen „chirurgischen Eingriff" hat sich der Vierzylinder jedoch gefallen lassen müssen. Durch die Umwandlung der Brennräume in sogenannte „3-Kugel-Wirbelwannen" und somit durch die Vergrößerung des Verdichtungsverhältnisses wird die Verbrennung des Gemischs optimiert. Dazu kommt etwas „Umwelt-Kosmetik". Für eine bessere Abgasregulierung – besonders bei Kaltstarts – sorgen die neuen Stromberg-Fallstromvergaser mit Startautomatik.

Trotzdem hapert es bei der Fitneß, denn der 115-PS-Motor benötigt nahezu 13 Sekunden, um das stattliche Gewicht von 1275 Kilo (bei der Automatik sind es 20 Kilo zusätzlich) von 0 auf 100 Stundenkilometer zu beschleunigen. Oben heraus geht es bis 175 Stundenkilometer weiter, und der Einspritzer mit 130 PS bringt es immerhin auf 183 km/h.

Verlängerter Radstand, verbreiterte Spur und Drehstab-stabilisatoren kommen dem bewährten Fahrwerk mit McPherson-Federbeinen vorn und einer Schräglenkerachse hinten so entgegen, daß nur noch etwas „Pediküre" notwendig ist, nämlich Feintuning bei der Federungsabstimmung. Gutmütige Kurveneigenschaften – leichtes Übersteuern kündigt sich frühzeitig an – und hoher Fahrkomfort sind Pluspunkte des 520.

Besonderes Augenmerk verdienen die sicheren Fahrgestelle mit verstärkten Holmen und besonderen Flankenversteifungen in der Bodengruppe. Computer haben errechnet, was bei einem Unfall geknautscht werden soll und was intakt bleiben muß.

Natürlich werden an einen Wagen, der 1972 ohne Extras knapp 15.000 Mark ab Werk kostet, auch Ansprüche gestellt. In dieser Hinsicht gibt sich das Interieur keine Blöße. Daß die Armaturen bei eingeschaltetem Licht orangefarben leuchten, ist eher nebensächlich. Außergewöhnlich hoch ist das Volumen der Frisch- oder Heizungsluft, die pro Minute bewegt werden kann.

Der Wagen, der auch mit Fünfganggetriebe oder Automatik erhältlich ist, und zu dessen Extras unter anderem Sicherheitsgurte zählen, bietet für seinen Preis offenbar so viel, daß allein 1973 über 45.000 neue 5er verkauft werden.

Une nouvelle génération de BMW voit la lumière du jour en septembre 1972. Son premier rejeton est la 520. Elle inaugure par la même occasion la série 5. Même si, sur le plan esthétique, elle s'inspire assez étroitement des grosses six-cylindres, on trouve sous son capot un moteur à quatre cylindres. Un moteur qui est d'ailleurs un peu lymphatique pour une voiture du segment intermédiaire supérieur. Il faudra attendre cinq ans pour que ce petit défaut soit réparé et que la BMW 520 reçoive un six-cylindres.

Le quatre-cylindres a cependant dû subir bon gré mal gré une petite «intervention chirurgicale». La combustion du mélange est optimisée par des modifications des chambres de combustion appelées «baignoires à tourbillons à trois sphères», ce qui permet d'augmenter le taux de compression. BMW en profite aussi pour faire quelque chose pour l'environnement. Les nouveaux carburateurs inversés Stromberg avec starter automatique régulent mieux les gaz d'échappement, en particulier lors des démarrages à froid.

Il n'y a que les muscles qui lui fassent défaut, car il faut près de 13 secondes au moteur de 115 ch pour faire passer de 0 à 100 km/h une voiture qui pèse 1275 kg (et même 20 kg de plus dans la version à boîte automatique). La vitesse de pointe se limite à 175 km/h, la version à injection de 130 ch atteignant tout de même 183 km/h.

Un empattement allongé, des voies élargies et des barres de torsion stabilisatrices complètent si bien les trains roulants éprouvés à jambes élastiques McPherson à l'avant et essieu arrière à bras obliques qu'il suffit d'affiner les tarages de suspension pour obtenir un comportement parfaitement équilibré. Le comportement sécurisant en virage – le léger survirage ne se manifeste jamais sans surprise – et le confort dynamique sont des atouts de la 520.

Une attention particulière a été consacrée à la cellule passagers de sécurité avec longerons renforcés et rigidification particulière des flancs de la plate-forme. Des ordinateurs ont calculé ce qui doit se déformer de façon programmée en cas de collision et ce qui doit rester intact en cas d'accident.

Naturellement, on pose certaines exigences à une voiture qui coûte près de 15 000 marks départ usine sans options en 1972. Et, à ce point de vue, le cockpit ne déçoit pas. Lorsque la lumière est allumée, les cadrans sont illuminés d'une couleur orange, mais ceci est plutôt secondaire. Inhabituellement élevé est, par contre, le volume d'air frais ou chaud que brasse l'installation par minute.

La voiture est disponible au choix avec une boîte manuelle à cinq vitesses ou une transmission automatique et la liste des options dans laquelle on trouve notamment des ceintures de sécurité en offre apparemment tant pour son prix que, rien qu'en 1973, plus de 45 000 nouvelles 520 seront vendues.

BMW 520 1972

The launch of the BMW 520 in 1972 heralded a new generation: the 5 series. Safety, comfort and good handling were the distinguishing characteristics of this automobile, which bears a slight external resemblance to the large BMW six-cylinder.

Mit dem BMW 520 läuft 1972 eine neue Generation an: die 5er Reihe. Sicherheit, Komfort und gutes Fahrverhalten kennzeichnen dieses Fahrzeug, das sich äußerlich leicht an die großen Sechszylinder von BMW anlehnt.

La BMW 520 de 1972 marque l'arrivée d'une nouvelle génération : la série 5. Sécurité, confort et bonne tenue de route sont les qualités de cette voiture qui, sur le plan esthétique, s'inspire légèrement des grosses BMW six-cylindres.

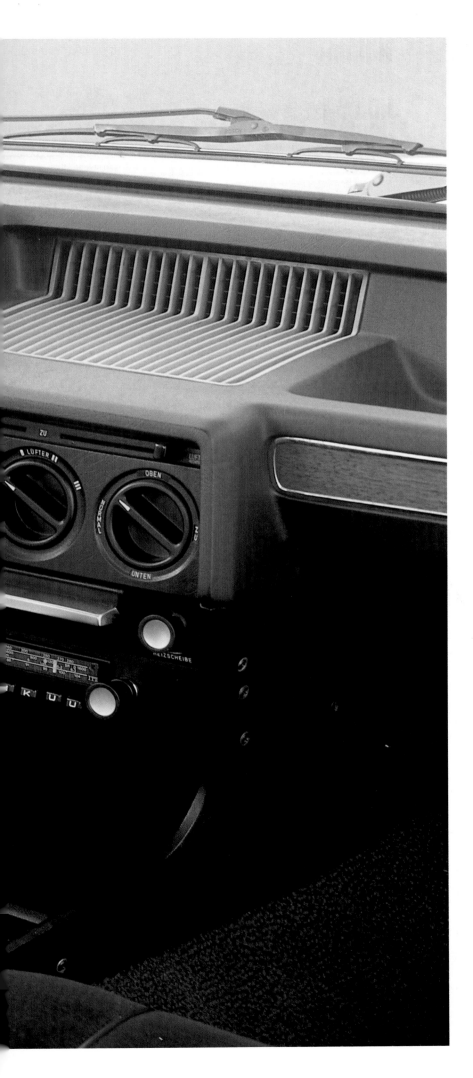

Vast quantities of fresh or heated air are forced into the car by the three controls on the center console. However, the car's engine was less impressive, being a four-cylinder affair developing 115 bhp.

Ein enormes Volumen an Frisch- und Heizungsluft wird von den drei Schaltern in der Mittelkonsole des Cockpits bewegt. Den Wagen selbst bewegt allerdings nur ein 115-PS-Vierzylinder.

Les trois commandes sur la console médiane brassent un volume énorme d'air frais ou réchauffé. Pour sa propulsion, la voiture elle-même se contente en revanche d'un quatre-cylindres de 115 ch.

BMW 520 1972

BMW M1 1978

M otor sport as a creative platform for engineers and the source of many innovative solutions for the series: that is how BMW Motorsport GmbH, founded in 1972, saw its task, which of course also had its commercial aspects. Ambitious plans, for the BMW personnel in Munich's Preußenstraße wanted more than simply to adapt production cars to the racetrack. With code E26, they certainly succeeded in proving their capabilities through a unique high-tech development.

This internal company code concealed a thoroughbred sports car. To use the car in motor sport, BMW had to prove that 400 road vehicles had been built within a two-year period. And that was their weak point. Due to a lack of capacity of their own, BMW trustingly turned to the sports car manufacturer Lamborghini, a thoroughly competent partner. But Lamborghini was hit by financial problems shortly after the first BMW prototype was completed.

BMW reacted quickly and switched the project to Baur coachworks in Stuttgart. As early as the Paris Motor Show of 1978, the E26 development, designed by Giorgio Guigiaro, was presented to the world as the M1. With the M1, BMW Motorsport GmbH created for itself a prestige visiting card for all subsequent products which utilized the prefix "M".

The M1, a mid-engine sports car without frills, was too functional for its target group. That certain something of a Ferrari was missing, although performance was adequate: six seconds from 0 to 62.5 mph (100 kph) and a top speed of 162.5 mph (260 kph). The four-valve M88/1 engine also proved itself durable, offering 277 bhp from a volume of 3.5 liters and

495 bhp for the racing version. Another technical treat was the chassis with independent suspension for each wheel and internally ventilated disc brakes.

Formula 1 had to provide this piece of BMW sports equipment with an adequate forum. Quickly — as always when the financial conditions are right - the godfather of Grand Prix racing, Bernie Ecclestone, and the BMW sports boss, Jochen Neerpasch, came to an agreement. BMW M1 races were to be held on Saturdays before the Grands Prix in Europe.

It was compulsory for all F1 drivers (except Ferrari and Renault) that the first five in Friday's F1 qualifying participate in the prestigious BMW series, called Procar. This was "huge fun" (said Procar driver Hans Stuck), and in 1979 and 1980 sometimes made the pulses of the crowd beat faster than the premier league Grand Prix on Sunday.

Altogether 50 racing versions of the M1 were built, partly with the assistance of Project Four Racing and Osella. Then there was a beefy group 5 version with turbochargers and approximately 900 bhp. All in all, the minimum required by the world association was met, but this limited number is probably the reason why the M1 is traded nowadays at higher prices than its new car values back then.

D ie 1972 gegründete BMW Motorsport GmbH definiert sich als kreative Bühne für Ingenieure und Ausgangspunkt vieler innovativer Lösungen für die Serie - eine hehre Aufgabe, die natürlich auch kommerzielle Aspekte hat. Die BMW-Mannen in Münchens Preußenstraße wollen mehr, als nur Serienwagen die Tauglichkeit für das Rennparkett zu verleihen. Dem selbstgestellten Anspruch, mit eigener High-Tech-Entwicklung einen eindrucksvollen Leistungsnachweis zu erbringen, ist die Abteilung mit dem E26 sicherlich gerecht geworden.

Hinter diesem firmeninternen Kürzel verbirgt sich ein reinrassiger Sportwagen. Um diesen im Motorsport einsetzen zu können, muß der Hersteller nachweisen können, daß er innerhalb von zwei Jahren mindestens 400 Straßenfahrzeuge dieses Typs gebaut hat. Und da liegt der Schwachpunkt. Mangels eigener Fertigungskapazitäten wendet sich BMW vertrauensvoll an den Sportwagenhersteller Lamborghini, einen durchaus kompetenten Partner, der jedoch kurz nach Fertigstellung der ersten Prototypen in wirtschaftliche Schwierigkeiten gerät.

BMW schaltet schnell und überträgt der Karosseriefabrik Baur in Stuttgart das Projekt. Bereits auf dem Pariser Autosalon 1978 wird der von Giorgio Guigiaro entworfene Wagen der Weltöffentlichkeit als M1 präsentiert. Mit dem M1 schafft sich die BMW Motorsport GmbH das Aushängeschild für alle Produkte, die sich hinter dem Buchstaben „M" verbergen.

Der M1, ein Mittelmotorsportwagen ohne Schnörkel, wirkt auf die Zielgruppe zu funktional. Das gewisse Etwas eines Ferrari fehlt, obwohl die Leistungen adäquat sind: sechs Sekunden von 0 auf 100 Stundenkilometer und eine Spitze von

260 Stundenkilometer. Auch in puncto Standfestigkeit bewährt sich das Vierventiler-Triebwerk vom Typ M88/1. Aus 3,5 Liter Hubraum werden 277 PS geholt und 495 PS für die Rennversion. Als technischer Leckerbissen erweist sich das Fahrwerk mit Einzelradaufhängungen und innenbelüfteten Scheibenbremsen.

Um diesem Sportgerät das angemessene Forum zu bieten, muß die Formel 1 herhalten. Schnell - wie immer, wenn die finanziellen Konditionen stimmen - werden sich Grand-Prix-Pate Bernie Ecclestone und BMW-Sportchef Jochen Neerpasch einig. An den Samstagen vor den europäischen Grand Prix soll ein BMW-M1-Rennen angesetzt werden. Bei der ohnehin hochkarätig besetzten Serie, genannt Procar, sollen jeweils die fünf Trainingsschnellsten aus dem Freitagstraining der Formel 1 starten. Ausgenommen sind lediglich die Fahrer von Ferrari und Renault. Diese Serie ist eine "Mordsgaudi", so Procar-Pilot Hans Stuck, und läßt 1979 und 1980 die Zuschauerherzen manchmal höher schlagen als der am Sonntag folgende Lauf der höchsten Klasse des Motorsports.

50 Rennversionen, teilweise unter Mithilfe von Project Four Racing und Osella, werden gebaut. Dazu kommt eine bullige Gruppe-5-Version mit Turboladern und rund 900 PS. Insgesamt wird das vom Weltverband geforderte Minimum gerade eben erfüllt, und deswegen liegt es wohl an dieser begrenzten Stückzahl, daß der M1 heute zu Preisen gehandelt wird, die weit über seinem damaligen Neuwert liegen.

La compétition automobile comme espace créatif pour les ingénieurs et source d'inspiration pour de nombreuses solutions novatrices en vue de la série est, pour la BMW Motorsport GmbH fondée en 1972, une noble vocation qui comporte, naturellement, aussi des aspects commerciaux. Les hommes de BMW de la «Preußenstraße» veulent plus que seulement conférer à une voiture de série l'aptitude à la compétition. Avec la E26, ils sont assurément parvenus à administrer la preuve de leur savoir-faire avec une véritable débauche de haute technologie.

Derrière ce nom de code se dissimule en effet une voiture de sport racée, un véritable étalon. Pour pouvoir l'engager en compétition, il faut prouver en avoir construit 400 en version routière en deux ans. Et c'est là que le bât blesse. Ne possédant pas elle-même les capacités de production nécessaires, BMW se tourne en toute confiance vers le constructeur de voitures de sport italien Lamborghini, un partenaire absolument compétent, mais qui, peu après l'achèvement des premiers prototypes, rencontre des difficultés économiques.

BMW n'hésite pas longtemps et confie le projet au carrossier Baur, à Stuttgart. Dès le Salon de l'Automobile de Paris de 1978, la M1 dessinée par Giorgio Guigiaro est présentée au public mondial. Avec la M1, la BMW Motorsport GmbH s'offre la carte de visite la plus représentative qui soit pour tous les produits qui arboreront plus tard le «M» magique.

La M1, une voiture de sport à moteur central sans fioritures, est trop fonctionnelle pour son groupe cible. Il lui manque le «petit quelque chose en plus» d'une Ferrari bien que ses prestations n'aient rien à lui envier: 6 secondes pour passer de 0 à 100 km/h et une vitesse de pointe de 260 km/h. En termes de fiabilité, également, le quatre-soupapes M88/1 est, lui aussi, au dessus de tout soupçon. Pour une cylindrée de 3,5 litres, il développe 277 ch, et même 495 ch dans la version course. Elle est aussi d'un grand raffinement technique: les trains roulants comportent une suspension à roues indépendantes et des freins à disques ventilés.

La seule scène digne de cette voiture de sport est la Formule 1. Vite - comme toujours lorsque les questions d'argent sont réglées - le parrain de la Formule 1, Bernie Ecclestone, et le directeur de course de BMW, Jochen Neerpasch, se mettent d'accord. Une course de BMW M1 aura lieu le samedi avant chaque Grand Prix de Formule 1 organisé en Europe. Tous les pilotes (sauf ceux de Ferrari et de Renault) doivent obligatoirement participer à cette série très relevée baptisée Procar dès lors qu'ils figurent parmi les cinq premiers des essais du vendredi. Pour le pilote Procar Hans Stuck, cette série est une «sacrée partie de rigolade» et, en 1979 et 1980, elle fait parfois plus frémir les spectateurs que la catégorie reine de la compétition automobile le dimanche.

50 versions course, dont certaines avec l'aide de Project Four Racing et d'Osella, seront construites - sans compter une puissante version groupe 5 à turbocompresseurs d'environ 900 ch. En fin de compte, BMW réussit tout juste à respecter la norme exigée par la Fédération mondiale et c'est bien en raison de ce nombre limité que, aujourd'hui, la M1 jouit d'une cote autrement plus élevée que son prix de vente comme voiture neuve.

The M1 allowed BMW to show its rivals a clean pair of heels. It provided BMW Motorsport GmbH with a mobile billboard for all its products bearing the letter "M" in their names.

Der Konkurrenz das Heck zu zeigen, ist BMW dank des M1 durchaus gelungen. Mit dem M1 schafft sich die BMW Motorsport GmbH ein Aushängeschild für all ihre Produkte, die sich mit dem „M" schmücken.

Montrer sa croupe à la concurrence, BMW y est parfaitement arrivée avec la M1. Avec la M1, BMW Motorsport GmbH donne un prestige envié à tous les produits qui arboreront ultérieurement le célèbre «M».

In order to satisfy international motor sport's homologation regulations and be able to race the car, BMW had to build 400 of the road version of the M1 over a two-year period.

Um sich motorsportlich mit diesem Wagen betätigen zu können, läßt BMW innerhalb von zwei Jahren die zur Homologation erforderlichen 400 M1-Straßenfahrzeuge bauen.

Pour pouvoir courir avec cette voiture, BMW fait construire en deux ans les 400 M1 de route nécessaires pour l'homologation internationale dans différentes catégories de voitures de course.

BMW M1 1978   273

Italian bodywork man Giorgio Guigiaro was responsible for the design of the M1. The front of the M1 is reminiscent of Frenchman Paul Bracq's 1972 prototype.

Für das Design des M1 ist der italienische Karosserie-Künstler Giorgio Guigiaro verantwortlich. Die Front des M1 erinnert an den Prototypen des Franzosen Paul Bracq aus dem Jahr 1972.

L'artiste carrossier italien Giorgio Guigiaro signe le design de la M1. La proue de la M1 rappelle le prototype du Français Paul Bracq de 1972.

The mid-engine automobile is a no-frills machine, with form very much secondary to function. High tech, particularly in the chassis area, and the reliability of the power unit are the dominant factors. The four-valve straight-six M88/1 engine produces 277 bhp (as against the 495 bhp of the racing version). And the cockpit would warm the cockles of any sports car driver. What more could the enthusiast want?

Der Mittelmotorwagen hat rundum keine Schnörkel, da seine Form der Funktion untergeordnet ist. High-Tech, besonders beim Fahrwerk, und Zuverlässigkeit des Triebwerks dominieren. Der Vierventilmotor, ein Reihensechszylinder des Typs M88/1, aktiviert 277 PS – bei der Rennversion sind es 495 PS. Das Cockpit: Sportfahrer-Herz, was willst Du mehr?

La voiture à moteur central possède une carrosserie sans fioritures, car sa forme suit la fonction. La haute technologie, en particulier pour les trains roulants, et la fiabilité de son moteur sont les éléments prédominants. 277 ch – mais 495 ch pour la version course – sont libérés par le moteur à quatre soupapes, un six-cylindres en ligne du type M88/1. Le cockpit: amoureux de la compétition, que souhaites-tu de plus?

BMW 323i 1978

With its completely new six-cylinder injection engine, the 323i was the Bavarian muscle in the 3 series, which was launched in May 1975. Two exhaust pipes draw visible and aural attention to the fact that here the monotone of the 3 series palette – from the 316 to the 320 – was relieved by the sound of a 143 bhp engine. With inlet manifold fuel injection (Bosch K-Jetronic) the mixture was precisely prepared. The 2.3-liter engine smoothly delivered its power with minimal vibration from a crankshaft held in seven bearings and civilized by a dozen counterweights.

Driving pleasure – not just in a straight line at a top speed of 122 mph (196 kph) – was assisted by strengthened springs and stabilizers. This was a compact car that did not have to be wrestled into corners, for the servo-assisted steering worked with pleasant ease and extreme precision.

Four disc brakes, the front ones internally ventilated, rein in the free-running temperament of the 323i on request. Offering acceleration of just nine seconds from 0 to 62.5 mph (100 kph) the 323i was a class leader – always assuming efficient use of the five-speed transmission, installed from September 1979 onwards. Those who preferred a little less sportiness and wished to change gear without hassle were provided with a ZF automatic transmission that featured an hydraulic torque converter and three-speed planetary gears.

Using a relatively high compression ratio of 9.5:1, this 3 series consumed many a liter of Super. Yet an average of 17 miles to the gallon (14 liters per 100 km) represented efficient performance in 1978 when compared against the high bhp figure. The competition from Alfa Romeo and Daimler-Benz was thirstier, but after some 260 miles (420 km) the tank of the Bavarian was empty.

The first 3 series (designated E21 for internal use) lived until 1983 and presented the white and blue BMW badge with a result previously thought impossible: 1.36 million cars sold, of which approximately 35 percent featured the six-cylinder engine.

As the top model, the 323i had collected a valuable cross-section of admiring customers: there were drivers with sporting ambitions, casual users of the accelerator, and people who valued reserves of power and effective brakes for everyday use.

Mit einem völlig neuen Sechszylinder-Einspritzmotor ist der 323i der „Kraftbayer" der im Mai 1975 aus der Taufe gehobenen 3er Serie. Zwei Auspuffrohre machen äußerlich, aber auch akustisch darauf aufmerksam, daß hier die „Eintönigkeit" der 3er Palette – beginnend mit dem 316 bis zum 320 – vom Sound eines 143 PS starken Triebwerkes unterbrochen wird. Mit einer Saugrohr-Benzineinspritzung (Bosch-K-Jetronic) wird das Gemisch gut dosiert aufbereitet. Laufruhig entfaltet das 2,3-Liter-Triebwerk seine Leistung: Keine Vibrationen, denn die siebenfach gelagerte Kurbelwelle weist ein Dutzend Gegengewichte auf.

Der Freude am Fahren – nicht nur geradeaus mit einer Spitzengeschwindigkeit von 196 Stundenkilometern – dienen verstärkte Federn und Stabilisatoren. Ein kompaktes Auto, das nicht mit Nachdruck in die Kurven gezogen werden muß, weil die Servolenkung angenehm leicht und äußerst präzise arbeitet.

Vier Scheibenbremsen – die vorderen innenbelüftet – zügeln bei Bedarf das Temperament des 323i, der mit einer Beschleunigung von knapp neun Sekunden von 0 auf 100 Stundenkilometer Primus in der Mittelklasse ist, gute Schaltarbeit mit dem ab September 1979 eingebauten Fünfganggetriebe vorausgesetzt. Wer es weniger sportlich mag und ohne Hakelei in die Gänge kommen will, dem steht eine ZF-Automatik mit hydraulischem Wandler und 3-Gang-Planetengetriebe zur Verfügung.

Mit einem relativ hohem Verdichtungsverhältnis von 9,5 : 1 stemmt dieser 3er eine ordentliche „Maß" Superbenzin. Doch 14 Liter im Schnitt sind 1978 gemessen an der PS-Zahl Bestwert. Die Konkurrenten von Alfa Romeo und Daimler-Benz schlucken

mehr Benzin. Nach rund 420 Kilometern ist der "Maßkrug" des Bajuwaren jedenfalls leer.

Die erste 3er Reihe (werksintern E21 genannt) läuft bis 1983 und beschert der weißblauen Marke ein bis dahin nicht für möglich gehaltenes Ergebnis: 1,36 Millionen Wagen, davon etwa 35 Prozent mit einem Sechszylinder bestückt, werden ausgeliefert.

Als Topmodell dieser Erfolgsreihe schafft sich der 323i einen ansehnlichen Freundeskreis: sportlich ambitionierte Fahrer, lässige Gasgeber und Menschen, die im Alltagsbetrieb Kraftreserven und wirksame Bremsen für schnelles und sicheres Vorankommen schätzen.

Avec son nouveau six-cylindres à injection, la 323i est la «Bavaroise musclée» de la nouvelle série 3 portée sur les fonts baptismaux en mai 1975. Extérieurement, deux pots d'échappement attirent bruyamment l'attention sur le fait que la «monotonie» de la série 3, qui va de la 316 à la 320, est interrompue par la sonorité d'un moteur de 143 ch. L'injection d'essence Bosch-K-Jetronic dans les tubulures d'aspiration garantit un bon dosage du mélange. Le 2,3 litres se distingue par une montée en puissance linéaire, sans vibration, car le vilebrequin à sept paliers comporte 12 contrepoids.

Le plaisir de conduire – et pas seulement tout droit à la vitesse de pointe de 196 km/h – est favorisé par des ressorts et stabilisateurs renforcés. Une voiture compacte qu'il n'est pas nécessaire de pousser dans les virages parce que la direction assistée est agréablement légère et extrêmement précise.

Quatre freins à disques, ventilés à l'avant, jugulent – si besoin est – le tempérament de la 323i, qui est la première de sa classe avec à peine 9 secondes pour les accélérations de 0 à 100 km/h, à condition de bien manier la boîte de cinq vitesses qui l'équipe à partir de septembre 1979. Celui qui préfère une conduite plus paisible a une excellente alternative avec une boîte automatique ZF à convertisseur hydraulique et boîte planétaire à 3 rapports.

Avec son taux de compression relativement élevé de 9,5:1, cette série 3 ne dédaigne pas le super. Mais, en 1978, une moyenne de 14 litres est un résultat inégalé compte tenu de la performance. Ses concurrentes de chez Alfa Romeo et Daimler-Benz consomment plus. Après environ 420 km, la Bavaroise doit rejoindre la pompe à essence.

La première série 3 (nom de code interne E21) est construite jusqu'en 1983 et rapporte à la marque à l'hélice bleue et blanche un succès commercial inédit à ce jour: 1,36 million de voitures vendues, dont un bon tiers de six-cylindres.

Le top model qu'est la 323i se constitue un enviable club d'amateurs: les automobilistes férus de conduite sportive, ceux qui aiment rouler vite et décontractés ainsi que ceux qui, dans la vie quotidienne, apprécient de bonnes réserves et des freins efficaces pour rouler vite et en toute sûreté.

The top model of the new 3 series, designated E21 within the company, is immediately recognizable from the front thanks to the 323i type plate next to the double headlamps. It proved so lively that it was fitted with a five-speed gearbox in September 1979.

Das Top-Modell der werksintern „E21" genannten neuen 3er Reihe, von vorn sofort an dem Typenschild 323i neben den Doppelscheinwerfern erkennbar, versprüht so viel Temperament, daß es im September 1979 mit einem Fünfganggetriebe belohnt wird.

Le top model de la nouvelle série 3, qui porte le code de production «E21» et est reconnaissable immédiatement au logotype 323i à côté des phares doubles, a un tempérament si débordant qu'il est récompensé, en septembre 1979, par une boîte manuelle à cinq vitesses.

A drive-free continuous fuel injection system supplies the smooth lively six-cylinder in-line engine, which develops 143 bhp, giving this mid-range model a 0 to 62.5 mph (100 kph) time of just under nine seconds.

Eine antriebslose, kontinuierliche Benzineinspritzung versorgt den drehfreudigen laufruhigen Reihensechszylinder, dessen 143 PS den flotten Mittelklassewagen in knapp neun Sekunden auf 100 Stundenkilometer beschleunigen.

Une injection d'essence continue sans entraînement mécanique alimente le six-cylindres en ligne soyeux et spontané dont les 143 ch permettent à cette rapide voiture de taille moyenne d'abattre le 0 à 100 km/h en neuf secondes à peine.

BMW 728i 1979

In accordance with the "law" governing series designations at BMW (3 series from 1975, 5 series from 1972 and 6 series from 1976), the new large sedan which appeared in May 1977 was designated the 7 series – right at the top of the BMW hierarchy. The objective was clear: to gain entry to territory occupied by the Mercedes-Benz S class. The 728i in particular, whose six-cylinder engine provided 184 bhp of performance, was unleashed on S class buyers in 1979. Its balanced cost-to-performance ratio determined that 33,700 marks had to be forked out for the luxurious one-and-a-half ton car.

The 2.8-liter engine materialized as flexible and willing, barely audible to the passengers. If the car was luxurious under the bonnet, the same was true of the interior with its armchair-like front seats and a back seat "sofa", on which just two headrests indicated that three should not try to squeeze inside. A quality interior and solid workmanship contributed to the good reputation of the sedan in the same memorable way as its performance.

From 0 to 62.5 mph (100 kph) with a manual transmission took 9.5 seconds and made the grade as "pretty speedy". The top speed of 125 mph (200 kph) corresponded to rival automotive upper-class standards. Chassis, brakes (discs all round), and the ball and nut type power steering gave this large car an amazing agility even on small country roads.

The 7 series was given four engines (170 to 218 bhp), and in 1984 the equipment was supplemented, as befitted its status, by ABS as standard. Armored 7 series cars for those "at risk", and a turbocharged 745i "Executive" for those with "ballistic salaries" concluded the range at the top. The 728 (with Bosch electronic fuel injection from 1979) achieved more than 100,000 units, if the production of BMW South Africa is included. In May 1986, BMW closed the initial and tasty 7 series chapter coded E23.

Nach dem BMW-spezifischen „Gesetz der Serie" (3er ab 1975, 5er ab 1972 und 6er ab 1976) wird die neue große Limousine, die im Mai 1977 erscheint, hierarchisch in der 7er Reihe – also ganz oben – angesiedelt. Die Zielrichtung ist eindeutig. Man will sich mit der S-Klasse von Mercedes-Benz messen. Besonders der 728i, dessen Sechszylindermotor 184 PS leistet, geht 1979 mit einem ausgewogenen Preis-Leistungs-Verhältnis auf die S-Klassen-Klientel los. 33.700 Mark sind für den luxuriösen Anderthalbtonner hinzublättern.

Das 2,8-Liter-Triebwerk erweist sich als elastisch und drehfreudig, kaum hörbar für die Passagiere. Kultiviert wie der Antrieb ist auch der Innenraum mit seinen fauteuilartigen Vordersitzen und der sofaähnlichen Rückbank, deren zwei Nackenstützen symbolisch andeuten, daß man sich hier nicht zu dritt hinzwängen sollte. Gediegenes Interieur und solide Verarbeitung tragen zum guten Ruf der Limousine ebenso bei wie die Fahrleistungen.

Die Beschleunigung in 9,5 Sekunden von 0 auf 100 Stundenkilometer (mit Schaltgetriebe) verdienen das Prädikat „recht flott". Auch die Spitze von 200 Stundenkilometern entspricht dem Niveau der automobilen Oberschicht. Fahrwerk, Bremsanlage – vorn und hinten Scheibenbremsen – und die Kugelmutter-Hydro-Servolenkung machen den großen Wagen auch auf kleinen Landstraßen recht beweglich.

Vier Motoren von 170 bis 218 PS werden der 7er Reihe spendiert, und 1984 kommt die standesgemäße Ausrüstung mit serienmäßigem ABS hinzu. Gepanzerte 7er für „Gefährdete" und ein 745i „Executive" für „unsinnig hoch Verdienende"

runden die Palette nach oben ab. Der 728 (ab 1979 mit der elektronischen Benzineinspritzung von Bosch) bringt es einschließlich der Produktion von BMW Südafrika auf mehr als 100.000 Einheiten. Im Mai 1986 schließt BMW das erfreuliche Kapitel E23 ab.

S elon la «loi» de la série chez BMW (série 3 à partir de 1975, série 5 à partir de 1972 et série 6 à partir de 1976), la nouvelle grosse limousine qui fait son apparition en mai 1977 se situe, hiérarchiquement, dans la série 7 – autrement dit tout en haut. L'objectif est sans équivoque : venir concurrencer la classe S de Mercedes-Benz. En particulier la 728i, dont le six-cylindres développe 184 ch, brigue les faveurs de la clientèle de la classe S en 1979 avec un rapport prix/prestations très équilibré. La luxueuse voiture de 1500 kg coûte 33 700 marks.

Souple, le moteur de 2,8 litres est friand de hauts régimes et reste pratiquement inaudible pour les passagers. La culture sous le capot se retrouve également dans le cockpit avec les sièges avant évoquant des fauteuils et un véritable divan à l'arrière où les deux appuie-tête signalent combien de personnes peuvent prendre leurs aises ici. Un intérieur soigné et une finition de grande qualité contribuent à asseoir la bonne réputation de la limousine au même titre que ses performances.

9,5 secondes pour le 0 à 100 km/h (avec boîte manuelle) sont un chiffre excellent dans cette catégorie. La vitesse de pointe de 200 km/h, est, elle aussi, tout à fait à la hauteur dans ce segment supérieur de l'automobile. Trains roulants, circuit de freinage (avec disques à l'avant et à l'arrière) et la direction hydraulique à écrou à billes confèrent une maniabilité inattendue à cette grosse voiture même sur des petites routes de campagne.

Quatre moteurs (170 à 218 ch) équipent la série 7 qui voit apparaître, en 1984, le montage en série d'un système ABS «digne de son rang». Une série 7 blindée pour hommes politiques et autres personnes «en danger» ainsi qu'une 745i «Executive» pour «ceux qui gagnent des sommes astronomiques» complètent la gamme vers le haut. La 728 (équipée d'une injection électronique Bosch à partir de 1979) est produite à plus de 100 000 exemplaires, y compris la production de BMW Afrique du Sud. En mai 1986, BMW ferme le passionnant chapitre E23 de sa typologie.

Launched in May 1977, the new BMW 7 series sedans were on an immediate collision course with the Mercedes-Benz S class. The 728i, which offered excellent value for money, was particularly successful.

Die neuen Limousinen von BMW, die im Mai 1977 „vom Stapel gelassen" und als 7er eingestuft werden, schwimmen auf Kollisionskurs mit der S-Klasse von Mercedes-Benz. Besonders erfolgreich, da preiswert, ist der 728i.

Lancées en mai 1977, les nouvelles limousines de BMW, cataloguées série 7, viennent marcher sur les plates-bandes de la classe S de Mercedes-Benz. La moins chère, la 728i, est aussi celle qui remporte le plus de succès.

After a "learning process" in the 733i, the electronic fuel injection system, indicated on the type plate with the letter "i", was introduced to all 7 series models in 1979.

Die elektronische Benzineinspritzung, äußerlich dokumentiert durch das Kürzel „i" hinter der Typenbezeichnung, wird nach einem „Reifeprozeß" im 733i ab 1979 in alle 7er Modelle implantiert.

L'injection d'essence électronique, documentée extérieurement par l'abréviation «i» derrière le logotype, équipe toutes les séries 7 à partir de 1979 après avoir fait ses preuves dans la 733i.

Kyalami, South Africa, 1983 Grand Prix: Alain Prost, Renault-Turbo, appears destined for the Formula 1 world championship. But the champagne mood of the French team goes up in a puff of turbocharger smoke. Not Renault, which pioneered Grand Prix turbo engine technology, but Brabham and BMW seized the prize as the "first Formula 1 turbo world champion" in motor sport history. Brazilian Nelson Piquet became the new world champion – if only by a narrow margin.

Piquet described the success of the Brabham-BMW cooperation: "A high level of technical expertise and professionalism. A team of such efficient mechanics that I consider them my life insurance, and a warm relationship between me, designer Gordon Murray, the team, and engine builder Paul Rosche."

Rosche, nicknamed "camshaft Paul" by insiders, had managed the impossible task of conjuring a standard four-cylinder block into an engine which in qualifying produced such performance that it went off the dial of the engine brake in Munich. That meant this M12/13 miracle engine produced more than 1280 bhp at full turbo-boost.

With newly developed electronic engine management for ignition and injection, Bosch contributed an innovation in monitoring which – a first – featured trackside telemetry. Yet no electronics help if the foundation is wrong. But quality was so solid from Rosche and his team that it could withstand 11,000 rpm and a temperature of 1100 degrees centigrade without complaint.

Special fuel from the BASF subsidiary Wintershall with a very high anti-knock value enabled the production of additional

power. BMW also notched up a PR success: it took barely two years from the decision to develop a Formula 1 engine to the world championship title – an achievement hitherto never attained.

Murray and his collaborator David North had succeeded in building unusually effective "ground effect" aerodynamics. The BT52, developed from the BT49, assembled an homogenous unit of chassis layout, driver position, aerodynamics and fine detail. This was a great challenge for the suppliers. A small example: Murray commissioned not only one, but three companies (Weismann, Alfa Romeo and Getrag) to work on the development of the transmission on a Hewland base, to choose the best.

That only the best materials were up to Murray's standards is shown by the use of carbon fiber panels and a special aluminium alloy for the monocoque, plus driveshafts of high strength alloys, special steels and miniature components of durable light alloys.

The result was a "fantastic" engine with a perfect racing car, guided by a gifted driving talent. No one should have been surprised by the world championship.

Kyalami, Südafrika, Grand-Prix-Finale 1983: Alain Prost, Renault-Turbo, scheint der Titel sicher zu sein. Doch die Champagnerlaune der französischen Equipe verpufft in einem Turboladerschaden. Nicht Renault, Vorreiter der Turbo-Motorentechnik in der Formel 1, sondern Brabham und BMW ernten den Ruhm des ersten „Turbo-Weltmeistertitels" in der Motorsportgeschichte. Der Brasilianer Nelson Piquet ist – wenn auch mit knappem Vorsprung – neuer Champion.

Piquet skizziert den Erfolg der Brabham-BMW-Liaison folgendermaßen: „Hohes technisches Niveau und Professionalität, eine so gut aufeinander eingespielte Mechanikertruppe, daß ich sie als meine Lebensversicherung betrachte, und eine herzliche Beziehung zwischen mir, Konstrukteur Gordon Murray, dem Team und Motorenmacher Paul Rosche."

Rosche, von Insidern „Nocken-Paule" genannt, hat das Unglaubliche geschafft, aus einem Serien-Vierzylinderblock ein Triebwerk zu zaubern, das im Endstadium mehr leistet, als die Meßskala der Motorbremse in München anzeigt. Das heißt, daß dieser M12/13-Wundermotor mehr als 1280 PS bei vollem Turbo-Boost freisetzt.

Mit einem neuentwickelten elektronischen Motormanagement für Zündung und Einspritzung steuert Bosch eine Innovation bei, die telemetrisch - ein Novum – überwacht wird. Doch alle Elektronik nützt nichts, wenn die Basis nicht stimmt. Diese ist bei Rosche jedoch derart solide, daß sie klaglos 11.000 Umdrehungen pro Minute und 1100 Grad Erwärmung aushält.

Spezialbenzin der BASF-Tochter Wintershall, dessen Klopffestigkeit weit über jener handelsüblicher Kraftstoffe liegt,

Brabham BMW BT52 1983

ermöglicht die Entfaltung zusätzlicher Power. BMW verbucht auch einen PR-Erfolg: Knapp zwei Jahre verstreichen von der Entscheidung, ein Formel-1-Triebwerk zu entwickeln bis zum Weltmeistertitel – eine bis dahin unerreichte Glanzleistung.

Kongenial ist das Chassis. Murray und seinem Mitarbeiter David North ist ein ungewöhnlich gut funktionierendes „ground effect car" gelungen. Der BT52, konsequent aus dem BT49 weiterentwickelt, bildet eine homogene Einheit aus Chassis-Layout, Fahrerposition, Aerodynamik und Feinarbeit im Detail. Da sind natürlich auch die Zulieferer gefordert. Kleines Beispiel: Murray setzt gleich drei Firmen auf die Weiterentwicklung des Getriebes auf Hewland-Basis an – Weismann, Alfa Romeo und Getrag –, um aus dem Vollen schöpfen zu können.

Daß nur die besten Materialien seinen Ansprüchen genügen, bezeugt die Verwendung von so futuristischen Werkstoffen wie Kohlefaserplatten und einer speziellen Aluminiumlegierung beim Monocoque, Antriebswellen aus hochlegiertem Edelstahl und Kleinstteilen aus stabilem Leichtmetall.

Das Ergebnis ist ein „Bombenmotor" in einem perfekten Rennwagen, pilotiert von einem begnadeten Fahrertalent. Wen wundert da die Weltmeisterkrone?

K yalami, Afrique du Sud, finale du championnat du monde 1983: Alain Prost, sur Renault-Turbo, semble prédestiné pour sacrer le titre. Mais l'équipe française qui se voyait déjà boire le champagne voit ses espoirs s'évanouir dans l'explosion d'un turbocompresseur. Ce n'est pas Renault, le pionnier de la suralimentation en Formule 1, mais Brabham et BMW qui récoltent les mérites du premier titre de «champion du monde de l'ère des turbos» dans l'histoire de la compétition automobile. Le Brésilien Nelson Piquet est sacré champion du monde, mais avec une avance infinitésimale.

«Une technicité élevée et un grand professionnalisme, une équipe de mécaniciens parfaitement rodés à la tâche que je considérais comme mon assurance-vie et des rapports cordiaux entre moi-même, l'ingénieur Gordon Murray, l'équipe et le motoriste Paul Rosche», déclare Piquet pour expliquer le succès du mariage Brabham-BMW.

Rosche, que les initiés surnomment «Paul la came» a réussi l'impossible, transformer un bloc de quatre-cylindres de série en un moteur qui, à son stade ultime, délivre plus de chevaux que le banc d'essais de Munich n'est capable d'en afficher. Cela signifie que ce merveilleux moteur M12/13 développe plus de 1280 ch à la pression de suralimentation maximum.

Bosch apporte son grain de sel avec une toute nouvelle gestion électronique du moteur pour l'allumage et l'injection, qui – ce qui est une nouveauté – est surveillée par télémétrie. Mais toute l'électronique ne sert à rien si la base n'est pas bonne. Or, avec Rosche, celle-ci est si inébranlable qu'elle supporte sans broncher 11 000 tr/mn et 1100 degrés.

Un carburant spécial de Wintershall, une filiale de BASF,

avec une limite de détonation très élevée permet d'obtenir quelques chevaux supplémentaires. Mais BMW remporte aussi un succès médiatique: il s'est écoulé à peine deux ans entre la décision de construire le moteur de Formule 1 et le sacre de la couronne de champion du monde – une brillante performance jusqu'à ce moment inégalée.

Tout aussi génial est le châssis. Murray et son collaborateur David North ont signé une «voiture à effet de sol» fonctionnant absolument à la perfection. La BT52, extrapolée systématiquement de la BT49, représente une entité homogène de châssis, position de conduite, aérodynamique et raffinement des détails. Mais les sous-traitants ont aussi dû jouer le jeu. Un petit exemple: pour perfectionner la boîte de vitesses (à l'origine une Hewland), Murray fait simultanément appel à trois firmes – Weismann, Alfa Romeo et Getrag – pour pouvoir choisir la meilleure.

Seuls les meilleurs matériaux satisfont aux critères de Gordon Murray, ce que prouvent l'utilisation de panneaux de fibre de carbone et un alliage d'aluminium spécial pour la monocoque, des arbres de transmission en alliage spécial et de minuscules pièces en alliage léger indestructible.

Résultat: un moteur qui est une «bombe» dans une voiture de course parfaite, pilotée par un talent béni des dieux. Qui s'étonnera donc que l'on coiffe la couronne de champion du monde?

Nelson Piquet, Brabham BMW BT50, Österreichring (A), 1982

Nelson Piquet, Brabham BMW BT53, Hockenheimring (D), 1984

Nelson Piquet, Brabham BMW BT54, Paul Ricard (F), 1985

Start number 1 for the first "turbo world champion" in the history of motor sport: Nelson Piquet in a Brabham BMW BT53 of 1984.

Startnummer 1 für den ersten „Turbo-Weltmeister" der Motorsportgeschichte: Nelson Piquet im Brabham BMW BT53 von 1984.

L'envié numéro 1 pour le premier champion du monde de l'ère des turbos dans l'histoire de la compétition automobile: Nelson Piquet dans la Brabham BMW BT53 de 1984.

The exhaust system, consisting of V2A steel pipes with single KKK turbocharger and relief valve (left). This turbocharger can withstand 2.9 bar boost pressure and 1100° centigrade. The racing version of these 1.5-liter "miracle engines" can easily achieve 800 bhp. The actual top performance of this engine, based on a production four-cylinder, lies off the 1280 bhp scale of the BMW test unit.

Das Auspuffsystem aus V2A-Stahl mit dem KKK-Einfach-Turbolader und dem Abblasventil (links).
2,9 bar Ladedruck und 1100° Celsius hält dieser Turbolader aus. Die 1,5-Liter-„Wundermotoren" der Rennversion kommen locker auf 800 PS. Die tatsächliche Leistung des Triebwerks, basierend auf einem Serien-Vierzylinderblock, liegt jenseits der 1280-PS-Meßskala der BMW-Motorbremse.

Le système d'échappement en tubes d'acier inoxydable avec le turbo KKK à un étage et la soupape de décharge (à gauche). Ce turbocompresseur résiste à une pression de suralimentation de 2,9 bars et une temperature de 1100° Celsius. En configuration course, les incroyables moteurs de 1,5 litre développent allègrement 800 ch. On ignore la puissance maximum développée par ce moteur dérivé d'un bloc quatre-cylindres de série, en tout cas bien plus que les 1280 ch jusqu'où va l'échelle de mesure du banc d'essais de moteurs de BMW.

Brabham BMW BT52 1983

"Don't choose a special car, choose your own standpoint", was the BMW advertisement theme for the 6 series, which could be admired at the Geneva Motor Show in March 1976. The special car (coded E24) turned out to be an elegant 6 series coupé for the discriminating. This was a quality guarantee from BMW which its partner Karmann apparently failed to satisfy, since final assembly was transferred early in its production life to the BMW factory at Dingolfing. Karmann was left with the production of the bare body.

Once more it was clear that coupé buyers make sporting comparisons of engine performance. The 630CS (3-liter carburetor engine) and the 628CSi (2.8-liter injection engine) sold a total 9642 units between 1971 and 1987. The 633CSi, whose 3.2-liter unit delivered a more generous 197 bhp, earned 20,234 buyers. Plenty, but nothing when compared to the 635CSi: 51,564 examples were built with its 3.5-liter engine, rated from 211 bhp (catalytic converter) to 286 bhp (M version). German membership figures of the "BMW 6 series club of Germany" are correspondingly high.

Externally the CSi appearance was hardly spectacular and characterized more by classical lines, typical for a BMW coupé. Aerodynamic aids such as front and rear spoilers to cut lift at high speeds were probably appearance items, considering the original kerb weight of 3290 lbs (1495 kg).

The technical innovations were more convincing, particularly as far as the electronics were concerned. There were digital engine electronics with manual gear change down to 1000 rpm. Or there was the option of total electronic control of engine and transmission via a four-speed automatic trans-mission using electronics and hydraulics. Unfortunately, the entry of electronics to the dashboard could not be avoided either. There was an on-board computer which played along with an "SI Service Interval Indicator" and "EC Energy Control". At 16 miles to the gallon of Super (15 liters per 100 km) this was a joke.

Also mechanically there was progress to report for the CSi of the 6 series. The new coupés eventually combined the advantages of the 7 series' double-jointed transverse control arm front axle and new 13-degree trailing arm angles inherited from the 5 series. For a car of this price class the issue of an ABS system as standard was no longer worthy of comment as early as the 1980s. From 1987 onwards it was supplemented by a rear suspension self-leveling device.

The voluminous coupé proved surprisingly rapid in motor sport, and won the European touring car championships three times (1981, 1983 and 1986) as well as the German national title in 1983. There was no lack of power potential in the racing version of the 3.5-liter engine with two valves per cylinder, peaking at a best of 380 bhp, but frequently having to win against rivals with V12 motors or turbochargers.

"Entscheiden Sie sich nicht nur für ein besonderes Automobil, sondern auch für einen eigenen Standpunkt." Mit diesem Slogan wirbt BMW für die 6er Reihe, deren Vorbote auf dem Genfer Salon im März 1976 zu bestaunen ist. Das „besondere" Auto der Baureihe E24 entpuppt sich als elegantes Coupé für Anspruchsvolle. Für BMW ist dies eine Qualitätsverpflichtung, der Partner Karmann offenbar nicht genügt, denn die Endmontage wird ins BMW-Werk Dingolfing verlegt. Karmann bleibt die Fertigung der Rohkarosse.

Einmal mehr zeigt sich, daß Coupékäufer den Vergleich mit Sportwagen suchen, wenn es um die Triebwerksleistung geht. Der 630CS mit 3-Liter-Vergasermotor und der 628CSi mit 2,8-Liter-Einspritzmotor bringen es von 1971 bis 1987 zusammen auf 9642 verkaufte Einheiten. Der 633CSi, dessen 3,2-Liter-Aggregat mit etwas üppigeren 197 PS aufwartet, findet 20.234 Käufer. Dies sind große Absatzzahlen und doch nichts gegen den 635CSi: 51.564 dieser Coupés mit 3,5-Liter-Motoren, deren Leistung von 211 PS (mit Kat) bis 286 PS (M-Version) reicht, werden gebaut. Entsprechend hoch ist die Mitgliederzahl im „BMW 6er Club Deutschland e.V."

Das äußere Erscheinungsbild des CSi, kaum spektakulär und eher von klassischer Linienführung geprägt, ist typisch für ein Coupé. Aerodynamische Hilfen wie Front- und Heckspoiler für mehr Abtrieb bei höheren Geschwindigkeiten dürften angesichts von 1495 Kilo Leergewicht in erster Linie der Optik gedient haben.

Überzeugender sind die technischen Innovationen, besonders im Bereich der Elektronik: Digitale Motorelektronik mit Schubabschaltung bis hinunter zu 1000 Touren oder – auf

BMW 635CSi 1982

Wunsch – eine elektronische Gesamtsteuerung für Motor und Getriebe durch eine Viergang-Automatik mit elektronisch-hydraulischer Arbeitsweise. Leider läßt sich der Einzug der Elektronik auch ins Armaturenbrett nicht vermeiden. Dort tobt sich ein Bordcomputer mit „SI Service Intervallanzeiger" und „EC Energie Control" aus – bei 15 Litern Super auf 100 Kilometer ein Witz!

Aber auch mechanisch gibt es beim CSi der 6er Reihe Fortschritte zu vermelden. Die neuen Coupés vereinen die Vorteile der Doppelgelenk-Federbeinvorderachse mit denen einer neuen 13-Grad-Schräglenkerhinterachse. Für einen Wagen dieser Preisklasse erübrigt sich schon in den achtziger Jahren die Frage nach einem serienmäßig eingebauten ABS-System. Ab 1987 kommt noch eine Niveauregelung hinzu.

Als erstaunlich wendig erweist sich das voluminöse Coupé im Motorsport. Dreimal immerhin holt es die Tourenwagen-Europameisterschaft (1981, 1983 und 1986) sowie 1983 den nationalen deutschen Titel. An Kraft mangelt es der Rennversion des 3,5-Liter-Motors mit zwei Ventilen pro Zylinder ohnehin nicht: 380 PS bringt er an die Hinterräder.

N'optez pas seulement pour une voiture particulière, optez aussi pour votre propre point de vue», déclare le slogan publicitaire de BMW pour la série 6 dont on peut admirer le modèle annonciateur au Salon de Genève de 1976. La voiture «particulière» de la gamme E24 se présente sous les traits d'un coupé élégant pour conducteur exigeant. Pour BMW, qualité oblige – une obligation à laquelle ne satisfait apparemment pas son partenaire Karmann, car le montage final est transféré à l'usine BMW de Dingolfing, Karmann conservant la fabrication de la carrosserie blanche.

Une fois de plus, on constate que les acheteurs de coupés jugent avec les mêmes critères que ceux de voitures de sport en ce qui concerne la puissance des moteurs. La 630CS (moteur à carburateur de trois litres) et la 628CSi (moteur à injection de 2,8 litres) représentent 9642 unités vendues de 1971 à 1987. La 633CSi, dont le 3,2 litres, plus puissant, développe 197 ch fait 20 234 adeptes, ce qui est beaucoup et pourtant rien par rapport à la 635CSi : 51 564 de ces coupés à moteur de 3,5 litres dont la puissance va de 211 ch (avec catalyseur) à 286 ch (version M) seront construits. Comme on peut l'imaginer, le nombre des membres du «BMW 6er Club Deutschland e.V.» est élevé.

Rejetant tout tape-à-l'oeil et plutôt empreinte de classicisme, l'allure extérieure de la CSi est typique d'un coupé. Compte tenu d'un poids à vide de 1495 kg, les expédients aérodynamiques tels que les becquets avant et arrière, censés générer l'appui nécessaire à haute vitesse, n'auraient sans doute guère eu d'efficacité.

Les innovations techniques sont plus convaincantes, notamment dans le domaine de l'électronique : gestion moteur numérique avec coupure de l'alimentation jusqu'à moins de 1000 tr/mn ou, sur demande, une gestion électronique globale du moteur et de la boîte de vitesses grâce à une transmission automatique à quatre rapports avec commande électronique et hydraulique. Malheureusement, l'omniprésence de l'électronique n'épargne pas non plus le tableau de bord. On y voit un ordinateur de bord avec affichage des périodicités d'entretien et contrôle de la consommation. A 15 litres de super aux 100 km, une aimable plaisanterie.

Mais, dans le domaine de la mécanique aussi, la version CSi de la série 6 peut se prévaloir d'avoir fait des progrès. Les nouveaux coupés allient les avantages d'un essieu avant à jambes élastiques à double articulation à ceux d'un nouveau train arrière à bras obliques inclinés de 13 degrés. Pour une voiture de cette catégorie de prix, il est superflu de poser la question de la présence en série du système ABS dès les années 80. Un correcteur d'assiette s'y ajoute en 1987.

Le volumineux coupé s'avère étonnamment maniable en compétition et remporte trois fois le championnat d'Europe des voitures de tourisme (en 1981, 1983 et 1986) ainsi que le titre national allemand en 1983. La version course du moteur de 3,5 litres ne manque en effet pas de chevaux avec ses deux soupapes par cylindre : elle a 380 ch sous le capot.

The orange dashboard illumination and displays are the outward signs that the computer age has dawned beneath the hood of the elegant 6 series coupé. 51,564 CSis were sold in total.

Armaturenbrett-Illuminierung in rot-orange und Displays signalisieren oberflächlich, daß unter der Haube des eleganten Coupés der 6er Reihe das Computerzeitalter Einzug gehalten hat. Vom 635 CSi werden 51.564 Wagen verkauft.

Un tableau de bord à cadrans à fond rouge et des écrans signalent au premier coup d'œil que l'ordinateur et les microprocesseurs commencent à se propager sous le capot de l'élégant coupé de la série 6. De la 635CSi, 51 564 exemplaires seront vendus.

BMW 635CSi 1982

BMW 635CSi 1982

The 3.5-liter power unit generates 218 bhp without the catalytic converter. Including its auxiliaries, the engine fills the 635CSi's engine space, though leaving sufficient space for the ever-increasing electronics. The age of digital motoring is heralded by such features as total electronic control of engine and transmission.

Das 3,5-Liter-Triebwerk mit 218 PS ohne Kat und seine Nebenaggregate füllen den Motorraum des 635CSi, lassen aber genügend Platz für die zunehmende Elektronisierung, beginnend bei der digitalen Motorelektronik mit Schubabschaltung bis hin zur elektronischen Gesamtsteuerung von Motor und Getriebe.

Le moteur de 3,5 litres et 218 ch sans catalyseur emplit le compartiment moteur de la 635CSi avec ses organes, mais laisse assez de place pour l'électronique qui se généralise de plus en plus, de la gestion moteur numérique avec coupure de l'alimentation à la gestion électronique complète du moteur et de la boîte de vitesses.

BMW 635CSi 1982 301

The M 635CSi, launched at the 1983 Frankfurt Motor Show, is both sporty and lavishly appointed, as befits a 156 mph (250 kph) coupé costing more than a Porsche S. The variety of accessories is impressive, and ranges from automatic electric controls and firmly-upholstered adjustable leather seats, whose adjustment options include the actual length of the seating surface, to the three-spoke sports steering wheel, also individually adjustable.

Im M 635CSi – Premiere auf der IAA 1983 in Frankfurt – geht es sportlich und nobel zu. Schließlich kostet das 250 km/h schnelle Coupé mehr als ein Porsche S. Auffällig sind die vielen Accessoires, die elektrischen Bedienungshilfen und die straff gepolsterten Ledersitze, deren Einstellmöglichkeiten auch die Länge der Sitzfläche einschließen. Ebenfalls individuell einstellbar ist das Dreispeichen-Sportlenkrad.

La M 635CSi, qui fête sa première au Salon de l'Automobile de Francfort de 1983, est aussi sportive qu'élégante. Ce coupé capable de croiser à 250 km/h coûte d'ailleurs plus cher qu'une Porsche S. Elle se distingue notamment par ses nombreux accessoires, ses asservisseurs électriques et des sièges cuir au capitonnage ferme dont les possibilités de réglage incluent aussi la longueur des coussins. Le volant sport à trois branches se règle aussi selon les besoins du conducteur.

BMW M 635CSi 1983

The M 635CSi power unit was borrowed from the M1. The six-cylinder four-valve engine with light alloy cross-flow cylinder heads generates a mighty 286 bhp at 6500 rpm, giving the one-and-a-half ton coupé stunning performance figures, for example 0 to 125 mph (200 kph) in just 30 seconds, a good 10 seconds less than the Mercedes 500 SEL.

Dem M1 entlehnt ist die Kraftquelle des M 635CSi. Der Sechszylinder-Vierventiler mit Querstromzylinderkopf aus Leichtmetall mobilisiert bei 6500 U/min stattliche 286 PS, die dem anderthalb Tonnen schweren Coupé zu beachtlichen Fahrleistungen verhelfen. Von 0 auf 200 km/h benötigt es knapp 30 Sekunden, gut 10 Sekunden weniger als ein Mercedes 500 SEL.

Le moteur de la M 635CSi s'inspire de celui de la M1. Le six-cylindres à quatre soupapes avec culasse cross-flow en alliage léger ne développe pas moins de 286 ch à 6500 tr/mn qui confèrent de brillantes performances à ce coupé de 1500 kg : à peine 30 secondes pour le 0 à 200 km/h, toutefois 10 secondes de moins qu'une Mercedes 500 SEL.

With its touring designation, BMW really presented a station wagon in August 1987: not the blend of coupé with a rear hatch and station wagon sedan, as had been the case for the 1971 touring on an 02 base. The customer demand was there, and thus deliveries started in March 1988 with four engine variants. There was also a 325iX, a designation which was neither secretive nor arbitrarily chosen.

The "X" meant 4-wheel drive (4x4). BMW had previously introduced this 325 name once in their 1939 standard light military vehicle for the German Army. The principle of driving all four wheels, revived by BMW in 1985, made more sense in a station wagon than a sedan – unless, of course, it was for a motor sport application.

Like all touring models, the 325iX was equipped with double-tube shock absorbers, disc brakes all round, headlights with ellipsoid dipped beams and a catalytic converter. The 170 bhp of the six-cylinder engine were sufficient to give the car a top speed of 130 mph (208 kph).

At the core of the four-wheel drive principle was a central transfer case with planetary differential and visco-locks. The additional power to the front axle was transmitted by a side drive, via a sprocket chain, and secondary shaft. A total 63 percent of power went to the rear axle and the remaining 37 percent drove the front wheels.

The 4x4 drive equipment, at about 176 lbs (80 kg), weighed heavily on the purchase price. The "X" cost an additional 8500 marks. Unsurprisingly production of the 4x4 drive version accounted for less than three percent of the touring output,

nevertheless 5273 "X"s were made. This is an indication of the success of the first station wagon from BMW.

In terms of equipment it was anything but your typical "workhorse". That is also why a loading rail directly above the bumper was left off. The rear lights only allowed sufficient opening for, say, golf bags, prams or a collapsible bicycle. Bulky chests, workmen's tools or building materials should kindly be transported by other means. That, at least, is how those who love this car see it – the speedy "three".

Mit dem touring stellt BMW im August 1987 einen echten Kombi vor, kein Verschnitt aus Coupé mit Heckklappe und Kombilimousine wie das gleichnamige Fahrzeug von 1971. Die entsprechende Nachfrage besteht, und so läuft im März 1988 die Auslieferung mit vier Motorvarianten an. Es gibt auch einen 325iX, eine Bezeichnung, die weder geheimnisvoll, noch x-beliebig gewählt worden ist.

Das „X" steht für Allradantrieb. Den hatte es bei BMW schon einmal gegeben: 1939 und ebenfalls bei einem 325er, dem leichten Einheits-Pkw für die Wehrmacht. Das von BMW 1985 wieder aufgegriffene Prinzip des Vierradantriebs macht bei einem Kombi eher Sinn als bei einer Limousine, es sei denn, man will diese im Motorsport einsetzen.

Wie alle Touringmodelle ist der 325iX mit Doppelrohr-Gasdruckdämpfern, Scheibenbremsen rundum, Scheinwerfern mit Ellipsoid-Abblendlicht und einem Katalysator ausgerüstet. Die 170 PS des Sechszylindertriebwerks reichen aus, um dem Wagen eine Spitzengeschwindigkeit von 208 Stundenkilometern zu verleihen.

Kernpunkt des Allradprinzips ist ein zentrales Verteilergetriebe mit Planetendifferential und Visco-Sperren. Der zusätzliche Antrieb zur Vorderachse wird durch einen Seitentrieb über Zahnkette und Nebenwelle erreicht. Zu 63 Prozent geht die Kraft an die Hinterachse, die restlichen 37 Prozent treiben die Vorderräder an.

Die rund 80 Kilo Allradtechnik liegen dem Käufer im wahrsten Sinne des Wortes schwer auf der Tasche: 8500 Mark Aufpreis kostet das „X". Kein Wunder also, daß der Produktionsanteil der Allradler unter den Tourings keine drei Prozent

BMW 325iX touring 1988

ausmacht. Absolut gesehen sind es immerhin 5273 „X". Daran läßt sich ermessen, wie erfolgreich der erste Kombi von BMW insgesamt ist.

Der Ausstattung nach ist er alles andere als ein typischer „Lastesel". Und deshalb wurde auch auf eine Ladekante direkt über der Stoßstange verzichtet. Die Heckleuchten lassen nur eine Durchreiche frei, etwa für Golfbags, Kinderwagen oder ein Klappfahrrad. Sperrige Kisten, Handwerkerzubehör oder Baumaterialien sollen gefälligst mit anderen Transportmitteln befördert werden. So sehen es jedenfalls diejenigen, die ihn lieben – den „flotten 3er".

BMW dévoile en août 1987 un authentique break: pas de croisement de coupé à hayon et de break-limousine comme la première voiture du même nom présentée en 1971. La demande ne se fait pas attendre et c'est ainsi que la commercialisation commence en mars 1988 avec quatre motorisations différentes. Il existe aussi une 325iX, une dénomination qui n'a rien de mystérieux et n'a pas été choisie fortuitement.

Le «X» signifie traction intégrale. BMW en avait déjà eu une en 1939 avec une 325, une légère voiture particulière pour le transport de personnels de la Wehrmacht. Reprendre, en 1985, le principe des quatre roues motrices a plus de sens avec un break qu'avec une berline, à moins que l'on ne veuille engager celle-ci en compétition.

Comme toutes les touring, la 325iX possède des amortisseurs à gaz bitube, des freins à disques sur les quatre roues, des phares à feux de croisement ellipsoïdaux et un pot catalytique. Les 170 ch du six-cylindres suffisent pour donner à la voiture une vitesse de pointe de 208 km/h.

La clef de voûte de la traction intégrale est une boîte distributrice centrale avec différentiel planétaire et viscocoupleurs. La prise de force supplémentaire pour l'essieu avant s'effectue de côté à l'aide d'une chaîne dentée et d'un arbre secondaire. 63 % du couple sont dirigés vers l'essieu arrière, les 37 % restants entraînant les roues avant.

Les quelque 80 kg de traction intégrale pèsent aussi sur le prix d'achat: la «X» coûte 8500 marks de plus que la version normale. Rien d'étonnant, donc, à ce que le taux des quatre roues motrices parmi les touring ne dépasse pas 3 %, ce qui,

dans l'absolu, se traduit tout de même par 5273 «X». Et cela indique le succès remporté par le premier break de BMW.

Son aménagement est tout sauf celui d'une bête de somme typique. Et c'est d'ailleurs la raison pour laquelle on renonce au seuil de chargement directement au-dessus du pare-chocs. Les optiques arrière n'autorisent en effet qu'une découpe de coffre limitée – par exemple pour un équipement de golf, une voiture d'enfant ou un vélo pliant. Que l'on se procure un autre véhicule pour transporter des objets encombrants, tout ce dont a besoin un artisan ou des matériaux de construction. Telle est en tout cas la philosophie de ceux qui l'adorent – la rapide série 3.

BMW identified a market niche and, to fill it, constructed a pure estate car based on the 3 series. The 325iX touring is driven by a 170 bhp engine and a transfer gear providing power to all axles. The design of the tailgate adds to the torsional rigidity, but is a nuisance when it comes to loading the trunk.

Eine Marktlücke: BMW baut, basierend auf dem 3er, einen reinen Kombi. Der 325iX touring wird von 170 PS über ein zentrales Verteilergetriebe an allen Achsen angetrieben. Das Heck, dessen Rücklichter wie bei der Limousine angeordnet sind, dient der Verwindungssteifigkeit, ist beim Beladen aber eher hinderlich.

BMW découvre un créneau et, sur la base de la série 3, construit un authentique break : la 325iX touring de 170 ch possède une traction intégrale avec boîte de distribution centrale. La découpe du coffre est favorable à la rigidité torsionnelle, mais n'est guère pratique.

The harmonious parallel roof and belt line give the touring an interesting appearance, while the BBS design alloy wheels lend a sporty note.

Der harmonische „Parallelschwung" aus Dach- und Gürtellinie macht den touring auch optisch interessant, wobei die Leichtmetallräder im BBS-Design eine sportliche Note hinzufügen.

Par leur harmonie, le parallélisme des lignes de toit et de ceinture rend la touring intéressante sur le plan esthétique aussi et les jantes alliage BBS y ajoutent une note de sportivité.

BMW M3 Sport Evolution 1990

The 1987 touring car world championship was in the bag — a unique title — and the European championship of 1988 too, both with Roberto Ravaglia. Still the engineers at BMW Motorsport GmbH saw stars. To be precise, one star in particular - that of Mercedes in Stuttgart. To shine in the German touring car championship as well, BMW had to make the racing version of its successful M3 undergo evolutionary changes. That meant evidence of 500 identical vehicles had to be presented to the governing body, the FIA, in Paris. Such machines contained the latest in knowledge from competition, gathered on the track.

However, competitor Mercedes-Benz was one step ahead and had approved the 190E 2.5-16 Evolution, a multi-wing creation which produced a rapid reaction from BMW. Sales problems with the tuned road version of the M3 Evolution (E30) did not cause much of a headache in Munich. Although 20,000 marks more than the usual M3, the "Evo" immediately sold out.

The product of this technology transfer in both directions rubbed off on the road and racing "Evo". The racing car, with almost 360 bhp, was given a catalytic converter and lambda sensor. Both "Evos" now possessed sophisticated engine electronics, large-diameter disc brakes made of high-alloy steel, an exhaust system of highest quality steel, and a rear spoiler with an adjustable lip.

The chassis ride stiffness was adjustable; three levels could be electronically selected – "Sport" – (here the "Evo" hugs the road), "Normal" and "Comfort". The latter was totally inappropriate for a stark racing platform chassis, one lacking electric windows and other normal refinements.

The bucket seats with guide slots for full harness seat belts befitted the sporty image of the "Evo". Why it was fitted with three-point inertia reel belts in red remains a BMW mystery. The warning tone which could be heard when the driver pre-set maximum speed was exeeded was a curious feature of this "road-runner" which could manage 145 mph (248 kph).

The manual adjustment of the front and rear spoilers — here owners were expected to handle the screwdriver themselves, according to the manual — was a bit of a nuisance for normal use, but essential for making aerodynamic adjustments for the racetrack. After all, the racing "Evo" could manage a good 187.5 mph (300 kph), depending on the transmission.

The driver of the showroom M3 Evo was provided with more than enough in terms of road holding and acceleration. Hold tight: the "Evo" was catapulted from 0 to 62.5 mph (100 kph) in 6.3 seconds, and the standing kilometer was achieved after just 26.7 seconds. Any sweat at such explosive acceleration was absorbed by a suede steering wheel.

At the end of six years of racing the M3 and its Evolution, the "M team" could be satisfied with more than 1500 wins and 50 international titles.

Da ist man nun Tourenwagen-Weltmeister 1987 - eine einmalige Titelvergabe - und Europameister 1988 mit Roberto Ravaglia, und dennoch sehen die Techniker der BMW Motorsport GmbH Sterne, genauer gesagt: Stern aus Stuttgart! Um auch in der Deutschen Tourenwagenmeisterschaft brillieren zu können, muß BMW den erfolgreichen M3 in Rennausführung einer Weiterentwicklung unterziehen. Das bedeutet, der Bau von 500 identischen Fahrzeugen, in die die neuesten Erkenntnisse aus dem Wettbewerb auf der Strecke einfließen, ist der obersten Automobilbehörde FIA in Paris nachzuweisen.

Doch mit eben diesem Schritt ist Konkurrent Mercedes-Benz zuvorgekommen und hat den 190E 2.5-16 Evolution homologieren lassen, eine mit viel „Flügelwerk" versehene Kreation, auf die BMW eilig reagiert. Über Absatzprobleme mit der aufgemotzten Straßenversion des M3 Evolution (E30) muß man sich in München keine Sorgen machen. Obwohl 20.000 Mark teurer als der „normale" M3, ist der „Evo" sofort vergriffen.

Das Produkt dieses Technologietransfers in beiden Richtungen färbt auf Straßen- und Renn-„Evo" ab. Das Rennauto, knapp 360 PS stark, bekommt KAT und Lambda-Sonde, und beide „Evos" verfügen jetzt über eine ausgefeilte digitale Motorelektronik, großdimensionierte Scheibenbremsen aus hochlegiertem Stahl, eine Auspuffanlage aus Edelstahl sowie einen Heckspoiler mit verstellbarer Lippe.

Verstellbar ist auch das gesamte Fahrwerk. Elektronisch wählbar sind die Stufen „Sport" - da liegt der „Evo" richtig gut auf der Straße - „Normal" und „Komfort". Letztere paßt

überhaupt nicht zu einer Fahrmaschine, bei der auf elektrische Fensterheber und sonstige Alltagshilfen verzichtet wird.

Zum sportlichen Image des „Evo" passen die Schalensitze mit Führungsrillen für Hosenträgergurte. Warum er dann mit Dreipunkt-Automatikgurten ausgerüstet wird, bleibt BMW-Geheimnis. Auch mutet bei einem „Straßenrenner", der 248 Stundenkilometer geht, der Piepton für selbst gesetzte Sollgeschwindigkeiten an wie das Geräusch einer Sirene beim Feueralarm.

Das manuelle Einstellen von Front- und Heckspoiler – hier darf man nach Betriebsanleitung selbst schrauben – ist für den Normalbetrieb eher lästig, für die aerodynamische Anpassung an eine Rennstrecke jedoch unerläßlich. Schließlich geht der Renn-"Evo" je nach Übersetzung gut 300 Stundenkilometer.

Dem Fahrer der „zivilen" Version wird in puncto Straßenlage und Beschleunigung schon genug geboten. Festhalten: In 6,3 Sekunden katapultiert sich der „Evo" von 0 auf 100 Stundenkilometer, und der stehende Kilometer wird bereits nach 26,7 Sekunden erreicht. Etwaige Schweißtropfen bei einem derartigen Adrenalinstoß saugt das Wildlederlenkrad auf.

Nach sechs Jahren Rennbetrieb des M3 und seiner Evolution dürfen sich die „M-Mannen" über 1500 Siege und 50 internationale Titel freuen.

Alors, on est champion du monde des voitures de tourisme en 1987 – un titre décerné une seule et unique fois – et champion d'Europe 1988 avec Roberto Ravaglia et, pourtant, les techniciens de BMW Motorsport GmbH ne voit que des étoiles: pour être plus précis, une étoile – celle de Stuttgart. Pour pouvoir briller également dans le championnat d'Allemagne des voitures de tourisme, BMW doit revoir et corriger la copie de sa M3 version course pourtant couronnée de succès. Et cela signifie 500 voitures identiques intégrant les derniers enseignements de la compétition pour obtenir l'homologation des instances suprêmes de l'automobile, la FIA, à Paris.

Mais son concurrent Mercedes-Benz ne se laisse pas prendre au dépourvu non plus et a déjà également fait homologuer une version plus sophistiquée, la 190E 2.5-16 Evolution. Une création dotée de nombreux appendices aérodynamiques à laquelle BMW réagit du tac au tac. A Munich, point n'est besoin de se perdre en conjectures sur les problèmes de vente de la version route «musclée» de la M3 Evolution (E30). Bien qu'elle coûte 20 000 marks de plus que la M3 normale, on s'arrache l'«Evo» jusqu'au dernier exemplaire.

Le produit de ce transfert de technologie dans les deux sens fait tache d'huile sur les «Evo» de route et de circuit. La voiture de course, avec ses près de 360 ch, reçoit catalyseur et sonde lambda tandis que les deux «Evos» possèdent maintenant une gestion électronique moteur numérique sophistiquée, des freins à disques de grandes dimensions en acier à alliage spécial, une ligne d'échappement en acier inoxydable ainsi qu'un becquet arrière à déflecteur réglable.

Réglable, ce qualificatif vaut aussi pour l'ensemble des trains roulants: on peut sélectionner électroniquement les niveaux «Sport» – l'«Evo» colle alors comme une ventouse à la route – «Normal» et «Confort». Ce dernier ne va absolument pas avec un tel engin qui renonce ostensiblement aux lève-vitres électriques et à tout autre gadget de cet acabit.

Les baquets avec ouvertures pour les harnais vont par contre fort bien avec l'image sportive de l'«Evo». Mais pourquoi l'équiper alors de ceintures automatiques à trois points? Cela restera pour toujours le secret de BMW. Pour un bolide roulant à 248 km/h, le bip sonore de dépassement de la vitesse que l'on s'est fixée est aussi incongru qu'un réveil dans une caserne de pompiers.

Le réglage manuel des ailerons avant et arrière – reportez-vous au mode d'emploi pour les déplacer vous-même – est quelque peu superflu en utilisation routière normale, mais, en revanche, absolument indispensable pour peaufiner les réglages aérodynamiques sur circuit. En effet, l«Evo» course atteint largement 300 km/h selon son rapport de pont.

Sur le plan de la tenue de route et des accélérations, les conducteurs de la version «civile» en ont de toute façon déjà pour leur argent. Mais il faut bien se tenir: l'«Evo» se catapulte de 0 à 100 km/h en 6,3 secondes et abat le kilomètre arrêté en 26,7 secondes à peine. Heureusement que le volant gainé de daim peut sécher les éventuelles mains moites que donne ce genre de poussées d'adrénaline.

Après six ans de compétition avec la M3 et son Evolution, les «hommes au M» peuvent se prévaloir de plus de 1500 victoires et de 50 titres internationaux.

Aerodynamic features such as spoilers with manually adjustable lips to increase downforce, so vital in motor sport, were here introduced into the small production run of 500 M3s – thus the name Sport Evolution.

Die im Motorsport erforderlichen aerodynamischen Attribute, wie Spoiler mit manuell verstellbarer Lippe für mehr Abtrieb, halten in der Kleinserie der 500 M3 Einzug – darum der Name Sport Evolution.

Des accessoires aérodynamiques indispensables en compétition, comme l'aileron à arête réglable à la main pour obtenir plus d'appui, font leur apparition dans la petite série de la M3 produite à 500 exemplaires et qui porte le nom Sport Evolution.

The chassis beneath the "plump cheeks" of the M3, which is equipped to take wide tires in a variety of sizes, had three electronically-adjustable suspension settings: a stiff sporty set-up, normal or comfortable.

Das Fahrwerk unter den „dicken Backen" des M3, der für Breitreifen unterschiedlicher Dimensionen gerüstet ist, läßt sich via Elektronik sportlich straff oder komfortabel einstellen. Dazwischen liegt noch die Stufe „Normal".

Sous les «grosses joues» de la M3 conçue pour recevoir des pneus larges de différentes dimensions, le châssis peut être électroniquement réglé, au choix, ferme ou confortable. Autre alternative, un réglage «normal».

The road version of the M3 Sport Evolution has impressive handling and performance, with a top speed of 155 mph (248 kph) and a 0 to 62.5 mph (100 kph) time of 6.3 seconds. The racing version won more than 1500 races and captured 50 international titles over a six-year period.

Die „zivile" Version des M3 Sport Evolution beeindruckt durch ihr Handling und ihre Leistung: 248 km/h Spitze, in 6,3 Sekunden von 0 auf 100 km/h. In der Rennversion bringt es der M3 innerhalb von sechs Jahren auf 1500 Siege und 50 internationale Titel.

La version Sport Evolution «civile» de la M3 stupéfait par sa maniabilité et ses performances: 248 km/h de vitesse de pointe, 0 à 100 km/h en 6,3 secondes. Dans la version course, la M3 remporte en six ans 1500 victoires et 50 titres internationaux.

BMW M3 Sport Evolution 1990

The super-functional cockpit features leather bucket seats with guide mechanisms for harness belts (though these do not come with the car) and a sports steering wheel with a suede grip area. Tests reveal a power output of 238 bhp at 7000 rpm for the four-valve four-cylinder engine with electronic fuel injection and a three-way catalytic converter.

In dem äußerst funktionellen Cockpit fallen die Lederschalensitze mit Führungen für Hosenträger-gurte (die freilich nicht mitgeliefert werden) und das Sportlenkrad mit Wildleder-Griffzone auf. Das Power-Stenogramm des Vierventil-Vierzylinders mit elektronischer Benzineinspritzung und geregeltem Dreiwegekatalysator lautet 238 PS bei 7000 U/min.

Dans le cockpit extrêmement fonctionnel, on remarque les baquets en cuir avec ouvertures pour le harnais six points (qui n'est toutefois pas livré avec la voiture) et le volant sport partiellement gainé de daim. La puissance du quatre-cylindres à quatre soupapes à injection électronique et catalyseur réglé à trois voies culmine à 238 ch à 7000 tr/mn.

BMW M3 Sport Evolution 1990

BMW 318i Cabrio (Kat) 1990

"Decapitating" BMW bodies and adapting them to open cars was fashionable at Baur in Stuttgart. Installing a Targa rollbar, effectively as a replacement to the B-pillar, also was a practical Baur tradition. At the Frankfurt Motor Show in September 1985, BMW demonstrated its willingness to do its own "beheading" to produce a full convertible. This car, which was much more elegant than the equivalent Baur version, was initially available based on the 325i and 320 .

It was only in 1990 – the new E36 3 series was poised on the brink of volume production – that the 318i was accompanied by a convertible version. The 318i with the new four-cylinder engine had a three-way catalytic converter and a lambda oxygen sensor. This was a sensible solution, particularly since the 113 bhp seemed to be perfectly capable of running for 21.5 miles on a gallon of normal lead-free petrol (11 liters per 100 km).

The price (less than 50,000 marks, back in 1993) was also attractive for those convertibles fans for whom a 325i was simply out of reach. The pleasure to be gained from driving under an open sky was never clouded with the four-cylinder engine. Employing the five-speed manual gearbox, acceleration from 0 to 62.5 mph (100 kph) came in just under 11 seconds, and with a top speed of 119 mph (190 kph), it was quite enough to lift your spirits without blowing your head off. Models with automatic transmission were almost as fast.

Narrow winding streets did not pose any problems to this convertible, provided that its driver had muscular arms, or spent the extra money and installed power-assisted steering.

The convertible only encountered problems in extreme cases of hard driving. Situations in which the rear drum brakes - discs at the front - could not cope did not generally appear in normal street driving conditions.

The finish and the folding mechanism of the fabric hood were of top quality. For those who did prefer something more substantial over their heads in winter, BMW also offered a hardtop cover. This item admittedly did not make the appearance of this 3 series more beautiful.

Das „Enthaupten" von BMW-Karosserien für den Umbau in offene Autos gehört bei Baur in Stuttgart zum Pflichtprogramm. Und traditionell bei Baur ist auch die Installation eines Targabügels, quasi als B-Säulen-Ersatz. Im September 1985 jedoch zeigt BMW auf der Frankfurter Automobilausstellung, daß man gewillt ist, selbst zu „köpfen", und zwar so, daß ein Vollcabriolet dabei herauskommt. Dieses Cabriolet – eleganter als die Baur-Version – ist zunächst auf Basis des 325i und des 320 erhältlich.

Erst 1990 - die neuen 3er der Baureihe E36 stehen bereits kurz vor der Serienreife - gesellt sich dem 318i ebenfalls ein Cabriolet zu. Der 318i mit dem neuen Vierzylindermotor verfügt über einen Dreiwegekatalysator und eine Lambda-Sonde - eine vernünftige Lösung, zumal sich die 113 PS mit knapp 11 Litern normaler bleifreier Flüssignahrung zufriedengeben.

Attraktiv ist auch der Preis für die Cabriolet-Fans, denen der 325i ein zu „starkes Stück" ist, kostet der 318i doch selbst 1993 noch unter 50.000 Mark. Auch mit dem Vierzylindertriebwerk bietet der offene 3er ungetrübten Fahrspaß unter freiem Himmel. Mit dem Fünfgang-Schaltgetriebe ist eine Beschleunigung von 0 auf 100 Stundenkilometer in knapp 11 Sekunden möglich, und die Spitzengeschwindigkeit von 190 Stundenkilometer genügt für viel Kopffreiheit. Nur geringfügig langsamer geht es mit der Automatik voran.

Auf engen kurvenreichen Straßen erweist sich dieses Cabriolet als sehr wendig, vorausgesetzt man hat kräftige Arme oder sich gegen Aufpreis eine Servolenkung einbauen lassen. Verwindungsprobleme kennt das 3er Cabrio höchstens im Extremfall, und Situationen, denen die hinteren Trommel-

bremsen – vorn hat das Cabriolet Scheibenbremsen – nicht gewachsen sind, treten im normalen Fahrbetrieb nicht auf.

Verarbeitung und Faltmechanismus des Stoffverdecks sind erstklassig. Wer im Winter jedoch mehr über dem Kopf haben möchte, dem bietet BMW einen maßgeschneiderten Hardtop-Aufsatz, durch den der 3er jedoch nicht verschönert wird.

Chez Baur, à Stuttgart, «décapiter» des carrosseries de BMW pour en faire des décapotables fait partie de la routine. Une tradition, chez Baur, est d'ailleurs le montage d'un arceau Targa qui remplace en quelque sorte le pied médian. En septembre 1985, au Salon de l'Automobile de Francfort, BMW veut montrer qu'à Munich aussi, on est parfaitement capable de «faire rouler des têtes». Et ce de telle façon que l'on obtienne un cabriolet à part entière. Celui-ci – plus élégant que celui de Baur – est tout d'abord disponible en version 325i et 320.

Ce n'est qu'en 1990 – alors que la nouvelle série 3 de la gamme E36 va bientôt être dévoilée au grand public – que l'on voit également apparaître un cabriolet 318i. Cette 318i propulsée par un nouveau moteur à quatre cylindres possède un catalyseur trois voies et une sonde lambda. Une solution raisonnable, d'autant plus que les 113 ch se contentent d'à peine 11 litres d'ordinaire sans plomb.

Le prix est aussi attrayant pour les amateurs de cabriolets (même en 1993, encore inférieur à 50 000 marks) pour lesquels une 325i est un trop «gros morceau». Avec le quatre-cylindres sous le capot, rouler les cheveux au vent sous les rayons du soleil est un tout aussi grand plaisir. La boîte manuelle à cinq vitesses permet d'accélérer de 0 à 100 km/h en 11 secondes à peine et la vitesse de pointe de 190 km/h est tout à fait suffisante pour une garde au toit illimitée. La version à boîte automatique n'est que légèrement plus lente.

Sur les routes étroites et sinueuses, ce cabriolet s'avère très maniable à condition que l'on ait suffisamment de biceps ou que l'on s'offre, contre supplément, une direction assistée. Le cabriolet de la série 3 ne connaît des problèmes de rigidité torsionnelle que dans les cas extrêmes et, en circulation normale, il ne se produit pas de situations dans lesquelles les freins à tambours à l'arrière – disques à l'avant – ne soient pas à la hauteur.

La finition et le mécanisme de fermeture de la capote sont «haut-de-gamme». Quiconque souhaite une protection en dur au-dessus de la tête durant l'hiver peut faire appel à BMW qui propose un hard-top taillé sur mesure, mais qui ne contribue pas particulièrement à embellir la série 3.

The convertible version of the 318i first arrived on the market in 1990. It is a highly economical convertible, its four-cylinder engine with three-way catalytic converter and lambda probe having a fuel consumption of around 21.5 miles per gallon (11 liters per 100 km).

Erst 1990 kommt der 318i auch „oben ohne" auf den Markt: ein äußerst preiswertes Cabriolet, dessen Vierzylindermotor mit Dreiwegekatalysator und Lambda-Sonde knapp 11 Liter Normalbenzin verbraucht.

Il faut attendre 1990 pour voir une 318i «décapitée» apparaître sur le marché: il s'agit d'un cabriolet au prix extrêmement intéressant, dont le quatre-cylindres à catalyseur trois voies et sonde lambda se contente de 11 litres d'ordinaire aux 100 km.

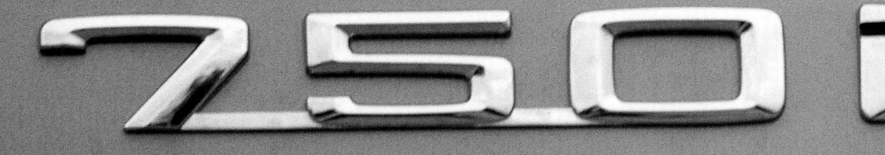

BMW 750iL 1987

Count Hans von der Goltz, supervisory board chairman of BMW AG, and his equally blue-blooded managing director, Dr Eberhard von Kuenheim, know what is right: "Noblesse oblige". BMW was to be among those who set the future tone in the highest sedan society, echoing Maybach in the 1930s. Expensive handbuilt labor, little high-tech and incredibly high prices handicapped the noble British convey-ance of aristocracy, Rolls-Royce. They were no competition for BMW – except that the name has that ring of royalty about it. The real competition in terms of numbers of cars registered was the S class from Mercedes-Benz. Stuttgart was convinced the S class would not lose any buyers to Munich.

Wrong! The new 750i – the first German twelve-cylinder luxury car since the Second World War – overtook the S class in new cars registered in Germany as early as May 1987. It was almost unheard-of that the Bavarians should steal the show from Stuttgart's Swabians in the luxury class. The only sound from Rolls was a surprised whisper. One was clearly "not amused".

This miracle of Bavarian engine technology had a block and twelve cylinder heads made of aluminium. That is why the 2500 or so refined engine parts together did not weigh more than 529 lbs (240 kg). The crankshaft of the V-engine had seven bearings. Since the two halves of the V had their own drive units and catalytic converters, total engine failure was almost unthinkable.

The 5-liter engine could only be heard when it delivered all 300 bhp – something which happened at an engine speed of 5200 rpm, so it was nobly restrained but powerful. Simply majestic. The most modern engine management and four-speed automatic transmission with drive programs "Sport" and "Economy" belonged to the magnicent and splendid Bavarian aristocrat. The 1.8 tons of unladen weight could be accelerated to 62.5 mph (100 kph) in less than eight seconds, and BMW was content to limit top speed electronically to 156 mph (250 kph). Higher speeds than that would reduce driving comfort. This, in any case, was equivalent to being carried in a sedan-chair due to automatic stabilization and electronic shock absorber controls.

Luxury reigned in the cabin, with five comfortable seats of the finest leather. And however hard you looked, not even the smallest technical refinement invented to make cars more comfortable was missing. Anyone wanting a drinks cabinet or a television would be advised to choose the 4 inches (11 cm) longer 750iL. In 1987 the 750i still cost a "modest" 102,000 marks, the stretched (L-badged) version demanded 17,000 marks more. The refined pleasure of being able to afford this ultimate limousine was enjoyed by almost 20,000 obviously well-heeled people in 1987/88.

Hans Graf von der Goltz, Aufsichtsratsvorsitzender der BMW AG, und sein ebenfalls blaublütiger Vorstand Dr.-Ing. h.c. Eberhard von Kuenheim wissen, was sich gehört: „Noblesse oblige!" BMW soll auch in der High society der Nobelkarossen künftig mit den Ton angeben – so wie Maybach in den dreißiger Jahren. Viel Handarbeit, wenig High-Tech und zu hohe Preise sind das Handicap der britischen Hochadels-Kutsche Rolls-Royce. Für BMW ist dieser Hersteller kein Konkurrent – nur der Name ist eben unvergleichlich vor-nehm. Die eigentliche Konkurrenz in der Zulassungsstatistik ist die S-Klasse von Mercedes-Benz. Und von der, so ist man zumindest in Stuttgart überzeugt, wird kein Käufer nach München abwandern.

Irrtum! Der neue BMW 750i – der erste deutsche Zwölf-zylinder-Luxuswagen nach dem Zweiten Weltkrieg – überholt bereits im Mai 1987 die S-Klasse bei den Fahrzeugzulassungen in Deutschland. Ein unerhörter Vorgang, daß die Bayern in der Luxusklasse den Schwaben die Show stehlen! Von Rolls-Royce hört man nur erstauntes Raunen: Man ist sichtlich „not amused".

Motorblock und Zylinderköpfe dieses Wunderwerks bayeri-scher Motorenbaukunst bestehen aus Aluminium, und deshalb wiegen die rund 2500 edlen Motorenteile zusammengenom-men nicht mehr als 240 Kilo. Die Kurbelwelle des V-Motors ist siebenfach gelagert, und da die beiden "Sechszylinder", aus denen er sich zusammensetzt, ihre eigenen Antriebsaggregate und Katalysatoren aufweisen, ist ein völliger Motorausfall kaum denkbar.

Erst wenn dieses 5-Liter-Triebwerk die vollen 300 PS entfaltet – und das geschieht bei 5200 Umdrehungen pro

Minute – ist auch der Sound vernehmbar: vornehm zurückhaltend, aber kraftvoll – majestätisch eben. Modernstes Motormanagement und eine Viergangautomatik mit den Fahrprogrammen „Sport" und „Economy" gehören zur Standardausstattung dieses bayerischen Prunkstücks, und wenn dessen Fahrer es wünscht, katapultiert die Urgewalt dieses Motors die 1,8 Tonnen Leergewicht in weniger als acht Sekunden auf 100 Stundenkilometer. Um den Fahrkomfort nicht zu schmälern, beliebt man werksseitig die Höchstgeschwindigkeit elektronisch auf 250 Stundenkilometer zu begrenzen. Mehr soll es nicht sein. Dieser Fahrkomfort wird ohnehin durch eine automatische Stabilisierung und eine elektronische Dämpferkontrolle auf Sänftenniveau gehalten.

In der „Sänfte" mit fünf komfortablen Sesseln aus feinstem Leder regiert der Luxus, und solange man auch sucht, es fehlt nicht die geringste jener vielen technischen Raffinessen, die für die Bequemlichkeit von Fahrzeuginsassen erfunden worden sind. Wer den Einbau einer Bordbar oder eines Fernsehers wünscht, sollte sich für den 11 Zentimeter längeren 750iL entscheiden.

1987 kostet der 750i noch „bescheidene" 102.000 Mark, die Langversion 17.000 Mark mehr. Das hochnoble Vergnügen, dieses Nonplusultra einer Limousine zu fahren – oder standesgemäß fahren zu lassen – gönnen sich 1987/88 fast 20.000 entsprechend betuchte Menschen.

Le comte Hans von der Goltz, président du Conseil de surveillance de BMW, et son collègue Eberhard von Kuenheim, lui aussi de la haute noblesse, docteur honoris causa en ingénierie, savent ce dont ils sont redevables: «Noblesse oblige!» A l'avenir, BMW donnera le ton dans le segment des limousines de très grand luxe – comme Maybach dans les années 30. Beaucoup de travail manuel, peu de haute technologie et des prix trop élevés sont le handicap de la grande noblesse automobile britannique qu'est Rolls-Royce: pour BMW, ce n'est pas un concurrent – seul le nom est d'une distinction royale. La concurrence proprement dite dans les statistiques d'immatriculations est la classe S de Mercedes-Benz. Et, à Stuttgart, chacun est convaincu qu'aucun client ne fera des infidélités pour passer dans le camp de Munich.

C'est une erreur! La nouvelle BMW 750i – la première douze-cylindres de luxe allemande depuis la Seconde Guerre mondiale – double la classe S pour les immatriculations de voitures neuves en Allemagne dès mai 1987. Il est absolument stupéfiant que les Bavarois volent la vedette aux Souabes dans le segment des voitures de grand luxe. De chez Rolls-Royce, on n'entend que des commentaires étonnés: on n'est manifestement «not amused».

Le bijou de la technique bavaroise en termes de moteur possède un bloc et des culasses en aluminium. Ce qui explique qu'à elles toutes, les quelque 2500 pièces prestigieuses du moteur ne pèsent pas plus que 240 kilos. Le vilebrequin du moteur en V est à sept paliers. Comme chacun des deux «six-cylindres» du moteur possède son propre groupe de transmission, il est pratiquement exclu que le moteur tombe totalement en panne.

Il faut que ce moteur de 5 litres libère la totalité de ses 300 ch – ce qu'il fait dès 5200 tr/mn – pour que l'on en perçoive la présence, d'une retenue discrète, mais non sans vigueur. Majestueux, tout simplement. Une gestion moteur ultramoderne et une boîte automatique à quatre rapports avec comme programmes «Sport» et «Economy» complètent la chaîne cinématique de cet étalon digne des haras des rois de Bavière. Côté performance, il est tout à fait possible de catapulter les 1,8 tonne à vide de la voiture en moins de huit secondes de 0 à 100 km/h et la vitesse maximum limitée électroniquement à 250 km/h laisse planer le mystère sur les possibilités réelles de la voiture. Cela suffit pour que l'on puisse jouir complètement du confort. Grâce à un contrôle automatique de la stabilisation et électronique des amortisseurs, on a de toute façon l'impression de rouler comme sur un nuage.

Le luxe règne en maître dans ce carrosse aux cinq fauteuils en cuir confortables. Et même si vous cherchez bien, vous ne regretterez l'absence d'aucun des plus infimes gadgets techniques inventés pour le confort le plus total des passagers. Celui qui souhaite faire installer un bar ou un téléviseur devrait opter pour la version 750iL allongée de 11 cm.

En 1987, la 750i coûte encore la somme «modique» de 102 000 marks, la version à empattement long, 17 000 marks de plus. En 1987/88, 20 000 personnes apparemment à l'aise financièrement peuvent se payer le luxe incomparable de posséder ce nec plus ultra de la technique automobile.

The renaissance of the German V12 engine (60°) – the 1929 Maybach "12", forerunner of the legendary "Zeppelin DS7", had one – was celebrated by BMW in 1987 with the introduction of the 750i/750iL. To mark this historic event, Niki Lauda was invited to test drive the blue-blooded Bavarian thoroughbred in Vienna.

1987 feiert BMW mit dem 750i/750iL die Renaissance des deutschen V12-Motors (60°). 1929 gab es ihn schon im Maybach „12", dem Vorläufer des legendären „Zeppelin DS7". Ein historisches Ereignis, das Niki Lauda zu einem Test des „noblen Bayern" in Wien bewegt.

BMW fête la renaissance d'un moteur V12 allemand (à 60°) en 1987 avec la 750i/750iL – le précédent remontait à 1929 avec la Maybach «12», le précurseur de la légendaire «Zeppelin DS7». Un événement historique qui incite Niki Lauda à faire un essai de cette «Bavaroise de prestige» à Vienne.

BMW 750iL 1987

Four and a half inches (11 cm) more legroom than the 750i: triple world champion Niki Lauda enjoys the unaccustomed comfort of the back seat. Barely audible is the noise of the 300 bhp engine, whose two cylinder banks have their own separate aggregate running from the injection unit to the catalytic converter. Boeing pilot Lauda samples the sumptuous driver area of the 7 series.

11 Zentimeter mehr Beinfreiheit als im 750i: Dem dreifachen Weltmeister, der hier Fondpassagier ist, behagt dieser Komfort. Kaum hörbar ist die „12-Ton-Musik" des 300-PS-Triebwerks, dessen zwei Zylinderreihen von der Einspritzanlage bis zum Kat beide über eigene Aggregate verfügen. Dem Boeing-Piloten Lauda ist das Cockpit des 7ers eine Laudatio wert.

11 cm de plus pour les jambes que dans la 750i : le triple champion du monde apprécie ce confort sur la banquette arrière. Le V12 de 300 ch est pratiquement inaudible ; de l'injection aux catalyseurs, chaque banc de cylindres possède son propre groupe de transmission. Lauda, le pilote de Boeing, ne tarit pas d'éloges sur le cockpit de la série 7.

BMW Z1 1988

"The roadster is focused, it embodies the core qualities of a BMW directly and unmistakably," was the comment of Dr Wolfgang Reitzle on the return of the BMW roadster in its most modern form. The Z1 was the surprise at the 1987 Frankfurt Motor Show. Pleasure could also be seen on the face of the rather distinguished and reticent BMW director for development and production as he invited the journalists for a test drive. Relaxed Reitzle wore a turtleneck pullover and a broad grin: "It might not be the most sensible car, but it's great fun."

This piece of fun was to cost more than 80,000 marks and was not originally planned as a production car, for it was designed and built as a high-technology demonstration vehicle for BMW Technik GmbH. So customer demand was all the more surprising. When the first Z1s went to the dealers, there were already 5000 orders. Assumed buyers' interest led to doubled and tripled production, reaching up to 18 Z1s per day. That was too much for a limited market. The Z1 could only be made affordable to roadster fans with discounts, and production ceased at 8000 cars in June 1991.

The marketing and pricing principle is missing from the Z1, and that was the crux of a roadster which was to serve as a test bed for new axles and trend-setting processed plastics in automotive construction. A galvanized sheet steel frame encloses the vehicle floor made of epoxy resin and PV plastics which were reinforced with glass fiber. This monocoque structure carried the external skin made of various thermoplastic compounds, and the relatively central, front engine, from the BMW 325i.

Virgin territory was entered with the doors: they retracted downwards. In view of the high sill, it is not easy for non-sporty people to get into the Z1, particularly when the folding top is closed. But anyone not of a sporty disposition has the wrong vehicle with the roadster anyway. Perfect handling, even with extreme load changes, is due to the chassis with independent suspension and the Z-axle at the rear. The "Z" signifies a "centrally articulated, spherical double wishbone axle" in German. Got that?

That the Z1 did without the usual spoilers, was due to the turbulence-free underbody, and a diffuser which – together with a lip on the trunk – ensured sufficient downward aerodynamic air pressure, even at a top speed of 141 mph (225 kph).

Just as Reitzle said, the maneuverability and easy handling of this roadster, which is less than 13 feet long (4 meters), makes it incredible fun to drive. It can only be fully enjoyed when the top is folded down, even if this increases the drag coefficient from Cd 0.36 to Cd 0.43. The irrationality of this car is due less to the fact that there is insufficient luggage space for longer journeys, or that it offers drivers with sporting ambitions a meager 170 bhp, than to its price. 10,000 marks less and the Z1 would have been a big seller for a decade.

Der Roadster bringt die Sache auf den Punkt. Er verkörpert die Kerneigenschaften eines BMW direkt und unmißverständlich", so kommentiert Dr.-Ing. Wolfgang Reitzle die Rückkehr zum Roadster, wenngleich modernster Prägung. Der Z1 ist die Überraschung auf der IAA 1987. Und man merkt dem eher vornehm zurückhaltenden BMW-Vorstandsmitglied für Entwicklung und Produktion die Freude über den gelungenen Coup an, als er die Journalisten zu Testfahrten bittet. Reitzle mit Rollkragenpullover und breitem Lausbuben-Grinsen: „Er ist vielleicht etwas unvernünftig, aber er macht ungemein Spaß."

Der Spaß soll mehr als 80.000 Mark kosten und war ursprünglich nicht für die Serie vorgesehen, sondern konzipiert und gebaut als Technologieträger der BMW Technik GmbH. Umso mehr überrascht die Nachfrage. In der Phase der Erstauslieferungen an die Händler liegen bereits 5000 Bestellungen vor. Spekulatives Käuferinteresse führt zur Verdoppelung und Verdreifachung der Produktion – bis zu 18 Z1 werden pro Tag gefertigt. Zuviel für einen begrenzten Markt. Nur mit Rabatten ist der Z1 letztlich an den Roadster-Fan zu bringen, und nach 8000 gebauten Wagen wird im Juni 1991 die Fertigung eingestellt.

Die Komponenten Marketing und Preispolitik haben bei der Konzipierung des Z1 keine Rolle gespielt, und das ist die Crux dieses Roadsters, der ursprünglich frei von Produktionszwängen zur Erprobung neuer Achsen und richtungsweisender Kunststoffverarbeitungsverfahren im Automobilbau dienen sollte. Ein Stahlblechgerüst, natürlich verzinkt, umschließt den Fahrzeugboden aus glasfaserverstärktem Epoxidharz und PV.

Dieses „Monocoque" trägt die aus verschiedenen Thermoplast-Verbindungen bestehende Außenhaut und den relativ zentrierten Frontmotor des BMW 325i.

Bei den Türen werden neue Wege beschritten: Sie sind nach unten versenkbar. Angesichts der hohen Schwelle bietet der Z1 unsportlichen Menschen keinen leichten Einstieg, besonders bei geschlossenem Verdeck. Aber für Unsportliche ist der Roadster sowieso nicht das richtige Auto. Sein perfektes Handling selbst bei extremen Lastwechseln verdankt der Z1 dem Fahrwerk mit Einzelradaufhängungen und der Z-Achse hinten. Das „Z" steht für eine „zentralpunktgeführte sphärische Doppel-Querlenkerachse". Alles klar?

Daß der Z1 ohne das übliche Spoilerwerk auskommt, verdankt er dem verwirbelungsfrei gestalteten Unterboden und einem Diffusor, der zusammen mit einer Lippe auf dem Kofferraum für genügend Anpreßdruck auch bei einer Höchstgeschwindigkeit von 225 Stundenkilometern sorgt.

Wendigkeit und Handlichkeit des nicht einmal vier Meter langen Roadsters machen, wie Reitzle richtig feststellt, wirklich ungemein Spaß – ein Vergnügen, das erst bei offenem Verdeck voll zu genießen ist, auch wenn dadurch der Luftwiderstandsbeiwert von Cw 0,36 auf Cw 0,43 steigt. Die Unvernunft des Wagens liegt weniger darin, daß er für längere Reisen nicht genügend Gepäckraum bereithält und sportlich ambitionierten Fahrern nur magere 170 PS bietet, sondern in seinem Preis. 10.000 Mark günstiger, und der Z1 wäre ein Renner für ein Jahrzehnt geworden.

Le roadster met les points sur les i, il incarne à la perfection les propriétés intrinsèques d'une BMW, immédiatement et sans ambiguïté», déclare l'ingénieur Wolfgang Reitzle pour commenter le retour du roadster même si celui-ci est ultramoderne. La Z1 est la surprise du Salon de l'Automobile de Francfort de 1987. Le plutôt discret et réservé membre du directoire de BMW, au titre du développement et de la production, ne peut s'en cacher lorsqu'il invite les journalistes à essayer la voiture. Reitzle, vêtu d'un col roulé et arborant un large sourire de gamin gouailleur, déclare: «Il n'est peut-être pas tout à fait raisonnable, mais il est vraiment amusant à piloter».

L'amusement est censé coûter plus de 80 000 marks et n'était, à l'origine, pas prévu pour la série: il a seulement été conçu et construit comme vitrine technologique de la BMW Technik GmbH. La demande est d'autant plus surprenante. Durant la phase des premières livraisons aux concessionnaires, 5000 commandes ont déjà été passées. La spéculation fait doubler puis tripler la production – jusqu'à 18 Z1 par jour. Chiffre trop élevé pour un marché restreint. En fin de compte, la Z1 ne trouve preneur parmi les fanas du roadster qu'avec une ristourne et la production est suspendue en juin 1991 avec 8000 voitures.

Les composantes marketing et politique de prix font défaut à la Z1 et c'est là le problème pour un roadster, libéré des contraintes de la production pour la mise à l'essai de nouveaux essieux et de matières plastiques novatrices dans la construction automobile. Un squelette d'acier, naturellement galvanisé, enserre la plate-forme en résine époxyde et PVC

renforcés de fibre de verre. Cette «monocoque» est coiffée de la carrosserie en matériaux composites et matière thermoplastique et héberge le moteur avant en position presque centrale de la BMW 325i.

Innovation également pour les portières: elles s'escamotent vers le bas. Compte tenu de la hauteur du seuil, l'accès n'est pas aisé pour un conducteur non sportif, a fortiori quand la capote est fermée. De toute façon, ceux pour qui le sport est un vain mot n'ont pas leur place dans le roadster. La Z1 doit son comportement parfait, même lors des transferts de charges extrêmes, à son châssis à suspension à roue indépendante et à son essieu en Z à l'arrière. Le «Z» signifie «double essieu transversal sphérique à guidage central». Tout est clair?

Si la Z1 peut se passer des ailerons traditionnels, elle le doit à son soubassement qui n'engendre aucun tourbillon et à un diffuseur qui, conjointement avec une lèvre sur le couvercle du coffre, génère suffisamment d'appui même à la vitesse maximum de 225 km/h.

La vivacité et la maniabilité de ce petit roadster de moins de quatre mètres de long sont, comme le disait Reitzle lui-même, vraiment amusantes et le plaisir est encore plus grand avec la capote ouverte même si, alors, le Cx passe de 0,36 à 0,43. Le caractère déraisonnable de la voiture réside moins dans le fait qu'il n'a pas suffisamment de place pour les bagages lors de longs voyages et, avec 170 ch, ne peut guère satisfaire les pilotes amateurs de conduite sportive, mais plutôt dans son prix. 10 000 marks moins cher, et la Z1 aurait été la vedette pendant une décennie entière.

For the roadster fan, the Z1 with its 170 bhp and retractable doors represents pure motoring fun. For BMW, its main purpose was to test new technology in the form of innovative synthetic components, aerodynamic details and the new Z-axle (centrally articulated, spherical double wishbone axle).

Für den Roadster-Fan ist der Z1 mit seinen 170 PS und den versenkbaren Türen ein „Spaßmobil". Für BMW ist er primär ein Technologieträger zur Erprobung innovativer Kunststoff-Komponenten, aerodynamischer Detaillösungen und der neuen Z-Achse (zentralpunktgeführte sphärische Doppel-Querlenkerachse).

Pour les fanas du roadster, la Z1 de 170 ch aux portières escamotables est une véritable voiture d'agrément. Pour BMW, il s'agit en revanche surtout d'une vitrine technologique qui permet de tester des matières plastiques novatrices, des solutions aérodynamiques de détail et le nouvel essieu en Z (double essieu transversal sphérique à guidage central).

BMW Z1 1988

Softtop compartment and trunk above, a turbulence-free underbody: the Z1 tail is fitted with a diffuser whose airstream is directed over a reverse airfoil fitted between the flat exhaust pipes.

Klappverdeckfach und Kofferraum oben, verwirbelungsfreier Boden unten: Das Z1-Heck verfügt über einen Diffusor, dessen Luftstrom über ein umgekehrtes Flügelprofil zwischen den flachen Auspuffrohren abgeführt wird.

Sous le compartiment à capote et le coffre se trouve un soubassement empêchant tout tourbillon: l'arrière de la Z1 comporte en effet un diffuseur dont le courant d'air est canalisé par un profil d'aile inversé entre les pots d'échappement aplatis.

BMW Z1 1988

BMW 850i 1989

In the 8 series coupé, BMW once and for all invaded the territory of the Mercedes-Benz luxury class. Launched in the autumn of 1989, it contained a synthesis of sportiness and comfort, advanced technology and all that is good and expensive. Opinions diverge as to whether this new upper-class car was exciting or just beautiful. Either way, it combined several styling elements which are typical of BMW.

Because of the extremely slim nose of the 850i, the BMW kidneys grills were made wider rather than high to remind us of the 1972 BMW Turbo study by Paul Bracq. The prominent lines of the fenders were borrowed from the M3 (E30), but both shape and height of the stub rear end are like those of other contemporary BMWs. Four exhaust pipes under a lip predict the power and splendor of a twelve-cylinder engine.

This V12 motor, shared by the 750i with aluminum engine block and cylinder heads, produced 300 bhp. That was increased in the 850CSi (from 1992 on) by a rise in cubic capacity from 4988 to 5578 cc to produce 380 bhp. The six-speed transmission is less popular than the optional automatic: a classic choice by the wealthy buyers of this coupé in favor of comfort. For sporty drivers, there are more agile models in the BMW range than this heavy coupé.

As far as maneuverability was concerned, the CSi entered a new dimension, for the wider back tire treads (265/40 ZR 17) and unique rear axle were responsive to steering inputs. The cost-benefit calculation for these expensive, active rear axle kinematics was a matter of debate. Yet expensive things – particularly when they concern electronics – have their enthusiastic supporters. Measured against the sales figures

(before the introduction of the Ci and CSi in 1992, some 16,000 coupés were sold), the price was probably not important. The CSi sold at 180,000 marks and more, but the demand was somewhat restrained.

The alarm bells rang immediately in BMW's marketing department: in 1993 the 840Ci appeared with an 286 bhp V8 engine, five-speed transmission and fewer electronics for 129,000 marks. This model did without the usual speed-limiting device at 156 mph (250 kph), for that was the actual top speed.

The sensual pleasure which BMW promises when driving the 8 series coupé is produced just by looking at the functional and extremely tasteful interior. It is quite simply "upper class", and the safety belts integrated into the seats are "safety first".

Eine Synthese aus Sportlichkeit und Komfort, Technik auf höchstem Niveau und allem, was gut und teuer ist, steckt im 8er Coupé, mit dem BMW im Herbst 1989 endgültig in die Pfründe der Mercedes-Benz-Luxusklasse eindringt. Die Meinungen darüber, ob das neue Nobelmobil aufregend oder nur schön ist, gehen auseinander. Immerhin vereint es mehrere BMW-typische Stylingelemente.

So erinnert die extrem flache Schnauze des 850i, dessen BMW-Nieren eher breit als hoch ausfallen, an die Turbo-Studie Paul Bracqs von 1972. Die ausladende Linienführung der Kotflügel ist dem M3 (E30) entlehnt, Form und Höhe der Abrißkante des Hecks gleichen den anderen Modellreihen. Vier wuchtige Auspuffrohre unter einer Lippe verkünden die Kraft und die Herrlichkeit eines Zwölfzylinders.

Dieses auch im 750i verwendete Kraftwerk mit Motorblock und Zylinderköpfen aus Aluminium bringt 300 PS und wird beim 850CSi ab 1992 durch eine Hubraumvergrößerung von 4988 ccm auf 5578 ccm auf 380 PS gesteigert. Das Sechsgang-Schaltgetriebe findet weniger Anklang als die wahlweise erhältliche Automatik – ein unmißverständliches Bekenntnis der wohlhabenden Käuferschicht dieses Coupés zum Komfort. Für eher sportliche Fahrer gibt es im Hause BMW wendigere Mobile als das schwere Coupé.

Das Thema Wendigkeit allerdings erfährt beim CSi eine neue Dimension, denn die breiten hinteren „Sohlen" (265/40 ZR 17) lassen sich lenken. Über die Kosten-Nutzen-Rechnung dieser aufwendigen aktiven Hinterachskinematik läßt sich freilich streiten. Dennoch findet Aufwendiges, besonders im Bereich Elektronik, Liebhaber. Angesichts der Verkaufszahlen – vor

Einführung des Ci und CSi 1992 wurden mehr als 16.000 Coupés verkauft – scheint in dieser Fahrzeugkategorie der Preis keine entscheidende Rolle zu spielen. Der CSi für 180.000 Mark ohne Extras findet ebenfalls Käufer, aber der Absatz ist verhalten.

In der Marketingabteilung läuten die Alarmglocken. 1993 erscheint der 840Ci mit 286-PS-V8-Motor, Fünfganggetriebe und etwas weniger Elektronik für 129.000 Mark. Dieses Modell benötigt keine Abriegelung bei 250 Stundenkilometer: Es ist seine Spitzengeschwindigkeit.

Der sinnliche Genuß, den BMW beim Fahren des 8er Coupés verheißt, kommt zumindest bei einem Blick auf das funktionelle, äußerst geschmackvoll gestaltete Interieur auf. Dieses ist einfach „upper class", und die in den Sitzen integrierten Sicherheitsgurte „safety first".

Une synthèse de sportivité et de confort, un summum de technicité et tout ce qui est bon et cher se dissimulent dans le coupé de la série 8 avec lequel BMW veut, à l'automne 1989, marcher définitivement sur les plates-bandes de la luxueuse Mercedes-Benz. Cette nouvelle voiture de prestige est-elle excitante ou belle? Les avis sont partagés. Elle réunit toutefois en elle plusieurs éléments de style typiques de BMW.

Ainsi le mufle extrêmement plat de la 850i, dont les naseaux BMW sont plus larges que hauts, rappelle-il le prototype de style qu'était la BMW Turbo de Paul Bracq de 1972. L'ample galbe des ailes s'inspire de la M3 (E30) tandis que la forme et la hauteur de l'arête de décrochement à l'arrière sont identiques à ceux des autres gammes. Quatre imposants pots d'échappement sous un becquet trahissent la puissance débordante et la magnificence d'un douze-cylindres.

Ce moteur à bloc et culasses en aluminium aussi utilisé pour la 750i développe 300 ch et voit sa cylindrée passer, pour la 850CSi (à partir de 1992), de 4988 à 5578 cm³ pour une puissance de 380 ch. La boîte manuelle à 6 vitesses remporte moins de succès que la transmission automatique proposée à titre alternatif: un aveu classique en faveur du confort de la part des riches acheteurs de ce coupé. Pour les amateurs épris de conduite sportive, il y a, chez BMW des engins autrement plus maniables que ce lourd coupé.

Le thème de la maniabilité prend une dimension nouvelle avec la CSi, car les larges gommes arrière (265/40 ZR 17) braquent. On peut toutefois se perdre en conjectures sur le rapport coût/utilité de cette sophistiquée cinématique d'essieu arrière actif.

La complexité, notamment dans le domaine de l'électronique, fait cependant des adeptes. Par rapport aux chiffres de ventes (avant le lancement de la Ci et de la CSi en 1992, le nombre de coupés avait déjà dépassé 16 000), le prix ne joue apparemment aucun rôle. Et c'est ainsi que la CSi trouve preneurs même à 180 000 marks et plus, quoique leur nombre soit réduit.

L'alarme sonne immédiatement chez les spécialistes du marketing: en 1993, BMW lance la 840Ci à moteur V8 de 286 ch, boîte manuelle à 5 vitesses et un peu moins d'électronique pour 129 000 marks. Ce modèle n'a pas besoin de rupteur à 250 km/h: c'est sa vitesse de pointe.

Le plaisir sensuel que BMW promet aux conducteurs des coupés de la série 8 transparaît déjà lorsque l'on jette un coup d'œil sur le cockpit fonctionnel, de bon goût. Il est tout simplement «upper class», et les ceintures de sécurité intégrées aux sièges sont «safety first».

BMW 850i 1989

Beneath the hood of the 850i we see a familiar sight: as in the 750i, a mighty 5-liter V12 engine does the business. The dashboard is restrained, but well-illuminated and ergonomic, and the center console features a trip computer and air conditioning system as well as the radio.

Unter der Haube des 850i bietet sich ein vertrautes Bild: Wie beim 750i verrichtet hier der starke 5-Liter-V12 seine Arbeit. Nüchtern, gut beleuchtet und im Blickfeld: Die übersichtlichen Armaturen und die Mittelkonsole mit Bordcomputer, Radio und Klimaanlage.

Sous le capot de la 850i se trouve une bonne vieille connaissance : le puissant V12 de 5 litres de la 750i. Sobre mais bien éclairé dans le champ de vision du conducteur : le tableau de bord bien agencé, prolongé par la console médiane avec ordinateur de bord, autoradio et climatisation.

The 850i's retractable headlights incorporate low beam and fog lamps. The parking lights and high beam are integrated into the fender area. The trunk has ample space for two people's baggage. The tail of the coupé conceals a novelty: thanks to a suspension system with five wheel suspension arms, the multi-link suspension, the wide rear wheels steer along with the driver, so to speak.

Die „Schlafaugen" des 850i: Klappscheinwerfer mit Abblend- und Nebellampen. Stand- und Fernlicht erstrahlen aus dem Stoßfänger. Für das Gepäck von zwei Personen gut bemessen ist der Kofferraum. Das Coupé wartet mit einer Besonderheit im Heck auf. Dank einer räumlich wirkenden Radaufhängung mit fünf Lenkern, der Integralachse, lenken die breiten Hinterräder sozusagen mit.

Les phares escamotables de la 850i renferment les feux de route et de croisement. Les feux de position et les longues portées se trouvent dans le pare-chocs. Le coffre est suffisamment généreux pour les bagages de deux personnes. Le coupé affiche une spécificité à l'arrière : grâce à une suspension agissant dans l'espace avec ses cinq doigts comme un essieu intégral, les larges roues arrière ont un effet directionnel.

BMW 850i 1989   345

BMW M5 1992

Just eight months after the launch of the 5 series (E34), the sporting version arrived in August 1988. It concealed, as always with BMW, massive performance behind a tiny abbreviation: M5. Externally, only the restrained aerodynamic aids on the lower body, the ventilated light alloy wheels and the badge indicated the M5. The power of the engine (315 bhp; from 1992 upped to 340 bhp) remained hidden.

Well then, raise the hood. "BMW M Power" stamped boldly on the valve cover could not be overlooked, and neither could the long funnels of the inlet tract with the unusual air intake. An electronically controlled flap was activated here in such an ingenious way that enhanced torque and performance were achieved right back in the intake area. "Resonance-tuned intake pressure charging" was BMW's name for this process.

Also at the back there were tell-tale signs that this engine was a powerful unit. After the catalytic converter, the exhaust gases exited by two mighty tail pipes. It is hardly necessary to mention that optimum combustion was achieved in the six cylinders with a total of 24 valves, and that the crankshaft with 12 counterweights was a metal-forging masterpiece.

A 25 bhp increase in power in 1992 boosted maximum torque from 360 Nm to 400 Nm at 4750 rpm, but had no effect on acceleration. This was powerful enough as it was, at 6.5 seconds from 0 to 62.5 mph (100 kph). That leaves the question of top speed. Not really relevant, for at 156 mph (250 kph) the Bosch Motronic intervened and prohibited further speed. This Motronic, initially the M1.2, and from 1992 the M3.3, managed the engine and regulated the lambda catalytic converter.

The M5 sat 0.7 inches (20 mm) lower than its brothers in the 5 series. Yet little adjustment was required to adapt the chassis to cope with the enhanced performance. Electronic shock absorber ride adjustment and hydropneumatic leveling were the magic technical words. As in the 750i, they stood for impressive roadholding and cornering, giving pleasure to those occupying the sporty and elegant cockpit. Whether a light inside the gearshift knob for the sporty five-speed transmission was really necessary is debatable.

In 1992, the year in which the M5 was upgraded again, including hot five-spoke star wheels, BMW also supplied its "M5 bullet" in a touring derivative. This sporting wagon cost 127,650 marks, and had particularly wide rear tires (255/40 ZR 17).

To blow away a Porsche or a Chevy Corvette on the highway with a four-door station wagon is most certainly not part of any driving test. But – leaving all morals aside – this might well be an uplifting moment.

Nur acht Monate nach der Vorstellung der 5er Reihe (E34) folgt im August 1988 das „Muskelpaket". Und dieses verbirgt, wie bei BMW üblich, seine große Leistung hinter einem kleinen Kürzel: M5. Äußerlich deuten nur dezente aerodynamische Hilfen im unteren Karosseriebereich, die Leichtmetallräder mit Lüftereinsatz und das Kürzel auf den M5 hin. Die Kraft (315 PS, ab 1992 sogar 340 PS) liegt im Verborgenen.

Also Haube auf! „BMW M Power" steht unübersehbar auf dem Zylinderkopfdeckel. Unübersehbar auch die langen Trichter des Ansaugtrakts mit dem ungewöhnlichen Luftmengensammler, in dem eine elektronisch gesteuerte Klappe derart geschickt arbeitet, daß sie schon im Ansaugbereich für mehr Drehmoment und Leistung sorgt. „Resonanzaufladung" nennt BMW diesen Vorgang.

Auch am hinteren Ende gibt es verräterische Anzeichen dafür, daß es sich bei diesem Motor um ein Kraftwerk handelt. Nach Passieren des Katalysators entweichen die Auspuffgase durch zwei gewaltige Endrohre. Daß in den sechs Zylindern mit insgesamt 24 Ventilen eine optimale Verbrennung erzielt wird und die Kurbelwelle mit 12 Gegengewichten ein Meisterstück der Schmiedekunst ist, braucht wohl nicht erwähnt zu werden.

Die Potenzsteigerung um 25 PS im Jahre 1992 hebt zwar das maximale Drehmoment von 360 Nm auf 400 Nm bei 4750 Touren, wirkt sich aber nicht auf die Beschleunigung aus, die mit knapp 6,5 Sekunden von 0 auf 100 Stundenkilometer ohnehin jenseits von Gut und Böse ist. Auch die Frage nach der Endgeschwindigkeit erübrigt sich, denn bei 250 Stundenkilometer greift die Bosch Motronic ein und untersagt weiteres

„Speeding". Diese Motronic – zunächst die M1.2, ab 1992 die M3.3 – steuert den Motor und die Lambda-Regelung des Kata-lysators.

Der M5 liegt 20 Millimeter tiefer als die Serienbrüder der 5er Reihe. Doch sind für die Anpassung des Fahrwerks an das neue Kräfteverhältnis nur geringe Einstellarbeiten erforderlich. Wie schon beim 750i heißen die technischen Zauberworte für gute Straßen- und Kurvenlage elektronische Dämpferkraftver-stellung und hydropneumatische Niveauregulierung – zur Freude der Fahrer, die sich in dem sportlich-eleganten Cockpit betätigen dürfen. Über den Sinn des von innen angestrahlten Schaltknopfes des sportlich abgestimmten Fünfganggetriebes läßt sich streiten.

1992, im Jahre der nochmaligen Aufrüstung des M5, unter anderem mit „heißen" Fünfstern-Rädern, liefert BMW das „M5-Geschoß" auch als Touring aus. Dieser 127.650 Mark teure Wagen steht hinten auf besonders breiten „Sohlen" (255/40 ZR 17).

Mit einem viertürigen Kombi auf der Autobahn einen Porsche oder eine Chevy-Corvette zu „verblasen", gehört gewiß nicht zur Reifeprüfung eines Autofahrers, dürfte aber – mal ganz unpädagogisch betrachtet – ein erhebender Moment sein.

Huit mois seulement après la présentation de la série 5 (E34), BMW en dévoile, en août 1988, la version «musclée». Et, comme cela est la tradition chez BMW, celle-ci dissimule son immense potentiel derrière une simple abréviation: M5. Extérieurement, seuls de discrets appendices aérodynamiques le long des bas de caisse, des jantes en alliage léger ressemblant à des ailettes de turbine et l'abréviation signalent que l'on est en présence de la M5. La puissance du moteur (315 ch et même 340 à partir de 1992) ne saute pas aux yeux.

Alors, ouvrons donc le capot. «BMW M Power» peut-on lire en grandes lettres sur la culasse et les longues tubulures du collecteur d'aspiration avec l'immense boîtier de filtre à air indiquent tout de suite à qui l'on a à faire. Dans ce boîtier, une soupape à commande électronique agit avec tant de raffinement qu'elle génère plus de couple et de puissance dès le collecteur d'aspiration. C'est ce que BMW appelle «suralimen-tation par résonance».

A l'arrière aussi, des signes sans équivoque trahissent que ce moteur n'est pas d'un gabarit courant. Après avoir franchi le catalyseur, les gaz brûlés s'échappent par deux énormes pots d'échappement. Point n'est besoin de signaler à ce propos qu'une combustion optimale est garantie dans les six cylindres avec au total 24 soupapes et que le vilebrequin à 12 contrepoids est un chef-d'œuvre de forge.

L'augmentation de puissance de 25 ch en 1992 fait passer le couple maximum de 360 Nm à 400 Nm à 4750 tr/mn, mais reste sans effet sur l'accélération: avec 6,5 secondes à peine pour le 0 à 100 km/h, elle est de toute façon fulminante. Quant à la question de la vitesse de pointe, elle est superflue. En effet, à 250 km/h, la gestion Bosch Motronic intervient et jugule effi-cacement toute autre poussée. Cette Motronic, tout d'abord la M1.2, puis la M3.3 à partir de 1992, gère le moteur et la régulation du catalyseur par sonde lambda.

La M5 est surbaissée de 20 millimètres par rapport à ses sœurs de la série 5. Mais bien peu de réglages de précision sont nécessaires pour adapter les trains roulants au nouveau rapport de forces. Des amortisseurs à réglage électronique et un correcteur d'assiette hydropneumatique comme pour la 750i sont la formule magique qui garantit une tenue de route à toute épreuve en ligne droite et en virage, pour le plus grand plaisir de celui qui a l'opportunité et le bonheur de se glisser au volant du cockpit aussi sportif qu'élégant. Les esprits sont partagés quant au bien-fondé de l'éclairage intérieur du pommeau de changement de vitesses de la boîte manuelle à cinq rapports à l'étagement sportif.

En 1992, année de la montée en puissance de la M5 – notamment avec de spectaculaires jantes en étoile à cinq rayons – BMW commercialise également sa «bombe M5» en une version touring. Ce break de 127 650 marks est garni de gommes particulièrement larges à l'arrière (255/40 ZR 17).

Donner la réplique sur autoroute à une Porsche ou à une Chevrolet-Corvette au volant d'un break à quatre portes n'appartient assurément pas au registre du commun des mortels parmi les automobilistes, mais – faisons pour une fois abstraction de toute morale – ceci est sans aucun doute un moment émouvant.

With the M5, the power – 315 bhp to begin with, then 340 bhp from 1992 – and the brilliance of a sports car are contained in a spacious sedan.

Beim M5 stecken die Kraft – zunächst 315 PS, ab 1992 dann 340 PS – und die Herrlichkeit eines Sportwagens in einer geräumigen Limousine.

Avec la M5, le ramage – tout d'abord 315 ch, puis 340 ch à partir de 1992 – vaut le plumage: il s'agit en l'occurrence d'une fougueuse voiture de sport sous les traits d'une spacieuse familiale.

BMW M5 1992

The extensively equipped cockpit of the M5 reflects well on this exclusive car. Its M-power means that a worthy "opponent" rarely appears in the aerodynamically shaped rear-view mirror.

So manchem Nobelgefährt zur Ehre gereicht das reichhaltig ausgestattete M5-Cockpit. Dank der M-Power taucht nur selten ein ebenbürtiger „Gegner" im aerodynamischen Rückspiegel auf.

Le cockpit richement équipé de la M5 ferait honneur aux voitures de sport de prestige. Avec le moteur «M Power», une rivale digne de ce nom se profile rarement dans le rétroviseur aéro-dynamique.

The M5 touring perfectly combines a load capacity of 1058 lbs (480 kg) with extreme performance: a top speed of 156 mph (250 kph) and from 0 to 62.5 mph (100 kph) in 6.5 seconds. The discreet spoilers in the lower body area are essential because of the wide tires and emphasize the aerodynamic shape of the car.

Der M5 touring kombiniert perfekt eine Transportkapazität von 480 Kilo mit extremen Fahrleistungen: 250 km/h Spitze und von 0 auf 100 km/h in 6,5 Sekunden. Das dezente Spoilerwerk im unteren Karosseriebereich ist wegen der Breitreifen unabdingbar und unterstreicht die aerodynamische Form des Fahrzeugs.

La M5 touring combine à la perfection une capacité de transport de 480 kg à des performances extrêmes: une vitesse de pointe de 250 km/h et le 0 à 100 km/h en 6,5 secondes. Les discrets artifices aérodynamiques le long du soubassement sont indispensables en raison de la largeur des pneus et soulignent la forme aérodynamique de la voiture.

BMW M5 1992

A sportily low chassis and wide tires – 255/40 ZR 17 at the rear – are essential to demonstrate
the M5 qualities.

Ein sportlich tiefer gelegtes Fahrwerk und „breite Sohlen" – hinten 255/40 ZR 17 – sind zur
Demonstration der M5-Qualitäten unerläßlich.

Un châssis surbaissé de voiture de sport et de larges gommes – 255/40 ZR 17 à l'arrière –
laissent entrevoir le potentiel et les qualités de la M5.

BMW M3 1992

Chosen as "Car of the Century" by American journalists, BMW is convinced that there are few other cars which have collected so many laurels as the M3 of the E36 series. In all modesty, the later M3 has undergone a considerable metamorphosis – transformed from a pure piece of sporting equipment to a cultivated high-performance car.

However, there was a major E36 M3 change from the 286 bhp 3-liter engine to a 3.2-liter engine with 321 bhp in 1995. The new aluminum six-cylinder engine of the 328i served as the basis for this powerful machine which possessed all the technical delicacies of BMW 's horsepower-generating kitchen: four valves per cylinder, continuously variable camshaft timing control of both intake and exhaust camshafts, plus the most modern digital electronic engine management with anti-knock control. The latter is, indeed, necessary as the M3 engine has such a high compression ratio that it demands Super-Plus fuel. On the other hand the top speed is electronically limited to 156 mph (250 kph). Petrol consumption is encouraging: average consumption above 19.7 miles per gallon (12 liters per 100 km) must be considered modest for a car which sprints from 0 to 62.5 mph (100 kph) in 5.5 seconds.

The elasticity of engine power delivery is considerable and the explosive performance starts as low as 2000 rpm, beginning an almost endless stream of power. The engine power of the M3 is supported by a six-speed transmission with a long sixth gear, so that the tachometer shows just 6000 rpm at 156 mph (250 kph).

Optionally, BMW offers a taste of the sequential gearboxes used in motor sport: clutch and the six forward gears are managed electro-hydraulically by computer. The gear lever has an automatic and a manual shift mode.

The chassis is optimized with a single-joint McPherson strut axle at the front and central trailing arm axle at the rear. Directional stability, handling and cornering stability could hardly be bettered. Driving comfort too deserves a "par excellence" rating.

A large trunk and 17-gallon (65 liter) tank mean that long legs can only be accommodated across the rear seats of the M3. Both M3 variants, coupé and convertible, have a large front spoiler. Standard equipment covers airbags, ABS, leather steering wheel, steering column adjustment and light alloy wheels with varied tire widths (225/45 front and 245/40 ZR 17 rear).

The convertible, on the market since May 1994, is a little softer than the coupé. Open air fun and rapid acceleration fit as well together as an open top and the euphoria of a 156 mph (250 kph) maximum in the rear of an M3 convertible.

Von amerikanischen Journalisten wird er zum „Auto des Jahrhunderts" gekürt, und BMW ist überzeugt, daß kaum ein Auto in der Vergangenheit so viele Lorbeeren wie der M3 der Baureihe E36 eingeheimst hat. In aller Bescheidenheit wird davon gesprochen, daß der M3 mit seiner Wandlung vom reinen Sportgerät hin zum kultivierten Hochleistungsauto eine starke Metamorphose erfahren hat.

Stark ist tatsächlich die Wandlung vom 286 PS starken 3-Liter-Motor zum 3,2-Liter-Triebwerk mit 321 PS im Jahr 1995. Der neue Aluminium-Sechszylinder des 328i dient als Basis des Kraftpakets, das über alle technischen Leckerbissen der BMW-PS-Küche verfügt: vier Ventile pro Zylinder, variable stufenlose Nockenwellenspreizung, Steuerung der Ein- und Auslaßnockenwelle und natürlich modernstes elektronisches Motormanagement mit Klopfregelung. Letztere ist auch erforderlich, denn der M3-Motor ist derart hoch verdichtet, daß er nach Super-Plus-Benzin verlangt. Andererseits wird die Höchstgeschwindigkeit bei 250 Stundenkilometer elektronisch abgeriegelt. Tröstlich ist der Benzinverbrauch: Für einen Wagen, der in 5,5 Sekunden von 0 auf 100 Stundenkilometer sprintet, darf ein Durchschnittsverbrauch, der unter 12 Litern liegt, als moderat gelten.

Die Elastizität des Motors ist beachtlich. Bereits bei 2000 Touren setzt der Schub mit Brachialgewalt ein, und es beginnt eine schier endlose Leistungsausbeute. Unterstützt wird die Durchzugskraft des M3 durch ein Sechsganggetriebe mit langem sechsten Gang, so daß der Drehzahlmesser bei 250 Stundenkilometer gerade 6000 Umdrehungen pro Minute anzeigt.

Auf Wunsch bietet BMW sogar das im Motorsport verwendete sequentielle Getriebe an: die Kupplung und die sechs Vorwärtsgänge werden computergesteuert hydraulisch geschaltet. Dabei verfügt der Wählhebel über eine automatisierte und eine manuelle Schaltgasse.

Optimal abgestimmt ist das Fahrwerk mit Eingelenk-Federbeinachse vorn und Zentrallenkerachse hinten. Geradeauslauf, Handling und Kurvenstabilität sind kaum noch zu übertreffen. Auch dem Fahrkomfort muß ein „par excellence" attestiert werden.

Zugunsten des großen Kofferraums und des 65-Liter-Tanks lassen sich lange Beine im Fond des M3 nur quer verstauen. Beide M3-Varianten, Coupé und Cabriolet, haben einen großen Frontspoiler. Serienmäßig sind auch Airbags, ABS, Lederlenkrad, Lenksäulenverstellung und Leichtmetallräder mit Mischbereifung (225/45 vorn und 245/40 ZR 17 hinten).

Das Cabriolet, seit Mai 1994 auf dem Markt, ist etwas weicher abgestimmt als das Coupé. Frischluftvergnügen und Querbeschleunigung passen eben genausowenig zusammen wie offenes Verdeck und der genußvoll erlebte „Rausch der Geschwindigkeit" bei 250 Stundenkilometer.

Les journalistes américains l'ont sacrée «voiture du siècle» et BMW est convaincue qu'une voiture aura, au cours du passé, rarement remporté autant de lauriers que la M3 de la série E36. En toute humilité, elle déclare que la M3 a, en se transformant de pure engin sportif en une voiture cultivée à haute performances, subi une métamorphose sans pareille.

La mutation est en effet impressionnante du 3 litres de 286 ch en un 3,2 litres développant 321 ch en 1995. Le nouveaux six-cylindres en aluminium de la 328i est la base de cette «grenade» qui renferme tous les raffinements techniques que connaissent les motoristes de chez BMW: quatre soupapes par cylindre, une distribution variable en continu des arbres à cames côté admission et échappement ainsi que, naturellement, une gestion moteur électronique ultramoderne avec régulation antidétonation. Celle-ci est d'ailleurs absolument indispensable, car le moteur de la M3 a un taux de compression si élevé qu'il doit consommer impérativement du super plus. En contrepartie, la vitesse maximum est régulée électroniquement à 250 km/h. Une consolation est sa consommation d'essence: pour une voiture qui abat le 0 à 100 km/h en 5,5 secondes, une consommation moyenne inférieure à 12 litres peut légitimement être qualifiée de modeste.

La souplesse du moteur est remarquable, et, dès 2000 tr/mn commence une montée en puissance qui semble ne jamais devoir finir. Les reprises de la M3 sont soutenues par une boîte à six vitesses à sixième longue, si bien qu'à 250 km/h, l'aiguille du compte-tours ne dépasse jamais les 6000 tr/mn.

En option, BMW propose la boîte séquentielle utilisée en compétition: l'embrayage et les six rapports avant sont actionnés par une commande électronique. Le pommeau trône alors au centre d'une double grille: automatique et manuelle.

Les trains roulants sont réglés optimalement avec des jambes élastiques à articulation unique à l'avant et un essieu arrière à bras guidés au centre. La tenue de cap, la maniabilité et la stabilité en virage sont pratiquement inégalées et le confort de conduite mérite lui aussi un prix d'excellence.

Le coffre de grande capacité et le réservoir de 65 litres obligent celui qui a de longues jambes à s'asseoir en biais à l'arrière de la M3. Les deux variantes de la M3, le coupé et le cabriolet, possèdent un généreux aileron avant. L'équipement de série comporte aussi des airbags, l'ABS, un volant cuir, une colonne de direction réglable et des jantes alliage chaussées de pneus mixtes (225/45 à l'avant et 245/40 ZR 17 à l'arrière).

Le cabriolet commercialisé depuis mai 1994 est un peu plus souple que le coupé. Il ne faut naturellement pas chercher à concilier les plaisirs du plein air et ceux des accélérations transversales, tout aussi peu que ceux de la capote rabattue et les «joies» de la décapotable à 250 km/h à l'arrière d'une M3.

The 286 bhp 3-liter engine of the M3 was replaced in 1995 by a 3.2-liter engine with 321 bhp. It was based on the aluminum six-cylinder engine of the 328i.

Der 3-Liter-Motor des M3 mit 286 PS wird 1995 von einem 3,2-Liter-Triebwerk mit 321 PS abgelöst. Er basiert auf dem Aluminium-Sechszylinder des 328i.

Le moteur de trois litres de la M3, qui développe 286 ch, est remplacé par un 3,2 litres de 321 ch en 1995. Il est extrapolé du six-cylindres en aluminium de la 328i.

A switch for the sports transmission and, on the console, various buttons for sound; the cockpit design expresses the idea of a refined high-performance car.

Ein Schaltknopf für das Sportgetriebe und auf der Konsole diverse Knöpfe für die akustischen Genüsse: Die Idee eines „kultivierten Hochleistungsautos" schlägt sich auch in der Gestaltung des Cockpits nieder.

Une touche de commande pour la boîte sport et, sur la console, divers boutons pour les plaisirs de l'ouïe: l'idée d'une «voiture cultivée à hautes performances» se reflète aussi dans l'agencement du cockpit.

With acceleration almost as fast as the M3 coupé, the M3 convertible accelerates from a standing start to 62.5 mph (100 kph) in 5.5 seconds, turning a drive with the top down into an exceptional experience.

Fast so sprintstark wie das M3 Coupé beschleunigt das M3 Cabrio in 5,5 Sekunden aus dem Stand auf 100 Stundenkilometer und läßt das Fahren mit offenem Verdeck zu einem besonderen Erlebnis werden.

Avec presque d'aussi bonnes reprises que le coupé M3, la M3 Cabrio abat le 0 à 100 km/h en 5,5 secondes. Dans cette voiture, rouler en décapotable est alors vraiment une sensation particulière.

As the basis for motor sport, the coupé is the "racer" in the M3 family. The appropriate wheel design for the road is also supplied.

Als Basisfahrzeug für den Motorsport ist das Coupé der „Renner" in der M3-Familie. Das passende Raddesign für die Straße wird mitgeliefert.

Comme voiture de base pour la compétition, le coupé est «la fusée» dans la famille M3. Le design des jantes de route est à l'unisson.

The individual and not quite so aggressive five-spoke star rims suit the M3 convertible particularly well.

Die individuellen und dennoch nicht aggressiv wirkenden Fünfstern-Felgen stehen dem M3 Cabriolet besonders gut.

Les jantes en étoile à cinq rayons, très personnelles mais pas agressives, vont particulièrement bien au cabriolet M3.

The large air intake on the M3 front spoiler is unmistakable; it ensures the necessary pressure at high speeds.

Unverkennbar ist der große Kühllufteinlaß des M3-Frontspoilers, der in den hohen Geschwindig- keitsbereichen für den nötigen Anpreßdruck sorgt.

Inconfondable: la grande prise d'air de refroidissement dans l'imposant aileron avant de la M3 qui confère l'appui indispensable à haute vitesse.

Even more elegant than its predecessor and full of technological gems, the E36 BMW 3 series convertible was unveiled in 1993. The aerodynamic wedge shape underlined the classic look of the open-top BMW which, according to its creators, was joy incarnated. From 1994, the advent of the 318i made this pleasure available to those with a more modest budget.

This tried and tested engine could deliver 115 bhp along with a few other innovations. For example, the maximum torque of 168 Nm could now be achieved at 3900 rpm. "DISA" was the name given by BMW to a new, high-tech component: the variable air intake unit controlled by the complex Digital Motor Electronics (DME). This unit delivered enhanced torque characteristics over the entire torque range by creating long intake tracts at low engine speeds, shortening as engine speed rises to develop full power at optimum revs. No distributor was left to interfere with radio and telephone reception, because the engine was controlled by the BMS 43 engine unit.

A reduction in fuel consumption to just under 29.5 miles per gallon (8 liters per 100 km) on the manual shift model was largely due to the introduction of the roller finger valve gear, which minimized friction between the camshaft and the fingers enormously. Despite the fun factor involved in driving convertibles, cost-effectiveness must be accorded high priority.

Although it was less nimble than its predecessor when accelerating, due to the extra 330 lbs (150 kg) of added technology carried, it had a higher top speed of 121 mph (194 kph). Overall, the four-cylinder convertible truly was value for money. The volume production model contained a plethora of

goodies. Under the letter "A" alone, you could find safety components such as ABS, airbags and ASC+T (Automatic Stability Control + Traction).

The properly reinforced car body with the strong windscreen frame contributed to the safety of the vehicle's occupants. Additional rollover protection was provided by an extended roll bar system, which shot up automatically behind the rear seats in emergencies.

As an alternative to the five-speed manual gearbox, there was an electro-hydraulic automatic transmission with a special winter program for setting off in snow and slush. This was a very useful feature, as the Bavarians knew only too well, and would probably come in handy for the rest of the world, too. Experience favored the usual E36 central control-arm type of rear axle of 3 series with squat and dip compensation as well as anti-dive control.

Convertible drivers normally have an individualist streak, which BMW catered for with its individual program, naturally provided the customer was willing to pay. This meant that even the most extravagant combinations of colors and interior variants could be specially ordered, such as yellow leather with black piping on the seats, carbon fiber finishers, azure blue and titanium silver on the outside.

Noch eleganter als der Vorgänger und vollgepackt mit technischen Leckerbissen stellt sich 1993 das Cabrio der 3er Reihe (E36) vor. Die aerodynamisch günstige Keilform unterstreicht den Chic des offenen BMW, den seine Schöpfer als ein Stück Lebensfreude anpreisen. Diese ist ab 1994 auch weniger Betuchten in Form des 318i zugänglich.

115 PS leistet inzwischen das bewährte Triebwerk, das mit einigen Innovationen aufwarten kann. So wird das maximale Drehmoment von 168 Nm schon bei 3900 Umdrehungen pro Minute erreicht. „DISA" nennt BMW eine neue High-Tech-Komponente: die differenzierte Sauganlage, gesteuert durch eine komplexe digitale Motorelektronik. Sie gewährleistet einen verbesserten Drehmomentverlauf über das gesamte Drehzahlspektrum durch lange Ansaugwege bei niedrigen Touren und kurze zur vollen Leistungsausbeute im Bereich der Höchstdrehzahl. Kein Zündverteiler stört mehr den Radio- oder Telefonempfang, denn schließlich hat das Triebwerk die BMS-43-Motorsteuerung.

Einen wesentlichen Beitrag zur Senkung des Benzinverbrauchs der handgeschalteten Version auf knapp 8 Liter pro 100 Kilometer leisten die erstmalig verwendeten Rollenschlepphebel, die die Reibung zwischen Nockenwelle und Schlepphebel enorm reduzieren. Hoch lebe die Wirtschaftlichkeit, die bei allem Cabrioletspaß nicht außer Acht gelassen werden darf.

Mit rund 150 Kilo mehr Gewicht im Anzug behäbiger als sein Vorgänger, aber in der Endgeschwindigkeit schneller (Spitze 194 Stundenkilometer), ist das Vierzylindercabriolet sein Geld allemal wert. Es beherbergt serienmäßige „Goodies" in

BMW 318i Cabrio 1994

Hülle und Fülle. Allein unter dem Buchstaben „A" finden sich Sicherheitskomponenten wie ABS, Airbags und die automatische Stabilitätskontrolle ASC+T (Automatic Stability Control + Traction). Zur Sicherheit der Fahrzeuginsassen trägt auch die gut verstärkte Karosserie mit stabilem Windschutzscheibenrahmen bei. Für zusätzlichen Überrollschutz empfiehlt sich ein Bügelsystem, das im Falle des Überschlags automatisch hinter der Rücksitzbank nach oben schnellt.

Alternativ zum Fünfgang-Schaltgetriebe gibt es ein elektronisch-hydraulisches Automatikgetriebe mit einer speziellen Anfahrstufe für Schnee und Matsch – aus bayerischer Sicht sehr nützlich, für den Rest der Welt zumindest kein Nachteil. Bestens bewährt hat sich die Zentrallenker-Hinterachse mit Anfahr- und Tauchreduzierung sowie Bremsnickausgleich.

Cabrioletfahrer sind gewöhnlich Individualisten, und denen kommt BMW mit sogenannten Individualangeboten entgegen. Gegen entsprechendes Aufgeld dürfen Farben und Interieurvarianten wild kombiniert werden – zum Beispiel gelbes Leder mit schwarzen Paspelierungen auf den Sitzen, Kohlefaserverblendungen, Azurblau und Titansilber außen.

Plus élégant encore que celui de la génération précédente et truffé de raffinements techniques, le cabriolet de la série 3 (E36) apparaît en 1993. Les lignes cunéiformes et aérodynamiques mettent en évidence le chic de la BMW décapotable qui, pour ses créateurs, contribue à la joie de vivre. Pour les portefeuilles moins bien garnis, cette voiture est disponible également à partir de 1994 sous la forme d'une 318i.

Le moteur éprouvé qui bénéficie de quelques innovations développe entre-temps 115 ch. Le couple maximum de 168 Nm est ainsi disponible dès 3900 tr/mn. BMW a baptisé «DISA» un nouveau dispositif à haute technologie: le système d'aspiration différencié commandé par les puces de l'électronique moteur numérique. Il garantit une meilleure courbe de couple sur toute la plage de régime grâce à des tubulures d'aspiration longues à bas régime, mais plus courtes à haut régime pour exploiter à fond tout le potentiel. Il n'y a plus de distributeur d'allumage qui puisse dégrader la qualité de réception de la radio ou du téléphone puisque le moteur possède une gestion électronique BMS 43.

Une innovation, les culbuteurs à rouleau qui diminuent considérablement la friction entre arbre à cames et culbuteurs, contribue de façon essentielle à faire baisser la consommation – 8 litres à peine aux 100 kilomètres pour la version à boîte manuelle. Vive l'économie qui, bien que l'on soit au volant d'un cabriolet, ne doit pas être réduite à la portion congrue.

Moins vif en reprise que sa devancière puisqu'il a pris environ 150 kilos d'embonpoint, mais plus rapide en pointe (maximum 194 km/h), le cabriolet quatre-cylindres vaut vraiment l'argent qu'il coûte. Il renferme en effet une pléthore

de raffinements proposés en série. Rien que sous la rubrique «A», on trouve des éléments de sécurité comme l'ABS, les airbags et l'ASC+T (Automatic Stability Control + Traction) – un dispositif automatique de contrôle de stabilité et de traction. La carrosserie renforcée avec une solide baie de pare-brise contribue également à garantir la sécurité des passagers. Un système d'arceau qui se met automatiquement en position derrière les appuie-tête arrière, dès qu'une situation critique se produit, offre une protection supplémentaire en cas de tonneaux.

En alternative à la boîte manuelle à cinq vitesses, BMW propose une boîte automatique à commande électronico-hydraulique avec un rapport de démarrage spécial pour la neige et la gadoue – qui a fait ses preuves dans les rigueurs de l'hiver bavarois. Pour le reste du monde, cela n'est assurément pas un inconvénient. Le train arrière à guidage central avec dispositif limitant la plongée au freinage et le cabrage aux accélérations a, lui aussi, parfaitement fait ses preuves.

Les conducteurs (et conductrices) de cabriolets sont généralement des individualistes et BMW va au-devant de leurs désirs avec des options individuelles. Ils peuvent ainsi choisir à volonté – contre espèces sonnantes et trébuchantes, naturellement – toutes les combinaisons possibles de couleurs de carrosserie et de décoration intérieure: des sièges de cuir jaune avec liseré noir, des panneaux de fibre de carbone, bleu azur et argent titane à l'extérieur.

The 318i Cabrio is visually very pleasing with its elegant and harmonious lines from the flat hood to the relatively low rear. It has 115 bhp at its disposal.

Das 318i Cabrio ist wegen der eleganten und harmonischen Linienführung von der flachen Motorhaube bis zu dem relativ niedrigen Heck optisch äußerst ansprechend. Es verfügt über 115 PS.

La 318i Cabrio est une très grande réussite esthétique en raison de l'élégance et de l'harmonie de ses lignes, étirées du capot moteur plat à l'arrière relativement bas. Elle est propulsée par un moteur de 115 ch.

BMW 318i Cabrio 1994

The fuel efficiency of the proven four-cylinder engine does nothing to reduce the feeling that there are no "constraints".

Der sparsame Benzinverbrauch des bewährten Vierzylinders mindert gewiß nicht das Gefühl der „grenzenlosen Freiheit".

L'économie du quatre-cylindres éprouvé ne minore assurément pas la sensation d'avoir une liberté illimitée.

In 1989, Gordon Murray revealed a secret. The South African had been a successful Formula 1 designer with Brabham in the BMW turbo engine era. Now Gordon worked with McLaren. His secret? It was a sketch of a racing-inspired road car to put anything else in the shade. Gordon predicted, "with McLaren, I can make my dream come true and design the ultimate sports car. Ron Dennis, the head of McLaren, and his partner Mansour Ojjeh are planning to launch a small, exclusive production series of this design."

BMW was selected from an exotic range of candidates as engine supplier. The reason for this was that the new BMW V12 (type S70/2) could produce at least 550 bhp from a six-liter engine. Equally impressive was that this power rating was achieved in the form of a gradual performance curve, not by the sudden surges of turbo power. Murray's friendship with Paul Rosche, the "High Priest" of BMW engines, meant that this new alliance took place smoothly. After all, they had pulled off the first Formula 1 "turbo title" in 1983 together.

The prestigious Monte Carlo Sporting Club and the 1992 Monaco Grand Prix were worthy venues for the car's debut to be staged. The McLaren BMW was baptized "F1" with performance which outstripped this aspirant name. In keeping with Formula 1 racing tradition, the F1 driver sat in the middle of the cockpit. However, two passengers, sitting slightly behind and to either side of the driver, also had the privilege of experiencing the sensation of this road rocket in action.

The countdown to this driving experience started in early 1993. Jonathan Palmer who, as a Formula 1 driver was deemed fit to test the first F1 prototype, spoke of driving characteristics

which were very similar to those exhibited by a Grand Prix car. A small difference: the aerodynamic body of the "F1 rocket" complete with its aerodynamic downforce configuration simply kept on accelerating past the 125 mph (200 kph) mark. The F1 reached – on a suitably long stretch of track and with no side winds – over 231 mph (370 kph).

One of the first to order the F1 (costing at least 1.6 million marks – then close to a million dollars) was former world champion Keke Rosberg, who was chauffeured around the Nürburgring by Ron Dennis in the supercar's first outing. Some 300 cars were planned, one a week from 1994. The chassis was just as elaborate as the 90 component concoction which made up the carbon fiber monocoque. One built to resemble a racing car, but adapted for the public highway. Preferably, a road without potholes was expected.

Unlike the racing version which won the 1996 GT Long Distance World Championship, the road version of the F1 did not need a spoiler. A rear flap was only electrically extended during braking. The normal F1 did not have the sequential gearshifts of the later racing F1 GTR; instead, shifts were in a six-speed H-gate. The rocker switches on the steering wheel only activated the headlights and the horn. Any remaining space contrasted with all the carbon, Kevlar and light-weight materials in the F1, for it was clad in deluxe leather, according to each customer's preferences. Anyway, there was little room left over for accessories.

1989 verrät Gordon Murray ein Geheimnis. Der Südafrikaner, in Brabhams Diensten erfolgreicher Formel-1-Konstrukteur und seit der Auflösung des Teams bei McLaren tätig, skizziert einen Straßensportwagen, der alles bisher Dagewesene in den Schatten stellen soll. „Ich darf mir bei McLaren einen Traum erfüllen und konstruiere den ultimativen Sportwagen, mit dem McLaren-Chef Ron Dennis und sein Teilhaber Mansour Ojjeh eine exklusive Kleinserie geplant haben."

Unter den in Frage kommenden Motorenlieferanten fällt die Wahl auf BMW. Ausschlaggebend dafür ist, daß der neue BMW V12 (Typ S70/2) aus sechs Litern Hubraum locker 550 PS und mehr holt, und das in einer stetigen Leistungskurve, also nicht durch plötzlich einsetzende Turbo-Power. Da BMWs „Motoren-Papst" Paul Rosche ein guter Freund von Murray ist – man hat 1983 gemeinsam den ersten „Turbo-Weltmeistertitel" der Formel 1 geholt, wird das neuerliche „Let's get together" erleichtert.

Der vornehme Sporting Club von Monte Carlo und der dortige Grand Prix 1992 sind der würdige Rahmen, um einen Wagen zu präsentieren, der „F1" heißt und diesem Namen alle Ehre macht. Wie in einem Formel-Wagen sitzt der Fahrer in der Cockpitmitte. Aber auch zwei Passagiere, seitlich und etwas nach hinten versetzt, dürfen dabeisein, wenn die „Rakete" gezündet wird.

Der Countdown zum Fahrerlebnis läuft im Frühjahr 1993 an. Jonathan Palmer, der als Formel-1-Pilot für tauglich befunden wird, die ersten F1-Prototypen zu testen, erklärt, daß das Fahrverhalten dem eines Grand-Prix-Wagens sehr nahe kommt. Der Unterschied liegt darin, daß die aerodynamisch

McLaren F1 1994

vollendet verkleidete F1-Rakete mit „Saugeffekt" auch jenseits der 200-km/h-Marke endlos weiterbeschleunigt und – eine entsprechend lange Gerade ohne Seitenwind vorausgesetzt – 370 Stundenkilometer erreicht.

Unter den ersten Bestellern des immerhin 1,6 Millionen Mark teuren F1 ist auch der frühere Formel-1-Weltmeister Keke Rosberg, der sich beim ersten „Outing" mit dem Supersportwagen von Ron Dennis über den Nürburgring chauffieren läßt. 300 Wagen sollen gebaut werden, ab 1994 pro Woche ein Exemplar. Aufwendig wie das aus 90 Teilen zusammengesetzte Kohlefaser-Monocoque ist auch das Fahrwerk: reinrassige Rennwagentechnik, aber straßentauglich. Schlaglöcher sind allerdings nicht eingeplant.

Im Gegensatz zur Rennversion, die 1996 die GT-Langstreckenweltmeisterschaft gewinnt, kommt der Straßen-F1 ohne Spoiler aus. Nur beim Bremsen wird eine Heckklappe ausgefahren. Und statt der sequentiellen Schaltung des F1 GTR wird die „Normalausgabe" manuell in einer Sechsgang-Kulisse geschaltet. Die Wippen am Lenkrad betätigen lediglich das Fernlicht und die Hupe. Was zwischen Carbon, Kevlar und Leichtmetall an Freiräumen bleibt, wird nach individuellen Wünschen mit feinstem Leder kaschiert. Viel Platz für Gepäck bleibt ohnehin nicht.

En 1989, Gordon Murray dévoile un secret. Le Sud-Africain et ancien constructeur génial de Formule 1 au service de Brabham, qui travaille pour McLaren depuis la dissolution de l'écurie, a conçu une voiture de sport routière destinée à éclipser tout ce que l'on connu à ce jour. «Chez McLaren, j'ai le plaisir de réaliser un rêve en construisant une voiture de sport au superlatif dont le P.-D.G. de McLaren, Ron Dennis, et son associé Mansour Ojjeh ont projeté une série confidentielle ultra-exclusive.»

Parmi les fournisseurs de moteurs envisagés, le choix se porte sur BMW. Un facteur déterminant est que le nouveau V12 BMW (type S70/2) développe allègrement 550 ch et plus à partir de six litres – et ce, selon une montée en puissance linéaire, autrement dit pas avec le «coup de pied au derrière» soudain d'un turbo. Le fait que le «pape» des moteurs BMW, Paul Rosche, soit un bon ami de Gordon Murray – ils ont en effet remporté en commun, en 1983, le premier titre de champion du monde de Formule 1 de l'ère du turbo – facilite bien évidemment le nouveau «let's get together».

Le sélect Sporting Club de Monte Carlo et le Grand Prix qui y est organisé en 1992 sont le cadre idéal pour présenter une voiture baptisée «F1» et qui roule encore plus vite que les monoplaces. Comme dans une monoplace, le conducteur se trouve au centre du cockpit. Les deux passagers, placés de chaque côté et légèrement décalés vers l'arrière, ont le plaisir d'être témoins de l'allumage de la «fusée».

Le compte à rebours pour sa commercialisation débute au printemps 1993. Jonathan Palmer, pilote de Formule 1 ayant la pointure nécessaire pour tester le premier prototype de la F1,

parle d'un comportement très proche de celui d'une voiture de Grand Prix. Détail d'importance, la «fusée F1» à l'aérodynamique parfaite et avec effet de sol accélère encore de façon apparemment infatigable même après avoir franchi le mur des 200 km/h et – à condition de se trouver sur une longue ligne droite correspondante et sans vent latéral – peut monter jusqu'à 370 km/h.

Parmi les premiers à signer le bulletin de commande de cette F1 qui coûte tout de même 1,6 million de marks figure aussi l'ancien champion du monde Keke Rosberg qui, pour le premier «roulage» de la super voiture de sport, se fait piloter sur le Nürburgring par Ron Dennis. Il est prévu de construire 300 voitures, une par semaine à partir de 1994. Aussi sophistiqué que la monocoque en fibre de carbone composée de 90 pièces, le châssis est digne de celui d'une voiture de course, mais à l'épreuve de la route. Les nids de poule ne sont évidemment pas prévus.

Contrairement à la version course qui remporte le Championnat du Monde d'Endurance des GT en 1996, la F1 de route ne comporte pas le moindre aileron. Il n'y a qu'au freinage que s'érige un becquet à l'arrière. Et, à la place de la commande séquentielle de la F1 GTR, l'édition pour le commun des mortels comporte de façon conventionnelle une coulisse à six vitesses. Les manettes au volant n'actionnent que les feux de route et le klaxon. Ce qui reste d'espace libre entre la fibre de carbone, le Kevlar et l'alliage léger est, selon les désirs personnels du client, drapé du cuir le plus luxueux. Il ne reste de toute façon pas beaucoup de place à bord pour les accessoires.

Getting into this unusual 1+2 seat cockpit of the McLaren F1, which can reach 231 mph (370 kph) on the appropriate track, in itself inspires the imagination of car freaks.

Bereits der Einstieg in das ungewöhnliche 1+2-Sitze-Cockpit des McLaren F1, der auf entsprechender Fahrbahn 370 Stundenkilometer erreichen kann, beflügelt die Phantasie jedes Autofreaks.

L'accès à l'extraordinaire cockpit 1+2 de la McLaren F1, capable d'atteindre 370 km/h lorsque les circonstances s'y prêtent, excite déjà l'imagination de tout amoureux de l'automobile.

In the F1, diverse flaps hide a lot of high tech. The action of the brakes is supported by an extendable air flap when the car is in motion.

Unter diversen Klappen verbirgt sich viel High-Tech. Während der Fahrt wird die Bremswirkung von einer ausfahrbaren Heckklappe unterstützt.

Une multitude de capots dissimulent la haute technologie omniprésente. Un aérofrein escamotable vient épauler le système de freinage conventionnel à haute vitesse.

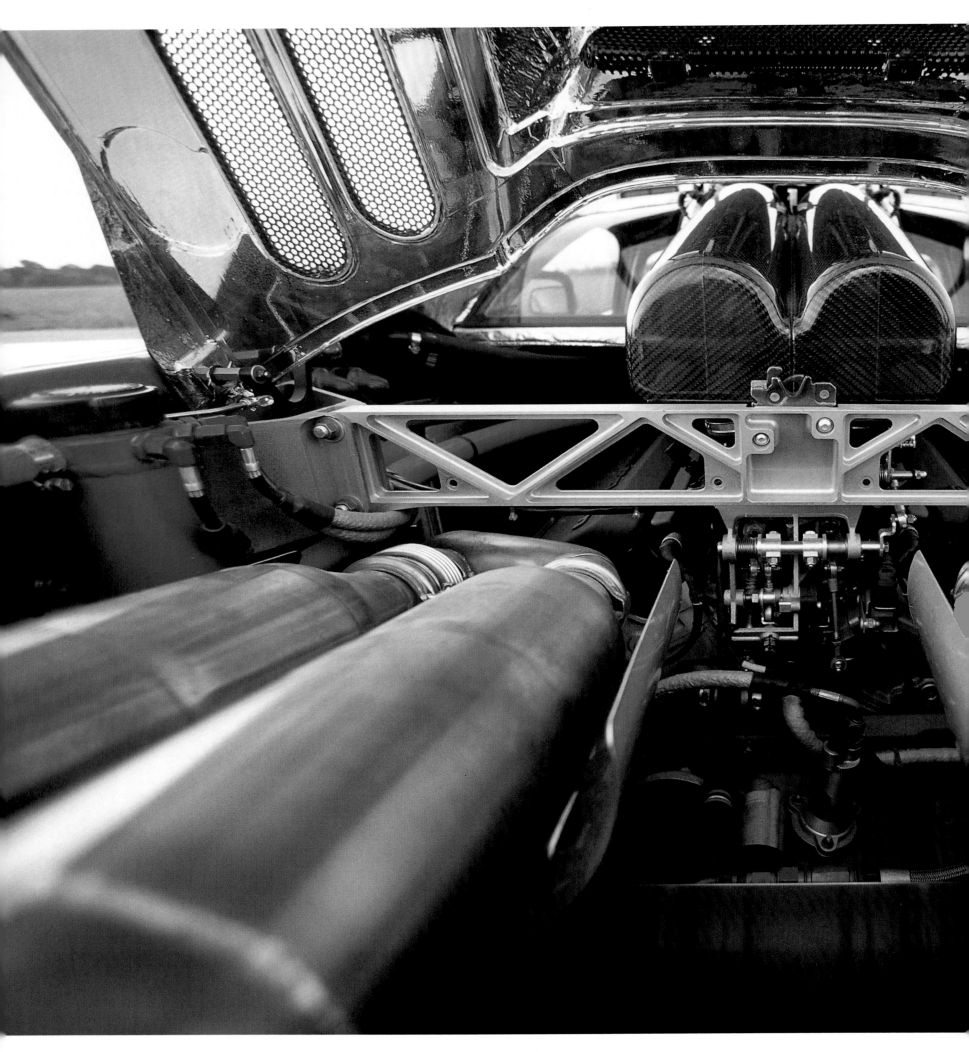

McLaren F1 1994

Powerful: the exhaust system with its four metal catalytic converters and the added carbon air intake of the BMW 12-cylinder engine. It produces a performance of 550 bhp and more from a capacity of six liters.

Gewaltig ist die mit vier Metallkatalysatoren bestückte Auspuffanlage und der aufgesetzte Karbon-Luftsammler des BMW-12-Zylinders, der mit sechs Litern Hubraum 550 PS und mehr leistet.

Impressionnant: la ligne d'échappement à quatre catalyseurs métalliques et le collecteur d'air en carbone coiffant le douze-cylindres BMW qui développe 550 ch ou plus à partir de six litres de cylindrée.

Dynamic: the wedge-shaped body of the McLaren F1 makes do without any noticeable spoilers or fins. The aerodynamically formed underbody ensures the necessary "suction".

Dynamisch: Die keilförmige Karosserie des McLaren F1 kommt ohne auffälligen Spoiler oder Flossen aus. Für den gewünschten „Saugeffekt" sorgt der aerodynamisch geformte Unterboden.

Dynamique : la carrosserie cunéiforme de la McLaren F1 ne possède pas le moindre aileron ou becquet disgracieux. Le soubassement à la forme aérodynamique calculée avec précision garantit l'effet d'aspiration souhaité.

McLaren F1 1994

Technical essentials are aesthetically implemented in the integration of various air intakes and outlets.

Bei der Integration diverser Lufteinlässe und -auslässe werden technische Notwendigkeiten ästhetisch umgesetzt.

Les contingences de la technique sont respectées et se concilient avec celles de l'esthétique, notamment dans l'intégration des diverses prises et sorties d'air.

The abbreviation "ti" (touring international) on a BMW badge symbolized from 1964 to 1975 the sportiness of a Porsche combined with space for a family. Drivers of a BMW "ti" or even a 130 bhp "tii" – the extra "i" denoted with fuel injection – had a youthful and dynamic image.

When BMW recalled these virtues in 1994, seeking its lost target customer group with the 318ti compact, those potential customers had largely swapped over to Volkswagen's Golf GTI. With spirited engine performance and driving manners, BMW became involved in the market of the GTI which was 1000 marks cheaper. Truly, the looks of the Bavarian with the short rear end compensated for the 7 mph (11 kph) missing at the top compared with the GTI.

Compared to other 3 series, 9 inches (23 cm) are missing from the rear end, but the large tailgate and individually folding rear seats provide excellent versatility on the inside. Those for whom this is not enough can allow themselves the open air variant — an electrically-operated fabric top, stretching the whole length of the roof.

Until 1996 the 318ti compact was powered by the four-valve engine from the 318ti coupé. This 1796 cc engine developed an unpleasant noise level at anything higher than 5000 rpm. BMW reacted with a larger capacity (1895 cc) to this single weakness. The alternative for power freaks was the 323ti compact: a six-cylinder of 170 bhp and 144 mph (230 kph) top speed.

That brings us back to the constant struggle of the "ti" with the GTI as to who is stronger, more maneuverable and faster, all whilst trying to achieve the most favorable consumption

figures. Since dedicated BMW drivers resist any comparison with the products from VW at Wolfsburg, the rear drive BMW ti should be looked at in its own right, and not in comparison to a GTI front-wheel drive car.

The strengths of the compact car from Munich lie in its maneuverability, neutral cornering behavior complimented by extremely precise steering, and the effective ABS brakes. The gear-change too is satisfying. Unfortunately the fifth gear is a little too short for cruising comfort. Impact safety, exhaust values and economy are to best BMW standards.

Nostalgia for the 2000tii Touring of 1971, which was 4 inches (10 cm) smaller all round and produced a mere 10 bhp less, arises from design similarities of the ti compact as a two-door with a large tailgate. The difference lies in the numbers produced. In this respect the 2002tii Touring was a rarity compared to its compact descendant.

Die Abkürzung „ti" (touring international) auf dem Typenschild eines BMW symbolisiert zwischen 1964 und 1975 die Kombination aus der Sportlichkeit eines Porsche mit dem Platzangebot einer familientauglichen Limousine. Die Fahrer eines „ti" oder gar eines 130 PS starken „tii" – also mit Einspritzung – gelten als jung und dynamisch.

BMW besinnt sich 1994 wieder auf diese Tugenden und sucht mit dem 318ti compact die verlorene Zielgruppe, die in der Zwischenzeit größtenteils auf den Golf GTI umgestiegen ist. Mit temperamentvoller Motorleistung und Fahrkultur mischt sich BMW in das Segment des 1000 Mark günstigeren GTI. Und gewiß macht die Optik des Kurzheck-Bayern die gegenüber dem GTI um 11 Stundenkilometer geringere Spitzengeschwindigkeit wett.

Gegenüber den anderen 3ern fehlen am „Hintern" 23 Zentimeter, doch durch die große Hecktür und die einzeln umklappbaren Fondsitze ist eine gewisse Innenraumvariabilität gegeben. Wem diese nicht ausreicht, der kann sich die Open-Air-Variante genehmigen – ein Stoffverdeck, das elektrisch über die ganze Dachlänge geöffnet werden kann.

Bis 1996 wird der 318ti compact vom Vierventiler des 318ti Coupé angetrieben. Dieser Motor mit 1796 ccm Hubraum entwickelt bei mehr als 5000 Umdrehungen pro Minute einen unangenehm hohen Geräuschpegel – seine einzige Schwachstelle, die BMW mit einem größeren Hubraum (1895 ccm) korrigiert. Die Alternative für Powerfreaks lautet 323ti compact: Sechszylinder, 170 PS, 230 Stundenkilometer Spitze.

Damit sind wir wieder beim „Golf-Krieg", dieser ständigen Auseinandersetzung des „ti" mit dem GTI über die Frage, wer

BMW 318ti compact 1994

nun stärker, handlicher und schneller ist, und das bei möglichst günstigen Verbrauchswerten. Da eingeschworene BMW-Fahrer jeglichem Vergleich mit den Produkten aus Wolfsburg abhold sind, sollte der BMW ti so gesehen werden, wie er ist, und nicht im Vergleich mit dem Fronttriebler GTI.

Die Stärken des kompakten Autos aus München liegen in seiner Handlichkeit, seinem neutralen Kurvenverhalten, einer äußerst präzisen Lenkung und den wirksamen Bremsen mit ABS. Auch das Getriebe läßt sich mit der bei BMW üblichen Präzision schalten. Leider ist der fünfte Gang etwas zu kurz geraten. Aufprallsicherheit, Abgaswerte und Wirtschaftlichkeit entsprechen BMW Standards.

Nostalgische Gefühle für den 2000tii Touring von 1971, der gerade 10 Zentimeter kleiner war und nur 10 PS weniger gebracht hat, kommen angesichts der ähnlichen Konzeption des ti compact als Zweitürer mit türähnlicher Heckklappe auf. Der feine Unterschied liegt in der Stückzahl. In dieser Hinsicht ist der alte tii Touring eine Rarität.

Avec l'abréviation «ti» (touring international) à l'arrière des voitures, BMW concilie, de 1964 à 1975, la sportivité d'une Porsche et l'habitabilité d'une limousine familiale. Les conducteurs de «ti» ou de la version à injection «tii» de 130 ch sont considérés comme jeunes et dynamiques.

Lorsque BMW reprend conscience de ses vertus en 1994 et cherche à retrouver son groupe cible perdu avec la 318ti compact, celui-ci a, en majorité, rejoint sans tambour ni trompette le camp de la Golf GTI. Avec une motorisation synonyme de tempérament et de douceur de fonctionnement, BMW s'engage dans le segment des GTI, moins cher de 1000 marks. Et, assurément, l'esthétique de la Bavaroise à l'arrière tronqué compense un peu les 11 km/h de vitesse de pointe qui lui manque par rapport à la GTI.

Par rapport aux autres série 3, elle a raccourci de 23 cm à l'arrière, mais le grand hayon et la banquette arrière fractionnée et rabattable lui confèrent une certaine polyvalence. Celui pour lequel cela ne suffit pas encore peut opter pour la variante «open air» - avec une capote s'ouvrant électriquement sur toute la longueur du toit.

Jusqu'en 1996, la 318ti compact est propulsée par le quatre-soupapes de la 318ti coupé. A plus de 5000 tr/mn, ce moteur de 1796 cm^3 de cylindrée développe une sonorité désagréable. C'est son seul point faible, mais BMW réagit en augmentant la cylindrée à 1895 cm^3. L'alternative pour les amateurs de performance a pour nom 323ti compact: six cylindres, 170 ch, une vitesse de pointe de 230 km/h.

Cela nous ramène à la confrontation permanente entre «ti» et les GTI sur la question de savoir lesquelles sont les plus puissantes, les plus maniables et les plus rapides tout en consommant le moins possible. Comme les inconditionnels de la BMW refusent toute comparaison avec son adversaire de Wolfsburg, il faut voir la BMW ti comme elle est et, donc, ne pas la confronter à une traction avant baptisée GTI.

Les points forts de la voiture compacte de Munich sont sa maniabilité, sa neutralité en virage avec une direction extrêmement précise et ses freins efficaces avec ABS. La boîte de vitesses se laisse manœuvrer avec la précision propre à BMW. Malheureusement, la cinquième a une démultiplication un peu trop courte. Sécurité en cas de collision, le taux de pollution et sobriété respectent la norme BMW, elles sont donc bonnes.

Compte tenu de la similitude de la conception de la BMW ti compacte à deux portes, avec hayon, on ne peut que ressentir de la nostalgie pour la 2000tii Touring de 1971, que BMW avait tout juste raccourcie de 10 cm et qui développait seulement 10 ch de moins. La seule différence, mais elle est de taille, réside dans les chiffres de production. La tii Touring est en effet une rareté.

Younger buyers in particular value this compact zippy BMW without a "rear", which is 9 inches (23 cm) shorter than the other 3 series cars.

Besonders jüngere Käuferschichten schätzen den kompakten spritzigen BMW ohne „Hintern", der 23 Zentimeter kürzer ist als die anderen 3er.

Les jeunes acheteurs, en particulier, apprécient la compacte et sémillante BMW sans «postérieur» qui mesure 23 cm de moins que les autres séries 3.

BMW 318ti compact 1994

The space in the two-door sedan with its sloping rear is quite acceptable. 930 lbs (422 kg) of additional load are allowed.

Das Platzangebot in der zweitürigen Schrägheck-Limousine ist durchaus akzeptabel. 422 Kilo Zuladung sind erlaubt.

L'habitabilité dans la berline deux portes à arrière tronqué est tout à fait acceptable. Elle peut transporter 422 kg.

Until 1996, the 318ti compact was powered by the 140 bhp four-valve four-cylinder engine of the 318ti coupé. Smart: the steering wheel with leather grip.

Bis 1996 wird der 318ti compact vom Vierventil-Vierzylinder mit 140 PS des 318ti coupé angetrieben. Schick ist das Lenkrad mit Ledergriffzone.

Jusqu'en 1996, la 318ti compact est propulsée par le quatre-cylindres à quatre soupapes de 140 ch de la 318ti coupé. Très chic: le volant avec emplacement de cuir pour les mains.

BMW 320i touring 1995

BMW has fond memories of the first Touring model, which as a two-door combination of estate car, sedan and coupé made a lively addition to the model range in 1971. The 3 series "touring" of the E36 generation, which was described by BMW as an "automobile for people who value individuality and have a mobile dynamic lifestyle," is more than a refined example of a four-door estate car.

The 320i, one of seven different engine configurations, has the now classic BMW format of the six-cylinder in-line 1991 cc engine. This power source with a three-way catalytic converter and a lambda sensor can deliver 150 bhp – exactly what could be expected from this "high-class beast of burden," which can take a load of half a ton. Laden only with the driver, the 320i can reach 132.5 mph (212 kph) and also does well in the sprint stakes, accelerating from 0 to 62.5 mph (100 kph) in approximately 10 seconds. The fuel tank has the same capacity for all touring variants of the 3 series: it only needs refueling every 375 miles (600 km) of mixed driving.

This sporting wagon's priority is a versatile compartment design which can accommodate the widest possible variety of loads. The loading volume of 1320 liters is enclosed by a large and retractable rear baggage cover. Practical hoops and other securing fixtures for loads ensure that nothing gets damaged when taking sharp corners. This sports wagon manages changes of direction and tight bends in an extremely smooth manner. Thanks to the Automatic Stability Control (ASC), wheel spin or sudden slides of the 320i touring's rear wheels are minimized. Like all models of the 3 series, the chassis is specified to optimum levels with the central control-arm rear axle.

Safety really does come first with this car: ABS, disc brakes (internally vented at the front), airbags including a side airbag for driver and front-seat passenger, plus impact absorption zones and the integrated side collision protection are all part of the standard equipment features.

In addition to those zones of passive and active safety, there are also extra features including some aimed specifically at the family. For example the 320i touring has electric circuit sockets that are integrated in the child seats at the rear of the car. Whether small children will use these plug-in points for reading lights or Walkman entertainment is another matter altogether.

The tasteful interior of the 320i displays a great deal of attention to practical details. In mass-produced automobiles, anything important appears exactly where you would expect. The answer to any extra individual requirements can be found in the BMW catalogs for special equipment, following their motto: "Anything developed and installed by us must be good."

Gern besinnt sich BMW auf den ersten Touring, der 1971 als zweitürige Mischung aus Kombi, Limousine und Coupé die Modellpalette belebte. Der 3er touring der heutigen BMW-Generation, von den Werbestrategen als „Automobil für Menschen, die auf Individualität Wert legen und einen mobilen dynamischen Lebensstil haben" beschrieben, ist mehr als ein viertüriger Kombi der besseren Art.

Der 320i, eine von sieben verschiedenen Triebwerkskonfigurationen, hat den mittlerweile schon klassischen Sechszylinder-Reihenmotor mit 1991 ccm Hubraum. Diese Kraftquelle mit Dreiwegekatalysator und Lambda-Sonde leistet 150 PS, genau das Richtige für einen „Edel-Lastesel", dem eine halbe Tonne Zuladung aufgebürdet werden kann. Nur mit dem Fahrer „beladen", erreicht der 320i eine Spitzengeschwindigkeit von 212 Stundenkilometer und zieht mit einer Beschleunigung von rund 10 Sekunden von 0 auf 100 Stundenkilometer recht ordentlich an. Der Tankinhalt, bei allen touring der 3er Serie gleich groß, reicht im gemischten Betrieb für eine Fahrtstrecke von rund 600 Kilometern.

Bei einem Kombi ist die Umsetzung eines variablen Raumkonzeptes wichtig, das Freiraum für die verschiedensten Formen der Zuladung schafft. Beim 3er verschließt eine große Heckklappe das Ladevolumen von 1320 Litern. Praktische Ösen und sonstige Ladeguthalterungen sorgen auch bei extremen Kurvenfahrten für Ordnung. Schnelle Richtungswechsel und enge Kurven meistert dieser Kombi ohne Schwankungen, denn dank der automatischen Stabilitätskontrolle werden ein Durchdrehen der Räder oder die Gefahr eines plötzlichen Ausbrechens des Wagenhecks auf ein Minimum reduziert. Wie

bei allen 3ern ist das Fahrwerk mit Zentrallenker-Hinterachse bestens nivelliert.

Das Thema Sicherheit wird großgeschrieben: ABS, Scheibenbremsen (vorn innenbelüftet), Airbags einschließlich Seitenairbag für Fahrer und Beifahrer und Stoßabsorbierungszonen gehören ebenso zum Standard wie der integrierte seitliche Aufprallschutz.

Neben diesen sinnvollen Bausteinen zur Verbesserung der passiven und aktiven Sicherheit gibt es natürlich auch viel Staffage und außerdem das sogenannte „Family"-Konzept, bei dem Kindersitze mit Bordstromsteckdosen in der hinteren Sitzbank integriert sind. Ob die Kleinen wohl mit Leseleuchten oder dem Anschluß für einen Walkman sehr viel anfangen können?

Viel Liebe zum praktischen Detail verrät das geschmackvolle Interieur des 320i. Alles Wichtige ist in der serienmäßigen Ausgabe dort, wo man es sich wünscht. Darüber hinaus gehenden individuellen Bedürfnissen setzen die BMW-Sonderausstattungskataloge keine Grenzen, frei nach dem Motto: Gut ist alles, was von uns entwickelt und eingebaut wird.

Ce n'est pas sans une certaine nostalgie que BMW se rappelle sa première Touring, née en 1971, qui était une espèce de cocktail à deux portes de break, berline et coupé – un authentique enrichissement de sa gamme, donc. La série 3 touring de l'actuelle génération de BMW, que Munich qualifie d'«automobile pour les hommes qui attachent de la valeur à la personnalité et cultivent un style de vie mobile et dynamique», est plus qu'un break à quatre portes – elle est d'une race supérieure.

La 320i, l'une de sept configurations de moteur différentes, possède le six-cylindres de 1991 cm³ qui est entre-temps devenu un grand classique. Ce propulseur à catalyseur trois voies et sondes lambda développe 150 ch, juste ce qu'il convient pour une «bête de somme prestigieuse» qui peut charger sur ses épaules une bonne demi-tonne de bagages. «Chargée» seulement du conducteur, la 320i atteint 212 km/h et accélère énergiquement puisqu'elle couvre le 0 à 100 km/h en environ 10 secondes. En conduite mixte, le réservoir de carburant dont la capacité est identique pour toutes les touring de la série 3 autorise une autonomie de 600 km.

Un aspect important pour un break est la transposition du concept de polyvalence qui donne carte blanche pour toutes les formes imaginables de transport. Un grand hayon donne accès à un coffre d'une capacité de 1320 litres. De pratiques œillets de fixation et diverses possibilités d'arrimage garantissent que tout reste bien en place même lorsque l'on franchit très rapidement les virages, car ce break maîtrise sans faillir à la tâche les changements de cap fréquents et virages étroits. Grâce au contrôle de stabilité automatique, tout patinage des

roues ou dérapage brutal de l'arrière est pratiquement exclu. Comme pour toutes les série 3, le châssis est parfaitement jugulé grâce à l'essieu arrière à guidage central.

Le thème de la sécurité n'a été négligé en rien: ABS, freins à disques (ventilés à l'avant), coussins gonflables avec airbags latéraux pour le conducteur et le passager avant et zones d'amortissement des chocs font partie de l'équipement de série au même titre que la protection anticollision latérale intégrée.

Outre ces éléments de sécurité passive et active, il y en a naturellement bien d'autres encore qui vont du gadget au concept «Family», selon lequel les sièges pour enfants intégrés à la banquette arrière comportent une prise de courant électrique. Mais que peuvent bien faire nos chères petites têtes blondes avec une veilleuse ou une prise de courant pour un baladeur?

Très bien conçu, le cockpit de la 320i fait preuve de beaucoup d'amour pour les détails pratiques. On trouve en série toutes les choses importantes là où on s'attend à les trouver. Le catalogue d'options de BMW, qui ne connaît pratiquement pas de limites selon la devise «tout ce que nous mettons au point et construisons est bon», répond aux besoins les plus personnels.

BMW 320i touring 1995

The 320i touring is well equipped with the 150 bhp 2-liter six-cylinder engine which can easily carry the burden of an extra half-ton load.

Mit dem 150 PS starken 2-Liter-Sechszylindermotor ist der 320i touring, dem ohne weiteres eine halbe Tonne Zuladung aufgebürdet werden kann, bestens ausgestattet.

Avec le six-cylindres de deux litres et 150 ch, la 320i touring qui peut transporter sans la moindre difficulté une bonne demi-tonne dispose d'un propulseur idéal.

BMW 740i 1996

This large BMW contains a multitude of useful small items with which BMW has done an excellent job. The 740i is a regal representative of the automotive upper class: technically perfect, luxuriously appointed, functionally thought through down to the smallest switch. Powered by the satin-smooth performance of the 4.4-liter V8 engine, whose long stroke characteristics mean the maximum torque peak for pulling power arrives at a remarkably low 3900 rpm.

What characterizes this latest generation of BMW eight-cylinder engines is not enhanced performance – 286 bhp does that job – but smoothness, a broad torque range and improved fuel economy. In figures, acceleration from 0 to 62.5 mph (100 kph) in 6.6 seconds says as much for the 740i as average fuel consumption of just 19 miles to the gallon of Super unleaded fuel (12.5 liters per 100 km). As usual for many bigger BMWs, top speed is electronically limited to 156 mph (250 kph).

In the manual transmission model, a sixth gear was added to the fifth to serve as an overdrive ratio, reducing engine revs by 17 percent and thus saving fuel. Anyone who loves luxury sedans will want to avoid straining his clutch foot, particularly as BMW offers an electro-hydraulically controlled five-speed automatic transmission as a popular optional extra. This is provided with technical refinements such as adaptive transmission control and Steptronic.

The BMW technical dictionary, which forms part of every 7 series brochure, reads at first sight like the manual for a space shuttle. There is reference to "Check Control", "Multi-Information Display" (MID), "On-Board Computer", "On-Board Diagnostics" and the optionally available satellite navigation

system which calculates the car's position through a "Global Positioning System" (GPS).

It is no doubt reassuring for the normal car user to know that the 740i (like all new 5 and 7 series cars) is equipped as standard with a head airbag, which has been fitted into the roof frame and usefully supplements the effect of the side airbag in the door. Naturally this system of tubed bags also has a catchy designation: "Inflatable Tubular Structure" (ITS). In comparison to the Mercedes-Benz S420, BMW have consciously dotted the "i" of the 740.

Im großen BMW steckt eine Fülle nützlicher Kleinigkeiten, bei denen BMW Großartiges geleistet hat. Der 740i ist ein souveräner Vertreter der Oberschicht unter den Automobilen: technisch perfekt, luxuriös im Interieur und funktionell durchdacht bis zum kleinsten Schalter. Er verwöhnt seine Passagiere mit der samtweichen Laufkultur des V8-Motors mit knapp 4,4 Litern Hubraum. Dank der langhubigen Auslegung dieses Triebwerks wird das maximale Drehmoment bereits bei 3900 Umdrehungen pro Minute erreicht.

Die jüngste Generation der BMW-Achtzylinder kennzeichnet nicht mehr brachiale Kraft und Leistung – 286 PS genügen – sondern Laufkultur, breiterer Drehmomentverlauf und gleichzeitige Senkung des Kraftstoffverbrauchs. In Zahlen ausgedrückt spricht eine Beschleunigung von 0 auf 100 Stundenkilometer in nur 6,6 Sekunden ebenso für den 740i wie ein durchschnittlicher Benzinverbrauch von 12,5 Litern Super. Wie bei BMW Usus, ist die Höchstgeschwindigkeit elektronisch auf 250 Stundenkilometer beschränkt.

Beim Schaltgetriebe wurde auf den fünften Gang noch ein sechster gesetzt – als Schongang, der die Motordrehzahl um 17 Prozent senkt und somit den Benzinverbrauch reduziert. Wer Luxuslimousinen liebt, schont meist den Kupplungsfuß, zumal BMW im Sonderausstattungspaket ein elektronisch-hydraulisch gesteuertes Fünfgang-Automatikgetriebe anbietet. Dieses ist natürlich mit technischen Raffinessen wie adaptiver Getriebesteuerung und Steptronic versehen.

Das BMW-Techniklexikon, Bestandteil jedes 7er-Prospekts, liest sich auf den ersten Blick wie das Handbuch eines Spaceshuttles. Da ist die Rede von „Check Control", „Multi-Informa-

tions-Display" (MID), „Bordcomputer", „On-Bord-Diagnose" und dem auf Wunsch erhältlichen Navigationssystem, das mit Hilfe des „Global Positioning System" (GPS) den jeweiligen Standort des Fahrzeugs errechnet.

Für den Normalverbraucher ist sicherlich beruhigend, daß der 740i (wie alle neuen 5er und 7er) serienmäßig mit einem Kopf-Airbag ausgerüstet ist, der, im Dachrahmen integriert, die Wirkung des in der Tür befindlichen Seiten-Airbags sinnvoll ergänzt. Natürlich trägt auch dieses Schlauchsystem eine werbewirksame Bezeichnung in unaussprechlichem Techniker-slang: „Inflatable Tubular Structure" (ITS). Mit dem 740i hat BMW dem Mercedes-Benz S420 jedenfalls das bewußte „i"-Tüpfelchen aufgesetzt.

La grosse BMW regorge de multiples petits détails pour lesquels BMW n'a pas regardé à la dépense. La 740i incarne la voiture de luxe par excellence qui choie ses passagers: parfaite sur le plan mécanique, avec un cockpit luxueux, conçue fonctionnellement jusqu'à la plus infime manette et animée par l'onctuosité d'un moteur V8 de 4,4 litres de cylindrée. Sa caractéristique à course longue permet à ce propulseur de délivrer son couple maximum dès 3900 tr/mn.

Ce n'est pas une débauche de puissance – 286 ch suffi-sent – qui caractérise la dernière génération des huit-cylindres BMW, dont les points forts sont en réalité la douceur de fonctionnement, la plage de couples et, simultanément, la diminution de la consommation. En chiffres, cela se traduit par des accélérations de 0 à 100 km/h en 6,6 secondes seulement ainsi que par une consommation moyenne de 12,5 litres de super aux 100 km. Comme il est de coutume chez BMW, la vitesse maximum est régulée électroniquement à 250 km/h.

La boîte manuelle a vu sa cinquième vitesse complétée par un sixième rapport – une démultipliée qui fait retomber le régime moteur de 17% et donc aussi la consommation. Le véritable amateur de limousines de luxe ne manie pas volontiers l'embrayage, d'autant plus que, dans sa liste des options, BMW propose une boîte automatique à cinq vitesses à commande électronico-hydraulique. Celle-ci comporte naturellement divers raffinements techniques comme une gestion adaptative et une commande Steptronic.

Le lexique de la mécanique d'une BMW, qui fait partie intégrante de tout prospectus de série 7, évoque à la première lecture le mode d'emploi d'une navette spatiale. On y parle de

«Check Control», de «Multi-Information Display» (MID), «Ordinateur de bord», d'«On-Board-Diagnostics» et du système de navigation proposé en option, qui indique l'endroit où l'on se trouve à l'aide du «Global Positioning System» (GPS).

Pour l'automobiliste de tous les jours, il est assurément tranquillisant de savoir que la 740i (comme toutes les série 5 et 7) comporte en série un coussin gonflable intégré dans le montant de pavillon et qui protège la tête, complétant efficacement à cette occasion les airbags latéraux se trouvant dans les portières. Mais pourquoi ce système de boudins gonflables a-t-il un nom qui risque de vous faire perdre votre latin: «Inflatable Tubular Structure» (ITS)? Avec la 740i, BMW a en quelque sorte placé la cerise sur le gâteau de la Mercedes-Benz S420.

The aesthetics of top-of-the-range cars find expression in the elegant lines of the 740i: a refined atmosphere with functional dashboard inside and a powerful eight-cylinder engine under the hood.

Die Ästhetik der „Oberschicht unter den Automobilen" drückt sich in der eleganten Linienführung des 740i aus: ein edles Ambiente mit funktionellem Armaturenbrett im Inneren und einem kraftvollen Achtzylinder unter der Haube.

L'esthétique du «grand chic automobile» s'exprime dans l'élégance des lignes de la 740i : une ambiance luxueuse avec un tableau de bord fonctionnel à l'intérieur et un puissant huit-cylindres sous le capot.

As flagship of the fourth generation of the 5 series (E39), which entered the automotive spring of 1997 with seven engine options, the 540i has been given a beefy but very modern 4.4-liter unit. This V8 aluminum engine with electronic engine management develops 420 Nm torque at a remarkably low 3900 rpm and even at very low engine revs it is surprisingly flexible. The 286 bhp provides acceleration of 6.2 seconds from 0 to 62.5 mph (100 kph) and a top speed of 156 mph (250 kph).

With reasonably restrained driving, not always easy given the premium road holding, the 540i does a good 19.2 miles to the gallon of Super (12.3 liters per 100 km). With the touring model, the higher weight of 3737 lbs (1695 kg) instead of 3494 lbs (1585 kg) becomes apparent with additional consumption of one tenth of a gallon. A carefully calculated six-speed manual transmission is designed for drivers who like to use the gears. Those who do not are happier with the modern adaptively controlled automatic transmission with five gears.

This new member of the 5 series stands out by its lightweight construction; thus the rigidity of the body shell has been considerably increased while maintaining the same weight as the previous model. The lightweight construction chassis components, mostly of aluminum, were a world first for a production model. Aluminum wheels were also standard on the 540i.

The integral rear axle, spatially effective suspension with acceleration and braking anti-dive mechanism, is taken from the BMW 7 series. Optionally, the aluminum integral axle can be combined with a pneumatic self-leveling mechanism.

That means that the suspension quality remains the same irrespective of the axle load.

ABS and ASC+T (Automatic Stability Control + Traction) are supplied as a matter of course for all members of the 5 series of this generation. And also present in this series is everything else necessary to provide safe and comfortable driving, even at high speeds.

Of course there is still room at BMW for a few special wishes such as automatic dip internal and external mirrors or a navigation system with TV monitor. Automatic air conditioning for the 540i became a standard part of 5 series equipment from the autumn of 1997 onwards.

The lines of this member of the 5 series can hardly be bettered in terms of aesthetics. Technical requirements and maximum interior space have been assembled in a shape to meet functional needs, which is seen as a trendsetter for further BMW models while producing good aerodynamic values.

Als Flaggschiff der vierten Generation der 5er Reihe (E39), die mit sieben Motorisierungsoptionen in den Autofrühling 1997 startet, ist der 540i mit einem bulligen, aber hochmodernen 4,4-Liter-Aggregat bestückt. Dieses V8-Aluminiumtriebwerk mit elektronischem Motormanagement entwickelt bereits bei 3900 Touren ein Drehmoment von 420 Newtonmetern und ist selbst bei ganz niedrigen Drehzahlen erstaunlich elastisch. Die 286 PS ermöglichen eine Beschleunigung von 0 auf 100 Stundenkilometer in 6,2 Sekunden und eine Spitzengeschwindigkeit von 250 „Sachen".

Bei nicht allzu forcierter Fahrweise, die sich angesichts der optimalen Straßenlage allerdings gern aufdrängt, schlürft der 540i lediglich 12,3 Liter Super. Beim Touring macht sich das höhere Gewicht von 1695 (statt 1585) Kilo mit einem Mehrverbrauch von knapp einem halben Liter bemerkbar. Ein sorgsam abgestimmtes Sechsgang-Getriebe kommt schaltfreudigen Fahrern entgegen. Schaltfaule freuen sich über das moderne, adaptiv gesteuerte Automatikgetriebe mit fünf Gängen.

Der neue 5er glänzt durch seine Leichtbauweise. So kann die Steifigkeit der Rohkarosse bei gleichem Gewicht gegenüber dem Vorgängermodell erheblich vergrößert werden. Weltpremiere bei einem Serienmodell feiert das weitgehend aus Aluminium gefertigte Leichtbaufahrwerk. Da ist es nur sinnvoll, daß auch die Alufelgen zur Serienausstattungt des 540i gehören.

Die Integralhinterachse, eine räumlich wirkende Radaufhängung mit Anfahr- und Bremsnickausgleich, wird der BMW-Oberklasse entnommen; auf Wunsch ist dieser

BMW 540i 1996

technische Leckerbissen auch noch mit einem pneumatischen Niveauausgleich kombinierbar. Das bedeutet gleichbleibende Federungsqualität unabhängig von der Achslast.

ABS und ASC+T (Schlupf- und Traktionsregelung) sind bei allen 5ern dieser Generation eine Selbstverständlichkeit. Auch sonst verfügt diese Klasse über alles, was sicherem und komfortablem Fahren dient – auch bei hohen Geschwindigkeiten.

Natürlich hat BMW noch Raum für ein paar Sonderwünsche gelassen, so zum Beispiel für automatisch abblendende Innen- und Außenspiegel oder ein Navigationssystem mit TV-tauglichem Monitor. Die Klimaautomatik indessen ist beim 540i ab Herbst 1997 bereits fester Bestandteil der Serie.

Die Linienführung dieser 5er ist an Ästhetik kaum zu überbieten. Technische Vorgaben und maximaler Innenraum werden funktionsgerecht in eine Form gebracht, die, neben guten aerodynamischen Werten, als richtungsweisend für künftige BMW-Modelle gilt.

En tant que navire amiral de la quatrième génération de la série 5 (E39) qui inaugure le printemps automobile 1997 avec une gamme de sept moteurs, la 540i est propulsée par un puissant et vigoureux, mais ultramoderne 4,4 litres. Ce V8 en aluminium à gestion moteur électronique développe déjà un couple de 420 Nm à 3900 tr/mn, même à bas régime, il fait preuve d'une souplesse étonnante. Les 286 ch lui permettent d'accélérer de 0 à 100 km/h en 6,2 secondes et d'atteindre allègrement les 250 km/h.

A conduite plus décontractée, qui ne met pas à contribution une tenue de route exceptionnelle, la 540i consomme seulement 12,3 litres de super. Dans la version touring, le poids supérieur, 1695 kg au lieu de 1585, se traduit par un supplément de consommation d'un demi-litre à peine. Une boîte à six vitesses bien étagée va au devant des virtuoses du pommeau. Les adeptes de la boîte automatique se féliciteront de la moderne transmission automatique à cinq vitesses et commande adaptative.

La nouvelle série 5 brille par la légèreté de sa construction : ainsi la carrosserie blanche offre-t-elle, à poids identique, une bien plus grande rigidité torsionnelle que l'ancien modèle. Les trains roulants en alliage léger, pratiquement tout en aluminium, représentent une première mondiale sur une voiture de série. Sur la 540i, les jantes alliage sont également de série.

L'essieu arrière intégral, une suspension qui agit dans l'espace avec compensation des mouvements de caisse à l'accélération et au freinage, est le même que celui qui équipe les BMW série 7 et les coupés. Sur demande, l'essieu intégral en aluminium peut être combiné à un correcteur d'assiette pneumatique. Cela signifie que la qualité de la suspension reste identique quelque soit la charge.

ABS et ASC+T (régulation antipatinage) vont de soi pour toutes les série 5 de cette génération. Et cette gamme comporte tout ce qui garantit une conduite sûre et confortable – aussi et surtout à haute vitesse.

Naturellement, BMW a aussi pensé à ceux qui ont des désirs particuliers, par exemple des rétroviseurs intérieurs et extérieurs anti-éblouissement automatiques ou un système de navigation avec écran de téléviseur. A partir de l'automne 1997, la climatisation automatique fait déjà partie de l'équipement de série pour la 540i.

L'esthétique de cette série 5 est difficile à surclasser. Les particularismes techniques et l'habitabilité maximum sont conciliés de façon fonctionnelle sous les traits d'une carrosserie qui, outre un bon coefficient aérodynamique, s'avérera novatrice pour d'autres gammes de BMW.

Under the 540i's stylistically successful, forward-extending hood with the BMW kidneys, there slumbers the same power source as in the 740i: a 4.4-liter aluminum V8 engine.

Unter der stilistisch gekonnt nach vorn gezogenen Haube mit den BMW-Nieren schlummert beim 540i die gleiche Kraftquelle wie beim 740i: ein 4,4-Liter-V8 aus Aluminium.

Sous le capot esthétiquement réussi de la 540i avec les traditionnels naseaux BMW ronronne le même propulseur que pour la 740i: un V8 de 4,4 litres en aluminium.

BMW 540i 1996

The monitor for on-board computer, navigation system and TV has been cleverly integrated into the central console of the stylishly thoroughbred 5 series.

Geschickt ist der TV-taugliche Monitor für Bordcomputer und Navigationssystem in die Mittelkonsole des schnittigen Edel-5ers integriert.

L'écran de l'ordinateur de bord, du système de navigation et de télévision est parfaitement intégré dans la console médiane de la rapide série 5 de prestige.

BMW M roadster 1997

Based on such beautiful two-seaters as the 328 and the postwar 507 and Z1 models, the first drawings for a new road sports car were created in Munich during 1989. It was to be a roadster, though not quite as spartan as in the originals. Modern technology, packaged in a sporting dress, with a touch of traditional BMW fashion at an affordable price: that is the profile of design priorities.

However, it is not in Bavaria's 1972 Olympic City, but near the site of the 1996 Olympic Games that the Z roadster begins to depart a production line. The newest BMW factory in America's Spartanburg, South Carolina, adjacent to Interstate 85 to Atlanta, offers the Z3 with various engines: 115 bhp 1.8-liter four-cylinder, 140 bhp 1.9-liter four-cylinder and the 192 bhp 2.8-liter six-cylinder.

Real roadster driving required even more power. This was acquired around the BMW resources that ring Munich's river, the Isar. Thus the M model with 3.2 liters and 321 bhp (as for the European M3) was developed for the "ultimate driving experience," as BMW put it. But the M roadster has to power 265 lbs (120 kg) less than the M3. This difference does not, however, show up in the enormous acceleration from 0 to 62.5 mph (100 kph): recorded 5.4 seconds for both.

A slightly longer wheelbase and a wider track at the front and rear, as well as significantly wider tire dimensions differentiate the M roadster from the Z3, as do discreet spoilers. At the end of the side cooling grills — surely a reminder of the 507 — the "M" badge of speed is displayed proudly, instead of the BMW roundel.

A roadster aura is also transmitted by the round chrome instruments for the clock, external temperature and oil temperature on the wide transmission tunnel, under which a five-ratio gearbox, geared like the Z3 2.8, does its duty. Dashboard and rich leather interior provide evidence of design imagination.

There is no spare wheel. The special shape of the light-alloy wheels is designed to prevent the tires coming off if there is a flat. Should a puncture occur, the driver operates an "M Mobility System" comprising a mini-compressor and quick sealant. If that does not help, nothing for it but a phone rescue: BMW breakdown service is famous for its good organization.

The electro-hydraulic activation of the fabric top comes as standard on the M, and as an extra on the four-cylinder models. The tonneau fabric must be manually buttoned over the folded top for that real roadster feeling.

The expensive chassis is not harsh, but well adjusted. Even under high acceleration this sports car dips only slightly. Performance, especially along roads with many bends and steering load changes, is a pleasure, for the steering stays precise. The vehicle amiably covers loose ground. The stunts which Pierce "James Bond" Brosnan did with the Z3 in the film "Golden Eye" do not require the driving skills of a Finnish rally star such as Rauno Aaltonen.

Given its enormous potential, the M roadster must have large-diameter ventilated disc brakes, measuring 12.4 inches (315 mm) front; the rears are 12.3 inches (312 mm). ABS braking and anti-dive mechanisms are BMW virtues of the 1990s.

Anknüpfend an so schöne Zweisitzer wie den 328 und die Nachkriegsmodelle 507 und Z1 entstehen 1989 in München erste Zeichnungen für einen neuen Straßensportwagen – ein Roadster, wenngleich die Ausstattung weniger spartanisch sein soll. Moderne Technik in sportlichem Anzug mit einem Hauch traditioneller BMW-Mode, dazu ein erschwinglicher Preis – so lautet das Anforderungsprofil.

Doch nicht in Bayerns Olympiastadt, sondern in der Nähe des Austragungsortes der Spiele von 1996 geht der Z roadster vom Band. Das jüngste BMW-Werk in Spartanburg, South Carolina (USA) ganz in der Nähe des Interstate Highway 85 nach Atlanta, bietet den Z3 in unterschiedlichen Motorisierungsvarianten an: 1,8-Liter-Vierzylinder mit 115 PS, 1,9-Liter-Vierzylinder mit 140 PS und 2,8-Liter-Sechszylinder mit 192 PS.

Richtiges Roadster-Running erfordert noch mehr Power, und die ist wiederum an der Isar zu haben. Dort gibt es für das „ultimative Fahrerlebnis", so BMW, die Variante „M" mit 3,2 Litern und 321 PS – analog zum M3. Allerdings wiegt der M roadster 120 Kilo weniger als der M3, was bei diesem Kraftpotential allerdings keine Rolle mehr spielt. In unglaublichen 5,4 Sekunden beschleunigen beide von 0 auf 100 Stundenkilometer.

Geringfügig längerer Radstand und die breite Spur vorn und hinten sowie wesentlich breitere Reifen und der dezente Spoiler unterscheiden den „M" vom „Z". Am Ende der seitlichen Kühlschlitze – sicherlich eine Reminiszenz an den 507 – prangt stolz statt des BMW-Emblems das „schnelle M".

Roadster-Feeling vermitteln auch die in Chrom gefaßten Rundinstrumente für Uhrzeit, Außen- und Öltemperatur auf

dem breiten Getriebetunnel, unter dem eine Fünfgang-Schaltung, abgestuft wie beim Z3 2.8, ihren Dienst verrichtet. Armaturenbrett und reichlich Lederinterieur zeugen von Einfallsreichtum.

Diesen vermißt man hingegen beim Reserverad – es gibt keines! Die spezielle Form der Leichtmetallfelgen soll ein Abspringen des Reifens im Falle eines „Platten" verhindern. Kommt es doch dazu, greift der Fahrer zum „M Mobility System", einem Kleinkompressor und Schnelldichtmittel. Hilft das nicht, muß der BMW-Notdienst anrücken, der bekanntlich gut organisiert ist.

Die elektrohydraulische Betätigung des Stoffverdecks gehört beim „M" zum Standard, bei den Vierzylindermodellen zu den Extras. Hier muß die Persenning von Hand über das zusammengefaltete Verdeck geknöpft werden – ein Rest von Roadster-Feeling.

Keineswegs hart, sondern gut abgestimmt ist das aufwendige Fahrwerk. Selbst bei hoher Querbeschleunigung neigt sich dieser Sportwagen nur geringfügig. Das Fahrverhalten ist eine Wonne, besonders auf kurvenreicher Strecke mit vielen Lastwechseln; die Lenkung ist präzise. Gutmütig bewegt sich dieses Fahrzeug selbst auf lockerem Untergrund. Was James-Bond-Darsteller Pierce Brosnan im Film „Golden Eye" mit dem Z3 anstellt, bedarf nicht der Fahrkünste eines Rauno Aaltonen.

Angesichts des enormen Leistungspotentials kann der M roadster auf belüftete Scheibenbremsen großen Durchmessers – vorn 315, hinten 312 Millimeter – nicht verzichten. ABS, Brems- und Anfahrnickausgleich gehören zu den BMW-Ausstattungsmerkmalen der neunziger Jahre.

C'est dans la tradition d'aussi jolies biplaces que la 328 et les 507 et Z1 d'après-guerre que sont faites, en 1989 à Munich, les premières esquisses pour une nouvelle sportive de route. Ce sera un roadster, mais pas aussi spartiate au sens propre du terme. Technicité et modernisme, une allure sportive et les arguments esthétiques traditionnels de BMW, un prix attrayant – tel est le cahier des charges.

Ce n'est pas dans la ville olympique bavaroise, mais à proximité du lieu des Jeux Olympiques de 1996 que la Z roadster sort de chaînes. La toute nouvelle usine de BMW à Spartanburg, en Caroline du Sud (Etats-Unis), près de l'Interstate Highway 85 qui mène à Atlanta, propose la Z3 avec trois motorisations: le quatre-cylindres de 1,8 litre et 115 ch, le quatre-cylindres de 1,9 litre et 140 ch et le six-cylindres de 2,8 litres et 192 ch.

Mais le vrai «roadster-running» exige encore plus de puissance que l'on n'obtient qu'à Munich. C'est là qu'est assemblée, pour «le plaisir de conduire à l'apogée», dit BMW, la variante «M» avec ce même moteur de 3,2 litres et 321 ch qui propulse la M3. Le M roadster pèse 120 kg de moins que la M3. Mais cela n'a aucune incidence sur les fantastiques accélérations de 0 à 100 km/h: 5,4 secondes pour toutes les deux.

Un empattement légèrement plus long et des voies plus larges à l'avant et à l'arrière, des pneus nettement plus volumineux et de discrets ailerons distinguent la «M» de la «Z». A l'extrémité des ouïes de refroidissement latérales – une réminiscence de la 507 – s'affiche fièrement, à la place de l'emblème BMW, le «rapide M».

Les cadrans circulaires cernés de chrome pour la montre, le thermomètre de température extérieure et le thermomètre

d'huile sur le large tunnel de transmission sous lequel se trouve une boîte à cinq vitesses avec le même étagement que pour la Z3 2.8 dégagent aussi une authentique sensation de roadster. Le tableau de bord et le cuir à profusion dans le cockpit témoignent de l'imagination des ingénieurs.

Ne cherchez pas la roue de secours – il n'y en a pas. La forme particulière des jantes en alliage est censée empêcher le pneu de s'échapper en cas de crevaison. S'il s'en produit toutefois une, le conducteur dispose du «M Mobility System», un mini-compresseur et une bombe d'agent d'étanchéification expresse. Si cela ne suffit pas, un coup de téléphone et le service de dépannage de BMW est là, toujours bien organisé.

La commande électrohydraulique de la capote est de série pour le M et en option pour les quatre-cylindres. Le couvre-capote doit être fixé à la main. N'est pas roadster qui veut!

Sophistiqués, les trains roulants ne sont absolument pas durs, mais bien réglés. Même en cas de fortes accélérations transversales, cette voiture de sport ne prend pratiquement pas de roulis. Le comportement, notamment sur route sinueuse avec de nombreux transferts de charges, est un délice et la direction est précise. Même sur revêtement peu adhérent, cette voiture ne perd rien de son tempérament bon enfant. Pour copier Pierce Brosnan qui a incarné James Bond dans le film «Golden Eye» avec la Z3, il n'est pas nécessaire d'être un artiste du volant comme Rauno Aaltonen.

Vu son potentiel énorme, le M roadster ne peut pas se passer de disques ventilés de grand diamètre (315 mm à l'avant, 312 à l'arrière). ABS et dispositif antiplongée au freinage et à l'accélération font partie des vertus des BMW des années 90.

With a display of consistency in the development of the BMW roadster tradition, the Munich company built the "ultimate driving machine": the M roadster – the 321 bhp power derivative of the US-built Z roadster.

In konsequenter Weiterführung der BMW-Roadster-Tradition bauen die Münchner das „ultimative Fahrerlebnis": den M roadster, der das 321-PS-Power-Derivat des in den USA gefertigten Z roadster ist.

Poussant à son paroxysme la tradition du roadster BMW, les Munichois offrent la «sensation de conduite à son apogée»: le M roadster qui est la version de 321 ch du Z roadster construit aux Etats-Unis.

A classic side profile with long hood and cooling vents. The front spoiler and a wide track with the corresponding tires clearly distinguish the M roadster from the basic version.

Klassisches Seitenprofil mit langer Motorhaube und Kühlschlitz. Der Frontspoiler und die breite Spur mit den entsprechenden „Walzen" heben den M roadster deutlich von der Basisversion ab.

Un profil classique au long capot moteur ponctué de fentes de refroidissement. L'aileron avant et les voies larges avec les gommes correspondantes distinguent le M roadster sans confusion possible de la version de base.

Open or closed, the driving characteristics of the M roadster with its sporty chassis and a power to weight ratio of 12.3 lbs (5.6 kg) per bhp are so convincing that many competitors see nothing but the rear end of the car.

Ob offen oder geschlossen: Die Fahreigenschaften des M roadsters sind angesichts des sportlichen Fahrwerks und einem Leistungsgewicht von 4,4 Kilo pro PS so überzeugend, daß viele Konkurrenten nur noch das Heck des Wagens sehen.

Que la capote soit ouverte ou fermée: les performances du M roadster sont si exceptionnelles, compte tenu du châssis sport et d'un rapport poids/puissance de 4,4 kg par ch, que beaucoup de ses rivales ne voient cette voiture que de l'arrière.

BMW M roadster 1997   409

Success through performance! Together with the BMW emblem, the M symbol not only stands for success on the racetrack, but also on the road.

Erfolg durch Leistung! In Verbindung mit dem BMW-Emblem steht das M-Symbol nicht nur für Erfolg auf der Rennpiste, sondern auch auf der Straße.

Tout travail est récompensé! Conjointement avec le logo BMW, le M emblématique est autant un symbole de succès sur les pistes des circuits que sur la route.

The 3.2-liter in-line six-cylinder engine with 24 valves provides a convincing display of power with a torque of 350 Nm, which is achieved at a speed as low as 3250 rpm.

Der 3,2-Liter-Reihensechszylinder mit 24 Ventilen überzeugt neben seiner Kraft durch ein Drehmoment von 350 Newtonmetern, das bereits bei 3250 Umdrehungen pro Minute erreicht wird.

Outre sa puissance, le six-cylindres en ligne de 3,2 litres convainc aussi par son couple de 350 Nm déjà délivré à 3250 tr/mn.

BMW M roadster 1997

The leather and chrome trim makes an essential contribution to the design of the cockpit, as can be seen on the wide central console above the five-speed transmission tunnel.

Daß Leder und Chromblenden zur Gestaltung des Cockpits wesentlich beitragen, zeigt die breite Mittelkonsole über dem Tunnel des Fünfgang-Schaltgetriebes.

La large console médiane sur le tunnel hébergeant la boîte manuelle à cinq vitesses témoigne de ce que le cuir et les applications de chrome contribuent joliment à la sportivité du cockpit.

The M roadster impresses with its looks and the comprehensiveness of its technical details down to components such as the electro-hydraulic fabric top.

Beeindruckend sind die Optik des M roadsters und die Summe all seiner technischen Details bis hin zu Komponenten wie dem elektrohydraulisch funktionierenden Stoffverdeck.

Tout aussi impressionnante que l'esthétique du M roadster est la somme de tous ses détails techniques, par exemple la capote à commande électrohydraulique.

"Errors are the rungs on the ladder to success. The trick is to detect them at an early stage of the design process, to eliminate them and to learn from them." That is what the American BMW design chief Christopher E. Bangle had to say about the development of the new 3 series. Five and a half years had elapsed between the first draft design and the car's market launch in April 1998.

Some 2.6 million working hours were invested in the E46, as it was referred to in-house. Over 2400 parts were completely redesigned and 130 prototypes handmade. The new model was to meet the highest standards of excellence right down to the last detail. The "small BMW" embodies the achievement of these exacting objectives.

"Corporate design" meant that this model had to bear at least some resemblance to the 5 series car, but on closer inspection, you can see that Chris Bangle has achieved stylistic high-precision work. The striking face of this car is characterized by the extended kidney-shaped grill on the hood, and the individually framed double round headlights. A harmonious effect is also created by the rear section, its rear lights wrapping around the trunk lid, surmounted by a wedge-shaped spoiler acting as an aerodynamic highlight.

Despite the high trunk compartment and the bulky appearance of the wide track body, the car does not seem to be out of proportion thanks to finely detailed artistic touches. For example, the elegant roof and seatbelt lines are supported by horizontal grooves, lips and rubber strips all round – stylish elements which also have a function.

This wonderful outline conceals an optimum use of space

and, most importantly, a great deal of technology. With 193 bhp, the 328i is the most powerful of the five engine variants with which the E46 BMW 3 series begins. The torque characteristics of this in-line six-cylinder engine – already silky smooth anyway – have been enhanced still further. "Double VANOS" is the latest entry in BMW's technical dictionary, stating: "Depending on the accelerator's position and the engine speed, the valve activation times of the intake and exhaust camshafts are adapted to the operating conditions of the engine in an infinitely variable manner." The electro-mechanical control of the throttle valve allows the engine to idle tranquilly, and ensures power is delivered in a smooth surge during acceleration.

"Putting your foot down" with the new 328i is always a pleasure because the 62.5 mph (100 kph) mark is reached by the high-precision speedo after a mere 7 seconds, and top speeds of 150 mph (240 kph) are not too bad either. Hans-Joachim Stuck put it in a nutshell in the BMW magazine: "The road-holding and power are phenomenal." As for the statement of his racing partner Johnny Cecotto, no one could have summarized the aesthetically-pleasing harmonious lines any better: "There is a unique synthesis of sportiness and elegance and the standard of active and passive safety is no less impressive. It is wonderful that so many familiar developments from larger BMW models have been incorporated into the new 3 series sedan, and that they are not only reserved for people who can afford larger models. All in all, the very comfortable driving characteristics, despite the car's enormous power capacity, mean that it is a truly charismatic drive."

Fehler sind die Sprossen auf der Leiter zum Erfolg. Die Kunst ist es, sie beim Designprozeß frühzeitig zu erkennen, auszumerzen und aus Ihnen zu lernen", so BMW-Chefdesigner Christopher E. Bangle über die Entwicklungsphase des neuen 3ers. Zwischen dem ersten Entwurf und der Markteinführung im April 1998 sind fünfeinhalb Jahre vergangen. 2,6 Millionen Arbeitsstunden werden in den E46, wie er firmenintern heißt, investiert. 2400 Teile werden völlig neu konzipiert und 130 Prototypen von Hand gefertigt. Höchsten Qualitätsansprüchen soll der Neue genügen, und diese erfordern Perfektion bis ins letzte Detail. Dafür ist der „kleine BMW" ein Musterbeispiel.

Zwar verlangt das „corporate design" nach einer gewissen Ähnlichkeit zum 5er, aber bei näherer Betrachtung stellt sich heraus, daß Christopher Bangle stilistische Feinarbeit geleistet hat. Die verlängerte Nierennase der Motorhaube und die Doppelscheinwerfer mit den Augenringen prägen das markante Gesicht. Harmonisch wirkt auch die Heckpartie mit den in den Kofferraumdeckel gezogenen Heckleuchten, über denen sich eine Abrißkante als aerodynamisches Attribut wölbt.

Trotz des hohen Kofferraums und der wuchtigen Wirkung des Breitfahrwerks stimmen die Proportionen dank kleiner, aber gelungener Kunstgriffe. So unterstützen horizontale Sicken, Lippen und rundum geführte Gummileisten die elegante Dach- und Gürtellinienführung – Stylingelemente, die auch eine Funktion erfüllen.

Unter dieser herrlichen Silhouette verbirgt sich eine optimale Raumausnutzung und vor allem viel Technik. Unter den fünf Antriebsvarianten, mit denen die Baureihe startet, ist

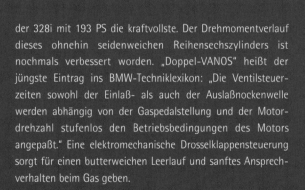

BMW 328i 1998

der 328i mit 193 PS die kraftvollste. Der Drehmomentverlauf dieses ohnehin seidenweichen Reihensechszylinders ist nochmals verbessert worden. „Doppel-VANOS" heißt der jüngste Eintrag ins BMW-Techniklexikon: „Die Ventilsteuerzeiten sowohl der Einlaß- als auch der Auslaßnockenwelle werden abhängig von der Gaspedalstellung und der Motordrehzahl stufenlos den Betriebsbedingungen des Motors angepaßt." Eine elektromechanische Drosselklappensteuerung sorgt für einen butterweichen Leerlauf und sanftes Ansprechverhalten beim Gas geben.

Es macht Spaß, beim neuen 328i zu beschleunigen, denn bereits nach 7 Sekunden zeigt der präzise Tacho 100 km/h an, und eine Spitzengeschwindigkeit von 240 Stundenkilometer lassen keine Wünsche offen. Hans-Joachim Stuck bringt es im BMW-Magazin auf den Punkt: „Straßenlage und Power sind phänomenal". Dem Statement seines Rennfahrer-Kollegen Johnny Cecotto ist wohl nichts mehr hinzuzufügen, wenn er diesem 3er ästhetische Harmonie bescheinigt und zusammenfaßt: „Die Synthese von Sportlichkeit und Eleganz ist einzigartig, der Standard der aktiven und passiven Sicherheit eindrucksvoll. Es ist toll, daß viele aus größeren Baureihen bekannte Entwicklungen in die neue 3er Limousine einfließen und nicht Menschen vorbehalten bleiben, die sich größere Modelle leisten können. Mein Fazit: Das trotz der Power sehr komfortable Fahrverhalten macht das Fahrzeug zu einem richtig sympathischen Wegbegleiter."

Les erreurs sont les barreaux sur l'échelle du succès. L'art consiste à les discerner à temps lors du processus de design, à les éliminer et à en tirer la leçon», déclare Christopher E. Bangle, chef styliste chez BMW, en évoquant les phases de développement de la nouvelle série 3. Avant sa commercialisation en avril 1998, cinq ans et demi se sont écoulés depuis le premier coup de crayon.

2,6 millions d'heures de travail sont investies dans la E46, comme on l'appelle au sein de l'entreprise. 2400 pièces sont conçues à partir d'une feuille blanche et 130 prototypes fabriqués à la main. La nouvelle doit satisfaire aux exigences de qualité les plus sévères et cela implique la perfection jusque dans les moindres détails. La «petite BMW» en est un exemple.

Certes, le «corporate design» exige une certaine similitude avec la série 5, mais, à y regarder de près, on constate que Christopher Bangle a réalisé un excellent travail esthétique. Le léger prolongement du mufle caractéristique de BMW et les phares doubles avec les «valises» sous les yeux lui donnent un visage caractéristique. Tout aussi harmonieuse est la poupe avec les phares arrière empiétant sur le couvercle de malle qui se termine sur une légère arête de décrochement aérodynamique.

Malgré la hauteur du coffre et l'effet massif des larges trains roulants, les proportions sont parfaites grâce à des astuces à peine perceptibles, mais efficaces: des coups de gouge longitudinaux, des arêtes et les bandeaux de caoutchouc cernant la voiture mettent en exergue l'élégance des lignes de toit et de ceinture – des éléments de style fonctionnels.

Sous cette silhouette magnifique se dissimule une utilisation optimale de l'espace disponible et surtout beaucoup de

technique. Des cinq série 3 fêtant leur première, la 328i est la plus puissante avec ses 193 ch. La courbe de couple de ce six-cylindres en ligne déjà réputé pour son onctuosité a encore été améliorée. «Double VANOS» est le nom de la dernière entrée au lexique de BMW: «Ce système permet d'adapter en continu la distribution des soupapes, aussi bien pour l'arbre à cames d'admission que pour l'arbre à cames d'échappement, en fonction de la position de l'accélérateur et du régime moteur et selon l'état de charge du moteur.» Une commande électromécanique de la vis papillon garantit un ralenti régulier et des réactions spontanées à l'accélérateur.

Quel plaisir l'on ressent à «enfoncer la pédale» de la nouvelle 328i, dont le tachymètre absolument exact indique 100 km/h au bout de seulement 7 secondes et qui satisfait tout à fait avec une vitesse de pointe de 240 km/h. Dans le magazine de BMW, le verdict de Hans-Joachim Stuck se passe de tout commentaire: «Tenue de route et puissance sont phénoménales». Il est tout aussi peu nécessaire d'ajouter le moindre commentaire à la déclaration de son collègue, le pilote de course Johnny Cecotto, qui atteste à cette série 3 une harmonie esthétique qu'il résume en ces termes: «La synthèse de sportivité et d'élégance est unique au monde; le niveau de sécurité active et passive est impressionnant. Il est intéressant de voir que de nombreuses innovations apparues avec les gammes supérieures soient reprises par la nouvelle BMW de la série 3 et ne soient pas réservées aux conducteurs qui peuvent s'offrir les modèles des segments supérieurs. Ma conclusion: le comportement très confortable malgré la puissance disponible fait de cette voiture un compagnon de route bien sympathique.»

A typical feature of the new face of the 3 series is the flat hood pulled down around the BMW kidney, with a space left for the flanking double headlights.

Typisch für das neue Gesicht der 3er Reihe ist die flache, über die BMW-Niere heruntergezogene Motorhaube, flankiert von Doppelscheinwerfern mit nach unten ausgesparten Masken.

Le capot moteur aplati descendant au-delà des naseaux BMW et cerné par les phares doubles avec découpe inférieure est typique du nouveau visage de la série 3.

F-NL 1046

BMW AG NIEDERLASSUNG FRANKFURT/M.

The coupé-like roof shape with the slight lip over the trunk is part of an overall aerodynamic concept which allows the 328i to achieve a top speed of 150 mph (240 kph) with 193 bhp.

Die Coupé-ähnliche Dachform mit leicht angedeuteter Abrißkante über dem Kofferraum ist Teil eines aerodynamischen Gesamtkonzepts, das den 328i mit 193 PS auf 240 Stundenkilometer bringt.

Le toit de style coupé avec arête de décrochement légèrement esquissée au-dessus du coffre fait partie d'un concept aérodynamique général qui permet à la 328i de 193 ch d'atteindre 240 km/h.

BMW 328i 1998

BMW 328i 1998

BMW V12 Le Mans 1998

oss of lubrication in the wheel bearings, something which was inexplicable and had not occurred during testing, made it impossible for the BMW V12 Le Mans to continue after only four hours in the 24-hour Le Mans classic race on the Sarthe. "I'm sorry for the whole team which put the BMW V12 Le Mans on its feet in a very short development time," Karl-Heinz Kalbfell, marketing boss of BMW AG and of BMW Motorsport Ltd. in England, commented.

The new sports racing car was created in the British former premises of Williams Grand Prix Engineering in Didcot (south of Oxford) in no time at all. It was an open two-seater with a 550 bhp V12 engine of 5990 cc, developed for the Le Mans Prototype Class 1 which prescribed a minimum weight of 1969 lbs (875 kg). Just try to imagine: in September 1997 the BMW engineers were standing in front of empty halls, waiting for their drawing boards and computers. Just nine months later their sports prototype started from the third row of the Le Mans grid.

This racing car with its carbon fiber chassis and aluminum honeycomb structure, as well as a crash-absorbent front section, possessed a potential which could not be exhausted in competition. The rear of the car also demonstrated modern and truly compact racing car design. The transmission, flange-mounted transversely at the rear of the engine to save space, also accommodated the engine oil tank. Engine and transmission were positioned together in a single sub-frame which was bolted to the chassis.

The center of gravity of the BMW was low and almost in the middle of the car. That is also where the driver sat. In place of the passenger seat – according to motor sport regulations, all that is required is an appropriate space – all kinds of essential equipment filled the area to the left of the driver. The only driver comfort concession was the servo-assisted steering, for ABS, traction control or automatic transmission were not allowed. Imagine 24 hours of manual labor changing six gears – even if the gear change was not in a tricky H-pattern but sequential as with a motorcycle.

Constant running for 50 hours, including all the load alternations and the rpm loads occurring at Le Mans, were completed by the V12 on the Munich test beds without problems. The engine, consisting of 600 components and weighing only 474 lbs (215 kg), was simultaneously powerful and economical.

The aerodynamics, too, were sophisticated. According to factory information, downward thrust on the car more than doubles the car's weight when track speed exceeds 162.5 mph (260 kph). BMW could not resist adding: "With grip like this the BMW V12 Le Mans could theoretically drive upside down on the ceiling."

The first action at Le Mans brought BMW firmly down to earth again. Kalbfell: "Today we were disappointed because of a defective component, but there will be another 24-hour race in Le Mans in 1999, and we are looking forward to that."

chmiermittelverlust an den Radlagern, unerklärlich und bei Testfahrten nie aufgetreten, macht eine weitere Teilnahme des BMW V12 „LM" am 24-Stunden-Klassiker an der Sarthe nach vier Stunden unmöglich. „Es tut mir leid für das gesamte Team, das den BMW V12 Le Mans innerhalb so kurzer Entwicklungszeit auf die Beine gestellt hat", erklärt Karl-Heinz Kalbfell, Marketingchef der BMW AG und der BMW Motorsport Ltd. in England.

In kürzester Zeit ist in den ehemaligen Hallen von Williams Grand Prix Engineering in Didcot südlich von Oxford der neue Sportwagen entstanden: ein offener Zweisitzer mit einem rund 550 PS starken BMW V12, entwickelt für die Le-Mans-Prototypenklasse 1, die ein Mindestgewicht von 875 Kilo vorschreibt. Man stelle sich das einmal vor: Da stehen die BMW-Techniker im September 1997 vor leeren Hallen und warten auf ihre Reißbretter und Computer und neun Monate später steht ihr Sport-Prototyp in der dritten Startreihe von Le Mans.

Dieses Rennfahrzeug mit Kohlefaserchassis, Aluminium-Wabenstruktur und einem Crash-absorbierenden Vorderwagen verfügt über ein Potential, das im praktischen Einsatz nicht ausgeschöpft werden kann. Auch das Wagenheck demonstriert modernen und deshalb kompakten Rennwagenbau. Das hinter dem Motor aus Platzgründen quer angeflanschte Getriebe beherbergt auch den Öltank des Motors. Motor und Getriebe sitzen zusammen in einem Rahmen, der mit dem Chassis verschraubt ist.

Der Schwerpunkt des BMW liegt tief und fast in der Fahrzeugmitte. Dort befindet sich auch der Arbeitsplatz des Piloten. Statt des Beifahrersitzes – nur der Platz dafür muß laut

Reglement vorgesehen sein - füllen allerlei Steuergeräte den Raum links des Fahrers. Einziges Zugeständnis an dessen Komfortbedürfnis ist die Servolenkung, denn ABS, Traktions-kontrollen oder gar Automatikgetriebe sind nicht erlaubt. Das bedeutet 24 Stunden lang Handarbeit beim Schalten, wenngleich nicht im H-Schema, sondern sequentiell wie beim Motorrad.

Einen 50-Stunden-Dauerlauf mit sämtlichen Lastwechseln und den in Le Mans auftretenden Drehzahlbelastungen absolviert der V12 auf dem Prüfstand in München klaglos. Das aus 600 Teilen bestehende, nur 215 Kilo schwere Triebwerk ist kraftvoll und sparsam zugleich.

Ausgefeilt ist auch die Aerodynamik. Laut Werksangaben übersteigt ab 260 Stundenkilometer der auf das Fahrzeug wirkende Anpreßdruck das Eigengewicht des Wagens. Man verkneift sich nicht den Zusatz: „Bei dieser Geschwindigkeit könnte der BMW V12 Le Mans theoretisch an der Decke fahren."

Der erste scharfe Einsatz in Le Mans hat die BMW-Mannen wieder auf den Boden der Tatsachen zurückgeholt. „Heute sind wir wegen eines defekten Einzelteils enttäuscht", meint Kalbfell, „aber es wird auch 1999 ein 24-Stunden-Rennen in Le Mans geben, und darauf freuen wir uns."

Une fuite de lubrifiant à hauteur des moyeux de roues, chose inexplicable qui ne s'est jamais manifestée lors des essais privés, cloue aux stands la BMW V12 Le Mans au bout de quatre heures à peine de la célèbre classique des 24 Heures de la Sarthe. «Cela me fait de la peine pour toute l'équipe qui a construit la BMW V12 Le Mans en une période de développement vraiment brève», déclare Karl-Heinz Kalbfell, le chef du marketing de BMW AG qui coiffe simultanément la casquette de directeur de BMW Motorsport Ltd. en Angleterre.

Une nouvelle voiture de sport est née en un très bref laps de temps dans les anciens ateliers de Williams Grand Prix Engineering, à Didcot (au sud d'Oxford) : il s'agit d'une biplace découverte propulsée par un V12 BMW d'environ 550 ch, mis au point pour les prototypes de la classe 1 du Mans qui prescrit un poids minimum de 875 kg. Imaginez-vous la situation : en septembre 1997, les techniciens de BMW se tiennent dans des ateliers désertiques et attendent leurs planches à dessin et leurs ordinateurs. Neuf mois plus tard, leur prototype sport occupe la troisième ligne sur la grille de départ du Mans.

Cette voiture de course à châssis en fibre de carbone et structure en nid d'abeille en aluminium avec une proue absorbant l'impact d'une collision possède un potentiel que l'on ne pourra jamais exploiter à fond en compétition. La partie arrière de la voiture, elle aussi, est une illustration du modernisme et de la compacité des voitures de course d'aujourd'hui. La boîte de vitesses montée en position transversale derrière le moteur pour économiser de la place renferme également la bâche à huile du moteur. Le moteur et la boîte de vitesses sont hébergés en commun dans un berceau auxiliaire boulonné au châssis.

Le centre de gravité de la BMW est très bas et se trouve presque au centre de la voiture. C'est également là que se trouve le poste de pilotage. A la place du siège passager – d'après le règlement en vigueur, seule la place prévue pour cela doit être respectée – se trouvent de multiples organes de commande occupant la gauche du conducteur. La seule concession au confort est la direction assistée puisque l'ABS, les contrôles de motricité ni les boîtes automatiques ne sont autorisées. Cela signifie 24 heures de changements de vitesses à la main, non pas avec une grille en H, mais avec une boîte séquentielle comme pour les motos.

Au banc d'essai, à Munich, le V12 a subi sans la moindre plainte un test de longue durée de 50 heures avec la totalité des transferts de charge et des changements de régime se produisant au Mans. Le moteur qui se compose de 600 pièces et ne pèse que 215 kg est à la fois puissant et sobre.

L'aérodynamique, elle aussi, est des plus raffinées. Selon ses constructeurs, l'appui qui agit sur la voiture à partir de 260 km/h dépasse son propre poids. On n'hésite pas à ajouter : «A cette vitesse, la BMW V12 Le Mans pourrait théoriquement rouler au plafond.»

Mais la première participation au Mans a ramené l'équipe de BMW les pieds sur terre. «Aujourd'hui», déclare Karl-Heinz Kalbfell, «nous sommes déçus en raison d'une petite pièce défectueuse, mais, en 1999 aussi, il y aura une course de 24 Heures du Mans et nous nous en réjouissons d'ores et déjà.»

Short pit stops – Hans-Joachim Stuck is being dispatched here – are as much a routine part of the work of the BMW Motorsport team as the test kilometers on the Paul Ricard track.

Schnelle Boxenstopps – hier wird Hans-Joachim Stuck abgefertigt – gehören ebenso zum Routineprogramm der BMW-Motorsporttruppe wie die Testkilometer auf dem Circuit Paul Ricard.

Les ravitaillements éclairs – ici, Hans-Joachim Stuck – font partie du programme de routine de l'écurie BMW Motorsport au même titre que les innombrables kilomètres de tests sur le circuit Paul Ricard.

The carbon fiber chassis, aerodynamically optimized in the wind tunnel of Williams Grand Prix Engineering – without rear lights during the tests – ensures a sufficient level of downward thrust that the car could in theory drive upside down on the ceiling at speeds faster than 162.5 mph (260 kph).

Die im Windkanal von Williams Grand Prix Engineering aerodynamisch optimierte Kohlefaseraußenhaut – hier bei den Tests noch ohne Rücklichter – sorgt für derart viel Anpreßdruck, daß der Wagen jenseits der 260 Stundenkilometer theoretisch auch an der Decke fahren könnte.

La carrosserie en fibre de carbone – encore sans feux arrière lors des tests – qui a été optimisée aérodynamiquement dans la soufflerie de Williams Grand Prix Engineering génère tant d'appui que la voiture pourrait théoriquement rouler au plafond dès qu'elle dépasse 260 km/h.

Front and rear axle have double control rods with spring/shock absorber units which are activated by connecting rods and rockers. For reasons of space, the transmission is set transversely to the direction of travel. Pictured is the test car with silencers.

Vorder- und Hinterachse verfügen über Doppel-Querlenker mit Feder-/Dämpfereinheiten, die über Schubstreben und Kipphebel betätigt werden. Aus Platzgründen ist das Getriebe quer zur Fahrtrichtung angeordnet. Hier das Testfahrzeug mit Schalldämpfern.

Les trains avant et arrière comportent une double triangulation transversale avec combinés ressort/amortisseur actionnés par des poussoirs et des culbuteurs. Par marque de place, la boîte est placée transversalement. Sur la photo, la voiture d'essai avec amortisseurs silencieux.

Driving aids other than servo-assisted steering are not allowed by the regulations. The on-board electronics to the left of the driver's seat may not transmit data by radio.

Außer einer Servounterstützung für die Lenkung sind laut Reglement keine anderen aktiven Hilfseinrichtungen erlaubt. Auch die Bordelektronik links des Fahrersitzes darf keine Daten per Funk übermitteln.

Le règlement n'autorise aucune autre aide à la conduite qu'une assistance de direction. De même, l'électronique de bord, placée à gauche du siège conducteur, ne doit transmettre aucune donnée par radio.

BMW Z3 coupé 2.8 1998

Opinion is divided between "as ugly as sin" and "stunning", attributes which would seem to be mutually exclusive. Whether or not you like the look of the Z3 coupé, which was unveiled on a rotating pedestal at the 1997 Frankfurt Motor Show, is a matter of taste. Yet technically it is very tasty. From the front, this sports car has the dynamic and powerful appearance of a roadster. From the back, it looks like a new Touring wagon of the 3 series, its extended fenders allowing an almost chubby-cheeked look. From the side, it does not seem to fit into any category. Perhaps "unconventional" is the best way of describing it.

You cannot help making certain comparisons - the elegant BMW 328 Mille Miglia or the Touring Coupé, or perhaps the MGB in its 1965 GT guise. It also seems as if the 1971 Volvo P 1800 ES sports wagon, transformed into the Volvo Coupé, has also provided some inspiration here.

This unmistakable Z3 coupé is offered only with powerful engines (2.8 liter, 192 bhp, and with the 321 bhp M-engine). Thanks to the fact that it is aerodynamically superior to the roadster, the 2.8-liter has a top speed of 144 mph (231 kph) and can reach 62.5 mph (100 kph) in less than 7 seconds from rest. The M version's power potential is phenomenal.

If you love unusual things, then price considerations normally take a back seat. Either you've got the cash, or you haven't! But even in terms of cost-effectiveness, BMW's Z3 2.8 coupé is worth every cent. Finding anything similar for 64,000 marks is difficult.

The chassis has a single-joint suspension taken from the 3 series at the front, and space-saving semi-trailing arms at the back with squat and anti-dip control. These are supported by ideal basic components: a long wheelbase with minimal body overhangs, a wide track and a relatively low center of gravity. Thanks to the ASC+T (Automatic Stability Control plus Traction), and the direct servo-assisted rack and pinion steering, Alpine mountain passes become a pleasurable challenge to Z3 coupé drivers. This roadrunner is capable of high levels of lateral acceleration without being prone to unexpected skids, and the limit can be appreciated and controlled.

A roll bar has been incorporated in the roof for rollover accidents, and the Z3 coupé's occupants are protected in extreme situations by four airbags. BMW always displays its good taste when it comes to the car's interior. Even the standard trim contains high-quality materials. The 410 liters of space created by the estate car body can hold two complete sets of golfing equipment so easily that it appears custom-built.

"The Z3 coupé 2.8 produces extreme reactions — love it or leave it," was how the BMW head of design Christopher Bangle was quoted in the special edition of the 1997 BMW magazine on the Frankfurt Motor Show. Unconventionality often creates its own attraction — on a second look.

Die Meinungen divergieren zwischen „potthäßlich" und „todschick" und anderen, ähnlich konträren Attributen. Das Z3 coupé, erstmals bei der IAA 1997 auf einer Drehscheibe zur Schau gestellt, ist zwar optisch Geschmacksache, in technischer Hinsicht aber ein Leckerbissen. Von vorn wirkt dieser Sportwagen dynamisch und kraftvoll wie ein Roadster, von hinten wie ein neuer 3er Kombi mit etwas pausbäckig geratenen Kotflügelverbreiterungen und von der Seite irgendwie undefinierbar. Vielleicht ist „eigenwillig" der richtige Ausdruck.

Vergleiche drängen sich auf zwischen dem eleganten BMW 328 Mille Miglia und dem Touring Coupé oder dem MGB und seiner GT-Version von 1965. Es scheint, als habe auch das zum Sportkombi P 1800 ES mutierte Volvo Coupé von 1971 in mancher Hinsicht Pate gestanden.

Der Unverwechselbare wird nur mit kraftvollen Triebwerken (2,8 Liter, 192 PS und mit dem 321-PS-M-Motor) angeboten. Dank seiner im Vergleich zum Roadster besseren Aerodynamik erreicht er in der 2.8-Liter-Version 231 Stundenkilometer und beschleunigt in weniger als 7 Sekunden aus dem Stand auf 100 Stundenkilometer. Das Leistungspotential der M-Version ist schlichtweg gigantisch.

Hat man eine Vorliebe für Ungewöhnliches, spielt der Preis meistens eine untergeordnete Rolle. Man hat es - oder man hat es nicht! Doch gerade beim Preis-Leistungs-Vergleich bietet BMW mit dem Z3 2.8 ein Coupé, das Zoll für Zoll sein Geld wert ist. Ein vergleichbares Auto für 64.000 Mark muß man erst einmal finden.

Das Fahrwerk, vorn die Eingelenk-Federbeinachse aus dem 3er, hinten die raumsparende Schräglenkerhinterachse mit

Anfahr- und Bremsnickausgleich, stützt sich auf ideale Basiskomponenten. Langer Radstand mit wenig Karosserieüberhängen, breite Spur und ein relativ niedriger Schwerpunkt tun ein übriges. Mit dem „Automatischen Stabilitäts- und Traktionssystem" (ASC+T) und der direkten servounterstützten Zahnstangenlenkung werden Alpenpässe zur vergnüglichen Herausforderung eines Z3-coupé-Fahrers. Auf hohe Querbeschleunigungen reagiert dieser „Roadrunner" mit wenig Seitenneigung, und im Grenzbereich bleibt er stets kontrollierbar.

Ein im Dach integrierter Überrollbügel und vier Airbags schützen die Fahrzeuginsassen im Extremfall. Geschmackvoll hat BMW das Interieur gestaltet. Schon das Standardoutfit beinhaltet edle Materialien. Das durch den Kombi-Anbau erzielte Volumen von 410 Litern ist wie geschaffen für zwei vollständige Golfausrüstungen.

„Die Formensprache des Z3 coupé 2.8 wirkt polarisierend – love it or leave it", wird BMW-Chefdesigner Christopher Bangle im IAA-Special des BMW-Magazins 1997 zitiert. Eigenwilliges wirkt oft sehr anziehend – auf den zweiten Blick!

Les esprits sont partagés entre «horriblement laid» et «absolument chic» ainsi que tous les qualificatifs opposés de ce genre. Le coupé Z3 dévoilé sur une plaque tournante au Salon de l'Automobile de Francfort de 1997 est en effet une question de goût sur le plan esthétique, mais il est très appétissant sur le plan mécanique. Vue de l'avant, cette voiture de sport diffuse dynamisme et énergie comme un roadster alors que, vue de l'arrière, elle évoque un break de la nouvelle série 3 avec des élargisseurs d'ailes un peu trop rebondis et, en vision latérale, est en quelque sorte indéfinissable. Peut-être le qualificatif «originale» est-il la bonne expression.

Des comparaisons viennent tout de suite à l'esprit – avec l'élégante BMW 328 Mille Miglia et le Touring Coupé ou la MGB dans sa version GT de 1965. Mais le coupé Volvo de 1971 métamorphosé en break de chasse P 1800 ES pourrait aussi lui avoir servi de modèle.

Particulière, elle n'est proposée qu'avec de puissants moteurs (un 2,8 litres de 192 ch et le moteur M de 321 ch). Grâce à une aérodynamique meilleure que celle du roadster, la version de 2,8 litres atteint une vitesse de pointe de 231 km/h et accélère de 0 à 100 km/h en moins de 7 secondes. Le potentiel de la version M est gigantesque.

Quand on est un véritable amoureux des voitures inhabituelles, le prix joue le plus souvent un rôle secondaire. On a de l'argent – ou on n'en a tout simplement pas! Or, pour le rapport prix/prestations, justement, avec le Z3 coupé 2.8, BMW propose une voiture qui vaut son argent jusqu'au bout des moyeux. Allez donc trouver quelque chose de similaire pour 64 000 marks.

Les trains roulants, avec l'essieu avant à jambes élastiques à une seule articulation de la série 3 et le compact train arrière à bras obliques avec compensation de la plongée à l'accélération et au freinage, sont montés sur une plate-forme idéale: un empattement long avec des porte-à-faux réduits, des voies larges et un centre de gravité relativement bas. Avec le dispositif ASC+T – contrôle automatique de la stabilité et de la traction – et la direction à crémaillère directe avec assistance, escalader les cols alpins devient un défi ludique pour tout conducteur de coupé Z3. Ce «roadrunner» réagit avec une prise de roulis réduite à sa plus simple expression face aux accélérations transversales élevées et la limite d'adhérence est toujours aisément contrôlable.

Un arceau de sécurité intégré au toit et quatre coussins gonflables protègent les passagers en cas d'accident. La réponse que BMW donne aux questions concernant l'habitacle sont guidées par le bon goût. La version standard, déjà, comporte tous les matériaux nobles que l'on puisse imaginer. Le volume de 410 litres disponible pour les bagages dans le vaste arrière break est comme prédestiné pour héberger deux équipements de golf complets.

«La langue formelle du coupé Z3 2.8 polarise les esprits – love it or leave it», déclara Christopher Bangle, le chef styliste de BMW, dans le numéro spécial du magazine BMW de 1997 lors du Salon de l'Automobile de Francfort. Ce qui est original récolte souvent l'amour – au second coup d'œil!

BMW Z3 coupé 2.8 1998

The coupé body, with its echoes of a station wagon and its large hatch, is particularly striking from the rear.

Der einem Kombi ähnliche und mit einer großen Ladeklappe versehene Coupé-Aufbau wirkt von hinten besonders markant.

La version Coupé qui rappelle un break avec son grand hayon est particulièrement personnelle vue de l'arrière.

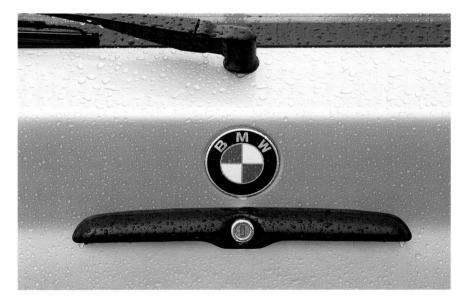

The usual Z3 styling elements, such as air vents and rounded rear-view mirrors, are supplemented by elements which are specific to the Z3 coupé.

Zu den üblichen Z3-Stylingelementen wie seitlichen Luftschlitzen und den abgerundeten Rückspiegeln gesellen sich Elemente, die typisch für das Z3 coupé sind.

Aux éléments de style traditionnels de la Z3, tels que les fentes d'aération latérales et les rétroviseurs arrondis, s'ajoutent des détails spécifiques au Z3 coupé.

BMW Z3 coupé 2.8 1998

The 2.8-liter engine with 192 bhp gives the Z3 coupé a top speed of 144 mph (231 kph) – the ideal transport for golfers in a hurry offers enough space for two complete sets of golf equipment.

Der 2,8-Liter-Motor mit 192 PS beschert dem Z3 coupé eine Spitzengeschwindigkeit von 231 Stundenkilometern. Eigentlich ein ideales Gefährt für Golfer in Eile, da der Kofferraum für zwei vollständige Golfausrüstungen Raum bietet.

Le moteur de 2,8 litres et 192 ch permet au Z3 coupé d'atteindre une vitesse de pointe de 231 km/h. C'est l'engin idéal, donc, pour les joueurs de golf pressés puisqu'il peut héberger deux équipements de golf complets.

The first press photos of the new BMW M5 were of symbolic character: they showed a miracle in blue – one available to drive from November 1998, at 400 bhp, 500 Nm torque and offering acceleration of 5.3 seconds from 0 to 62.5 mph (100 kph)!

The "ultimate performance machine" from Munich is outwardly unassuming. It is distinguished subtly from the usual 5 series by a larger air intake, oval fog lights, aerodynamically designed external mirrors which can be folded away, shiny chrome light alloy wheels with fat tires (245/40 ZR 18 and 275/35 ZR 18) and the four stainless steel exhausts of the eight-cylinder engine.

A special Bosch Motronic manages the throttle flaps, the temperature-sensitive lubrication oil supply, and fully automatic variable timing of the intake and exhaust camshafts. This increases torque at lower and middle engine speeds. As well as this double VANOS system, patented by BMW M GmbH, the accelerator action can also be electronically adjusted. Power with an instant "blast" or a comfortable power surge: the press of a button is all it takes.

Clever aerodynamic design of the subframe and a taut sporty chassis enable the M5 to achieve lateral acceleration loads of 1.2 g. When the color drains from drivers' faces in fast bends, the engine oil also experiences an unhealthy centrifugal force. Instead of a racing dry sump system, the M5 counters such oil surges with a lubrication system that reacts to lateral force.

Compound disc brakes, which BMW uses in motor racing, ensure better heat diffusion when braking through their "floating" construction. In addition, they are longer lasting than normal brakes. The conventional six-speed transmission has short precise shifts. Those who are averse to changing gear can console themselves with the fact that the M5 — rolling comfortably along in fourth gear — can manage to spurt from 50 mph (80 kph) to 75 mph (120 kph) in less than 5 seconds.

Be it elegantly restrained or sporty and dynamic, there are no design limits for the M5 interior. Everything is simply perfected in this sporty five-seater 5-liter car. The only problem is being able to afford this superlative sedan. The M5 has had a firm customer base since 1985, and approximately 1000 automotive individualists acquire this wolf in sheep's clothing every year.

Die ersten Pressefotos des neuen BMW M5 haben Symbolcharakter: Zu sehen ist ein blaues Wunder, und das kann man seit November 1998 auch erleben – bei 400 PS, 500 Newtonmeter Drehmoment und einer Beschleunigung von 0 auf Tempo 100 in 5,3 Sekunden!

Das „ultimative Kraftpaket" aus München gibt sich äußerlich unaufdringlich. Vom „normalen" 5er unterscheidet es sich nur durch einen größeren Kühllufteinlaß, ovale Nebelscheinwerfer, aerodynamisch gestaltete und elektrisch wegklappbare Außenspiegel, chromglänzende Leichtmetall-räder mit „dicken Puschen" (245/40 ZR 18 und 275/35 ZR 18) und die vier Edelstahl-Auspuffrohre des Achtzylinders.

Eine spezielle Mototronic regelt die Drosselklappen, den thermischen Ölniveau-Geber und die vollautomatische Spreizung der Ein- und Auslaßnockenwellen zur Drehmoment-steigerung im unteren und mittleren Drehzahlbereich. Neben diesem von der BMW M GmbH patentierten Doppel-VANOS-System läßt sich auch das Gaspedal elektronisch beeinflussen. Ob plötzliche Kraftentfaltung oder komfortables Anschwellen der motorischen Leistung - ein Druck auf den Schalter genügt!

Geschickte aerodynamische Gestaltung des Unterbodens und ein straffes sportliches Fahrwerk erlauben dem M5 Querbeschleunigungen von 1,2 g. Wenn einem Fahrer in schnellen Kurven die Farbe aus dem Gesicht weicht, verspürt auch das Motoröl den „ungesunden" Drang nach außen. Statt mit einem Trockensumpf begegnet der M5 solchen „Strö-mungen" mit einem querkraftgesteuerten Schmierungssystem.

Sogenannte „Compound-Scheibenbremsen", wie sie BMW im Motorsport verwendet, sorgen durch ihre „schwimmende"

BMW M5 1998

Bauweise für eine bessere Ableitung der Reibungswärme. Außerdem sind sie haltbarer als die üblichen Bremsen. Eher konventionell ist das Sechsganggetriebe mit kurzen präzisen Schaltwegen. Schaltfaule können sich damit trösten, daß der neue M5 – gemütlich im vierten Gang dahinrollend – einen Zwischenspurt von 80 auf 120 Stundenkilometer in weniger als 5 Sekunden schafft.

Ob vornehm zurückhaltend oder sportlich dynamisch – der Gestaltung des M5-Interieurs sind keine Grenzen gesetzt. An diesem sportlichen 5-Liter-Wagen mit fünf Sitzen ist eben alles perfekt. Man muß sich diesen Superlativ einer Limousine nur leisten können. Doch der M5 hat seit 1985 eine feste Käuferschicht: Pro Jahr legen sich rund 1000 Individualisten diesen „Wolf im Schafspelz" zu.

Les premières photos de presse de la nouvelle BMW M5 ont un caractère symbolique : au diapason de la couleur de la carrosserie, du sang bleu s'écoule dans ses veines. C'est un cocktail détonant que l'on peut déguster depuis novembre 1998 : une puissance de 400 ch, un couple de 500 Nm et 5,3 secondes pour les accélérations de 0 à 100 km/h !

Extérieurement, la «nouvelle reine de Bavière» est presque trop discrète. De la série 5 «normale» elle ne se distingue que par de plus grandes prises d'air, des phares antibrouillard ovales, des rétroviseurs extérieurs plus fins aérodynamiquement et rabattables électriquement, des jantes alliage chromées avec de «larges boudins» (245/40 ZR 18 et 275/35 ZR 18) et les quatre sorties de pot d'échappement chromées du huit-cylindres.

Une gestion Mototronic spéciale orchestre la symphonie des vis papillon, du capteur de niveau d'huile thermique et de la distribution variable automatique des arbres à cames d'admission et d'échappement aux régimes inférieurs et intermédiaires qui augmente le couple. Outre ce système breveté par BMW M GmbH sous le nom de «double VANOS», elle régule aussi l'accélérateur électronique. Montée en puissance avec «coup de pied au postérieur» ou envol progressif et linéaire de la performance : pour choisir, il suffit d'appuyer sur le bouton.

Une configuration aérodynamique intelligente du soubassement et un châssis sportif d'une fermeté de bon aloi permettent à la M5 d'encaisser des accélérations transversales de 1,2 g. Quand le visage du conducteur commence à se déformer dans les virages rapides, l'huile moteur a elle aussi la propension «malsaine» à succomber aux effets de la force centrifuge. En alternative à la lubrification à carter sec, la M5 combat un tel laisser-aller avec un système de lubrification commandé par la force transversale.

Grâce à leur montage «flottant», les freins à disques en composites, utilisés par BMW en compétition, garantissent une meilleure évacuation de la chaleur de friction, ce qui leur donne accessoirement beaucoup plus d'endurance que les freins usuels. La boîte à six vitesses est, quant à elle, plutôt conventionnelle avec ses débattements courts et précis. Que les paresseux du changement de vitesse se consolent, la nouvelle M5 – même si elle flâne distraitement en quatrième – peut toujours accélérer instantanément en moins de 5 secondes de 80 à 120 km/h.

Que l'on opte pour une élégance discrète ou une sportivité dynamique, on n'a que l'embarras du choix pour la décoration du cockpit de la M5. Avec cette sportive de 5 litres pour cinq passagers, tout est tout simplement parfait – sauf que tout le monde n'a pas les moyens de s'offrir cette limousine au superlatif. Depuis 1985, la M5 a son club d'individualistes amoureux de l'automobile : chaque année, environ 1000 d'entre eux s'offrent cette authentique grand tourisme aux allures de berline bourgeoise.

Tremendous power, discreetly packaged, speedy light alloy wheels, M sports seats and a well-built interior: the 400 bhp M5 is a high-performance sedan of that special type which sets new standards.

Gewaltige Power, diskret verpackt, rasante Leichtmetallräder, M-Sportsitze und ein gediegenes Interieur: Der 400-PS-M5 ist eine Hochleistungs-Limousine der besonderen Art, die neue Maßstäbe setzt.

Une puissance pléthorique, une allure de paisible familiale, d'excitantes jantes en alliage léger, des sièges sport M et un cockpit soigné: la M5 de 400 ch est une berline à hautes performances d'une race particulière. Elle fera incontestablement date.

BMW X5 1999

Although it was built in Spartanburg, South Carolina, it was a German car that was the highlight of the North American International Auto Show 1999, right in the Mecca of the US automobile industry, Detroit. The search for new market niches – something which BMW was pursuing as long as 30 years ago with the 02 series – produced the so-called SAV (Sports Activity Vehicle) segment, resulting in the BMW X5.

The X5 was neither intended as competition for the Range Rover within the BMW group, nor represented a "tuned" 5 series touring. On the sidelines at the debut of the X5 BMW announced: "Like other BMW automobiles, the X5 is defined by well-known classic BMW characteristics, such as aesthetics, dynamism and safety. But the X5 in addition places great emphasis on a completely new feel for the driver, produced in particular through the high seating and the excellent road-holding on all the highways and byways of this world."

The most modern all-wheel drive technology with anti-skid regulation by brake action, as well as some BMW high-tech goodies such as automatic and dynamic stability control, lend the X5 on-road qualities which allow for an emphatically sporty drive. But off-road the X5 also makes a strong impression – a powerful mountaineer which has no difficulties with returning to earth due to "hill descent control".

The range of engines for the X5 contains not only the well-known eight-cylinder V-engines, but also offers six-cylinder inline petrol and diesel engines with direct fuel injection. On the subject of safety, BMW powers ahead too with its "F.I.R.S.T." safety package. Strong beams, well-designed crumple zones, and up to ten airbags provide protection in a crash.

As far as equipment and driver comfort is concerned, the range stretches from a sports package via a multi-function steering wheel to a great many items that are electrically controlled, plus diverse seating "furniture" alternatives on to a navigation system and practical roof and rear rack storage systems.

There is enough space between the beefy 19-inch wheels for excursions into uneven countryside. On the other hand there is calculated ground clearance to prevent aerobatics during cornering. As the 23/1998 edition of *auto motor und sport* stated, this BMW, in meeting the dynamic requirements for this brand of car, was designed to lap the north loop of the Nürburgring in less than nine minutes. We can safely assume that the new Z7 roadster, which BMW is planning for autumn 2000, will be able to lap Germany's most famous track in less than eight minutes.

For the people of Spartanburg, the X5 was the second piece of good luck after the Z3. The factory doubled in size and the number of employees rose by 50 percent in January 1999. This commitment to the US is seen by BMW as a further step in consolidating the position of their group through the globalization policy.

Ausgerechnet ein deutsches Auto, wenngleich in Spartanburg, South Carolina, gebaut, ist das Highlight der „North American International Auto Show 1999" im US-Automobil-Mekka Detroit. Das Entdecken neuer Marktnischen – von BMW schon vor mehr als 30 Jahren mit der 02er Serie propagiert – brachte das sogenannte SAV-Segment (Sports Activity Vehicle) hervor und resultiert im BMW X5.

Am Rande der Premiere dieses Wagens, der weder innerhalb des Konzerns dem Range Rover Konkurrenz machen soll, noch einen „aufgebockten" 5er Touring darstellt, läßt BMW verlauten: „Der X5 definiert sich wie die anderen BMW-Automobile über die bekannten klassischen BMW-Eigenschaften wie Ästhetik, Dynamik und Sicherheit. Im Falle des X5 ist darüber hinaus ein völlig neues Fahrgefühl, insbesondere durch die hohe Sitzposition und das exzellente Fahrverhalten auf allen Straßen und Wegen dieser Welt stark ausgeprägt."

Modernste Allradtechnologie mit Schlupfregelung durch Bremseingriff sowie einige High-Tech-„Bonbons", zu denen auch eine automatische und dynamische Stabilitätskontrolle gehört, verleihen dem X5 On-Road-Qualitäten, die eine durchaus sportliche Fahrweise ermöglichen. Aber auch im Off-Road-Betrieb hinterläßt der X5 einen starken Eindruck – ein kräftiger Bergsteiger, dem der Abstieg dank „hill descent control" leicht gemacht wird.

Die Motorenpalette für den X5 sieht nicht nur die bekannten Achtzylinder-V-Motoren vor, sondern umfaßt auch den Reihensechszylinder als Benziner und als Diesel mit Direkteinspritzung. Auch beim Thema Sicherheit rüstet BMW mit dem „F.I.R.S.T."-Safety-Paket auf. Starke Holme, gut angelegte

Knautschzonen und bis zu zehn Airbags bieten bei einem Crash Schutz.

Hinsichtlich Ausstattung und Fahrkomfort reicht das Angebot vom Sportpaket über ein Multifunktionslenkrad, vielen elektrisch verstellbaren Komponenten und diversen Sitzmöbeln bis zum Navigationssystem oder praktischen Dach- und Heck-Trägersystemen.

Zwischen den bulligen 19-Zoll-Rädern befindet sich genügend Freiraum für Exkursionen in unebene Botanik. Andererseits reicht der Bodenabstand noch aus, um in Kurven nicht abzuheben. Denn – so *auto motor und sport* 23/1998 – sollte dieser BMW in Erfüllung markentypischer Dynamikanforderungen in der Lage sein, die Nordschleife des Nürburgrings in weniger als neun Minuten zu umrunden. In weniger als acht Minuten schafft es bestimmt der neue Z7 Roadster, den BMW für den Herbst 2000 vorgesehen hat.

Für die Spartanburger ist der X5 nach dem Z3 der zweite Glücksfall: Vergrößerung des Werks und Anhebung der Mitarbeiterzahl im Januar 1999 um 50 Prozent. Mit diesem US-Engagement sieht BMW einen weiteren Schritt, die Position des Konzerns durch Globalisierung zu festigen.

Le monde à l'envers: c'est une voiture allemande, quoi que construite à Spartanburg, en Caroline du Sud, qui est la vedette du «North American International Auto Show 1999» à Detroit, la capitale nord-américaine de l'automobile. Le segment des SAV (Sport Activity Vehicle) a permis de découvrir de nouvelles niches – un exercice que BMW avait déjà pratiqué il y a plus de 30 ans avec la série 02. Le résultat en est la BMW X5.

En marge de la première de cette voiture, qui n'est pas appelée à concurrencer le Range Rover au sein du groupe et n'est pas non plus une touring série 5 à échasses, BMW déclare: «La X5 se définit, au même titre que les autres automobiles de BMW, par les propriétés classiques bien connues de BMW, telles l'esthétique, la dynamique et la sécurité. Dans le cas de la X5, on a en outre des sensations de conduite absolument différentes, caractérisées, en particulier, par la position de conduite élevée et l'excellent comportement sur la totalité des routes et chemins de ce monde.»

Une technologie de traction intégrale ultramoderne avec régulation antipatinage par intervention sur les freins ainsi que quelques raffinements à haute technologie chers à BMW, parmi lesquels figure également un contrôle automatique et dynamique de la stabilité, confèrent à la X5 des qualités de franchissement qui autorisent parfaitement un style de conduite sportif. Mais, en tout chemin aussi, la X5 fait forte impression. C'est un véritable chamois, qui n'a pas de problèmes en descente non plus grâce au «hill descent control».

La gamme de moteurs pour la X5 ne comporte pas seulement les huit-cylindres en V bien connus, mais aussi le six-cylindres en ligne en version essence et diesel à injection directe. Sur le plan de la sécurité, BMW ne lésine pas non plus avec son pack de sécurité «F.I.R.S.T.». De solides longerons, des zones de déformation programmée bien calculées et jusqu'à dix coussins gonflables offrent une protection optimale en cas de collision.

Dans le registre de l'aménagement et du confort, on n'a que l'embarras du choix: du pack Sport au système de navigation ou aux pratiques systèmes de portage sur le toit et à l'arrière en passant par un volant multifonctions, de nombreux asservissements électriques et divers fauteuils.

Entre les généreuses roues de 19 pouces, on dispose de suffisamment de marge pour les excursions hors des sentiers battus. D'un autre côté, la garde au sol est suffisante pour garder sa stabilité dans les virages. En effet, comme le constate le numéro 23/1998 d'*auto motor und sport,* cette BMW, pour respecter les propriétés dynamiques typiques de sa race, devrait être en mesure de couvrir la boucle nord du Nürburgring en moins de neuf minutes. Moins de huit minutes, c'est un temps que réussira sans aucun doute le nouveau roadster Z7 que BMW a l'intention de dévoiler à l'automne de l'an 2000.

Pour les citoyens de Spartanburg, la X5 est, après la Z3, la deuxième bonne nouvelle: l'usine a été multipliée par deux et les effectifs majorés de 50 % en janvier 1999. Avec cet engagement aux Etats-Unis, BMW considère franchir une nouvelle étape dans la voie de la consolidation du statut dont jouit le groupe par la globalisation.

An extensive range of equipment with up to ten airbags and many extras is as much a part of the X5's SAV (Sports Activity Vehicle) segment as are the BMW engines for the different markets. The X5 performs well on dirt tracks due to its ultra-modern four-wheel drive technology. It is exemplary with regard to driving dynamics and safety.

Eine reichhaltige Ausstattung mit bis zu zehn Airbags und viele Extras gehören ebenso zum SAV-Segment (Sports Activity Vehicle) des X5 wie die BMW-Motoren für die jeweiligen Märkte. Auf unbefestigtem Untergrund macht der X5 dank modernster Allradtechnologie eine gute Figur. Hinsichtlich der Komponenten Fahrdynamik und Sicherheit ist er vorbildlich.

Un équipement presque sans lacune avec jusqu'à dix coussins gonflables et de nombreuses options caractérise le segment de la SAV (Sports Activity Vehicle) auquel appartient la X5, au même titre que les moteurs BMW pour les marchés respectifs. Hors des routes asphaltées, la X5 fait bonne figure grâce à la technologie ultramoderne de sa traction intégrale. Elle est exemplaire dans les registres de la dynamique et de la sécurité.

Specifications
Technische Daten
Spécifications

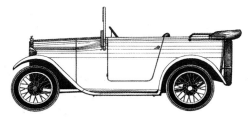

Baureihe		Wartburg Motorwagen
Baujahre		1898–1900
Modell		Wartburg Kutschierwagen 1898
Motor	Konfiguration	2-Zylinder (luftgekühlt)
	Hubraum	479 ccm
	Bohrung x Hub	66 x 70 mm
	Kraftstoffversorgung	Oberflächenvergaser
	Leistung	3,5 PS bei 1100 U/min
Getriebe		2-Gang
Chassis	Rahmen	Stahlrohrrahmen
	Aufhängung vorn	Einzelradaufhängung mit gekapselten Schraubenfedern und hochliegender Querfeder
	Aufhängung hinten	ungefederte Starrachse
Maße	Radstand	1600 mm
	Länge x Breite x Höhe	2300 x 1250 x 1450 mm
	Gewicht	315 kg
Fahrleistung	Höchstgeschwindigkeit	40–45 km/h

Dixi 3/15 PS
1927–1929
DA1
4-Zylinder in Reihe
748,5 ccm
56 x 76 mm
1 Solex-Flachstromvergaser
15 PS bei 3000 U/min
3-Gang
U-Profilrahmen aus Preßstahl
Starrachse mit Querfeder

Starrachse mit Ausleger-Viertelfedern

1905 mm
2800 x 1170 x 1625 mm
440 kg
75 km/h

Baureihe		Wartburg
Baujahre		1930–1931
Modell		DA3 Sport-Zweisitzer
Motor	Konfiguration	4-Zylinder in Reihe
	Hubraum	748,5 ccm
	Bohrung x Hub	56 x 76 mm
	Kraftstoffversorgung	1 Solex-Flachstromvergaser
	Leistung	18 PS bei 3500 U/min
Getriebe		3-Gang
Chassis	Rahmen	U-Profilrahmen, Karosserie in Holz-/Stahlbauweise
	Aufhängung vorn	Starrachse mit Querfeder
	Aufhängung hinten	Starrachse mit Ausleger-Viertelfedern
Maße	Radstand	1905 mm
	Länge x Breite x Höhe	3100 x 1150 x 1400 mm
	Gewicht	410 kg
Fahrleistung	Höchstgeschwindigkeit	90 km/h

3/20 PS
1932–1934
AM 4
4-Zylinder in Reihe
782 ccm
56 x 80 mm
1 Solex-Flachstromvergaser
20 PS bei 3500 U/min
4-Gang
Zentralkasten-Niederrahmen
achslos, Querfeder

Pendelachse mit 2 Querfedern

2150 mm
3200 x 1420 x 1550 mm
650 kg
80 km/h

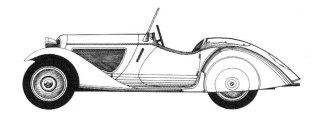

Baureihe		303
Baujahre		1933–1934
Modell		303
Motor	Konfiguration	6-Zylinder in Reihe
	Hubraum	1173 ccm
	Bohrung x Hub	58 x 80 mm
	Kraftstoffversorgung	2 Solex-Vertikalvergaser
	Leistung	30 PS bei 4000 U/min
Getriebe		4-Gang
Chassis	Rahmen	Leiterrahmen, Stahlrohrlängsträger, 4 Kastenquerträger
	Aufhängung vorn	Querlenker unten, Querfeder oben
	Aufhängung hinten	Starrachse mit Halbfedern
Maße	Radstand	2400 mm
	Länge x Breite x Höhe	3900 x 1440 x 1550 mm
	Gewicht	820 kg
Fahrleistung	Höchstgeschwindigkeit	90 km/h

315
1934–1936
315/1 Sport-Zweisitzer
6-Zylinder in Reihe
1490 ccm
58 x 94 mm
3 Solex-Flachstromvergaser
40 PS bei 4300 U/min
4-Gang
Leiterrahmen, Stahlrohrlängsträger, 4 Kastenquerträger
Querlenker unten, Querfeder oben

Starrachse mit Halbfedern

2400 mm
3800 x 1440 x 1350 mm
780 kg
130 km/h

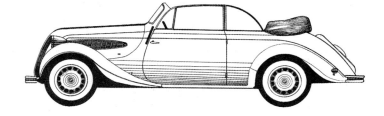
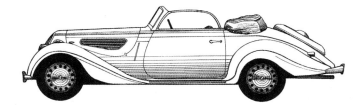

Baureihe		326	327
Baujahre		1936–1941	1937–1941
Modell		326 Cabriolet	327 Cabriolet
Motor	Konfiguration	6-Zylinder in Reihe	6-Zylinder in Reihe
	Hubraum	1971 ccm	1971 ccm
	Bohrung x Hub	66 x 96 mm	66 x 96 mm
	Kraftstoffversorgung	2 Solex-Vertikalvergaser	2 Solex-Vertikalvergaser
	Leistung	50 PS bei 3750 U/min	55 PS bei 4500 U/min
Getriebe		4-Gang	4-Gang
Chassis	Rahmen	Tiefbett-Kastenrahmen	Tiefbett-Kastenrahmen
	Aufhängung vorn	Querfeder unten, Querlenker oben	Querfeder unten, Querlenker oben
	Aufhängung hinten	Starrachse mit Halbfedern	Starrachse mit Halbfedern
Maße	Radstand	2750 mm	2750 mm
	Länge x Breite x Höhe	4600 x 1600 x 1500 mm	4500 x 1600 x 1420 mm
	Gewicht	1100 kg	1100 kg
Fahrleistung	Höchstgeschwindigkeit	115 km/h	125 km/h

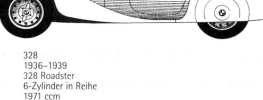
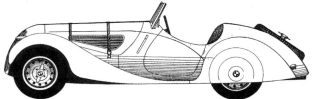

Baureihe		328	328 Mille Miglia
Baujahre		1936–1939	1940
Modell		328 Roadster	Roadster
Motor	Konfiguration	6-Zylinder in Reihe	6-Zylinder in Reihe
	Hubraum	1971 ccm	1971 ccm
	Bohrung x Hub	66 x 96 mm	66 x 96 mm
	Kraftstoffversorgung	3 Solex-Fallstromvergaser	3 Solex-Fallstromvergaser 30 IF, auf 32 mm aufgebohrt
	Leistung	80 PS bei 5000 U/min	130 PS bei 5750 U/min
Getriebe		4-Gang	4-Gang
Chassis	Rahmen	Rohrrahmen mit Kastenquerträger	Rohrrahmen, Kastenquerträger
	Aufhängung vorn	Einzelradaufhängung, Querlenker unten, Querblattfeder oben	Querlenker unten, Querfeder oben
	Aufhängung hinten	Starrachse	Starrachse mit Halbfedern
Maße	Radstand	2400 mm	2400 mm
	Länge x Breite x Höhe	3900 x 1550 x 1450 mm	3850 x 1490 x 1060 mm
	Gewicht	830 kg	700 kg
Fahrleistung	Höchstgeschwindigkeit	150 km/h	200 km/h

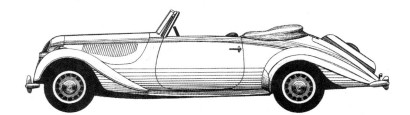

Baureihe		335	325
Baujahre		1939–1943	1937–1940
Modell		335 Cabriolet Graber	Leichter Einheits-Pkw, 3türig mit Gerätekasten
Motor	Konfiguration	6-Zylinder in Reihe	6-Zylinder in Reihe
	Hubraum	3485 ccm	1971 ccm
	Bohrung x Hub	82 x 110 mm	66 x 96 mm
	Kraftstoffversorgung	2 Solex-Vertikal-Doppelregistervergaser	2 Solex-Steigstromvergaser 26 BFLV
	Leistung	90 PS bei 3500 U/min	50 PS bei 3750 U/min
Getriebe		4-Gang	5-Gang
Chassis	Rahmen	Tiefbett-Kastenrahmen	Kastenrahmen mit Ganzstahlkarosserie
	Aufhängung vorn	Querlenker und Querfeder oben	Doppelquerlenker mit 2 Schraubenfedern pro Rad
	Aufhängung hinten	Starrachse, 2 Längsfederstäbe	Doppelquerlenker mit 2 Schraubenfedern pro Rad
Maße	Radstand	2984 mm	2400 mm
	Länge x Breite x Höhe	4988 x 1700 x 1685 mm	3900 x 1690 x 1900 mm
	Gewicht	1300 kg	1775 kg
Fahrleistung	Höchstgeschwindigkeit	145 km/h	80 km/h

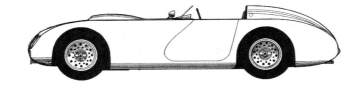
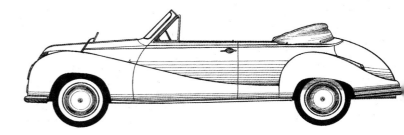

		Veritas Rennsportwagen	502
Baureihe			
Baujahre		1949	1954–1956
Modell		Veritas RS	502 Cabrio 2/2 (Baur)
Motor	Konfiguration	6-Zylinder in Reihe	8-Zylinder V 90°
	Hubraum	1971 ccm	2580 ccm
	Bohrung x Hub	66 x 96 mm	74 x 75 mm
	Kraftstoffversorgung	3 Solex-Vergaser 32 PBIC	Zenith-Doppel-Fallstromvergaser 32 NDIX
	Leistung	125 PS bei 5500 U/min	100 PS bei 4800 U/min
Getriebe		4-Gang	4-Gang
Chassis	Rahmen	Gitterrohrrahmen, Kastenquerträger	Kastenrahmen mit Längs- und Rohrquerträgern
	Aufhängung vorn	Einzelradaufhängung, Dreieckslenker unten, Querblattfeder oben	Doppelquerlenker und Längslenker
	Aufhängung hinten	Starrachse, Längsblattfeder	Banjo-Achse an Federhebeln und Dreieckslenker
Maße	Radstand	2250 mm	2835 mm
	Länge x Breite x Höhe	4200 x 1430 x 1030 mm	4720 x 1780 x 1530 mm
	Gewicht	800 kg	1400 kg
Fahrleistung	Höchstgeschwindigkeit	200 km/h	170 km/h

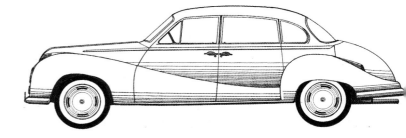

		Isetta	502
Baureihe			
Baujahre		1956–1962	1957–1961
Modell		Isetta 300	502 3,2 Liter Super
Motor	Konfiguration	1-Zylinder Viertakt	8-Zylinder V 90°
	Hubraum	298 ccm	3168 ccm
	Bohrung x Hub	72 x 73 mm	82 x 75 mm
	Kraftstoffversorgung	1 Bing-Schiebervergaser	2 Zenith-Doppel-Fallstromvergaser
	Leistung	13 PS bei 5200 U/min	140 PS bei 4800 U/min
Getriebe		4-Gang	4-Gang
Chassis	Rahmen	Stahlrohr mit Ganzstahlkarosserie	Kasten-, Längs- und Rohrquerträger, mit Karosserie verschweißt
	Aufhängung vorn	geschobene Längsschwingen, Schraubenfedern	Doppelquerlenker, Längsfederstäbe
	Aufhängung hinten	Starrachse (Schmalspur), Viertelelliptik-Auslegerblattfedern	Starrachse, Dreieck-Schublenker, Längsfederstäbe
Maße	Radstand	1500 mm	2835 mm
	Länge x Breite x Höhe	2285 x 1380 x 1340 mm	4730 x 1780 x 1530 mm
	Gewicht	360 kg	1500 kg
Fahrleistung	Höchstgeschwindigkeit	85 km/h	175 km/h

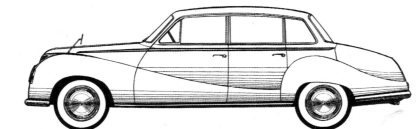

		502	507
Baureihe			
Baujahre		1963	1956–1959
Modell		3200S (Staatslimousine)	507
Motor	Konfiguration	8-Zylinder V 90°	8-Zylinder V 90°
	Hubraum	3168 ccm	3168 ccm
	Bohrung x Hub	82 x 75 mm	82 x 75 mm
	Kraftstoffversorgung	2 Doppel-Fallstromvergaser	2 Zenith-Doppel-Fallstromvergaser
	Leistung	160 PS bei 5600 U/min	150 PS bei 5000 U/min
Getriebe		4-Gang	4-Gang
Chassis	Rahmen	Kasten-, Längs- und Rohrquerträger, mit Ganzstahlkarosserie verschweißt	Kasten-, Längs- und Rohrquerträger, mit Karosserie verschweißt
	Aufhängung vorn	Doppelquerlenker, Längsfederstäbe	Doppelquerlenker, Stabilisator, Längsfederstäbe
	Aufhängung hinten	Starrachse, Dreieck-Schublenker, Längsfederstäbe	Starrachse
Maße	Radstand	2835 mm	2480 mm
	Länge x Breite x Höhe	4870 x 1780 x 1530 mm	4380 x 1650 x 1300 mm
	Gewicht	1490 kg	1330 kg
Fahrleistung	Höchstgeschwindigkeit	190 km/h	200 km/h

Specifications

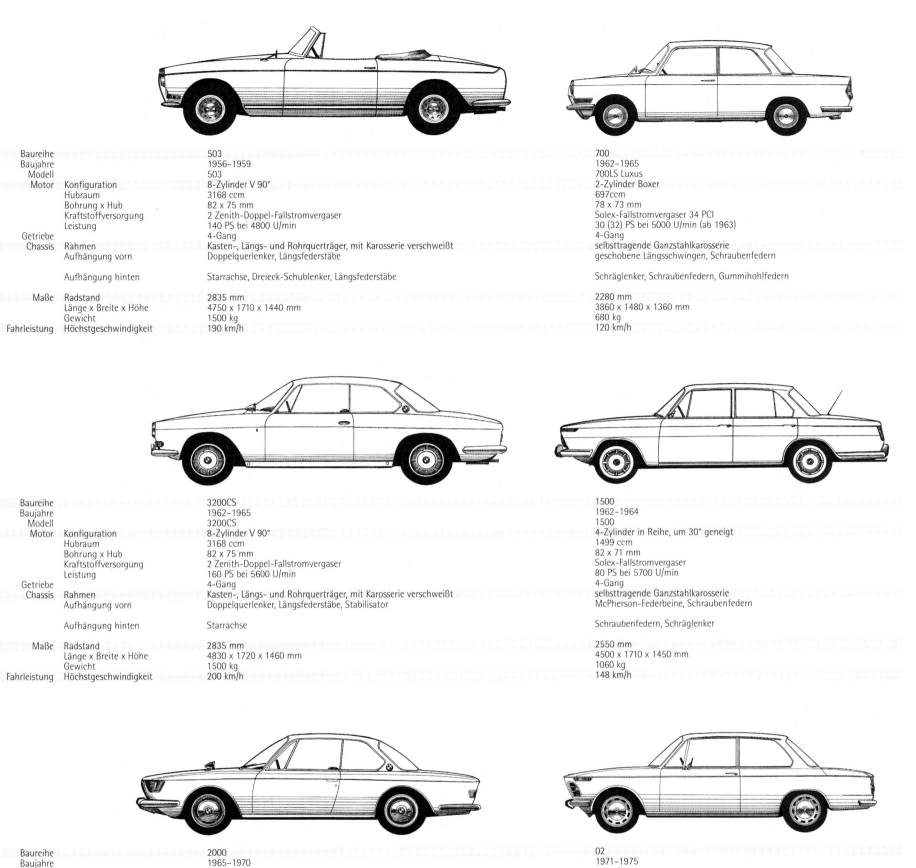

Baureihe		503	700
Baujahre		1956–1959	1962–1965
Modell		503	700LS Luxus
Motor	Konfiguration	8-Zylinder V 90°	2-Zylinder Boxer
	Hubraum	3168 ccm	697ccm
	Bohrung x Hub	82 x 75 mm	78 x 73 mm
	Kraftstoffversorgung	2 Zenith-Doppel-Fallstromvergaser	Solex-Fallstromvergaser 34 PCI
	Leistung	140 PS bei 4800 U/min	30 (32) PS bei 5000 U/min (ab 1963)
Getriebe		4-Gang	4-Gang
Chassis	Rahmen	Kasten-, Längs- und Rohrquerträger, mit Karosserie verschweißt	selbsttragende Ganzstahlkarosserie
	Aufhängung vorn	Doppelquerlenker, Längsfederstäbe	geschobene Längsschwingen, Schraubenfedern
	Aufhängung hinten	Starrachse, Dreieck-Schublenker, Längsfederstäbe	Schräglenker, Schraubenfedern, Gummihohlfedern
Maße	Radstand	2835 mm	2280 mm
	Länge x Breite x Höhe	4750 x 1710 x 1440 mm	3860 x 1480 x 1360 mm
	Gewicht	1500 kg	680 kg
Fahrleistung	Höchstgeschwindigkeit	190 km/h	120 km/h

Baureihe		3200CS	1500
Baujahre		1962–1965	1962–1964
Modell		3200CS	1500
Motor	Konfiguration	8-Zylinder V 90°	4-Zylinder in Reihe, um 30° geneigt
	Hubraum	3168 ccm	1499 ccm
	Bohrung x Hub	82 x 75 mm	82 x 71 mm
	Kraftstoffversorgung	2 Zenith-Doppel-Fallstromvergaser	Solex-Fallstromvergaser
	Leistung	160 PS bei 5600 U/min	80 PS bei 5700 U/min
Getriebe		4-Gang	4-Gang
Chassis	Rahmen	Kasten-, Längs- und Rohrquerträger, mit Karosserie verschweißt	selbsttragende Ganzstahlkarosserie
	Aufhängung vorn	Doppelquerlenker, Längsfederstäbe, Stabilisator	McPherson-Federbeine, Schraubenfedern
	Aufhängung hinten	Starrachse	Schraubenfedern, Schräglenker
Maße	Radstand	2835 mm	2550 mm
	Länge x Breite x Höhe	4830 x 1720 x 1460 mm	4500 x 1710 x 1450 mm
	Gewicht	1500 kg	1060 kg
Fahrleistung	Höchstgeschwindigkeit	200 km/h	148 km/h

Baureihe		2000	02
Baujahre		1965–1970	1971–1975
Modell		2000CS	2002tii
Motor	Konfiguration	4-Zylinder in Reihe, um 30° geneigt	4-Zylinder in Reihe, um 30° geneigt
	Hubraum	1990 ccm	1990 ccm
	Bohrung x Hub	89 x 80 mm	89 x 80 mm
	Kraftstoffversorgung	2 Solex-Doppel-Flachstromvergaser	Kugelfischer-Einspritzpumpe
	Leistung	120 PS bei 5500 U/min	130 PS bei 5800 U/min
Getriebe		4-Gang	4-Gang (5-Gang gegen Aufpreis)
Chassis	Rahmen	selbsttragende Ganzstahlkarosserie	selbsttragende Ganzstahlkarosserie
	Aufhängung vorn	McPherson-Federbeine, Schraubenfedern, Stabilisator	McPherson-Federbeine, Schraubenfedern, Drehstab-Stabilisator
	Aufhängung hinten	Schraubenfedern, Stabilisator, Schräglenker	Schraubenfedern, Drehstab-Stabilisator, Schräglenker
Maße	Radstand	2550 mm	2500 mm
	Länge x Breite x Höhe	4530 x 1675 x 1360 mm	4230 x 1590 x 1410 mm
	Gewicht	1200 kg	1010 kg
Fahrleistung	Höchstgeschwindigkeit	185 km/h	190 km/h

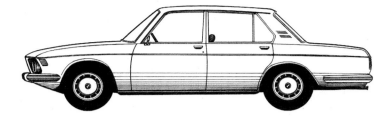

Baureihe		02
Baujahre		1973
Modell		2002 turbo
Motor	Konfiguration	4-Zylinder in Reihe mit Abgas-Turbolader
	Hubraum	1990 ccm
	Bohrung x Hub	89 x 80 mm
	Kraftstoffversorgung	mechanische Kugelfischer-Benzineinspritzung
	Leistung	170 PS bei 5800 U/min
Getriebe		4-Gang
Chassis	Rahmen	selbsttragende Ganzstahlkarosserie
	Aufhängung vorn	Einzelradaufhängung an Federbeinen und Querlenkern, Stabilisator
	Aufhängung hinten	Einzelradaufhängung an Schräglenkern, Schraubenfeder mit Gummizusatzfeder
Maße	Radstand	2500 mm
	Länge x Breite x Höhe	4220 x 1620 x 1410 mm
	Gewicht	1080 kg
Fahrleistung	Höchstgeschwindigkeit	210 km/h

		2500 (E3)
		1968–1977
		2500
		6-Zylinder in Reihe, um 30° geneigt
		2494 ccm
		86 x 71,6 mm
		2 Fallstrom-Registervergaser
		150 PS bei 6000 U/min
		4-Gang
		selbsttragende Ganzstahlkarosserie
		McPherson-Federbeine, Schraubenfedern, Gummizusatzfedern, Drehstab-Stabilisator (ab 1971)
		Federbeine, Schraubenfedern, Gummizusatzfedern, Boge-Nivomat mit Stabilisator
		2692 mm
		4700 x 1750 x 1450 mm
		1360 kg
		190 km/h

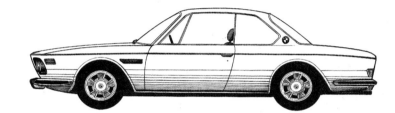
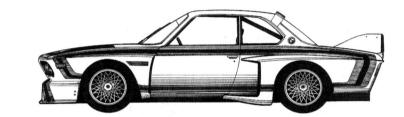

Baureihe		3.0CS
Baujahre		1971–1975
Modell		3.0CSi
Motor	Konfiguration	6-Zylinder in Reihe, um 30° geneigt
	Hubraum	2985 ccm
	Bohrung x Hub	89 x 80 mm
	Kraftstoffversorgung	elektronische Bosch-Einspritzung
	Leistung	200 PS bei 5500 U/min
Getriebe		4-Gang
Chassis	Rahmen	selbsttragende Ganzstahlkarosserie
	Aufhängung vorn	McPherson-Federbeine, Schraubenfedern, Drehstab-Stabilisator
	Aufhängung hinten	Federbeine, Schraubenfedern, Drehstab-Stabilisator, Schräglenker
Maße	Radstand	2625 mm
	Länge x Breite x Höhe	4630 x 1730 x 1370 mm
	Gewicht	1400 kg
Fahrleistung	Höchstgeschwindigkeit	220 km/h

		3.0CS
		1975
		3.0CSL (IMSA)
		6-Zylinder in Reihe
		3498 ccm
		94 x 84 mm
		elektronische Einspritzung
		430 PS bei 8500 U/min
		5-Gang
		Stahlrahmen mit Überrollkäfig, Aluhauben/-türen, Kunststoff-Aerodynamikteile
		Magnesium-Radträger für Federbeine, Gelenklager, verstellbarer Stabilisator
		Dreieckslenker, verstellbarer Stabilisator
		2625 mm
		4630 x 1730 x 1366 mm
		1062 kg
		280–300 km/h (je nach Übersetzung)

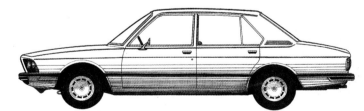

Baureihe		5er Reihe (E12)
Baujahre		1972–1977
Modell		520
Motor	Konfiguration	4-Zylinder in Reihe, um 30° geneigt
	Hubraum	1990 ccm
	Bohrung x Hub	89 x 80 mm
	Kraftstoffversorgung	1 Fallstromvergaser
	Leistung	115 PS bei 5800 U/min
Getriebe		4-Gang
Chassis	Rahmen	selbsttragende Ganzstahlkarosserie
	Aufhängung vorn	McPherson-Federbeine, Schraubenfedern, Drehstab-Stabilisator
	Aufhängung hinten	Federbeine, Schraubenfedern, Drehstab-Stabilisator, Schräglenker
Maße	Radstand	2636 mm
	Länge x Breite x Höhe	4620 x 1690 x 1425 mm
	Gewicht	1275 kg
Fahrleistung	Höchstgeschwindigkeit	175 km/h

		M1 (E26)
		1978–1981
		M1
		6-Zylinder in Reihe
		3453 ccm
		93,4 x 84 mm
		mechanische Kugelfischer-Einspritzung
		277 PS bei 6500 U/min
		5-Gang
		Stahlrohr-Gitterrahmen mit Kunststoffkarosserie
		Doppelquerlenker, Schraubenfedern, Drehstab-Stabilisator, Gasdruckdämpfer
		Doppelquerlenker, Schraubenfedern, Drehstab-Stabilisator, Gasdruckdämpfer
		2560 mm
		4360 x 1824 x 1140 mm
		1440 kg
		260 km/h

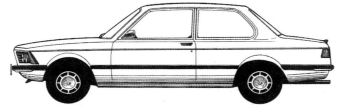
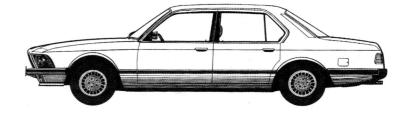
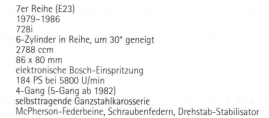

Baureihe		3er Reihe (E21)	7er Reihe (E23)
Baujahre		1978–1982	1979–1986
Modell		323i	728i
Motor	Konfiguration	6-Zylinder in Reihe, um 30° geneigt	6-Zylinder in Reihe, um 30° geneigt
	Hubraum	2315 ccm	2788 ccm
	Bohrung x Hub	80 x 76,8 mm	86 x 80 mm
	Kraftstoffversorgung	Bosch-Saugrohr-Einspritzung	elektronische Bosch-Einspritzung
	Leistung	143 PS bei 6000 U/min	184 PS bei 5800 U/min
Getriebe		5-Gang	4-Gang (5-Gang ab 1982)
Chassis	Rahmen	selbsttragende Ganzstahlkarosserie	selbsttragende Ganzstahlkarosserie
	Aufhängung vorn	McPherson-Federbeine, Schraubenfedern, Gummizusatzfedern, Drehstab-Stabilisator	McPherson-Federbeine, Schraubenfedern, Drehstab-Stabilisator
	Aufhängung hinten	Federbeine, Schraubenfedern, Gummizusatzfedern, Drehstab-Stabilisator, Schräglenker	Federbeine, Schräglenker, Schraubenfedern
Maße	Radstand	2563 mm	2795 mm
	Länge x Breite x Höhe	4355 x 1610 x 1380 mm	4860 x 1800 x 1430 mm
	Gewicht	1180 kg	1530 kg
Fahrleistung	Höchstgeschwindigkeit	192 km/h	200 km/h

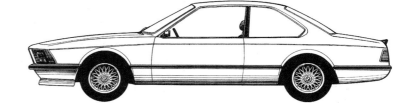

Baureihe		Brabham BMW	6er Reihe (E24)
Baujahre		1983	1983–1989
Modell		BT52	M 635CSi
Motor	Konfiguration	4-Zylinder in Reihe mit Turbolader	6-Zylinder in Reihe, um 30° geneigt
	Hubraum	1499 ccm	3453 ccm
	Bohrung x Hub	89,2 x 60 mm	93 x 84 mm
	Kraftstoffversorgung	elektronische Einspritzung	elektronische Bosch-Einspritzung
	Leistung	bis 790 PS bei 3,5 bar	286 PS bei 6500 U/min
Getriebe		6-Gang	5-Gang
Chassis	Rahmen	Monocoque aus Kohlefaserplatten und Alulegierung	selbsttragende Ganzstahlkarosserie
	Aufhängung vorn	innenliegende Feder-/Dämpfereinheit, zwei Dreieckslenker mit Doppelquerlenkern	McPherson-Federbeine, Schraubenfedern, Drehstab-Stabilisator
	Aufhängung hinten	innenliegende Feder-/Dämpfereinheit, zwei Dreieckslenker	Federbeine, Schraubenfedern, Drehstab-Stabilisator, Schräglenker
Maße	Radstand	2860 mm	2626 mm
	Länge x Breite x Höhe	4323 x 2108 x 990 mm	4755 x 1725 x 1354 mm
	Gewicht	540 kg	1510 kg
Fahrleistung	Höchstgeschwindigkeit	325–350 km/h (je nach Übersetzung)	250 km/h

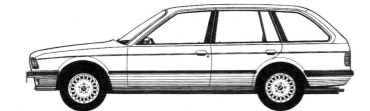
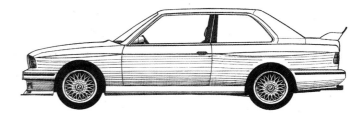

Baureihe		3er Reihe (E30)	3er Reihe (E30)
Baujahre		1985–1991	1990
Modell		325iX touring	M3 Sport Evolution
Motor	Konfiguration	6-Zylinder in Reihe, um 20° geneigt	4-Zylinder in Reihe, um 30° geneigt
	Hubraum	2494 ccm	2467 ccm
	Bohrung x Hub	84 x 75 mm	95 x 87 mm
	Kraftstoffversorgung	elektronische Bosch-Einspritzung	elektronische Bosch-Einspritzung
	Leistung	171 PS bei 5800 U/min	238 PS bei 7000 U/min
Getriebe		5-Gang	5-Gang
Chassis	Rahmen	selbsttragende Ganzstahlkarosserie	selbsttragende Ganzstahlkarosserie
	Aufhängung vorn	McPherson-Federbeine, Schraubenfedern, Drehstab-Stabilisator	McPherson-Federbeine, Schraubenfedern, Drehstab-Stabilisator
	Aufhängung hinten	Schräglenker, Schraubenfedern, Drehstab-Stabilisator	Schräglenker, Schraubenfedern, Drehstab-Stabilisator
Maße	Radstand	2570 mm	2565 mm
	Länge x Breite x Höhe	4325 x 1645 x 1400 mm	4345 x 1680 x 1370 mm
	Gewicht	1330 kg	1200 kg
Fahrleistung	Höchstgeschwindigkeit	210 km/h	248 km/h

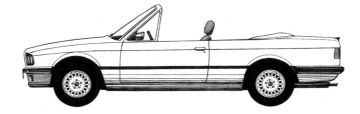

Baureihe		3er Reihe (E30)	7er Reihe (E32)
Baujahre		1990–1993	1987–1994
Modell		318i Cabrio (Kat)	750iL
Motor	Konfiguration	4-Zylinder in Reihe, um 30° geneigt	12-Zylinder V 60°
	Hubraum	1796 ccm	4988 ccm
	Bohrung x Hub	84 x 81 mm	84 x 75 mm
	Kraftstoffversorgung	elektronische Bosch-Einspritzung	elektronische Bosch-Einspritzung
	Leistung	113 PS bei 5500 U/min	300 PS bei 5200 U/min
Getriebe		5-Gang	4-Gang Automatik
Chassis	Rahmen	selbsttragende Ganzstahlkarosserie	selbsttragende Ganzstahlkarosserie
	Aufhängung vorn	McPherson-Federbeine, Schraubenfedern, Drehstab-Stabilisator	McPherson-Federbeine, Schraubenfedern, Drehstab-Stabilisator
	Aufhängung hinten	Minibloc-Schraubenfedern, Schräglenker, Drehstab-Stabilisator	Federbeine, Präzisions-Schräglenkerachse, Drehstab-Stabilisator, Niveauregulierung
Maße	Radstand	2570 mm	2947 mm
	Länge x Breite x Höhe	4325 x 1645 x 1380 mm	5024 x 1845 x 1400 mm
	Gewicht	1230 kg	1930 kg
Fahrleistung	Höchstgeschwindigkeit	190 km/h	250 km/h

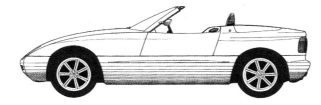

Baureihe		Z1	8er Reihe (E31)
Baujahre		1988–1991	1989–1992
Modell		Z1	850i
Motor	Konfiguration	6-Zylinder in Reihe, um 20° geneigt	12-Zylinder, V 60°
	Hubraum	2494 ccm	4988 ccm
	Bohrung x Hub	84 x 75 mm	84 x 75 mm
	Kraftstoffversorgung	digitale Bosch-Motronic	elektronische Bosch-Einspritzung
	Leistung	170 PS bei 5800 U/min	300 PS bei 5200 U/min
Getriebe		5-Gang	6-Gang/4-Gang Automatik
Chassis	Rahmen	verzinktes Stahlblechgerüst mit Kunststoff- und Verbundstoffteilen	selbsttragende Ganzstahlkarosserie
	Aufhängung vorn	McPherson-Federbeine, Schraubenfedern, Drehstab-Stabilisator	Doppelgelenk-Federbeinachse, Querstabilisator, Querkraftausgleich
	Aufhängung hinten	Z-Achse (zentralpunktgeführte sphärische Doppelquerlenker-Achse) mit Längs- und Querlenker, Schraubenfedern, Drehstab-Stabilisator	Integralachse mit fünf Lenkern, Querstabilisator
Maße	Radstand	2450 mm	2684 mm
	Länge x Breite x Höhe	3925 x 1690 x 1248 mm	4780 x 1855 x 1340 mm
	Gewicht	1290 kg	1840 kg
Fahrleistung	Höchstgeschwindigkeit	220–225 km/h	250 km/h

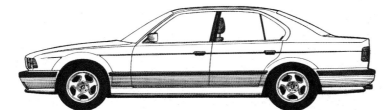

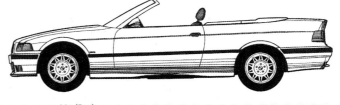

Baureihe		5er Reihe (E34)	M3 (E36)
Baujahre		1988–1995 (ab 1992*)	1992 –>
Modell		M5	M3 Cabrio
Motor	Konfiguration	6-Zylinder in Reihe, um 30° geneigt	6-Zylinder in Reihe
	Hubraum	3535 ccm (3795 ccm*)	3201 ccm (ab 1995)
	Bohrung x Hub	93,4 x 86 mm (94,6 x 90 mm*)	86,4 x 91 mm
	Kraftstoffversorgung	digitale Bosch-Motronic	elektronisches Motormanagement MSS 50
	Leistung	315 PS (340 PS*) bei 6900 U/min	321 PS bei 7400 U/min
Getriebe		5-Gang	6-Gang
Chassis	Rahmen	selbsttragende Ganzstahlkarosserie	selbsttragende Ganzstahlkarosserie
	Aufhängung vorn	Doppelgelenk-Federbeinachse mit Querkraft- und Bremsnickausgleich, Querstabilisator	Eingelenk-Federbeinachse mit Vorlaufversatz, Querkraftausgleich, Bremsnickreduzierung
	Aufhängung hinten	Schräglenkerachse mit Anfahrtauchreduzierung und Bremsnickausgleich, Querstabilisator	Zentrallenkerachse mit Längslenker und Doppelquerlenker, Anfahr- und Bremsnickausgleich
Maße	Radstand	2761 mm	2710 mm
	Länge x Breite x Höhe	4720 x 1751 x 1396 mm	4433 x 1710 x 1355 mm
	Gewicht	1720 kg	1460 kg
Fahrleistung	Höchstgeschwindigkeit	250 km/h	250 km/h

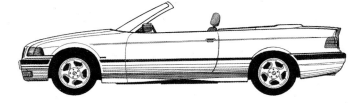

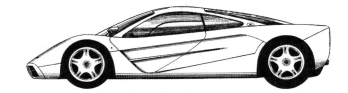

Baureihe		3er Reihe (E36)	McLaren F1
Baujahre		1993 —>	1994 —>
Modell		318i Cabrio	McLaren F1
Motor	Konfiguration	4-Zylinder in Reihe	BMW 12-Zylinder V 60°
	Hubraum	1796 ccm	6064 ccm
	Bohrung x Hub	84 x 81 mm	86 x 87 mm
	Kraftstoffversorgung	elektronisches Motormanagement BMS 43	elektronisches Motormanagement
	Leistung	115 PS bei 5500 U/min	ca. 600 PS bei 7000 U/min
Getriebe		5-Gang	6-Gang
Chassis	Rahmen	selbsttragende Ganzstahlkarosserie	Kohlefaser-Monocoque
	Aufhängung vorn	Eingelenk-Federbeinachse mit Vorlaufversatz, Querkraftausgleich, Bremsnickreduzierung	Einzelradaufhängung, Dreiecksquerlenker oben und unten, Stabilisator
	Aufhängung hinten	Zentrallenkerachse mit Längslenker und Doppelquerlenker, Anfahr- und Bremsnickausgleich	Einzelradaufhängung, Dreiecksquerlenker oben und unten
Maße	Radstand	2700 mm	2718 mm
	Länge x Breite x Höhe	4433 x 1710 x 1348 mm	4287 x 1920 x 1120 mm
	Gewicht	1370 kg	1016 kg
Fahrleistung	Höchstgeschwindigkeit	194 km/h	bis 370 km/h (je nach Übersetzung)

Baureihe		3er Reihe (E36)	3er Reihe (E36)
Baujahre		1994 —>	1995 —>
Modell		318ti compact	320i touring
Motor	Konfiguration	4-Zylinder in Reihe	6-Zylinder in Reihe
	Hubraum	1895 ccm (ab 1996)	1991 ccm
	Bohrung x Hub	85 x 83,5 mm	80 x 66 mm
	Kraftstoffversorgung	elektronisches Motormanagement M 5,2	elektronisches Motormanagement MS 41.0
	Leistung	140 PS bei 6000 U/min	150 PS bei 5900 U/min
Getriebe		5-Gang	5-Gang
Chassis	Rahmen	selbsttragende Ganzstahlkarosserie	selbsttragende Ganzstahlkarosserie
	Aufhängung vorn	Eingelenk-Federbeinachse mit Vorlaufversatz, Querkraftausgleich, Bremsnickreduzierung	Eingelenk-Federbeinachse mit Vorlaufversatz, Querkraftausgleich, Bremsnickreduzierung
	Aufhängung hinten	Einzelradaufhängung an Schräglenker, getrennte Feder und Dämpfer, Anfahr- und Bremsnickausgleich	Zentrallenkerachse mit Längslenker und Doppelquerlenker, Anfahr- und Bremsnickausgleich
Maße	Radstand	2700 mm	2700 mm
	Länge x Breite x Höhe	4210 x 1698 x 1393 mm	4433 x 1698 x 1391 mm
	Gewicht	1200 kg	1365 kg
Fahrleistung	Höchstgeschwindigkeit	209 km/h	230 km/h

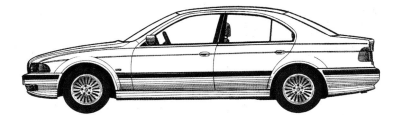

Baureihe		7er Reihe	5er Reihe (E39)
Baujahre		1996 —>	1996 —>
Modell		740i	540i
Motor	Konfiguration	8-Zylinder V 90°	8-Zylinder V 90°
	Hubraum	4398 ccm	4398 ccm
	Bohrung x Hub	92 x 82,7 mm	92 x 82,7 mm
	Kraftstoffversorgung	elektronisches Motormanagement M 5,2	elektronische Benzineinspritzung M 5,2
	Leistung	286 PS bei 5700 U/min	286 PS bei 5700 U/min
Getriebe		6-Gang	6-Gang
Chassis	Rahmen	selbsttragende Ganzstahlkarosserie	selbsttragende Ganzstahlkarosserie
	Aufhängung vorn	Doppelgelenk-Federbeinachse mit Vorlaufversatz, Querkraftausgleich und Bremsnickreduzierung	Druckstreben-Doppelgelenk-Federbeinachse (Aluminium), Querkraftausgleich, Bremsnickreduzierung
	Aufhängung hinten	Integralachse, räumlich wirkende Radaufhängung mit Anfahr- und Bremsnickausgleich	Integralachse (Aluminium), räumlich wirkende Aufhängung mit Anfahr- und Bremsnickausgleich
Maße	Radstand	2930 mm	2830 mm
	Länge x Breite x Höhe	4984 x 1862 x 1435 mm	4775 x 1800 x 1435 mm
	Gewicht	1800 kg	1585 kg
Fahrleistung	Höchstgeschwindigkeit	250 km/h	250 km/h

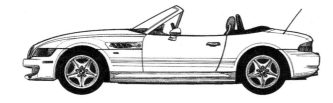

Baureihe		Z3	3er Reihe (E46)
Baujahre		1996 —>	1998 —>
Modell		M roadster	328i
Motor	Konfiguration	6-Zylinder in Reihe, 4-Ventil	6-Zylinder in Reihe
	Hubraum	3201 ccm	2793 ccm
	Bohrung x Hub	86,4 x 91 mm	84 x 84 mm
	Kraftstoffversorgung	elektronisches Motormanagement MSS 50	elektronisches Motormanagement
	Leistung	321 PS bei 7400 U/min	193 PS bei 5500 U/min
Getriebe		5-Gang	5-Gang
Chassis	Rahmen	selbsttragende Karosserie	selbsttragende Ganzstahlkarosserie
	Aufhängung vorn	Eingelenk-Federbeinachse, Querkraftausgleich, Bremsnickreduzierung	Eingelenk-Federbeinachse mit Bremsnickausgleich und Stabilisator
	Aufhängung hinten	Einzelradaufhängung am Schräglenker, getrennte Feder und Dämpfer, Anfahr- und Bremsnickausgleich	Zentrallenkerachse mit Längslenker und Doppelquerlenker, Anfahr- und Bremsnickausgleich
Maße	Radstand	2459 mm	2725 mm
	Länge x Breite x Höhe	4025 x 1740 x 1266 mm	4471 x 1932 x 1415 mm
	Gewicht	1350 kg	1470 kg
Fahrleistung	Höchstgeschwindigkeit	250 km/h	240 km/h

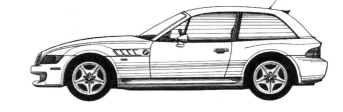

Baureihe		BMW V12 Le Mans	Z3
Baujahre		1998	1998 —>
Modell		BMW V12 Le Mans (LMP1)	Z3 coupé 2.8
Motor	Konfiguration	12 Zylinder V 60°	6-Zylinder in Reihe
	Hubraum	5990,5 ccm	2793 ccm
	Bohrung x Hub	86 x 85,94 mm	84 x 84 mm
	Kraftstoffversorgung	elektronische Einspritzung, eine Einspritzdüse pro Zylinder	elektronisches Motormanagement MS 41,0
	Leistung	550 PS bei 4500 U/min	192 PS bei 5300 U/min
Getriebe		6-Gang, sequentiell	5-Gang
Chassis	Rahmen	Kohlefaser-Monocoque mit Aluminium-Befestigungsblöcken	selbsttragende Karosserie
	Aufhängung vorn	Doppel-Querlenkerachse, Feder-/Dämpfereinheit, über Kipphebel und Schubstangen betätigt	Eingelenk-Federbeinachse mit Vorlaufversatz, Querkraftausgleich, Bremsnickreduzierung
	Aufhängung hinten	Doppel-Querlenkerachse, Feder-/Dämpfereinheit, über Kipphebel und Schubstangen betätigt	Einzelradaufhängung an Schräglenker, getrennte Feder und Dämpfer, Anfahr- und Bremsnickausgleich
Maße	Radstand	2790 mm	2446 mm
	Länge x Breite x Höhe	4650 x 2000 x 1020 mm	4025 x 1740 x 1293 mm
	Gewicht	875 kg	1280 kg
Fahrleistung	Höchstgeschwindigkeit	ca. 350 km/h	231 km/h

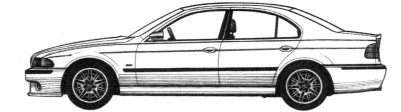

Baureihe		5er Reihe (E39)	E 53
Baujahre		1998 —>	1999 —>
Modell		M5	X5
Motor	Konfiguration	8-Zylinder V 90°	wahlweise V8, 6-Zylinder in Reihe oder 6-Zylinder-Diesel mit Direkteinspritzung
			Keine Werksangaben bei Redaktionsschluß
	Hubraum	4941 ccm	s. o.
	Bohrung x Hub	94 x 89 mm	s. o.
	Kraftstoffversorgung	elektronische Benzineinspritzung MSS 52	s. o.
	Leistung	400 PS bei 6600 U/min	
Getriebe		6-Gang	6-Gang
Chassis	Rahmen	selbsttragende Ganzstahlkarosserie	selbsttragende Ganzstahlkarosserie
	Aufhängung vorn	Druckstreben-Doppelgelenk-Federbeinachse (Aluminium), Querkraftausgleich, Bremsnickreduzierung	Allradantrieb mit Vierrad-Bremseingriff mit ASC+T, DSC3 (automatische und dynamische Stabilitätskontrolle)
	Aufhängung hinten	Integralachse (Aluminium), räumlich wirkende Aufhängung mit Anfahr- und Bremsnickausgleich	
Maße	Radstand	2830 mm	2880 mm
	Länge x Breite x Höhe	4784 x 1800 x 1432 mm	4660 x 1870 x 1720 mm
	Gewicht	1720 kg	Keine Werksangaben bei Redaktionsschluß
Fahrleistung	Höchstgeschwindigkeit	250 km/h	je nach Motorvariante bis ca. 230 km/h

Glossary / Glossaire

English	Allgemein	Généralités
General	**Allgemein**	**Généralités**
since	ab	depuis
on	an	à
on	auf	sur
made of	aus	en
twin	Doppel-	double
electronic	elektronisch	électronique
for	für	pour
rear	hinten	arrière
per	je	par
no	kein/e	aucun(e)
no factory information at time	keine Werksangaben bei	pas d'indications de l'usine au moment
of going to print	Redaktionsschluß	de la clôture de la rédaction
with	mit	avec
above	oben	supérieur
per	pro	par
see above	s. o.	voir ci-dessus
via/by	über	par
below	unten	inférieur
adjustable	verstellbar	réglable
front	vorn	avant
Series	**Baureihe**	**Gamme**
Years of Production	**Baujahre**	**Millésimes**
Model	**Modell**	**Modèle**
light standard-type passenger vehicle,	Leichter Einheits-PKW, 3türig mit	VP légère uniformisée, 3 portes avec
3-door with tool box	Gerätekasten	malle à équipements
state limousine	Staatslimousine	limousine de représentation
Engine	**Motor**	**Moteur**
Configuration	**Konfiguration**	**Configuration**
exhaust gas turbocharger	Abgas-Turbolader	turbocompresseur entraîné par les gaz d'échappement
direct fuel injection	Direkteinspritzung	injection directe
inclined block	geneigt	bloc incliné
in-line	in Reihe	en ligne
air-cooled	luftgekühlt	refroidi par air
in-line six-cylinder engine	6-Zylinder in Reihe	six-cylindres en ligne
six-cylinder diesel	6-Zylinder-Diesel	six-cylindres en version diesel
turbocharger	Turbolader	turbocompresseur
four-stroke	Viertakt	à quatre temps
optional	wahlweise	à titre alternatif
cylinder	Zylinder	cylindre
Cubic capacity	**Hubraum**	**Cylindrée**
cc	ccm	cm³
Bore x stroke	**Bohrung x Hub**	**Alésage x course**
Fuel supply	**Kraftstoffversorgung**	**Alimentation en carburant**
fuel injection	Benzineinspritzung	injection d'essence
digital engine electronics	digitale Motorelektronik	électronique du moteur
dual-throat downdraft carburetors	Doppel-Fallstromvergaser	double carburateurs inversés
injector	Einspritzdüse	buse d'injection
injection pump	Einspritzpumpe	pompe d'injection
injection	Einspritzung	injection
electronic engine management	elektronisches Motormanagement	gestion moteur électronique
downdraft register carburetor	Fallstrom-Registervergaser	carburateur inversé à registre
downdraft carburetor	Fallstromvergaser	carburateur inversé
sidedraft carburetor	Flachstromvergaser	carburateur horizontal
mechanical	mechanisch	mécanique
surface carburetor	Oberflächenvergaser	carburateur à surface
inlet pipe injection	Saugrohr-Einspritzung	injection dans les tubulures d'aspiration
sliding carburetor	Schiebervergaser	carburateur à coulisse
updraft carburetor	Steigstromvergaser	carburateur vertical
vertical double register carburetor	Vertikal-Doppelregistervergaser	carburateur vertical à double registre
vertical carburetor	Vertikalvergaser	carburateur vertical
Output	**Leistung**	**Puissance**
bar	bar	bar
at	bei	à
to	bis	jusqu'à
bhp	PS	ch
at ... rpm	bei ... U/min	à ... tr/mn
Transmission	**Getriebe**	**Boîte de vitesses**
2-stage	2-Stufen	à deux rapports
4-speed	4-Gang	à quatre vitesses
four-wheel drive	Allradantrieb	traction intégrale
automatic	Automatik	automatique
at extra cost	gegen Aufpreis	contre supplément
sequential	sequentiell	séquentielle
Chassis	**Chassis**	**Châssis**
Frame	**Rahmen**	**Cadre**
aerodynamic parts	Aerodynamikteile	éléments aérodynamiques
aluminum tops and doors	Aluhauben/-türen	capots et portières en aluminium
aluminum alloy	Alulegierung	alliage d'aluminium
aluminum fastening blocks	Aluminium-Befestigungsblöcke	blocs de fixation en aluminium
all-steel body	Ganzstahlkarosserie	carrosserie tout acier
multi-tubular spaceframe	Gitterrohrrahmen	châssis tubulaire
bodywork	Karosserie	carrosserie
box-section cross beams	Kastenquerträger	poutres transversales
box-type frame	Kastenrahmen	châssis à caisson
carbon fiber	Kohlefaser	fibre de carbone
carbon fiber panels	Kohlefaserplatten	panneaux en fibre de carbone
plastic	Kunststoff	matière plastique
plastic and composite material parts	Kunststoff- und Verbundstoffteile	matières plastiques et composites
longitudinal beam	Längsträger	poutre longitudinale
ladder frame	Leiterrahmen	châssis en échelle
pressed steel	Preßstahl	acier embouti
cross beam	Querträger	poutre transversale
tubular frame	Rohrrahmen	cadre en tube
integral	selbsttragend	autoporteuse
sheet steel frame	Stahlblechgerüst	squelette d'acier
steel tube	Stahlrohr	tube d'acier
steel frame	Stahlrahmen	châssis en acier
tubular steel spaceframe	Stahlrohr-Gitterrahmen	châssis en tube d'acier
steel tubular frame	Stahlrohrrahmen	cadre tubulaire en acier
drop base box frame	Tiefbett-Kastenrahmen	châssis surbaissé à caisson
rollovercage	Überrollkäfig	arceau de sécurité
U-section	U-Profil	profilé en U
welded	verschweißt	soudé
galvanized	verzinkt	galvanisé
central box-section low frame	Zentralkasten-Niederrahmen	châssis surbaissé à caisson central
two	zwei	deux
Drive/undercarriage	**Antrieb/Fahrwerk**	**Transmission/trains roulants**
automatic	automatisch	automatique
dynamic	dynamisch	dynamique
stability control	Stabilitätskontrolle	contrôle de la stabilité
four-wheel brake action	Vierrad-Bremseingriff	freins sur les quatres roues
Suspension front/rear	**Aufhängung vorn/hinten**	**Suspension avant/arrière**
axle	Achse	essieu
four-wheel drive	Allradantrieb	traction intégrale
aluminum	Alu/Aluminium	aluminium
anti-dive mechanism	Anfahrtauchreduzierung	réduction de la plongée au démarrage
anti-squat and anti-dive mechanism	Anfahr- und Bremsnickausgleich	compensation du tangage au démarrage et au freinage
cantilever quarter-spring	Ausleger-Viertelfeder	quart de ressort cantilever
banjo axle	Banjo-Achse	essieu en banjo
controlled	betätigt	actionné
anti-dive mechanism	Bremsnickreduzierung	diminution du tangage au freinage
absorber	Dämpfer	amortisseur
double-jointed McPherson strut axle	Doppelgelenk-Federbeinachse	essieu à jambes élastiques à double articulation
double control rods	Doppelquerlenker	double bras transversaux
anti-roll bar	Drehstab-Stabilisator	stabilisateur à barre de torsion
wishbone	Dreieckslenker	bras triangulaire
wishbone	Dreieck-Schublenker	poussoir triangulaire
wishbone	Dreiecksquerlenker	triangle transversal
constant velocity double-jointed McPherson strut axle	Druckstreben-Doppelgelenk-Federbeinachse	essieu à jambes élastiques à double articulation et bras de pression
single-joint McPherson strut axle	Eingelenk-Federbeinachse	essieu à jambes élastiques à une articulation
independent suspension	Einzelradaufhängung	suspension à roues indépendantes
strut	Federbein	jambe élastique
spring/absorber unit	Feder-/Dämpfereinheit	unité ressorts/amortisseurs
spring lever	Federhebel	levier de ressort
five	fünf	cinq
pressurized gas shock absorber	Gasdruckdämpfer	amortisseur à gaz
wishbone	Gelenklager	levier triangulé
enclosed	gekapselt	encapsulé
slide-action longitudinal swing axle	geschobene Längsschwingen	bras oscillants longitudinaux poussés
separate	getrennt	séparé
rubber hollow spring	Gummihohlfeder	ressort creux en caoutchouc
auxiliary rubber spring	Gummizusatzfeder	ressort supplémentaire en caoutchouc
semi-elliptic spring	Halbfeder	ressort semi-elliptique
integral axle	Integralachse	essieu intégral
rocker arm	Kipphebel	culbuteur
longitudinal leaf spring	Längsblattfeder	ressort à lames longitudinaux
longitudinal spring bars	Längsfederstäbe	barres de torsion longitudinales
longitudinal swing arm	Längslenker	bras longitudinal
arm	Lenker	bras
McPherson strut	McPherson-Federbein	jambe élastique McPherson
magnesium wheel bearing	Magnesium-Radträger	palier de roue en magnésium
Minibloc coil spring	Minibloc-Schraubenfeder	ressort hélicoïdal Minibloc
level control	Niveauregulierung	correction d'assiette
swing axle	Pendelachse	essieu oscillant
precision angled control bar axle	Präzisions-Schräglenkerachse	bras oblique à haute précision
transverse leaf spring	Querblattfeder	ressort à lames transversal
transverse spring	Querfeder	ressort transversal
lateral force compensation	Querkraftausgleich	compensation des accélérations latérales
transverse arm	Querlenker	bras transversal
transverse antiroll bar	Querstabilisator	barre stabilisatrice transversale
wheel	Rad	roue
spatially effective	räumlich wirkend	agissant dans l'espace
narrow track	Schmalspur	à voie étroite
diagonal arm	Schräglenker	bras diagonal
diagonal control arm axle	Schräglenkerachse	essieu à bras diagonal
coil spring	Schraubenfeder	ressort hélicoïdal
connecting rod	Schubstange	poussoir
spherical	sphärisch	sphérique
antiroll bar	Stabilisator	barre antiroulis
rigid	starr	rigide
rigid axle	Starrachse	essieu rigide
adjustable	verstellbar	réglable
quarter elliptic cantilever leaf spring	Viertelelliptik-Ausleger-Blattfeder	ressort à lames à quart d'ellipse cantilever
tracking offset	Vorlaufversatz	déport de chasse négative
Z-axle	Z-Achse	essieu en Z
centrally articulated axle	Zentrallenkerachse	essieu en guidage central
centrally articulated	zentralpunktgeführt	guidage par point central
Dimensions	**Maße**	**Dimensions**
Wheelbase	**Radstand**	**Empattement**
Length x width x height	**Länge x Breite x Höhe**	**Longueur x largeur x hauteur**
100 mm = 3.937 inches	mm	mm
Weight	**Gewicht**	**Poids**
1 kg = 2.205 lb	kg	kg
Performance	**Fahrleistung**	**Performances**
Maximum speed	**Höchstgeschwindigkeit**	**Vitesse de pointe**
depending on engine up to c.	je nach Motorvariante bis ca.	selon les options du moteur jusqu'à
depending on ratios	je nach Übersetzung	selon rapport de pont
1 km/h (kph) = 0.625 mph	km/h	km/h

Bibliography · Bibliographie

Jürgen Lewandowski: BMW Typen und Geschichte, Steiger Verlag, Augsburg 1998

Horst Mönnich: BMW, eine deutsche Geschichte, Piper, München 1991

Werner Oswald: Alle BMW-Automobile seit 1928, Stuttgart 1993

Halwart Schrader: BMW, 2 Bde., Bleicher Verlag, Gerlingen 1994

Usines & Industries 85/1989, Bayerische Motoren Werke, Brüssel

Auto und Sport

auto motor und sport

BMW-Magazin

rallye racing

BMW-Presseabteilung

BMW Mobile Tradition / Archiv

BMW-Veteranen-Club Deutschland e.V.

Photographic credits · Fotonachweis · Crédits photographiques